S
Patchogue-M

The Historic King Arthur

THE HISTORIC KING ARTHUR

*Authenticating the Celtic
Hero of Post-Roman Britain*

by FRANK D. RENO

McFarland & Company, Inc., Publishers
Jefferson, North Carolina, and London

942.4
0.4
REN

British Library Cataloguing-in-Publication data are available

Library of Congress Cataloguing-in-Publication Data

Reno, Frank D., 1937–
    The historic King Arthur : authenticating the Celtic hero of post-
Roman Britain / by Frank D. Reno.
        p.   cm.
    Includes bibliographic references and index.
    ISBN 0-7864-0266-0 (library binding : 50# alk. paper) ∞
    1. Arthur, King.   2. Great Britain — Antiquities, Celtic.
3. Heroes — Great Britain — Biography.   4. Great Britain —
History — To 1066.   5. Arthurian romances — Sources.   I. Title
DA152.5.A7R46   1996
942.01'4 — dc20   96-22231
                                                            CIP

Manufactured in the United States of America

McFarland & Company, Inc., Publishers
  Box 611, Jefferson, North Carolina 28640

To my wife Lavinia
who remained encouraging, enthusiastic,
optimistic, steadfast, and supportive
during this entire adventuresome quest

Acknowledgments

Although many organizations, colleagues, and personal friends contributed in some way to the accomplishment of this book, I would specifically like to express my deepest gratitude to the National Endowment for the Humanities and their promotion of pure scholarship for the love of learning, to Dr. Michael Curley of the University of Puget Sound as an outstanding mentor who kindled within me the intense passion for discovery, and to Nancy Langmaid from Somerton, England, who helped plan our itineraries.

Table of Contents

List of Illustrations

Except when otherwise indicated in a caption, all maps, tables, drawings, and photographs are by the author.

List of Abbreviations
of Works Cited in the Text

AA	*The Age of Arthur*
AB	*Arthur's Britain*
AoA	*Arthur of Albion*
AoB	*Arthur of Britain*
AC	*Annales Cambriae*
AKB	*Arthur, King of Britain*
ALMA	*Arthurian Literature in the Middle Ages*
ASC	*The Anglo-Saxon Chronicle*
ASCP	*Two of the Saxon Chronicles Parallel with Supplementary Extracts from the Others*
BH	*British History*
CÆ	*Chronicle of Æthelweard*
CAGE	*Cronica sive Antiquitates Glastoniensis Ecclesie*
DA	*De Antiquitate Glastonie Ecclesie*
DE	*De Excidio Britanniæ*
DKA	*The Discovery of King Arthur*
GRA	*Gestis Regum Anglorum*
HB	*Historia Brittonum*
HECP	*A History of the English Church and People*
HKB	*The History of the Kings of Britain*
KAA	*King Arthur's Avalon*
QAB	*The Quest for Arthur's Britain*

Preface

Whenever the name King Arthur arises, the majority of enthusiasts think only of the romances. It is the lure of these tales which stirs the imagination: his noble knights of the Round Table, the chivalric code, the formidable Merlin, jousting, courtly love, damsels in distress, war, honor, and the quest for adventures. Never has there been such an outpouring of stories about such an imposing figure based upon such scanty historical evidence.

Few enthusiasts, however, are aware of the chasm of eight centuries splitting Arthur's origins and the later romances. Bridging that intervening span of 800 years is a difficult engineering feat. The "Dark Ages" from which he emerged is in itself a term of vague, suggestive meanings. *Dark* can imply mystery and intrigue; it can imply obscurity because of the scarcity of historical information; and it can suggest a brutish, ignorant time. However the term might be interpreted, it denotes here a period of history so obscure it is phantasmagoric, yet from it a near-deified idol paradoxically materializes from its shadows. Through isolated, intellectually seductive passages, Arthur's specter appears, vanishes, and reappears, leaving one with a disquieting sense of hallucination.

Because details about his origin are so meager, explanations are painfully elusive. Trying to answer any one question leads to a chain reaction of other questions which must be addressed because they affect so inherently the response of a previous inquiry. Not only does the search grow in profundity, but it becomes progressively difficult to extricate the historical material from the early literary sources since they are so intertwined.

In writing about the Arthurian romances, even John Steinbeck experienced the frustration of chasing shadows. He had just begun *The Acts of King Arthur and His Noble Knights* in November of 1956 when he wrote, "I have a feeling that this will go very fast,"[1] thinking that his pursuit of King Arthur would be a short-term project. However, by January of 1957 Steinbeck's attitude had already changed to "I have known for some time that this is not a job to whip out."[2] And by April of 1957 he related that, "People ask me when I will have the Artu thing ready and I choose a conservative figure and say ten years."[3] As if this does not sound depressing enough, by August 27 of 1959, almost three years after he had begun, he wrote:

> This field and subject [of King Arthur] is so huge, so vague, so powerful and eternal, that I can't seem to mount it and set spurs. ... For the deeper I go, the more profound the subject becomes, always escaping me so that often I feel that I am not good enough nor wise enough to do this work. They seem puny in the face of a hideous subject, and I use the word in a Malorian sense.[4]

Steinbeck does not communicate anything more about Arthur in his letters from 1959 until May of 1965.

Yet, as John Steinbeck would have eventually discovered had he lived, patience conquers adversity. An incidental value of the present book is its chronological compilation of a great deal of Arthuriana from a hodge-podge of sources, which heretofore had not been done. However, one of the innovative end-products is a 100-year history of the Dark Ages, accurate even with the exclusion of Arthurian detail. The major contributions in this respect are:

  I. Emendations in the *Annales Cambriae*— not only of the Arthurian 19-year lunar adaptations for entries 516 and 537 to 497 and 518, but a later insertion for Saint David's birth-year which was erroneously transposed from 548 to 458, meaning his lifespan is a more realistic 50 years instead of 140 years;
 II. Emendations of misleading headings in the *Historia Brittonum*, including
      A. THE KENTISH CHRONICLE, PART 1, which mistakenly lists Hengist and Horsa as Saxon leaders for Saxon *Adventus* One and incorrectly infers that they are actually Kentish Saxons;
      B. THE KENTISH CHRONICLE, PART 2, and its confusion of geographic locales, namely
          1. Tanat is misconstrued as Thanet, and its locale is set at the mouth of the Thames River rather than in the northeastern part of Wales;
          2. "insula Oghgul" is incorrectly translated as "Angeln," leading readers to believe that Hengist consults *his* council of elders from *Anglia* rather than *Vortigern's* council of elders (the expelled Dessi tribe) from Ireland;
          3. (Guoyrancgono) Gwyrangon is listed as the displaced Kentish king but his name is obviously Welsh;
          4. Octha is sent to the north, near the wall called Guaul, wrongly assumed to be near Hadrian's Wall instead of Wall-by-Lichfield (Caer Luit Coyt);
          5. Hengist's tribe migrates to the "regionem Cantorum," a reference to the region of Cantlop or the River Caint in Wales three miles south of River Tanat, not the kingdom of Kent;
      C. THE KENTISH CHRONICLE, PART 3, which continues its erroneous connection with the southeast through references to
          1. one of Vortimer's battles against the Saxons at Darenth instead of Darwent or Darwen in northern Wales;
          2. another by the Inscribed Stone (oghams which are *Irish*) near the Gallic Sea (Gallici maris) rather than near the Gaelic Sea;
      D. The introduction to THE CAMPAIGNS OF ARTHUR, which should read that Octha came down from the north after Horsa's death, not Hengist's.
III. Emendations in the *Anglo-Saxon Chronicle* for the entries of

A. 465, 473, 477, 485, 495, and 508, in which distinctions should be made between the Welsh and the Britons, and between Cerdicesora and Cerdicesford;

B. Hengist's death and Octha's sole succession in 473;

C. Octha's 24-year reign beginning in 473 instead of 488;

D. Octha's death in 497;

IV. And, most important, a reconciliation of dates between the *Anglo-Saxon Chronicle* and its Genealogical Preface, a discrepancy first noted by Plummer and Earle in 1899 and deemed "impossible to harmonize."[5]

Arthur can be set into this historically accurate milieu. As part of the third facet of the *in corporalis* triad with Ambrosius Aurelianus and Riothamus, he joins the ranks of verifiable people of his era: Cunedda, Enniaun Girt, Owein Dantguin, Cerdic, Hengist, Octha, Vortigern, Anthemius, Aetius, Ægidius, Syagrius, and Euric. Just as their authenticity is undeniable, so is his, and through contemporaneous interweaving, Arthur's origins are verified by association.

In spite of depressing odds, scholarship mandates that theories be proposed and risks be taken when they are built upon a firmly documented base confidently established by the researcher. John Morris in *The Age of Arthur* writes that

> He [the historian, pupil, interpreter] has to sum up like a judge, and decide like a jury. He may not blankly refuse to decide, but he cannot proclaim certainty. He must give an informed opinion on what is probable and improbable, and return an open verdict when the balance of evidence suggests no probability.[6]

In this context Morris is referring specifically to historians, pupils and interpreters, but his statement easily applies to the Arthurian researcher. He admonishes the researcher to curb belief or disbelief and at the same time to present evidence leading to clear objective conclusions that embody informed opinions. He stresses that the important outcome is to make a decision, knowing that the conclusion might not be a proclamation of certainty.

I want no more than for readers to appreciate the Arthur of *fact* behind the Arthur of *legend*, thus intensifying even more the lure of the twelfth and thirteenth century tales D'Artu. In more ways than one, Arthur is the phoenix king, not only of Britain, but of the Dark Ages. He arises as Ambrosius Aurelianus from the devastation left by Rome's withdrawal, and from the smoldering ashes of his country, he salvages the Briton nation. When Ambrosius Aurelianus passes into history, from his dust Riothamus transmutes on the continent as the "king from across the Ocean" to deflect the immediate death-throes of the Bretons and Burgundians. After many successes, however, lacking Rome's help, Riothamus finally suffers defeat dealt by the barbarians and disappears from history into Burgundy. Yet from his embers, he reasserts Briton supremacy once more on the island as Arthur. As a result, this heroic king of human origin is exalted from Ambrosius to Riothamus to Arthur, signifying levels beyond mere mortality and rising from reality into legendary and godlike omnipotence. The phoenix survives the evanescence of time.

Chapter 1
Introduction

People of the Western world have been caught up in the intriguing romances of King Arthur for well over a thousand years. Throughout Great Britain, continental Europe, and North America, the escapades of Arthur and his noble knights know no ethnic or nationalistic bounds. A host of translations have practically eradicated language barriers, creating Arthur as a universal heroic figure in every sense of the word. Allied to his name are all traits good and worthy and honest. His spirit epitomizes morality disciplined by ethics, truth triumphant through justice, might submitting to right, compassion blending with sensitivity, chivalry governed by courtesy, and love tempered by forgiveness.

At the mere mention of this king among kings, people of different ages, nationalities, and backgrounds can recall at least one story of the famed adventures surrounding him. They can name his wizard, his sword, his queen, and at least several of his knights. The name King Arthur arouses a fascinating appeal, a mixture of the awe of fantasy and the spice of reality. Most who are tantalized by Arthur are caught up in the knightly adventures of the romantic Middle Ages — the excitement of the court, the intrigue of courtly love, knights in search of adventurous quests, jousting and the display of manhood. Yet even with these enthusiasts, there is an absorbing interest in Arthur's reality. The magic of Arthur spills over into history and the Dark Ages where intriguing mysteries are locked in the mists of time.

Although this arena of history, archaeology, and speculation is not as well-known to the buffs of the romanticized Arthur, the interest in Arthur's historicity is as intense as the interest in his knightly accomplishments recorded in literary tradition. Folktale heroes serve as role models to nourish cultural values as they pass from one generation to the next. King Arthur was one of the greatest cultural heroes of all times, an embodiment of all enviable values. He was imbued with powers that bordered on wizardry, resurrected not once but twice, and saved his country from annihilation for over a half century. Accounts of his deeds evolved into medieval romances, entering modern times laden with embellishment, fabrications, ingenious inventions, and sometimes deliberate deception.

Originally, "Arthuriana" referred to a chapter titled "The Campaigns of Arthur" in the *Historia Brittonum* by Nennius. Of the 12 battles ascribed to Arthur, only the last — the Battle of Badon — appears in two other early manuscripts. One, which predates Nennius, is by Gildas, who records the victory at Badon but does not attribute leadership to a man named Arthur. The second is an entry in the *Annales Cambriae*, which, like Nennius, binds Badon to Arthur. The *Annales Cambriae* also records a separate entry linking Arthur to the fatal Battle of Camlann, a battle not listed by either Nennius or Gildas. From this skeletal framework, the term *Arthuriana* has become generalized to include any allusion, real or fantastic, which transmits information about King Arthur.

The deluge of Arthuriana in the twentieth century has made it difficult to distinguish between the *legendary* Arthur, buried under layers of exaggeration, and the historical *reality* of a national hero. Theories, therefore, on the authenticity of King Arthur are almost as numerous as the scholars who have researched him, particularly in their attempts to anchor his activities chronologically and geographically. In the quest for the reality of King Arthur, some researchers have erred in believing that any reference to Arthur in manuscripts during the first millennium was to a single individual. This error has led to a great deal of frustration. By mistakenly combining several figures with the same name, scholars imply an Arthur who spans a period from the 420s to the opening decades of the 600s, foiling any attempt to pinpoint him chronologically.

Richard Barber, among other researchers, however, believes that within this 200-year period, there were at least three distinct Arthurs — a northern, a western, and a southern — reflected in different literary works or histories of the times. He places Arthur of Dalriada in northern Britain near the Antonine Wall. The setting is in the thin neck of northern Britain bounded by the Irish and the North Seas, the Kilpatrick Hills, and the Firth of Clyde during the 570s and into the seventh century when the Saxons had been steadily advancing to the north. History records that near Catterick, the Britons met the Saxon army and engaged them in battle. All except a few of the Britons were massacred. Aneirin, the *Gododdin* poet, managed to escape and later wrote his famous poem, a literary depiction in which several Briton warriors are mentioned by name and title. Aneirin refers to Arthur when writing that "[Gwawrddur] glutted (?) black ravens on the rampart of the stronghold, though he was no Arthur."[1]

Assuming that the Arthurian reference is to a contemporary of the poet, Richard Barber names this Arthur as the son of Aedan. Aedan rose to the throne in the mid–570s, but Arthur did not succeed to the kingship; he and his brother were killed in a battle with a tribe called the Miathi. This Arthur, then, is the Arthur of Dalriada, leading some scholars to ascribe the "real" Arthur to the north, the son of a Scottish chieftain, of Irish descent, who died at an early age in a battle with *northern* barbarians, not Saxons. There is no doubt, as Richard Barber avers, that this northern Arthur "flourished within a mere decade or so in time and a mere fifty miles in space of the milieu in which the *Gododdin* was written,"[2] and he was evidently somewhat of a local hero. However, it is unlikely that a figure of this minor stature could have risen to national recognition unless he had been linked to some cataclysmic event threatening the entire structure of Britain.

Aneirin might have been writing about Arthur son of Aedan, but the comparison between Gwawrddur and Arthur shows Arthur to be a much more prestigious figure. Aneirin's use of Arthur's name is far from conclusive proof that the Arthur in this source is a contemporary of the poet. If, for example, a poet of the 1990s claimed that Ulysses S. Grant was a great president and warrior, but he was no George Washington, this would in no way suggest that the poet, Ulysses S. Grant, and George Washington were all contemporaries. Similarly, Aneirin could have been referring to a heroic Arthur of nearly a century earlier.

Nevertheless, Barber leans toward the northern Arthur, claiming, "The reference [in *The Gododdin*] to [Arthur] comes from an early and reliable source, which, as we shall see, cannot be said of the rival and generally accepted [southern] candidate."[3] In a terse rejection of a southern Arthur, Barber dismisses the *Annales Cambriae* and the *Historia Brittonum,* plus the Arthurian implications associated with Gildas' *De Excidio* and the *Anglo-Saxon Chronicle.* Barber claims that evidence for the true Arthur must be weighed on the merit of who wrote what and why, and what some of the prevailing attitudes were (of the writer specifically and the society in general), thus implying that the proponents of a southwestern Arthur have not considered these same influences.

Barber's Arthur of Dalriada may be the same far-northern Arthur advocated by American professor Norma Goodrich, who claims that Camelot can be traced to Creenan Castle near Ayr on the Firth of Clyde and that Arthur's Round Table is a rotunda on the banks of the Carron River near Stirling, approximately 60 miles northeast of the Camelot site as the raven flies. A template of Barber's Dalriada superimposed on a modern map would show the precise geography which Goodrich describes. She also makes two other claims. One is that King Arthur's burial place is near Gretna Green, 72 miles southeast of her proposed Camelot site. The second is that the Battle of Camlann was fought at Camboglanna near Gilsland, 20 miles even farther east of Arthur's burial site and therefore 90 to 95 miles from Camelot. According to her account, Arthur's fort on the south shores of the Solway Firth, near his burial site, is now under water; this fort likewise would be situated 70 to 75 miles from where Goodrich places Camelot.

A different Arthur suggested by Barber is the western one, whom he calls the Arthur of Dyfed, after an ancient district in southwestern Wales. The evidence establishing this Arthur as a separate individual from the southern one is shaky because it is based on a charter called *The Expulsion of the Dessi,* allegedly written in the seventh century but almost certainly a twelfth century forgery. One questionable interpretation of the story is its chronological placement. Barber puts the birth for the Arthur of Dyfed between 580 and 620,[4] minimizing the importance of the date, which is in fact crucial. At odds with the date Barber assigns,

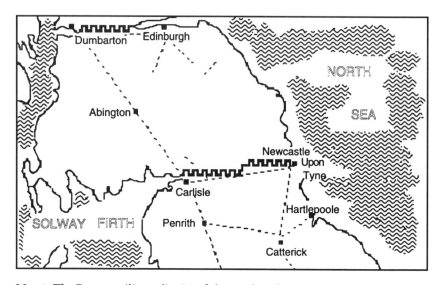

Map 1. The Roman military district of the north. When comparing characteristics of the midlands and southern Britain, the theory of a northern King Arthur is not supportable. The Antonine Wall was abandoned early in the Roman occupation because of its isolation, rugged terrain, and harassment from the Picts. Territories about 100 miles south of Hadrian's Wall were much more strategically important.

two of the major ancient documents — the *Historia Brittonum* and the *Annales Cambriae*— refute his opinion.

Based on the abundant details in the *Historia*, the geographic locations for Arthur's activities on the island are encompassed in the Snowden area of northern Wales, the northern midlands and Britanniae Maxima, the ancient Cornovian territory bordering Britanniae Prima, Wiltshire and Avon, Bridgwater Bay, the River Severn, and southern Wales. The continuous references to Irish incursions and Welsh settlements leave no doubt that the manuscripts were not interpolated for the sake of increasing status. Cunedda's migration to the Carlisle area, the colonization along the western seaboard, and the major locales of Arthur's activity — the Battle of Badon, the Battle of Camlann, his fortress, his burial site, the eventual disputes with the Saxons, and Vortimer's battles — lie within this circumference. Combined with details from other sources all this background material in the *Historia Brittonum* provides accurate information about King Arthur's placement within this arena. In conjunction with the geography, the *Annales Cambriae* (and its link with its parent manuscripts, the Irish Annals) sets the Arthurian chronology at the end of the fifth century and beginning of the sixth. Gildas hints at a general time frame for Arthur's battle at Badon, Nennius supplies the milieu, and the *Annales* supplies a date.

Advocates for a southern Arthur claim the same time frame but vary considerably on the geographic locations. During Romano-Britain times, and then in King Arthur's era after the abandonment, the heartland of southern Britain

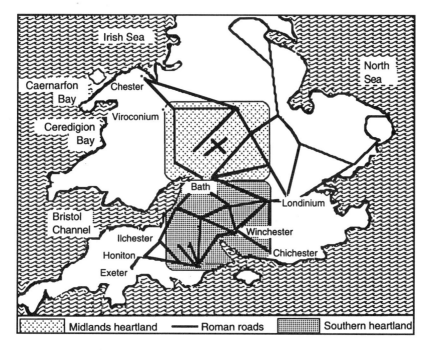

Map 2. The Roman civil districts of southern and central Britain.

was delineated by an oval encompassing the area from Bath and Swindon in the north, Roman Town in the east, Chichester and Dorchester in the south, and Ilchester in the west, creating a southern sanctuary of civilized activity. Although this perimeter was extensive, the area is much smaller than the massive Roman military confines protecting it from the surrounding barbaric pressures. Within this civilian area of security, unlike the sparsely settled north, a maze of Roman roads connected several important hubs for political, commercial, industrial, and agricultural purposes.

One of the major intersections, built upon the ruins of an Iron Age hillfort near the southern coast, was Badbury Rings, a purported site for the Battle of Mount Badon which marked Arthur's major victory against the Saxons. As a surveillance lookout, this ancient hillfort protected Wimbourne and Poole Harbor, visible a short distance to the south. Because encroachment from across the Channel could be detected early, Briton warriors could send an alarm inland and engage the enemy. Roads to the east led to Cadnam and Winchester, and beyond that, Chichester, protecting Southampton Water and Portsmouth. Roads to the northwest pointed to South Cadbury and connected with others leading north. Off the beaten track in the southern heartland, a western road pierced Dorchester (Durnovaria of Roman times) and continued its arrowed course to Axminster and Honiton, embracing one of the Cadbury sites, a possible Camelot location, six miles north of Exeter.

Sixty miles to the northeast of Badbury Rings was Roman Town, another hub with six roads fanning out in a ring-shaped pattern, connecting Icknield Way to the north, Caesar's Camp to the East, Winchester and Chichester to the south. Andover lies to the southwest, and a different Badbury, also a possibility of the Badon site, lies to the west. This southern perimeter protected the coast from Selsey Bill on the eastern border to the Vale of the White Horse near Swindon in the northeast.

A third major convergence was Cirencester, southeast of Wales. In a northern arc, roads ran to Gloucester, Leicester, and Bicester; to the south they pointed the way to Roman town and Bath. The webs here formed the northern borders of the civilian district, incorporating the Hwicce territory and the later West Saxon kingdom. Bath or the neighboring hillfort of Little Solsbury Hill near Batheaston is a third possible location of the Badon battle associated with the southern Arthur, and Gloucester reflects the connection to the western Arthur of Dyfed.

Within these boundaries, the webbing of Roman roads connects all the important sites of the south-central area, including the major ones associated with Arthurian history and lore. Old Sarum — called Sorviodunum by the Romans — is the strategic center, protected during the decades of Arthur but then invaded by the Saxons around 552. Stonehenge, one of the major mysterious wonders of the country, lies a short distance to the north, designated in legend as a burial place for such memorable figures as Aurelius Ambrosius and Utherpendragon. Little Solsbury Hill, Liddington Castle near Badbury, and Badbury Rings — three possible sites for Arthur's victorious Badon battle which catapulted him to fame — are nestled within the perimeter. Other familiar names such as Camelot, Avalon, and Camlann are also set in this protected arena where Arthur made his heroic stand against the continuous German Saxon onslaughts from across the Channel.

That there were continuous Saxon onslaughts from across the Channel is the trap which baits southern–Arthur advocates. Saxon incursions from the continent have been viewed in typical sequences first up the Thames Valley inland, then along the southeastern Kentish coast to Chichester and Portsmouth, and finally through the Solent and up Southampton Water, a route of the West Saxons. That Saxons comprised the major British adversaries must be accepted as true; Gildas (with Bede reiterating the information) writes of the ravages by the Saxons after they were invited in by Vortigern. Prior to the battle list in Chapter 56 of the *Historia Brittonum*, Nennius states outright that *all* the battles are fought by Arthur *against the Saxons*. Although Nennius' manuscript is sometimes a copy and thus not a verification of Gildas, in this instance he not only provides Badon as the last in a series, but he also gives 11 earlier battles not recorded anywhere else.

Nennius' details cannot be attributed to sly invention; to criticize Nennius for using skimpy pieces of historical information or to suggest that Nennius manipulates Gildas to build up Arthur's prestige as a national hero is to criticize all Arthurian scholars, since only the barest vestiges of historical material about Arthur exist. Nennius' own introduction of himself indicates that he is not a nefarious prevaricator. Literary tradition, antiquarians, and modern historians concur that the major Briton enemy after the Roman abandonment was the Saxons, on the island as well as in their homeland.

The identification of Saxons as the major adversaries not only points to the southern Arthur but also narrows the geographic possibilities of the battlesites listed by Nennius. Calculating mileage between locations in Goodrich's book, distances from one site to another for a northern Arthur would have been unmanageable. From a geographic regard this is a major difference between a northern and a southern Arthur. As a comparison, based upon the orthodox sites established by proponents for a southern Arthur, distances are much shorter and more feasible, especially when considering the network of Roman roads in southern Britain. In the south, Camelot (South Cadbury) is a distance of 16 miles via Roman roads to Arthur's burial site at Glastonbury; from Badon (Badbury Rings) to Camelot past Hod Hill and Hambledon Hill is 24 miles. Because no location has been solidified for Camlann, a comparison cannot be made between the southern Camelot and the Battle of Camlann. Hence, a southern Arthur would be in close proximity to Saxons from across the sea, whereby if Arthur is considered northern, near the two Walls, encroachment would require a journey of over 200 miles.

Yet accepting a southern Arthur solely on the premise of continental Saxon proximity ignores Arthur's Welsh roots and his name in Welsh annals, his enigmatic connections with Ambrosius the Emrys Gwledig whose title reflects Welsh heritage, and all the Welsh locales appearing in the *Historia.* This inspires a comparison of the southern and western Arthur. Intriguing clues suggest the two are actually a composite, once the seeming inconsistency — that Arthur cannot be Welsh and proximate to Saxons simultaneously — is reconciled. While archaeology affirms that Saxon penetration from the southern coast to Salisbury did not occur until 552, half a century after Badon, it also attests to heavy Saxon settlements and burial grounds near Gloucester, Cirencester and Cheltenham in the heart of Gewissae/Cornovii/West Saxon territory. Leslie Alcock writes:

> It is natural to believe therefore that the people whom Arthur fought against were either the Saxons in general, or specifically the kings of Kent. ... [I]t would be difficult to reconcile warfare [between Arthur and Octha] in south-eastern England [Kent] with such information as we have about Arthur.[5]

That Arthur fought against the Saxons is true; that Octha was a king of *Kent* is false. In the *Historia,* misleading headings added by later scribes improperly placed Octha in the southeast rather than in central Britain, near Caer Luit Coyt, where the main text of the *Historia* locates him. Octha was part of the Saxon settlements in the midlands, established there during the second Saxon *Adventus* when Saxons were still considered Briton allies.

In conjunction with the heavy Saxon settlements in the midlands, Alcock explains,

> Whereas the story in the *Chronicle* is of a band of adventurers landing in Southampton Water and battling their way inland over some three generations, archaeology demonstrates that the nucleus of Wessex was a peasant settlement in the mid and upper Thames valley, *going back a generation before the Chronicle date for Cerdic's landing* [italics mine].[6]

The middle Thames Valley cuts through West Saxon territory, and as a matter of fact, the upper Thames Valley and the source of the River Thames is only two miles southwest of Cirencester.

Alcock's crucial observation has several implications. One is that the ethnic group "Saxons" is not limited to continentals who persistently tried to invade Britain. "Saxons" can also refer to the prior two generations who settled in Britain, sanctioned not only by the Romans but later by the Britons themselves. The present text later distinguishes between the English Saxons (who were settlers on the island) and the German Saxons (continentals who are newcomers). The second implication is equally enlightening. Although the West Saxon dynasty is portrayed as *German* Saxons assailing Britain from the Southampton Water *northward*, Cerdic's tribe were *English* Saxons trying to pierce the civilian heartland *southward*. Wales and Gewissae are neighboring territories whose leaders are motivated by different goals, inevitably leading to continuous *internal* conflicts.

Saxons as the major Briton enemy as far to the west as Wales is at first difficult to reconstruct without in-depth scrutiny, but the Saxon threat in Wales is just as logistically defensible as a Saxon threat along the southern coast, and much more defensible than Saxon invasions near the Antonine Wall during the waning decades of the fifth century. Arthur, Beli Mawr, Coel, Cunedda, Vortigern, Ambrosius Aurelianus, and Octha are all listed in Welsh geneaology, but whereas the latter have been accepted as historical figures, Arthur is not accorded the same distinction, which in itself is puzzling.

Soundly formulated conjectures, then — built upon a foundation of authoritative histories, ecclesiastic records, archaeology, topography, philology, and etymology — tip the scale in favor of a southwestern Arthur. Details from literary tradition combine with those validated resources to substantiate further the general circumstances of his era; the northern counterpart cannot be verified with the same conviction as the southwestern Arthur, who became a renowned king and evolved into the central figure of the knightly tales. Using Barber's words, the merits of an acceptable conclusion must be based upon who wrote what and why, plus what prevailing individual and societal attitudes were.

The evidence places Arthur in the southwest between A.D. 420 and A.D. 520, beginning shortly after the Roman withdrawal from the island and ending at the Battle of Camlann when Arthur is "summoned from human activity." All (except one) of the historically significant characters appear in the *Historia*: Emrys Ambrosius, Vortigern, Vortimer, Vitalinus, Hengist, Octha, Cunedda, Owein Dantguin, and Cerdic. Judging by length and excluding the passages on Saints Germanus and Patrick, Vortigern and Ambrosius are the major figures. The pertinent narrative revolves around Vortigern the usurper and young Ambrosius; this "Tale of

Map 3. The five Britains of the Romans.

Emrys" emphasizes the important connection between these two individuals and Arthur, requiring a close inspection of their relationship. The background on Hengist and his Saxon clan ranks next in importance; Octha occupies a minor niche, but when details are gleaned from the *Anglo-Saxon Chronicle,* "Culhwch and Olwen," the "Dream of Rhonabwy" and the *History of the Kings of Britain,* his role becomes a major one, first as Arthur's ally and then as an enemy. Cerdic appears in two roles, both of which seem even more incidental than Octha's, but when he is linked as interpreter/son of Cunedda *and* the West Saxon king, his roles swell to mammoth proportions as Octha's comrade, as Arthur's friend and eventual arch-rival, and as a powerful English-Saxon leader. Details about Vortimer and Arthur in the *Historia* are about equally balanced, which is perhaps one of the reasons why some scholars claim that Vortimer is the Briton counterpart of the Roman Ambrosius and conclude that the two are doubles. And last, Vitalinus has a direct bearing upon the true identity of King Arthur, while Owein Dantguin plays a minor though important role.

The only significant historical *figure* who does not appear in the *Historia* is Riothamus. This is neither surprising nor unexpected, however, since Riothamus' operations take place on the continent. Because the *Historia* does not recount Arthur's Gallic encounters, Riothamus is passed over as an essential link to Arthur. Jordanes and Gregory of Tours verify Riothamus as a Briton king from beyond the Ocean fighting in Gaul, battles which Monmouth incorporates into his story, but under the leadership of Arthur. Between the Battle of Badon and the Battle of Camlann, Monmouth inserts a battle against King Gilmaurius of Ireland, a battle in Iceland, warfare in Norway, and then finally conflicts in Gaul, none of which are borrowed from Welsh sources. With this much emphasis on continental warfare, Arthur emerges more as a Gallic warrior, pointing to the possibility that Geoffrey's certain ancient source (as he claims) may be a Breton manuscript now lost, which could have had its basis in a bonafide Latin original.

This Gallic insertion by Monmouth led Geoffrey Ashe to perceive a connection between Riothamus and Arthur and to write a book postulating that Riothamus was a continental title referring to Arthur. This connection cannot be lightly dismissed or totally ignored. It is a valid concept, enhancing the portrayal of Arthur and offering a theory which parallels the hypothesis of this book — that Ambrosius and Arthur are terms referring to a single individual.

This possibility relates to several uncanny twists in Monmouth's narrative. Although Monmouth does not supply many dates, he does place Arthur's Gallic episodes between the 450s and the 480s, during the reign of Leo I, thus tying Arthur to a verified Roman emperor on the continent. Arthur's enterprises, therefore, fit into a coherent pattern when overlaid with Riothamus' voyage to the continent. Arthur's reign would continue to the end of the fifth century and beginning of the sixth. A second interesting item is that Monmouth confused Arthur and Ambrosius. According to his account, Arthur and Ambrosius would be uncle and nephew. Arthur is further described as having a sister, Ana, who marries Loth and has two sons, Gawain and Mordred. In a later section, however, Monmouth indicates that Ana was married to King Budic of a territory in Brittany and had a son named Hoel. Madeleine Blaess suggests that instead of Ana being Arthur's sister, she should be considered as Aurelius' (i.e., Ambrosius') sister. This leads to the speculation that, as Monmouth scrutinized "his ancient source," he overlooked the possibility that Arthur and Aurelius were both references to a single individual. This oversight would have caused the confusion over who Arthur's sisters are, and (important in the later romances) it would have provided grounds for the suggestion that there was an incestuous relationship between Arthur and a sister.

That Arthur is the same historical figure as both Ambrosius Aurelianus and Riothamus* is the major theory of this text, meaning that although not under the *nomen* of Arthur, the great king makes his debut over a century before Aneirin writes of a northern leader by that name. One of the requirements for seeking the "correct" Arthur who lies beneath the thick strata of the legendary romances is the investigation of any probable association between his name and a certain Lucius Artorius Castus in the histories, since several researchers suggest that Arthur's name might have derived from this individual's *nomen*, or middle name, normally indicating in Latin a person's *gens* or clan. The name of "Artorius" is rare during this era, but there is enough of a philological connection to explore the forms *Arthur, Artu, Artr, Arthu, Arddu,* and *Artorius.* The challenge becomes one of determining whether these appellations are proper names or epithets.

If the term "Arthur" is accepted as an epithet, then the link between the legendary king and Ambrosius Aurelianus must be the strongest in the chain. Gildas Badonicus does not name Arthur in the *De Excidio*, but just prior to writing about the Battle of Mount Badon, he records the name Ambrosius with very rare praise. The question of whether Gildas was ignoring Arthur as an individual or simply referring to him by his proper name instead of his title is answered by their associations depicted in the *Saints' Lives* and tales in literary tradition. Nennius, on the other hand, not only mentions Arthur by name but also attributes 12 battles to him. Yet he allots as much space to Vortimer and his four Saxon battles and describes Ambrosius Aurelianus in even more detail, increasing Ambrosius' stature by narrating his power as a wizard.

Richard Barber hints at the connection between Arthur and Ambrosius by writing that "On Gildas' evidence, it would be more reasonable to call [Badon] 'the *Ambrosian* fact.'"[7] The suggestion is that Arthur is more than just a natural successor to Ambrosius; his power, prestige, leadership qualities, and right to the throne stem directly from his ancestry. Gildas Badonicus does not refuse deliberately or with rancor to name Arthur as the Badon leader; instead, he identifies

*For want of a better term, "homolog" is used later in this text in an explicit, narrow context to express this idea. Homo- and -logo(s) are both Greek derivatives, the first meaning "same." The second suggests one word or thought embodying the essence of a separate word referring to the same nature or substance. For example, the word "Arthur" is similar to "Riothamus" in that they are both epithets for the historical figure Ambrosius Aurelianus. During the Arthurian era there was an overlap of four major languages — Latin, British, Welsh, and Saxon — so that one individual might be identified by four different names, plus perhaps several epithets; hence, those names and epithets may be termed homologs.

the leader by a proper name rather than an epithet, a man whom he respects, not disdains. Nennius handles the Arthurian material as a copyist; judging from his Preface, he is simply heaping together all manuscripts he found, from the Annals of the Romans and from the Chronicles of the Holy Fathers.

Through analysis of events on the continent during the same time frame, a similar equation indicates that Riothamus is not a name either, but is another title referring to Ambrosius Aurelianus. Accepting Ashe's theory that Riothamus is Arthur, the hypothesis in this text ventures further by proposing that Ambrosius Aurelianus is Riothamus; the result is a triumvirate that blends Ambrosius Aurelianus, Riothamus, and Arthur, in that order. This not only gives a chronological span for the 12 battles listed by Nennius, but it ties into literary sources which relate that Arthur became king at age 15 (as Ambrosius Aurelianus), fought battles on the mainland against the Saxons (as Riothamus), and returned to Britain where he continued to engage the Saxons in battle until his death at Camlann (as Arthur), a progression that makes these circumstances chronologically feasible.

The Battle of Camlann is the only significant *event* that does not appear in either the *Historia* (which does not even hint at it) or the *De Excidio* (which suggests it very vaguely in Chapter 26.3). The *Annales Cambriae* gives only its typical brief notice (eight words long in its original Latin) before moving to an equally brief entry of the plague in Britain and Ireland. One problem of the Camlann entry is that its mystery is intensified by the mention of Medraut, whose introduction creates a tempting sidetrack to determine whether this figure really existed as Arthur's son by incest, whether he was a traitor, or whether he died as Arthur's ally. But because Arthur's verifiable historicity is the main target, this text does not elaborate on Medraut.

Much more difficult than calibrating Camlann's date, since there is a chronological starting point supplied by the *Annales Cambriae*, is its geographic location. There are two equally plausible possibilities. One, already suggested and analyzed by previous researchers, is Camboglanna at the western end of Hadrian's Wall, a probability because Cunedda migrated from the north to this location, and his offspring could logistically have fought a desperate battle there. The second is equally logical; after the 12 battles recorded in the *Historia*, the narration relates that the English sought help from the German Saxons, implying that the battle might have been fought on the southern coast, specifically near Charford as recorded in the *Anglo-Saxon Chronicle*. Both locations fit snugly into the historical scheme; both centralize the hotspots of action; both fit philologically the name of Camlann.

Though the geographic issue remains unresolved, the reality of Camlann is not negated. The scanty obituary of a king as renowned as Arthur is sometimes cited as proof that this king was not historical or authentic. Fortunately, the second part to the same entry is a disclaimer to that contention: the plague listed so briefly in this Camlann entry (and also the one listed in the Maelgwn entry of 547) killed thousands of people, but the brevity of the entry cannot deny its reality. The nature of annal entries — the *Anglo-Saxon Chronicle* and the Irish Annals in addition to the *Annales Cambriae*—is their brevity; the unusual ones are longer, a cause for suspicion. However, there are two other mysteries that shroud Arthur's passing: why the word "death" is not used in the *Annales* or in Geoffrey of Monmouth's account, and where Monmouth got his detailed information if it were not simply a figment of his imagination. There are postulations about his death and his burial, but the secrets remain secrets.

In structuring the quest for King Arthur's historicity, one difficulty was determining proper approaches that would give a comprehensive view of his era. One obvious possibility was chronology, using Gildas as a discrete launching point, even though his clue was confusing. Using the year he suggests for the Battle of Badon was the first step through a maze of Arthur's Dark Ages. By methodically substantiating other cardinal and ordinal years — two terms coined for this text to validate calibrations according to specific conditions — events were strung together based on enough evidence to formulate a defensible chronology. Each date had to be corroborated by a separate historical source or a reliable, ancient literary work. Upon completion of the chronology, the second process — termed "spatial order" or "order of location"—was to validate geographic locations by analyzing cause-and-effect relationships. Migrations up the Thames Valley and eastward, plus coastal movements from the Saxon Shores to Southampton Water, were the prime considerations for this approach.

Added to these two methods which are more objective by their nature, the last technique — termed "order of importance"—begins with general information followed by specific details producing a formula that the whole is the sum of its parts. Because Arthur was the central focus of the search, it was best to begin with the broad information about him, and then to fill in specific details from any of the available sources, including literary tradition. This approach was used for all of the major and minor figures associated with him; floruits and lifespans were devised for each, after which specific events from different sources were set into a sociometric chart. This revealed the sequence binding these personalities together and showed whose lives touched Arthur's. Some references supply background for Arthur only in an incidental way, but they are crucial in establishing an accurate historical milieu for Arthur and his contemporaries; the individuals who had no factual relevance (such as Utherpendragon) were not included. What crystallizes is a solid epic figure based firmly in time and space rather than an apparition of wispy substance.

In spite of the enigma of his death, the birth and life of a southwestern Arthur can be constructed from documented evidence, even within the procedural confines and ramifications of scientific inquiry. The result is an explicit chronology of an authentic post–Roman Welsh figure of the mid–fifth century whose meteoric rise to fame is attributed to two things. The first is his Roman heritage, expertise, and his inextricable link to the bonafide figures of Ambrosius Aurelianus and Riothamus; the second is his allegiance to the idea of the survival of the Britons. His major foes after the Roman withdrawal were English Saxons on the island plus the German Saxons and Visigoths in Gaul, and his allies were the Britons, the Bretons, the Gauls, and the Romans. And last, his geographic theaters of operation are identified as Wales and the midlands, the southern coast of the island, Brittany, and Gaul.

With the acceptance of these documented premises, a clear, composite panorama of historical happenings and the people who shaped those events emerges. Historical threads braid themselves into one continuous tale; seemingly unrelated entries in chronicles and annals become parallel or identical occurrences; literary references become storehouses of historical gems; philology contributes its share by revealing that many names — as symbols — can point to the same locale.

As an end result, the mists enveloping this great king are slowly dissolving to reveal a more complete, unembellished image of the legendary figure. Although the chronological and geographical precepts are absolutely essential, the most significant element is the definitive blend of Arthur–Ambrosius Aurelianus–Riothamus. In conjunction with their interrelationships with other figures, their milieu turns out to be a 100-year history of the Dark Ages, since it is impossible to piece together the Arthurian era without deciphering ancillary historical events. The quest for Arthur's historical authenticity does not deal with twelfth and thirteenth century portrayals of chivalrous knights. There are no Walt Disney productions of Excalibur; Lancelot and Guinevere do not form two sides of a love triangle with the king; Merlin does not wrap Utherpendragon in magical mists so that the king can seduce Igraine; the Holy Grail and the bleeding lance are not introduced as profound symbols. Instead, the excitement comes from discovering the roots of this magnificent figure and what accomplishments assured him a place in immortality.

Chapter 2
The Ancient Manuscripts

In spite of discouragement because most of the material on Arthuriana is several centuries removed from Arthur's time, there are several documents in combination which can still give dependable historical data of that period. Four major ones, the closest sources to the historic King Arthur, are accepted as historically rooted and most reliable. The first is the *De Excidio* by Gildas Badonicus, the surname added to distinguish him from Gildas Albanius, a near-contemporary to the author who died in France around 512. The second, the *Annales Cambriae*, is published most of the time along with the third, the *Historia Brittonum*, since both are part of the *Harleian MS 3859*. The *Historia* has 18 variant manuscripts or fragments, dating from the 900s through the 1300s. The last is actually a combination of the *Anglo-Saxon Chronicle* and its Genealogical Preface. Whereas the first three of these ancient sources are Briton/Welsh, this is English/German Saxon. There are six versions of the *Chronicle*, plus two fragments; more than likely, a Genealogical Preface was attached to Manuscript B, as with Manuscript Ā.[1]

There are other important though minor sources used, two which are supplements. The first is Bede's manuscript, *A History of the English Church and People*, dated to the middle of the eighth century. Bede used other sources heavily, particularly Gildas, and as Morris writes,

> Before 597, Bede is a secondary writer; all the sources that he knew are extant, known to us independently; and many other texts are known which were not available to Bede. ... [Bede's readers] can learn nothing from his introductory chapters that they could not also learn elsewhere.[2]

Bede, like Gildas, does not name Arthur and mentions Ambrosius Aurelianus only once; nevertheless, he offers a slightly different perspective and gives a slight variation of details. One of his main contributions to historical writing is his standardized use of the Dionysiac Table for reckoning; he used some of the regnal years for Roman emperors or British kings where it seemed best, unifying some of the calibrations from his sources.

The second supplement is *The Chronicle of Æthelweard*. At first it appears to be a duplicate of the *ASC* with a slight tinge of the Genealogical Preface, but there are crucial variances. Specifically, some one-year discrepancies show up not in a numerical date but in the introductory sentence of the succeeding entry. Additionally, some facts are not recorded in other sources, such as entry 500 suggesting "acquisition" and not "conquest" of Wessex, and entry 519 adding the detail of the River Avon. Other than the one-year shortcomings, a more serious flaw is his failure to distinguish between Briton and Welsh.

Gildas Badonicus

The full title for Gildas' work from the old translation is *The Epistle of Gildas the most ancient British Author: who flourished in the yeere of our Lord 546. And who by his great erudition, sanctitie, and wisdome, acquired the name of Sapiens.*[3] The manuscript has 110 "chapters." Chapter 1 is a fairly long General Preface, and similar to Nennius he decries his writing talents before giving a preview of castigations. Chapters 2 through 26 are generally labeled "The History of Britain" and include the coming of the Saxons and the Briton victory at Mount Badon. Chapters 27 through 65 are termed "The Complaint About Kings," and 66 through 110 comprise a counterpart titled "The Complaint About Clergy."

Most of the manuscript is basically irrelevant for the purpose of tracing Arthur, but the fragments of useful information gleaned from it are major keys for unlocking the historicity of King Arthur, which may seem surprising since Gildas does not allude to that name. His contributions to Arthuriana are based upon four segments:

A. Chapters 19, 20, and 21 narrate the Roman withdrawal from the island and the encroachment of *barbarci* tribes to the Wall from the north, the significant letter to Aetius, famine, a respite from Irish and Pictish attacks, prosperity, and then a plunge into licentiousness.

B. Chapters 23, 24, and 25 are a sweeping history of the pre–Arthurian period beginning with the advent of the Saxons, the devastation they wrought on the island, and the salvation by Ambrosius Aurelianus who salvaged a country on the brink of total destruction. Under the banner of Ambrosius, the wretched survivors attained a victory.

C. Chapter 26 is the core of the Arthurian chronology. Gildas writes about the Battle of Badon (Badonici montis) in which his countrymen are victorious and, equally important, gives a brief history of the conditions on the island, making a distinction between foreign and domestic wars.

D. Chapters 33 through 36, although exclusive of specific references to Arthur, furnish information about Maglocune. These chapters contribute to a general chronological framework establishing Arthur's historical relevance.

From the outset it is important to remember that although Gildas was writing during the sixth century, the translation of the manuscript being used as a reference is the oldest actual manuscript in existence, termed the Cottonian MS Vitellius A VI dating from the *eleventh* century. Both O'Sullivan and Alcock allude to this particular version.[4] There are later manuscripts of the twelfth and thirteenth centuries, plus the Cambridge manuscript of circa 1400. Nothing, however, is older than the eleventh century version except witnesses to Gildas' original in the form of quotations and paraphrases from Bede, and glossaries dating to the late eighth century.[5]

The interpolations and postulations about Gildas are prolific. Thomas O'Sullivan lists Gildas as a Welsh-Breton saint "who flourished in the first half of the sixth century," yet as straightforward as this statement appears, even it is open to debate. O'Sullivan gives a later suggestion that the *De Excidio* is not of the sixth century but of a significantly later date. He also cites Thomas Wright, who believed that this particular manuscript sounded like Aldhelm of Malmsbury and dated the work as having been written in the latter part of the seventh century,[6] which would mean that Gildas is further charged as being a forgerer.[7] There are other criticisms by Alfred Anscombe, who believes that the manuscript was written by an anonymous monk of Gwynedd around 655,[8] and by Arthur Wade-Evans who attacks Gildas' accuracy by claiming that 547 is far too late for Maelgwn's death and should be altered to 502.[9] In a meticulous, scholarly manner, O'Sullivan documents all of these assertions, each of which offers validity for its claim.

Much of the controversy, however, can be bypassed, since it deals with finer points of scholarship which do not affect Arthurian matter. For example, the charge that Gildas is a forgerer is insignificant; whether Aldhelm of Malmsbury was the author or some anonymous monk penned the manuscript is a complex issue obscuring the important emphasis of structuring a chronology that establishes Arthur's historicity. However, substantiating the accurate year of Maelgwn's death, the Aetius letter, and the Battle of Badon are integral components for Arthur's claim to reality; without a reliable chronology, the figure of Arthur crumbles.

There are many reasons the Badonicus manuscript is so important in the Arthurian quest. Although the passage in the *De Excidio* about Gildas' birth-year is difficult to interpret, using it to calibrate the penning of the manuscript is important. Most scholars agree that it dates to the mid–sixth century. Ashe set the date "somewhere about 545"[10]; Leslie Alcock states that "The date of the *De Excidio* itself has usually been placed about 530 and certainly no later than 540, give or take five years."[11] Further on, Alcock verifies that the *DE* has a customary date "that we must place before 549."[12] In *Was It Camelot?*, Alcock lists the date (inadvertently off by a century in the original edition) of the *DE* as A.D. 542.[13] John Morris gives a similar date when he writes, "About 540, the priest Gildas published [sic] a forthright attack on the princes and bishops of his day."[14]

Dates given by scholars, then, are reasonably close to the mid 500s; giving a chronological fix on Gildas and the writing of the *DE* also allows a fix on two of Arthur's battles, the Battle of Mount Badon and the Battle of Camlann. Additionally, it coordinates with information from the *ASC* so that parallel entries can be compared to the two battles listed in the *AC*, with the verification of at least one (Badon) provided also by Gildas. In the next chapter, the validity of these dates are verified by establishing a cardinal year for the penning of the *DE* as well as one for Maelgwn's death.

Another important reason for examining Gildas is satellite historical information. In Chapter 23 Gildas writes,

> Then all the councillors, together with that [*superbus tyrannus*] were so blinded, that, as a protection to their country, they sealed its doom by inviting in ... the fierce and impious [*Saxones*], a race hateful both to God and men, to repel the invasions of the northern nations.[15]

Typical of Gildas, he uses only the terms *superbus tyrannus* (proud tyrant, supreme ruler), *Saxones*, and the common expression, "northern tribes"; later translators of the *De Excidio*, the *Historia Brittonum*, and the *Anglo-Saxon Chronicle* supply more explicit names. Vortigern is the name assigned to the *superbus tyrannus*, and the word *Saxones* is an early Latin generic term for strangers who had arrived from the continent, not in reference to a single nation, but generally Germanic tribes including "Old Saxons," Angles, and Frisians. Even the names "Scots " and "Picts" have to be assigned as the proper names for the northern tribes. Hengist and Horsa, named in later manuscripts as the Saxon leaders, displace history by about 15 years; these two Saxons did not arrive until the second *Adventus*.

However, the names for the northern tribes — the Scots and the Picts — provide the cue that Chapter 19, where Gildas *does* refer to the hordes of Scots and Picts ravaging the island right up to the high wall, must be viewed as a parallel to chapters 23 and 24. Gildas first writes in broad generalities (Chapter 19), then becomes more specific (Chapter 23) when he narrates the same events of the Britons handling the invasions from the northern tribes once the Romans leave: they curb the northern attacks by recruiting Saxons from the eastern part of the island (Britannia Secunda), whom he equates with the "sacrilegious easterners" (orientali sacrilegorum) in Chapter 24, the rebellious pagan traitors.

This sequence can be simplified:

1. The Romans abandon Britain because of their crumbling empire and troubles on the continent. (Chapter 19)
2. The Scots and the Picts pillage the north up to Hadrian's Wall. (Chapter 19)
3. The British appeal to Aetius for help, but none is forthcoming. (Chapter 20)
4. Famine ravages the land; the Britons finally succeed in resisting not only their northern attackers but the Irish; peace and prosperity return. (Chapter 21)
5. By very vague inference (which is analyzed later), the English Saxons, hired as guards and allies, have contributed to the peace and prosperity. (Chapter 23)
6. But vice flourishes beside luxury, even among the kings. (Chapters 21, 22)
7. Quarrels and hatred spring up between the Britons and the Saxons and there is a revolt by the sacrilegious easterners. (Chapters 23, 24)

By A.D. 455 (*ASC* reckoning) war broke out between Vortigern and the two brothers Hengist and Horsa. The entry relates that Horsa was killed, and although no suggestion is made of Vortigern being killed, his name does not appear any more in the *Chronicle*.

This gives rise to the next important part of Chapter 25 from Gildas:

> After a time when these cruel robbers had gone home, ... the poor remnants of our nation took arms under the conduct of Ambrosius Aurelianus a modest man, who of all the Roman nation was then alone in the confusion of this troubled period by chance left alive. His parents, who for their merit were adorned with the purple, had been slain in these same broils, and now his progeny in these our days, although shamefully degenerated from the worthiness of their ancestors, provoke to battle their cruel conquerors, and by the goodness of our Lord obtain the victory.[16]

Near the 460s, then, Ambrosius Aurelianus was victorious over the rebellious English Saxons, who returned to their homeland (apparently to Britannia Secunda) since they were second or third generation on the island and not Germanic.

Victories then alternated back and forth until the Battle of Badon. Gildas writes that this state of affairs

> ... lasted right up till the year of the siege of Badonici montis which was ... forty-four years and one month after the landing of the Saxons, and also the time of my own nativity.[17]

Both the Saxon landing and Gildas' birth-year are appropriately postponed until the analysis of the *Annales Cambriae* and their calibration as cardinal or ordinal years, but the omission of Arthur's name is a focal point. As already shown, the omission of names in the *DE* is not at all uncommon, but in this instance it is important to clarify the omission because of the confusion between Gildas Albanius and Gildas Badonicus.

As Alcock points out, because Vortigern's and Ambrosius' historicity has never been questioned, neither should Arthur's be; he attests to their genuineness:

> Their claim to historicity is based on contemporary or near-contemporary notices: of Ambrosius by Gildas, of Vortigern in the *calculi* at the head of the British Easter Table compiled in 455, and of Arthur in the British Easter Annals. ... There would have been no occasion for later ages to attribute the victory to Arthur, still less to invent Arthur for the purpose. In this sense, Ambrosius is the touchstone to prove the genuineness of Arthur.[18]

The passage avers that even though Gildas does not use Arthur's name, Arthur is nevertheless a real person, yet this still evades the issue of who the leader was at Badon. The *Annales Cambriae* and the *Historia Brittonum* list Arthur as the leader, but the *De Excidio* does not. Why?

Geoffrey Ashe offers an explanation for why Gildas does not name the victorious Briton leader:

> Arthur was unmentionable, a deliverer who he [Gildas] could not attack yet would not praise. The Welsh Life of St. Gildas, by Caradoc of Llancarfan, at least hints at

strained relations. According to this, Gildas was a northern Briton, one of the many sons of Caw, who lived near the Clyde. Most of them were driven by Pictish raids to migrate to Wales. The eldest, however, named Hueil, stayed in the north. The brothers fought against Arthur — described as a tyrannus and rex rebullus claiming to rule all Britain — until Hueil was captured and put to death. Gildas was the family spokesman in demanding compensation, and Arthur had to pay.[19]

This, however, becomes a moot defense, since it is a reference to Gildas Albanius. There might have been "bad blood" between Arthur and Albanius, but it would have had no effect on the author of the De Excidio.

There is, of course, a simpler explanation: Ambrosius Aurelianus is in fact the leader at the Battle of Badon. In the last sentence of Chapter 25, Gildas writes that Ambrosius Aurelianus was victorious against the enemy. In the first sentence of Chapter 26 Gildas then indicates that ensuing victories alternated. In the sentence immediately following, he writes of the Battle of Mount Badon. Unquestionably Ambrosius was the victor in the initial battle and the back-and-forth successes after that; there is no other leader who could have intervened. Even so, one might think, like Alcock, that if Ambrosius had been the leader at Badon, Gildas would have magnified that hero's success by re-mentioning his name. Yet because the sequence is so rapid, it is not unreasonable to assume that Ambrosius retained leadership, particularly after his initial victory, and that Gildas did not use the name Ambrosius again because the transition from one sentence to the next was obvious. One could easily — and correctly — assume that Ambrosius was the famous leader.

There are two separate items which will be detailed later but which merit notice here. One is Giles' translation of "Badonici montis," Bath-hill. Some translations refer to the scene of the battle as Badonis, Badonicus, Badon, and Mount Badon, which suggest etymological connections with locations bearing the root "Badbury": Badbury Rings, Badbury Hill, or Baumber. Other translations use the terms Baddon, Bathon, Vaddon, and Vathon, suggestive of an association with "Bath," since all the associations with the latter are pronounced with an unvoiced "th-." Giles' interpretation, therefore, supports the connection with Bath. The second noteworthy detail is Gildas' wording about the "last almost" battle, which will later be superimposed on material in the ASC. The Britons defeated the English, and a period of peace followed, but Badon was not the last battle between the the the two; the Chronicle records subsequent skirmishes and attacks.

Another item worthy of note because of Arthurian connections is Gildas' castigation of British princes. Maglocunus plays a very important role not only in helping to calibrate the date for the penning of the De Excidio, but also because of his lineage. Of all the kings, Gildas denounces him most severely. As the affix in his name suggests, he has kindred ties with Cuneglasus (one of the other kings whom Gildas reviles), Cunedda, Cunorix (whose marker was discovered at Viroconium), and Cunobelinus. Another interesting revelation is that three of the five tyrants have kingdoms in Wales: Constantine of Dumnonia, Vortipor of Dementae, and Maglocunus of Gwynedd. A third important fact gleaned from the denunciations of the kings is the verb tense in which this section is written. At the time the *De Excidio* was written, all five of the tyrants were living.

The last piece of information, although garbled because of its grammatical structure, calibrates Gildas' birth year. If Gildas was born in the same year as the Battle of Badon, then he is writing the *DE* 42 years later. The only difficulty, of course, is confirming a date for the Battle of Mount Badon, considering the chronological differences among the Dionysiac Table, the Victorian Table, and the possible discrepancies between the Easter Tables and their transcriptions into the Easter Annals. This is the third item which will be proposed in more detail later.

Bede offers several different perspectives. In Book I, Chapter XV, he writes

> In the year of our Lord 449 Marcian, forty-sixth from Augustus, became emperor with Valentinian and ruled for seven years. At that time the race of the Angles or Saxons, invited by Vortigern, came to Britain in three warships and by his command were granted a place of settlement in the eastern part of the island, ostensibly to fight on behalf of the country, but their real intention was to conquer it.[20]

He puts the coming of the Angles and Saxons at about 446: Maurice becomes emperor in 582; the fourteenth year of this emperor was 150 years after the coming of the Angles and Saxons to Britain (582 + 14 - 150 = 446 [page 69]). In Book II, Chapter XIV, Bede indicates that the year of our Lord 627 was about 180 years after the coming of the English to Britain, bringing the date to about 447 (page 187). In Book V, Chapter XXIII (page 561), he writes, "This is the state of the whole of Britain at the present time, about 285 years after the coming of the English to Britain," giving the year of 446. These passages do exemplify Bede's care and accuracy in transcribing important factual information.

His *History* uses Pliny and Constantine as sources other than Gildas. For the part which concerns Arthur at the end of the Roman rule when the Britons were responsible for their own protection, however, Bede draws upon Gildas, although as Colgrave and Mynors point out, there are many additions and explanatory notes of his own.[21] To give a flavoring of Bede and a comparison to Gildas, this translation of Chapter XVII deals with the Arthurian period:

> When the army of the enemy had exterminated or scattered the native peoples, they returned home and the Britons slowly began to recover strength and courage. ... Their leader at that time was a certain Ambrosius Aurelianus, a discreet man, who was, as it happened, the sole member of the Roman race who had survived this storm in which his parent, who bore a royal and famous name, had perished. Under his leadership the Britons regained their strength, channeled their victors to battle, and, with God's help, won the day. From that time on, first the Britons won and then the enemy were victorious until the year of the siege of Badonici montis, when the Britons slaughtered no small number of their foes about forty-four years after their arrival in Britain.[22]

This passage indicates that Bede, like Gildas, minimizes the importance of Arthur and is not explicit about the Saxon homeland, but it additionally shows how information can be extrapolated from one copy to the next. For example, he sets Badon according to the landing of the Saxons and makes no reference to Gildas' birth. Second, going back to Gildas, Gildas writes that Ambrosius had progeny who were extant in Gildas' day and that Ambrosius' progeny were not honorable in the way their father had been but instead had degenerated from the worthiness of their ancestors. When Bede transcribes this, he makes no mention that Ambrosius had offspring, nor that his offspring's ethics and morals had deteriorated. And last, he relates that the Angles (Saxons) joined with the Picts to try to overcome the Britons, but he does not clarify the term English Saxons or acknowledge their intermingled culture and alliance with the Britons prior to a split.

The Annales Cambriae

Along with the *Historia Brittonum* (material attributed to Nennius), the *Annales Cambriae* is a part of the compilation titled the *British Harleian MS 3859*, or the *British Historical Miscellany*. The segment *AC* is sometimes termed the *Welsh Annals*, the *Easter Annals*, or the *British Easter Annals*.

The *Annales Cambriae* is very interesting because it provides crucial historical references to Arthur while at the same time being the origin for characters in the literary sources of 600 to 700 years beyond Arthur's historical roots. In the ancient manuscripts there are two entries which relate directly to Arthur's historicity: the Badon entry of his victory over the English Saxons, and the Camlann entry which tells of Arthur's summons from human activity. For reference, the Badon entry and its translation are

516 an. Bellum Badonis, in quo Arthur portavit crucem Domini nostri Jhesu Christi tribus diebus et tribus noctibus in humeros suos et Brittones victores fuerunt.[23]

516 The Battle of Badon, in which Arthur carried the Cross of our Lord Jesus Christ three days and three nights on his shoulders [shield] and the Britons were victorious.

The Camlann entries are

537 an Gueith Camlann in qua Arthur et Medraut corruerunt, et mortalitas in Britannia et in Hibernia fuit.[24]

537 The Battle of Camlann, in which Arthur and Medraut fell; and there was death in Britain and Ireland.

Other entries tie to the romances of the thirteenth and fourteenth centuries. One of the latter entries for the year 573 states in part, "Merlinus insanus effectus est,"[25] translated as "Merlin went mad." Two entries later, for the year 580 is "Guurci et Peretur (filii Elifer) moritur,"[26] translated as "Gwrgi and Peredur, (sons of Elifert) died." Both Merlin and Peredur (who probably becomes Percival) appear in the medieval romances as Arthur's trusted allies. The name Belin appears at entry 627, describing his death, but this is almost a century after the Camlann entry, and there is no real evidence that Belin might refer to Balin who was one of Arthur's knights. Almost 300 years after Camlann, the name of Owain (Eugein in the original) appears in entry 811 as an obituary. This particular Owain, though, is not the same Owein who appears in *The Mabinogion* since the *Tales* relate that Owein was son of Uryen, while the Owain in the *Annales* was the son of Maredudd. There seems to be, however, a connection between Owein of the *Mabinogion* and Yvain of the later romances, but evidently there is no connection with Owain. The name Uryen as Owein's father draws attention to the early decades of the 600s in the *AC*. Entries 617 and 626 contain the name of Edwin (Etguin) as the son of Urien, but again the connection between Urien and Uryen as Owein's father is vague. All of this signifies the necessity for extreme caution in making associations between the later romances and the reality of Arthur's era.

In listing these *Annales* as a primary source for the historicity of Arthur, it should be underscored that this is not just one source but a conglomerate of previous sources upon which it is based. Most often, too, it is printed with Nennius' *Historia Brittonum* appearing first. David Dumville writes that the *AC*

> ... seem to take their origin at St. Davids in Dyfed at the end of the eighth century. The earliest text, "A," is a version created, probably also at St. Davids, in the middle-years of the tenth century: it survives only in a copy (very likely made directly from a Welsh manuscript of that date) by an Anglo-Norman scribe active *ca* 1100 at an as yet unidentified church. Since the compiler of the A-text of *Annales Cambriae* was working no later than the middle of the tenth century ... he had access to an Irish annalistic manuscript substantially older than any directly available to us.[27]

This observation reinforces the present text's claim that the chronology in Arthuriana must remain adaptable by a few years since the texts used by modern scholars are copies of copies open to scribal errors, and hence "it is not to be wondered at that chronological discrepancies of a very few years might be found."[28]

Therefore, an excellent launching point for any study addressing the chronology for Arthur is the section of *Harleian MS 3859, Annales Cambriae,* an offshoot of the Easter Tables. Originally these tables were ecclesiastic manuscripts devised from necessity because Easter was a holy day which varied on the calendar. Church scholars prepared the tables to show the dates when Easter would fall for a number of years so that the churches could celebrate the Christian year correctly. The *anni Domini* (Years of our Lord) were listed in columns, either three or four to a page. An actual year was recorded every decade, followed by *an. (anno)* with a blank to the right for recording information. Calibration for these *Annales* was originally based upon the Great Cycle Easter Table of 533 years, established from the calculations of Victorius of Aquitaine, which therefore is reckoned from the Passion of Christ based upon astronomical *desiderata.*[29] On the Paschal question, Dumville is also of the opinion that "the stress in the *Annales Cambriae* on the correct mode of calculating Easter has suggested that it took shape soon after the resolution of the Easter-question."[30]

Anni Domini	Incid-tiones	Epactae	Concur-rentes	Ciccli lunares	Dies XIIII lunae	Dies paschae	Luna ipsius [diei]	
DCCCCLXIX	XII	Nulla	IIII	XVII	Non. aprelis	III id. aprelis	XX	
DCCCCLXX	XIII	XI	V	XVIII	VIII id. aprelis	VI kal. aprelis	XVI	
DCCCCLXXI	XIIII	XXII	VI	XIX	Idus aprelis	XVI kal. mai	XVII	
B DCCCCLXXII	XV	II	I	I	IIII non. aprelis	VII id. aprelis	XIX	
DCCCCLXXIII	I	XIII	II	II	XI kal. aprelis	X kal. aprelis	XV	
DCCCCLXXIIII	II	XXV	III	III	IIII id. aprelis	II id. aprelis	XV	
DCCCCLXXV	III	VI	IIII	IIII	III kal. aprelis	II non. aprelis	XIX	
B DCCCCLXXVI	IIII	XVII	VI	V	XIIII kal. mai	IX kal. mai	XIX	Obitus eadgari regis
DCCCCLXXVII	V	XXVIII	VII	VI	VII id. aprelis	VI id. aprelis	XV	
DCCCCLXXVIII	VI	VIII	I	VII	VI kal. aprelis	II kal. aprelis	XVIII	
DCCCCLXXIX	VII	XX	II	VIII	XVII kal. mai	XII kal. mai	XIX	Hic interemtus est rex eadweardus
B DCCCCLXXX	VIII	I	III	VIII	II non. aprelis	III id. aprelis	XXI	
DCCCCLXXXI	IX	XII	V	X	IX kal. aprelis	VI kal aprelis	XVII	
DCCCCLXXXII	X	XXIII	VI	XI	II id. aprelis	XVI kal mai	XVIII	
DCCCCLXXXIII	XI	IIII	VII	XII	Kal. aprelis	VI id. aprelis	XXI	
B DCCCCLXXXIIII	XII	XV	II	XIII	XII kal. aprelis	X kal aprelis	XVI	
DCCCCLXXXV	XIII	XXVI	III	XIIII	V id. aprelis	II id. aprelis	XVII	Depositio adelwoldi episcopi
DCCCCLXXXVI	XIIII	V	IIII	XV	IIII kal. aprelis	II non. aprelis	XX	
DCCCCLXXXVII	XV	XVIII	V	XVI	XV kal. mai	VIII kal. mai	XXI	

Table 1. Easter Table, late tenth century.†

†*Fredrick E. Warren, ed.,* The Leofric Missal, *page 50.*

Year of Our Lord	Golden Number	Epact	Sunday Letter	Sunday After Epiphany	Septuagesima Sunday	First day of Lent	Easter day	Rogation Sunday	Asension Day	Whitsun Day	Sundays After Trinity	Advent Sunday
1875	XIV	23	C	Two	Jan. 24	--10	Mar. 28	--2	--6	--16	26	--28
1876	XV	4	BA	Five	Feb. 13	Mar. 1	Apr. 16	--21	--25	June 4	24	Dec. 3
1877	XVI	15	G	Three	Jan. 28	Feb. 14	--1	--16	--10	May 20	26	--2
1878	XVII	26	F	Five	Feb. 17	Mar. 6	--21	--26	--30	June 9	23	--1
1879	XVIII	7	E	Four	--9	Feb. 26	--13	--18	--22	--1	24	Nov. 30
1880	XIX	18	DC	Two	Jan. 25	--11	Mar. 28	--2	--6	May 16	26	--28
1881	1	0	B	Five	Feb. 13	Mar. 2	Apr. 17	--22	--26	June 5	23	--27
1882	II	11	A	Four	--5	Feb. 22	--9	--14	--18	May 28	24	Dec. 3
1883	III	22	G	Two	Jan. 21	--7	Mar. 25	--2	--3	--13	27	--2
1884	IV	3	FE	Four	Feb. 10	--27	Apr. 13	Apr. 29	--22	June 1	24	Nov. 30
1885	V	14	D	Three	--1	--18	--5	May 18	--14	May 24	25	--29
1886	VI	25	C	Six	--21	Mar. 10	--25	--30	June 3	June 13	22	--28
1887	VII	6	B	Four	--6	Feb. 23	--10	--15	May 19	May 29	24	--27
1888	VIII	17	AG	Three	Jan. 29	--15	--1	--6	--10	--20	26	Dec. 2
1889	IX	28	F	Five	Feb. 17	Mar. 6	--21	--26	--30	June 9	23	--1
1890	X	9	E	Three	--2	Feb. 19	--6	--11	--15	May 25	25	Nov. 30
1891	XI	20	D	Two	Jan 25	--11	Mar. 29	--3	--7	--17	26	--29
1892	XII	1	CB	Five	Feb. 14	Mar. 2	Apr. 17	--22	--26	June 5	23	--27
1893	XIII	12	A	Three	Jan. 29	Feb. 15	--2	--7	--11	May 21	26	Dec. 3
1894	XIV	23	G	Two	--21	--7	Mar. 25	Apr. 29	--3	--13	27	--2
1895	XV	4	F	Four	Feb. 10	--27	Apr. 14	May 19	--23	June 2	24	--1
1896	XVI	15	ED	Three	--2	--19	--5	--10	--14	May 24	25	Nov. 29
1897	XVII	26	C	Five	--14	Mar. 3	--18	--23	--27	June 6	23	--28
1898	XVIII	7	B	Four	--6	Feb. 23	--10	--15	--19	May 29	24	--27
1899	XIX	18	A	Three	Jan. 29	--15	--2	--7	--11	--21	26	Dec. 3
1900	I	0	G	Five	Feb. 11	--28	--15	--20	--24	June 3	24	--2

Table 2. Easter table, Anglican Church, *Book of Common Prayer.*††

††*John H. Blunt,* Book of Common Prayer, *The Church of England, page 84.*

Table 3. *Harleian Manuscript 3859*, Folio 190A. By permission of the British Library.

Table 4. Harleian Manuscript 3859, Folio 190B. By permission of the British Library.

The fill-ins to the right contained more than just ecclesiastic data; scribes inserted births and deaths of saints and kings, lengths of kings' reigns, wars, natural phenomena, epidemics, and other current events. Frequently, the details were interpolated by later scholars, sometimes causing problems for accurate calibration because it was impossible to differentiate between the original entry and later modifications. Nevertheless, the *Annales* is an excellent resource for chronological study. In addition to the obvious importance of the two entries which specifically name Arthur, the other historical and religious events are functionally essential for calibrating the Arthurian period.

Tables 3 and 4 exemplify the *Annales'* format, and Table 6 transcribes not only the format but also explains the shortcomings which give rise to errors. Note, for instance, in Table 3 that near the end of column 2, the beginning decade of lx (60) is marked, and carries over to column 3, two years prior to the Badon entry. However, there are eleven years assigned to that decade, a difficulty compounded because the very first entry on the page crosses all three columns. Similarly the 40th decade (xl) has only nine years following it. The two errors balance out over three decades, but sometimes the resolution is not that simple. The Badon entry is recorded two years after *anno* lxx (year 72), and the Camlann battle three years after xc (year 93).

The shocking realization is that for an entire *century* (444 to 544) the *Annales Cambriae* records only eight entries, including the two which name Arthur. Not only does this drive home the profound significance of Arthur in the entries, but it stresses the importance of other dates contributed by the *Annales*. The most important for calibrating the Arthurian span are, of course, Badon and Camlann, plus the death-years for Maelgwn and Gildas because these dates allow calibrations for the entire panorama of Arthur's span: Vortigern, the Saxon *Adventi*, Ambrosius, Cunedda's migration, Hengist, Cerdic, Octha. The *AC* celebrations of Easter are noted three times, at years ix, ccxxi, and cccxxiv. O'Sullivan lists these as Roman, Saxon, and Welsh respectively, apparently recording the years in which the annalists believed that the correct Easter cycle was introduced among the Romans, followed by the Saxons and the Welsh.[31]

Hence the Paschal controversy — which O'Sullivan indicates "erupted ... in the early days of the Canterbury mission ... during the sojourn of Saint Columban, around the first years of the seventh century" — assumes a major role in attempting to establish some sense of accuracy in tracing Arthur's chronology.[32] Bede, in Book V, Chapter 21, devotes approximately eight pages to the controversial issue surrounding Easter.[33] In a letter to Nechtan, King of the Picts, he writes:

> This calculation of Easter ... depends upon a cycle of nineteen years, which began to be observed by the Church long ago in the time of the Apostles, especially in Rome and Egypt, as I mentioned earlier.[34]

The 19-year cycle occurs frequently in all of the sources attached to the search for Arthur. Bede goes on to enumerate other names which play a role in determining a chronological base: Eusebius reduced the cycle to a clear system so that it could be understood by everyone because the fourteenth day of the moon fell in regular sequence; Theophilus drew up an Easter Table for the ensuing 100 years; Cyril drew up a Table for 95 years; Dionysius Exiguus added others which extended to Bede's day. These cycles can be configured for 532 years, after which a new cycle occurs.

Eusebius, as the deviser of the 19-year tables, became an exemplar by his work in the fourth century. His chronicle, the *Historia Ecclesiastica*, not only

> ... synchronize[d] the historical tradition of Rome with the legends of Greece, of the Near East, and of the Old Testament, [but] thereafter his chronicle of world history was [also] continued by many other writers. The Irish set themselves a comparable task, of synchronising the stories of their own pagan past with the world chronicles of Eusebius and of his successors. The earlier surviving versions preserve many of the European entries that were used to fix the dates of native events, but the later recensions omit them, copying only the native entries.[35]

John Morris explains further that Eusebius was the main manuscript for Bede's *History*, plus a source for the *AC*, since both quote from it independently and use passages which do not recur in other sources.[36]

Plummer supports this position by extending the definitions and distinctions of "chronicle" and "history" given just below in the section on the *ASC*. Sometimes there are other circumstances when a chronicle is put together as keys to unlock knowledge from other sources which have stored the information, but the source lacks the coordination to compile it in a logistic form. In clarifying the Eusebius chronicle, Plummer adds:

> So Eusebius' Chronicle serves as a key to his Ecclesiastical History. "In the chronicle the required facts are tabulated in proper sequence; in the history they must be sought out here and there with much pains, and pieced together."[37]

Bede used this approach in his *History*, which is why in Chapter 24 of Book V he expends the time and energy to devise a chronological summary. As an aside, this text takes the same viewpoint in coordinating historical with literary origins. It lends a repetitive nature to the chronologies of the later sections, but the process of adjusting, modifying, and developing is easier to trace to the final goal.

This leads to the question of chronological reliability as recorded in the *AC*. The *Annales* should not be viewed as sacred and untouchable in the conversion of dates from pagan times, through the other annals of its source, to the Victorian method of reckoning based upon the Passion of Christ, into the Paschal controversy, and beyond to the Dionysiac system based upon the Incarnation of Christ. As Easter tables and annals, these Cambrian works have an imputed rather than genuine accuracy. In addition to O'Sullivan and Dumville cited above, O'Sullivan refers to H.M. and N.K. Chadwick who suggest that behind the chronology of the *Annales Cambriae* are the Paschal Tables of Victorius of Aquitaine,[38] and Alcock in his research recognizes that an Easter Table may lie behind the dates in the Cambrian manuscript.[39] Morris retrogresses one more step and relates that

> The study of the Irish Annals does not concern Ireland alone. The English and the Welsh Chronicles derive both their form and their earlier entries directly from their Irish Exemplars. The "Cambrian Annals" are, for the fifth and sixth centuries, a transcript of the Irish Annals; of the first 22 entries, 18 are copied from the Irish, and only four British notices are inserted among them....[40]

This agrees with Chambers who writes "Their [the Badon and Camlann entries in the *Annales Cambriae*] general dating gets a good deal of support from the Irish annals...."[41] Of the first 22 entries that Morris refers to, with 18 of the 22 copied from the Irish, the only four which cover Arthur's time span are for the years 447, 458 (which is the passage on St. David and Patrick), the entry of 565 on the voyage of Gildas to Ireland, and 569 about the Synod of Victory between the Britons.

These difficulties in the *Annales*, although not insurmountable, are inherent in all aspects of the Arthurian search. In referring to the Paschal controversy specifically, O'Sullivan epitomizes the general problems. He writes,

> The literature of the Paschal question is, in short, not merely consistent but maddeningly insistent (to the taste of the modern reader) in its use of terminology and argumentation when it deals with this crucial problem of computation.[42]

Yet with the groundwork already laid by modern scholarship, there is no need to reconstruct repetitively some of the sound foundations which have been erected. Fortunately, the starting point is not from square one; the foundation need only be modified; then new structures can rise to complete the architectural design. The constructs of modern scholarship are utilized specifically in later chapters; here only the general contributions will be touched upon.

In establishing an overview for dating in the *AC*, Leslie Alcock calculated an *anno Domini* date,[43] but then discovered a possible two-year discrepancy by the time the Pelican edition of his book came out; this is a minor variation when considering the obstacles to accuracy.[44] In *British History* John Morris makes a two-year adjustment in his translation of the *Annales*, which accounts for the difference between the year he gives and the one given by Alcock.[45]

There are several other adjustments which must be checked. One other possibility is a 28-year differential between calculations based upon the Passion (Death) of Christ rather than the Incarnation (Birth). A second variation accounts for a 19-year difference because of lunar adjustments. Both of these changes, either a 19- or a 28-year variation in reckonings would create a significant difference. To further complicate matters, there is the ever-present possibility of scribal errors or interpolations. The further a manuscript is from its original source, the more these mistakes and incorrect additions are confounded. Once

Pre-Christian		Christian		Pre-Christian		Christian	
Arabic	*Roman*	*Arabic*	*Roman*	*Arabic*	*Roman*	*Arabic*	*Roman*
YEARS							
0	nulla	444	CDXLIV	30	xxx	474	CDLXXIV
1	i	445	CDXLV	35	xxxv	479	CDLXXIX
2	ii	446	CDXLVI	40	xl	484	CDLXXXIV
3	iii	447	CDXLVII	45	vl	489	CDLXXXIX
4	iv	448	CDXLVIII	50	l	494	CDXCIV
5	v	449	CDXLIX	55	lv	499	ID
6	vi	450	CDL	60	lx	504	DIV
7	vii	451	CDLI	65	lxv	509	DIX
8	viii	452	CDLII	70	lxx	514	DXIV
9	ix	453	CDLIII	75	lxxv	519	DXIX
10	x	454	CDLIV	80	lxxx	524	DXXIV
11	xi	455	CDLV	85	lxxxv	529	DXXIX
12	xii	456	CDLVI	90	xc	534	DXXXIV
13	xiii	457	CDLVII	95	vc	539	DXXXIX
14	xiv	458	CDLVIII	100	c	544	DXLIV
15	xv	459	CDLIX	105	cv	549	DIL
16	xvi	460	CDLX	110	cx	554	DLIV
17	xvii	461	CDLXI	115	cxv	559	DLIX
18	xviii	462	CDLXII	120	cxx	564	DLXIV
19	xix	463	CDLXIII	125	cxxv	569	DLXIX
20	xx	464	CDLXIV	130	cxxx	574	DLXXIV
21	xxi	465	CDLXV	135	cxxxv	579	DLXXIX
22	xxii	466	CDLXVI	140	cxl	584	DLXXXIV
23	xxiii	467	CDLXVII	145	cxlv	589	DLXXXIX
24	xxiv	468	CDLXVIII	150	cl	594	DXCIV

Table 5. Reckoning variations. Conversions for reckonings and systems.

the Badon entry is fixed, then the Camlann entry would be analyzed to determine its place in the scheme of things, related to but independent of the Badon entry. This format will be applied to any entry about Arthur, a slow but rewarding methodical process.

In spite of all this, establishing the reckonings of the *AC* is an excellent point of inception. Once an initial chronology is completed, those dates can be reconciled with other events. This will be done in the culminating chapters of this text, and after the analysis of all the methods of reckoning and the possibility of scribal errors or interpolations, then any adjustments, both historically and literarily, will be made in the final chronology.

The cautionary advice from Dumville and Morris, as well as others, is well

an † 444 — Days as dark as nights
an
an
an
an
an
an
an
an-453 — Easter altered by Pope Leo
an-X — 454 — St. Brigid is born
an
an
an-457 — St. Patrick goes to the Lord
an-† 458 — St. David is born   ◆
an
an
an
an
an-XX — 464
an-
an
an
an-468 — Death of Bishop Benignus   ◆
an.
an
an
an
an
an-XXX — 474
an-475
an
an
an
an
an
an
an
an-XL — 484
an-485
an-486
an-487
an-488
an-XC — 534
an
an
an-537 — Battle of Camlann
an
an
an
an
an

an-489
an-490
an-491
an-492
an-L — 494 (noted 1 yr. early)
an-L — 494 should be herein
an
an
an
an
an
an-501 — Bishop Ebur dies 350 yrs old
an
an
an-LX — 504 (noted 1 yr. early)
an-LX — 504 should be herein
an
an
an
an
an
an
an
an
an-LXX — 514
an
an-516 — Battle of Badon
an
an
an
an
an-521 — St. Columba born; St. B died
an
an
an-LXXX — 524
an
an
an
an
an
an
an
an
an
an
an
an
an-558 — Death of Gabran
an
an
an
an-562 — Columba went to Britain
an

an	an-CXX — 564
an-C—death of Ciaran	an-565 † Gildas Badonicus to Ireland ♦ ♦
an	an
an-547 — Plague; Maelgwn's death	an
an	an
an	an-569 † the Synod of Victory ♦ ♦ ♦
an	an-570 — Death of Gildas Badonicus ♦ ♦
an	an ♦ ♦ ♦
an	an
an	an
an	an-CXXX — 574
an-CX — 554	

Table 6. Transcription of Tables 3 and 4, Harley folios 190A and 190B. Because the Easter Annals in 190A and 190B are difficult to read, this transcription saves time and effort. The entries with daggers (†) are not entries in the original 190A and 190B folios, but are later additions. The three daggered entries marked with black diamonds ♦ (entries 458, 565 and 569) show a variance from Morris' transcription of the *Annales Cambriae* in *British History*, page 85. In Morris, the year heading of XX is followed by three *anno* blanks and then the entry on St. David's birth, which would technically be at the same year which lists the death of Benignus; the heading CXX is followed by five *anno* entries before the Voyage of Gildas; then comes the Synod entry with no intervening *anno* markings. In this adjusted table those three entries are properly placed at their *anno* markings. In Morris' transcription, a single diamond indicates where the entry for Saint David's birth appears; a double diamond denotes where the Gildas voyage is, and a triple diamond indicates the Synod entry. The value of this transcription, in addition to showing how difficult the three-column run-on entries are to read in the Easter Annals, is to indicate how few entries were recorded from the years 444 to 574.

taken. Dumville is referring to the death-year for Maelgwn, but his caution can be generalized for other entries of the *Annales*:

> In short, it would be most unwise to rely too heavily on the entry in the *Annales Cambriae*. It is a tenth-century Welsh adaptation of an Irish annal, of uncertain date, with the aid of information derived possibly — indeed probably — from an oral source. The Welsh text, into which the information is incorporated, itself has no detectable history as a text before the 790s.[46]

The 790s is a date close to Arthurian history, but even so, it does not nullify the important niche which must be accorded to the *Annales*. It nevertheless reinforces the necessity to verify a hypothesis with as many other sources as possible. From the onset, this is one of the basic premises of this text; a date or a location will be verified by as many other sources as possible. By establishing a chronological and geographic framework and then modifying it as many times as necessary may seem circular, spiral, evasive, or irresolute, but that built-in flexibility is an important requisite in the search for the historical Arthur.

Nennius

The work attributed to Nennius is the *Historia Brittonum*, a part of the *Harleian MS 3859*, sometimes catalogued as the *British Historical Miscellany*. According to Josephus Stevenson, the *Historia Brittonum* has two independent Prologues and no fewer than 18 variant manuscripts, including L_1 and L_2, dating from the tenth century through Manuscript R at the end of the fourteenth century.[47] It is also important to recognize Stevenson's three major propositions: one, that the *Historia* is the production of an unknown writer, sometimes attributed to Gildas or Mark the Hermit; two, that the *Historia* is ascribed to Nennius upon the sole authority of Prologues which cannot be traced to an earlier period than the twelfth century; and three, the variations in the different manuscripts show that the work has undergone several recensions.[48] Therefore, gleaning details from the various manuscripts and using that information in conjunction with other sources and verifications should not be considered a travesty when creating a chronological framework that confers a historical reality upon Arthuriana. The accounts of Germanus, plus Vortigern's incest with his daughter, seem to have formed no part of the original work, but

> the arrival of the Saxons, the manner in which they gained a footing in this island, the marriage of Vortigern with the daughter of Hengist [unnamed], and the surrender of Kent, have the appearance of genuine British traditions of considerable antiquity.[49]

The version which has been used for the present investigation is of the tenth century, "that text which ... is least vitiated by (such) extraneous matter."[50]

CHRONOLOGY

In his Preface to the *Historia*, Nennius apologizes for his ineptitude at trying to set down a record left incomplete and obscure by previous scholars and copyists. The first 30 chapters then concentrate upon details such as the six Ages of the World, an explanation of British and Irish origins including the reign of Brutus, plus a history of Roman Britain. These chapters—19 through 30—also give some background information to set the stage for material which directly relates to the Arthurian data.

Chapter 16, particularly in conjunction with his Prologue, is of interest because Nennius calculates various dates based upon the coming of the Saxons to his present year. In section 16 he writes, "From the year when the Saxons first came to Britain to the fourth year of king Mervyn [Mervin, Merfyn, Mermin, Mermini, Mermenus, Meruin, Meruini], 429 years are reckoned."[51] At this point, no "fourth year of king Mervyn" is given but can be reckoned from the two other pieces of information. First, the accepted date for the advent of the Saxons given by historians and scholars is the year 428; Mervyn's fourth year can be calculated easily by adding 429 years to the Saxon advent, giving the year 857. As a check, the last segment that Nennius lists in Chapter 16 gives calculations based upon the 19-year lunar cycles. He indicates that there has been a total of 45 lunar cycles of 19 years each, plus two years into the new cycle. That is $45 \times 19 = 855 + 2 = 857$, which Nennius lists as "this present year."[52] This gives a good verification for the year 857.

In this section Nennius not only indicates his method of reckoning — mentioning that his calculations are from the birth of the Lord and that he is calculating in 19-year lunar cycles — but he also reflects, specifically through his use of the word *ogdoad*, that he is fully aware of the Paschal controversy which had been debated vehemently and extensively in Britain and on the continent during the 600s and 700s. Nennius confirms his awareness of historical events to his era and earlier by his message in his Prologue. He writes

> I have presumed to deliver these things in the Latin tongue, not trusting to my own learning, which is little or none at all, but partly from traditions of our ancestors, partly from writings and monuments of the ancient inhabitants of Britain, partly from the annals of the Romans, and the chronicles of the sacred fathers, Isidore, Hieronymous, Prosper, Eusebius, and from the histories of the Scots and Saxons, although our enemies....[53]

Of the people Nennius names, Eusebius was a leading scribal scholar who wrote ecclesiastical histories and devised a system for the calculations of Easter in 19-year cycles.

The British king Mervin recurs in two other places. One is in Nennius' Prologue in a passage which reads

> This history therefore has been compiled ... in the 858th year of our Lord's incarnation, and in the 24th year of Mervin, King of the Britons....[54]

The year 858 is strikingly close as a further verification for the date of 857 in Chapter 16. Additionally, two other details of a chronological nature reveal themselves. One is that Nennius specifically uses the word "incarnation," a reference that his calculations for 858 were based upon Christ's *birth*, and not His Passion [death]. This indicates that a 28-year adjustment (the difference in reckoning between Christ's birth and death) does not have to be made for modern-day chronological reckoning. In other words, the reader is given a marker to indicate which system of reckoning has been used. As a matter of fact, this must be what John Morris did when he adjusted that date to 829.[55] A difficulty arises, however, with the phrase "in the 24th year of Mervin." The resolution here, with the support from Chapter 16 should be that the "24th year of Mervin" be emended to the "4th year of Mervin." This is not attributed lightly to scribal error — whether from Nennius or a later copyist — but after a host of other calculations, nothing else correctly manifests itself as the workable chronology.

The only other listing for Mervin is in the *AC*, year 844, which reads, "Merfyn dies. The battle of Cetill."[56] This, too, presents an inconsistency, but one which is not as difficult to resolve. If Mervin died in year 844, then it would be impossible for him to be in the fourth year of his reign in 857/8. Nennius leaves no doubt that he is basing his calculations on 19-year lunar cycles. However, the compilers of the *AC,* whomever they were, gave no hint of their form of reckoning. Assuming that the year is based upon the Incarnation of Christ, then the discrepancy is easily explained. If that entry is adjusted to the lunar cycle or the Passion of Christ, then the date would change Mervin's death from 844 to somewhere between 863 and 872. If the fourth year of his reign was in 857/8, then his reign would have ended somewhere between his ninth and eighteenth year.

All of the preceding calculations exemplify what has to be done to verify or authenticate each date in an Arthurian chronology. The process is a painstaking, tedious task. Each time one date is established, it must be verified, if that is possible, and then set into a milieu of other events to determine its workability. The information, plus the methods for calibration, exemplify why Nennius is a repository of crucial data. If this kind of analysis is true for items which relate only indirectly to Arthur, a reader can well understand the procedural involvement required for those things connected to him.

The Arthurian material in Nennius begins in Chapter 31. This section through Chapter 55 furnishes the backdrop for Vortigern, the Saxons, Cerdic, Vortimer, Vitalinus, and Ambrosius Aurelianus before naming Arthur in Chapter 56, in actuality the only chapter where the name Arthur is given in a historical context. His name also appears in Chapter 73, but that is in a legendary format under a section labeled "The Wonders of Britain." As part of *British Harleian MS 3859,* a reference to Arthur also appears in the *Annales Cambriae,* the third source of ancient manuscripts.

GEOGRAPHY

In the opening paragraph of his Preface, Stevenson writes that

The information which is extant ... of the work entitled "Historia Britonum" is so scanty, and the literary history ... is so obscure and contradictory, that we may despair of being able to decide, with any degree of accuracy, either as to the age, the historical value, or the authorship of this composition.[57]

He then goes on to enumerate, among other shortcomings, that

1. the "Historia Brittonum" is the production of an unknown writer, but conveniently ascribed to Nennius;
2. the work has undergone several recensions, obscuring its original form;
3. the miracles of Germanus seem to have formed no part of the original;
4. Vortigern's incest with his daughter is not derived from an early ms;
5. the St. Patrick Legend is unconnected with the context;
6. the genealogies of the Saxon monarchs and the *Miracles* formed no part of the original work.

An initial dejection would cause a researcher to reject the work as a useless resource, but upon closer examination, it is an invaluable key in unlocking the

Dark Ages. In spite of its shortcomings — including its jumble of some historical events which cannot be attributed to Nennius, even though he criticizes his own ineptitude — it offers a great deal. One is its "genuine British traditions of considerable antiquity"[58] through an array of historical figures and events, even though it lacks a precise chronology. Additionally, those historical figures and events, in conjunction with other ancient sources, do provide an accurate chronology.

And most important of all, the *Historia* is also an invaluable repository of proper names which, when deciphered, unveil the secrets of geographic locations hidden for so long. Alcock expresses interest where the Saxons were marauding in 428-29. The *HB* not only provides general answers but specifically sets the stage geographically for the entire Arthurian saga while at the same time providing an accurate analysis of an ancient manuscript independent of the renowned king. Both southern and northern Wales, plus a strip of provinces east of Offa's Dyke, provide the geographic groundwork for the advent of Arthur through the historical figures of Vortigern, Ambrosius Aurelianus, Vitalinus, Cerdic, Hengist, and Octha.

Sir Ifor Williams, who believes that an original of the *HB* was written just before A.D. 800, offers this information as underpinnings for his claim:

> Welsh has arrived pretty definitely by 800. Corroboration is provided by the Welsh extracts and glosses in an Oxford manuscript in the Bodeleian (Ox. I) written in A.D. 820; as well as by the Welsh form of all the royal names on the Pillar of Elisedd, near Llangollen, set up probably about 810-20. … If neither Nennius, the disciple of the great Bishop Elfoddw, nor the royal scribe of Powys felt any qualms about writing these Welsh names about the year 800, it is safe to assume that the language by this time was well established, and we may say that the British inflexions had been shed a century earlier, to say the least.[59]

Some of his citations date from the fifth century to the early sixth. He then bases further claims on the "many names in their Welsh form, and common nouns as well."[60] Through careful analysis of the poems of Llywarch Hen, he reaches a conclusion which becomes crucial in being able to identify the geographic locations provided in the *Historia*. He writes:

> Most of these names, if correctly identified, belong to the border districts from Kerry, Berriew up to Oswestry. On the other hand, the Lywarch tales are staged at first in the Rheged district of south-west Scotland; then the scene shifts to Powys… Rhyd Forlas is a stream running into the River Ceiriog. … *Sawyl* … was buried at Llangollen.[61]

Neither the geographies for the Nennius battlelist nor the site for Arthur's court called Celliwig are pursued in the present search for the great king's authenticity in this text, but Sir Ifor provides some interesting clues for these sidelights. One appears in the above quote; Killibury or sites with the prefix *kelli-* have been suggested by previous scholars as Arthur's court, but Kerry, only six miles within the Welsh borderland of Offa's Dyke and around 25 miles west of Viroconium, invites speculation. A second name provided in the above quote by Sir Ifor is Rhyd Forlas, similar to a site considered below in relation to battles allegedly fought by Vortimer, the battle of Rit Hergabail sometimes translated to Rhyd yr afael.

At one point Sir Ifor is proposing his thesis that the Llywarch Hen englynion are pre–Norman, but in doing so, he gives a panoramic picture of the last half of the fifth century and the beginning of the sixth through the lingual content of stories, tales and sagas. From his ascriptions, these cycles take place in northeastern Wales, in the eastern part of Powys bordering on England, on the boundary of modern Wales, portions of Herfordshire and of Shropshire including Shrewsbury, and in the border country.[62] The locales are reflected in the *HB* which also outline the war zones for both Ambrosius Aurelianus as depicted by Gildas and the later campaigns of Arthur as reported by Nennius. The two manuscripts also provide the setting for Vortigern's activities.

Vortigern has two strongholds in Wales, one south and one north. Both are mentioned in a difficult passage dealing with the life of Saint Germanus. The passage sounds as if Vortigern flees to his northern fortress, then flees again to his southern fortification. Considered in a sequence of events, however, his original fortress was in Dementia, later called Dyfed, adjacent to the province of Glvessig:

> Again Vortigern ignominiously fled from St. Germanus to the kingdom of Dimetæ [Dementia], where, on the river Towy [Teibi, Teifi], he built a castle.[63]

After the treachery of his Saxon allies, he follows the advice of his wizards and travels to the farthest borders of his kingdom to build a northern stronghold at Beddgelert. His attempts are foiled and after giving Beddgelert and all of Dementia to his dreaded adversary Ambrosius, he and his wizards go to the northern part of Wales

> ... in the region named Gueneri [Gwynessi, Guunessi, Gwynedd], where he built a city which, according to his name, was called Cair Guorthegirn [Gwrtheyrn].[64]

Each of these sites is a capsulized story of its own. When Vortigern attempts to build his fortification in the north, three times he assembles masons and material, and three times they disappear. His wizards tell him that he must sprinkle the site with the blood of a fatherless child.

> ... [T]he king [Vortigern] sent messengers throughout Britain, in search of a child born without a father. After having inquired in all the provinces, they came to the field of Ælecti [Maes Eleti, Maes Eledi] in the district of Glevesing [Glouising], where a party of boys were playing at ball.[65]

Understanding this sequence of events is possible because of etymological tracings of place-names. According to Ekwall, the prefix *Maes-* means "on the boundary, boundary marker, border, or border district."[66] *Maes* is an Old Welsh term, and every town — ten of them — with this prefix is located in Welsh territory. Of the ten, eight are west of Offa's Dyke, and the other two are no more than a mile east, all indicating Wales (or the districts and kingdoms of antiquity) as border districts. Of that number, two are in the district of Glevissig. *Elledi* or *Elleti* provides the clue to a *specific* location. Roberts listed this

> to be the village called in Welsh "Maesaleg," i.e., campus Electi called at present "Bassaleg," upon the river Ebwith, in Monmouthshire.[67]

The present name of the river is Ebbw, and Bassaleg is three miles due west of Newport, and about the same distance south to the Mouth of the Severn.

This agrees with the *general* locale of Glevisig (Glywysing, Glesuissing), which is a province bordering Dementia, listed on maps of ancient territories such as that provided by John Morris. Stevenson notes that

> The district [of Glevissig] comprehended the tract of land between the rivers Usk and Rumney, in Monmouthshire; and derived its name from Gliwisus, father to the celebrated Welsh saint Gundlaeus.[68]

The present-day name on maps for the Rumney river is the Rhymney, which passes along the eastern edge of Cardiff and empties into the Mouth of the Severn. There is also a small suburb named Rumney, about a mile from the coast.

Section 42 is at first geographically confusing. At the chapter's opening, there are several vague references to "this [Vortigern's] fortress," that is, the one which is to be built. At the end of the section, Ambrosius tells Vortigern to leave "this fortress" and he himself will stay. Vortigern gives him "this fortress" and all the kingdoms of the *western* part of Britain, and Vortigern goes to the *northern* part and there builds a city. The confusion is resolved by backtracking to Section 40, which explains that Vortigern and his wizards at last found a suitable place in a country called Guined, atop a summit in the mountains of Hereri, also called Snoudune, where the king could build a citadel so that he would be safe against the barbarians and those who opposed him. Stevenson explains that (Guined) Gwynedd encompasses the whole of northern Wales, in the Snowdonian mountains which, of course, suggests the hillfort Dinas Emrys, named after Ambrosius, just outside the present village of Beddgelert.[69]

Then, at the end of Section 41, the wizards deliver Ambrosius to that spot, the proposed site of Vortigern's northwestern fortress, the future location of Dinas Emrys, which Ambrosius inherits in addition to Dementia and other kingdoms in southern Wales:

> Then the king [Vortigern] assigned him [Ambrosius] that [fortress, Dinas Emrys], with all the western provinces of Britain.[70]

and Vortigern goes farther to the north and east where

> ... he built a city which ... was called Cair Guorthegirn.[71]

Alcock expresses doubt that Vortigern could have any personal connection with Gwrtheyrn.[72] He makes a puzzling reference to Gwrtheyrn in Carmarthenshire, but putting that aside, Vortigern's link with Gwrtheyrn fits well into the historic pattern of the period. At the beginning of Vortigern's reign, his kingdom was Dementia. After the Romans withdrew from the island, all of Britain — including Wales — was on the brink of destruction. Vortigern was concerned not only with a Roman return, but with harassment by the Picts and the Irish. He was also in dread of other Britons of rank, particularly Ambrosius Aurelianus, vying for kingship. He recruited help from the Saxons, but this exacerbated the conditions. Some Britons were outraged by the alliance with the Saxons, and the Saxons themselves were demanding and treasonous. Vortigern additionally had profligate tendencies, and the combined pressures caused him to desert his throne and flee to the north, hoping to fortify himself and save his life. He abdicated to Ambrosius and sought seclusion at Gwrtheyrn. His final demise is obscure.

Vortigern is entrenched in Welsh history and tradition, but Alcock voices the belief accepted by scholars that

> In the *Historia Brittonum* the doings of Vortigern ... [show] he is active both in Kent and in Wales.[73]

However, Vortigern's Kentish connection is contradictory to what a close analysis of the *Historia* relates. Vortigern's activities were limited to Wales, and he did not reign freely between the territory of northern Wales and Kent. After Vortigern covets Hengist's daughter, he opens negotiations for her by offering up to half of his kingdom. The next segment of that chapter is the basis for the judgment that Vortigern rules over Kent, but the passage is laden with incongruities. Nennius records that

> Then Hengist, who had already consulted with the elders who attended him of the Oghgul race, demanded for his daughter the province, called in English Centland, in British Ceint ... This cession was made without the knowledge of the king, Guoyrancgonus, who then reigned in [Ceint], and who experienced no inconsiderable share of grief, from seeing his kingdom ... resigned to foreigners.[74]

This is the first time that the name Kent appears in the *Historia Brittonum*, and it is misidentified partly because of the translated term "Angeln" for "Oghgul." "Angeln" is one of two places: it is the modern-day word for the landmass base of the Schleswig-Jutland Peninsula, or it is a part of Britannia Flavia in eastern Britain, either of which, by its use in the translation, implies that Hengist is taking counsel with his own tribe, the Angles and the Saxons from his homeland. However, Manuscript *A* uses the Latin expression *insula Oghgul*, and Manuscript *a* uses *Oehgul*, both of which are ancient terms for Ireland, additionally verified by its being called an island (insula). Historically, the dynasty of the *Dési* migrated from Ireland specifically to Dementia, the later province of Dyfed, known as one of Vortigern's strongholds. The difference between the translated word *Angeln* and the original word *Oghgul* shifts attention from the Anglo-Saxon peninsula of Britannia Flavia in Hengist's homeland to Wales where the Dési migrated.

This confusion of terms restructures several important pieces of information. One is that Hengist is negotiating with *Vortigern's* counsel, not with Saxons. The second is that Vortigern's counsel is part of the Dési tribe, suggesting that Vortigern himself migrated from Ireland to Wales. Vortigern and Hengist, therefore, are negotiating for provinces in or near Wales.

More important, it exposes the misleading assumption that the Latin equivalent Cantguaraland is equated with Kent (Chent). When Nennius writes — or more accurately copies — that the country in *their* language was known as Cantguaraland, the pronoun seems to be a reference to *Hengist's* language — that is, Saxon. However, the root of the word —*guoralen*—is undoubtedly Welsh, which leads to a closer inspection of its prefix. Ekwall has this to say about *Cant-* which is too quickly misjudged as Kent:

> Cant is an Old Britain river-name, which may be related to Caint R (Wales) and KENN D, So.[75]

He suggests that the prefix *Cantewar-* means "people of Kent" in place-names such as Canterbury and Canterton. But Canterbury in Arthurian times was known instead by the name of *Darovernon*. Other sites such as Cantlop, Cantsfield, Canwell, and Canwick are in the midlands: Derbyshire, Shropshire, Lancashire, Staffordshire. This could point to areas where former Kentishmen settled, but it does not signify that it isolates the reference to Kent. *Cant-* rather than *Cantewar-*, more closely represents a region in Wales, especially as it ties to other place-names provided by the *HB*. The Nennius translation therefore incorrectly equates *Chent* with the affix *Cantewar-*. When Vortigern indicates that he will relinquish up to half of his kingdom, he is referring not to Kent but to Wales, which is his to give away.

Stevenson verifies that Cantguaraland is *not* in the province of Kent. Manuscript *a* of the *Historia* for this passage reads

> ... quæ vocatur Anglice Centland, Britannice autem Cæint.[76]

which translates as "which is called Centland in English, Cæint in Brython." This much more closely parallels *Caint* in Wales than it does *Chent* in Kent.

Another inconsistency in the segment is the alleged name of the Kentish king, Guoyrancgonus. Stevenson explains that this word is generic, not a proper name, meaning a governor or sub-king.[77] More important, however, is the segment (-guora-) from both his name and the territory which he rules, showing that the names are Welsh, not Briton. The inconsistency would be a Welsh king ruling a British territory, just as there is an inconsistency in one of the citations above where both Chent and Cantia are translated as Kent. In the Arthurian period of A.D. 500 there was a distinction between the Wilsc (Welsh) and Briton tongues, and they were not historically or literarily blended until later centuries.

One other misleading translation occurs in the last sentence of Chapter 38:

> But Hengist continued, by degrees, sending for ships ... and whilst his people were increasing in power and number, they came to the above-named province of Kent.[78]

But the original Latin in Manuscript *a* reads as

> ... venerunt ad supradictam regionem.[79]

This translates as "... they came to the aforesaid province." The oldest extant copy of the *Historia*, then, does not name a city in the land of Kent but simply makes a generic reference to "that province," which is somewhere near the borders of the Picts.

This also has a direct bearing on Hengist's genealogy. As mentioned earlier, the genealogies of the Saxon kings apparently did not appear in the original work, according to Stevenson, but they remain an important contribution because of their remote antiquity. Once again, the misinterpretation lies in the translations. These genealogies have been superficially headed, beginning at Section 57 as "The Northern History, Part I." Section 58, only one sentence showing Hengist's progeny, has two superficial headings, "Southern English Genealogies" and "The genealogy of the Kings of Kent." If these two headings are eliminated (as they should be since they appear in only a single manuscript added by a later hand[80]), then Hengist's genealogy blends into its proper place in the *northern* genealogies, followed by those of the East Angles.

The confusion between Wales and Kent also has a direct bearing on the interpretation of four battles fought against the Saxons by Vortimer. In the first,

> At length Vortimer, the son of Vortigern, valiantly fought against Hengist, Horsa, and his people; drove them to the isle of Thanet, and thrice enclosed them within it.[81]

Kent is naturally the first location to come to mind, especially since attention was focused on the Kent area in earlier Nennius chapters. Nennius uses the word *Tanet*, and in context with Kent it makes sense. Ekwall gives the derivative of the word as a brilliant river, and the mouth of the Thames could certainly be called that name with an island nestled in its glow. However, if the assumption is made that Thanet is in Kent, Vortimer would have accomplished an unbelievable feat: from Dementia, his army chased the Saxons over 250 miles across Britain.

When perceived in a chain of events linked to geographic adjacency in Wales, a different explanation fits the pattern much better. In more detail, the information by Ekwall is this:

> A British river-name identical with Old Welsh *tanet* in personal nouns and meaning "brilliant river." Old Welsh *tanet* is derived from *tan* "fire."[82]

As in this entry, Old Welsh etymologies recur regularly in all the alleged "Kentish" references. Of particular interest in this instance is a river named Tanat in northern Wales, adjacent to all the sites associated with Vortigern. The Tanat River is west of Offa's Dyke, about ten miles south of Llangollen in Wales; it joins the Severn River in its destination to Bridgwater Bay.

Vortimer's second battle was on the river Darenth. Morris, in *The Age of Arthur*, picks up on Darenth, since there is a small village of that name in Kent, and sets the scene of the battle there. As with so many place-names, however, this one is not what it seems. Because of the skepticism created in earlier chapters of Nennius, Kent is an unlikely site for battles between the Welsh and their ex-compatriots.

Once again, Ekwall supplies a lucid explanation. He gives the etymology of Darent as

Identical with Derwent. On the Darent is Darenth.[83]

A further check for Derwent reveals that Bede first used the term, which is based upon

A British river-name *Derventio,* found as the name of a place on the Yorkshire Derwent … derived from Brit *dervā* oak, Welsh *derw* … The name means "river where oaks are common."[84]

Darenth, Derwent, Darent, Dart, and Darwen all go back to the term *Derventio.* Derwent is a major river in the region of Wales, but more explicitly there is a village named Derwen located strategically in northern Wales. It is located between Vortigern's Castle (Gwytherin) twelve miles to the northwest and Llangollen nine miles to the southeast. In the immediate vicinity of Llangollen is Eliseg's Pillar, linked not only to Vortigern but to Cunedda and Cerdic's ancestry. Additionally, Derwen is only three miles from the Roman road connecting the northern Welsh coast to the Thames Valley nearly 300 miles away.

The next battle is the most intriguing. Because Horsa's death is listed, Nennius' entry can be equated with the *Anglo-Saxon Chronicle*'s entry of year 455, which in turn means that information can be cross-checked. Unfortunately, the comparison creates more mystery than it solves. To begin, Nennius attributes Briton leadership to Vortimer, while the *Chronicle* relates that the battle was between Hengist and Vortigern. Second, the first impression is that the geographic names will point to specific locales. The *Chronicle* provides the name Agælesthrep (Ægelesthrep), which scholars have translated as

the Ford, in their language … Epsford, … in ours [Rithergabail].[85]

Morris equates Episford with Aylesford, a small village near Maidstone in Kent, following a tendency among researchers to suggest a pattern that these battles took place in southeastern Britain. The Nennius manuscript also gives the *Welsh* name Rithergabail. Morris translates that as Rhyd yr afael, but makes no attempt to pinpoint a location, undoubtedly because he has already labeled Kent as the locus. A village named Rhyd-foel exists on the northern Welsh coast. It, too, fits within a different pattern of battles, in northern Wales, only nine miles from Vortigern's Castle and eighteen miles from Derwen. If this does not offer enough intrigue, about six miles north of Bolten is a large city named Darwen, and it has an immediate suburb named Ryal Fold. Furthermore, the confusing search for specific geographic locations is compounded because there is also a Welsh locale named Agglethorpe, farther north than other Vortimer battles which can be set in the Cornovii area but still within a reasonable arc of the River Ribble, Ribblesdale, and Ripon.

The alternate spelling provided by the *Chronicle*, Ægelesthrep, also offers possibilities without an extreme stretch of the imagination. Gele is a river in northern Wales emptying into the Irish Sea. On the coast, Abergele is a small modern city (incidentally only about two miles from Rhyd y foel) whose name is derived from the River Gele. Ekwall gives an extensive definition to the affix -*threp*,[86] but in simple terms it means a locale, such as a hamlet, which is attached to a mother village. Ægelesthrep, then, could have been a small hamlet on the River Gele near an important port such as Rhyl, on a bay where the River Gele and the River Clwyd merge.

Vortimer's last battle fits into the same kind of pattern when northern Wales and Derbyshire are considered as Vortimer's territory. It

> ... [was] fought near the [Inscribed] stone on the shore of the Gallic [Gallici] Sea.[87]

The first inclination is to interpret the shore of the Gallici sea as Gaul, but with the other amassed information, the reference is undoubtedly to the *Gaelic* Sea off the coast of Wales. Alcock verifies this via his discussion of inscribed stones, disconnected from a vested interest of proving the historicity of Arthur. In his study of inscribed stones of Britain, he writes this of the stones in Group I, of special interest because they are dated from the fifth, sixth, and seventh centuries, spanning the Arthurian age:

> [Of nearly two hundred inscribed stones in Group I], Wales has the overwhelming bulk, some 140 concentrated in Gwynedd, Dyfed, and Brycheiniog.[88]

He also postulates

> a Roman element in the ancestry of the Group I stones, but their overwhelming distribution pattern is away from the lowland heart of Roman Britain, and lies instead in the Irish Sea zone.[89]

In addition to the sizable number in the three provinces Alcock mentions in southern Wales, another concentration is in northern Wales. There are ten

Group I stones on the Lleyn Peninsula slightly southwest of Dinas Emrys, and clustered around Dinas Emrys and Gwytherin are at least ten more. There are also three in the immediate vicinity of Rhyd-foel. It has already been pointed out that Dinas Emrys was Ambrosius' stronghold, Gwytherin was Vortigern's northern fortification, and Rhyd-foel was a possible site for one of Vortimer's battles. Derwen, a possible site for another of Vortimer's battles, is within perhaps five miles of an inscribed stone, excluding Eliseg's Pillar, which is also about five miles away. With this degree of proof, there should be no remaining doubt that the battle at the Inscribed Stone would be in this same vicinity.

The final segment in Chapter 31 of *British History* is a Mommsen addition to Morris' translation, marked by daggers (†). The proper noun, *Ripum*, emerges as the last item of interest, although it is etymologically obscure. *Ripum* is a Latin word applied to a *civitate*, the seat of administrative function. Ekwall does not list Ripum, but under the entry Ripon, he lists

> Hrypis, Hripis ... OE Bede *Hyrpsætna* ... *Onhripum* ... *Hryopan* ... Ripun. Ripon is the dative plural of OE Hyrpe, a tribal name, found also in Repton.[90]

Under the entry Repton is the following information:

> *Hrypadun* ... *Hreopandune* ... *Rapendune* ... *Rependun* ... *Repedon*. "The hill of the *Hrype* tribe." The same tribe gave its name to Ripon and probably some places near Ripon (see Ribston, Ripley). The etymology of the tribal name is obscure.[91]

Bede uses *in-Hrypum* only once (page 187), and all of these possibilities except one lead to a dead-end. However, because an intervocalic change of *p* for *b* is found in other names, the interesting revelation comes from the history of the word *Ribston*.

> No doubt *Hrypa stan* "the stone of the *Hrype*." The stone may have been a boundary stone marking the territory of the *Hrype* tribe, or a stone at the meeting-place of the tribe.[92]

This intervocalic change is also the root for the Rib River, the Ribble River and Ribchester. The Ribble River in Lancashire, for example, flows southwesterly from its source to the Irish Sea, and this, too, could have been a boundary marker for the *Hrype* tribe. This presumption for Ribchester is even stronger. Morris, even though he writes about this fortification in a different set of circumstances, contributes influential information. Ribchester was a principal fortified town in Lancashire shortly preceding Cunedda's migration to the south, where the territories of this region remained intact just prior to the end of the fifth century, Arthur's period.[93]

Archaeologist Peter Clayton also makes an indirect contribution. About Ribchester, he writes:

> This was a small cavalry fort in the territory of the Brigantes tribe. When a group
> of Sarmatian cavalry veterans were given land to settle here on their retirement about
> 200 it was Brigantian land taken from the tribe.[94]

Historically, Ribchester was not only a *civitas* but was a demarcation point and could have functioned as such in setting future divisional boundaries.

The most interesting picture which emerges, however, is not based upon verification of *specific* locations, but is instead a *general* pattern which manifests itself. Ekwall claims that the etymology of the tribal name *Hrype* is obscure, but it is suspiciously similar to Hwicce. The Old English transcription would be pronounced as a voiced or unvoiced "th-" sound, *Hrythe*. Plotting only those place-names positively associated with the root *Hrype* onto a map splits Britain in half, from the mouth of the Ribble on the west to the River Humber on the east. Ribble, Ribchester, Ribble Head, Ripley, Ripon, and Riplingham form a jagged boundary across the country, a testimony in themselves to the borders of the *Hrype* tribe. The same is true down the center of the country to the south coast: Ripponden, Ripley, Repton, Ribberford, Ripple, and Ripley could be border markers for *Hrype* territories.

Scholars and historians do not equate *Hwicce* and *Gewisse*. Morris, for example, labels the Hwicce territory mainly the present province of Gloucestershire, and Ashe sets the Gewisse territory mainly in Dorset and Hampshire, with the later empire of the West Saxons superimposed between the two to show the eventual combined kingdom of the West Saxons. Yet there are clues within their own work to show that the two synonyms refer to the same kingdoms. Ashe cites Geoffrey of Monmouth as reporting that Vortigern was "the ruler of the Gewissei."[95] Morris writes that "Gewissae was the earlier name of the Middle Thames Saxons,"[96] adding in footnotes that they were "probably" confederates "of the Berkshire English of the middle Thames about Abingdon."[97]

On a map showing the *seventh* century English kingdoms,[98] Morris not only misses chronologically on the ancient nature of the Hwicce people, but he concentrates the Hwicce tribe solely in the area of Gloucestershire, rather than having the kingdom extend eastward as far as Abingdon in Oxfordshire. Ashe is trying to prove that Arthur is a fifth century figure by interpreting Geoffrey of Monmouth, and sets the Gewisse in Dorset and Hampshire, even though Vortigern (of Dementia) is labeled as their ruler but has no historical associations with the south.

Very early in the Dark Ages, Hrype/Hwicce/Gewisse was a massive territory granted to, or perhaps taken by, the Saxon compatriots invited in by Vortigern. It extended from the River Ribble to at least Ripon and Ripley in the north, bounded roughly by Offa's Dyke to the west, all the *Hrype* place-names on the east, and two similar place-names in Hants and Surrey to the south. This massive kingdom germinates sometime after Vortigern's succession to kingship in the fourth decade of the 400s. The West Saxon conquests of 50 years later play an important role in the development of these kingdoms from their inception to Arthur's death in the second decade of the 500s.

The Anglo-Saxon Chronicle/ *Genealogical Preface*

It is important to distinguish between the *ASC* and its Genealogical Preface because they give contradictory information which has to be resolved. The edition of the *Chronicle* (actually a collection of variable copies) cited in this text was prepared by Whitelock, Douglas, and Tucker. As supplements, the translation by G.N. Garmonsway and the work of Charles Plummer were used, particularly the entries dealing with the time periods from 381 through 560. The associated chronicles of Ethelwerd and Asser, edited by J.A. Giles, round out the references. Any study of the *Chronicle* is highly complex; Charles Plummer is the authoritative source, and any question or verification to be resolved should be checked through his work, since he scrutinizes details more thoroughly than anyone else.

As introductory expectations for our purposes, Plummer defines the difference between a history and a chronicle. History is an arrangement of facts which have undergone a new arrangement after those facts have been reexamined, criticized, distributed, and grouped; once it is woven and interlocked in this way, then modifications are unwelcome since additions and subtractions will destroy its integrity. On the other hand, chronicles are the simplest form of history but admit alterations indefinitely; they can accommodate insertions at any part.[99] At this point Plummer is raising a precautionary flag warning that chronicles, although they should be deemed history, are more interpretive and not as inflexible as history, but both are set within limited parameters.

The effect of the Paschal Tables upon the *Annales Cambriae* is also an important consideration in a study of the *ASC*. Plummer is of the opinion that the Paschal Tables had a powerful effect on the formation of many chronicles, but he says, "I do not see any direct trace in our Chronicles."[100] Morris indicates that, like the *Annales Cambriae*, the *Anglo-Saxon Chronicle* follows the Irish form, explaining that "... in its earlier entries, concerning the first century, it makes the same selection as the Irish made from Bede, or from his source, and shares with the Irish half a dozen items not found in Bede."[101]

The difference lies, however, in what Morris says next: "But from the fifth century on, it copies only native entries, as in the later texts of the Irish Annals; for it is preserved in a relatively late version, edited in Wessex in the 9th century."[102] Morris is evidently referring to the Alfredian Chronicle through 892, which was compiled under the supervision of Alfred the Great, and the continuation of that chronicle from 894 to 924. The basis of this Alfredian material is Manuscript $\overline{A}$ in both instances.[103] And the importance of this must be underscored and repeated. Plummer has no doubt whatsoever that the chronicles themselves ran a sequence of $\overline{A}$ = æ = Æ, with the earliest form of a national chronicle attributed to Alfred. (Alfred's birth is listed for the year 848, with him succeeding to the throne at 23 years old, in the year 871. See Plummer, page 79.) Plummer asserts:

> I have no hesitation in declaring that in my opinion the popular answer (of who gave the earliest form of a national Chronicle) is in this case the right one: it is the work of Alfred the Great. ... The idea of a national Chronicle as opposed to merely local annals was his, that the idea was carried out under his direction and supervision, this I do most firmly believe.... I have chosen the symbol Æ for this original Chronicle partly because it is the initial of the great king's name, and partly because it expresses the fact that this original stock branches out on the one side into our Ⱥ, and on the other into our E, the two Chronicles which are the furthest apart from one another in character, as they are in time, of all our existing Chronicles.[104]

This means that special significance must be granted to the Genealogical Preface of Manuscript Ⱥ. Plummer emphasizes that "we have the strongest evidence that the preface to Ⱥ was drawn up in the reign of Alfred, and was intended for a Chronicle compiled in that reign."[105]

That preface becomes crucial for looking at chronological possibilities because some of the information is different from what the actual *Chronicle* gives. The Preface not only confirms the relationship of Alfred to the Anglo-Saxon manuscripts, but it further strengthens its pre–ninth century reliability. Nothing is said of Alfred's reign "for the excellent reason that when the Preface was written the length of [his] reign could not be known; and later scribes, with more self-restraint than they sometimes manifest, have refrained from supplying the deficiency."[106] That means that the Preface avoids interpolations that could be attributed to scribal errors. This gives additional evidence that it was drawn up closer to Arthur's time period, since it was used in Alfred's time, and the closer the source to Arthurian times, the less liability there is for scribal inconsistencies or incompatibilities. Plummer suggests that it is an offshoot of the Orosius translation dating to the years 890–893.[107]

As an extra bonus of crucial consequence, the Genealogical Preface gives specific information about the nature of the West Saxon genealogies and "probably supplied the chronological framework when the West Saxon traditions came to be written down."[108] This becomes invaluable in this text by establishing Arthurian connections with Cerdic, Creoda, and Cynric of the West Saxons while at the same time helping structure the chronology of the period and determining how Arthur fit into the scheme. The Preface is not subject to the same criticisms as the entries in the *Chronicle* for the entries from 465 to 544, an analysis which occurs later at the appropriate time.* One can ask for no more reliability and accuracy for a source that close to Arthur's time.

An offshoot is a chronicle by Ethelwerd, a descendant of Alfred. Ethelwerd has some details from a source independent of the Ⱥ manuscript of the *ASC*, plus some details peculiar to himself. Ethelwerd becomes important, not only because his work relies upon the prestige of Manuscript Ⱥ, but also because of clues that he was working from chronicles now lost.[109]

The main criticisms center around the artificial arrangement of the chronological dates in fours and eights, plus the aetiological characters in many of the entries. The Preface is exonerated because it does not give specific year entries as are given in the body of the Chronicle, *plus there are significant variances of dates. The key is to conclude the correct date in conjunction with other crucial data.*

In his analysis of the various other manuscripts of the *ASC*, Plummer writes:

> It is commonly stated that the *ASC* is contained in seven MSS., those which are here denoted by the letters Ᾱ, A, B, C, D, E, F. It would be truer to say that these MSS. contain four Anglo-Saxon Chronicles. A is a transcript of Ᾱ; B, as far as it goes, is identical with C, both having been copied from the same MS.: F is an epitome of E. But Ᾱ, C, D, E, have every right to be considered distinct Chronicles.[110]

Other clarifications are mandatory on these manuscripts. Plummer explains that "... up to 892 Ᾱ, B, C, and also those parts of D, E which are common to them with Ᾱ, B, C, must be traced back to a common original which I have called æ."[111] And there is still more depth to what Plummer does with the chronicles. He states that the æ copies were sent to different monasteries[112] and became the basis for the Ᾱ manuscripts, which confirms that the Ᾱ manuscripts are a copy of a copy and not the original.[113] Plummer quickly points out, however, that this should not lower the prestige of the Ᾱ manuscripts.

Plummer explains that the dating of the Ᾱ manuscript is perplexing because of the number of scribes involved, but as pointed out earlier, he ascribes the original Æ manuscript to a date of 892, with a possible range to 900.[114] Manuscript A is dated in the first quarter of the eleventh century,[115] and E is dated in the first quarter of the twelfth century.[116] Similar to the Preface, the Ethelwerd chronicle is important to the analysis of Arthur because, as Plummer points out, "Ethelwerd used a Chronicle which was not our Ᾱ, but was closer to it than any other of our existing Chronicles."[117]

The Asser Annals are

> of great importance for the criticism of the *ASC*; for, while founded largely on that Chronicle, they have preserved the true chronology, which in all our MSS. is disjointed.[118]

Only the first segments of these two chronicles are crucial to the Arthurian search. The First Book of Ethelwerd gives rare information for an entry date 500, separate and distinct from the year 501 which appears in the body of the *ASC*. The wording of the entry for 500 is of supreme importance in its implication with the geographic location for the Battle of Badon, with the Battle of Camlann, and with the *ASC* entry for 519. Whitelock refers to the Ethelwerd chronicle as being close to the original, having "authentic details of its own, especially in relation to south-western affairs."[119] The first 22 lines of Giles' translation of Asser are important because it, too, uses the Preface of the *ASC* (or some other lost source) which differs from the body of the *ASC* itself, echoing the name of Creoda as part of the West Saxon Genealogy, which is so vital in establishing dates for the Arthurian era.

Whitelock lists the manuscripts through "H," but for the sake of simplicity, in order not to get too bogged down with details which can become incredibly specific, this text will deal only with manuscripts "A" through "E" in addition to the ones specifically emphasized above, many times not giving the difference among the versions. For the sake of background information, however, the various other manuscripts are capsulized.†

THE RELIABILITY OF THE *ANGLO-SAXON CHRONICLE*

Before we leave the ancient manuscripts, we must check one more question on the reliability of the *ASC*. Gildas gives one chronological fix — the year of his writing of the *De Excidio* — and the *Annales Cambriae* gives three clues on dates — the Battle of Mount Badon, the Battle of Camlann, and the death of Gildas. It is necessary now to check the sources of this last major manuscript.

According to Leslie Alcock, the *Chronicle* as we know it follows the example of Bede and uses an *anno Domini* system of dating. Alcock explains how these dates were computed:

> In some cases, no doubt, annals were entered retrospectively in Easter Tables which stretch back before each individual English kingdom was converted. Much stress has been laid on the fact that, even before the conversion of Kent in 597, a significant proportion of the annals follow a four-year cycle. It has been suggested that this is because events were entered, long after they had actually occurred, in an Easter Table in which the leap years had been specially indicated. There are entries for the years 540, 544, 547, 552, 556, 560, 565, and 568, but none for the intervening years. All of these, except for 547 and 565, are of course leap years, and it was certainly common practice to mark off the leap years in an Easter Table, so the hypothesis seems sensible. It immediately exposes the artificiality of much of the pre–Christian chronology of the *Chronicle*.[120]

Looking at the crucial dates in Arthur's time span and how other dates from other sources relate to the *Chronicle*, the leap years for Arthur's time would be 496,

†*Manuscript A, referred to as either Corpus Christi College, Cambridge MS 173, or the Parker manuscript, is the oldest, dating to 891, written in one hand of the late ninth or very early tenth century. It covers events up to about 920. Even though it is the oldest (and therefore might be considered the most reliable) its age as a pitfall must be avoided. Sometimes it is carelessly written, with certain detectable errors, making it clear that this manuscript was at least two stages removed from an earlier compilation.*

Manuscript B (British Museum Cotton Tiberius A. vi), picking up at the end of "A," covers until 977 and is closely connected with "C." Both "C" and "B" are very close from 491 to 652, with 652 being the date where manuscript "B" omits annal numbers. It cannot be coincidence, incidentally, that this juncture marks changes henceforth between "B" and "C."

Manuscript C, which gives an excellent record of Ethelred the Unready, manifested in the excavation of South Cadbury by Leslie Alcock in the late 1960s and early 70s. This manuscript dates to the mid–eleventh century, up until the entry of 1056. Manuscript C differs from "B" by omitting the West Saxon genealogy and regnal lists. It changes from "B" at 653, but not totally; there are still relationships to "B" until "B" stops.

Manuscript D, like "C," provides an excellent record of Ethelred the Unready, but it is more parallel with manuscript E until 1031. Manuscript D has more of a northern interest, drawn from Bede and northern annals. It covers the tenth and eleventh centuries, and ends in 1079, at the beginning of the first millennium.

Manuscript E again gives an excellent record of Ethelred the Unready, but it ceases to be northern when it branches off from "D" in 1031. Manuscript E continues the longest, with its final section running from 1132 until 1154.

500, 504, 508, 512, 516, 520, 524, 528, 532, 536, and 540. The dates actually listed in the *Chronicle* over that time span are 495, 501, 508, 514, 519, 527, 530, 534, and 538. Only one entry, that of 508, actually falls on a leap year. The answer, then, is emphatically no — these dates do not reflect that portion of the annals that follow a four-year cycle and therefore they do *not* fit into Alcock's hypothesis that it was common practice to mark off leap years in an Easter Table. This means that Alcock's hypothesis, although it might be generally true for other parts of the *Chronicle*, is not applicable when looking at the significant Arthurian period from 499 to 520 and beyond; there is none of the pre–Christian artificiality.

Further, the erratic spacings of the entries in the *Chronicle* (that is, leap years being one year after the 500 entry, two years after the 512 entry, three years after the 516 entry, three years after the 524 entry, two years after the 528 entry, etc.) indicates that this particular segment from the *Chronicle* was not miscalculated, or else the entries would indeed have been spaced at four-year intervals. It seems unjustified, therefore, to accept the statement used in Alcock which reaches the conclusion that the accuracy of sequence in the *Chronicle* for the period of 449 to 500 or even later is artificial and untrustworthy. On the contrary, the *Chronicle* seems to fit a reliable chronology with other sources, although there are some inconsistencies elsewhere, as suggested by Plummer. The few entries which are essential to provide a firm fix for Arthur, particularly those dealing with the Wessex kingdom and the Preface addition to the actual *Chronicle*, are the stronger and more reliable dates according to the indications provided by the scholars.

DECIPHERING THE DISCREPANCY BETWEEN THE *CHRONICLE* AND ITS GENEALOGICAL PREFACE

The final step prior to accepting the *Chronicle* is to analyze its Genealogical Preface as an integral overview to properly modify certain entries and delete doublets within the *Chronicle*. The two documents must be compared and adjusted, since they record such divergent views on almost all of their entries pertaining to Cerdic and his progeny. Based upon material from Plummer, Table 7 was devised to show the discrepancies pertaining to the kings' length of reign as recorded in the body of the *Chronicle* and its Preface. Once these inconsistencies are resolved, the adjustments, which are historical in nature but have a direct bearing on Arthurian context, will be used to modify chronologies in the chapters to follow. In our area of concern, Plummer points out that the *Chronicle* gives the entry of

495 — In this year two [ealdormen], Cerdic and Cynric his son, came to Britain with five ships at the place which is called *Cerdicesora*, and the same day they fought against the Welsh.[121]

The *Chronicle* later records the entry of

519 — In this year Cerdic and Cynric succeeded to the kingdom of the West Saxons; and in the same year they fought against the Britons at a place called Charford.[122]

However, the Preface gives the West Saxon genealogy by relating a different sequence:

> In the year of Christ's Nativity 494, Cerdic and Cynric his son landed at *Cerdicesora* with five ships. ... Six years after they had landed they conquered the kingdom of Wessex. These were the first kings who conquered the land of Wessex from the Welsh.[123]

Whereas the *Chronicle* gives a span from 495 to 519 and offers an equation to the Badon and Camlann entries of the *Annales*, the Preface with its span from 494 to 500 denies that similarity. Plummer writes about these disparities in this way:

> It is a small matter that the Preface puts the invasion of Cerdic and Cynric in 494, while the Chronicle places it in 495; it is more serious that the Preface places the foundation of the kingdom of Wessex six years after their arrival, *i.e.* in 500, while the Chronicle places it in 519.[124]

Unfortunately, he then writes about Ceawlin's reign and does not offer possible reasons for the discrepancy, and equally unfortunate, no succeeding scholar has addressed the problem or attempted to resolve the issue. Although scarce, clues exist and the divergent reports can be reconciled. Plummer redeems himself in a rambling, indirect way when he analyzes two *Chronicle* entries unrelated to the discrepancy between the *Chronicle* and its Preface, although one of the entries involves the year 519. He compares this particular entry (year 519) with the entry for year 527 in the *Chronicle*. In tandem they appear as:

> 519 — In this year Cerdic and Cynric succeeded to the kingdom; and in the same year they fought against the Britons at a place called Charford.
> 527 — In this year Cerdic and Cynric fought against the Britons in the place which is called *Cerdicesleag*.[125]

About entry 527 he writes

> "Cerdicesford" for "Cerdicesleag" is peculiar to [MS]. E. It is followed by H[enry of] H[untingdon] but not by Fl[orence of] W[orcester]. It is due to the influence of the preceding annal 519, of which in truth this looks very like a doublet.[126]

Plummer identifies entry 527 as a duplicate of the 519 entry and this observation encouraged a closer look at entries not only in the *Chronicle* but also in the Preface. An analytical approach suggests the possibility of doublets with several other entries in the *Chronicle* (Whitelock, page 11). Compare, for instance, the following two entries:

> 495 — In this year two ealdormen, Cerdic and his son Cynric, came with five ships to Britain at the place which is called Cerdicesora, and they fought against the Britons on the same day.

514 — In this year the West Saxons came into Britain with three ships at a place called Cerdicesora; and Stuf and Wihtgar fought against the Britons and put them to flight.

The differentiation between the two dates is 19 years, the same span for a lunar adjustment. This seems too bizarre to be a mere coincidence, especially in light of the lunar adjustments made for other entries. Likewise, if the generic term of "West Saxons" is used instead of proper names, the entries are almost identical. An additional peculiarity of the entry for 514 — a skepticism which Plummer expresses on etiological grounds[127] — is the names of Stuf and Wihtgar, two alleged West-Saxon names which do not appear in the West-Saxon genealogical trees.[128]

This supports the hypothesis that entry 514 is a doublet of 495, but even more evidence can be evinced by a closer comparison with entry 519 because this latter date inspires an even more interesting inquiry about its origins. Plummer has already expressed suspicion that this date is a doublet, and his doubts are modified by what he calls an "artificial system of chronology" for some entries in the *Chronicle* during this time span.[129]

Together the Ethelwerd chronicle and the Genealogical Preface offer a channel for analyzing the date of 519 by looking at similarities and parallels of dates in pairs. Plummer gives the details of Ethelwerd's relation with the *ASC*, explaining that

> Even in the earlier period [of the Ethelwerd chronicle], however, he has many details peculiar to himself, the source of which it would be interesting to learn. I do not think, however, that they oblige us to suppose that Ethelwerd used a Chronicle differing very widely from those which have come down to us. These details probably come from some independent source. ... On the whole, the conclusion seems to be that Ethelwerd used a Chronicle which was not our Ā, but was closer to it than to any other of our existing Chronicles.[130]

The Genealogical Preface is an integral part of the Ethelwerd chronicle and must be viewed as such in searching for dates as reflected in the *ASC*. Plummer explains the connection:

> The view taken above of the relation of Alfred to the [*ASC*] derives some confirmation from the Genealogical Preface in Ā. The genealogy is carried down to Alfred, and there it stops; and nothing is said as to the length of his reign for the excellent reason that when the preface was written the length of the reign could not be known. ... We thus have the strongest evidence that the preface to Ā was drawn up in the reign of Alfred, and was intended for a Chronicle compiled in that reign.[131]

He later adds details about the West Saxon house given in the Genealogical Preface, which is crucial to this search. He writes:

> The West Saxon Genealogical Preface to Ā may give us a fair idea of the nature of these [Alfred's scheme for a national Chronicle] records; and they probably supplied the chronological framework when the West Saxon traditions came to be written down.[132]

The question of Saxon succession to Wessex and its possible placement in 519 can be viewed from a different perspective by tracing Ethelwerd's likely procedure when creating his chronicle. He includes the following in his manuscript:

> 495 — After the lapse of three more years [from 491], Cerdic and his son Cynric, having arrived in Britain with five ships at the port called *Cerdicesora* [Cerdicesoran], joined battle against the Britons the same day, and they were victors in the end.[133]
>
> 500 — In the sixth year from their arrival they encircled that western area of Britain now known as Wessex.[134]
>
> 514 — When the sixth year was completed [from 508], Stuf and Wihtgar touched land in Britain at *Cerdicesora*, and soon pressed an attack against the Britons, and they put them to flight and were themselves the victors, and from the time that Hengest and Horsa arrived in Britain, the number of fifty-six years was almost completed.[135]
>
> 519 — Then after five years, Cerdic and Cynric attacked the Britons at the place called Charford [Cerdicesforda] on the river Avon [Auene], and in the same year they began to rule.[136]

Doubtlessly, Ethelwerd was using a forerunner to the Ā manuscript because there is an oddly unique mixture of details from both the *Chronicle* and the Preface. Ethelwerd's entry for 495 states that Cerdic and his son Cynric landed with five ships at Cerdicesora, which agrees with the Preface (for 494), the Parker Chronicle (Ā), and the Laud Chronicle (E). However, the Preface adds no more details, while the Ethelwerd chronicle, the Parker, and the Laud add the key piece that Cerdicesora is in Britain. All three chronicles assert that a battle was fought on that same day, but Ethelwerd deviates from that information. Both the Parker and the Laud label the battle against the *Welsh*, but Ethelwerd lists the conflict against the Britons, and then adds that the West Saxons were the victors of the battle.

The word *Welsh* must be critically noted. Upon checking Whitelock, none of the manuscripts — A, B, C, D, E, F, or G — make any reference to the entry of 495 reading "Cerdic and [Creoda] fought against the Welsh on the same day." Instead, the manuscripts convey that "Cerdic and [Creoda] fought against the *Britons* on that day." Whitelock provides a footnote about Ethelwerd's variation but does not comment on the term "Welsh" as opposed to "Briton." However, in light of more recent research, the translation of the *ASC* by G.N. Garmonsway lists both the Ā and the E manuscripts as reading, "In this year two princes, Cerdic and Cynric his son, came to Britain in five ships [arriving] at the place which is called *Cerdicesora*, and on the same day they fought against the Welsh." A check of Plummer's analysis of that entry reveals nothing; Plummer concentrated on the use of the word "Cerdic," since that was a Briton name and not an English name. Only after close reading of Plummer does the discrepancy resolve itself and clarify the issue, epitomizing how important a single word can be.

The difference between "Briton" and "Welsh" is a geographically crucial distinction. In what is an obscure explanation, evidently not considered important by either Plummer, Whitelock, or any successor for that matter, Plummer gives this explanation in a different context, which makes an astounding difference in the history and geography of the Arthurian period. Plummer is writing about the five languages in Britain:

> [Manuscript] E, by breaking up D's "Brytwylsc" into "Brittisc-Wilsc" has apparently made six. ... "Wilsc" as opposed to "Brittisc" E probably means Cornish as opposed to Welsh. In Bede's time the dialectic difference would be hardly apparent. We find "Brytland" for Wales in 1063 D, E, 1065 C, D, 1086, p. 200.[137]

Plummer is saying that by Bede's time there was no distinction between words like "Brittisc" and "Wilsc." Instead, the word "Briton" had become a generic term, and therefore it, rather than the more precise term "Welsh," was used in the ancient manuscripts. "Wales," in Manuscript E as elsewhere, was a reference not to *Cornish* as Plummer suggests, but to *Cornovii*, which is the earlier Roman term for part of Vortigern's kingdoms and for the Gewissae territories just east of Offa's Dyke.

Plummer gives the variations for the terms Briton/British/Britain and Welsh/ Wales and indicates that Briton/Wilsc was used more in the entries up to about the middle of the sixth century, and thereafter, in the later entries, the Welsh terms began to blend with the British.[138] Plummer suggests that the terms Briton/ British/Britain as opposed to Welsh were used in the specific sense for entries 449, 457, 501, 508, 514, 519, 552, and 556. He then makes a distinction that Wessex was conquered from the *Welsh* and that Wilsc was one of the languages of Britain.

G.N. Garmonsway seems to be the most accurate in his translations of the *Chronicle* by making a distinction between Briton and Welsh. For example, in the Genealogical Preface, he writes that Cerdic and [Creoda] were the first kings who conquered the kingdom of Wessex from the *Welsh*, and at the end summarizes that the kingdom of Wessex was originally *Welsh*. As it applies to Cerdic, he likewise uses the term *Welsh* in the Parker Chronicle for entries 495 and 508, but in contrast uses the term *British* in entry 519. The implication is that the reference is to two entirely different locales in Britain, one in the west (Cerdicesora), and the other in the south (Cerdiceford).

Continuing the comparison/contrast with Ethelwerd's chronicle and the other versions plus the Preface, a second curiosity is his introduction to the year 500, labeled as the sixth year after their arrival. Because the span between 495 and 500 is only *five* years instead of six, attention focuses on the one-year discrepancy. At first this might seem that Ethelwerd was simply guilty of a scribal error. But Ethelwerd, as suggested by Plummer, must have been copying a manuscript different from what was currently available, since the *ASC* itself did not have an entry for 500. The most jarring oddity, however, is the nature of entry 500. The Preface explicitly states that six years after Cerdic and Cynric landed at Cerdicesora (494 + 6) they conquered the kingdom of Wessex from the Welsh. But Ethelwerd's chronicle does not use the expression "conquered the kingdom"; Giles' translation says that they "sailed round the western part of Britain, which is now called Wessex,"[139] and Campbell's version relates that "they encircled that western part of Britain now known as Wessex."[140] Two key inferences emerge. One is that Wessex is adjacent to Welsh territory in the west and therefore associated with *Cerdicesora*, and the other is that a battle ending in a Saxon victory is not what necessarily led to "conquering the Wessex kingdom."

We will set aside the possibility that 527 and 519 may be doublets (as inferred by Plummer) because 527 lies beyond the Arthurian interest. I will also suspend the 514 entry to avoid confusing the issue. The relationship among the dates of 494/495, 500, and 519, however, remains to be resolved. As Plummer writes, the difference between 494 and 495 is a small matter, but their connection with the other two is important.

The confusion can be eliminated by the following associations. The *ASC* entry of 495, the Preface entry of 494, and the Ethelwerd entry for 494 should all be equated, listing only that the West Saxons (Cerdic and Cynric) arrived at Cerdicesora in western Britain, in the Wales/Gewissae area. But no battles were fought.

Unfortunately, the Preface entry of 500 has been equated with the *ASC* entry and the Ethelwerd entry of 519, occurring because the Preface uses the expression "conquered the kingdom" and identified that as the West Saxons "beginning to rule" and "succeeding to the kingdom." But two things deny that connection: the Preface is specifying the Welsh, not the Britons, and the Preface is likewise suggesting Cerdicesora, not Cerdicesford. The word "conquered" in the Preface must therefore be emended to something like "granted" or "obtained."

Instead, the Ethelwerd entry of 500 should be equated with the *ASC* entry of 495 and the Preface entry of 494. All of those entries make reference to Cerdicesora and the western part of Britain known as Wessex, and a battle at Cerdicesora against the Welsh can be recorded. It is important to note, however, that no victory for the Saxons is claimed. Based upon this, then, the Ethelwerd entry of 519 can be equated with the *ASC* entry also of 519, the year in which the Saxons fought against the *Britons* at Cerdicesford and obtained (or reigned over) the kingdom. The Preface does not list anything for the year 519, but instead points to the year 516 as the end of Cerdic's reign (494 + 6 + 16).

Structuring a chronology based upon the Genealogical Preface verifies the version of events just given. Whitelock's genealogical tree — following the founders of Cerdic, Creoda, and Cynric — lists the divisions of three major lines for the West Saxon royal house,[141] but the Preface is in a more simplified format. However, several modifications, in addition to the insertion of Creoda's generation, are absolutely essential before accurate evidence can be gleaned from the Preface. The Preface segment below is given with sentence numbers added in parentheses for easy reference; everything else reflects how the information is relayed in translations.

(1) Six years [i.e., in the year 500] after they [Cerdic and Cynric, his son] landed they conquered the kingdom of Wessex. (2) These were the first kings who conquered the land of Wessex from the Welsh. (3) He held the kingdom sixteen years,

and when he died his son Cynric succeeded to the kingdom and held it <twenty-six years. (4) When he passed away, his son Ceawlin succeeded and held it >seventeen years. (5) When he died Ceol succeeded to the kingdom and held it six years. (6) When he died his brother Ceolwulf succeeded and ruled seventeen years, and their ancestry goes back to Cerdic.[142]

The most significant segment of the passage focuses on the derivational signs (< >) signifying a crucial footnote which must be properly interpreted in order to understand the passage. No matter which translation is used, the information within these symbols is the same. The footnote states:

> Supplied from ß. Material lacking in any MS, and supplied from other sources.[143]

As clarification, this is saying that the material in brackets is being added from the ß version of the *ASC*; the material in brackets is lacking in all manuscripts of the Genealogical Preface, and therefore the addition was supplied from some other source. This is the *opposite* of the Preface's purpose, which is an overview listing the specifics which are to follow in the more detailed body of the work. The Preface of the *Chronicle* begins with the West Saxon house of Cerdic and lists the succession of the kings until the end of the ninth century, a prelude of what the *Chronicle* will supply, particularly in relation to the West Saxon house. To take a piece of information from the body of some other manuscript several copies removed from the original, and to add that information to any preface without explanation is misleading and inaccurate, creating a deceptive calibration for the *Chronicle* itself. This is what has happened between the Genealogical Preface and the *Chronicle*. The difference in calibration between the two manuscripts has been a source of misinformation for literally centuries.

Fortunately, Charles Plummer offers a partial solution. For one, he is correct in assuming a scribal error in the Preface based upon Manuscript ß listing *Cynric's* reign as only 17 years instead of 26 years, citing support from Manuscript ß and Bede's copy.[144] Secondly, he points out that in the Preface, the reign of Ceawlin is omitted altogether, which jumps to Ceol's reign, listed as six years in the Preface and five years at entry 591 in the *Chronicle*. Plummer explains Ceawlin's omission in this way

> But a comparison of Napier's MS shows that this too [in addition to the shortness of Cynric's reign] has its origin in a scribal error. Ceawlin's name seems to have been written Ceolwin, then abbreviated to Ceol; this gave two Ceols apparently reigning in succession. The next scribe not unnaturally treated this as mere dittography and omitted the former Ceol (=Caewlin) altogether.[145]

Plummer is correct in labeling this second instance a scribal error by saying that Ceawlin was omitted in the Preface for the reason which he states.

The effect of these errors which compound themselves eventually led to the discrepancy which Plummer noted. Table 7 displays Plummer's divergence of dates in an easy-to-read format. In Plummer's parallel, every single entry shows

Preface		Chronicle
Cerdic	500+16	519×534=15 years
Cynric	516+27 (17)	534×560=26 years
Ceawlin	[543+31]	560×591=31 years
Ceol	574+6	591×597=6 years
Ceolwulf	580+17	597×611=14 years
Cynegils	597+31	611×643=32 years
Cenwalh	628+31	643×672=29 years
Sexburg	659+1	672×673=1 year
Æscwine	660+2	674×676=2 years

Table 7. Plummer's contast of dates from the Preface and the *Chronicle*.

a disparity, notwithstanding the adjustments he has already made, and he concludes that "It is impossible to harmonise the two series of dates."[146] Alcock, as a modern researcher, echoes this sentiment, claiming that "we must therefore accept the position that no reliable chronology is possible in Wessex before the reign of Cynegils."[147]

However, in the above instance, Plummer compounds the scribal error by two miscalculations. For one, Ceawlin's reign was followed by Ceol's, but the next scribe who copied the work did not *omit* Ceol's reign; he combined the two into 31 total years. Plummer then assigns the 31-year combined reign of the two West Saxon kings to only Ceawlin and adds an additional six years for Ceol's reign, giving a total span of 37 years for the two rulers. This miscalculation causes divergent calibrations between the Preface and the *Chronicle*. Ceol's reign is listed as six years, not only in the Preface, but also in manuscripts E and A of the *Chronicle*, so that in order to correctly interpret Ceawlin's reign, six years must be subtracted from the 31 total years normally attributed to him. That would give Ceawlin's true reign of 25 years, omitted from the Preface, which would mean that the Preface should be emended to read as follows:

(1) Six years after they landed they conquered the kingdom of Wessex. (2) These were the first kings who conquered the land of Wessex from the Welsh. (3) He held the kingdom sixteen years, and when he died, his son Cynric succeeded to the kingdom and held it twenty-seven years. (4) When he died, Ceawlin succeeded to the kingdom and reigned for twenty-five years. (5) When he died Ceol succeeded to the kingdom and held it six years. (6) When he died his brother Ceolwulf succeeded and ruled seventeen years, and their ancestry goes back to Cerdic.

Plummer's major oversight, however, is that the Creoda generation is also missing in the Preface. Plummer himself recognizes the missing Creoda generation and that Creoda is Cynric's son,[148] which Whitelock also verifies in the genealogy of the West Saxon royal house,[149] yet Plummer does not account for it. This means that other changes and additions must also be made to the above passage beginning with the first line, which has to be adjusted to "Cerdic and

	Preface	Chronicle
Cerdic	500+16=516	34 years: 500–534
Creoda	517+17=534	
Cynric	534+26=560	26 years: 534–560
Ceawlin	560+25=585	31 years: 560–591
Ceol	585+6=591	
Ceolwulf	591+17=608	14 years: 597–611
Cynegils	608+31=639	31 years: 611–642
Cenwalh	639+31=670	29 years: 643–672 Parker Chronicle A̅
		641–670 Mss A, B, C, E
Sexburg	670+1=671	1 year: 672–673
		670–671
Aescwine	671+2=673	2 years: 673–675

Table 8. Reconciliation of discrepancies between the *Anglo-Saxon Chronicle* and its Genealogical Preface. The bold-faced dates show the striking similarities of dates. Compare to Plummer's chart.

Creoda his son." In order to add that omission, other modifications must then be made. There follows between sentence (2) and sentence (3) enigmatic pronoun references. Sentence (2) is referring to *two* kings, but then sentence (3) contains two *singular* pronoun references of "he." There is no scribal error possible of the singular pronoun "he" being substituted *twice* for the plural pronoun "they." Sentence (3) would make no sense if it were to read "*They* held the kingdom sixteen years and when *they* died ...." The only other possibility is that the pronoun reference is to Cerdic, because he is the leader, and his son Creoda is a prince. That pronoun reference "he," therefore, needs an antecedent which is "Cerdic," so that sentence (3) would change to "*Cerdic* held the kingdom sixteen years, and when he died his son *Creoda* succeeded to the kingdom." The name "Cynric" would have to be changed to "Creoda" because Cerdic did not have a son named Cynric, but a *grandson* by that name. On the other hand, if the pronoun reference is to Creoda as the chief, then the proper name "Cynric" could remain as is and the sentence would change to "Creoda held the kingdom sixteen years, and when he died his son Cynric succeeded to the kingdom." This would imply, however, that Cerdic was killed in the year 500 in the battle for the West Saxon kingdom. It could be argued that Cerdic may have been killed in 494, but there is no battle in the entry for that year in the Preface. According to the *Chronicle*, a battle between the West Saxons and the Welsh occurred in the year 495, but the Preface is silent about a conflict earlier than the year 500. Additionally, if this were the case, Cerdic's length of reign would be passed over in the Preface; therefore, the passage would be more accurately rendered in the following way:

> In the year of Christ's nativity 494, Cerdic and Creoda his son landed at Cerdiscesora with five ships. (1) Six years after they landed they conquered the kingdom of

494—Cerdic and *Creoda* his son landed at Cerdicesora with five ships.

500—Six years after they landed they conquered the kingdom of Wessex. These were the first kings who conquered the land of Wessex from the Welsh. Cerdic holds the kingdom for 16 years. 516—*Cerdic* held the kingdom 16 years, and when he died his son *Creoda* succeeded to the kingdom.

534—*In this year Creoda died.* Cynric inherited the kingdom of the West Saxons and ruled for 26 years. 560— *When Cynric passed away, his son Ceawlin succeeded to the kingdom and held it 25 years.* 585—When *Ceawlin* died, Ceol succeeded to the kingdom and held it for 6 years. 591—When Ceol died his brother Ceolwulf succeeded and ruled 17 years, and their ancestry goes back to Cerdic.

608—Then Cynegils, Ceolwulf's brother's son, succeeded to the kingdom and ruled 31 years, and he was the first of the West Saxon kings to receive baptism. 639—Then Cenwalh succeeded and held it 31 years; and that Cenwalh was the son of Cynegils. 671—Then Cenwalh's queen Seaxburh held the kingdom one year after him.

495—In this year two princes, Cerdic and *Creoda* his son, came to Britain in five ships at a place which is called Cerdicesora. 500—[Ethelwerdian chronicle] In the sixth year after their arrival they conquered the western part of Britain which is now called Wessex: Whitelock, footnote 5, page 11. 519—In this year Creoda obtained the kingdom of the West Saxons; the same year they fought against the Britons at Cerdicesford.[1] 534—In this year Creoda died and his son Cynric ruled for 27 years.[2]

560—In this year Ceawlin succeeded to the kingdom in Wessex; Ælle to the kingdom of the Northumbrians.

591—In this year Ceol reigned for six years. [MSS E and A give six years instead of five.] 593—In this year Ceawlin, Cwichelm, and Crida perished. 611—In this year Cynegils succeeded to the kingdom in Wessex, and held it for 31 years. Cynegils was the son of Ceol, the son of Cutha, the son of Cynric.[3]

641—And Cenwalh succeeded to the kingdom of the West Saxons and held it for 31 years.[4] 672—In this year Cenwalh died, and his queen Seaxburh reigned one year after him.

---

1. Based upon the clue from the Preface, Cerdic dies or is killed at this point, and the name Creoda should replace the name Cerdic in all entries until entry 534.

2. The name Cerdic should be replaced with the name Creoda to account for the lost generation. This would mean that Creoda ruled for 18 years.

3. *611 + 31 = 642, but Cynegils' death is given as 641. This one-year discrepancy gives credence to the date of 609 in the Preface for Cynegils' succession.

4. **At this point manuscripts A, B, C, E are two years behind $\bar{A}$.

Table 9. Contrast of dates from the *Anglo-Saxon Chronicle* and the Genealogical Preface, resolved by this text.

Wessex. (2) These were the first kings who conquered the land of Wessex from the Welsh. (3) Cerdic held the kingdom sixteen years, and when he died his son Creoda succeeded to the kingdom and held it until his death. (4) When Creoda passed away, his son Cynric succeeded to the kingdom and held it twenty-seven years. (5) When he died, Ceawlin succeeded and held it twenty-five years. (6) When he died Ceol succeeded to the kingdom and held it six years. (7) When he died his brother Ceolwulf succeeded and ruled seventeen years, and their ancestry goes back to Cerdic.

What this means is that the year 494 in the Preface is accurate because it is based upon the Dionysiac method of reckoning (the year of Christ's nativity), and the Preface had the derivational information added later as an incorrect interpolation, most likely for the reason that, since *two* generations had been omitted, there had to be an explanation of what transpired during that time frame. If the derivational information is ignored, and both the Creoda/Ceawlin generations are inserted, then the assumption from sentence (4) accurately reflects that Cynric's reign should be listed as 27 years long.

Summarized, Cerdic's son is Creoda, not Cynric. Cerdic dies in the year 516, and upon the insertion of Creoda's generation, the *ASC* and Ethelwerd entry of 534 should record Creoda's death, not Cerdic's. According to the Preface and the *ASC*, Cynric reigns for 26 years, and Ceawlin's reign is 25 years, separate from Ceol's short reign of six years. Then, as shown in Table 8, once the four basic modifications are made, the Genealogical Preface and the *Chronicle* meld the way they should; a surprisingly accurate calibration emerges for Cerdic, Creoda, Cynric, Ceowlin, and other successors even beyond that.

The emphasis is on the *reigns* of the West Saxon kings, *not* upon the actual events which were earlier resolved. Modifications made in the Preface are indicated by bold italics, while modifications in the *Chronicle* are underlined, with a bracketed commentary following the entry. So that the table can be tabulated in its totality, some of the entries are footnoted directly below the chart rather than being included in the brackets as commentary.

Accepting the modifications at the beginning of the genealogy shows how amazingly similar the Genealogical Preface and the *ASC* have become. If Creoda's generation is added with his death in 534, and if Ceawlin's and Ceol's generations are added with the respective reigns of 25 and 6 years, and if Cynric's reign is left intact at 27 years, then with few exceptions, the other entries fall into place, with either identical dates or dates within one year of each other. Tables 8 and 9 are tabulations of the same information in different formats. Compare the surprising accuracy of these matching chronologies with the one given by Plummer in Table 7.

Chapter 3
The Cardinal and
Ordinal Years for the
Arthurian Chronology

As revealed in Chapter 2, modern attempts to chronologically date manuscripts from the early centuries presents a difficult hurdle. The reckoning process nowadays is so automatic that no one gives it a second thought. With the entrenchment of the Gregorian calendar, the attitude toward its developmental stage is nonchalant and the inherent difficulties of early dating are viewed apathetically. Once a way to mark time is established, indifference sets in for all except those who deal with early reckonings. Historically, the Gregorian calendar is quite recent, with countries applying the Gregorian reform at various times as recently as 1752 in England and Sweden. There are not too many difficulties with Julian calendar leftovers for September, October, November, and December as our ninth, tenth, eleventh, and twelfth months, even though *Sept-*, *Octo-*, *Nove-*, and *Decim-* literally mean seven, eight, nine and ten respectively. Of parenthetical interest is the reformation of the Roman calendar by Julius Caesar. Julius sent for a Greek astronomer by the name of Sosigenes to serve as his advisor. When the calendar was changed in 46 B.C., that year supposedly became known as the last year of confusion.

Unfortunately it was not truly so; it would make the placement of Arthur so much easier. As soon as a question is formulated, "When did Arthur ...," the method of chronology becomes important. Without belaboring the point, prior to a Christianized chronology, calibration was sketchy at best; one can rely on genealogies, with the lineal descent of emperors, kings, and nobles giving some sort of historical feel; tribal laws can also function as a source; the law itself— and then any amendments and changes — also reflects a sequence of events.

Nevertheless, even with the advent of Christianized reckonings the problem was not solved. As with the easy acceptance of modern-day calendars, there is a misconception of what early Christian books were. One tends to think of clean, crisp, printed material packaged by a hard cover, one entire unit, but of course the manuscripts, normally printed on a coarse vellum, are piecemeal. They are sometimes torn, fragmented, stained, blackened by fire, pierced by wormholes, mildewed, and difficult to read not because of the language choice, but because they are not formatted with sentences, punctuation, capitalization, or paragraphing. Johannes Gutenberg was to the printed word what Dionysius Exiguus was to temporal calibration.

Arthur's era was an age of continuous turmoil and conflict. The struggle for basic necessities left no time for more refined pursuits, and daily demands in order to survive generated isolation because of deprivation and distrust. Recording history for posterity was not a high priority; most of the writing was done by ecclesiastics to take care of day-to-day business or to disseminate religious doctrine, and history for the most part was an incidental consequence. Annals, journals, records, and diaries were written for express purposes, and it was not until centuries later that the inherent history of the records was deemed important enough to preserve. Civilized empires like Rome knew the value of the written word, but the ravages of time have left meager legacies.

The making of only one copy of a manuscript was costly, tedious work, and of course, accuracy suffered. Miscopying was not uncommon, and that coupled with a scribe trying to embellish or improve upon the original has led to present-day difficulties in trying to distinguish what parts are the original manuscript and what parts are later interpolations added by a scribe copying the manuscript. The problem is compounded when there is, for instance, a manuscript from the fifth century that was copied by a scribe in the eighth century, with a later scribe in the tenth century copying the manuscript from the eighth century. The tenth century copy is twice-removed from the original, with two different sets of interpolations, and if scribe number two added incorrect information which scribe number three thought was accurate, and additionally wanted to insert a personal hypothesis, information became jumbled beyond recognition.

This is true of Arthurian history and the Dark Ages. As Leslie Alcock mentions, no fifth or sixth century manuscripts which are directly relevant to Arthurian study have survived. This kind of probe into the history of 1,500 years ago requires the scholar to rely upon an incomplete copy of a copy of a copy. As Alcock points out, that means many times the only source of information is a tenth century manuscript written by an eighth century scribe about events in the fifth century.[1] Another interesting example is given by G.N. Garmonsway. There are six variant copies of the *Anglo-Saxon Chronicle*, and in one of them, the Parker Chronicle, the handwriting of 13 or possibly 14 scribes can be traced. It is wondrous that the ancient manuscripts came down through the ages with the accuracy they did.

Nevertheless, even though the number of errors is proportionately minimal, the researcher must be vigilant. The process of repeated copying, aside from interpolations, leads to other problems, too, in the transmissions. Simple, honest errors by the scribes have led to complex contradictions for the modern scholar, especially if these scribal errors cannot be resolved by modern scholars through a separate work on the same subject. If, for instance, a scribe transposed the Roman "XL" to "LX," it meant a difference of 20 years to the historian; omissions such as "DD" for "DDD" meant a century difference. Already discussed, too, if the Victorian method of reckoning were used instead of the Dionysiac, then an event would be displaced by 28 years.

Another possible chronological aberration complicates the reckoning process even further. This last disparity centers on the transfer of information from the Easter Tables to the Easter Annals and the ensuing 19-year discrepancy because of possible miscalculations of the lunar cycle, a pitfall encountered in Alcock's pursuit of calibrations. Chapter 2 of the present text should also have made evident the difficulty of discussing the calibration of a singular event like the Battle of Badon without also interweaving it with a series of other events such as the writing of the *De Excidio*, the birth of Gildas, the *Adventus* of the Saxons, and Maelgwn's death. Inherent in the linkage of these series of events is the counterbalancing necessity of deliberately postponing the scrutiny of other events, such as ignoring the identities of the Briton and Saxon leaders at Badon, or the role of Ambrosius Aurelianus in the Saxon rebellion against Vortigern, to maintain a sharp focus on the issue at hand.

Because causal relationships are confusing enough in a morass of dates, variances, and overlaps, some information must be pigeonholed and postponed for later development in order to isolate specific events for sharp clarification. The drawback of this procedure is linked with an advantage: there may be repetition, but this could be beneficial in order to imprint important data on the memory. Chapter 1 indicated that an eclectic approach is the best way to piece the puzzle of the historical Arthur together. One does not assemble a jigsaw by working left to right, or right to left, up to down or down to up; instead the puzzle-solver begins with the parameters — the general borders — and then works randomly first with one side of the picture, then sometimes for no apparent reason, switches to a different segment. The single individual pieces are important only in the way in which they relate to the entire panorama.

Last, a scribe's personal background is another important factor which affected manuscript reproduction. If the scribe was copying information from an original which he did not understand, or perhaps only partially understood, then the likelihood of errors increased. If he was fluent in a language such as Latin but was not aware of Welsh nuances and did not know Saxon at all, then clues for geographic place names or etymological subtleties were lost, and those connotative differences in words are inestimable to present researchers.

Chronology is the essential base for verifying the authenticity of Arthur. The sequence of events demonstrates his role in history and must be as detailed as possible in order to extricate Arthur from the realm of figmentary imagination. To accomplish this goal, several basic pieces of the puzzle — termed the cardinal and ordinal years in this chapter — will be set into place. The primary concerns exclusive of Arthur concentrate on Gildas' birth-year, the three Saxon *Adventi*,

Maelgwn's death, the Cunedda migration to the south, Cerdic's role in the Arthurian saga, the penning of the *De Excidio*, and Gildas' death-year. The Arthurian matter of Badon and Camlann as they appear in the *Annales Cambriae* must also be analyzed as they relate to the milieu of other verified events. As examples, Gildas' birth has a direct bearing on establishing the year for the Battle of Badon; the penning of the *De Excidio* occurred during Maelgwn's lifetime, and hence is directly linked to Maelgwn's recorded death-year; Cunedda's migration cannot be calibrated without knowing when Maelgwn's reign began; reckoning the beginning of Vortigern's cannot be accomplished without knowing the year of the first Saxon *Adventus*; and the date for the Badon battle must be reconciled with Camlann's. And so it goes with the first serial of dates; once these basic cardinal and ordinal years are calibrated, others will follow until the sequence is complete.

Systems of Calibration

The three systems used to calibrate dates sprang from ecclesiatical needs. The initial system was the one devised in 457 by the scribal scholar Victorius of Aquitaine based upon Christ's death-year, referred to by clerics as the Passion of Christ.[2] He devised an Easter Table giving the dates for Easter for every year from the Passion of Christ down to his writing of the Table. But instead of stopping there, he calculated the dates into the distant future and discovered that 533 years after Christ's Passion, Easter would fall on the same day of the same month and in the same moon phase as in the year of the Passion itself. This repetition, which became known as the 532-year Great Cycle was the subject matter for the *computi*.

Sixty-eight years later Dionysius Exiguus used a system calibrating dates, based upon the birth of Christ, called the Incarnation.[3] From that point onward Christ's Incarnation as the base for calibration spread throughout the church, and it was used instead of the Victorian method of chronological fixing. Ecclesiastical scribes not only calibrated entries according to the Dionysiac Table but also began to replace computations which were done according to the Victorian table. Unfortunately, however, the replacement was neither methodical nor documented, so that as time passed there was no record to show which calculations had been done according to the Victorian Table and which had already been emended according to the Dionysiac system.

The difference between the two creates a 28-year span. In his book *Arthur's Britain*, Alcock was at first aware of only these two systems of reckoning in calibrating his two proposals of chronologies. He equates year 9 with A.D. 455, the Easter change by Pope Leo,[4] and then uses that beginning to compute the *AC* date for Badon as A.D. 518, since 518 is in year 72 of the cycle.[5] The calculation therefore follows this process: if year 9 = 455, then year 72 = 518. The span between years 9 and 72 equals 63, and hence 455 + 63 = 518, the date provided by Alcock's version of the *AC*. However, other computations have different starting points. John Morris, for example, picked up on this differential when he edited and translated *British History.* The dates which he provides for the *AC* begin the cycle with A.D. 444. In comparing that with Alcock's calculations for Badon, year 9 = A.D. 453 and year 72 (the Badon date) = 453 + 63 = 516.

Subsequent to the publication of *Arthur's Britain,* Alcock discovered the 19-year lunar cycles and wrote in the Preface:

> I now think that my discussion of the irreconcilable dates which the Welsh Easter Annals give for Badon and Maelgwn Gwynedd (pp. 22-4, 53-5) is too elaborate. Confusion between Incarnation and Passion dating is not the only way in which chronological errors can occur in the records of the period; another cause of error is confusion between successive nineteen-year Easter cycles. ... Secondly, my suggestion that the *computus* dates to A.D. 455 cannot be wholly correct because it contains a reference to Constantinus and Rufus, who were consuls in A.D. 457.[6]

He included addenda in two later books, *Cadbury/Camelot* and *Was This Camelot?*, about the Easter cycle. In searching for a computational adjustment for the Battle of Badon, he writes:

> The answer [for a Badon date] lies in a further consideration of the character of Easter Tables. Modern tables, like that, for instance, in the Book of Common Prayer, have *Anno Domini* dates in their left-hand column, and this has been the practice for well over a thousand years. But the system of A.D. dates, so familiar to us, was not invented until A.D. 525; so when we find such dates applied to events before then, they have been calculated from figures which had originally been expressed in terms of some other era.
>
> ... Now early Easter Tables sometimes covered a period of nineteen years only. The reason for this is that the date of Easter is governed by the phases of the moon, and nineteen years is a lunar cycle. It is probable that Badon was originally entered in a nineteen year table, with no further indication of date. Subsequently, some monk with historical interests copied the Badon entry into a table covering a longer span. But he misidentified the lunar cycle, and placed the battle exactly nineteen years too late.[7]

Accordingly, Alcock lists three logistic dates for Badon: 518 as it appeared in his version of the *AC*, 499 if the lunar adjustment is made, or 490 if the Dionysiac system is applied.

It should be noted, however, that Table 6 in the last chapter records the Battle of Badon in 516 because it is based upon Morris' two-year variation in *British History*, which is different from Alcock's reckoning. Alcock is aware of the difference and accepts that a variation of a year or two either way is the highest degree of chronological accuracy that may be expected during this period. Nevertheless, it causes confusion since both Alcock and Morris are such heavy contributors to the Arthurian material. Arbitrarily, for purposes of simplification in references, the dates from Morris are retained throughout this book when a cardinal date is being established. The postulations given by Alcock do not conflict with these reckonings, because any specific date proposed in this text has the ±

variation built into it without having to use expressions or symbols such as *circa*, *ca*, ©, <, or >.

Hence, as material was transcribed from the single Easter Tables to the Great Cycle Easter Annals, there was even more confusion because of the uncertainty of whether the Victorian Table or the Dionysiac Table had been used, compounded by the problematic discrepancy of the 19-year lunar cycle. For instance, the Badon battle is listed at year 516. If the calculation has been made according the Dionysiac Table based upon Christ's birth, then the calibration can stand as is with our modern method of reckoning. However, if the Victorian Table has been employed, then by modern reckoning, the correct year would have to be adjusted to year 488. The third possibility, a lunar adjustment, would establish the battle in 497. The question of which date is correct, of course, poses a major problem.

The resolution is by no means simple. If the manuscript itself did not explain the method it used, there were limited ways to verify any conversion. The best, though rare and difficult to determine, would be cross-checks of any parent manuscripts. Next would be obvious references to the same event from some other reliable work. And last, if at all possible, would be setting the questionable event into a milieu of other established circumstances. If enough data is available, the conclusion will point accurately to one of the three choices.

There are even more difficulties to chronicling. What has been mentioned so far applies only to the three systems of post–Christian reckoning. Summarizing the information on the Easter Tables into a compact format gives a fairly comprehensive picture of what transpired because Christianized calibrations at least give a standardized pattern in dealing with problems of chronology. But prior to Victorius of Aquitaine, dating was characterized by regnal listings, genealogies and family trees, natural phenomena, diseases and disasters, and sometimes local or regional laws, with major differences in the reckonings or very vague references which have become more and more obscure with the passage of time. The Arthurian epoch balances between these two eras.

The quest for Arthur begins with his historical entrance, the Battle of Badon which is listed in the *Historia Brittonum* and the *Annales Cambriae*, but the latter is the only source which records a year. His passing at the Battle of Camlann appears only in the *AC*, also with a year attached. Several scholars might object to this span on the grounds that Badon is not Arthur's first battle, nor was Camlann his last. Some researchers set his military activities from 446 to approximately 470, suggesting that he died in his forties; others begin his career around 446 at an age of approximately 15 and list his last battle as the Battle of Camlann, when as a centigenarian he was finally released from his earthly duties in this life. The premise of this book — which will be echoed several times in the course of its search — is to begin as closely as possible to the actual era of Arthur using authentically based data about Badon and Camlann, and from there branch out into literary tradition.

At this point it is crucial to keep uppermost in mind that there are only the four major sources listed earlier which can be drawn upon for information. Gildas' *De Excidio* is chronologically important because of the following:

1. the passage about the Battle of Bath-hill attached to his birth-year;
2. the Saxon landing;
3. cross-referencing the *De Excidio* with the other three historical sources, plus the Irish Annals as a parent reference.

Gildas gives no dates, but by using the procedures outlined above, calibrations can be made from other sources to determine Gildas' birth-year, the date of his writing the *De Excidio*, and his death-year, all of which are fixed (not variable) dates in the three proposed chronologies to be established in this chapter.

One of the other indispensable sources mentioned, the *AC*, is important for the Easter Tables and Easter Annals. In looking at this information it is vital to remember that dates from the Easter Annals and Easter Tables can involve discrepancies because of ecclesiastic variations. This is why, in the formulation of the Arthurian chronology in this chapter, that some calibrations from whatever the source remain fixed, but certain dates such as entries referring to the Battle of Badon and the Battle of Camlann vary, since they derived from some manuscript other than a known parent source.

The third major manuscript is the *Anglo-Saxon Chronicle* that "narrates an account of the fifth and sixth centuries which is largely independent of the other two."[8] It provides

1. events of Britain's primary enemy during the Arthurian period;
2. reckonings for those events;
3. an affirmation of battles listed elsewhere with the Britons;
4. a cross-reference check with other major and minor sources;
5. a very keen possibility of determining not only the chronologies for specific battles, but also the geographic locations and the persons involved in the events.

There is justification, therefore, for some dates remaining fixed while others are subject to modification. The four major sources must provide a comprehensive base for dealing with the historic Arthur, followed by later medieval records, whether it be from Geoffrey of Monmouth, antiquarians, ancient literature, or the romances. This does not negate the importance of these later sources, nor does it ignore Leslie Alcock's comments that for the ancient manuscripts there are no extant originals, but only copies or copies of copies which survived from the sixth century. All manuscripts play a role, but each must be weighted for its contribution.

Cardinal Years for the Arthurian Chronology

Although some calibrations might seem discouragingly unattainable, enough manuscripts have survived to trace human endeavors, thanks to the previous work by antiquarians, historians, scribes, monks, scholars, researchers, and scientists in all fields. An example of this accomplishment is evidenced by Table 6 in the previous chapter. In verifying the historical Arthur, the Herculean task begins with this matter of chronology; the first exigency for a strategic plan is to anchor each substantive year which will function as a cardinal reckoning for all other dates. By definition, this text has coined the term *cardinal year* if it meets the following conditions:

1. the source is one of the ancient manuscripts which implicitly or explicitly gives a time frame;
2. the implicit or explicit date can be verified from a separate historic (not literary) source;
3. The date which is confirmed in this way must have direct bearing on Arthur.

If more than one other document offers a cross-check for the established date, that makes it still better. Similarly, from the onset the underlying tenet for a cardinal year must convey that any date thus established remain fluid; that is, even if a specific year is conscripted, there is the basic understanding that a standard deviation of at least two years will be factored into the computation of that cardinal date. If there is a correlation of two dates from two separate reliable sources, and those dates are within a two- to three-year limit, that is viewed as more than satisfactory. There must be concessions for chronologists calibrating dates from 1,500 years previously; precision-reckoning is an unrealistic expectation, especially when considering the scarcity of documents that survived 15 centuries of destruction, the primitive techniques of transcription and distribution, the ravages of change, the shrinkage of civilization during the early medieval ages counterbalanced by the rise of apathetic barbarism, and a host of other setbacks.

This does not mean that just any fanciful date is acceptable for cardinal years in the chronology. A full treatise does not follow every suggestion of a year, but there must be a balance between blind acceptance and justifiable suppositions. Whenever a postulation is proposed, as many defensible details as possible will be given, in addition to verification by other researchers, scholars, and sources for checks and balances. The procedure is somewhat cumbersome in its detail, but one of the primary purposes of this text is to create a resource-book on Arthurian history. So that the documentation is as close to a scientific method of inquiry as possible, other sources are often quoted verbatim, with close monitoring to safeguard against misinformation or misinterpretation. One other advantage of the prolific use of other sources is the elimination of the need to expound upon theories that previous experts have already synthesized. If a reader wishes to exhaust other viewpoints, a detailed bibliography is provided.

The one exception to the above conditions for a cardinal year is the Easter date which immediately follows. The Easter change does meet the condition of an explicit date given in historic manuscripts, verified by a separate historic source, but it really does not have a *direct* relevance to Arthur's milieu. Even though it has this shortcoming, however, it is listed as a cardinal year because of its pervading influence on the entire chronology which follows its adjustment.

THE EASTER CHANGE: CARDINAL YEAR #1

The first cardinal year evolves from the calibrations computing the year in which Pope Leo I changed the day of Easter. Alcock explains

> Fortunately year 9 deals with an event which we can date because of its general Christian significance: "Easter is changed on the Lord's Day by Pope Leo, bishop of Rome." This is known to have happened in A.D. 455. If the ninth year is A.D. 455, the first year is A.D. 447. Whenever this calibration can be tested against dates known from other sources it appears to work within a year or two either way, which is the highest degree of chronological accuracy that may be expected in this period.[9]

The process allows conversion from pagan reckoning to the Christianized dating. Fortunately, because there are no major discrepancies — that is, Alcock listing A.D. 455 when Pope Leo altered Easter as opposed to Morris listing that Easter change in year 453 — this cardinal date is not controversial or extensively debated by scholars. In his option for the date, Alcock gives some background on the format for the Easter Tables and Easter Annals. He terms the prefaces to these church manuscripts as the *computus* or a set of *calculi* which summarized the cycles for determining when the celebration for Easter should be.

In turn, the acceptance of this date strengthens the faith for other entries in the Easter Annals, since in the fifth and sixth centuries the British Annals were using cyclical tables in striving for uniformity. This would reinforce the dates in the *AC*, since the Easter and Irish Annals are the base for them. Alcock has similar convictions, leading to his judgment that the Easter Annals are a reliable source which can aid in authenticating Arthur.[10] He stresses the role of the Easter Annals in formulating an accurate chronology for Arthur; after indicating their importance and his awareness of the additional confusion of successive 19-year Easter cycles, he explains:

> Much more detailed study will be required before we can make a sound assessment of the sources that lie behind these records [the Easter Annals] and of their historical value. ... I would not rush to conclude that this [his calculation of year 455 for the Easter change] vitiates my entire use of the *computus* and the Annals.[11]

By extension that means if the Easter Annals themselves are a reliable source for authenticating Arthur, then the *Annales Cambriae* and the Irish Annals as parent manuscripts can be viewed in the same way.

BATTLE OF BADON/BIRTH OF GILDAS: CARDINAL YEAR #2, AND SAXON LANDING: CARDINAL YEAR #3

Cardinal years #2 and #3 actually tie three events together — the Battle of Badon, the birth of Gildas, and the Saxon Landing. Only two early sources — the *Historia Brittonum* and the *Annales Cambriae* — name Arthur as the Briton leader in the Battle of Badon, which exemplifies why it is mandatory to use the documents cited in Chapter 2 in conjunction with each other. Gildas, although he does not refer to King Arthur in the *De Excidio*, offers a clue for unlocking the date for the Battle of Badon, which is the major area of interest at this point and not whether Arthur was the leader. Once established, this particular battle becomes the singular, most important key to the entire Arthurian chronology. This *anno Domini* will supply the lifeblood for the entire structure of calibration, obviously not running sequentially from Arthur's birth to his death.

The Battle of Badon is an excellent starting point to establish the historical Arthur in the scheme of things for several reasons. First, it establishes an objective date for an important battle independent of Arthur's involvement, which is beneficial since there is no vested interest which can be claimed. Second, because three sources are involved, the verification of the date is strengthened. A specific date is not given by Gildas, but in spite of garbled grammatical structure, a calculation can be made for a particular year. This can then be compared to the specific year given in the *Annales*. Devising a chronology for Arthur using this technique, unlike some genealogical searches, will begin with the Battle of Mount Badon and work in either direction, sometimes toward his death, and sometimes toward his birth. By the end of the search, however, it will become evident why the calibration of cardinal dates makes sense in what at first appears a random selection of years. The result will give a solid picture from approximately 420 until 560.

Earlier, as an example, the three possible dates for the Badon battle were given: 488, 497, and 516. Each scholar has given good reasons why one of those particular dates makes more sense than the other two — a difficult, slow, laborious process when it comes to extracting one tiny piece of information which finally tips the scale of one in favor of the others. Alcock goes through the same process; although his parallel dates are 490, 499, and 518 (an acceptable variation since they are within the standard deviation) the technique is the same. He sets the latest Badon possibility (the Victorian reckoning of 516/518) by explaining that this particular battle, according to the *AC*, occurred in "... year 72 of the cycle, which may be reckoned as A.D. 518."[12] Ashe follows suit in *The Quest for Arthur's Britain* by writing that

> An early Welsh source, the *Annales Cambriae*, dates the "battle of Badon" with a slight ambiguity in 516 or 518.[13]

This is the Morris/Alcock variation of two years, but Ashe is speaking generally of Badon and does not pursue a date; instead, he talks of Arthur as a Celt who may have been born in the 470s, with the possibility that later Arthurs were named after the British hero of the earlier date. Similarly, in the same book Ashe does not address a date for Badon because his theory implants Arthur two to three decades before the end of the fifth century. With Arthur's career ending in the 470s, Ashe concludes that Arthur could not have fought at either Badon or Camlann. As an explanation of Arthur's linkage to these battles, he offers the possibility that there were two Arthurs, the real one and a synthetic hero, or perhaps the leader of Badon was *like* Arthur, or like Arthur's men. Ashe's speculations are offered for comparison, but this text earlier established the southwestern Arthur, meaning that the battle at Badon has already been accepted as a foregone conclusion; the remaining problem is calibrating its date.

Of this year for the Battle of Badon and the birth of Gildas, Alcock writes:

> ... when all the allowance is made for the chronological vagueness of the *De Excidio*, it is difficult to believe that there was any long interval between the initial Ambrosian victory some time before 475 and the triumph of Badon. If this view is sound, then it becomes difficult to think of Badon as late as 518.[14]

As Alcock suggests, the Gildas material in Chapter 23 relates Vortigern's invitation to the Saxons, in Chapter 24 the Saxon treachery and slaughter of the Britons, and in Chapter 25 the rise of Ambrosius Aurelianus, followed in Chapter 26, the Battle of Badon when the slaughter of the Britons ended. This format indicates that one event closely followed the other.

For the second possibility, the date using the Dionysiac system would be 28 years earlier, emending the date to 488 according to Morris' translation of the *AC* in *British History* or to 490 according to Alcock's reckoning. Alcock adds a last segment to the quotation above, concluding succinctly that, "In other words, a consideration of the possible dates for Ambrosius leads us to favor the alternative earlier date for Badon, namely A.D. 490."[15] He reaffirms the date later in the same text; it is important, however, to keep in mind that at this point in his research and discoveries, Alcock had not yet proposed the lunar-cycle discrepancies.

The third possibility, if the lunar cycles are considered, would be 19 years earlier than the Victorian system and 9 years later than the Dionysiac format, emending the year to 497/499. Once this discovery was made by Alcock, he altered what he had said earlier in *Arthur's Britain*. In an appendix entitled "The Battle of Badon" in *Cadbury/Camelot*, he writes:

> If this is so, then Badon should not be placed at year 72 of the British Easter Annals, A.D. 518, but at year 53, A.D. 499. To check this we add 43 for Gildas' lifetime, to arrive at A.D. [Alcock meant A.D. 542 and A.D. 549 respectively.] 442 for the time he was writing, seven years before Maelgwn's death in A.D. 449.[16]

If we emend Alcock's new proposal according to Morris' adjustment, the year becomes A.D. 497 with the 19-year lunar correction.

On this issue, Ashe writes that

> Alcock virtually abandoned his defense of the *Annales* entries about [the dates for Badon and Camlann] in his British Academy lecture. These [Badon and Camlann entries] are now discounted as historical evidence, and the chief question is where they come from.[17]

Ashe's text is more recent than either the edition of Alcock's *Arthur's Britain* or his *Cadbury/Camelot* but because no specifics are given by Ashe, the conclusion cannot be drawn that Alcock abandoned the Badon and Camlann entries based solely upon his not mentioning them in a lecture. As a matter of fact, earlier in the chapter of *Arthur's Britain*, Alcock avers that he will pursue studies of the Easter Annals, suggesting that he considers the two entries of Badon and Camlann are crucial and indispensable to the study of the Arthurian material. Applying more reservation and caution, then, the two entries should stand on their own merit, and only after all facets are applied should they be judged. If the Badon entry in particular were to be abandoned, then both Gildas and Nennius would be negated, two absolutely monumental and vital ancient documents. In any case, both entries must be judged in relation to a host of other criteria.

One way the issue of the precise year in the *AC* can be cross-checked and resolved is by analyzing the Gildas passage as a separate event which can be historically verified. The Badon passage from Gildas which continuously receives widespread attention from scholars reads:

> After this [the slaughter of the Britons by the Saxons followed by Ambrosius Aurelianus arising as savior and obtaining a victory], sometimes our countrymen, sometimes the enemy won the field, ... until the year of the siege of Bath-hill, when took place also the last almost, though not the least slaughter of our cruel foes, which was (as I am sure) forty-four years and one month after the landing of the Saxons, and also the time of my own nativity.[18]

This passage, skimpy in its information, raises myriads of questions and leads to as many conjectures so that many references will be made to it in a search for answers. For now, interest is concentrated on calibrating a date for the Badon siege. The way in which Gildas words this particular passage could be interpreted in different ways because of its syntactic structure. In addition to the obvious question which arises — "What was the year of the siege of Bath-hill?" — a second is, "When was the Saxon landing?" Gildas does not make things easy by giving a date, nor does he help by being grammatically precise. Unlike Nennius or the *Anglo-Saxon Chronicle*, he does not supply the names of Hengist or Horsa in reference to the Saxon *Adventus*, although he does mention a *surperbus tyrannus* who invited the Saxons in.

The Saxon landing is a major obstacle. However, Alcock in *Arthur's Britain* clearly extrapolates that in reality there were *three* distinctive Saxon landings, not just one. To maintain the proper focus of establishing Cardinal year #2 for Badon, the most commonly accepted Saxon landing will be used as Cardinal year #3, and then later, when more appropriate, the two other Saxon landings will specifically be established as other cardinal years. For conformity, this means that the cardinal years for the Saxon landings will be in reverse chronological order, since the year of the last landing will be established first.

Hence it is with full knowledge that merely accepting the date of 449 as listed in the *Anglo-Saxon Chronicle* is simplistic. Nevertheless, it is the launching point which can be modified later if it is shown to be inaccurate. One of the interpretations of the Gildas passage could be that Gildas was born in the same year as the landing of the Saxons, in 449, when the *Chronicle* places Hengist and Horsa's invitation into Britain by Vortigern to help defeat the Picts. This possibility can be eliminated quite quickly, particularly in conjunction with the three possible dates of Gildas' death. At the most realistic, he would be 93 years old at his death; at the least realistic, 123 years old.

The *Chronicle* offers a clue which helps fix not only the cardinal date for Badon but also one (the last) of the Saxon landings. In addition to names such as Hengist, Horsa, and Vortigern, there are two undoubted historical figures in the *Chronicle* entry who clinch the date for the last Saxon *Adventus*: the Roman emperors Marcian and Valentinian. Any standard encyclopedia gives Marcian's rise to the throne as 450 by his agreeing to marry the sister of the deceased emperor Theodosius II, and his death on January 26, 457. Valentinian III is listed as Emperor of the West, who died in 455. Morris does not write much about these two emperors, but he does include both in his Table of Dates, with the same information.[19] Bede gives the date 449 as listed in the *Chronicle* but then adds that

> Martian [Marcian] became Emperor with Valentinian, the forty-sixth in succession from Augustus, ruling for seven years. In his [Marcian's] time, the Angles or Saxons came to Britain at the invitation of King Vortigern in three long-ships.[20]

Like his source Gildas, he does not link Hengist or Horsa with Vortigern in the passage, but approximately a page later he adds, "Their first chieftains are said to have been the brothers Hengist and Horsa." At the end of that chapter, Bede also paraphrases Gildas by stating that the Battle of Badon took place about 44 years after the Saxon arrival in Britain.

This information does not give a specific year, but the the known reigns of Marcian and Valentinian set the Battle of Badon between the years 450 and 457, with the median year being 453. Accepting this year with its ± standard deviation of one year, by mathematical calculation both the Battle of Badon and Gildas' birth would have taken place 44 years beyond 453, giving the cardinal year of 497. As a cross-check from the year 516 given for Badon in the *AC*, if the discrepancy of a 19-year lunar cycle is subtracted as Alcock proposes from the date of 516, the year 497 resurfaces. This means that 497 is a secure lock-in as the date for the Badon battle and for Gildas' birth.

Unfortunately, there is no other source which can verify unconditionally 497 as Gildas' birth, but there is a source — the *Anglo-Saxon Chronicle*—which can offer a reasonable and sensible check for the Battle of Badon. Nennius relates that Arthur's major battles are against the Saxons with the twelfth battle being a victorious Briton encounter against the enemy. Gildas, too, verifies this by writing that Badon was the "last almost" battle in which the Britons were victors and stopped encroachment and foreign wars even though some civil troubles still remained.

The closest *Chronicle* entry to the date of 497 is the entry of 495, which records that two Saxon chieftains came into Britain and fought against the Britons on the same day. Unlike some of the other *Chronicle* entries, this particular entry does not indicate a Briton flight, devastation, or defeat, and the Saxons do not record or even imply a victory. Even though five ships invaded the island, there is no Saxon domination. Ethelwerd in his chronicle does add that the Saxons were finally victorious, but the emphasis must be on the word "finally," because he is making reference that ultimately, six years after their arrival, the Saxons conquered the western part of Britain, which is now called Wessex. Admittedly, six years between the Battle of Badon and the establishment of the West Saxon kingdom is not a generation as given by Gildas. For now, however, the focus must remain on the Badon battle, and in subsequent analyses, the issue of Wessex and the West Saxon kingdom will be resolved. The date of 497, however, has been established as the most probable date for the Battle of Badon, and the *Chronicle* entry for 495 offers the best verification to support this conclusion. From the *De Excidio*, the *Annales Cambriae*, and the *Anglo-Saxon Chronicle*, then, the year which marks the crucial Badon battle is 497. This is a firm lock-in date for Badon and becomes a stationary pivotal point to be used as a well-defined, unshakable reference for all other chronological reckonings hinging upon it. The same is true from the date established for the writing of the *AC*; all of the historical data rests on the stability of this foundation.

In the interest of impartiality, the two other Badon dates should be cross-checked with the *Anglo-Saxon Chronicle* to determine if it reports any battles which might fit the characteristics of the Badon encounter. The Victorian reckoning of 516 is the year as translated by Morris in the *Annales Cambriae*. The nearest entries to that date recorded in the *Chronicle* is for the years of 514 and 519, the former recording that in this year the West Saxons came into Britain with three ships and Stuf and Wihtgar put the Britons to flight, and the latter reporting that in this year Cerdic and Cynric succeeded to the kingdom of the West Saxons.

The word "flight" in entry 514 suggests Briton defeat rather than victory. The 519 entry is undeniably a Saxon victory, clinching a kind of permanence in the suggestion that the Saxons were now in control of the kingdom, particularly since manuscripts A and E of the *Chronicle* add "and the Princes of the West Saxons ruled from that day onward," and another adds that "Sunset stopped the slaughter." This indicates a major battle with a great deal of death and devastation, but the *Saxons* are the victors.

Opponents of the 497 date can assert that Saxon chronicles are for Saxon glorification and would therefore not contain entries of Briton success, therefore omitting any reference to the Badon battle. This is a supportable contention; in a historical record to aggrandize their nation, the Saxons would never admit to or record a defeat, nor would chroniclers deliberately lie about an event which contemporaries of that era could easily check. Quite a few entries attest to the techniques of a scribe omitting the entry or maximizing the accomplishment of his ancestors without claiming victory, rather than misrepresenting history.

If there is the possibility that the Battle of Badon was fought in 516 but unrecorded in the Saxon *Chronicle*, the 519 entry in which the tables turned drastically seems unlikely; the Gildas manuscript conveys an extended sense of Briton elation from a victory, not a brief interlude followed by depression from a Saxon victory only three years after the Briton success. In this section Gildas is writing in the past tense and specifically states that a new race that cannot remember the past troublesome era has succeeded to the Briton kingdom. It is evident, too, that this new Briton race, this new generation, is a reference to Briton dominion — not a Saxon one. Gildas is relating that the Briton victory of the Battle of Badon offered a generational respite from foreign conflicts. The new generation cannot remember the pride and virtue of the Badon victory because there has been relative peace in that interim. None of this suggests a mere three-year passage of time. Nothing here, then, really verifies (but in fact denies) the year of 516 for the Battle of Badon.

The last possible date for Badon, with the Dionysiac adaptation to the chronology applied to the *Annales Cambriae* entry, is 488. A check for a parallel entry in the *Anglo-Saxon Chronicle* also turns up an entry for 488, which records that the (East) Saxons succeeded to the kingdom and Aesc became the king of the people of Kent. Again, this does not suggest a Briton victory, nor even a stand-off as might have been reported by the Saxons. Instead, when compared to the Gildas account, this period seems to reflect a time when the Saxons established a stronghold in the east prior to their raging from sea to sea, destroying lands and towns, and exterminating the Britons. And just when utter devastation seemed to be at hand, Ambrosius Aurelianus arose from the ashes and obtained a victory. The 488 date, followed by the entry of 491 that describes the siege of Andre-desceaster in which all the Britons were killed, does not imply the victorious battle at Badon, but reflects a Saxon time of domination just prior to massive incursions into the island.

Furthermore, the 488 date for Badon does not coordinate as well with other dates as proposed by the *AC*. If Gildas had been born in that same year, his death-year at 570 would have made him 82 years old, a more unrealistic figure than age 73. Morris lists the beginning of Maelgwn's reign as 520, and if Gildas' penning of the *De Excidio* occurred 44 years after his own birth, then the writing would be in the year of 532, within Maelgwn's reigning years. However, Gildas' invectives against Maelgwn reflect a later period in the king's reign. Gildas castigates Maelgwn for his offenses as a youth, his contrition and reform in his later years, and then a reversion to his old lascivious ways, all of which would indicate a period in the declining years of the king's tenure.

POSTULATIONS FROM SCHOLARS: CARDINAL YEAR #2: BADON BATTLE AS ASSOCIATED WITH BIRTH OF GILDAS AND SAXON LANDING

A summary is in order to determine how previous scholars view the cardinal date of 497 for the Battle of Badon. Thomas O'Sullivan is an excellent example of a scholar who scrutinizes all sides of issues as proposed by a variety of writers, weighs the evidence, and then establishes what seem to him the most plausible conclusions. All his information is pertinent to this Arthurian search, and

O'Sullivan's exactitude gives a perceptive idea of what other researches consider reasonable dates for the specified events. In addition to the O'Sullivan material, there are also citations from other sources.

Because Gildas' syntactic structure is hazy — as reflected in the 490 Dionysiac reckoning for Badon given earlier — it is necessary to look at the possibility of Gildas' birth not only at the *second* landing of the Saxons, but also at the Battle of Badon. The results of the three separate possibilities are interesting to compare, especially when looking at other postulations which have been proposed at various times.

Listing Gildas' birth-year at this second landing of the Saxons while keeping the Battle of Badon at the year 497 produced some curious results. By a statement in Gildas' own passage, he would have been writing the *De Excidio* 44 years later, which would have put his writings in the year 522, right in the middle of events when Britain was being devastated. The Britons were in their death-throes and the Saxons were poised to infiltrate the island for the next several decades; Cerdic's actions had established the kingdom of the West Saxons (including Wessex) and Saxon supremacy. Gildas would have been directly embroiled with the most significant events in the British Isles since the Roman conquest several centuries earlier. But the writings themselves indicate that time had elapsed and that Gildas was remembering things past.

The adjustment to the second Saxon landing also makes the time spans too long. From the writing of the *De Excidio* to Gildas' death would have been a span of 48 years. That would be an extraordinarily long period of silence unless Gildas had become even more reclusive and withdrawn. As outspoken as he was, this seems unlikely; if Gildas was incensed by the profligate Britons immediately after Camlann, he would have been even more outraged by what happened to Britain after the Saxons began coming into the country as victors. Another change would be his age (92) at the time of his death. That advanced age during this era is highly unlikely; other ages from other chronologies seem much more reasonable.

O'Sullivan indicates that "Plummer accepted the statement of Bede about the date of Badon, as a precise chronological reckoning, and assigned the siege to A.D. 493."[21] John Morris, in "Dark Age Dates" states, "... its plain meaning [Chapter 26 of Gildas] is that the wars ended more than a generation since, something like forty years or more ago, that Badon was fought about 500, or a little before. It is to be preferred to brittle manipulations or crude figure dates."[22] O'Sullivan himself accepts "... that the siege of mons Badonicus (and the birth of Gildas the Wise) took place ca. 490-500."[23] Alcock, fully aware of the discrepancies of dating, gives the most thorough presentation in offering the alternatives in the dating of Badon. In Chapter Three of *Arthur's Britain*, his introductory stance supports the possibility that Gildas' birth-year occurs simultaneously with the Battle of Mount Badon, in the year 518.[24] In the same chapter, he explains how the dates of 490 and 533 can be determined for the Battle of Badon and the Battle of Camlann respectively.[25] In Chapter Four, he explains in more detail why he feels that the 490 date is more probable than the 518 date for the Badon conflict.[26] It is not until after the publication of this particular edition that Alcock, in his Preface to the Pelican text, suggests the Badon date as 499.[27]

Other notable scholars have also recognized as a possibility the Battle of Badon was fought at the turn of the century. David Dumville lists very cautiously, and "at the risk of foolish over-simplification," the Battle of Mount Badon and Slaughter of the Saxons as ca. 500+.[28] Geoffrey Ashe, in *The Quest for Arthur's Britain*, puts the Badon siege tentatively at 516 or 518,[29] but he is not concerned with Badon in *The Discovery of King Arthur*, since the setting for that book is a different century and era. Kenneth Jackson, though, writes, "516 [for Badon] is probably too late by as much as ten or fifteen years," then extrapolates a date of 500.[30]

A summary of these sources, then, fixes the date for the Battle of Badon at either 493, or about 500 or a little before, or between 490 and 500, or 499 if the lunar cycle discrepancy is taken into account, or circa 500+, or 500. Although not using the same terminology, five of the seven scholars cited above point to the lunar cycle plus or minus only three years. All of this agreement circa the 497 cardinal year for Badon is logical, since the research is based upon these very scholars; that date, therefore, is not just a haphazard guess; it is one which, because it is well-based, will now be used to formulate other accurate chronological fixes within the lunar-adjusted chronology.

The other chronological calibrations now become simpler to propose. It is a short step to Gildas' birth-year. O'Sullivan relates the connection:

> But it is conceded that Gildas the Wise was himself born in the year of the siege of mons Badonicus. That is the premise with which we began. Few propositions about this period of history are more widely accepted, although there are exceptions.[31]

ADVENTI OF THE SAXONS: CARDINAL YEARS #4 AND #5

When the *Adventus* (third landing) of the Saxons was discussed earlier in this chapter in conjunction with the Battle of Badon to establish Cardinal year #3, the premise was retained for purposes of simplification that there was only one coming of the Saxons. At this point, to become more explicit, the focus must once more settle upon the expression "The coming of the Saxons." As the above heading suggests, instead of only one *Adventus*, three major comings, or, to coin a new Arthurian term, *Adventi*, have been accurately identified. This distinction is crucial because of its far-reaching implications. Although three major landings creates some intricate analytical complexities, they will be simplified because of the groundwork already laid. Alcock is the primary source; he indicates that the long-standing concept of a single Saxon *Adventus* might be hard to relinquish, but armed with archaeological evidence, the hypothesis can be formulated that there were at least three "comings of the English" in the second quarter of the fifth century and adds, "it is becoming apparent that the English settlement was much more complex, both in its chronology and in its character, than Bede would suggest."[32]

The "first" coming of the English occurs in 428 at the invitation of Vortigern. Unfortunately, because of the "compacting" of history in the early documents — the technique of including several historic events in a short passage which gives the impression that the events were concurrent or only a short period apart — scribes hooked together Vortigern, the first coming of the Saxons, and the names Hengist and Horsa. Gildas is not guilty of this, since he writes about Vortigern and the invitation to the Saxons but does not assign Hengist and Horsa as the Saxon leaders. Nennius, however, makes the Vortigern/*Adventus*/Hengist connection throughout the *Historia* after an introduction in Chapter 31 which ties together the three aspects and adds the donation of land to the incoming Saxons. Bede assigns the *Adventus* to the year 449 and then writes that in the time of Martian three long-ships of Saxons came into Britain at the invitation of King Vortigern. He later says that "[t]heir first chieftains *are said to have been* the brothers Hengist and Horsa [italics added]."[33] The *Anglo-Saxon Chronicle* picks up on the same information and in manuscripts B and C state succinctly, "In their days Hengest and Horsa, invited by Vortigern, king of the Britons, came to Britain at the place which is called Ebbsfleet, first to the help of the Britons, but afterwards fought against them."[34] Manuscript E gives more information, but the connection between the two events is still there: the first coming of the Saxons and Hengist/Horsa as their leaders are tied together by the ancient documents.

This connection has created a great deal of consternation for chronographers. Trying to establish sequential events with Hengist and Horsa linked to the first coming creates a task of trying to put square pegs into round holes. Vortigern invites the Saxons in — even Gildas, the earliest source, relates that fact in the opening passage of Chapter 23 — but nowhere in Gildas is there an implication that the Saxon leaders of that first coming were Hengist and Horsa. He relates only that "[The Saxons] first landed on the eastern side of the island, by the invitation of the unlucky king, and there fixed their sharp talons, apparently to fight in favour of the island."[35]

How, then, was the date of 428 for the *first* coming formulated? Some thorough researchers list this date, but they make the error of associating Hengist and Horsa with it. Alcock explains the confusion as well as anyone, which relates to the Dionysiac system. He begins his explanation by saying that the earliest reference to Vortigern is given in the *computi* of the Easter Annals of the *British Historical Miscellany*. The important part reads, "Vortigern held rule in Britain in the consulship of Theodosius II and Valentinian III. And in the fourth year of his reign the Saxons came to Britain in the Consulship of Felix and Taurus, in the 400th year from the incarnation of Our Lord Jesus Christ." Alcock then clarifies what this means:

> There is one major blunder in these calculations (as well as other minor ones in parts of the computations which are not discussed here). The consulship of Felix and Taurus was in fact in 428 A.D. and therefore four hundred years not from the Incarnation but from the conventional date for the Passion. We have already seen that until the general acceptance of the Dionysiac system of dating from the Incarnation, confusion between Passion and Incarnation of Christ eras was not uncommon. If

therefore we emend "Incarnation" to read "Passion," we obtain a consistent series of dates. The first consulship of Theodosius and Valentinian was in 425 and an earlier, partly bungled calculation already equated the start of Vortigern's reign with that of Valentinian, again 425. So the fourth year of Vortigern's reign would be 428, which was the consulship of Felix and Taurus. So the Saxons — at least, those with whom Vortigern had dealings — came to Britain in 428.[36]

This year of 428, therefore, becomes a foundation for a distinctive cardinal year of the *first*—not the third — Saxon landing, though more clarification is needed. The extant histories of Theodosius II and Valentinian III — particularly Valentinian — are broad, indicating a life-span for Valentinian III from ca. 419 to 455, but it is narrowed by a reference to the first consulship of Theodosius and Valentinian in the year 425. This is followed by the statement that Theodosius II, emperor of the East, seated Valentinian on the throne of the West in 425, which conveys that Valentinian was seated as emperor of the West when he was about six years old, seemingly a contradiction. However, historic sources do explain that Valentinius III ascended to the throne as a child, and the actual rule fell to his mother, Galla Placidia, until around 440. Morris provides the broad outlines of Theodosius' reign from approximately 408 to 450 and Valentinian from approximately 423 to 455,[37] but in spite of year 423, which he assigns in his Table of Dates, he accepts the year of 425 for the calculation of Valentinian's rise to the throne. Both Valentinian's death in 455 and his appointment to the Western throne by Theodosius in 425 are reliable.

The first coming of the Saxons is tied directly to the reign of Vortigern, and Nennius — supported by an explanation by Alcock — fulfills the dual function of verifying the first Saxon coming and the reign of Vortigern. Nennius writes:

> *Guorthigirnus autem tenuit imperium in Brittannia,*
> Vortigern held reign in Britain
>
> *Theodosio et Valentiniano consulibus, et in quarto*
> in the consulship of Theodosius and Valentinian, and in the fourth
>
> *anno regni sui Saxones ad Brittanniam venerunt,*
> year of his reign the Saxons came to Britain,
>
> *Felice et Tauro consulibus, quadringentesimo anno ab*
> in the consulship of Felix and Taurus, four hundred years from
>
> *incarnatione Domini nostri Jesu Christi.*[38]
> the Incarnation of our Lord Jesus Christ.

Alcock interprets this information by his references to the different calibrations for reckonings so familiar at this point. Through his explanation given above, there are verifications for two dates, the beginning of Vortigern's reign and the first coming of the Saxons.

About 11 years later, around 440, was a second coming of the Saxons. Both Alcock and Morris concur in their research that two years prior to this, in 437, Ambrosius Aurelianus had a falling out with Vortigern. Technically, according to Section 66 in the *Historia*, the quarrel is between a certain Vitalinus and

Ambrosius. The word "quarrel" is used in translation by both Morris and Giles. At one point Alcock gives the term "dissension," then uses the synonyms "conflict" and "clash."[39] The original term in Nennius' Latin is *discordiam*,[40] discord, which literally means "hearts which are apart." The connotations are important, since discord implies a lack of harmony while conflict indicates an encounter in arms, to literally and physically strike as in battle or war.[41] "Discord" in its definition is nowhere close in degree to the implications of the word "conflict." In this particular context, it means that Vitalinus and Ambrosius were in disharmony, but does not indicate a cleavage which led to actual warfare.

Another important issue that is skirted is the relationship between Ambrosius Aurelianus and Vitalinus, who is referred to as Guitolinus in the original Latin. Morris, Alcock, and Fletcher assume that Ambrosius and Vitalinus are opponents or rivals, Ambrosius representing a pro–Roman faction and Vitalinus representing a Briton faction allied with Vortigern. Morris strengthens the connection between Vitalinus and Vortigern by suggesting that the two names refer to the same individual.[42] However, there is nothing in the ancient manuscripts prior to Geoffrey of Monmouth to support this assumption.

It is more likely that Vitalinus and Ambrosius were allies but disagreed on how to avert Vortigern's manipulations for the kingship after the Roman withdrawal. Although both sets of names (Vitalinus/Ambrosius and Guithelinus/Ambrosius) are unquestionably Roman, there are no other contextual clues in the *Historia* to show whether they were friends or enemies. Alcock mentions the name of Vit[a]linus/Guitolini but says nothing critically interpretive; Barber, Lindsay, and Ashe do not refer to anyone by the name of Vitalinus or Guitolini. On the other hand, Fletcher and Chambers not only specify Guithelinus, but express a strong possibility that Guitolini from Nennius and Guithelinus from Monmouth refer to the same individual, a connection which is explored later.

These considerations tie into the second coming of the Saxons established by Alcock. Morris then asserts that in 442 the Saxon Revolt occurred. This is not to imply that these were the only momentous events which occurred, nor does it mean there was no back-and-forth movement between the island and the continent. For example, a decade after the Roman withdrawal, much Briton urban life was still recognizably Roman, and so was some structure of Roman military and civilian administrative organization. In this intervening period, in the beginning at least, the Saxons did keep their bargain in defending the Britons from the marauders of the north, which led to a period of co-existence and recovery. But with the passage of time and the influx of Saxons, demands increased from the Saxon allies, and fears grew in the Britons.

Alcock, Morris and Wade-Evans cite two early chronicles which set the date for the Saxon Revolt between the years 442 and 443.[43] Alcock does not address the time lapse between the Saxon Revolt and the letter to Aetius; Morris dates the letter between 446 and 454, then explains why Gildas erroneously misplaced the chronology. Accepting the Saxon Revolt in 442 and the Aetius letter in 456, the traditional explanation that Britons were making a plea to the Romans to aid in repelling the second *Adventus* becomes moot; a letter dated *after* the Saxon uprising would be valueless in summoning aid from Aetius for a revolt which had already taken place.

Although Wade-Evans also agrees with the letter's date as 446, he perceives the motive behind it differently. Based upon the *Chronica Gallica a. CCCCLII*, he points out several relevant things. For one, the entry does not say that the Britons were "conquered" by the Saxon, but instead that the English ascendancy was accomplished by diplomatic expedience. Second, not all five of the British provinces were involved. And third, the entry does not imply invaders from overseas — that is, German Saxons — but internal troubles as a spin-off from Roman abandonment. This is the milieu that Ambrosius Aurelianus inherited when the Romanitas rallied to his banner.

The Aetius letter of appeal here plays an important role in establishing the date of a second coming. In relation to this letter, Alcock once again clarifies a confusion inherent in the complexity of rooting out specifics in the early manuscripts. Gildas uses the spelling "Agitius," which is most reasonably associated with Ægidius of Gaul, put in charge when Avitus went to Rome. However, Gildas also uses the title "the third consul of Rome," and Alcock points out that Ægidius was never a consul. Ægidius was appointed a commander with the actual title of *magister militum per Gallias* by Avitus.

A review of the two extant Gildean manuscripts[44] supplied by Josephus Stevenson shows that a late edition by Polydore Vergil — "who either may have employed materials unknown to us, or may have altered and amended the text upon [his] own responsibility"[45] — used the name Aetius. This edition, which was printed in London in 1525, claims to have used two manuscripts to form the text, but the reliability and antiquity of those two manuscripts are unknown.

With no explanation, Bede makes the change from "Agitius" to "Aetius," and history relates that Aetius accepted the third consulship in 446. Morris is definite about the date of 442 for the Saxon Revolt but then adds that the letter of appeal was sent to Aetius *immediately* after the revolt, yet he does not record Aetius' third consul until four years later, in 446.[46] Wade-Evans relates that in 443 Aetius was the main Roman power of the West on the continent, and the letter of appeal was not written until his third consul three years later, in 446.

Wade-Evans goes on to give the most explicit information about the letter, which is generally known from the *De Excidio* as *gemitus Britannorum*, the "groans of the Britannians." More important, he explains what is meant by the term Britannians:

> It was long the fashion to regard the pre–Roman inhabitants of Britain as ... "Ancient Britons" ... [an] idea [which] derives from the *de excidio* ... which equated the *Britanni* (i.e., the general name given to the pre–Roman inhabitants of the Island of Britain in its most extended sense) with the self-styled Britons of [Gildas'] own day. ... For though the *Britanni* ... were all of them Romans (Walas), they were by no means all of them "Britons."[47]

In continuing the clarification and significance of the Aetius letter, he writes that interpretations of the events of the fifth century have missed the mark. Wade-Evans believes that

... by the year 443 the distinction between "Saxons" and "Britons" (in modern terms, English and Welsh) is established, recognized, and confirmed, the "Saxons" towards the east and the "Britons" towards the west.[48]

Wade-Evans reconfirms this three pages later; according to him (and supported by Anscombe) the territories southeast of Wales (Cornovii area) were placed under Saxon authority while Wales was considered "Briton" (i.e., Welsh) domain, as he writes, "no doubt at the instance of Aetius," a diplomatic arrangement as a carry-over from 442 to 443.[49]

This, of course, leads to Wade-Evans' view that the letter of appeal to Aetius has been misinterpreted down through the ages. Using the Gildas manuscript to rectify this, he identifies the Barbarians as the Picts and Scots and the Britanni as Roman provincials, including "Saxons" (i.e., English) and "Britons." He explains that

> The author of the *de excidio* mistook the term *Britanni* in the Letter to Aetius, to signify the "Ancient Britons," in which he has been universally followed. The Letter was evidently intended to emanate from all the Five Britains as they then were, all England and Wales as we may say; in short, the final appeal of the provincials of Roman Britain for imperial aid against their old enemies, the Northern nations. Or to put it more strikingly, the final appeal of what was now becoming England and Wales for Roman assistance against "Scotland" and Ireland.[50]

The dating and purpose, therefore, of the Aetius letter has undergone a great deal of scrutiny, particularly since there are so many errors and emendations attached to it. The difficulty arises from its inception in Gildas where Gildas misplaces the event chronologically, and compounds the problem by using the incorrect name of Agitius. Bede inherits the error, but makes emendations of his own.

In order to make a more accurate adjustment for the date of the Aetius letter, the conflicts during the time of Aetius must be looked at more closely. Aetius rose to power shortly after the reign of Honorius, the Emperor of the West whose reign from 395 to 423 overlapped that of Theodosius II, who ruled in the East from 408 to 450. Honorius' tenure was plagued by invasions, conflicts, and loss of Roman territories to the barbarians. However, Constantius III, a member of the noble Roman family, distinguished himself in Gaul by overcoming usurpers, by driving the Visigoths from the area, and by reclaiming Galla Placidia, Honorius' sister, who had been held hostage for four years by the Visigoths following their sack of Rome in 410. Constantius III married Galla Placidia in 417, and because of his brilliant leadership in Gaul, Honorius elevated him to co-emperor in 421. He died, however, in that same year, and was followed in death by Honorius only two years later. After Honorius' death in 423, Valentinian III, son of Constantius III and Galla Placidia, succeeded to the throne, but because of his age, Galla Placidia acted as her son's regent in Gaul, a position she actually held as ruler until around 440. After Honorius' death and Galla Placidia's rise, Aetius aligned his allegiance with the usurper Joanna, along with a mercenary army of Huns, in opposition to Galla Placidia. Joanna was defeated, the Huns were bribed

Province	Roman Name	Medieval Name	Modern Province
Britannia Prima: West (Britannia, *Brython* Britons)	Dumnonii	Cornovian Welsh	Cornwall, Devon,
	Belgae		Dorset, Hampshire
	Durotriges		Dorset
	Dobunni, Atrebates	Wessex, Hwicce	Wiltshire, Hampshire, Somerset, Gloucester
	Ordovices, Dementia, Dobunni, Silures	Gwynedd, Powys, Dyfed, Gwent	Gwynedd, Dyfed, Clwyd, Shropshire, Hereford, Worcester, Glamorgan
Britannia Secunda: Southeast (Saxonia, *Saxoniaid*, Saxons, Saeson)	Trinovantes	Essex	Essex
	Catuvellauni	Middlesex	Hertfordshire, Bedfordshire
	Atrebates	West Saxon	Berkshire
	Regenses	South Saxon	Sussex
	Cantii		Kent
Britannia Flavia: East Midlands (Anglia, *Eingl*, Angles)	Iceni	East Anglia	Norfolk, Suffolk, Cambridgeshire
	Coritani	Middle Anglia, Lindisse	Leicestershire, Lincolnshire
	Southern Brigantes	Mercia	Derbyshire, Nottinghamshire
Britannia Maxima: Beyond the Humber (Deira, *Dewr*, Deifr, Gwyr y Gogledd)	Brigantes, Parisi	Elmet, Deira, Eburacum, Northumbria, Rheged	Humberside, Yorkshire, Lancashire, Cumbria, Northumberland, Durham
Valentia: Beyond Antonine Wall (Nordi)	Damnonii, Novantae, Selgovae, Votadini, Epidii	Strathclyde, Rheged, Bernicia, Gododdin, Dalriada	Central, Tayside, Grampion, Highland, Fife, Strathclyde

Table 10. The five provinces of Britain.

to vacate Gaul, and a shaky reconciliation was established between Aetius and Galla Placidia. During the third and fourth decades of this period, there was a great deal of upheaval in the entire Roman Empire, East as well as West, and Aetius faced troubles in the West from the Huns, from the Visigoths, from the Salian Franks under the rule of King Clodion from 428 to 448, and not in the least from Valentinian III, the weak ruler, filled with jealousy toward Aetius, who began assuming more power in 440. It was during this period when Valentinian was acquiring more power from Galla Placidia that Aetius received the letter of appeal from the Britons.

The date of the third Saxon *Adventus* goes back to Bede. In Chapter 15 he writes,

> In the year of our Lord 449, Martian became Emperor with Valentinian III, the forty-sixth in succession from Augustus, ruling for seven years. In his time the Angles or Saxons came to Britain at the invitation of King Vortigern in three long-ships and were granted lands in the eastern part of the island on condition that they protected the country.[51]

That means between the years of Martian's rule, 449–456, the Saxons came once more. *The Anglo-Saxon Chronicle* partially picks up on Bede, but manuscripts A, B, and C spell Bede's "Martian" as Mauritius, while manuscripts E and F spell it correctly as Martianus. Likewise, the *Chronicle* lists the name "Valentinus." Rather than this being just a corruption in copying, the *Chronicle* might have had a different source with these names listed. This would put the *Chronicle* entry of 449 pretty much on track, independent of, but verifiable by, at least one other source. Using Morris' caution that an absolute and specific date is dangerous, with the range between 449 and 456 as the possibility, the compromise date of approximately half of that — somewhere around 453 — would be reasonable.

More accurately, then, *three* major Saxon arrivals, or the *Adventi* of the Saxons must be considered accurate, as suggested by Alcock, rather than the one *Adventus* previously deemed acceptable. For archaeological evidence he offers

> some pagan Anglo-Saxon cemeteries [which] contain pottery vessels closely similar to urns found in the continental homelands of the English and dated on the continent to the decades before 450. From this it appears that the English had already ceased to raid and had started to settle in Britain significantly before Bede's date for the third *Adventus*. Again, the recognition on Roman military sites in south-east England of sword-belt buckles ornamented in a mixed Roman-Provincial and Teutonic taste argues for a large deployment of German troops for the defense of Britain in the late fourth and early fifth centuries.[52]

If one subscribes to this idea of Alcock's on the three comings of the Saxons, with Hengist appearing on the scene in the mid-450s rather than in the late 430s, then the entire time frame must change. First there is a contradiction between the *Chronicle* and Nennius; the *Chronicle* entry of 455 specifically records a battle between Vortigern and Hengist/Horsa in which Horsa was killed. Nennius, however, writes that Vortigern had gone to the north because of a confrontation with Saint Germanus, and Vortimer, not Vortigern, encountered Hengist and Horsa in battle where Horsa was killed.

The second difference is the inversion of the two battles. Morris claims that the Battle of Creacanford preceded the Battle of Ægelsthrep, with the sequence suggesting that the battle at Creacanford was an English victory which caused the

Britons to flee Kent, and after the Britons had fled, there was then the Battle of Ægelesthrep which secured the kingdom for Hengist and the Saxons. According to Morris, the next battle in the series would have been several years later, when the Britons were victorious at Wippedesfleot.

In contrast, if one follows what the *Historia* and the *Chronicle* both report, then Ægelesthrep was the site of the first battle, Creaganford the second, and Wippedesfleot the third. If this is the order, how can the issue be resolved that the first battle would allow Hengist to succeed to the kingdom when even the *Chronicle* does not claim a victory? The answer lies in the way the phrase "succeeded to the kingdom" is interpreted. This expression does not have to mean "won the battle," but might mean "the death of one leader and the succession of someone else." Several examples of succeeding entries in the *Chronicle* will suffice. In the four consecutive entries which follow the Battle of Ægelesthrep, *none* of the four equate the victory in a battle with the succession to the kingdom. The entry of 488 does not designate a battle; Entry 519 does, but specifically states that Cerdic succeeded to the kingdom, and then *afterwards* fought a battle in that same year. The entries for both 547 and 560, similar to that of 488, do not indicate any battles. All of those entries are declaring outright that a leader died and a successor took his place. The entry for 455 is no different. Horsa is killed, and *after that* Hengist's son Octha (Æsc) took Horsa's place as a leader. The expression "succeed to the kingdom" can be interpreted in a variety of ways.

More important than "succeeding to the kingdom," though, is the change in chronology. If Alcock's postulation is accepted, then several other sequences become locked into positions differing from Morris' time frame. By retaining the "Kentish Chronicle, Part 1," the three chapters of the "Kentish Chronicle, Part 2," and the "Kentish Chronicle, Part 3," but passing over both Part I and Part II of the "Life of Saint Germanus," and the three chapters of the "Tale of Emrys," a fairly comprehensive sequence of events can be strung together through chapters 31, 36, 37, 38, 43, 44, 45, and 46.

Chapter 31 gives an overview of the era. After the Roman Empire crumbled in Britain, the Britons

> … were in alarm forty years. … Vortigern then reigned in Britain. In his time, the natives had cause of dread, not only from the inroads of the Scotti [Irish] and Picts, but also from the Romans, and [especially] their apprehensions of Ambrosius. … In the meantime, three vessels, exiled from Germany, arrived in Britain.[53]

This information is echoed in the Laud version of the *Anglo-Saxon Chronicle*, entry 449. By picking up on the clue from Nennius that the British went in fear for 40 years and attaching that to the last mention of Vortigern in the *Chronicle* at entry 455, the Roman withdrawal from the island occurred around 415, a date close to that verified by other sources.

However, the Laud Chronicle deviates from what Nennius records next. Nennius indicates that Hengist and Horsa were leaders of the three keels, but the *Chronicle* does not list leaders in this first wave. Rather than the keels being driven in exile, the entry states

In their days Vortigern invited the Angles hither, and they then came hither to Britain in three ships. ... King Vortigern gave them land to the south-east of this land on condition that they fought against the Picts.[54]

An incidental notation is that "south-east of this land" is to the southeast of Wales (Vortigern's territory) in the southern midlands, a more logical location where they would be fighting Picts, but more important is the absence of the leaders' names. After the first wave victoriously fought the Picts, *then* a larger force led by Hengist and Horsa came over.

The logistic sense of sequence breaks down in Chapter 36 as a crossover from Chapter 31 to 37. This gap supports Alcock's assertion that the initial influx of the Saxons was *not* led by Hengist and his brother Horsa. In Chapter 31 Vortigern gives the island of Thanet to the first wave, referred to as "land to the south-east" in the *Chronicle*. Chapter 36 gives more detail about this first coming of the Saxons, correctly omitting any reference to Hengist. After the Saxons successfully fight the Picts, they send for larger numbers from their homeland, which causes Vortigern to become fearful enough to break his pact. In Chapter 37, Hengist is correctly identified as the Saxon leader, but the *Historia* does not correctly pinpoint the second entry. The beginning of a new chapter in itself suggests a new time period, but the transition is weak in concluding the first wave.

Vortigern's response to Hengist in Chapter 37 is the warning bell which rings a discordant tone. When Hengist asks for more Saxon warriors and fighting men so that the number who fight for Vortigern may be larger, Vortigern "ordered that it be done." If the situation in Chapter 36 is the same one as in 37, then Vortigern would be issuing contrary commands, first telling the Saxons to go away, then immediately turning about and ordering even more to come over. This points to a flaw in the supposition (by Nennius?) that Hengist was the leader as reported in Chapter 31. Hengist is correctly named in Chapter 37 as the leader of the second *Adventus*.

There is no logistic sense in Vortigern's inviting in additional hordes of Saxons if there were only one *Adventus* and he already felt overwhelmed by them. The advent of the Saxons was a slow-paced event, supported by the archaeological evidence which Alcock sites, that, "at least in 428–429, town life in a recognizable Roman sense was still continuing," and several lines later reinforcing the concept that the influx of Saxons was gradual by writing, "But it would be very rash to infer from this [the time passage between St. Germanus' first visit and his second] that between 429 and 446 there had been any marked disintegration or even weakening, of the fabric of romanized administrative arrangements," a remark which is echoed by several other specialists.[55]

What is attributed to Hengist in this Nennius segment should be transferred to the second and third waves in the fourth and fifth decades of the fifth century, a reckoning based on the historical data of Aetius. Morris gives the reign of Aetius from 433 to 454, with the third consulship beginning in 446. This in turn means that in determining the third coming, two events can be correlated. One is the span of time of Aetius' third consulship, between 446 and 454. If this is combined with the *Chronicle* information that Marcian and Valentinian were rulers during this same era, then the time span of 450 to 457 can be established. The time span from 446 through 449 can be eliminated, since the third wave would have to overlap Aetius' third consulship and the reign of Marcian and Valentinian. The time span is narrowed down to a surprising limitation between the years of 450 and 454. The date of 454 can be selected as a realistic date, since the date, in addition to being in that range, would be the same date of Morris' rule of thumb when we look at 450 to 457 as the reign of Marcian and Valentinian III.

DEATH OF MAELGWN: CARDINAL YEAR #6

Cardinal year #6 for the Arthurian chronology is the *Annales* entry for Maelgwn.* According to Morris' interpretation, the *Annales* records the year as 547, when

> A great death [i.e., plague] in which Maelgwn, king of Gwynedd died. Thus they say "The long sleep of Maelgwn in the court of Rhos." Then there was yellow plague.[56]

A great many opinions have been expressed about this particular entry. One is that Maelgwn's death was entered here not because it was factually known as his death-year but because it happened to be the year of the Great Death, and since thousands literally died in this year, then Maelgwn was allegedly listed as also dying at this time. The plague is listed not only as an introduction to the entry but also its conclusion. Interestingly, Maelgwn's name also appears twice in the entry and both incidents seem to suggest some interpolation from the original entry. Another opinion is that only the first sentence was the original entry. A third suggests that this addition came from folklore. Still another indicates that the last sentence was an addition made by some scribe to specify the particular plague, because there were several during the era. The most enigmatic opinion concentrates upon the name of Maelgwn.

This singular entry has spurred a controversy almost as complex and detailed as the Gildas passage about his birth-year. Dealing with the Maelgwn entry, the simplest item is the term "Rhos" in sentence two. This is a province, or perhaps more accurately a separate territory, of eastern Gwynedd where Gawain's grave was allegedly discovered. William of Malmsbury reported on it and Geoffrey of Monmouth carried on the tradition of Gawain in the province of Wales called Ros.[57] Dumville cites a "very late pedigree-text"[58] in pointing out that Maelgwn's line belonged to the Cantref of Rhos in eastern Gwynedd, and therefore with the three citations, sentence 2, although it might have been a later addition, seems to be accurate in expressing that Maelgwn was buried in Rhos, and that Maelgwn was a historical figure of some importance.

This name also appears in other works in a variety of ways: Maglocunus, Maglo, Maelchu, and Mailcun, with his kingdom referred to as Gwynedd, Guenedota, Gwendota, and Venedotia.

The use of the word "plague" (or at least its translation) presents more of a problem. In the antecedent sources of the *Annales Cambriae*, the Irish Annals, the words used for A.D. 548 are "mortalitas magna," the Great Death,[59] the same terms retained in the *Annales*. O'Sullivan gives an adequate clarification of the generic definition for the term *plague*, attached to an equally detailed explanation of why the term *plague* normally associates with the Bubonic one but does not necessarily have to be associated with the entry on Maelgwn.[60] Even if the term "plague" *was* used in its specific sense of the *Bubonic* plague in the Maelgwn entry, the date of 547 would still be workable. The Great (Bubonic) Plague of the Justinian reign began in the East around 542, and assuming approximately five years for the disease to spread through Europe and across the Channel, the year 547 would not be unreasonable as to when its effect would be felt on the island.

However, the Maelgwn entry itself does not specifically name the Bubonic Plague, but instead the Great Death is translated as the plague. Because the last sentence names the Yellow Plague and is suspected of being a later inaccurate interpolation, it becomes necessary to follow O'Sullivan's advice of discovering any source which would verify the epidemic which killed Maelgwn. O'Sullivan devises such a search. Some accounts in the Welsh vernacular texts relate how Taliesin was deprived of certain property and because of his loss, he cursed Maelgwn and all his possessions whereupon "Vad Velen came to Rhos, and whoever witnessed it became doomed to certain death. Maelgwn saw the Vad Velen through the keyhole, in the Rhos church, and died in consequence."[61] Without going into the specific reasons of acceptance/rejection but instead briefly stating that this material passed through known, unreliable hands, it is highly suspect and therefore not acceptable as corroborative evidence here. Furthermore, the format in the present section of this text distinguishes between the ancient historical manuscripts and those of tradition. The Taliesin material here, because it is literary tradition, is therefore misplaced.

Fortunately, there is evidence from other sources. The *Saints' Lives* as ecclesiastical documents many times give accurate historical information not only because their main interest lay in precise recording of contemporary and previous events, but also because of the privileged access to church data and church methods created more reliable reckonings. Saint Teilo, sometimes appearing as Teiliavi and Latinized by Geoffrey of Monmouth as Thelianus, offers a secondary source on the Maelgwn entry as a verification. O'Sullivan cites the Evans-Rhys edition of the *De vita sancti Teiliavi*:

> Pestis autem illa flava vocabatur, eo quod flavos et exangues efficiebat universos quos persequebatur ... Traxit enim Mailconum regem Guenedotiae, delevit et patriam suam ...[62]

This passage basically describes the universal (universos) outbreak (exangues) of the affliction (persequebatur) called the Yellow Pestilence (pestis flava). Maelgwn, the king of Gwynedd is delivered to our Father on High by this epidemic.

Unlike the Taliesin source listed above, which was tainted by an intervening source,[63] this source from Saint Teilo, although it dates to the 1100s, appears "clean." Teilo established several monasteries in south-central Wales and then allegedly crossed the Channel to Brittany in hopes of escaping the Yellow Pestilence at the end of the fifth decade of the 500s. Where this scribe of the 1100s got his information is unknown, but Saint Teilo was an important bishop who probably oversaw all of Dementia, and Maelgwn was a major king, so that it would not be unusual to have important segments about either figure in ancient manuscripts. This kind of hagiographical information offers a strong parallel to pure historical data.

The Irish Annals as previous sources for the *Annales Cambriae* record the Great Death as the Yellow Pestilence. William MacArthur, who devoted time to the study of some of the epidemics given in the Irish Annals, indicates that the Yellow Pestilence in Welsh was referred to as the "buidhe" (or "cron") choniall.[64] He also calls this jaundice epidemic as characteristic of the relapsing or famine fever. The Irish term used during the great Potato Famine of 1845, supposedly still used today, is the "fiabhras buidhe," the yellow fever. The accumulation of data, therefore, indicates that the Yellow Pestilence did occur in the Gwynedd/Rhos/Ireland area around 547/548. The *Annales Cambriae* and the manuscript *De vita sancti Teiliavi* as an independent source link that pestilence with the death of Maelgwn, and no other source denies the validity of that connection.

Wade-Evans cites the *pestifera lues* recorded in Chapter 22 of Gildas as the epidemic which killed Maelgwn, since he places Maelgwn's floruit in the middle of the fifth century rather than the middle of the sixth as recorded in the *Annales Cambriae*.[65] However, evidence is overwhelming that Maelgwn died from the Yellow Pestilence, while the *pestifera lues* in Chapter 22 of Gildas is the plague of 442, verified by Stevens in the *Chronicon*.[66] This is the plague which swiftly spread across Britain about the time of the Saxon Revolt.

While on the subject of the parallels between the *Annales Cambriae* and the Irish Annals as its parent document, it is worthwhile to relay some attempts made to establish a death-year for Maelgwn of the *Annales* through the identification of a supposed Pictish son of the north recorded in the Irish Annals. This son appears in the ancient manuscripts as Brude, Brudeus, Bruide, Brodjos, Bride, Bridei, or Bridius, linked to another name, Saint Columba, also appearing in the *AC*. Bede writes of the Picts receiving the faith of Christ, but his passage reflects the parallel which has emerged between the ancient documents. He relays, "Columba arrived in Britain in the ninth year of the reign of the powerful Pictish king, Bride son of Meilochon."[67] If Meilochon = Maglocunus = Maelgwn, connected with Columba's trip to Britain already established as post-563, then Brude as Maelgwn's son and Maelgwn's death-year are all within the realm of confirmation. But this still remains unsettled, ambiguous, and general. John Morris in his major history unconditionally accepts the premises that Meilochon = Maelgwn and that Bridei = Maelgwn's son and devotes a section of his chapter on the Picts and the Northerners to this connection.[68] On the other hand, O'Sullivan cites John Rhys' belief that the Irish Maelchon and the Welsh Maelgwn were two quite different names, further indicating that O'Rahilly at first thought that the two names Maelchon and Maelgwn were distinctive, but then later reconsidered and decided that the identification of the two names was reasonable; O'Sullivan further points out that Kenneth Jackson felt that "Bruide mac Maelchon or Mailcon was a Pict, and his father's name cannot be regarded as Goidelic, still less Irish, in which the genetive would be Malchon," but at the same time saying, "The Celtic Maglocu is well-known in Welsh ... but there are no Irish equivalents." Lastly, O'Sullivan also cites Dillon and Chadwick who indicate that the two names are basically identical.[69] The connection leans toward the verfication of a connection between Maelochon and Maelgwn and is therefore noteworthy, but it is tenuous.

In pursuit of a date for the penning of the *De Excidio*, which would hopefully also firm up the date of Maelgwn's death, O'Sullivan devotes a 46-page chapter on the five Gildasian princes. After all the detailed exploration, however, he concludes "we see mostly just mechanical repetition of the 547 obit of Maelgwn Gwynedd."[70] Nevertheless, the date as it appears in the *AC* can stand on its own merit given the evidence on which it was written, leading to the conclusion that the content of the Maelgwn entry is accurate: Maelgwn was spirited from this earth by the Yellow Pestilence and buried in the province of Rhos in the year 547.

CERDIC OF FACT

Another association must now be probed to reach further historic milestones in the Arthurian chronology. This focuses upon Cerdic's enigmatic connection to Arthur as his arch-enemy in a historical as well as literary context. In the ancient documents, Cerdic is mentioned in five different circumstances: this name is first recorded in Chapter 37 of Nennius' *Historia Brittonum* identifying the interpreter for Vortigern; then at the end of the Welsh Genealogies in the *British Historical Miscellany* this name is listed as Cunedda's fifth son.[71] In the *Anglo-Saxon Chronicle* the renowned West Saxon king is named Cerdic, and in the *Annales Cambriae* one of the kings of Elmet is Cerdic. In a last veiled reference from other histories, Coroticus, king of Strathclyde, is also referred to as Cerdic. In regard to the Arthurian milieu, two of them can be set aside. The obit for Cerdic, king of Elmet, appears in year 616, which is outside the parameters of the Arthurian chronology; this particular Cerdic was killed by Edwin during the invasion of Wales. Coroticus is outside the geographic parameters of the Arthurian setting; Strathclyde is too far north for heavy Saxon entanglements during this period. Very little is known of this king except through Saint Patrick's letter to him, but there are no direct or implied references connecting him with King Arthur.

The remaining three, however, all fall into the Arthurian age. For precision, each Cerdic must be discussed separately, even though the references might be to the same individual. This means that establishing a cardinal or an ordinal year, floruits, and lifespans for Cerdic is not a simple process. If each Cerdic is a separate individual and at least one year is established for each separate entity, then this means that at least three separate ordinal years would have to be established. On the other hand, if the three Cerdics point to a single personality, then the establishment of his role and the listing of any of the years would be in the much stronger category of cardinal years, since his existence would be verified by at least one other independent historical source. This precludes, too, Cerdic in literary tradition, which would strengthen even more his impact in an Arthurian role.

Of concern here, because interest lies with him as a historic, verifiable figure, is the role of each Cerdic in the Arthurian saga. For a resolution to this difficult problem, this book has established a dual-pronged hypothesis. The first is that Cerdic the West Saxon king flourished during the Arthurian Age, a six-decade span from 460 to 520. This postulation, not a contentious one, has already forged itself through the merger of the *Anglo-Saxon Chronicle* and its Genealogical Preface. The second dimension, however, has never been proposed and is more radical: genealogically, Cerdic the West Saxon King is son of Cunedda and historically, he is also Vortigern's interpreter. Each conjecture will be handled as a cardinal year. Cerdic the West Saxon king was recorded in what was two separate historical documents, the Genealogical Preface and the *Anglo-Saxon Chronicle*, and the two other Cerdics link the *Historia Brittonum / British Historical Miscellany* to the *Chronicle*.

CERDIC THE WEST SAXON KING: CARDINAL YEAR #7

Cerdic as the West Saxon king presented in the *Anglo-Saxon Chronicle* is the most obvious and the least controversial of the Cerdic trio; a review of all the literature on Arthur showed that no researcher objected to the date in the *Anglo-Saxon Chronicle*, which places Cerdic's first entry in 495. The versions, at least manuscripts A̅ and A through E, do not offer variations, although there is the one-year discrepancy between the Preface date of 494 and the actual *Chronicle*. With the deviation being only ± one year, this date has evidently not created controversy. No other annal or ancient manuscript deals with this event, but as explained just above, because it is to be associated with other material from the *HB* as a separate source, it appears here as a cardinal rather than an ordinal year.

Earlier in this chapter under the subheading establishing the cardinal year for the Badon battle, the *Anglo-Saxon Chronicle* entry for 495 was offered as a verification for that significant Briton/Saxon encounter, but the same year is offered here in a slightly different context. Earlier, the point was being made that there was a link between the years 495/497 and the Badon conflict, whereas in this context the emphasis shifts to the *person* who molded a massive and powerful kingdom on the island. The purpose here is solely to mark the year of Cerdic's entry into Wales and to devise a general time frame which will aid in structuring other cardinal or ordinal years in the Arthurian chronology.

Scholars agree that Cerdic is not a Saxon name. This in itself points to his authenticity in the *Chronicle*, since no Saxon would add a Briton name to its regnal lists. Researchers generally concur, too, that the genealogy for Cerdic's ancestry is made up. Yet Cerdic's genealogy must not be viewed too simply, since it gives some very intriguing clues about where he came from. Several times in the *Chronicle* one of his ancestors is listed as "Gewis," strikingly like the term "Gewisse," a word applied to the West Saxon people meaning "allies" or "compatriots." This could logistically mean, that Cerdic was a Briton who had Saxon leanings, a Briton genetically but a Saxon politically, hence a West Saxon ally. It might even suggest, as Ashe pointed out, a genetic connection, a man of mixed blood, an ethnic mixture of Briton and Saxon.

Because the term *Gewissae* appears as bonafide information in the ancient histories, not attempting to prove or disprove Arthur, and not suggesting a vested interest by the scribes, information about any term in a genealogy must be analyzed. In reading the early histories, it is easy to overlook the important implication of the word *Gewissae* as it applies to the term which evolved, the *West Saxons*. With some researchers concurring that Cerdic's genealogy in the *Chronicle* is bogus, one tends to accept unthinkingly that the ancestry for Cerdic was probably made up; the names of Elesa and Esla seem to have no particular significance to Saxon history, and the last name of Woden in Cerdic's family tree taints the entire pedigree with mythological fantasy. By generalizing that the family tree is the figment of the imagination, the name of Gewis becomes buried until the nagging similarity between *Gewis* and *Gewisse* becomes too obvious to ignore. This gives rise to evidence that the connection between Cerdic of the West Saxons and Cerdic of Briton/Welsh heritage is much more profound than first realized or anticipated.

The terms specified in Chapter 2 — Gewissae, Hwicce, and Hyrpe — are synonymous. "Hrype" is an ancient term describing an early tribe; Bede uses the term "Hwiccas,"[72] the word later surfaces as "Gegwis" in Asser's Annals of the Reign of Alfred the Great[73] and is echoed as "Gewissei" at least four times by Geoffrey of Monmouth.[74] As suggested earlier, Morris in *The Age of Arthur* explains the term in detail. He relates that English tradition gave the name "Gewissae" to apply to "federates" or "confederates" who eventually accepted the description of West Saxons.[75] He gives more information by explaining that the Gewissae "burial rite attests [to] a mixed origin"[76] and continues later that the term

> was more probably the earlier name of the Berkshire English ... [who] were known to the British as Saxons, as were all other English ... Thereafter "West Saxon" was the common and usual national name, though for centuries the old name Gewissae occurs as an occasionally literary variant in Bede, Asser and elsewhere.[77]

This territory in Britain is verified by others attempting to pinpoint the area. Abingdon is in Oxfordshire near Oxford and in close proximity to the locale identified by Charles Plummer. Using the term from Bede, Plummer describes the Hwiccas (in Manuscript E) or the Hwiccias (in Manuscript A) as "a tribe in Worcestershire and Gloucestershire."[78] This territory of Gewisse is visualized in Map 4 and shows Cerdic's ties as a West Saxon king to Briton dominions.

This area verifies some very important data. For one, it suggests that the

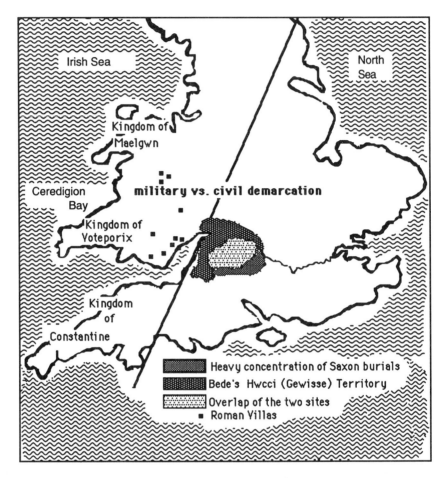

Map 4. The territory of Gewisse and Saxon burial grounds. The depiction of two over-lapping areas, Gewisse and an area heavily dotted with Saxon cemeteries. The implication of these factors as they tie together indicate the heavy Roman population in this area just prior to the Arthurian age, the location of conflict — specifically the Battle of Badon — between the Britons and the Saxons near the line of demarcation between the military and the civilian districts, the heavy concentration of Saxon occupation in a mainly Briton locale, and Cerdic's ancestral connection to the Gewisse territories.

Gewissi as an ethnic group is a mixture of British and Saxon, specifically Britons who were confederates or allies with the Saxons invited in by Vortigern, with the leader of those confederates or allies being the Cerdic who later acquired the title of West Saxon king. This would resolve the mystery of where Cerdic, the most important king of the West Saxon kingdom, came from. There would no longer be a perplexing problem needing an elaborate explanation of Cerdic's phantas-magoric appearance out of thin air. Second, the Gewisse area of Worcester,

Gloucestershire, and Oxfordshire incorporates Bath as a region of general Briton/Saxon conflict, and points to a specific Badon site. Third, not only is the geographic location accurate for Cerdic as a Briton, but the time frame is precise. Cerdic as the West Saxon king, with no evident heritage as a Saxon, appears in the chronicles during the decades after Roman withdrawal and just at the point when Britons and Saxons are struggling in their rise to supremacy on the island.

And last, John Morris unknowingly gives a subsidiary clue about Creoda. Morris does not make the connection that Creoda is the son of Cerdic according the Preface of the *Anglo-Saxon Chronicle*. Instead he indicates that Creoda is a descendant of Icel. According to Whitelock and others, however, the Creoda listed as a descendant of Icel in the *Chronicle* is the son of Cynewold (Cenwealh).[79] This particular Creoda as defined by Whitelock, since his father reigned from 641 to 672, would be an ealdorman of the *seventh* century, not of the fifth and sixth. Morris nevertheless establishes an important connection between Creoda and the Gewisse. Morris writes, "[Creoda's] kingdom was a federation of very small peoples ... [whose territory was] on the borders of northern Oxfordshire and Worcestershire, with the main territory coinciding with that of the former Roman *civitas* of the Coritani."[80] There are several important implications from this information. Coritani is just north of the area described as Gewisse, adjacent to it if not a small segment of it. Morris identifies Creoda with Icel, which in itself is interesting because Icel's reign is listed approximately from 460 to 480, although it is miscalculated.[81] Neither the name Icel nor the name Creoda son of Cynewold fits the Arthurian-age chronology, but the name Creoda as son of Cerdic does fit the time frame. This not only aligns Creoda with the Gewisse, but it puts both Creoda and Cerdic in the right place at the right time. That is, geographically and chronologically Creoda can be tied to Cerdic as his son, and both would be West Saxon leaders vying for the West Saxon kingship in Britain.

At this point the similarity between Elesa and Esla[82] of the *Chronicle* entries and Eliset/Eliseg[83] inscribed on the pillar at Valle Crucis near Llangollen in north-central Wales must be reiterated. In *The Discovery of King Arthur*, Ashe gives Cerdic's ancestry by writing

> The *Chronicle* gives Cerdic a Saxon pedigree which is clearly bogus. It comes down to a father called Elesa. A real fifth-century Saxon father would never have given his son a British name, so Elesa can be discounted; he and his forebears have been grafted on to Cerdic to give him desirable ancestors.[84]

What makes the pedigree seem bogus is the tracing of Cerdic ultimately to Woden, but just because that segment is mythological, we need not dismiss the entire entry. It has already been shown that the term Gewis in the middle of Cerdic's lineage cannot be passed over; the same is true of Elesa being listed as Cerdic's father.

Ashe is correct in claiming that a Saxon father would never have given his son a British name. Cerdic's father, then, is an important key to this puzzling dilemma. Cerdic is unquestionably a Briton name bestowed upon an important Saxon king. The most obvious path to an answer is this: a Saxon father would never have given his son a British name, but a Briton father *would* have. This means, then, that one must look to Elesa as a name having *Briton* roots.

It has been established that Gewisse is a term meaning "compatriots" or "allies," referring to an intermixed people of Saxon and Briton descent in Wales who emerged from an era when there was peace between the two during the first part of Vortigern's reign before the debacle. The next name from the *Chronicle* which comes under scrutiny is Elesa. That particular name in the West Saxon genealogy aligns itself with the Eliset/Eliseg inscribed stone in Valle Crucis, near Llangollen in northeastern Wales just east of Offa's Dyke. The Pillar, one of the most famous of the Ogham stones, commemorates Eliseg, an adversary of Offa's. The inscription is now illegible, but it was allegedly copied in 1696 by a Welsh antiquarian, Edward Lhuyd.[85] Unfortunately, both Eliseg's and Offa's genealogies are obscured by mythological references. The name Offa appears regularly in the *Anglo-Saxon Chronicle*, but Eliseg and its possible connection to Elesa appears only three times. There are two entries in the *AC*, years 814 and 943, which give the name Elized. The 943 entry is traceable back to the Clonmacnoise Chronicle which adds that Elized and his father Idwal (Iudgual) were killed by the West Saxons.[86] The name Idwal is also a dead-end. The strongest confirmation which Dumville can give about the entry's authenticity is that

> We may suspect that the *Annales Cambriae* were compiled in the early 950s. We may therefore give to the composition of the "Clonmacnoise Chronicle" the dates 911 x 954 with some confidence that they cannot be undermined.[87]

Both the Saxon and the Briton genealogies are indistinct. Elise ab Idwal is the closest similarity to Elesa of the *Chronicle*, but Eliseg does directly relate to Vortigern and his Saxon compatriots, the Gewissae. If the equation of Elesa = Eliset/Eliseg is retained, then Elesa is the Saxon term and Eliset/Eliseg is the philological Briton counterpart. Approaching the equation in reverse, if Elesa is Cerdic's father in Saxon terms, then Eliset/Eliseg is Cerdic's father in Briton terms. Based upon 1) Cerdic the West Saxon king's mystical past; 2) the term *Gewisse* for the tribe occupying a specific geographic space in Britain and its counterpart *Gewis* in the *Chronicle*; 3) the time frame for Cerdic's rise to kingship; and 4) the probable connection among the three Cerdics of the era, then the equation of Elesa/Eliset = Cerdic's father is defensibly accurate.

Before concluding with any type of cardinal year for Cerdic the West Saxon king, it is necessary to comment about the life-spans as they are recorded in the *Anglo-Saxon Chronicle*/Genealogical Preface, particularly as they pertain to this Arthurian era and to Cerdic and his offspring. This problem, which other scholars have noted, has to be resolved before any type of reliable chronology can be established for the events which encompass Arthur. The *Chronicle* entry for 495, which has already been cited a couple of times, reads, "Two ealdormen Cerdic and Cynric, came to Britain with five ships at the place which is called

Cerdicesora, and they fought against the Britons on the same day." (Ethelwerd adds, "and finally were victorious.")[88] The entry of 556 reads, "In this year Cynric and Ceawlin fought against the Britons at Barbury [Barbury Castle, Wilts]" followed by the entry of 560, "In this year Ceawlin succeeded to the kingdom in Wessex."[89] With all of these entries strung together, Cynric first appears in entry 495 with his death implied in 560, when Ceawlin succeeds to the kingdom. Logically assuming that Cynric would have been at least 18 years old at the entry of 495 in order to go on a warring expedition, that would make him 83 at his death.

Cerdic's age presents a similar problem. If Cerdic was approximately 18 when Cynric was born, and Cynric was 18 in 495, then Cerdic's birth would be in the year 459. His death is listed in the *Chronicle* at 534, which would make him at least 75 years old.

Ashe discusses this problem in *The Discovery of Arthur*, saying of these lifespans:

> The *Anglo-Saxon Chronicle* supplies us two cases of life-prolongation very close to Arthur. It says that the founder of the West Saxon dynasty, Cerdic, brought his expedition to land in 495 with his son Cynric. Both are called ealdormen, "princes." Cynric would hardly have been mentioned if he had been a child, and by implication he is adult. Cerdic, therefore, is likely to have been in his forties and was certainly not much younger. Yet in 530 he is named as chief conqueror of the Isle of Wight, therefore still an active warrior, and he lives on till 534. Cynric, born probably in the 470s, is still fighting in 556 and does not die till 560. These lives of a father and son are theoretically possible, but under early Saxon conditions they are beyond reasonable belief.[90]

The "reasonable age" concept has been proposed by some scholars also in relation to Gildas. Following the sensibility of what Alcock and Ashe write, and putting their postulations into a mathematical formulation, Cerdic's and Cynric's ages are unreasonable. If the 495 entry is correct, that Cerdic and Cynric are father and son, and that they are both chieftains, a logical assumption would be that Cynric would be 18 to 24 years old, and Cerdic between 38 and 42. Using years in the middle of those spans would mean that in 534, Cerdic died when he was nearly in his eighties. In 556 Cynric would have been in his eighties when he and Ceawlin fought against the Britons, and he would have been nearing his nineties in 560 when the kingdom passed to Ceawlin. As with the Badon entries proposed by the Dionysiac system, which would mark Gildas' age in the 90s, the dates given for Cerdic and Cynric and their ages are irreconcilable; it is not logical that so many men in this era would live that long during a period which lacked medical technology and skills.

It is surprising that Plummer was aware of the missing Creoda generation but did not take it into account in trying to reconcile the differences between the *Chronicle* and the Preface. The *Chronicle* itself lists Cynric as Cerdic's son (entries 495 and 534) but the Preface lists the genealogy as Cerdic — (Creoda*) — Cynric — Ceawlin.[91] Plummer notes this (hence the asterisk) by explaining that Creoda is omitted by Manuscript A both in the *Preface* and at 855 in the *Chronicle*. Creoda is likewise omitted by A, B, C, at the years 552, 597, 674, 685, 688. He is inserted by ß in the *Preface* and by B, C, D at 855.[92]

He also lists Creoda as "father of Cynric, son of Cerdic."[93] Whitelock, too, lists Creoda in the genealogies of the chief dynasties and noble houses in the family tree[94] and inserts Creoda in the index as "s(on) of Cerdic, Pref. ß, 855–858."[95] However, since Whitelock is dealing mainly with manuscripts A and E, Creoda does not appear in the body of the text. Garmonsway, on the other hand, provides the information that manuscripts B, C, and D give in their genealogical listings, "Cynric, the son of Creoda, the son of Cerdic."[96]

Combining all that Alcock, Ashe, Plummer, Whitelock, and Garmonsway have written, a chart reflecting floruits and lifespans is important for structuring a general outline for a Cerdic/Creoda/Cynric chronology. Even though Creoda and Cynric may seem incidental to the major focus upon the life-span and floruit of Cerdic the Saxon king, the scheme of the general genealogical tree from Cynric back to Cerdic's father is relevent in relation to Arthur's involvement with the West-Saxon line. Since the discrepancy between the Preface and the *Chronicle* has been reconciled, there are several specific dates and some other pieces of information that provide a stable base for structuring the floruits and life-spans:

1. Cerdic established the West-Saxon kingdom in 500 and ruled for 16 years. In addition to his length of reign, it provides the year 516 for the end of his life-span.
2. Creoda's length of reign provides us with two dates: 517 when he begins his kingship, and 534 which marks his death.
3. Cynric's rule is 27 years long, begun in 534 and ending 26 years later in 560.

As a clarification, a floruit normally marks a span of 30 years characteristic of a generation. This 30-year span would be considered the same as a slice of life during a prime time, with 15 years prior to the first mark of the floruit and 15 years after the last mark to give a range for a general lifetime. The floruits, then, for father-son would be distinctive, with the last year of one touching the first year of the other, but lifespans would be overlapping. By their very nature, the floruits and lifespans do not get specific for a cardinal or ordinal year with a ± deviation of one or two years, but they do give general guidelines for establishing birth- and death-years. Both the death-year and the birth-year in the lifespans are, of course, obvious, but the interesting rule-of-thumb calculation is the birth-year for a succeeding generation. Although floruits and life-spans by their nature are general, there are some solid specifics revealed by the table. The discoveries are surprising, but even more gratifying, they are directly related to the Arthurian matter. The relationship between Cerdic and Arthur which has been vaguely sensed by scholars has become more vivid. Cerdic entered western Britain in 494/495, very close to the time of the Badon battle. In 500, also very close to the Badon battle, he in some way obtained western territories and succeeded to the West Saxon kingdom. He died or was killed in 516, near the time of the Camlann battle. Creoda succeeds to the throne at this time, and in the true sense

	Cerdic	*Creoda*	*Cynric*
Floruit	465–495	495–525	525–555
Life-Span	450–510	480–540	510–570
Years of Reign	16: 500–516	17: 517–534	26: 534–560
Age at Onset	50 (?)	37	24
Age at Death	66 (?)	54	50

Table 11 — **Floruits and lifespans for West Saxon kings.** Statistical probabilities for initial West Saxon kings based upon floruits and lifespans. According to the reconfiguration of the *Anglo-Saxon Chronicle* and its Preface, the **Years of Reign**, highlighted by bold type, are accurate. The base used for the configuration of the floruits, **495**, is also accurate as Cerdic's entry into Britain.

of the term, the West Saxon conquered the kingdom. The solidification of these specifics comes later, but here they serve the purpose of demonstrating that the Cardinal/Ordinal years in the chronology are soundly substantiated and logical. Even though history sometimes shows that kings may be young when crowned (such as Valentinian III at the age of six), the floruits and life-spans for each of these West Saxons are not questionable exceptions. They succeeded to the kingdom at a reasonable age, and their lives were not abnormally long.

CERDIC, THE SON OF CUNEDDA: CARDINAL YEAR #8

Distinguishing between categories on Cerdic son of Cunedda and the Cunneda generation is difficult and will cause some unavoidable repetition, but for accurate analysis they should be considered as separate issues. The name of Cerdic as son of Cunedda in a Briton context during the Arthurian era occurs once, in Sections 193A to 195A of *Harleian MS 3859*, called the Welsh Genealogies.[†] Section 62 of the *Historia Brittonum* echoes Cunedda's migration to the south with his eight sons but does not list his offspring. The Welsh Genealogies give more specific information:

> These are the names of the sons of Cunedda of whom the number was 9. ... 5 Ceretic, 6 Abloyc, 7 Enniaun Girt [grandfather of Maelgwn and Cinglas], ...[97]

The difference in the number of sons listed by Nennius as opposed to the Welsh Genealogies is accounted for by Nennius' not listing Cunedda's first-born, Typipaun, who died in the north.

The Welsh Genealogies do not appear as part of the *Historia Brittonum*, but the information which they convey is very important to Arthuriana. In addition to providing the name of Cerdic as Cunedda's fifth son, they give information about Cunedda's migration in the late fourth or early fifth century and list specific

†*See Appendix B.*

territories granted to him, from the River Dee to the River Teifi plus regions in western Britain. Some researchers consider this material historically weak, as if written in an attempt to explain geographic place-names, but Alcock writes:

> [A]gainst this [criticism] it can be asserted first, that names like Ceretic and Etern are well attested as personal names; and second, that Welsh territorial names were regularly formed by adding possessive or territorial suffixes -*ing* or -*iog* to personal names. There is nothing inherently improbable about part of west Wales being called Ceredigion after an early ruler Cerdic, nor is there any reason why the account of Cunedda and his sons should be anything other than a record of fact.[98]

Accepting this information on those grounds, Ceredigion is a bonafide place-name derived from Cerdic. But a study of a map on the ancient territories of Wales (see Map 5) proves to be even more interesting. Within the dominion of Deheubarth in southwestern Wales there is a smaller kingdom just north of Ceredigion called Creuddyn, which is a far more significant place-name. In a different context Alcock has clarified that documents about various dynasties passed through a British or Welsh phase of transmission which is evidenced by Welsh spellings of Saxon names.[99] What makes this so crucial and unique is a comparison of the place-name Creuddyn (pronounced Cray-oo-thin) with the lost Creoda generation from the *Anglo-Saxon Chronicle*. Creuddyn is a Welsh form of the Saxon name Creoda. As Cunneda's son, Cerdic, a Gewisse or "Saxon compatriot" but a Briton by ancestry, inherits a large territorial tract in Wales, and in turn, he bequeaths a segment of his kingdom to his son Creoda. This not only gives credence to the territory of Ceredigion granted to Cerdic by his father Cunedda, but as a more profound impact it directly connects the Welsh Genealogies with the *Anglo-Saxon Chronicle*.

The floruits and life-spans for the West Saxon kings of Cerdic and Creoda apply therefore to Cunedda's offspring Ceretic and his son Creuddyn. The floruits bridge the years 465 to 555, and the lifespans are from 450 to 560. This places the West Saxons Cerdic/Creoda and Cunedda's offspring Ceretic/Creuddyn at a geographic and chronologic crossroads with other key figures: Vortigern, the Saxon allies who were termed the Gewissae, Hengist, and Octha. O'Sullivan provides chronological verification. After resolving the issue of a Ceredig of Strathclyde and a Ceredig of Cardigan, O'Sullivan concludes:

> On the whole, however, it seems far more likely that Ceredig of Strathclyde and Ceredig of Cardigan were two different men. In any case, the chronology would be relatively unaffected, for a Cunedda son and a Cunedda lieutenant would fall into much the same era.[100]

Earlier in his text, he was more specific about a time span. O'Sullivan writes that "if the expedition of Cunedda took place ca. 400 A.D. ... and if Maelgwn Gwynedd flourished towards the beginning of the sixth century, ... then the floruit of Cerdig of Cardigan would be roughly the same as that of Ceredig of Strathclyde (ca. 420–450, as we have seen)."[101]

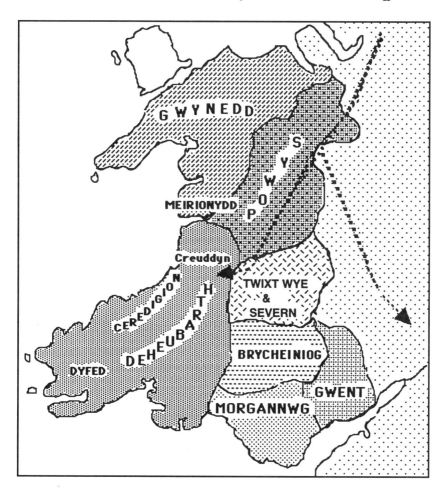

Map 5. The ancient kingdoms in Wales. The path of the Cunedda migration is indicated by the arrows from the north into Wales and to the Hwicce/Gewissae territories.

He bases the floruit for Cerdic of Cardigan on the two assumptions that Maelgwn flourished at the beginning of the sixth century and Cunedda migrated to the south at the beginning of the fifth century. However, as already established as a cardinal year, Maelgwn flourished in the *middle* of the sixth century, and, to be analyzed in detail in the next section of this chapter, Cunedda's migration was precipitated by the Saxon revolt in the *middle* of the fifth century. If the displacement of the two assumptions is corrected by 50 years from his generalized dates, the floruit for Cerdic of Cardigan becomes 470–500. This might appear "manipulating the figures, as scholars delight to do,"[102] but this text deals with the *specific* assignation of dates rather than the general place of at the beginning, or in the middle or toward the end of certain centuries. This, plus the concession that no historian can point to Cunedda's migration other than somewhere between 383 and 490, means that circumstantial evidence must be amassed so that a researcher is entitled to calculate specifically limited time frames. The floruit for Cunedda will be used to calibrate his migration in a succeeding section of this text.

It is necessary to look at one more microcosm on Cerdic as the son of Cunedda. Geoffrey Ashe binds the historical packet on this crucial figure, even though his material at first seems to be misplaced in a section on Cerdic as Cunedda's son. In his pursuit of a similar puzzle seeking to reveal that Cerdic the West Saxon king was Arthur's adversary at the Battle of Badon, he, like so many other researchers, notes that Cerdic is a Briton and not a Saxon name and concludes that there was

> ... a phase of British-Saxon fraternisation and intermarriage in the fifth century, before the debacle. ... Later that century, at all events, we seem to be confronted with a man of mixed blood who bears a British name, has a title which establishes an obscure link with a British family, yet leads a Saxon war-band against the Britons. ... [These cryptic hints] show the need for collation of facts from many sources.[103]

The collation of that information leads to Cunedda as Cerdic's father. Cunedda is an important and powerful Briton chieftain who fraternizes with Saxon allies. His offspring — Cerdic and *his* progeny — lead Saxon armies against the Britons. It is time now to turn to Cunedda and his role.

CUNEDDA: CARDINAL YEAR #9

In the process of establishing the year for Maelgwn's death, O'Sullivan devotes approximately eight pages to specifics about Cunedda, since Cunedda is directly and closely tied to Maelgwn as an ancestor who can also be used to verify Maelgwn's death.[104] Because of the complexity of the relationship in establishing dates, Cunedda was not used to establish Cardinal year #6 on Maelgwn in the preceding section, but he is important in his own right for establishing another cardinal year in the Arthurian chronology. In addition to the date of the Cunedda migration as another primary historical fact which must be evaluated to confirm the Arthurian chronology, Cunneda's relationship to Cerdic must be probed.

The name Cunedda appears three times in the ancient British manuscripts — twice in the *Historia Brittonum*, and once in the Welsh Genealogies. The brief entry in Chapter 14 relates that

> The sons of [Liethan] obtained the country of Dimetæ ... and [other provinces] ... till they were expelled from every part of Britain, by Cunedda and his sons.[105]

Chapter 62 continues that

> The great king, Mailcun, reigned ... in the district of Guenedota [Gwynedd] because his great-great-great grandfather, Cunedda, had come before from ... Manau Gustodin

[Gododdin], one hundred and forty-six years before Mailcun reigned and expelled the Scots [i.e., Irish] ... from those countries.[106]

The Welsh Genealogies conclude by supplying the names of his nine sons (including the one who perished in Manau Gododdin), by mentioning that Maelgwn and Cinglas were grandsons to Enniaun Girt, Cunedda's seventh son and therefore brother to Cerdic, and by giving a specific boundary of their territories from the "river which is called Dubr Duiu up to another river Tebi," plus general holdings in "many regions in western Britain."[107]

Without interpolation, the Cunedda saga offers these details: Cunedda and his eight sons came from the north, from the country called Manaw Gododdin 146 years before Maelgwn reigned in Gwynedd. He originally had nine sons, but his first-born, Typipaun, died in the region of Manaw Gododdin, and therefore did not come hither with his father and aforesaid brothers, all of whom are specifically named, in addition to two of Cunedda's great-grandsons, Maelgwn and Cinglas. Cunedda expelled the Kindred of Eight and all their race, plus Istoreth and all his people who held Dal Riada, plus Bolg and his people who held the Isle of Man and other islands, plus Liathan and his sons who prevailed in the country of the Dementians. Once the Irish were expelled with great slaughter from these countries and all countries in Britain never to return to inhabit them again, Cunedda and his sons held territories from the River Dubr Duiu to the River Tebi and many regions in western Britain.

Surprisingly, the story about him is quite detailed. However, this story of the fifth century, being copied and recopied over a span of four to five centuries, has presumably come down to modern times with omissions, deletions, insertions, modifications, misinterpretations, and miscopyings. It is the researcher's arduous task to cull those items that corrupt the text so that what is retained reflects history as factually and accurately as possible.

The narrative supplies a number so that Cunedda's migration can be calculated, but the task is much more difficult than that. In Morris' translation of Section 62 of the *Historia Brittonum*, he writes and then clarifies the passage by adding

> Cunedag, ancestor of Mailcunus, came with his eight sons from the north ... CXLVI years before Mailcunus reigned ... [Cunedda] was the great-grandfather of Mailcunus, or Maelgwn. ... The figure of 146 years is given in Roman figures, that are easily corrupted in copying. It conflicts with the evidence of the genealogies that place Cunedda in the 430s.[108]

Morris misleads on two major points. The first is that what he translates as the original varies from what Josephus Stevenson writes. Stevenson, who is probably the foremost translator of both Nennius and Gildas, expresses the 146 years between Cunedda's migration to the south and Maelgwyn reign as "centum quadraginta sex annis,"[109] contradicting what Morris claims were numerals in the original Latin.

Alcock has this to say about the possibility of scribal error in recording that particular time span:

> The apparent precision of the figure "one hundred and forty-six years" has a strong attraction. Because it is spelt out in our source — Centu[m] quadraginta sex, not cxlvi — it is difficult to claim that there has been a scribal error.[110]

If a person rejects that figure, then, it must be done for reasons other than a scribal error.

This does not mean, however, that the choices are to accept the 146 years as correct or abandon the search. The Welsh Genealogies do trace Cunedda to his son Enniaun Girt, to his grandson Catgolaun Lauhir, to his great-grandson Mailcun. Section 62 of the *HB* uses the word *atavus*, which can mean ancestor in a generic sense, or great-great-great grandfather in a specific sense. O'Sullivan discusses this term, explaining that it does not actually mean great-grandfather, but in Roman law it is a technical term indicating great-great-great grandfather. He then points out that in the passage, "which was hardly drawn up by a Roman lawyer, the word [atavus] most likely means simply 'ancestor,' not at all excluding a great-grandfather."[111] The Genealogies rule out the specific definition, which means that 146 years is too long a span for that number of generations. Reconfiguring the time span between Cunedda and Maelgwn,

> On the conventional reckoning of thirty years to a generation, Maelgwn should have flourished between 90 and 120 years after Cunedda. It can be argued that even this interval is too long, because the thirty-year generation seems quite unrealistically long in the conditions of fifth- and sixth-century Britain.[112]

Alcock has written about his own calculations, setting up three possible times for the Cunedda migration, each based upon a justifiable motive for the move. If it occurred around 380, then the move was "an act of Roman policy"; if it was around 450, it may have been organized by "some sub-Roman authority like that which brought in the Anglo-Saxons as allies"; if it were as late as 490 based upon three generations of twenty years, then his migration was "certainly an act of private enterprise."[113]

Alcock does not go into detail or give much credence to the first possibility, prior to the Roman withdrawal, because Nennius records Cunedda's expulsion of the Irish. The Irish were settled in Wales until the Roman withdrawal, and it would have been afterwards when they were expelled from Britain. Apparently following Alcock's lead, Graham Webster gives an accurate rendition of the period's events. Toward the end of Rome's reign on the island, even though there were skirmishes between the Romans and the settlers, the Irish had already settled in Wales. It had been an accepted Roman practice to allow barbarian tribes to settle in captured territory in return for protection around the Roman borders, and in the death-throes of the Romano/Briton empire, the Romans did not have the resources to expel the Irish. Rome instituted a practice of giving posts to tribal chieftains who could pass titles and responsibilities on to their heirs in return for their fealty as border guards. But the concept "... was not successful. The Irish invaders gradually gained command and another drastic reorganisation was needed by 430 with the transfer to North Wales of Cunedda."[114] After some juggling, Morris also sets the migration in the 430s. Logistically, this is Alcock's point for writing that the migration was organized in the middle decades of the fifth century by some sub–Roman authority, and the expulsion of the Irish from the territories of Wales was followed immediately by wars to drive the traitorous Saxon allies from Briton soil. In 490 Cunedda would have been acting as an independent, but by that late date, new kingdoms had already been delineated and settlements had sprung up.

However, the date around 450 (442 specifically) provides two ideal motives for Cunedda's migration: the Irish who were warring with the weakened Roman forces just prior to the withdrawal, and the Saxon Revolt which occurred just shortly thereafter. As compatriots, there were Saxons in the north under the leadership of Octha, and Hengist had been procured as a mercenary. When treachery and deceit, probably motivated by greed, split the alliance, Vortigern as the sub–Roman king solicited help from a renegade Briton who had already helped drive the Irish from the country. The conflicts with the Irish shifted to conflicts with the Saxons. The island was still in upheaval and in grave peril of being ravaged; only the enemy had changed.

By borrowing Alcock's piece of information and settling on the mid-point between 90 and 120 years, and by setting the date into a milieu of events just discussed, Maelgwn can be placed realistically 105 years after Cunedda. Using Maelgwn's death established as a cardinal year in 547, that means Cunedda flourished in 442. This is in the ideal range for Cunedda's floruit and lifespan building upon what has already been set up for Cerdic. Cunedda's floruit would be 435–465, calculating to a lifespan from 420 to 480. Cunedda therefore would be a young man in his thirties when he migrated from the north to fight against the Irish and rebelling Saxons.

One other implication that has not been addressed yet is the term *Cymry*. It is similar to the word *Gewissae* and is defined by Wade-Evans as "compatriots," a synonymous definition of "federates" applied by Morris to *Gewissae*.[115] Both are tribal terms associated with "countrymen" and "allies," the latter applied to Vortigern as a king of these people and to Cerdic's heritage. *Cymry* derives from *Kymery*, a common noun "as old as the Welsh language itself."[116] This term carries back to the time when the Welsh language was emerging from Old British, some time during the period around the Roman withdrawal. It seems to apply to the *Cymru* in Wales and specifically attaches itself to Cunedda's diverse forces, mostly British. Morris writes that "Cymry is still the national name of the Welsh and the northwestern Britons"[117] and links the name Cymry with *Combrogi*, a cavalry force that battled English infantry. An independent observation is parallel between the word Cymry and Emrys: both applied to tribes and chiefs in the northern and western territories vacated by the Romans and then occupied by Cunedda and his countrymen.

In *The Age of Arthur* Morris gives detailed material on Cunedda, recording
that because of Cunedda's arrival, his conquest of Wales, and the later kings who
claimed descent from him, the history of Wales changed. In his later discussion
of inheritances, Morris writes that upon Cunedda's passing, Cerdic inherits Wales.
He also draws a parallel between Cunedda's migration and the Cornovian movement to Dumnonia. He relates that there is no date given for the Cornoviian
migration, but based upon Docco and Gerontius plus the similarity of "military
tradition," he estimates that it occurred in the first half of the fifth century. He
concludes that

> The Dumnonian end of the migration suggests the same context as the movement
> of the Votadini, for it also presupposes a strong central government. ... No evidence
> suggests that either the predecessors or the immediate successors of Vortigern enjoyed
> such authority, and it was therefore probably he who organised the migration of the
> Cornovii, as of the Votadini.[118]

Irish colonists had also settled in Roman Dumnonia, which highlights not only
the expulsion of the Irish from that territory but also explains why the old Roman
name of Dumnonia was replaced with Cornwall, the peninsula of the Cornoviian Welsh.

According to what the histories report, four important events can pinpoint
Cunedda's floruit as a Votadinian: the Roman abandonment in the 420s, Cunedda's
migration in the early 440s, the Irish expulsion from the island in the latter part
of the third decade in the fifth century, and the Saxon Revolt in 442. For comparison, when the cluster of dates near 442 are superimposed on Cunedda's floruit
as the father of Cerdic the West Saxon king, the match is ideal, especially when
considering the general nature of floruits. Stated differently, Cerdic's floruit supports the postulation that he is Cunedda's son who becomes the West Saxon king.
Cunedda, the southern migration, Cerdic as his son and subsequent West Saxon
king, the Irish expulsion, and the Saxon Revolt are undoubtedly intertwined.
Alcock writes that the dropping out of two generations in the early manuscripts
is not an impossible happening,[119] so a match this close is much better than anticipated. Vortigern's role as the post–Roman authority who sanctioned the migration points to the next consideration, Cerdic as Vortigern's interpreter.

Interestingly, this takes us full circle to the opening quotation by Nennius
beginning the section on Cunedda's cardinal year:

> The sons of Liathan prevailed in the country of the Dementians ... and in other
> countries ... until they were expelled by Cunedda, and by his sons, from all coun-
> tries in Britain.[120]

Morris provides the history of the *Ui Liathan* which documents Liathan's initial
migration from southeastern Ireland to Dementia:

> [Liathan and his sons] were driven out of [Dementia's] eastern borders, about Kid-
> welly, by Cunedda, in the middle of the fifth century, but both British and Irish texts

prolong their rule in the rest of Dementia for another two generations, until Agricola's [father of Vortipor[121]] campaign ended their independence and their dynasty, in Arthur's time.[122]

The emergent history not only embraces the withdrawal of the Romans, Cunedda's migration, the vacating of Cornovii, the explusion of the Irish, the Saxon Revolt, the rise of the Cymry, the origin of the Gewissae, and the advent of the Saxon kingdoms, but it also ties together the manuscripts of Gildas, the *Historia Brittonum*, the Welsh Genealogies, the Irish Annals, and the *Anglo-Saxon Chronicle* into an unprecedented packet. Cunedda's migration from the north was a military maneuver to expel first the Irish and then the Saxons.

CERDIC AS VORTIGERN'S INTERPRETER: CARDINAL YEAR #10

Plummer, the foremost authority on the manuscripts of the *Chronicles*, has this to say about the entry of 495, the very first entry in which Cerdic makes an appearance. The quotation follows, with underlining and brackets added to focus attention on relevant parts which are then discussed below it:

> 495 — The coming of the West Saxons; the foundation, as it proved of England. It is curious to find the traditional founder of the West-Saxon kingdom, the source to which all West-Saxon pedigrees are traced, bearing a name Cerdic, Certic, so like the Welsh Ceredig, Ceretic. [It is worth noting that in Nennius, Chapter 37, Ceretic is the name of Hengist's interpreter.][123]

After several re-readings of this passage, it is more than just Plummer's choice of the word *curious* which draws attention. In particular, what Plummer had in parentheses labeling Cerdic as *Hengist's* interpreter was confusing because there are no clues in the *Historia* to indicate that Cerdic must be aligned with Hengist. Nennius relates:

> When the keels had arrived, Hengist held a banquet for Vortigern, and his men and his interpreter, whose name was Ceretic, and he told the girl to serve their wine and spirits. They all got exceedingly drunk. When they were drinking, Satan entered into Vortigern's heart and made him love the girl. Through his interpreter he asked her father for her hand, saying "Ask of me what you will, even to the half of my kingdom."[124]

Clarifying the grammatical structure, and thus explaining the meaning, but definitely not manipulating the facts, the passage reads this way:

> Hengist held a banquet for Vortigern, and for Vortigern's men, and for Vortigern's interpreter, whose name was Ceretic, and Hengist told his daughter Rowena to serve their wine and spirits. They all got exceedingly drunk. When they were drinking, Satan entered Vortigern's heart and made him love the girl. Through Vortigern's interpreter, Vortigern demanded of the father Hengist Rowena's hand, saying, "Ask of me what you will, even to the half of my kingdom."

The confusion stems not necessarily from the translations of the passage, but from Nennius' original Latin, in the segment which reads

> Illis autem bibentibus, intravit Sathanas in corde Gurthigirni ut amaret puellam, et postulavit eam a patre suo per interpretem suum...[125]

Giles' translation is the most confusing: "... Vortigern, at the instigation of the devil, and enamoured with the beauty of the damsel, demanded her, through the medium of his interpreter, of the father, promising...."[126] This sounds as if the interpreter is with the father of the damsel, or in other words, is with Hengist. However, in the original passage Nennius states that Vortigern through his interpreter demands the father's daughter. The antecedent for the pronoun *his* is what causes the confusion; is the pronoun referring to the father (Hengist), or to Vortigern? The nearest antecedent is *Vortigern*: "Through Vortigern's interpreter, Vortigern asked Rowena's father Hengist for Rowena." Furthermore, because Cerdic is an undeniable Briton name, it is illogical to assume that the interpreter has arrived with Hengist. The interpreter is *not* Hengist's interpreter, but Vortigern's, and the implications of this one little change shed a profoundly different light on the history of that period. For one, it instantly clarifies Plummer's quotation, and eliminates the curiosity of it: Cerdic the interpreter is not a Saxon; he is a Briton, portending the appearance of a Briton Cerdic in the *Anglo-Saxon Chronicle.*

Richard Barber supports the contention that Cerdic is Briton. His text, *The Figure of Arthur*, gives the following addendum about Ceredic:

> No other Briton among the Britons knew Saxon except this man; and he applied himself to acquiring a knowledge of it (or reading it) until he was able to understand the Saxon speech.[127]

Barber does not state outright whose interpreter Ceredic is, but the implication is undeniable; nothing would indicate a Saxon having a Briton interpreter. Barber is evidently following an original untranslated source very carefully.

Not only is it important at this juncture to establish Cerdic as a Briton who is Vortigern's interpreter, but it is also crucial to identify his association with Hengist. Cerdic, of course, is directly linked to Hengist and Vortigern in Nennius. A firm fix has been detailed for Cerdic son of Cunedda and Cerdic the West Saxon King: now Cerdic as the interpreter has to be set in a time frame at a crossroad with Hengist and Vortigern. Octha, too, is inextricably bound to Hengist's time frame, and therefore his role has to be viewed simultaneously. The son of Hengist is referred to as Æsc in the *Chronicle*, but for continuity, the name Octha will be used. It has already been calibrated that there were three Saxon *Adventi*, but the emphasis was upon Saxon entries into Britain, not upon the leaders.

Framing a composite chronology for Hengist, Octha, and Vortigern is not as elementary as interlacing events from the two separate sources of the *Brittonum* and the *Chronicle*. Placement of the three major Saxon ingressions was relatively easy. Evidence was amassed establishing Cardinal year #2 which directly affected

Cardinal year #3, the third Saxon *Adventus.* Setting the third Saxon *Adventus* at 453 simplified the placement of the second *Adventus* within those parameters. However, conciliating the floruits of Hengist, Octha, and Vortigern is more complicated. The only entry in the *Chronicle* which records them simultaneously is 455. The Saxons are no longer allies with the Britons, Horsa is killed in the battle, and Octha succeeds to the kingdom and reigns with his father.

This starting base is simple, but when viewed as one item in a composite picture, the general chronology is extremely obscure. Vortigern is not recorded again, Hengist's last appearance is in entry 473, and 488 is given as the year of Octha's succession to the kingdom, reigning for 24 more years. There is no information in the historical documents giving dates for Octha's entry into Britain, Rowena's encounter with Vortigern, or Vortigern's birth- or death-years. The scant information is provided by the *Chronicle,* and during this time segment it is unreliable in any attempts to calibrate events particularly from the second half of the fifth decade to the first half of the seventh, and carrying on even to the end of the eighth decade when Octha's succession to the throne is listed.

Only silhouettes of possibilities can be sketched. Manuscript A̅ does not record an entry for 456, but Manuscript E does, actually listed as 457 in A̅, A, and the Ethelwerd chronicle. Manuscripts A̅, A, E, and Ethelwerd record a battle at Wippedesfleot in 465, but Manuscript B places it in year 461 and Manuscript F in 466. Additionally, all manuscripts for either 456 or 457 indicate that the Saxon battle is against the Britons. But entry 465 in manuscripts A̅ and E record the battle of the Saxons against the Welsh, while Manuscript A, the variant B of 461 and the variant F of 466 record the battle as being against the Britons. The entry for 473 indicates in manuscripts A̅ and E that the Saxons fought the Welsh, while A, B, and C record the enemy as the Britons.

However, entry 488 causes the most difficulty. Manuscript A̅ relates that Octha succeeded to the kingdom and ruled for 24 years, while Manuscript E lists the length of rule as 34 years. Which of these is a scribal error is a moot point, since either would put Octha's lifespan beyond the "reasonable age" concept. For the first, if Octha reigned for 24 years, then his death-year would have been 512. Assuming that he inherited the kingdom with his father in 455 and he was 18 at that time, his birth-year would have been 437, making him 75 years old at his death. Figuring the 10-year discrepancy, he would have died at 85.

Octha succeeds to the kingdom twice — once when he inherited the kingdom shared with his father, and later as the sole ruler — which could be legitimate. What seems most likely is that Octha's first succession to the throne did in fact occur in 455 upon the death of Horsa, but his sole succession should be added to the entry of 473, the last entry where Hengist is mentioned. This common practice in the *Chronicle* of listing simultaneously a succession but only implying the predecessor's death puts Octha's life-span into alignment, while at the same time making Hengist's span more reasonable. If Hengist's death is set in year 473, his floruit/lifespan would be 428–458 and 413–473, with 473 surprisingly marking the last entry mentioning his name. This means that Hengist's age would be 29 when he led the second expedition into Britain, overlapping Vortigern's and

Event	Vortigern	Hengist	Octha	Cerdic
	407(?) –	413–473	437–497	465–495
				450–510
Saxon Revolt, 442	35	29	5	(-8)
Octha's succession, 455	48	42	18	(5)
Horsa's death				
458–464	51–57	45–51	21–27	8–14
Death of Hengist, 473		60	36	23
Death of Octha, 497			60	47

Table 12 — Overlap of four historical figures of the Arthurian period.

Octha's. Based upon Octha's death in 497, if he ruled for 24 years from 473, his floruit/lifespan would extend beyond Hengist's from 452 to 483/437 to 497. This means that Octha would have been approximately 18 when he first succeeded to the kingdom and somewhere around age 36 when Hengist died and he became the sole ruler. Interestingly his projected death-year occurs during the same year as the Battle of Badon.

If Rowena made her appearance before Vortigern about the same time that Octha succeeded to the throne with his father and she was either two years older or younger, since her floruit and her brother's would be very close, then the superimposition of Cerdic's floruit/lifespan indicates that Cerdic's life would have touched these other figures of history, whether it was as an interpreter in his earlier years or as a Saxon king in later years. In a simplified format, the events involving these people is recorded in Table 12 above.

The information about Octha's first succession to the kingdom leads to one other matter which must be clarified. The *Anglo-Saxon Chronicle* records that Octha and Hengist succeed to the kingdom after Horsa's death. Nennius in the *Historia* reports that upon Hengist's death, Octha came down from the north. This can be interpreted in one of two ways. One, is that Octha came down from the north in 473, the year of his *second* succession, using the more reasonable adaptation already established for the *Chronicle* entry. Had Octha stayed in the north until 473, then he and his father would not have fought the battles together against the Britons and the Welsh in 456, 465, or 473 as reported in the *Chronicle*. This leads to the second interpretation, that there is a scribal error in the Nennius manuscript: the beginning of Chapter 56 should read that on *Horsa's* death, Octha came down from the north. Accepting this latter case, the *Chronicle* entries could stand correctly as they are for 456, 465, and 473, and Hengist's directives to Vortigern in Chapter 38 would fit well contextually:

  1. shortly after Vortimer was killed, the Saxons, led by Hengist, returned in force (Chapter 45, *HB*) in the third Saxon *Adventus* in 452;
  2. the suggestion that Octha fought against the Irish is chronologically and geographically

correct. Cunedda and his sons, including Cerdic, had filled the void in the Cornovii territory and were fighting the Irish, Vortigern's main concern;

3. within a general time frame Cerdic, son of Cunedda, could have also functioned as Vortigern's interpreter since he was in close contact with the Saxon compatriots and would know their language well, and as the fortunes of warfare shift, his allegiance could have shifted as well, leading to a kingship which was called Saxon;

4. the shaky reconciliation between Vortigern and Hengist breaks down and the emphasis shifts from the Irish wars to the strife between the Welsh and the treasonous Saxons.

In a separate context Octha's name is linked to Arthur and not to Cerdic in the *Historia Brittonum.* Chapter 56 relates a straightforward occurrence that Octha comes down from the north and fights against Arthur. An interesting link which has been suggested is that Octha's death-year is the same as the date for the Battle of Badon, which is also tied to Arthur, but specific comments will be postponed because of contributions from the literary segment.

THE BATTLE OF CAMLANN: CARDINAL YEAR #11

Camlann is next in line, which can be verified by looking at one other cardinal year already calibrated. The entry for the Badon date was adjusted because evidence showed that it was displaced by a 19-year lunar cycle; that adjustment moved the year from 516 to 497, the latter year being verified within a minor deviation by the *Anglo-Saxon Chronicle*, year 495, which records that Cerdic came to Britain in that year. Evidence also showed that both the Badon and Camlann entries were later insertions in the *Annales*, without parent roots in the Irish Annals. Since they were paired in that way, the date between the two battles remains a constant rather than a variable, separated by a 21-year span.

Previous scholars have speculated that perhaps the 21-year span was incorrect, based upon the discrepancy between the dates in the *Anglo-Saxon Chronicle* and its overview manuscript, the Genealogical Preface. Those speculations analyzed the possibility that only four to five years separated the battles based upon Cerdic's entry into Britain in 494 (Badon) and succeeding to the West Saxon kingdom six years later in 500 (Camlann). However, since this text reconciled the discrepancy between the *Chronicle* and the Preface, the 21-year span between Badon and Camlann can stand, particularly in view of the evidence which Gildas' manuscipt offers.

The Camlann entry in the *Annales*, then, must be adjusted by one 19-year cycle, from 537 to 518. Like the Badon adjustment, this date can be verified by entries in the *Chronicle*. Camlann would be the final major victory of the Saxons over the Britons and their succession to the West Saxon kingdom. That date is given for year 519 in the *Chronicle* and implied with a minor deviation in the Preface in giving Cerdic's reign of 16 years and Creoda's succession in 517.

Another procedure for verifying the Camlann date at 518 is checking other sources which might offer enlightenment on the milieu of the period. Nennius provides no clue of the Arthurian/Camlann connection, since his Chapter 56 on the campaigns of Arthur lists only the 12 battles culminating with Badon; he relates that Arthur was victorious in all the campaigns, but then makes no reference to the campaign in which Arthur was defeated. However, he does provide a crucial clue of Arthur's enemy after the 12 campaigns. He writes:

> The more the [English] Saxons were vanquished, the more they sought for new supplies of Saxons from Germany [i.e., German Saxons]; so that kings, commanders, and military bands were invited over from almost every [German Saxon] province. And this practice they continued till the reign of Ida.[128]

After the Badon victory, then, the major enemy still remained the Saxons, with more and more of the foreigners assaulting the shores of Britain. This points naturally in the direction of Saxon records, with the *Anglo-Saxon Chronicle* as the primary source.

It is interesting to compare the Welsh (or Briton) point of view reported in the *AC* with the Saxon one in the *Chronicle*. The *Chronicle* provides more information and is of course biased, but Henry of Huntingdon is more objective in his record:

> ... [T]hat same year some of the most powerful of the British chiefs joined battle against [Cerdic]. It was fought bravely and obstinately on both sides; when the day was declining, the Saxons gained the victory; and there was great slaughter that day of the inhabitants of Albion [Britain], which would have been still more terrible had not the setting sun stayed it.[129]

Emphasis is on the severity of the conflict. This war is the apex of a long-standing rivalry between two unrelenting foes, the outcome of which will finally settle the claim for supremacy on the Island, and Camlann becomes a lock-in for the year 518.

Ordinal Years of the Arthurian Chronology

There are several other entries in the *Annales Cambriae* deserving mention because they function well as background filler for the Arthurian chronology, although they are not directly associated with Arthuriana. As a distinction, this book has also coined the term *ordinal years*, with two differences from cardinal years. Ordinal years must also have as their source one of the four ancient manuscripts listed in Chapter 2 with an implicit or explicit date, similar to the cardinal years. Ordinal years must also have that implicit or explicit date verified from a separate source, but that separate source does not have to be a historic one; instead, it can come from literary tradition. The second variant is that the confirmed date does not have to have direct pertinence to Arthur. These three additions as ordinal years signify a specified order in a general series for reckoning, but they are not elevated to cardinal years because they are of subsidiary importance in the search for Arthur's historicity.

These ordinal dates are relatively simple to insert, since the verification of their dates is straightforward. In addition to their inclusions in the *AC*, two are easily traceable to the parent manuscripts of the Irish Annals and also appear in various manuscripts of the *Saints' Lives*. The one exception is the dating of the Gildean manuscript. One major and two minor ordinal calibrations spring from the reckonings of the cardinal years. The important one is the year in which the *De Excidio* was written.

THE PENNING OF THE DE EXCIDIO: ORDINAL YEAR #1

Calibration of this date requires some back-tracking to show why the date A.D. 516 for the Battle of Badon would create some irreconcilable discrepancies in conjunction with the penning of the *De Excidio*. If 516 had been accepted as the year for the Battle of Badon and therefore the year of Gildas' birth, then Gildas himself is indicating in his manuscript that he is penning the words in the forty-fourth year after his birth, which would place the year at 516 + 44 = 560. This indicates in turn that Gildas would have been writing the *De Excidio* approximately 13 years *after* Maelgwn's death.

But Michael Winterbottom amply verifies in his Preface (borne out through his translation) that Gildas gives a history of Britain in the past tense, but when he begins his admonitions of the five British kings, he switches to present tense.[130] Gildas' specific vilification of Constantine applies equally to the other tyrants when he writes, "I know full well you are still alive, and I charge you as though you were present."[131]

When the 19-year lunar adaptation for Badon is accepted, the formula shifts dramatically. The year 497 is the date of Badon and therefore the birth of Gildas, and Gildas is penning the *De Excidio* 44 years later. Hence, the calculation becomes 497 + 44 = 541, approximately six years prior to Maelgwn's death, which has already been entrenched as a cardinal year. This time span was also verified in calibrating Cunedda's migration and floruit which pointed out that both Maelgwn and Cuneglas were his great grandsons. Their generational spans would have fallen between the years of 516 and 546, precisely during the era when Gildas was castigating the five rulers of Britain. This would make Gildas approximately 50 years old at Maelgwn's death, and accepting the *Annals* death-year in 570, it further means that Gildas would have been 73 years old when he died. Ensuing scholarship also attests to a date near 541 for the penning of the *De Excidio*. Plummer gauges a year very close to the lunar adaptation proposed by this book: "Hence Gildas wrote the *De Excidio* c. 539. ... the occurrence of the same number, 44, in both cases is a mere coincidence."[132] In the latter part of this quote, Plummer is saying that 44 years from the first landing of the Saxons and 44 years from Gildas' birth to his writing the *De Excidio* is coincidence. Morris, too, believes that Gildas wrote the *De Excidio* around 540.[133] Alcock also computes that if Badon is placed at year 53, then "[t]o check this, we add 43 years to Gildas' lifetime, to arrive at A.D. [542] for the time when he was writing."[134] Although O'Sullivan accepts the birth of Gildas in the same year as the Badon battle, he then states that "As a young man, no older than *twenty-five or thirty* [author's italics], Gildas would then have written the *De Excidio* ca. 515-530."[135] This ignores the obvious, that Gildas was born in the same year as the siege of Badon, which is *44* years earlier, meaning he is writing at age 43.

David Dumville verifies in an oblique way this chronology with a couple of rhetorical questions in his essay "The Chronology of *De Excidio Britanniae*, Book I." He asks, "Where in Britain could Gildas or his [Gildas'] *ciues* have lived such that they could not travel by a westerly land-route to Carleon?"[136] Because Dumville seems not to be working from a comparative set of several different chronologies, he questions that Gildas would have trouble traveling a land-route by encountering Saxons so far west. But after posing this problem which "urgently demands a solution," Dumville answers his own question: "It suggests that much of western England was in Anglo-Saxon hands in Gildas' day."[137] This is exactly the case; the writing of the *De Excidio* takes place 23 years after Arthur's fatal Battle of Camlann where he was defeated by Cerdic the Saxon, who succeeded to the kingdom of the West Saxons. This in turn means that Gildas lived the later years of his life under Saxon rule.

Dumville remains puzzled, however, by this problematic contradiction:

> If Gildas' *ciues* cannot reach Carleon because of barbarian annexation of territory, we must suppose either that Anglo-Saxon settlement extended much farther westwards at that time than we have ever supposed, or that his meaning is that the normal route is impeded by Anglo-Saxon settlements and that political rivalries of the Britons make it impossible for the *ciues* of Gildas' own area to travel through the British kingdom(s) between there and *legionum urbs*.[138]

Dumville's first supposition is correct: the Anglo-Saxon settlements did extend much further west than originally supposed because Saxon domination was complete and there was only minor resistance on the part of the remaining Britons.

Gildas' own writings affirm that he is writing a little over two decades after the defeat and death of Arthur and Medraut at the Battle of Camlann, and the gradual establishment of the Saxon kingdom. He is detached from the heat of action, so to speak; his manuscript shows its separation from the immediacy of Camlann:

> And yet *neither to this day* are the cities of our country inhabited as *before* but being forsaken and *overthrown* still lie desolate; *our foreign wars having ceased*, our civil troubles still remaining. For as well as the *remembrance* of such a terrible desolation of the island, as also of the unexpected recovery of the same, *remained in the minds of those who were eye-witnesses of the wonderful events of both*. ... But when these [orderly kings, public magistrates, and private persons, with priests and clergymen] *had departed out of this world and a new race succeeded, who were ignorant of this*

troublesome time ... that not so much as a vestige ... or *remembrance of these virtues remained.*[139] [Author's italics]

This passage gives important insights into Gildas' emotions at this time, as well as crucial clues of the era. The Britons have been overthrown as a result of the Battle of Camlann and the Briton hero Arthur is dead; the Saxons have finally overrun the Britons, and the country still lies forsaken and uninhabited. The foreign wars with the English have ceased because they (the Saxons) are now the victors, but in spite of that, there are still civil troubles between the victors (Saxons) and the vanquished (Britons). Remembrances remain in the minds of those eyewitnesses who can recall the era of Badon and the 21 years of relative peace which ensued. But after that generation had passed from this world, not even the remembrance of that generation's virtue remained. The Britons, who had become the servants to the barbaric Saxons, had now become as wicked as their conquerors.

SAINT COLUMBA: ORDINAL YEAR #2

Ordinal year #2 is the entry which lists Saint Columba, who founded several monasteries, notably the one on Io (Iona) of the Inner Hebrides, near the shores of the old territory called Dalriada, where he passed away.[140] Because it was this particular monastery which helped achieve much of the permanent Christianization of Britain, a great deal of information anchors Columba in authenticity. Alan Orr Anderson and Marjorie Ogilvie Anderson — in their Introduction to Adomnan's biography, based upon three Irish Annals — give a death date of Sunday night of Pentacost, June 9, and then capsulize the three entries which occur in the *AC* on Columba:

> 9 June was a Sunday in 597, and that may be accepted as the year in which Columba died. According to Adomnan's figures, Columba's pilgrimages in Britain would have begun in 563, and the year of his birth would have been 521 or 522. Adomnan gives no year-numbers, but inclines to use battles as dating points.[141]

The three entries for Saint Columba in the *AC* list his birth-year as 521, his voyage to Britain as 562, and his death-year as 595. Since one of the years, 521, in the *Annales* matches the material from Adomnan, this year should stand in the chronology which is formulated later in this chapter. There is only the minor one-year difference in the two reports of his voyage to Britain, and a two-year difference in the report of his obituary. Although there are not major variants and there is a commitment to the fluidity of dates, the voyage year and the death-year for Columba will be labeled as 563 and 597 respectively because they derive from earlier sources. In addition to the Adomnan source, Columba's migration to Britain can be found in the Annals of Ulster at entries 562/63, and his death-year at age 76 likewise in the Annals of Ulster at entry 595.[142]

SAINT DAVID, THE SYNOD OF VICTORY: ORDINAL YEAR #3

Another ordinal date of interest is tied to Saint David of Wales. The *Annales* lists his birth-year as 458, which is a later insertion in that chronicle. Saint David is entered in the *Catalogue of Saints of Ireland*, a manuscript dating to about 730, and in the *Martyrology of Oenegus*, a manuscript from around 800. Another principal source of information is his biography, written about 1090 by Rhygyfarch, son of Sulien. Rhygyfarch's account does not give a birth-year or a death-year, but Saint David is reputed to have taken part in two synods, one at Brefi about 560 and another at Caerleon about 569.[143] The interesting link is the *Annales* entry of 569, another later insertion, which reads, "The 'Synod of Victory' was held between the Britons."[144] If this is the synod attended by Saint David — and there is no reason to believe that it is not — then his birth-year is a corruption which cannot be used as an ordinal year. That is, Saint David's birth in the *AC* was inserted in the blank at year 24, which was actually the blank for year 468, yet Saint David's birth-year was listed by the A.D. date of 458. The Synod at Caerleon was also a later addition, but it was more properly placed. (See tables 3 and 6 in the previous chapter for a visual representation of this.) His alleged death-year — not listed in the *AC*—is set as 598. Considered with his birth-year in 458, his attendance at the Synod in 569, and his death in 598, this would give him the impossible lifespan of 140 years. There is a possibility that his birth-year was transposed from 548 to 458, in which case had he been born in 548, he would have attended the Synod in 569 at age 21 and would have died in 598 at age 50. But this is all supposition, and supposition without evidence cannot be used as an ordinal year. This means that neither Saint David's birth-year nor his death-year can be used as ordinal dates. However, in that indirect way, the Synod of Victory at Caerleon does have verification for an ordinal year.

Summary of Cardinal and Ordinal Years, Arthurian Chronology

Using not only the *AC* and their parent manuscripts the Irish Annals as the springboard but the other ancient manuscripts in conjunction with relevant scholarship, a list of the basic cardinal and ordinal years for the Arthurian Chronology has now been established. Prior to the cardinal year of 453 the Annals of Ireland recorded the collection and compilation, the purification and the writings of the old books of Ireland in year 438. According to O'Donovan, the significance of this is a collection of records that are remarkable for their accuracy, and he cites two other experts who acclaim the authenticity and historical importance of these records that are several centuries older than other nations' monuments to the written word.[145] By implication, the reliability of the *AC* has been established. The following chronological table will therefore function as the primary base for historical material appearing in the ancient manuscripts and relating to the search for King Arthur, since each item has been checked and verified. With this much of a chronology established, other entries can now be added, item by item, after a determination is made of how each of those items relates to what has already been established, plus how each of those items is verified by some other source.

The cardinal years can be summarized in a list as follows:

Cardinal Year 1 = 453 — the year in which Easter was altered by Pope Leo I
Cardinal Year 2 = 497 — the Battle of Badon
                              the birth of Gildas Badonicus
Cardinal Year 3 = 453 — by a surprising coincidence, the third Saxon landing (one of
      them), same as the alteration of Easter
Cardinal Year 4 = 440 — the second Saxon landing
Cardinal Year 5 = 428 — the first Saxon landing
Cardinal Year 6 = 547 — Great Death
                              Death of Maelgwn
Cardinal Year 7 = 495 — the advent of Cerdic the West Saxon king
Cardinal Year 8 = 455+ — Cerdic son of Cunedda
Cardinal Year 9 = 440 — Cunedda migration
Cardinal Year 10 = 465+ — Cerdic the Interpreter
Cardinal Year 11 = 518 — The Battle of Camlann

In the same format, the list for the ordinal years that have been established so far reflects these chronologies:

Ordinal Year 1 = 541 — the penning of the *De Excidio*
Ordinal Year 2 = 521 — the birth of Saint Columba
Ordinal Year 3 = 563 — Saint Columba's voyage to Britain
Ordinal Year 4 = 569 — The Synod of Victory in Caerleon
Ordinal Year 5 = 597 — The Death of Saint Columba

In the format of a table, that same information is reflected below, with the addition of the pre–Christian reckoning of that date. In any of the subsequent tables presented in ensuing chapters, a single bullet (•) will signify a cardinal year and a double (••) will indicate an ordinal year to show that these dates are entrenched in the chronology.

A survey of Manuscript A of the *Annales Cambriae* entries from 453 to 570 reveals some interesting generalizations. The first of these is that if an entry appears in the *AC* and can be traced back to the parent Irish Annals, those dates are surprisingly accurate and needed no chronological adjustment. Based upon this generalization are two other ordinal years which appear in Table 13. One is the the death of Bishop Benignus entered in the *AC* at year 468, with an entry in the Annals of Ulster at year 467.[146] The other is the death of Gildas Badonicus, entered in the *AC* for the year 570, and also appearing in the Annals of Ulster for year 569.3, in the Annals of Roscrea for year 570, and in the Annals of Inisfallen for the year 567.1.[147]

The second generalization, a comparison between Manuscript A and the

Anno Domini	Pre-Christian	Event
•428	Nulla	The first Saxon landing
438	Nulla	The compilation, purification, and writing of the Annals of Ireland
•440	Nulla	The second Saxon landing
•		Cunedda migration
•453	ix	Easter was altered by Pope Leo I
•		The year of the (third) Saxon landing
467	xxiii	The death of Bishop Benignus
•455–516	Nulla	Cerdic son of Cunedda
•455–516	v/xiv	Cerdic the interpreter
•497	liii	The Battle of Badon, in which Arthur and the Britons were victorious
••		Cerdic and Cynric came in five ships to Britain and fought against the Britons
•		The birth of Gildas
•518	lxxxiv	The Battle of Camlann, death of Arthur
••		Cerdic and Cynric succeed to the kingdom of the West Saxons
••521	lxxvii	The birth of Saint Columba
••541	iiic	The penning of the De Excidio, Gildas age 44
•547	ciii	The Great Death
•		The death of Maelgwn, King of Gwynedd
••563	cxix	Saint Columba's voyage to Britain
••569	cxxv	The Synod of Victory at Caerleon
••570	cxxvi	The death of Gildas Badonicus, age 73
••597	cliii	The death of Saint Columba

Table 13. Cardinal/ordinal years for the Arthurian chronology.

additions found in Manuscript B of the Cambrian Annals, indicates that the additions in Manuscript B reflect a mixture of unreliability and accuracy. There is a transpositional error in the entry of Saint David's birth, and there is no verification of Gildas' trip to Ireland; conversely, the recording of the Synod of Victory and the additions of Maelgwn's death by the Yellow Pestilence and burial at Rhos are accurate.

The third observation shows that the two Arthurian references, both later entries, are the only ones requiring an adaptation of lunar adjustment. At this point, without the literary data analyzed, the Camlann entry is the weakest only in that it cannot be traced to a parent manuscript and does not appear in the Nennius manuscript. However, in its support, it aligns itself with the Badon entry by virtue of the association with King Arthur, it does attach itself to an entry in the *Anglo-Saxon Chronicle*, and it does have the support of the Gildas manuscript by virtue of the battle's occurrence after a generation of peace.

At this point, however, it would be an unfair assumption to conclude that those items not needing adjustment are more accurate (though of course they are more reliable) than those which need recalculation. The Badon and Camlann entries still pre-date the *Annales Cambriae*, and their original source, though unknown, could have been correctly dated in a pre–Christian system, then miscalibrated by the Christianized method. Nevertheless, a close and critical eye will still be maintained on items such as these, and if analyses warrant it, any item will be recalibrated in light of the new evidence.

Chapter 4
Hillforts and Roman Roads

The Roman Empire and Conquest of Britain

In order to correlate the information on hillforts and their refortification by the Romans who occupied Britain, with their profound consequences on the Arthurian period, it becomes necessary to note the Roman invasions, establishments, and effects in Britain. This influence was not cursory or short-lived; it continued for nearly four centuries and became ingrained in all the succeeding history of the island, symbolized as a bastion of civilization in the midst of barbarity from the Picts, the Irish, the Scots, the Saxons, the Franks, the Visigoths, and the Huns.

The important segment of Roman history which directly influenced the Arthurian period is approximately from A.D. 425 to A.D. 550. One of the emperors of this period was Theodosius I, who reunited the empire briefly and increased the prestige of the church by banning infidelity and paganism and embracing Christianity as the Empire's religion. Between 379 and 382 he made peace with the Ostrogoths and the Visigoths on the continent and permitted them to assimilate into the empire, one of the factors which led to the downfall of the Roman civilization. Near the end of the fourth century just before his death, Theodosius divided the sovereignty between his two sons, Arcadius who received the Eastern Empire, and Honorius who ruled the Western Empire, which included, among other countries, Italy, Britain, and Gaul.

The relevant sequence of events was as follows:

I. 395–423 was Honorius' rule, spanning among other things, a Visigoth army led by Alaric defeated in 402, a Visigoth defeat by Honorius' general Stilicho in 405, Honorius' murder of Stilicho in 408 followed by Alaric staging a comeback and sacking Rome in 410, and a Visigoth invasion of Gaul in 412;

II. in the early 5th century Roman Legions were withdrawn from Britain;

III. 425–455 marked Valentinian III's reign as Honorius' successor, during which Aetius, Valentinian's general, defeated Visigoths in Gaul in 436, and won his last important Roman victory over Attila and the Huns in 451, followed by several disasters including Attila's invading Italy in 452, Valentinian's killing Aetius and his own death at the hands of Aetius' guards in 454, and Galla Placidia, Valentinian's mother, re-assuming rule in 455.

For several more decades men unfit for office ruled and were at the mercy of barbarian chiefs in imperial service. One of the chiefs was Ricimer, a Suevian who successively deposed and raised five emperors. Another was Orestes, former equerry of Attila, who in 475 placed the crown upon his own son, Romulus, a child of 14.

By the seventh decade of the 400s, little remained of the Western Empire except Italy. The peninsula itself fell in 476, when another barbarian general, Odovacer, king of the Heruli overthrew Orestes and deposed Romulus. The empire of the West had deteriorated long before, but the date — 476 — marks the traditional end of the Western Roman Empire, though the Eastern was to continue until the mid–1400s.

Rome's invasion of Britain is usually viewed as negative, and indeed, much death, destruction, and oppression occurred in the early stages of the take-over. Yet once the Romans established themselves, Britain was a haven of civilization in an uncivilized world. Everyday comforts of life, modes of travel, and the arts were incorporated into the Britons' lives as a carry-over from what the Romans provided. The Roman offering was much better than the alternative; the Empire rescued the Britons from invasions by the barbarians and secured internal peace for them.

Collingwood, in his first edition of *Roman Britain* published in 1923, describes the invasion succinctly and effectively:

> Britain before the Romans came was a wild country of marsh and woodland inhabited by Celtic-speaking barbarians who lived in rude huts, made up in blue paint what they lacked in clothing, and spent most of their time fighting each other. They had a kind of barbaric tribal organization, and offered human sacrifices, at the instigation of Druids, in places like Stonehenge.[1]

Collingwood, like Haverfield, who also wrote of the Roman conquest of Britain, agrees that the meshing of the two cultures over a period of about four centuries was, overall, beneficial for the conquered as well as the conqueror. Particularly during the first century of the occupation, assaults and retaliations were frequent and violent, but as time passed the Britons won a more equal footing. The Romans were still in control, having superior power and military might, and they were still the invaders, but there were mutual benefits in the latter half of the occupation. Briton enemies were held in check — the Picts, Irish, and Scots from the North, and the Angles, Saxons, and Jutes from across the Channel.

Because of the peace that the establishment of the Empire brought with it, the level of amenities rose; language — both written and oral communication — improved, giving rise to a process of recording and transmitting records; political structures created stable forms of government and led to a feeling of self-sufficiency;

city life was established, along with trade and a sense of social identity; cultural refinements were cultivated. Civilization established nationalism. The defined culture of Rome took hold of the uncivilized provincials and instilled in them the desire to learn its language and share in its benefits. The provinces lost their hostility toward their conquerors, and instead, the two began to meld. The provincials became civilized enough to realize the value of what Rome had to offer.

Under the Roman rule, Britain was basically divided into five provinces and two halves. The provinces, called the Five Britains were created for political and commercial expedience; the sections were general divisions of military and civil. The northern section was composed of military districts — the outland, which would be the frontiers protecting the Empire from the marauding barbarians of the north and west. Haverfield asserts that there were three legions at York, Chester, and Carleon[2]; Collingwood verifies that the legions were quartered in fortresses some distance back from the actual frontier. The legions were divided into cohorts and centuries, and on the outlying fringes, a brigade of about 6,000 troops was commanded by a *legatus ligionis* who represented the Emperor as commander-in-chief.[3] The Roman auxiliaries, estimated to be 30,000 to 35,000 men,[4] were scattered in *castella*, little forts close to the very limits of the Roman boundaries. These auxiliaries were divided also into cohorts and *alae*, cavalry 500 to 1,000 strong, commanded by prefects or tribunes.[5]

The midlands and southern lowlands comprised the civilian district. This division is exemplifed by the status of not many artifacts existing from the northern provinces, but the south (including the midlands) reflecting the influence from Rome almost everywhere.[6] In these districts there were five municipalities of the privileged Italian type:

1. Camulodunum (Colchester) and
2. Verulamium (St. Albans), both southeast sections established soon after the Claudian conquest of A.D. 43.
3. Lindum (Lincoln) which was established in the early Flavian period, A.D. 70-80.
4. Glevum (Gloucester), established A.D. 96–98.
5. Eburacum (York), established at the end of the second or beginning of the third century.[7]

The local magistrates were classified like the magistrates of a municipality, using the same titles, including *ordo* or senate. Because of the way these districts were divided which corresponded with the territories of the Celtic tribes — each with its capital, its magistrates, and its senate — the Romanization was made easier. The whole of Britain was governed by a man appointed by Rome's Emperor, and titled *legatus Augusti pro praetore*, Imperial Viceroy with the rank of Praetor.[8]

Collingwood asserts, "There is no difficulty in believing that almost every Briton in the third and fourth centuries spoke Latin."[9] And Haverfield verifies that "portions of Kent, Sussex, Essex, and Somerset are 'thick-set' with ruins of country houses and similar vestiges of Romano-British life, and Roman influence even in the most secluded villages of the upland regions."[10]

An assumption might be made that the wealthy, upper-class Britons were the only ones to benefit from the civilizing influence of Rome, including language use and literary refinements, but this is unfounded. Haverfield shows that a town such as Silchester (Calleva Atrebatum) used Latin as its public language, even in ordinary conversation of the lower class of Callevans:

> When a weary brickmaker scrawls SATIS (enough) with his finger on a tile, or some prouder spirit writes FECIT TVBVL(um) CLEMEMTINVS (Clementinus made this box tile); when a bit of Samian is marked FVR (thief), presumably as a warning from the servants of one house to those of the next, or a brick shows the word PVELLAM, part of an amatory sentence otherwise lost, or another brick gives a Roman date, the "sixth day before the Calends of October," we may be sure that the lower classes of Calleva used Latin alike at their work and in their more frivolous moments.[11]

Even knowledge of Aeneid was not out of place. In the 20 years' excavation in this same town, no *Celtic* inscription has emerged. Although the rural country-houses and farms are ill-explored and ill-recorded, there is evidence of *Roman* inscriptions. This indicates that the owners-occupiers of the houses knew Latin. Furthermore, even peasants were eventually affected:

> Turn now to the dwellings of the peasant poor. There we know mainly in one corner of Southern England, but within this limit we know them well. ... In plan their villages are not Roman; ... but Roman civilization soon reached and absorbed them. The ditches were filled up; hypocasts, odd but unmistakable, wall-plaster painted in Roman fashion, roofing of Roman tiles, came into use; the villagers learned to eat and drink from Samian dishes and cups of glass and even to keep their clothes in wooden chests of drawers; some of them could read and write. Meanwhile, they utterly forgot their Celtic fashions; there is no sign of the Late Celtic Art in any of Pitt-Rivers multitudinous illustrations. To these men the Roman objects which they used were the ordinary environment of life; there were no "delicate exotic varnish," as one eminent writer has called them.[12]

There is further affirmation that Plutarch includes in his tract on the cessation of oracles: one Demetrius of Tarsus, a "grammarian" was teaching in Britain (A.D. 80) and his teaching is recorded as nothing out of the ordinary.[13]

The effects of Rome on Britain, then, were profoundly rooted in political, social, religious, and military soils. There was nothing superficial in the assimilations of both cultures. Gildas Badonicus himself, one of the most well-known Britons, was well-acquainted with Latin and called it "nostra lingua," our language. He viewed the Roman occupation as positive and was aware of the beneficial influences from the Empire which raised the island from the mire of barbarity.

A nagging question which arises is why Britain was unable to carry on all the assimilated traditions even though the Romans withdrew. Collingwood answers:

> ... Britain had more and deadlier enemies, who succeeded in destroying her civilization. Gaul defeated Attila and absorbed the Franks; her Romanized population weathered the storm and their Latin speech developed quietly and steadily into the

dialects of French. ... The shock was administered by the triple invasion of Saxons, Picts, and Scots, enemies more dangerous, because harder to crush, than Attila himself.[14]

Because of these continuous attacks toward the end of the Roman occupation, the Romano-British strength weakened. Milecastles along the Wall were abandoned, towns shrank, and civilization began decaying. Written records — so common under Roman rule — were eroded along with all the other legacies from Rome. The Dark Ages inexorably began the destruction of what Rome had built over three and a half centuries of occupation.

The Vestigial Remnants of a Civilization

Two legacies — not paltry anachronisms — carried into Arthurian times, both of which molded Britain's history not only immediately afterwards in Arthur's era but have continued to shape that history into the twentieth century as well. The first was the Roman refortifications of the Iron Age hillforts which have a direct bearing on the Arthurian quest. From Nennius' battlelist, seven of the sites are at or near river-crossings, while only two specify tors, but of those two, Badon in particular suggests several possible Arthurian locations. In the south are Badbury Rings and Badbury near Liddington Castle, while farther north and east are Little Solsbury Hill near Bath and the Wrekin near Wroxeter.

The second legacy is Roman roads. The importance of the highways constructed during the Roman occupation — and their vital role in establishing geographic credibility in capturing the reality of Arthur — cannot be overstated. Not only do these roads demonstrate an incredible, advanced technology of an ancient Empire, but their foundations have also marked indelibly the modern countryside; for nearly 2,000 years these roads have continued to be the chief means of communication within the island. Some are still in almost total perfect condition, while only portions of many more serve as foundations for roads currently in use. Unfortunately, something as commonplace as a road does not capture the romantic imagination like such remains as Hadrian's Wall, Stonehenge, Avebury, or Silbury Hill. Nevertheless, "when the extent and the permanent nature and effect of these roads are considered, they may claim a foremost place among the remains of Roman work in the country."[15]

HILLFORTS

To accurately grasp the authenticity of King Arthur as a historical figure, there must be a bridge of factual information between British history and its effect specifically upon Arthur and Ambrosius Aurelianus during the late fifth and early sixth centuries. The impact of Iron Age hillforts refortified by the Romans has a pervading effect upon Arthurian geography and history. The link between Iron Age hillforts and Arthur requires a glimpse backward of more than a millennium.

In *Was This Camelot?*, Alcock aligns himself with a particular dating:

> It has usually been considered in the past that the construction of hillforts in south-
> ern Britain did not begin before the Iron Age: the earliest ones may have been built
> in the fifth century BC, but the majority were works of the third century or later.
> Recently, however, some doubts have been cast on this chronology by the recogni-
> tion that hillforts were being built well before the fifth century on the continent,
> and probably — on the evidence of radio-carbon dating — in Scotland and Wales as
> well.[16]

Because pattern analysis and phases of development can differ among experts
by several centuries, dating of certain artifacts is particularly difficult. But with
advances being made in archaeology, more precision is becoming possible. This
relates to the Arthurian interest, since recently

> The recognition of imported pottery of the same types as that found in western
> Britain — Classes A, B, and E — has brought rather more precision into the chronol-
> ogy of the fifth and subsequent centuries.[17]

The important emphasis is, of course, the fifth and subsequent centuries, within
the time frame for Arthur's rise to power. These Iron Age hillforts, then, have an
extensive history and long-lasting influence on Britain's development and the
outcome of events as they apply to Arthur's era.

These hillforts are known by several other terms. They are occasionally
referred to as "ring-forts" because of their tendency to be in concentric patterns
atop tors for a view of the surrounding countryside. Janet and Colin Bord sometimes call them contour forts, plateau forts, promontory forts, and cliff castles.[18]
More commonly they are also known as "raths" or "cashels." Alcock elaborates
on the distinction:

> By far the largest class of site … is that of the circular enclosures, known usually as
> raths when they are surrounded by an earthen bank with external ditch and as cashels
> or cahers when the enclosure is a dry-built stone wall usually without a ditch.[19]

It is astonishing that Britain is so heavily dotted with these hillforts. As a
matter of fact, if they are plotted on a map of Britain, some of them are so close
to each other that they would no longer be distinctive as separate pinpoints.
Although used by John Morris for a different reason to describe the Demetian
campaign in Wales, Map 6 exemplifies the number of hillforts in western Wales.
It is estimated that there are between 30,000 and 40,000 of these "ring-forts" scattered more or less throughout the island; this figure "must be set against the long
period of time during which they were being built and occupied,"[20] but nonetheless in retrospect their influence cannot be minimized.

There are three distinctive characteristics of these hillforts; one is the geographic location, the other is the shape of the hillforts, and the third is the varying sizes of the different sites. Situated as they are, atop tors, the first reason that

suggests itself for this configuration is defense. The raths with their deep ditches and the cashels with their high walls would repel or at least discourage any invaders from easy access. Any outside force could be viewed sometimes at a distance of four to five miles, and this in itself would allow preparation time when an attack or siege seemed imminent.

The shapes of the dwellings within the hillfort are also distinctively British, based evidently in a cultural tradition. Unlike the continental counterparts — the Hallstatt houses of Europe — which were invariably rectangular, those of Iron Age Britain were almost always circular. Since the houses of the British Bronze Age were also circular, the Iron Age round-house must reflect the continuity of native traditions.[21] This implies that not only was Britain peculiar in this respect, but also that there was a carry-over from one age to another; that is, there was a continuity from the Bronze Age to the Iron Age.

Size, on the other hand, suggests more than just defenses. Sizes vary from raths as small as 60 feet in internal diameter to the great triple-banked forts, 150 feet internally and perhaps 400 feet overall. Morris describes a rath in this manner:

> A rath is commonly a roughly circular enclosed area, about 100 feet in diameter, [which] contained a barn, a few querns, occasionally a kiln, and a house, with a superficial area of between 100 and 200 square feet, enough for the parents and children of a single family; it might accommodate the cattle of the bo-aire, when weather or danger constrained him to congregate them within his defences.[22]

A well-preserved cashel may have walls 15 feet high with flights of steps leading up to the wall-walk and chambers built into the thickness of the walls. The great majority of ring-forts must be thought of as defensible dwelling places, fairly small according to Alcock, but "suitable for a prince and his war-band, together with his personal retainers, servants and craftsmen."[23] The medium and large hillforts, which enclose more than eight acres of ground atop a tor, suggest more than just defensible homesteads; they fulfilled a communal purpose as a tribal settlement and accommodated a much larger sociometric unit. These "extended" hillforts, therefore, are of interest as possible courts or headquarters for Arthur and his retinue. Of these large hillforts, Alcock writes:

> ... [T]hey emphasize the unusual character of Cadbury-Camelot among British strongholds, in terms both of strength of its post–Roman refortification and of its large extent. It seems unlikely that this eighteen-acre fort was intended as a prince's defended homestead, and it is unthinkable that it was a tribal centre on the pre-Roman model. It seems most likely to have served as the base for an army that was large by the standards of the time.[24]

The implication is that in addition to location, size suggests the stature of the chieftain; these are the ones which stir the most curiosity in regard to Arthur's strongholds. The contiguity and size of two clusters — South Cadbury, Badbury Rings, and Glastonbury or South Cadbury, Bath, and Glastonbury — invite the

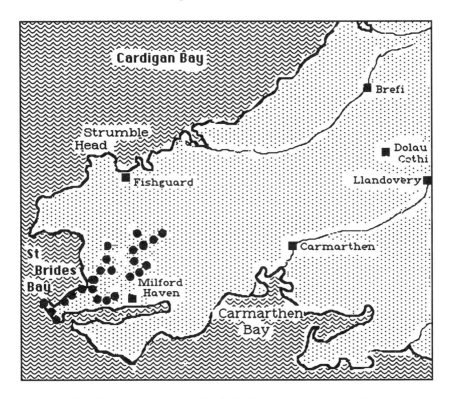

Map 6. Wales, showing the number of raths in the western section. As the text reports, there are thirty to forty thousand of these sites dotting the island.

alluring endorsement of a southern Arthur. In addition to the size Alcock gives for South Cadbury, Badbury Rings also has an interior of 18 acres and Little Solsbury Hill almost 20. Using South Cadbury as center, none of the sites is more than 27 miles distant.

There is the same alluring support for the southwestern Arthur. The Wrekin, as the center, was probably the "tribal capital of the Cornovii who were later resettled at Wroxeter. The fort … covers just over 10 acres, but the central strongpoint area is only 7 acres."[25] Unlike Badbury Rings and Little Solsbury Hill, massive evidence has been unearthed showing that this entire area was an important hub during Arthur's time. To the south is the elongated Herefordshire Beacon hillfort perched atop the Malvern Hills. It grew in size from an initial 8 acres to a total of 32 between the first century B.C. and its Norman history, but little is known of its interim time. Kerry, a possible court of Arthur, lies only 30 miles to the west of the Wrekin. Literary tradition often records "Celliwic" or "Kelliwic" as Arthur's court, and "Kerriwic" becomes a supportable contender. The name Kerry itself achieved recognition from J.G. Evans in his *The Poetry from the Red Book of Hergest*, in which he repeatedly writes of Powys and makes reference to Kerry. Powys is listed in historical sources as Arthur's kingdom after the Roman abandonment, and Kerry is located in that province, only a few miles west of Offa's Dyke and Clun Forest. Literary tradition places Kelliwic in Cornwall, but Kerriwic bordering Cornoviian territory is much more accurate. Ekwall explains that the suffix is "an early loan-word from Latin *vicus*, [which] means 'dwelling, dwelling-place; village, hamlet, town.'"[26]

The Wrekin area is flavored with even more folklore. In an arc from the south to the west, between the Herefordshire Beacon hillfort and Kerry is Arthur's Stone, a 25-ton glacial boulder balanced on nine rock supports, forming two burial chambers. One legend lists it as a tomb for a giant whom Arthur killed; another claims that it is a tomb for a king Arthur slew in battle. This is only one of several sites known as "Arthur's Stone."

Between Kerry and Llangollen in the same arc are two other sites, one legendary and the other historical. Old Oswestry hillfort is near a later entrenchment. Wats Dyke was dug in the eighth century as a boundary between Wales and Mercia, followed by Offa's Dyke. Clayton writes of its complicated history which "goes back through several stages from its origins in the mid–third century BC"; it was abandoned after the Roman conquest, but there is evidence of squatters moving in during the Dark Ages before it was deserted again.[27] It has Arthurian ties through Gogyrfan, Guinevere's father, but there is no solid evidence that the squatters might have been part of his band. The other one, Breiddin Hillfort, is just west of Shrewsbury in Cornoviian territory near the Severn River. There was no evidence until the early 1970s[28] that this site was refortified, but during the excavations some elaborate timber defenses were discovered dating to the late fourth century, with some possible spill-over into the fifth.

Last in the arc is Valle Crucis, the site of the Eliset Pillar. If these locations — the Eliset Pillar, Old Oswestry, Powis Castle, Kerry, Arthur's Stone, and Herefordshire Beacon — were connected by a dotted line on a map, it would mark the western and southern boundaries almost perfectly for the Cornovii territory. With the Wrekin as its axis, no point would be further than 40 miles away.

ROMAN ROADS

The other lasting legacy is Roman roads. One of the distinguishing characteristics is their straight direction with very little deviation except to avoid escarpments, steep ascents or descents, or a variance either to intersect with another road or to approach a fort. For instance, the Roman road running from Badbury Rings to Old Sarum has almost disappeared and is now almost indistinguishable near the River Ebble, but at Bishopstone is an interesting jog from a straight line. In that vicinity is a steep-sided valley, dropping about 200 feet. The road diverted to keep to the high ridge, and after it deflected from the valley, it again picked up its straight course. On modern-day roadmaps, the Roman roads are marked with dotted lines, but where the lines disappear, the direction is still easy to follow because modern roads laid upon the Roman bases are straight rather than meandering.

A destination, too, is easy to project because of the road's straight-line persistence. At Badbury Rings, the Roman road splits, one branch eventually going to Dorchester and the other more southerly leading to Poole Harbor. A third forming a V from Old Sarum heads northwesterly toward Ashmore on Cranborne Chase. Codrington describes Badbury Rings, a major crossroads for this cluster of Roman roads:

> ... [F]or six miles north of Badbury the direction of the Roman road from Old Sarum is straight towards the east side of that earthwork, and with a slight turn, passes more to the east of it, as if in the first place the road was laid out to communicate with the south rather than the west, and the road branching off towards the west was afterwards laid out.[29]

In the Arthurian era, locales and their layouts would be consistent with a south/southwestern emphasis. Additionally, the branch heading to the west points to the Gewissae territory of Saxon compatriots (or ex-compatriots) in western Wales or to the Camelot region.

The importance of destination is also stressed in another segment on road-building which Codrington discusses:

> A Roman road leaving Badbury at or near the point where the road from Old Sarum divides has been traced northward to Donhead, by Hemsworth Down. Traces of that road can still be seen to Monkton Deverill, where it intersects with another Roman Road that headed almost due west from Old Sarum.[30]

No traces of the continuation of that road can be found north of Monkton Deverill, but the projection on a map shows that the road would lead directly to Little Solsbury Hill in the vicinity of Batheaston, slightly north and east of Bath.

J.A. Giles, in his appendix to the *Six Chronicles*, gives a great deal of valuable information about Roman roads. He states,

> Posts or towns are placed on them at nearly regular distances, seldom exceeding twenty miles, the length of a single march, and also at the point where two roads intersect each other, or where several roads diverge.[31]

By providing this kind of detail, Giles has given information with both intrinsic and extrinsic value. First, he has provided details which show the technical Roman thoroughness in road-building. But equally important are military posts along the roads at regular intervals of about 20 miles so that troops could make it from one station to the next in a day's march. Applied to King Arthur's time, this is crucial in silencing the critics who point out that Arthur could not have moved his armies the distances which he supposedly moved them. Giles suggests a day's march between posts or stations; mounted warriors could travel that distance on straight, unwavering roads in a fraction of that time.

A clarification is needed here of what constituted a Roman mile as a standard of measurement in compiling the *Itineraries*. Bianchini used a measurement of the Roman foot, "still preserved in the capitol," for the exact length of the miles between the military columns on the Appian way, and Danville estimates the Roman mile at 755 toises, or 1,593 yards, English measure.[32] However, when English antiquaries measured distances on the British roads, the measurements between any two known stations conflicted in almost every instance with the numbers listed in the *Itineraries*. Horsley states that the

> Romans measured only the horizontal distance, without regarding the inequalities of the surface, or that the space between station and station was ascertained from maps accurately constructed. Itinerary miles bear a regular proportion to the English miles on plains, but fall short of them in hilly ground.[33]

The course of the roads was evidently planned with skill and laid out by Roman road-builders who had a complete grasp of the general features of the country. Taking into account, of course, the number of centuries the Romans occupied Britain, and the thousands of miles of Roman roads that were built, the construction was carried out under many masters at different times. Many of the roads were built with the middle section separated from the sides of the road by flat stones set on edge, suggesting that the middle was used by wheeled vehicles, and the sides served for footsoldiers and horsemen, being wide enough to allow cavalry and infantry to pass easily.[34]

In conclusion, the Roman roads were always well-constructed in addition to being superbly maintained. With the web of these roads crisscrossing the island, military movement as well as commercial trade routes unified the municipalities so that distances could be covered in short amounts of time. The roads were well-traveled, and with posts and way-stations every 20 miles, mobility was relatively safe. Life in the south and southwestern midlands was secured against serious invasions, and this is the legacy which was left to Arthur after the Romans withdrew to protect the Empire on the continental European front.

Collingwood and Myres have this to say about the revival of Rome's legacy:

> About the middle of the fifth century, Roman Britain is thus turning into congeries of warring states, each dependent for its existence on the prowess of the man at its head. These men are drawn not altogether from the most romanized class of its population, but largely from the Celtic peoples of the less romanized fringe, in which case their political traditions are not those of the city but those of the tribe.[35]

As decades of the late fifth century and early sixth century passed, the Romanization of Britain began to fade, and the island entered a new phase:

> The culture of the romanized upper classes has sunk into discredit and fades away, now that its owners have confessed their inability to control the political situation, and abdicated in favour of what today would be called a dictatorship. Roman Britain is now rapidly dying, and we are reaching the "sub–Roman" period, when men lived on the relics of Romanity diluted in a pervading medium of Celticism.

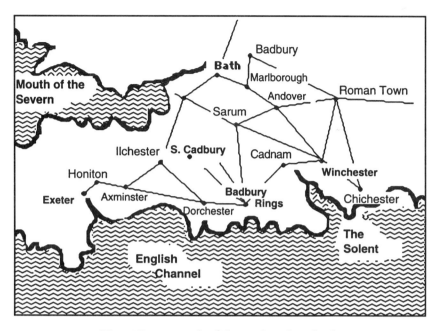

Map 7. Roman roads of the southern heartland.

Thus, from the middle of the century onwards, the general tone of Romano-British society became more and more barbarized. As the Saxon settlements grew in strength, the Roman civilization of their lowland zone was declining into a Celto-Roman civilization where Celtic elements were more and more prevailing over Roman. Latin must have been less and less used. Rome was becoming a memory.[36]

Although maps 7 and 8 are not precisely to scale, they give an accurate representation of the Roman roads in the south-central part of Britain. These maps give different overviews of two separate areas; they contain a variety of information leading to some interesting speculations, particularly when considering the interrelation of those facts. Roman roads, for instance, even though there may be no present evidence of their original courses, can pretty safely be plotted by: 1) using the segments of Roman roads where evidence is positive; and 2) plotting the projection in a straight line, taking into account deviations for natural geologic formations such as unfordable rivers, lakes, chasms and cliffs, or changes in course to intersect with other roads. These two segments of Britain have the highest concentration of Roman roads used during the Arthurian period, one of the archaeological as well as historical reasons why Arthur's historical arena of operation is listed as central Britain.

One item of particular interest on Map 7 is the projected course between Badbury Rings and South Cadbury. The remaining traces of Roman road indicate a deviation from a straight line because of the peculiar alignment of Badbury Rings and Hod Hill. After a short angle, the road resumes its unswerving

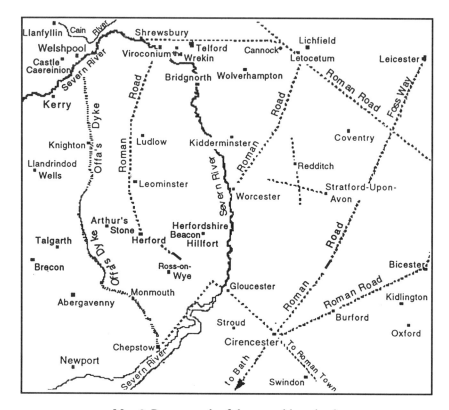

Map 8. Roman roads of the central heartland.

northwesterly direction until it crosses the river Stour, at which point the National Trust maps show the road veering off to the left, then making a bowl curvature to intersect with Foss Way between Ilchester and Axminster.

Knowing the characteristics of Roman roads, one obvious question that arises is, "Why does the road from Badbury southwesterly to Hod Hill and beyond take an unexpected course after crossing the River Stour?" An on-site study of the topography immediately provides the geographic reason for the diversion: following the known course of the Roman road after passing Hod Hill in that northwesterly direction, within a short distance of perhaps under a mile is a cupped valley called Blackmoor Vale, which marks, additionally, the confluence of the rivers Stour and Cale. Even today this is a low-lying area, and in Roman times might have been prone to flooding and marshlands. Furthermore, the River Yeo lies just farther to the north and west, and this particular course proposed by the National Trust maps could circumvent the River Yeo near Sherbourne and then connect with Foss Way several miles southwest of Ilchester.

One other interesting projection is drawn on the map: the dotted line (after crossing the River Stour) on a straight course, which, even if only coincidence,

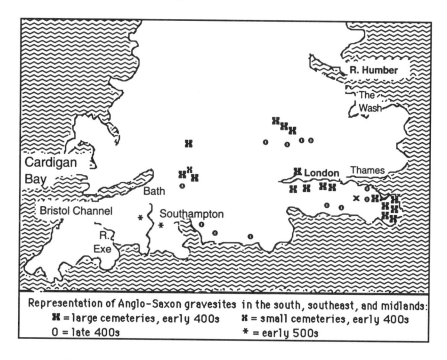

Map 9. Saxon cemeteries of the south, southeast, and midlands.

intersects perfectly with South Cadbury, thus giving a direct route from South Cadbury to Badbury Rings. This route crosses Blackmoor Vale, but no other obstacles bar a road to South Cadbury. Unfortunately, no traces of a Roman road indicate either route. The evidence showing certainty of the road from Badbury Rings northwest stops a short distance past Hambledon Hill. Only one other thing remains certain: Roman roads did not simply stop. Thus, this particular road would have had a destination. Hod Hill was not its terminal point, because a visible portion of road goes beyond it; likewise, Hambledon Hill was not the end station, since the remnants of the existing road show that it went at least a mile beyond Hambledon Hill. The surety is that somewhere this road connected with Foss Way, whether it was through South Cadbury or south of Ilchester.

Whichever conjecture is accepted is of little importance in tracking Arthur's chronology and geographic movements; what is significant is the proximity to South Cadbury and a direct route via Roman roads to Badbury Rings. If the route is as the National Trust suggests, the distance would be a little over 40 miles, which would be a more circuitous route than South Cadbury–Camelot to Kelsey Down, the intersection on the Roman road from Badbury Rings toward Bath. This second route from South Cadbury–Camelot to Kelsey Down and thence to Badbury Rings would be a distance of approximately 30 miles. If, however, the Roman road was an extension from Badbury Rings past Hod and Hambledon

Hills directly to South Cadbury–Camelot, the distance would be only about 24 miles. Either of the latter two distances would give Arthur quick access from his headquarters to Badbury Rings as a hot-spot of Saxon invasion, particularly if he and his army were traveling on horseback along roads still in good repair from the Roman era.

The comparisons between the alleged Arthurian sites of southern Britain and those of the midlands are interesting. One similarity is the capability to project a road's course even though there are not any present-day traces. An example is the road from Cirencester to Gloucester, which can be projected to cross the Severn and connect with Hereford. A second parallel is the major intersection of roads from five directions. In the south, Silchester (Roman Town) is the major hub of Roman roads running to Cirencester, London, Chichester, Winchester, and Andover; the similarity in the midlands is Cirencester, which has spokes radiating to Leicester via Foss Way, Bicester, Silchester, Bath, and Gloucester. Each has easy access in any direction, but Silchester establishes an affinity with the south, while Cirencester aligns itself with the midlands.

One of the distinguishing characteristics in the midlands, however, is the massive "X" that marks the island. Watling Street, traversing the island from London to Holyhead in Anglesey, and Foss Way, running from Seaton on Lyme Bay to Lincoln in the northeast, intersect near a small village named Wibtoft in the west midlands. As general markers, this intersection to the east, plus Cirencester to the south and Ludlow to the west, would be boundaries for the Cornovian territories.

South Cadbury as the Camelot of the south has easy ingress to either Bath or Badbury Rings as the Badon battlesite, especially for cavalry troops; additionally, it is only about a dozen miles from Glastonbury, the commonly named site of Arthur's burial. Kerry, the Camelot of the midlands, is likewise only a short distance (about 30 miles) from its Badon locale, the Wrekin. Based upon literary tradition, however, the midlands connection between the two sites is more justifiable. For one, Kerry is in Powys territory just west of Offa's Dyke, and the Wrekin is the major stronghold in the Gewissae dominion, part of the Roman Cornoviian territory. Second, in keeping with material recorded by Gildas and Nennius, the battle was not indicative of foreign invasion from across the Channel but instead viewed as an internal conflict. Third, Arthur's cavalry had to ford the Severn River to get to the battle on a hill near the baths, at Wroxeter. In a straight-line approach from Kerry, Arthur's troops could cross the Severn at the ancient crossing of Buildwas. And last, Octha would not have been the Saxon leader nor Arthur's enemy at Badbury Rings; he made his entry into Britain about 30 years earlier (in itself a significant fact) and was sent north to Wall-by-Lichfield (near Hadrian's Wall and not the Antonine) by his father Hengist.

A separate graphic, Map 9, provides a comparative analysis of southern Britain with the midlands on locations, dates and sizes of Saxon cemeteries. Of particular interest are the early 400s, the period when the first Saxons were invited in by Vortigern and began to occupy the Gewissae region, according to the *De Excidio* and the *Historia Brittonum*. As expected, there is a heavy concentration of large Saxon cemeteries in Kent, along the northern shores of the Thames. As Alcock explained, however, archaeological finds of large Saxon cemeteries in the Upper Thames Valley seem surprisingly misplaced for this period of time. Upon reflection, however, this locale is not as extraordinary as it initially appears. There is no confirmation that the Saxon movement originated in the Thames Valley and moved up the Thames River, nor is there evidence that the Saxons arched around Kent to Southampton Water and pushed inland for 60 miles, somehow miraculously passing over the Salisbury area in the process, which was not conquered by the Saxons until 552.

Of these seemingly "dislocated" burial grounds, Alcock writes that one of the points deserving special emphasis is the very large size of the cemeteries. This in turn led him to conclude that the

> [archaeological evidence] may encourage us to ... make possible a thorough-going amplification or even correction of the scanty accounts of the English settlement given by Gildas and Bede, or the circumstantial but chronologically uncertain narrative of the *Anglo-Saxon Chronicle*.[37]

He then points to Wessex (the Gewissae kingdom encompassing Cirencester) as an area of Saxon settlements in the early 400s, followed by an admonition that attempts to rewrite the *Chronicle* should not be carried too far.

In stark contrast to this, there is only a scattering of Saxon burial sites along the southern coast near Southampton Water during the second half of the 400s and even fewer along the banks of the Avon River in the early 500s. Based upon this and the further evidence that the Saxons did not make inroads to Salisbury until 552, there is a strong case confirming that Saxons, by invitation, first settled in the midlands of Britain very early in the fifth century, and it was not until the end of the sixth century that ingressions were made from the southern coast.

Chapter 5
The Geography
of Mount Badon

General Geography

Before discussing the specific battles attributed to Arthur in the ensuing chapters, it seems beneficial to structure a base for the geographic information. The milieu for Arthur (a combination of Richard Barber's "western" Arthur of Dyfed and the "southern" Arthur) has been determined as west-central and southern Britain, encompassing two specific areas, although these do not necessarily reflect the areas in which all or even most of the battles took place. The southern circumference accurately indicates the heartland and why this particular piece of geography was important to the barbarians encroaching on the land. Just prior to and after the Roman withdrawal, as the Empire began receding from the north to protect its interests in the civilian districts of the south, one of the last acts of the Roman emperors, as Pitt-Rivers observed,

> ... was to post a force on the east coast of England which was called the Saxon Shore to repel these invaders, but no sooner was that force withdrawn than the full tide of westerly migration set in again direct upon southern Britain with results that are well-known to us all.[1]

Some of that movement was at the request of the Britons, but as the three successive Saxon waves began gathering momentum, the Briton fear of invasion shifted from the Pictish north to southeastern Wales and the Hwicce territory of their restless and rebellious English Saxon allies. In the beginning when the Saxons had been recruited, the concern of the Britons was to maintain a resistance to incursions from areas other than the continent, but as the alliance between the Britons and Saxons deteriorated, the Britons had to guard against reprisals from their ex-compatriots already inhabiting the interior of Britain in addition to shifting attention back to the southern shores.

History highlights these two geographic areas in the course of events which followed. Briton salvation was counterbalanced by the successful defense of two regions, one oval of land called Cornovii running from the mouth of the Severn eastward and northward from Wales, and the other along the southern coast, including Southampton Water. Some geographic references — such as Arthur's Seat, Arthur's Stone, and Arthur's Footprint — suggesting Arthurian involvement do not play a historical role, nor is Arthur factually based with some of these site-names. In this respect, General Pitt-Rivers indicates the unreliability of tales centered around these types of sites:

> I have been greatly deceived at times by the external appearance of earthworks, as for example in the case of Caesar's Camp, near Folkstone, (supposedly) named after Caesar, in the days of our greatest ignorance of the subject, and since found to be entirely Norman. Also is the case of Dane's Dyke at Flamborough, assumed to be Danish by popular tradition, but proved by a section cut through the rampart to be much earlier.[2]

Some locations are so difficult to deduce as authentic Arthurian locations that even a wild guess seems silly. The first battle at the River Glein and the second through fifth battles on the River Dubglas from the Nennius battlelist fall into this category. Giles offers two suggestions for the first battle either as the Glem in Lincolnshire or the Glen in Northumberland. For the second through the fifth battles he gives Dunglass as a boundary of Lothian, but neither suggestion can be substantiated. Other battles in that list, though, invite speculation because of clues and innuendos. In addition to the battlelist, an original theory is proposed in this text for the battle of Camlann, Arthur's last battle, associated with the regeneration motif.

The confusion about geographic location is magnified even more because some regions in Britain and Brittany have identical names. When a statement is made in the early manuscripts that Arthur retired to Kelliwig in his homeland of Cornwall, its content seems elementary: Celliwig was a village or a stronghold and Cornwall was a region. Both locations, however, are difficult to identify because of possible mixtures of language derivatives, spelling variations, phonological and etymological changes. Celliwig can begin with a "K," and both spellings can end in a "c"; it can also be separated into two words; it is further identified with Killibury, Kelly Rounds, Callington, Kerry, or Egloshayle. The term for the general area of Cornwall, however, is what compounds the difficulty. Webster notes three tribes in Britain bearing the name Cornovii. Each is well-evidenced by inscriptions and manuscripts but the three are widely separated.[3] One was the huge territory with Wroxeter as its capital.

To get an impression of the extensiveness of this territory, one must look historically at manuscripts which recorded the Cornovii name. Cirencester was referred to as Corinium Dobunnorum, Wroxeter as Viroconium or Cornoviorum, Wansborough in Wiltshire (the Cornovii stronghold) as Durocornovium, and Troggy Brook near Monmouthshire as being in Cernyw. Interestingly, Wroxeter was the only canton which failed to carry on its identity after the Roman departure. Unlike the others, it was split into smaller communities, all bearing English (Saxon) names, suggesting that this territory was in upheaval during this era, most likely a warring arena.

The second Cornovian area, the entire peninsula west of the Tamar River, acquired its dynastic name, according to Morris, from the Cornovian Welsh who migrated into the region.[4] The third, not as well-known, is simply labeled as being somewhere in northwestern Scotland, probably a reference to the Strathclyde area. There is also a fourth, along the coast of southwestern Brittany. This means that in addition to present-day Cornwall, the name could be a reference to one of the former Roman Cornovii or to the Franco/Breton Cornouailles, pronounced remarkably similar to "Cornwall." One of Arthur's courts, then, is a wooded area (Kelliwig) somewhere in the present Cornwall, in southeastern Wales, in central Britain, or in southwestern Brittany. This accentuates emphatically why the process of formulating a postulation begins by extracting clues from numerous sources, correlating the information with other data, and then drawing an impartial conclusion by eliminating the improbabilities.

A similar example is the area of Dumnonia in Britain, now called Cornwall, and the region of Dumonoie in northeastern Brittany. Arthur could have been fighting one of the eleven battles either in the southwestern corner of the island or in the northeastern segment of Armorica. To complicate the location even further, in this post–Roman transitional period there was still another territory of Dumnonii (or Damnonii) just south of the Antonine Wall and east of the Firth of Clyde, in the area where Norma Goodrich sets her northern–Arthur's Camelot. Peter Berresford Ellis was aware of the confusion of these areas.

From an archaeological point of view, Collingwood and Myres fill in some of the geographic changes of this period, using the refortification of an old Roman hillfort at Cissbury on the South Downs as an example of what generally transpired. Although they indicate that some archaeologists call this era the end of the Roman period, they more precisely label these refortifications not as Roman *civitates*, but as strongholds for war lords, when Vortigern tried to protect the south with Saxon help.

One of the general impressions these co-authors wish to convey is what ultimately became of Roman civilization in Britain. After the Roman abandonment, the Celtic influence returned very slowly; it was not as if the Saxons besieged a Roman town as that town would have been in the full glory of Roman occupation. When the Saxons began moving in, the culture was actually more sub-Roman than Roman. Collingwood and Myres give varying perspectives of what the area was like and sensibly settle on middle ground. They write,

> Some have thought that it [The Roman Empire in Britain] came to an end by the destruction of cities, the burning of villas, the massacre of villagers, and in a word the extermination of the people, except so far as their remnant fled into the west or were enslaved by the English; ... [o]thers have believed that it stood firm, conquered its conquerors, and brought England within the circle of the countries whose historical tradition is based on Rome. Neither view is wholly right. The truth is too

complex for such crude generalizations; if they are posited as the horns of a dilemma, the facts of history slip between them.[5]

They explain how at times neither archaeology, nor anthropology, nor philology can relay to us the physical characteristics or the survival of traditions, the "feel" of the era. But then they make one very important point: the change-over from Roman to sub–Roman, and from sub–Roman to Saxon was mainly peaceful. Archaeological evidence shows that this is so:

> In the case of the smaller towns, evidence of complete desertion is the rule rather than the exception. In the case of the villas, it is a rule to which exceptions are unknown. Not a single villa in the country has been found underlying a Saxon dwelling or has yielded evidence of permanent occupation in the Saxon period. ... [T]here are large tracts of country ... where population-maps of the two periods [Roman and Saxon] have been compiled with great thoroughness, and where the two are mutually exclusive at almost every point.[6]

They conclude:

> But let us keep our hold on the archaeological facts. All four of the deserted major towns, and several minor ones, have been excavated; and the excavators have in every case looked for evidence that the towns finally perished in some such way. The results are decisive. These towns came to an end, not by fire and sword, but by decay and evacuation. They were abandoned and left to fall down.[7]

Two other writers offer insight into what transpired after the Romans evacuated the island. One writes,

> Initially after the Romans abandoned the island, the Britons still engaged in a multiplicity of industries that the Romans had left: potters, carpenters, builders, tanners, and so on. But slowly the remains of Roman civilization in Britain crumbled and were eventually forgotten by time and man.[8]

The importance of the land was of course an ever-present influence, but the Romans had left behind the results of technology, including that of mining, rock and lead quarrying, the construction of canals and waterways, the superb laying of roads, and the comfort and luxury of villas. Without the masterminds, however, the results were doomed to disintegrate; skills such as mortar-making, landscaping, drainage, heating and cooling, bridge-building, and the hundreds of little things which had been taken for granted, began to fade and disappear. The Britons had begun to fend for themselves, not only militarily, but economically and politically. Some settled elsewhere, since the thriving villages could no longer sustain themselves through bartering. Life moved down to the basics: farming, raising livestock, furnishing themselves with clothing and shelter, and maintaining what communications they could with neighboring communities, sometimes banding together for protection.

Various archaeologists turned attention to villages and hamlets. Aston writes

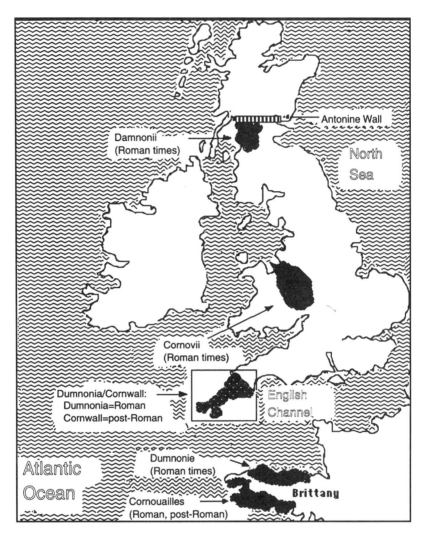

Map 10. The geographic confusions of the areas of Cornwall and Dumnonia. The blackened left-to-right diagonal area plus the blackened meshed diagonals signify the Cornwall locations. The Dumnonia territories are the blackened right-to-left diagonals plus the blackened meshed diagonals, since the shaded meshed diagonal area signaled both Cornwall *and* Dumnonia at different times in history. See also Map 14 in this chapter for the names of the older Roman territories.

about deserted and shrunken settlements during the immediate post–Roman period, providing some idea of the changes in settlement patterns. Nether Adber and Mudford Terry have virtually disappeared, and West Mudford, Mudford Sock, and Up Mudford are severely shrunken, with only Mudford itself intact.[9]

That there was a peaceful transition should not be taken to mean that there was no devastation and destruction. Gildas Badonicus attests to the slaughter, and Morris records some of the carnage. Alcock and Pitt-Rivers, too, can verify violence by some of the archaeological finds. The battles were not only with the English Saxons but with their counterparts across the sea and with raiders from Ireland and the north. But then, as Collingwood points out, the end was brought about by the victories of Ambrosius; he guesses the date slightly later — in 470 to 480 — but the name is correct.

Natural landscape was changing, too. Selsey Bill, an important landing spot listed in the *Chronicle*, disappeared into the sea. Inland draining and the natural changing of river courses dried up the area of Somerset Levels, and water receded so that Glastonbury could no longer be called an island. Some hillforts which the Romans had used (and some they had not) were reestablished, rebarricaded and used for protection, as outposts or as observation points. As time passed, the natural erosion process filled in valleys and built up fertile farmland. In medieval Somerset, Arthur's home ground, Aston reports that

> Roger Leech has shown that there was a Romano-British settlement about every one kilometer across the landscape. This is particularly evident around Somerton, but can also be seen in the Bath area.[10]

Leech concludes that many of the settlements in this region survived from the Roman era.

In the several centuries following the Roman withdrawal from Britain and the Saxons filling the void, many major changes took place. Even now, fifteen centuries later, however, there is visible evidence of a civilization at its height, and anyone standing on a wind-swept moor, if he knows what to look for, can envision the earlier way of life on the island. There were wars — evidently fierce ones — but there is firm evidence that during this period, too, the Saxons and the Britons had something akin to an uneasy truce to protect themselves against other common enemies. Dumville gives a little different perspective of the events of this era. Speaking of the Saxon assault specifically, his comment would fit into the events right after this uneasy truce. He writes:

> The second important point is that their assault [the Saxon Revolt] on their former employers' territory was a raid. They had said [Chapter 23 of Gildas] that they would plunder the whole island: ... [T]hey did just that. However damaging, indeed disastrous, the raid was, it was nonetheless a raid.[11]

He continues that Gildas himself does not explain the intention of this raid, but Dumville inserts that the description of the raiders appears to indicate booty as a primary concern. Then he adds,

> The point to grasp ... is that no intention to annex and settle territory is noted; ... whatever the motives of the assault, ... the Saxons withdrew, having inflicted the most terrible wounds on their opponents' country.[12]

This view is distorted, based upon the definition of "homeland." After some devastating raids, the *English* Saxons withdrew and returned to their homeland, but this was in the Gewissae/Cornovii territories. And in truth, there were Saxon settlements that were encroaching upon Wales and the southern territories.

Badon: Badbury Possibilities

The location of the Battle of Mount Badon is just one of the many enigmas one encounters when researching material on Arthur. Proposals by various scholars indicate that as many as five sites have been proposed as Badon possibilities, excluding the second Battle of Badon listed in the *Annales Cambriae* at year 665. Analyzing the word *Badon* etymologically is a helpful prelude to examining some of the theories.

Badon — along with its variations of Baddon, Badonis, Badonicus, Bathhill — is associated with the present name of Badbury. Checking the etymology of the word invariably leads to some complex problems; in Ekwall's text on placenames, Badbury has the variations of Baddanbyrig, Baddeburi, Badeberi, and Badeberie, all leading to the possibility of Badda's Burg.[13] One of the suffixes, -*burgh*, is very common in English, generally from -*burg*, meaning "fort." In some cases, Ekwall explains, the suffix refers to a Roman fort, but in most cases the reason for the name is not obvious; the suffix with an "h" on the end might also refer to a fortified manor.[14] The Old English -*burgh* also associates with -*beorg*, meaning hill or mound.

The suffixes, then (-*burg*, -*burgh*, -*byrig*, -*beri*, -*buri*, and -*berie*), all tie to -*bury*, with a fair latitude of meanings: a mound, a hill, a fort, or a fortified manor.[15] John Morris strongly emphasizes the word *mons* in the writings of Gildas and Nennius, relating the inherent meaning in the suffix of -*bury* as "hill," "mound," or "mount," but it is important to note that this *excludes* the inference of a hillfort or fortification. Alcock points out that

> There is in fact nothing in our earliest sources to suggest that the battle [of Badon] was fought at a hill-fort rather than on an open hilltop — the idea of a fort is a spurious element.[16]

On the other hand, the idea of Badon as a *hillfort* is supported by references to it as "Din Badon."[17] Referring to Ekwall again, the prefix *din-* is Early Welsh, meaning a "fortified hill, a fort."[18]

Assuming that Badon is attached to the word "Badbury," then -*bury* (associated with the Old English -*beorg*) labels the locale as a hill, further verified by the term *mons*, meaning hill, used in the Gildas and Nennius manuscripts. The term *Din* for Badon would carry the "hill" aspect one step further and label it as a fortification. Of the five possible sites, three are based on the element of *Badbury*.

BAUMBER

At first glance, the name Baumber does not seem to be a possibility. It is northeast on the peninsula formed by the Wash and the River Humber, near

Lincoln in Lincolnshire. It is listed in the *Domesday Book* as "Badeburg," reappears in *The Lincolnshire Survey* as "Baburc" around the year 1115, and emerges in later charters as "Baumbur." Ekwall clarifies the connection by listing its etymology as "*Bada's* or *Badda's* BURG, translating to Badbury."[19] This "Badbury" is on a ridge (hence meeting the criterion of "hill" or "mount") near a Roman road running in a west-northwesterly direction, only about 22 miles from the North Sea. It was also enclosed with a wall during Ida's time,[20] putting it into the classification of a fort.

One reason this has traditionally been considered a Badon site is its association with Lincoln, a distance of only 15 miles from Baumber. Lincoln is an important consideration because of its early reference as Lindum, an area listed by Nennius for Arthur's second through fifth battles, a possibility that elevates Baumber's importance in the scheme of Arthuriana.

On the other hand, however, the evidence against Baumber as the Badon site is overwhelming. One problem is its isolation. The German Saxons would have had to traverse the Strait of Calais and sail quite a distance north past the Wash to land near Ingoldmells point. Because this would have been so difficult, they would have penetrated the island at easier, more strategic points. For the English Saxons, this is outside the realm of Cornovii; their settlements were farther to the west.

Even more unassailable is the argument provided by the *Anglo-Saxon Chronicle*. In 547, Ida is credited with building Baumburgh, and Nennius continues the history by supplying the details that after Ida died,

> Eadred Flesaurs [Aethelfert the Artful, Aethelfrith in the *Chronicle*] ... gave to his wife Bebba the town of Dynguoaroy, which from her is called Bebbanburg [Baumburgh].[21]

The word "Din" of "Dinas" reinforces Baumburgh as a fortification, but the chronology puts it outside the framework of Arthur. Arthur's passing takes place prior to the second decade of the sixth century, more than 30 years prior to Ida's initial construction and more than 60 years prior to Æthelfrith's accession to the kingdom.

LIDDINGTON CASTLE: BADBURY/BADBURY HILL

Liddington Castle as the battlesite of Badon presents its own set of difficulties. Although Liddington Castle is a fortification on a hilltop, it only indirectly associates with the word Badbury. This problem compounds itself because there is a village named Badbury approximately half a mile from Liddington, but the village is neither fortified nor elevated. Adding to the confusion is Badbury Hill. Obscure and virtually unresearched, approximately ten miles almost due north of Liddington, some scholars consider this site a possibility distinctively separate from Liddington. This area, however, fits into a general Arthurian scheme; it lies within the Hwicce/West Saxon territories and could relate to the Saxon compatriots who were invited into the vicinity by Vortigern. Arthur's successful battle in this area could have been the routing of the Hwicce Saxons.

General Pitt-Rivers — sometimes referred to as Fox-Pitt-Rivers — did a great deal of work on both the Wansdyke, which addresses the Badon issue at Liddington Castle, and Bokerly Dyke, near Badbury Rings, the other major possibility of the Badon site. His excavations cover both Dykes plus adjacent areas of each near the turn of the nineteenth century. In Volume I of his notes, he emphasizes the thoroughness of his archaeological diggings by writing that he delegated no authority without personal supervision and that no excavations were ever conducted unless he was present. Because his major concern was the accuracy of his archaeological finds, he was impartial in his approach to Arthurian controversies, addressing the issues from a reserved scientific viewpoint rather than ignoring or skirting them.

These two significant lines of defense — the Wansdyke and the Bokerly Dyke — are the major pieces of physical evidence which create the differences of opinion among scholars as to how the Saxons attempted to pierce the heart of the island — by moving from eastern Wales southward toward Bath and the 40-mile, east-west stretch of the Wansdyke, or by gaining access from Poole and thrusting northward toward Salisbury. These alternatives have a direct bearing on where the Battle of Mount Badon was fought: was it fought near Bath, indicative of a Saxon invasion from the inland Gewissae area where the Saxons had already been granted a stronghold by invitation from Vortigern, or was it fought near the southern coast by Saxons who had crossed the Channel and were attempting to penetrate the heartland from Poole Bay and thus to Badbury Rings?

In *King Arthur's Avalon*, Geoffrey Ashe proposes two possibilities for the Badon site:

> There are two favorite candidates, Badbury Rings in Dorset, and Liddington Castle just south of Swindon. ... The objection to the first is political. Arthur might have come there to defeat a foray by Cerdic, but the West Saxons were not yet important enough for their vicissitudes to affect the position as a whole.
>
> ...These facts transfer the focus of our attention to the Liddington Badon. It is far over, but not too far. ... The enormous defensive line called the Wansdyke was almost certainly constructed under Ambrosius, to defend the south-west against an army marching from the Thames Valley. ... Ambrosius apparently feared that Hengist would move up from Kent to reinforce these advanced posts, and then swing left into Wilts and Somerset, the heartland of British territory.[22]

Within these few short paragraphs, there is a great deal of conjectural material to be explored. Before looking at the brief explanation of why Badbury Rings was so summarily dismissed as Mount Badon because of "political" reasons, it is important to look at the reasons why Liddington Castle is presented as a possible site. Ashe describes Liddington as "far over, but not too far."[23] Presumably he means that Liddington Castle is far to the west of the Thames Valley, but not too far. The first hordes of Saxons who made an entry into Britain came at the invitation of Vortigern. History, as well as archaeological digs, bear out that Saxon

Liddington Hill, a proposed site for the Battle of Mount Badon. The site lies south of Swindon and 25 miles north of Old Sarum.

artifacts and Saxon burial grounds dot the landscape heavily, particularly along the southern shore of the Thames River, from the eastern coast of Kent right up the Thames River to Crayford. Additionally, in the early 400s there is heavy evidence of settlement in Anglia and Mercia; there is likewise evidence of settlement even farther north, in the fifth to seventh century province of Lindsey, the present county of Lincolnshire.

But there is no evidence of heavy settling between London and Swindon. Oddly enough, however, between Swindon and Bath, archaeological finds indicate a heavy concentration of Saxon cemeteries and burial grounds. But the "not-too-far" distance from Crayford, on the Thames, to Liddington Castle in an almost perfectly western direction, is approximately 80 miles. Similar to Greek times and early Roman times, any kind of travel overland was considered much more hazardous and slower than travel by water. The story of Theseus, for instance, depicts the treacherous evils lurking at every turn, behind every tree, atop every rise, at the base of every chasm in land travel. Theseus was repeatedly advised to travel to Athens by sea, but he elects to show his strength, manhood, and fearlessness by overland travel. This, too, would typify the German Saxon infiltration of the island. Their homeland on the continent was south and east of the mouth of the Thames, with the Kentish shores being the shortest distance between the island and the continent. The surest, swiftest, safest way for these seafarers to travel was by boat, exploring the coastline in hopes of finding coves, bays, harbours, channels, and river-mouths to move farther inland in the most expedient way. Their first such discovery was the entrance allowed by the Thames River; from the mouth of the Thames, the Saxons could travel inland another 20 or 25 miles to Crayford. They could have made it even farther inland to Londinium, but it would be unrealistic for them to begin an 80-mile overland trek whether it be to conquer, plunder, or settle, especially considering that the fertile, southern heartland was the most coveted and protected of the territories.

Furthermore, it is uncertain how Liddington Castle fits into the "strategic picture." It is true that Liddington lies at an intersection of Roman roads running from the hub at Cirencester (Corinium) to Andover and intersecting with the Roman road running from Badbury to Silchester, but Badbury at Liddington is not very strategic. In fact, Silchester, 30 miles or so to the east-southeast, is much more important. It was the site of a major Roman town with five major roads converging there. A Saxon advance from Londinium to the west would put them on a collision course with one of the major strongholds of the southern territories.

Ashe also alludes to the "enormous defensive line called the Wansdyke [which] was almost certainly constructed under Ambrosius, to defend the southwest against an army marching from the Thames Valley."[24] The beginning of the Wansdyke is approximately ten miles due south of Liddington Castle, visible near the Savernake Forest and snaking its way directly west for about 36 miles, disappearing just beyond Bath.

Leslie Alcock has this to say about Wansdyke:

> Excavation has shown that the dyke is late Roman or later, while its very name, Woden's Dyke, shows that it was in existence before the conversion of Wessex in the 630s. All else about its history is conjecture. It is disputed for a start whether the two separate halves, East and West Wansdyke, are part of the same scheme. East Wansdyke may have been a defensive frontier for the Britons of Salisbury Plain against early Saxon settlements in the Thames Valley; or it may be a creation of the Saxons themselves in the course of some internal struggle. ... There is at present no evidence to help us decide between these hypotheses, but even if there were we would still be left with the tactical problem: how were the dykes used? ... It is difficult to believe that the infantry of Wessex, whether attacking Britons or fellow–Saxons, would have found the ditch and bank an insuperable obstacle. ... It is of course typical of our period that one of its major archaeological monuments should defy attempt to date it, to set it in its political context, or to understand its tactical function.[25]

It seems an overstatement, then, for Ashe to claim that the Wansdyke (West or East?) was almost certainly constructed under Ambrosius to defend the southwest against an army marching from the Thames Valley. If the dyke had been constructed to protect the southwest from armies approaching from the west, the axis of the dyke would have been *diagonal*— from northwest to southeast — rather than east-west.

Though aware of these other possibilities,[26] Pitt-Rivers suggests that there is no evidence to disprove the supposition that "the Wansdyke could have been thrown up by the West Saxons as a defence between them and the Mercians."[27] When he completed his archaeological test sections in the Wansdyke just north of Devizes, he was able to satisfy himself "that it contained Roman material and so could not have been thrown up before late Roman times."[28] The additional discovery of iron cleats which formed part of leather fastenings or sole guards for sandals led Pitt-Rivers to conclude also that "It is only reasonable to suppose that the periods of these two Dykes [Wansdyke and Bokerly] could not be very remote from one another."[29]

He became even more specific as his excavations continued. He began his work on the Wansdyke in April of 1889, while he was still excavating Bokerly; it was therefore propitious timing that allowed him to conduct excavations on both dykes simultaneously. He worked for only a very short time on the Wansdyke before falling to an illness which almost claimed his life, but then when he renewed his excavations about a year and a half later, he researched Sir Richard Hoare who had traced a branch of the Wansdyke for nearly five miles along the Berkshire Hills and to the east of Chisbury Camp. Hoare was trying to determine if the Wansdyke continued from Inkpen and originally ran to Silchester but was unsuccessful in finding traces of it.[30]

Pitt-Rivers observes that the Wansdyke seemed at times little more than a road, but at other times such as near Morgan's Hill and Sheperd's Shore near Devizes, it was a large defensive work. He observes that: "The ditch [of Wansdyke] is always to the north, showing that it was thrown up against a northern enemy."[31] This is in direct contradiction to Ashe's postulation. German Saxons coming from the Thames Valley and moving inland would have been invading this particular area from the east, not the north.

The length of the Wansdyke is another feature that prevents a simplified determination of its construction date. The Wansdyke runs from a point close to the Bristol Channel near Bath to an area by the Savernake Forest where it hooks in the direction of Andover. This means that it extends for a distance of nearly 40 miles, or about six times the length of Bokerly Dyke, even if one makes the supposition that Bokerly used abatis through the dense forests and continued to the northwestern side of White Sheet Hill. Because of the Wansdyke's great extent, Pitt-Rivers states that "The evidence [of when it was constructed] leaves open a wider field for conjecture."[32] This also leads him to hypothesize that "although the Wansdyke is not certain of construction at one time, though it was one continuous line, evidence is much in favor of it having been one work of defense."[33] He goes on to say that

> We must consider the possibility of the Wansdyke having been constructed by the Romanized Britons, after the departure of the Romans.[34]

This agrees with Ashe's theory, but in the same sentence Pitt-Rivers reiterates that it was a defense against the Picts and Scots when the Britons were driven into the southwest corner of the country, whilst Bokerly, at a somewhat different time, may have served to protect them against the Saxons.[35]

BADBURY RINGS

With the determination of why Liddington Castle is *not* feasible as the Badon site, attention must now focus on why Badbury Rings is a better choice. Surprisingly, the ASC provides important data for geographic locations, specifically in entries 477, 491, 495, 501, 508, 514, 519, and 552. Year 477 records two places, Cymenesora and Andredeslea, the first a location now covered by the sea near Selsea Bill, just south of Chichester in Hampshire. The second is the Weald, where the Britons were driven in a northeasterly direction. Year 491 lists Andredesceaster, the Roman Anderida, near Pevensey, a coastal area in Sussex. The entries for 495 and 514 name Cerdicesora while 508 and 519 name Cerdicesford, two locations which some scholars postulate too hastily are identical; Giles lists the site as Hamble on the Hamble, a short distance up the Southampton Water. Entry 501 names Portsmouth. Year 527 names Cerdicesford or Cerdicesleag, depending upon the version. Entry 552 mentions Salisbury, interpreted from Searoburh, the ancient name for Sarum.

The pattern of progression noted by these entries offers some interesting possibilities. In the days of Hengist, Horsa, and Vortigern, and for a short period thereafter, the Saxon activity in Britain was mainly in the Thames Valley and Kent. Beginning in 477, activity increased along the southern coastal areas and the English Channel: Ælle battles at Selsea Bill; Ælle besieges Pevensey; Cerdic fights the Britons at Hamble; Port lands at Portsmouth; Cerdic has a great battle and claims land near Charford; Stuf puts the Britons to flight at Hamble; Cerdic succeeds to the kingdom of the West Saxons by winning a major battle at Charford; and last, with the Saxon objectives accomplished, Cynric fights the Britons at Old Sarum.

In *King Arthur's Avalon*, just prior to Ashe's claim that Badon is Badbury at Liddington, he says this about the *Chronicle* picture:

> The invaders [Saxons] overrun Kent. ... They inaugurate Sussex, but fail to push far beyond the Downs, or to break through toward London along the Roman road from Chichester. They establish an embryonic Wessex, ... and in 477 Ælle tries Sussex. Ælle's last success is in 491, and in 495 Cerdic tries Hampshire.[36]

Wessex might initially have been only a nuisance on the British flank, but by the time Cerdic asserts himself, the confrontations are major conflicts. The important focus here is that the Britons are attempting countermeasures not only along the southern shores of the Thames, Kent, Sussex, and Hampshire, but also along the shores of Southampton Water.

This emphasizes the strategic importance of Badbury Rings as the Badon site. Badon at Liddington is relatively isolated, actually in the military rather than civilian district, an outpost like Hadrian's Wall would be, though not as extreme. These were the outlying areas north of Old Sarum. The civilian areas, on the other hand, lay to the south of Old Sarum — the farmlands, the settlements, the centers of the civilization — as opposed to the perimeters protecting that heartland.

A view of the northern ramparts of Badbury Rings. The three rings of the ramparts are quite evident.

Badon at Liddington actually had one Roman road running through it, north and south, with an intersection connecting it to Londinium.

As a contrast, Badbury Rings has a maze of Roman roads intersecting there, accentuating the area as a crucial heartland. Roads directly connect Badbury Rings with Poole Harbor, Winchester, Old Sarum, South Cadbury, and Dorchester, making it a hub of commerical and civilian vitality as opposed to the inactivity at Liddington Castle. Of four archaeological sources — James Dyer, Courtland Canby, Peter Clayton, and M.W. Thompson — only Dyer lists Liddington Castle Hillfort, whereas all list Badbury Rings. Their work is independent of Arthur, but the Roman connection allies itself strongly with the Arthurian post-Roman period, attesting to the importance of its location.

Just as Wansdyke was used to verify or nullify the Liddington site as Badon, the same must be done for Bokerly Dyke and Badbury Rings. Bokerly is a much smaller system than the Wansdyke; if the obvious line of Bokerly is measured, excluding the assumption that it continues to the northwestern ridge of White Sheet Hill, its length is only 6 miles compared to the 40-mile extension of the Wansdyke.

Looking at its physiography, Bokerly runs in a northwesterly direction after a hooked beginning in Blagdon Hill Wood. Pitt-Rivers looked for traces farther southeast in Martin Wood, but found no evidence that it continued.[37] For reasons he disclosed for other structures, he suggests that perhaps the dense forests of those days, along with the construction of abatises, were incorporated with the

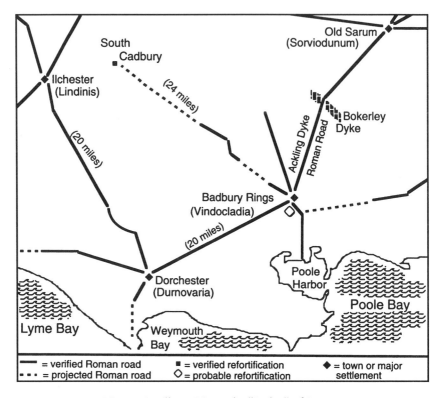

Map 11. Bradbury Rings, the "Badon" of Dorset.

dykes for defensive protection. If this is true, one interesting projection is possible: following the contour of the Dyke, plus the Blagdon Hill Wood, Martin Wood, and Boulsbury Wood in its southeasterly direction, the line intersects the Charford-Cadnam-Southampton Water areas. These barriers could feasibly hamper invaders attempting to move north from the coastal areas.

After the dyke exits Blagdon Hill Wood, it begins its ascent up Blagdon Hill almost immediately. On this side of the hill the ascent from the valley is steep, affording protection and a panoramic view of the northern and eastern countryside. It then runs along the crest of the hill, and as it nears the top, it becomes higher. Even with erosion over the centuries, it is still obvious that there was a deep ditch backed by a high ridge along this entire area. As the Dyke turns west before beginning its descent, there is perhaps a 250-degree view of the northern and eastern sections of the country. The view to the southwest is blocked by Pentridge Hill, which is about 100 feet higher than Blagdon Hill.

The Dyke then crosses the lowland segment of Martin Down, and at about its center, the Dyke bulges outward, but not for defensive purposes. Pitt-Rivers concludes that, "because of the comparative verdure of the crops and the fertile ground, there was the former existence of a spring at this spot,"[38] and that the

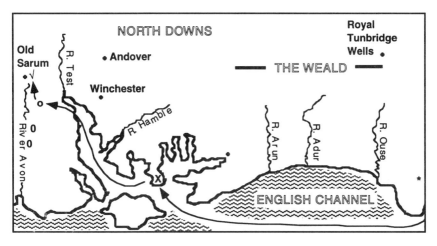

Map 12. A depiction of the Saxon movement along the southern coast of Britain according to the progression theory derived from entries in the *Anglo-Saxon Chronicle*.

  * = Pevensey (Andredesceaster), 491
  x = Portsmouth, 501
  o = Charford, 519
  √ = Sarum (Searoburh), 552

Special note: Entries 495, 508, and 514 are not listed because they are recorded in the *ASC* as battles against the Welsh, not the Britons, and 514 is possibly a doublet.

Dyke assumes that course to incorporate the spring behind its line of defenses. Because there is not much natural defense on Martin Down, the dyke's high rampart and wide ditch are very obvious. It continues northwesterly for about a half-mile, to Bokerly Gap, where it switches to a slight westerly direction before it hooks to the south very near its intersection with the Roman road running from Old Sarum to Badbury Rings.

Several important features occupy this area. One is the man-made structure which Pitt-Rivers refers to as the Epaulement, just west of Bokerly Gap. He says:

> The use of the Epaulement has been frequently discussed; my excavations show that the Dyke to the westward of it is probably more recent, and that it may have been a part of the bank thrown back to guard the flank of the Dyke, at a time when it extended no further to the westward.[39]

After completing several exploratory cuts, he verifies that the Dyke to the west of the Epaulement is a more recent construction, dating to the immediate post-Roman period. Additionally it indicates that the Dyke, because it runs almost parallel to the Roman road for about 300 yards, protects the road at its weakest point from northern and western assaults.

There is a peculiarity in the Dyke as it crosses the Roman road and extends westward. A very short distance to the north, running parallel to Bokerly Dyke, is a man-made feature called Grim's Ditch. Whereas Bokerly Dyke has its rampart to the south and its ditch to the north, Grim's Ditch is reversed; it has its ramparts to the north and the ditch to the south. Pitt-Rivers' conclusion is that "If the Grim's Ditch ever was a defensive entrenchment, and of the same period as the Dyke, it must have been erected in opposition to the defenders of Bokerly Dyke."[40] The evidence, though, of Grim's Ditch being a counter-defensive structure to Bokerly Dyke is inconclusive.

Pitt-Rivers made some interesting archaeological discoveries west of the Dyke's intersection with the Roman road. Just south of a Romano-Briton settlement, a segment of the Dyke continues almost due west before angling southwest. After about 300 yards, it cuts through Hill Copse and continues its course to Denbose Wood, where traces of it disappear. Excavations along this left flank show an earlier defense which Pitt-Rivers calls the Rear Dyke. He concludes that the more recent Fore Dyke was constructed to replace the rear section, because the Fore Dyke

> runs along the most suitable ground for defence and command, topping the gentle slope in its rear and explains probably the reason, or one reason, for the change of the line of defence from the Rear to the Fore Dyke.[41]

From this, he drew several important inferences. For one, it

> made it evident that a settlement must have existed on the ground before the Entrenchment was thrown up, but no trace of such a settlement could be seen on the surface, the greater part of which, at this spot, was in fallow.[42]

This not only led to the discovery of the settlement, but because of lost coins thrown up into the rampart, it further showed that "clearly the Roman road must have continued in use after the Rear Dyke had been filled in."[43] The left flank, therefore, was not a double defense, but the Fore Dyke was built to obtain a better defensive line, since the old segment had rotted away and was no longer as effective for protection.

Pitt-Rivers observed that the Dyke took advantage of natural contours of the land, leading into primeval forests of dense growth that were therefore impenetrable, supporting his position that Bokerly was a defensive system to protect the southwest from invasion: "Bokerly Dyke everywhere occupies strong ground, if viewed from the standpoint of an enemy advancing to attack it from the northeast."[44] Additionally he dates it during the era of Arthur's reign. The discovery of 584 coins from the rampart and silting of the ditch just north and west of Bokerly Junction proves that this segment of the Dyke

> must have been made at the time or subsequently to the departure of the Romans from the British Isles in 407. This was no longer a matter for conjecture — it was a proved fact.[45]

He further supports his stand by adding that

When the people advanced to a higher state of civilization, and several tribes combined for the defence of a district, it was not by detached forts, but by continuous entrenchments, that they accomplished that object. They threw up continuous lines of ditch and bank, the latter probably surmounted by a stockade, running for miles along the open country from an inaccessible position on one flank to some other natural defence on the other flank. And although it may be true ... that these long entrenchments ... would be difficult, or impossible to defend at all points, yet we know as a fact, that this system was adopted, and that the Romans used it, not only for the north of Britain, as a defence against the Picts and the Scots, but also in the more extended defence of their German frontier.[46]

This strategy had held true not only in earlier warfare, such as battles fought along the Great Wall of China, but also in the recent past with the Maginot Line of World War II. With the amassed evidence supporting his viewpoint, he also rejects the possibility that these dykes were elaborate systems for funneling wild game into pens.[47]

The last item to consider is the layout of the Roman roads and why Codrington states that the road to Old Sarum was "laid out to communicate with the south rather than the west."[48] The major intersection of roads is to the south and east of Badbury Rings, and as Codrington points out, the road is heading more to the east before it makes a peculiar, angular diversion just before intersecting with the Roman road running from the southeast to the northwest. Codrington further suggests that the Roman road to the west was laid out at a later time, meaning that the road to Dorchester and then Exeter post-dated the more important area to the east of Badbury Rings. This implies, too, that the road to Hod Hill and beyond was also constructed at a later date.

Simplified, this draws attention to the indications of another road from Badbury Rings to Hod Hill, near the present site of Blandford Forum. At Hod Hill there are remains of a Roman encampment within early entrenchments. Codrington writes,

A parish boundary in a straight line along a belt of trees for a mile and a quarter points to Hod Hill eight miles off, and there are tracks onwards in the same line.[49]

This further stresses the strategic location of Badbury Rings as Badon. Not only would it function as a frontier stronghold to the west, but it would offer control of the southeast and connect it to Arthur's headquarters, just 24 miles to the northwest, in South Cadbury.

Likewise, where Bokerly Dyke intersects with the Roman road, about 10 miles northeast of Badbury Rings, stations "occur at 10- or 12-mile intervals along Roman roads."[50] Other sources have suggested that the distances between stations was no more than 20 miles, but Pitt-Rivers, in this area at least, fixes the space at 10 to 12 miles, which would further substantiate the importance of this area.

The extensive evidence is funneled to Badbury Rings as one of the primary probabilities of the Badon site. A battle at this deep south-central outpost conforms in detail to defenses which the Britons would have devised against the Saxons. If the enemy crossed the Channel and sailed up the Southampton Water,

Bokerly Dyke would, in fact, be a defense system. Similarly, if the Saxons landed at Poole Harbor and pushed inland along the Roman road leading from Wimbourne Minster, Badbury Rings would be the objective. A Briton victory here would discourage attempts to conquer the heartland. The acceptance that Badbury Rings is the best choice for the Battle of Badon, however, is based on two assumptions. One is that the Saxons were invading and attempting to capture the heartland by sailing across the Channel, and the other is that the Britons were the defenders of Badbury Rings and the Saxons the attackers. Neither assumption is resolved by the entry in the *AC* or explained by any evidence to date.

Badon: Bath Possibilities

Other contentions show that Badon does not necessarily have to be linked to the term Badbury. Gildas describes the site of this famous battle as *Mons Badonicus*, leaving no doubt that the siege took place on a hill, though history does not detail who besieged whom. As Alcock pointed out, a hill need not be equated with a hillfort, and when Bath is considered as a possibility, there is no suffix in the word to suggest a hillfort. However, the term *mons* does not exclude a hillfort, so that if the hill is an occupied refortification, its justification as a possibility is strengthened. In this context, Badon is interpreted as a reference to Vadon and its variables Vathon and Vaddon, in which the "double d" is pronounced as an unvoiced "th-." This would naturally lead to a translation of "Bathon," but the term is not necessarily restricted just to the area of modern-day Bath, particularly in light of the name Aguae Sulis which was its ancient designation.

LITTLE SOLSBURY HILL

Little Solsbury Hill, just outside Batheaston, is another strong probability for a variety of reasons. As a point of fact, Morris is one of the few Arthuriana researchers who refers to Solsbury Hill by name in association with Badon. Morris prefers this site by explaining that

> There are many hills and hillforts in the neighborhood of Bath. Most are defended spurs, easily attacked from the rear, or forts placed on the flat tops of large hills. One hill only is a separate *Mons*, sharply escarped on all sides, small enough to be defended with ease by a body of dismounted cavalry, Solsbury Hill by Batheaston. Though there are endless possibilities, this site best fits both Gildas' choice of words and the nature of the campaign.[51]

An interesting sidelight, the subject of later scrutiny, is Morris' statement that "Wessex tradition places the death of Cerdic at the same time as the death of Oesc [Æsc, Octha] and the Battle of Badon."[52] Not only does this establish the rivalry between Cerdic, Octha, and Arthur, but it sets the scene at Badon, relating that one and perhaps two Saxon leaders are killed in that encounter, and it locks it in a time frame to account for Arthur's spectacular rise to fame.

Leslie Alcock vacillates on the possibility of the Bath area as the Badon location, but avoids the specific name of Solsbury Hill. He writes, "In strategic terms, given the mobility of war at the time, there is nothing to exclude Bath as the site of either the first or the second Badon."[53]

Although Alcock does not commit himself to a hillfort as a condition for the Badon location, neither does he completely reject that the battle of Badon could not have been in the vicinity of Bath, rather than the south-central coast of the island. In his summary, however, he does lean toward the area of Bath as the Badon site. He concludes, "His [Arthur's] major victory, the siege of Mount Badon, was fought against the English about 490, most probably on a hill outside Bath."[54] The date has already been modified to 497 in this text, but now the question of geographic locale for Badon has been raised.

Further support for the Bath area is derived through philology, which explains that the Latin writers of that period who were spelling British placenames wrote the word as Badonis, with the "d" not gutturally pronounced as in the word "bad," but unvoiced as a "th" in the word "thing." In Old English this particular sound had its own letter, which looked like a peculiar "d" with the crossed stem at an angle, giving the word the modern pronounciation of "Bathonis." Bathonis, then, is later identified in Welsh tradition with Caer Vathon, the Roman Aguae Sulis. Bath itself is not on a promontory, nor is it a hillfort, but this candidate is just northeast of Bath, in Batheaston, called Solsbury Hill, not to be confused with Silbury Hill or Salisbury. Morris asserts that Solsbury is specifically a *mons*, and it was an Iron-Age hillfort.

Plummer's analysis of the *Anglo-Saxon Chronicle* indicates that for the entry of 577, the West Saxons captured Bathanceaster and interpreted it as Bath.[55] The date not withstanding, this entry is important in that the prefix in Bathanceaster points out the likelihood that the Saxons equated Bathon with their legendary hero or semigod, *Baddan*, which adds a peculiar but supportive twist to Ekwall's explanation. The date itself of 577, of course, does not suggest a battlesite during Arthur's era, since the equation here is that the Battle of Badon was fought in the year 497 and this entry refers to the Battle of Dyrham. In addition to being 80 years later, this was a battle against northern enemies, with movement north in the direction of Gloucester. However, the setting of Bath — specifically Solsbury Hill in Batheaston — as a possible site for the Battle of Mount Badon could be correct geographically, chronologically, and historically.

The only reference to Solsbury Hill comes from John Morris. After a time-consuming survey of archaeological excavations on British hillforts, one source — unrelated to Arthurian material — was uncovered, provided by Barry Cunliffe, who relates that Little Solsbury Hill was excavated and analyzed first in 1957 and then again in 1962 by W.A. Dowden.[56] In Volume 8, W.A. Dowden reported on the excavations of Little Solsbury Camp during 1955 and 1956, and in Volume 9 he reported on the excavations from 1958. An original excavation was conducted in 1935 by Falconer and Adams, which Dowden also reviews.

The objectives for the excavations were to carry out trial digs to determine the range of time and the sequence of occupation of the hillfort. In 1955, three trial pits, each about 10 feet square, were dug; the deepest hit bedrock at three feet. In 1956, hampered by bad weather, one pit was dug to determine the zone of occupation within the rampart. In 1958, three squares of 10 feet were dug parallel to the 1956 trench and at right angles to the rampart wall. The significant findings were as follows:

1. two phases of occupation were shown, the first period clearly starting in a period of peace with some evidence of burning which might have been accidental and ending with a partial collapse or throwing down of the rampart;
2. the second phase was a relatively long one, lasting from approximately 150 B.C. to about 50 B.C., offering no clue as to why the site was completely abandoned;
3. in the 1956-1957 report, echoed in the 1958 discussion, the hillfort appears "to have been abandoned well before the Roman period, for there is no trace of Roman influence."[57]

A.H.A. Hogg in an index of *British Hillforts* gives some technical information about this particular site; the scarce data on Solsbury indicates its area is approximately eight hectares, about the same size as South Cadbury. Dowden elaborates on its size:

The site itself covers nearly 20 acres. It is an island hill mass at the south end of a long spur, and there are a number of good springs around the hill, only a matter of a few yards down from the edge of the plateau. In all, this would have been a very good site for a tribal *oppidum*. So far only a tiny fraction of the area of occupation has been tackled; an area scarcely larger than that lost annually by natural slip and by the depredations of treasure hunters.[58]

The National Trust adds that Solsbury Hill was a walled village that came into existence during the early Iron Age, occupied from about 300 B.C. to 100 B.C. According to published information from the Trust, at first the area near the edge of the hilltop was cleared to a rock base on which substantial timber-framed and wattle huts were built. A 20-foot-wide rampart was then made, faced inside and outside with well-built dry stone walls and infilled with loose stones. The outer face was at least 12 feet high. After a period of occupation — with no evident reoccupation by the Romans or post–Roman Britons — some huts burned down and the rampart was overthrown.

These details have important implications for the Arthurian period. Even if one assumes the site was never rebuilt or reoccupied as an active hillfort during the Roman or post–Roman period, this does not negate the possibility of Badon in this vicinity. As an *oppidum*, with literally nine water springs just below the lip of the plateau, an army on the move could use this site as an interim haven. Or, another possibility could be what Alcock himself suggested: Bathon could well have been in the vicinity of Bath, but Caer Vathon does not necessarily have to be limited to either Bathampton Down or Solsbury Hill at the exclusion of the other possibilities surrounding Bath. In giving the general geography of the

Little Solsbury Hillfort, westward toward the Mouth of the Severn, with Bath to the southwest. The defense was a wide rampart faced by a drystone wall, slightly visible because of light erosion on the eastern slope. The ramparts were fronted by a deep ditch. The weakness of it as a consideration of Badon is its distance from the River Severn and its accessibility from Wales, over 20 miles to the west.

area, Barry Cunliffe illustrates other hilltops, including Lansdown, Charmy Down, and Odd Down. Unlike South Cadbury which was extensively excavated, only 4,000 square feet of Solsbury's 1,271,200 square feet has been explored, and even though there may be more probes, Solsbury Hill is presently an enigma.

Whereas Badbury Rings would have been an outpost along the southern border of the heartland, Bath, 40 miles distant, would have been an outpost on the northern border. The Hwicce and a segment of the West Saxon territories lie to the north, and Bath as a fortification, in conjunction with the Wansdyke, could allow the Britons immediate defense of Somersetshire, Avon, and Wiltshire. One inference, of course, is that the Saxon compatriots (Gewissae) and the West Saxons were occupying a vast inland region east of the Severn.

This inference is validated by the *Historia* as a historical source. In a section titled the "Wonders of Britain," totally disconnected from Arthurian material and the Kentish Chronicles, Nennius records the third wonder, which is "... the Hot Lake, *where the Baths of Badonis are*, in the country of the Hwicce."[59] The impact of this information is that Nennius actually equates Bath with Badonis, but even more significant, he reveals that Badonis is in *Saxon* territory. It is important to recall that Saxon compatriots were granted the region called the Hwicce Territory in Britain after Vortigern's invitation. This changes the entire historical scenario because the English Saxons would be entrenched in their own territory *defending* Badonis, and Arthur's warriors would be the aggressors trying to oust them from Briton soil.

VIROCONIUM

Of the three major sites detailed above — Liddington Castle near Badbury, Badbury Rings, and Bath — two are associated with the term Badbury, and one is more closely linked to the term Bathonis. The last one (as implied by Nennius) is the one cited most often by scholars as the location for the Battle of Mount Bathonis. When compiled, clues provided by historical and literary sources are very specific about Badon's geography:

1. By its nature, the Badonis location would be important strategically from military and civil standpoints. (All sources literary and historical, including the *De Excidio*, the *Historia*, and *Annales Cambriae*.)
2. It is on a hill in or near a place renowned for its Roman baths. (Gildas: Badonici montis; Nennius: Monte Badonis; Dream of Rhonabwy: at the base of Caer Vaddon; Geoffrey of Monmouth: Kaerbadum)
3. Arthur and his army must ford the River Severn to attack Mount Badon. (Dream of Rhonabwy)
4. The hill is occupied by the Saxons. (Dream of Rhonabwy, Monmouth)
5. Both the hill and the baths are adjacent to the River Severn. (Dream of Rhonabwy)

These major considerations have pointed to Bath, since Bath meets several of the conditions. Although Bath itself is not located atop a tor, several hillforts occupy the immediate vicinity, either at Little Solsbury Hill or the hillfort on Bathampton Down. Likewise, it is about 20 miles from the Mouth of the Severn via the River Avon, perhaps even less than that in Arthurian times. Furthermore, it is close to the Hwicce territories and, of course, dating from Roman times, it was a commercial trading center with an easy access to the mouth of the Severn, necessary to defend militarily.

A closer look, however, leads to a serious rethinking of the Badon location, perhaps from inadvertent misinterpretations, or maybe because of some deliberate deception. Bath (Aguae Sulis) as the sole unquestionable location associated with Vathon does not meet all of the requisites gleaned from history and tradition. Plummer's analysis cited above sets 577 as the date when Bathanceaster was captured. If this date is accurate, then Aguae Sulis did not come under West Saxon control until 80 years *after* the Badon battle was fought, at which time it would have been assigned a Saxon name. Although it is possible that West Saxons did attack Bath in 497, it contradicts evidence not only from the the *Anglo-Saxon Chronicle* but also the "Dream of Rhonabwy." In 497 Bath would still be under Welsh control and would *not* have been named after a Saxon semigod; thus, a site named Baddon in 497 after a Saxon semigod would be in *Saxon* dominions, somewhere in Gewissae or Cornovii provinces, associated with a different Bath. In turn, the English Saxons would be in control of the area and the Welsh would be the attackers, as narrated in the "Dream of Rhonabwy."

The pronunciations for Baddon and Vaddon have already been touched upon, but Alcock builds upon that and writes:

> Later Welsh tradition identifies the Badon of the battles with Caer Vadon, or Bath. It is generally considered that the English [Saxons] gave the name Bath to a decayed Roman spa-town because traces of the Roman hot baths were still visible when the Wessex dynasty captured the area in A.D. 577. Certainly the English name owed nothing to a Roman predecessor, for the Romans knew the spa as *Aguae Sulis*, "Waters of the Sul."[60]

He, too, points to the generally accepted pattern that Badon is equated with Bath but expresses suspicions that Bath as the battle site is a misfit. It is his last sentence which induces the need for a reassessment.

It is specifically known, then, that Bath was *not* a proper name used for Aguae Sulis until at least 80 years after the inception of the Wessex dynasty. Attention turns immediately, of course, to the *Historia* and the third "Wonder of Britain" listed in Chapter 67. The *Historia* seemingly validated a connection between Aguae Sulis, Bath, and Baddon by a passage which states, "... the Hot Lake, *where the Baths of Badon are*, in the country of the Hwicce."[61] For some reason, Morris inserted italics in his translation. Because this technique usually signifies an interpolation, this led to the inspection of a copy of the original Latin manuscript which he used. It states, "... stagnum calidum *in quo balnea sunt Badonis*, quod est in regione Huich."[62] The significant segment in italics is a serious transgression. *None* of the *Historia* manuscripts edited and compiled by Josephus Stevenson contain the italicized passage *in quo balnea sunt Badonis*. One wonders where Morris acquired this information. According to Stevenson on page 56 of his Nennius text, the passage in any of the extant manuscripts simply reads "... stagnum calidum quod est in regione Huich, et muro ambitur ex latere et lapide facto."[63] This translates as "hot lake which is in the Hwicce territory, and surrounded by a wall made of brick and stone." Neither the word Badon nor Bath appears in the passage. There is a generic reference to men bathing, but in that sense the word "bath" would be a common noun and not a reference to a city. Furthermore, the wall is made of brick and stone, an indication that the structure was Roman. The Hot Lake, therefore is in Gewissae territory, originally enclosed and used as baths by the Romans. Although "Bath" (Aguae Sulis) would be on the fringes of the Gewissae territories, probably 10 or 20 miles farther south, this again shows that it would be excluded as a Badon site in English Saxon territory.

In spite of Morris' translation, then the *Historia* provides no evidence to indicate that there was a location named "Bath" equated with the Aguae Sulis of Roman times, nor is there an equation between Aguae Sulis and Badon. The association between Bath and Aguae Sulis may have been made by the English 80 years after the Badon battle was fought, but during the Arthurian era in 497 there was not a city by that name where Romans bathed. "Roman baths," therefore, is a general term applicable to several sites. The justification for some hillfort near the modern site of Bath as Badon is thus considerably diminished.

Viroconium as a site of Roman baths becomes the most practicable because it meets *all* of the conditions for the historical and literary Badon as set forth above.

In the same vein, the historical role of the Wansdyke becomes crucial. As Ashe writes, the Wansdyke might have been constructed by Ambrosius, but it would not have been as protection from Saxon infiltration from the Thames Valley. It could likewise be as Pitt-Rivers contends, that it could have been thrown up by the West Saxons as a defense between them and the Mercians. Or it could be as Alcock suggests, that the East Wansdyke was either a defensive barrier built by the Britons against the English Saxons from the Upper Thames Valley or a creation of the Saxons themselves in the course of some internal struggle. In any event, two archaeological finds remain inflexible: the dyke was built in late-Roman or post–Roman times, and it was a barrier with the ditch always to the north, showing that it was thrown up against a northern enemy.

To arrive at a viable answer, the focus must first shift to a leader who would be powerful and influential enough to manage such an undertaking. Only three names of historical significance surface. The first is Vortigern, but he is most unlikely. He is part of the Desi tribe exiled to Wales, whose dominion is originally the Glouising[64] (a name which eventually evolves to Gewissae). He flees farther north, and is therefore not associated with the southern regions of Britain. Ambrosius Aurelianus is another possibility. He is also associated with the Glouising province and is Welsh-related, associated with the midlands, but not explicitly named as the Badon leader. The third is Arthur. He is considered a king of the south, with southwest roots, and is also named in the *Historia* as the Badon victor, virtually the only one who could have authorized or initiated such an undertaking. Circumstantially, his historicity is the most tenuous, a proposition which will be explored in more detail later.

Why Arthur would expend the time, money, and manpower is also answerable. As the emergent Briton king from the south, he would want to protect the southern heartland from the marauding north, namely the remainder of the Picts and the Irish, and also the English Saxons who were still settled in Britain after the Battle of Badon. South of the east/west Wansdyke about 30 miles was South Cadbury, his Camelot court, and about 40 miles away was Badbury Rings, the southern site of the Badon battle, where he could have won his nationally recognized victory against the German Saxons.

Based upon the preceding discrepancies for the other sites, Wroxeter, the Roman Viroconium, when set in the milieu of the period, fits the geography of Badon better historically and logistically than any other proposal. In its general nature, Bath would have been commercially significant because of trade routes and militarily important because it was the northwestern gateway to the heartland of southern Britain from the Gewissae territories. But the importance of Wroxeter overshadows even these considerations. Even though Nennius' list of British cities has been open to a great deal of speculation and no clear-cut conclusions have been drawn about certain locations, the name of Wroxeter (Guricon) invariably appears, whereby Bath (Aguae Sulis) is not mentioned even once.

In its heyday, Wroxeter was the fourth largest city in Roman Britain and important for its consideration as an Arthurian battlesite:

> Following periods of growth and decline, in the second, third, and fourth centuries, a remarkable resurgence of activity took place after A.D. 400 at a time when the Roman administration began to withdraw from Britain, leaving the country vulnerable to conquest and settlement by Germanic peoples.[65]

Originally, there was a legionary fortress on the site. Many military buildings have been unearthed in addition to the rampart, the western gate, and the northern section of the fort, each with a distinctive difference from subsequent development which reflects a change from military to civil status. Webster writes that

> It is thus likely that the fortress had changed function to become a depot for administration, storage and training, while the fighting strength was engaged in the northern campaign under Agricola.[66]

When the military establishment moved, the site became the seat for civil authorities, and Wroxeter became a tribal center with some local autonomy, attracting Britons so that the city became "a well-established and very mixed community, several thousand strong."[67] Retired legionnaires remained behind when the military camps moved, and the families became the nucleus of citizens who became subjects of Rome, governed by their own town council.

From its inception after the military fortress was relocated, the city expanded and experienced heavy political and economic growth throughout the second and into the third century. Defensive banks and ditches were built around the city paralleling the cliff edge near the River Severn and enclosing the village to the south. Webster and Barker explain that "the total length of this massive defence was about 2 miles (3.7 km); no mean enterprise in itself, [enclosing] the fourth largest area of any Roman city in Britain."[68] Within a radius of 35 miles there were two legionary forts (Viroconium itself and Chester to the north), four large forts including one at Penkridge (Pennocrucium) and another at Wall (Letocetum) along Watling Street, 18 regular forts circling the entire province, 16 marching camps, 4 military sites of unknown function, and 2 strongpoints, one at Wall where there was a fortress and another near Red Hill (Uxacona).[69] Additionally, Wroxeter is connected to London by the most direct Roman road, Watling Street. In one of his itineraries, Richard of Cirencester gives a comprehensive description of this highway and its importance. It runs from Richborough on the coast of Kent to Canterbury and directly to Rochester. He continues:

> It left that city to the right, passed the Medway by a ford, and ran almost straight, through lord Darnley's park, to Southfleet. It bent to the left to avoid the marshes near London, continued along a road now lost to Holwood Hill, the capital of the Rhemi, and then followed the course of the present road to London. Having crossed the Thames, it ran by Edgeware to Verulam; and from thence, with the present great Irish road, through Dunstable and Towcester to Weedon. Hence, instead of bending

to the left, with the present turnpike, it proceeded straight by Dovebridge, High Cross, Fazeley, Wall, and Wellington, to Wroxeter.[70]

He further explains that in its northwesterly course it forks just past Bala before finally connecting at Holyhead on the coast. Although this direct land route was traveled heavily by the Romans during their occupation, more than likely it was not the route used initially by the Saxons, since they were seafarers and the *Historia* records that they came in ships. Instead, their route was probably Bridgwater Bay to the mouth of the Severn, and up the navigable River Severn.

Information about Wall, only about 30 miles due east of Viroconium, is equally important in verifying this locale as the Badon site. The Nennius manuscript describes Hengist's proposal to Vortigern that Octha be given provinces in the north, "juxta murum qui vocatur Guaul,"[71] near the wall called Wall. By capitalizing the "W" on the first wall and by translating a passage which states that Octha was fighting the Irish in the north, John Morris implies a site near Hadrian's Wall. Giles proposes that Guaul is near the Antonine Wall. But both interpretations are set too far to the north, even though seemingly supported by Chapter 38 in the *Historia* which claims that Octha fought the Picts, wasted the Orkney Islands, and occupied districts beyond an obscure "Frenessican" Sea. However, Wade-Evans points out that chapters 37–38 and 40–46 in the *Historia* contain some distinctive stories or romances told by professional storytellers

> out of which Nennius is trying to make history to harmonize with Bede's disastrous misunderstanding of a "Saxon advent" as told in the *de excidio* and with all the guesswork he expended on it.[72]

In keeping with other historical details, Octha went approximately 50 miles farther north than his father was (from Gloucestershire to Wall-by-Lichfield), but still nearly 150 miles *south* of Hadrian's Wall. There is a settlement of Wall on Hadrian's Wall, but evidence disputes that Nennius' history makes reference to this location. For one, Guaul is a variation of Gwawl, a distinctively Welsh word that would be misplaced in its application to an area so far removed to the north. Ekwall mentions that the Wall in Northumbria and the one in Staffordshire both trace back to the same root, but the emphasis must be focused on the importance of the site in relation to its surroundings. Wall-by-Lichfield is verified by both John Morris and Graham Webster as Cair Luit Coyt[73] from Nennius' list of cities; Giles identifies Cair Luit Coyt as Lincoln, evidently borrowing that information directly from Geoffrey of Monmouth's Kaerluideoit without further documentation. Cair Luit Coyt, Wall-by-Lichfield, is also near a "wall that is called Wall." Webster describes Wall (Wall-by-Lichfield, Letocetum) in this way:

> The modern name Wall appears to have been derived from a long stretch of masonry ... which was presumably part of the late defence system. ... It was a two-mile ribbon strip of development along the main road and occupation has been noted at points along this length.[74]

As a faction of Vortigern's compatriots, Octha would have been in precisely the right location, driving out the Irish from the vacancy left by the Romans who abandoned Cornovii. Then later, after the traitorous Saxon reversal, Octha would be entrenched in an area where Arthur would have to expel the English Saxons. Only a few modern scholars concentrate efforts upon Octha because at first glance he appears a minor figure in the Arthurian saga. But information proposed by the major researchers, combined with other details which have been gleaned by this text, assign to Octha a major role in Arthuriana. Alcock says little of this figure, but what he does contribute offers important insights. He writes:

> It is natural to believe therefore that the people whom Arthur fought against were either the Saxons in general, or specifically the kings of Kent. In fact, there are no other grounds for accepting the second suggestion, and indeed it would be difficult to reconcile warfare in southeastern England with such information as we have about Arthur.[75]

Arthur is fighting the *English* Saxons in general and Octha as a king of the midlands (not Kent) specifically. In this instance Alcock is misled by the erroneous scribal heading inserted in the *Historia* which lists Octha's kingdom as Kent. What Alcock writes in the second sentence is true; all the evidence points to the mistaken alignment of Hengist and Octha with Kent, and Alcock corroborates what has been established so far in this text about the activities of Arthur: it would be impossible — not just difficult — to accept warfare between Octha and Arthur in Kent.

Alcock himself resolves the objection to Octha's and Arthur's warfare taking place in Kent by indirectly denying the possibility of an Arthur of the north. He writes:

> It has been claimed that, although the *British Historical Miscellany* in which we find the information is a Welsh manuscript, none the less the actual origin of those sections which interest us lies among the Britons of the north. Their language, no less than that of the sixth century inhabitants of Wales, was British in the process of becoming Welsh. When their lands were overrun by the Angles, and the Welsh language disappeared from the north, poems and tales about historic personages were carried to the west and preserved in Wales simply because that land was not anglicized. ... All this is beyond dispute because of the clear-cut nature of the evidence.[76]

His reasoning, however, still prevents him from emending the Octha/Arthur battles from Kent to the midlands. He is convinced that Arthur is not of the far north, but for some reason he does not consider the midland borderlands just to the east of Wales, even though this is precisely the territory he is referring to. Battles were fought in the old territories of Powys and Cornovii, and this tract of Britain encompassing the Severn, Viroconium, the Wrekin, and Caer Luit Coyt was the center of activity.

Morris, in combining several events in the middle decades of the fifth century including Cunedda's migration to the south and reasons for it, expresses a military tactic used either by Hengist or by Vortigern, which sent Octha to the north with English *federates* into the same vicinity of the Votadini where Cunedda operated prior to his migration.[77] Morris reinforces this tactic by later writing that

> It is at this point that the Kentish Chronicler inserts the expedition of Octha and Ebissa to the lands about the wall. ... [T]heir settlement may have had an additional purpose. Placed on the flank of the northern armies, it may have helped to deter any possibility of their intervention in the affairs of the south on behalf of Vortigern's enemies.[78]

The basics are accurate, except that Morris interprets the "wall" as Hadrian's Wall, whereas this text places it at Wall-by-Lichfield (Caer Luit Coyt). Once again, because the information about Octha and Ebissa appears in the "Kentish Chronicler," the location is misconstrued.

The second condition, that Bathon was a battle fought on a hill in or near a place renowned for its Roman baths, is easily fulfilled by Wroxeter. A remarkable amount is known about the baths of Wroxeter. Built by Hadrian, the perimeter of the baths enclosed an area of 5,600 square yards, 600 square yards larger than a modern-day American football field. The north bath basilica, an exercise hall called the palaestra, measured almost 32 by 82 yards, "about equal to the nave of one of the larger English Cathedrals of the Middle Ages."[79] It led to a frigidarium, the cold room with a cold plunge bath, and from there to a tepidarium (the warm room), a caldarium (the hot bath), two mild saunas and two intense ones. To the west, split by a separate entryway, were the latrines, civil offices, and a three-story market hall called the macellum.

The baths were later extended, with alterations to the western saunas, which were

> extended to form a separate wet-heat bath suite, entered from the frigidarium. The laconica [sauna] became tepidaria, with a newly built caldarium beyond. Furnaces to the west and south replaced the earlier one.[80]

The western extension encroached upon the open area of the piscina, an open, shallow bathing pool in a lounge area. Together with the forum, which represented the administrative and trading activities of the city, Webster and Barker explain that

> the baths were equally important, as a social center. Here, the citizens met informally in a relaxed atmosphere. Both sexes used the baths, but were segregated, normally women in the morning, men in the afternoon and evening.[81]

The additions and extensions may have been made as a possible extra bath house for a merchant guild or perhaps because the main bath could no longer accommodate the population. Webster and Barker conclude their description of the Wroxeter bath complex by writing that "With the bath opposite [the administrative offices], which also had a colonnade fronting the street, it was among the most impressive examples of civic planning in Roman Britain."[82]

The baths at Wroxeter. The tile stacks supported the floors to allow hot air from the furnaces to pass below and thus heat the rooms.

In addition to the massive bath complex at Wroxeter, Wall-by-Lichfield had its own mansio and bath complex. Although more modest, the bath house including its colonnade and basilica but excluding the mansion measured approximately 560 square yards. There is no archaeological evidence to determine whether the bath-house was a civil one or a late military one. However, "the visible remains ... form a very complicated sequence of walls and floors which cannot be fully understood," and in its final form some of the entryways were sealed, "suggesting that when the building ceased to function as a bath-house, it was divided into small tenements."[83] Besides its own baths, Wall-by-Lichfield is a hub in its own right. It is the strategic center for the Cornovii territory, adjacent to the Wrekin and river fords, and at the crossroads of Watling Street (the vital link to the southeast) and Ryknild Street (a quick passage to the north). It also had direct access northwest to Chester on the coast and south to Gloucester as an important port.

The hillfort adjacent to these baths provides even more intrigue. Unlike Little Solsbury Hill skirting Bath, the Wrekin hillfort here has produced evidence of a revival after the Roman withdrawal. Webster and Barker have written that a British tribe, the Cornovii, had a fortress on the top of the Wrekin, an imposing promontory rising over 1,300 feet and shadowing Wroxeter and Wall below. After the Romans left Viroconium, the city slowly began to decline and decay, the baths cracking from subsidence and falling into ruins beyond repair. The colonnade along the east side was pulled down, and the basilica was gradually

The Roman city of Wroxeter. Foreground left shows the circular bases for the massive columns of the basilica, depicted by Ivan Lapper in Drawing 2; foreground center is the remaining wall called the Old Works with the extensive bath area to the immediate right. In the background is the massive shadow of the Wrekin, a hillfort used in Arthurian times.

dismantled, with tiles and blocks of stone used for other structures, a process carrying on into the fifth century. The disappearance of Roman technology and the gradual influx of the Cornovians changed the features of the civilization's superstructures. Webster and Barker write that

> The nineteenth-century excavators found charred grain on the floor of the frigidarium and there is evidence to be seen of blocking of the entrances to the tepidarium. Thus parts of the baths were used for storage and possibly living quarters.[84]

Ivan Lapper has effectively depicted the site of the exercise hall as it may have appeared in the fifth century after the baths had gone out of use.[85]

There is a great deal of archaeological evidence of a phenomenal and unforeseen revival of the city beginning shortly after A.D. 400. The northern section of the basilica was demolished, cleared of rubble, and restructured. The new buildings were timber rather than stone, with the redevelopment centering upon a massive winged building just north of the basilica. An addition continued from it to Watling Street, which was still the main north-south street of the settlement. An old east-west street paved with cobblestones was replaced by gravel, and small shops and cubicles sprang up along its length. The market in front of the macellum was still used and more than likely spread northward in a series of small buildings.

Webster and Barker offer some interesting comments about the impetus behind this revitalization:

The whole of this late development seems to have been private rather than public in character. ... This seems to have been the demesne of a great man with energy, determination and resources to replan and rebuild the city centre at a time when public life in Roman towns had changed drastically. It is not known who was responsible for this rebuilding but it may have been one of the local "tyrants" who emerged from the chaos of the early fifth-century — a petty king reviving the city as the capital of the region.[86]

The word "tyrants" immediately evokes the name of Vortigern from Nennius and the "superbus tyrannus" recorded in Gildas' manuscript. Webster and Barker have already asserted that a British tribe, likely of mixed origins and more provincial than tribes to the south and east, had a fortress on the top of the Wrekin and their farmsteads were probably scattered over the fertile lands bordering the Severn. This links, then, not only to the figure of Vortigern, but to his Saxon confederation leading to compatriation and intermarriage and a new designation as the Hwicce or Gewissae. Upon the collapse of that alliance, another offshoot is the invitation for Cunedda to migrate from the north.

The story actually continues to unfold. The authors reinforce that the rejuvenation could hardly be fitted into the fourth century and is likely to have lasted well into, if not to the end of, the fifth. But the most important archaeological find turns out to be the tombstone of Cunorix, the stone of an Irish chieftain dating to the second half of the fifth century. The affix *-cun-* as in Cunedda, Cuneglas, and Maglocunus is akin to the Welsh *cyn-* where the "y" has an $\overline{oo}$ sound, creating the words Cymru and Cymri, Wales and Welsh. As mentioned earlier in this text, these inscribed stones were very common throughout Wales, but according to Alcock there are only ten in "northern Britain between the walls of Hadrian and Antonine,"[87] which aids in accurately pinpointing the migration period.

The changes and discoveries at Wroxeter lead Webster and Barker to conclude that

> As the pressures of the barbarian peoples on the northern frontier increased, Rome was forced to make a positive pragmatic decision. This was to allow selected groups of these peoples to settle on frontier lands on the condition that they acted as the defenders against other barbarians attempting to cross the frontier.[88]

This was a common practice throughout the Roman empire, including the eastern part of Britain, and would therefore have been a policy in the west, using Irish settlers and migrators from the north. It logically follows, too, as a common military practice even at the end of Roman reign in Britain, that the tribal kings would continue doing the same thing to protect their frontiers. It is not known when the city of Viroconium disappeared, but Webster and Barker claim that

> Such evidence as exists suggests the date was somewhere between *c* A.D. 500 and the mid seventh century. The whole complex seems once again to have been systematically dismantled — there was no evidence of fire or other violent destruction or hurried evacuation. It may be that the city, with its vast perimeter, was too large to be

defended by the dwindling numbers of men available and that the whole population moved to another, more easily defensible, site, perhaps one of the hillforts in the vicinity.[89]

This verifies that upon Ochta's entry into Britain, this area would have been politically, administratively, and militarily important, a shrewd selection made by Hengist for his son.

Attention must now focus on the role of the River Severn in this area to further confirm the Wrekin as Mount Bathon. In addition to Little Solsbury Hill lacking firm archaeological evidence during the Arthurian period, one of the other major shortfalls in labeling Bath as the site for the Bathon site is the unfordability of the River Severn in that area. Twenty-three miles directly to the west is the mouth of the Severn, which could be easily traversed by ship from southern Wales. Thirty-three miles to the north is a ford at Gloucester, but that ford is not near the baths or the shadow of a hillfort. The "Dream of Rhonabwy" relates that Arthur's army is crossing a ford shallow enough to keep dry, except that Avaon, son of Taliessin, splashes water on Arthur and the Bishop. Caer Vaddon is very close to the crossing, because by the time Arthur's troops ford the Severn, Arthur was at the base of the hillfort.

The only locales which ideally meet these conditions are the crossings at Wroxeter with the Wrekin hillfort adjacent to it. There is a ford crossing the Severn at Bewdley 25 miles to the southeast, plus important crossings even farther south at Worcester and Gloucester, but two important crossings are situated near Wroxeter. One, a mere mile and a half directly south of the Wrekin, is at Buildwas, "a route that would have connected the Wrekin with sites to the south by means of a ridgeway along Wenlock Edge."[90] The other, Atcham, is the crossing where Telford chose later to build a bridge.[91] These both attest to the importance of placing a legionary fort at Wroxeter to not only control east-west routes, but also to control the river, an indispensable link with the seaway from Bridgwater Bay.

Arthur's crossing of the Severn to fight the battle of Badon could have been at either location, but Buildwas seems the most likely for reasons that Graham Webster gives totally independent of the Arthurian saga. In explaining the layout of the Roman roads of the region and importance of controlling the River Severn and its crossing points, Webster talks about supply routes, military and civilian transport, mining and timbering, and then makes an important observation:

> Finally, there is the other military road plunging into the heart of central Wales up the Severn Valley to the forts at Forden Gaer and Caersws, which was a nodal point for the routes controlling this great central mountain massif.[92]

He mentions Caersws several more times, each emphasizing the importance of this location in the general scheme of the area. He writes, too, that "The network as at present so imperfectly known leaves enormous gaps, like that in the rectangle Wroxeter, Caersws, Caer Gai, and Chester." He then infers that "such

The River Severn in the vicinity of Wroxeter and the Wrekin.

Drawing 1. The walled city of Wroxeter as it may have looked in the early third century, by Ivan Lapper. Copyright English Heritage, #A900156.

1=Dumnonia   2=Dyfed   3=Cornovii   4=Hwicce

5=West Saxon   6=Dalriada

Map 13. Present-day counties, overlaid with Arthurian-age territories. Note the heavy concentration in the south-central area called the heartland.

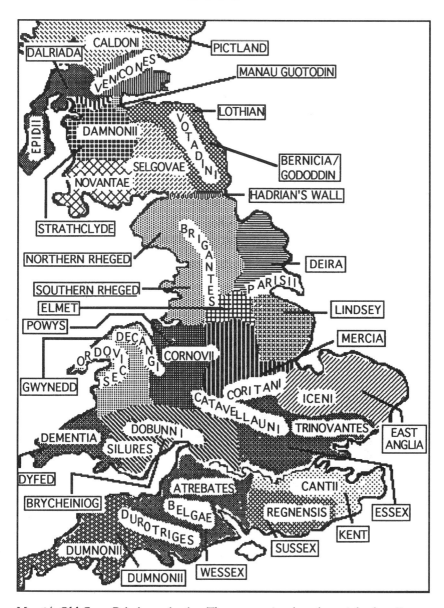

Map 14. Old Great Britain territories. The names printed on the mainland are Roman names for the territories used for the first century A.D. The names in the boxes are the territories of the fifth to seventh centuries A.D. With this overlay it is possible to pinpoint a territory during Arthurian times even though earlier Roman names might be used.

Drawing 2. The basilica (palaestra) of the public baths at Wroxeter, a conjectural reconstruction by Ivan Lapper. Copyright English Heritage, #A900161.

a road [as that for transporting copper] ... may also have had another connection with Caersws along the north side of the valley."[93] These comments point out the importance of Caersws in Wales as a nucleus of activity protecting the northern central section of Wales and show that it ranked in importance with Wroxeter and Chester in a rectangular plot of the territory.

This leads to a reverse speculation. At this point, there should be no doubt about Arthur's destination in his confrontation with Osla at Bathon. Where, though, would his point of origin be? The "Dream of Rhonabwy" narrates that after the truce, Arthur was returning to Cornwall, but both Cornwall and Cornovii are vast provinces with no specific clues for a point of origin. It is a certainty that Arthur is not coming from Cornwall or anywhere east of the meandering Severn, because of distance and time, and he had no reason to cross the Severn to reach the Wrekin. His point of origin, then, would have to be south of the Severn as it makes its east-west arc, and west of it in its north-south flow. Caersws falls within the realm of probability; there is a small, east-west, three-mile section of Roman road near Caersws, tilting slightly to the north, and an arrow following that path leads almost directly to Buildwas, where Arthur would have to cross the Severn.

However, just about any site in Wales or the western midlands would be a probability. There is no indication in the "Dream of Rhonabwy" how far Arthur has had to travel; there is only the clue that Arthur wants to be at Bathon by noon. To echo Webster, the network of information is so imperfect with enormous gaps that labeling Caersws as Arthur's point of origin is sheer speculation based on intuition. Kerry, only six miles to the east and slightly to the south of Caersws, is an even better possibility, since it is south of the River Severn and could be associated with Celli Wig just as well as Kelly Rounds is.

The proof, however, points to Viroconium and the Wrekin as the baths and the hillfort of Badon. Webster provides more information about the Wrekin:

> Working from the old Welsh name of the Wrekin, Cair Guricon, and the later Anglo-Saxon form, Wreocen, Professor Kenneth Jackson has suggested Uriconon as a possibility, changed by the Romans, for ease of pronunciation and with a proper Latin ending, to Viroconium.[94]

Following the same pattern of Wall-by-Lichfield borrowing its proper name Cair Luit Coyt from a neighboring site, this name, Viroconium, was then applied to the nearby legionary fortress, but the original name can be attributed to the Wrekin. Both the Wrekin and Wroxeter, then, appear as Cair Guricon in Nennius' list of major cities in the whole of Britain, stressing even further the importance of this region.

O'Sullivan cites Baring-Gould and Fisher in relating that "Badon was a defeat suffered by the nascent kingdom of the Gewisse in Hampshire under Cerdic and Cynric"[95] and assigned it a date of A.D. 520. This single statement contains several truths: it was a defeat, it was suffered by the nascent kingdom of the Gewissae, and Cerdic was a Gewissi king. Three other claims are wrong: the Gewissae/Hwicce/Hyrpe territory covered a much vaster area in the midlands (Cornovii and eastern Wales), and did not take place in the Hampshire area of the south; it has been resolved that *Creoda* was Cerdic's son, not Cynric; and the date is wrong because Baring-Gould and Fisher did not adapt the *Annales Cambriae* date by a lunar cycle. And lastly, three other items have to be clarified. One is that the term Gewissae embraces Saxon compatriots and therefore Cerdic is considered a Saxon/Briton involved in internecine strife. The second is that by "nascent" the authors are talking about a province that had been founded approximately 60 years earlier. Third, Cerdic is defeated in the conflict, but he is not killed; he lives to engage Arthur in another battle.

O'Sullivan also points out that "the *Chronicle* says nothing about Badon."[96] Again, this is true, because the *Chronicle* is interested in recording Saxon successes and victories, not their defeats. But even so, the manuscript provides a great deal of inferential evidence. In 494–495 Cerdic arrives at Cerdicesora, in the Gewissae territory, although it is not accurate to say that he came from the mainland of Europe. In 500 he sails to the western area of Britain known in Ethelwerd's time as Wessex. This marked encroachment upon Briton soil and culminated with the Battle of Badon.

To recapitulate: the narration leading up to the Battle of Mount Bathonis is as follows. According to Nennius, once an alliance between Hengist and Vortigern is forged, Hengist sends for his son Octha who goes north to the region of Wroxeter, the Wrekin, and Wall-by-Lichfield to war against the Irish who have been encroaching upon the Cornovian territory abandoned by the Romans. The alliance between Vortigern and the Saxons disintegrates, and the Briton king solicits the aid of Cunedda not only to curb the influx of the Irish but to stem the Saxon expansion. Internecine wars ravage Britain over several decades that witness the massacre of Vortigern's council, the eventual deaths of Vortimer, Vortigern, Horsa, and Hengist. Octha assumes the leadership of the Saxons almost simultaneously with Arthur's rise to the kingship after Vortigern's deposal. Arthur and the Saxons struggle for supremacy of the island, the fortunes of war leaning first one way and then the other, until the battle of Bathon.

The "Dream of Rhonabwy" picks up the tale from there. Arthur leaves his fortress and travels to the east. On an islet near the ford across the Severn, Arthur awaits the assembly of his massive army where Avaon, son of Taliessin is reprimanded for splashing water on the king. As Iddawg and his rider Rhonabwy reach the middle of the ford, they turn and survey the Severn Valley. Arthur crosses, and the troops amass at the base of Bathon by noon, in order to fight against Osla Big Knife. The battle ebbs and flows until Osla Big Knife asks for and is granted a truce to the end of the month and a fortnight. Arthur leaves with a retinue that wishes to follow him to "Cornwall" and all are to meet Arthur at Bathon at the end of the truce. Other sources, historical and literary, reveal that the truce fails, the battle at Bathon resumes, and the Britons are victorious. Interestingly, the resolution of date discrepancies between the Preface and *Chronicle* marked Octha's death-year at 497, the identical year set by this text for the battle of Badon, a strong implication that Octha was killed during the siege after the truce. This Briton victory is an auspicious turning point because it dislodges the Saxons from their entrenched position. It is a dawn of hope for the beleaguered Briton empire.

Chapter 6
The Geography of Camlann

The Heartland

In Arthuriana, the term "heartland" has been used in conflicting ways. The *Anglo-Saxon Chronicle* relates in entry 449 that Hengist informed the German Saxons of the "excellence of the land," evidently describing the southeast section of the island, in Kent. The land was eventually referred to as the "heartland," but the term seems improperly applied. Traditionally, Hengist has been understood as the leader during Saxon *Adventus* #1 instead of *Adventus* #2 carrying over into #3, thus creating the misconception that Hengist is associated with Kent. The "heartland" soon came to be linked to the figure of Arthur in south-central Britain, also part of the former Roman civil district with Silchester as its hub and locations such as South Cadbury, Glastonbury, and Badbury Rings acquiring Arthurian connections.

However, the Arthurian "heartland" has become obscured. Because of the overwhelming evidence that the *Historia Brittonum*, the *De Excidio*, and even entries in the *Anglo-Saxon Chronicle* are Welsh in nature, Arthur's heartland shifted slightly to the north and west. The circumference included Cirencester as the hub, Viroconium as Rome's significant legacy, Kerry as Arthur's court, Wall-by-Lichfield as Octha's first settlement, and the entire Cornovii territory as a tempestuous battleground for the Britons and English Saxons. History blends with literary tradition, and instead of Badbury Rings or Bath, the Wrekin emerges as the location for the *Annales Cambriae's* most crucial entry.

Judging from the archaeological data showing the Wansdyke as a defensive system protecting the south, and the history relayed by the *Historia Brittonum*, the action shifted once more to the south-central part of the island and across the channel to the mainland. While Britain was being assaulted, their leaders were at the same time trying to stem the Saxon incursions by attacking the source. Their mainland alliances with Gaul, Burgundy, and Rome were at first successful, but with the decay of the Western Empire, the Britons' attempts were doomed

179

to fail. The return to the island and the victory at Badon reversed the destructive tide. The English Saxons, after their defeat and retreat, sought aid from the German Saxons, and a fresh round of battles and conflicts continued for the next two decades. The "heartland" became even more obscure.

Camlann's role is even more perplexing to unravel than Badon's. Both the *De Excidio* and the *Historia* are weak in their inferences, and the *Annales Cambriae*, the only source to supply the word, offers nothing beyond the date and Medraut's name alongside Arthur's. The only anomalous clues come from the *Anglo-Saxon Chronicle*. By looking at the broad, historical picture, it is possible to spin a gossamer filament connecting Camlann with one of two tentative locations.

If the *Chronicle* entries for the Arthurian period from 449 to 560 are arranged on a continuum with the Camlann date as a chronological demarcation point and the Wansdyke as a geographic one, the two separate segments do manifest two distinctive locales. Of the fourteen entries between 449 and 508, after misplacements, doublets and unrelated events have been purged, eleven entries remain. Six[1] of that number signify northern locations, specifically Welsh, two[2] are dubious, and three[3] are southern. Of the ten entries between 527 and 560, after doublets and unrelated events have been extracted, seven entries remain. Four[4] of that number signify southern locations, one[5] is northern, and two[6] are dubious. From this division it is obvious that events prior to the Battle of Camlann are mainly concentrated in the north, but after Arthur's death, the infiltration begins in the south.

The specifics of some of the entries support the generalizations. Although the entry for 449 was listed as noncommittal, Hengist and Horsa as the leaders were also involved in the second *Adventus*, and their role was to fight against the Picts and Irish invading from the north; logic dictates that this could not be accomplished if Kent was their base. The battle in 455 was fought at Agælesthrep, which Bede places in "orientalibus Cantiae." The misidentification of *Cantiae* as the Kentish kingdom has already been pointed out.

In this instance several intriguing pieces of information coincide. There is a small village by the name of Agglethorpe, near the southern fringes of the old Northumbrian and Deira territories. Over the centuries, this site has slipped into oblivion, but at the end of the Arthurian era it was just reaching its historical significance. Plummer pointed out that "-threp" means "edge" or "brink,"[7] which could refer to the boundary of the Pictish territory, or the area subjected to continuous Pictish raids. By itself this deduction is far-fetched, but in Bede's work Agælesthrep is identified as "eastern Kent." Agglethorpe in northern Britain is about 30 miles east of the Kent river, which flows through Kendal and into the Irish Sea nine miles to the south.

Additionally, Agglethorpe is not as isolated as it first seems. It is a mere seven miles to Catterick Bridge, the Cataractonium of Roman times which had sprung from the site of the original fort. Just as Viroconium was occupied by the natives after the Roman withdrawal, Cataractonium with its massive ramparts was a perfect fortification for the local tribes. This historical site entered literary tradition as Catraeth through the *Gododdin* of Aneirin. In praise of a Gododdin warrior who is godlike in battle, Aneirin alludes to an Arthur, the son of Aedan who was a Scottish chieftain. This is the figure dubbed Arthur of Dalriada by Richard Barber. Prior to the event recorded in the *Gododdin*, Catterick as a fortification in the 450s would have been even more formidable than in Aedan's era when he was fighting the Pictish Miathi.

Another curiosity focuses upon Ælle. Scribes from 500 years later, antiquarians after that, and modern scholars have traditionally listed Ælle as a South Saxon, establishing his locale as Sussex in the area of Selsey Bill, the Weald, and Andreida. Yet of the three entries about Ælle — 477, 485, and 491 — only the last uses the term "Briton" as his enemy. The other two use the term "Welsh" and then offer other undoubted Welsh information associated with the Cymry: Cymen and Cymenesora. This by itself might be dismissed as inconsequential, but there is one other item that supports the contention.

That item is expressed well by John Morris; in tracing the movements of the German Saxons, he writes of Ælle's alleged Sussex territory:

> But in West Sussex, the first English [Saxon] graves are more than a hundred years [after Ælle's landing]. ... [T]he earliest English object in the area is a brooch, found in the Roman cemetery of St. Pancras, that dates to the time of Ælle's grandchildren. Its isolation suggests a Saxon woman who lived and died in a British community rather than a Saxon settlement. The absence of pagan burial grounds in west Sussex argues that the English did not reach Chichester until more than a hundred years after Ælle's time.[8]

He mentions the lack of Saxon settlements in western Sussex again later, in referring again to the brooch:

> One brooch ... cannot people an otherwise empty region. In Hampshire, a few fifth-century objects have been found ... but these few objects are more than a generation earlier that any others ... and until they are confirmed by future discoveries they cannot by themselves demonstrate isolated settlement at so early a date.[9]

There is another puzzling aspect about Ælle. He is titled as the first *Bretwalda*, yet he occupies a miniscule niche in Saxon history. The South Saxon house is an obscure kingdom that fades from recognition. This, similar to the lack of West Sussex settlements, likewise confuses Morris:

> Ælle's authority can only have been voluntarily bestowed. At the end of the fifth century, Sussex was the smallest of the southern English kingdoms, but Ælle was the eldest of their kings. These notices suggest that the English force comprised the armies of King, and of the south and west Saxons, under the overall command of Ælle. There is no hint that the Angles took part. Had they done so, it is unlikely that the high claims of their kings could have admitted the supremacy of Ælle, however senior his age. Moreover, if East Anglian expansion had been checked by Arthur's victory in Lincolnshire, recent defeat is likely to have deterred them from further adventure.[10]

Because his kingdom is small and so far away from the chaos and conflict occurring at the time, the questions arise of why he was one of only eight kings in the Saxon histories bestowed with the honor of *Bretwalda*, and how, if he held imperium over the English, he was able to assert his military might.

In relation to this passage, "Arthur's victories in Lincolnshire" is an allusion to Arthur's second through fifth battles as listed in the *Historia* as in the country of Linnuis, which Morris has interpreted as Lincolnshire battles fought in the late 470s and early 480s. Arthur's battles at the River Dubglas, however, are extremely difficult if not impossible to pinpoint, which hardly seems justifiable as reasons for Ælle's inactivity and the infrequent reference to him in Saxon history. The assumption, too, that the East Anglians were not involved in the conflicts of the period is weak. The Ælle entries in the *Chronicle* heavily suggest, in addition to this king being labeled as a *Bretwalda*, that his activities are somewhere in the midlands. Gildas Badonicus writes of this specific period as a time of continuous internal conflict, with victories going first one direction and then another; the East Anglians under the generic term of English Saxons more than likely *would* have been involved.

One last generalization that suggests the limitation of Camlann to two possible locales is Plummer's comment about the connection of Bernician and Wessex pedigrees. As commentary on entry 547, he writes:

> [The entry] marks the beginning of the kingdom of Bernicia; the beginning of that of Diera is marked by Ælle's accession. Owing to the fact that both kingdoms were ultimately united in the line of Ida, he is often spoken of as the founder and King of Northumbria. ... It may be noted that neither Bede nor the *Chronicle* give even *traditions* with reference to the conquest of Northumbria; nor does either of them give any countenance to the later idea that Ida came from the continent.[11]

Of the genealogical association, he points out that

> It is noteworthy that the Bernician genealogy is traced up to the son and grandson of Woden from whom the house of Wessex comes. In the later part of the pedigree also West-Saxon names, Cuthwine, Cutha, Ceowulf, occur. We know too little of the settlement of Northumbria to say whether any historical fact underlies this tradition.[12]

His allusion to Ælle in entry 560 is to a person evidently different from Ælle the South Saxon, and although there is a genealogy for this second Ælle of Deira, there is no association or link given in any other genealogical tracts between the two Ælles. Only one other enticing tidbit surfaces about Ælle, the alleged king of Sussex: at the entry for 827 in all *Chronicle* manuscripts except one (Cotton MS. Domitian A viii), he is listed as the king of Sussex, but in Manuscript F he is listed as a king of the West Saxons.[13] This could be nothing more than a scribal error, but if it is beyond that, Ælle as a *Bretwalda* and as a king preceding Cerdic makes more sense.

The connection between Northumbria and the West Saxon dynasty is only slightly more definitive. When the West Saxon tree branches after Cynric, two of the three splits are Ceawlin and Cutha. Cutha also appears in the Ceawlin division because of the possibility that this could be a shortened form of Cuthwine or Cuthwulf. Plummer's reference, however, is to early origins, Bældæg and Brand, who are named in both the West Saxon and the Bernician dynasties. These names, though, are too close to the mythological source of Woden to be of much historical significance.

The only abstruse link with Camlann generated from these excerpts is that from the Cornovii territory, the English Saxons were pushed both north towards Hadrian's Wall and south near Gloucester and Cirencester after the Badon victory at the Wrekin. The internal conflicts over the next two decades were waged over the intervening territories. According to the *Historia*, the English Saxons sought help from the continent, importing German kings to rule over them. When the two sides finally engaged in the fatal battle, it could have been either near Hadrian's Wall because that was the English Saxon homeland, or at Charford in 519 as suggested in the *Anglo-Saxon Chronicle*, because the Britons were trying to stem the influx of German Saxons. The latter possibility means that there would be an emphatic shift of attention from the midlands to the southern heartland.

The Annales Cambriae

Of the many geographic sites that have elicited controversy in Arthuriana, Camlann probably remains the most obscure and ambiguous, obscure because the meaning of the name Camlann is veiled, and ambiguous because of the multiple roots for the term. To fuel the mystery, particularly since it is the battle in which Arthur is mortally wounded, Nennius does not include the Battle of Camlann in his noted list of Arthur's conflicts. Because Gildas does not write of Arthur, he of course does not include Camlann, and because Bede is a close echo of Gildas nothing appears in his writings. Camlann makes its only *historical* appearance in the *Annales Cambriae* where only eight words are devoted to the demise of Arthur:

> an. Gueith Camlann in qua Arthur et Medraut corruerunt, et mortalitas in Brittannia et in Hibernia fuit.[14]

In Chapter 3 the *chronological* determination for Camlann was set at year 518 because of its link with the Battle of Badon in the *Anglo-Saxon Chronicle* and verified by the year 519 in the *Anglo-Saxon Chronicle*. That is, through the use of cardinal years Camlann was validated by a milieu of events leading to a culminating consequence, not in isolation. Likewise, this same process of association should point to the identification of Camlann's location. In isolation, the entry implies succinctly the death of Arthur and another individual named Medraut at the Battle of Camlann. There are no clues of geographic location, Arthur's adversaries, who was on the offensive, or what circumstances surrounded the conflict. Because Medraut is only incidental to this inquiry, attention will focus on the word "Camlann," plus any historical and literary source which can aid in pinpointing the battle's circumstances.

This mystery of Camlann's location has been discussed in some detail by Alcock, who gives the following etymological possibilities:

> It has been suggested that the name might derive from the British *Camboglanna* which would give Camlann in the Middle Welsh. In Early Welsh, however, the form should have been *Camglann,* and therefore if the battle had been entered contemporaneously in an Easter Table we would expect *gueith Camglann.* The fact that we have *gueith camlann* may mean either that there never was a contemporary entry in the Primitive Welsh — and so the credibility of the Arthurian entries in the Welsh Easter Annals would be destroyed — or that, in the process of copying and recopying, some scribe had modernized the spelling.[15]

That the original *Annales* entry was *gueith Camglann* but interpolated as *gueith Camlann* is a reasonable explanation. As evidenced in many other entries, scribal errors, whether deliberate or inadvertent, were common occurrences. The elimination of a "g" might at first seem inconsequential, but its subsequent importance would be immeasurable.

Alcock then continues his connection between *Camboglanna* and Camlann:

> The main reason for favouring *Camboglanna* [as a possible site for Camlann] is that we do know a place of this name, the Roman fort of Birdoswald which stands above the Irthing Valley towards the western end of Hadrian's Wall.[16]

Other scholars in addition to Alcock also suggest Camlann as a derivative of *Camboglanna* and similarly identify Camlann as Birdoswald above the Irthing Valley. Although there have been quite a few proponents for this equation, no one has heretofore justified it by explaining explicit circumstances.

There is a different explanation of a Camlann/*Camboglanna* connection, not as a specific site near Hadrian's Wall, but as an etymological focus upon a general place-name reference. Once again, Alcock supplies the basic, correct information: "*Camboglanna* means 'crooked bank,' *Cambolanda* is 'crooked enclosure.'"[17]

Hence, Camlann is not necessarily a specific reference to Birdoswald, but generically, it is somewhere on the crooked banks of a river. Unfortunately, this is not as gratifying as a precise identification, but combined with material from other sources, this piece of information, that seems at first useless, aids in pinpointing a particular locale, or at least in minimizing substantially the probabilities.

In *The Quest for Arthur's Britain,* Geoffrey Ashe mixes two diverse possibilities in his presentation of Camlann. First, he writes that "the River Camel [in Cornwall near Slaughter Bridge on the river] is often stated to be the scene of the battle of Camlann."[18] Then, on the very next page, he selects — as the best of three possibilities for the Camlann site — Camboglanna in Cumberland, "better

Hadrian's Wall at Camboglanna, looking northward; the midlands Camlann.

than the other two etymologically but perhaps not historically."[19] The first is a reference to literary tradition and Geoffrey of Monmouth, the second a speculation offered by a number of different scholars.

In a different book, *The Discovery of King Arthur*, which embraces the thesis that Arthur was a fifth rather than a sixth century figure, Ashe follows the same pattern of mixing literary tradition and historical speculation without making a clear distinction. After some initial hesitation, he becomes more explicit about the location of Camlann, voicing a different possibility from that in *The Quest for Arthur's Britain*:

> The real location is not clear. *Camlann* probably means "crooked bank," and more than one river has the "crooked" element in its name. The only place called Camlan today is a valley in Merioneth in northwestern Wales with a small river flowing down it.[20]

More than likely, he means that *Camboglanna* (not Camlann) should be defined as "crooked bank," and that Merioneth is the territory adjacent to Gwynedd. He refers to a valley by the name of Camlan — spelled with one "n" rather than two — unlocatable on modern maps, although there is an Afon Gamlan about five miles *north* of Dolgellau.

However, his theory to establish Arthur (and the king's death) in the seventh decade of the fifth century requires that he abandon both the Badon and Camlann entries in the *Annales*. He acknowledges Alcock's support of the Camlann entry in particular, for which afterwards both Alcock and Morris were "savaged by David Dumville," who claimed that "the Welsh matter was worthless as history."[21] Alcock maintained that the Camlann entry, although it appears in the *Annales Cambriae* which generally dates to the tenth century, had a much earlier beginning, which Ashe criticizes by saying that "In the end it has to be recognized that a book like Nennius's, put together so long after the event, *may* give facts but cannot alone be proved to do so."[22] However, this is exactly the trap that Ashe himself falls into by trying to validate a fifth century Arthur mainly through Geoffrey of Monmouth. Monmouth's manuscript is later still than the *Historia* or the *Annales*, which means that no pre–fourteenth century source should be totally discarded.

According to Ashe's innovative proposal, he links *an* Arthur — but not *the* Arthur — to a Camlann 50 or 60 years after the death of *the* Arthur. His disclaimers of Camlann appear in several passages:

1. It [Camlann] hangs in a void, with nothing to show where it came from, no means of checking it against history, and an almost incredible date.[23]
2. No linkage of Arthur's name with Camlann — indeed no Camlann — can be proved before the *Annals* in the tenth century.[24]
3. Here [in Camlann] if anywhere is the case for a second, lesser Arthur, who came to be confused with the first.[25]

The first passage is an interesting charge: Camlann hanging in a void, nothing to show where it comes from, no means of checking it against history, and an almost incredible date. All of what Ashe says is true if a person is establishing a theory which sets Arthur in the *fifth* century. However, from the perspective of a *sixth* century Arthur, everything changes. First, Camlann does not have "an incredible date"; if Arthur is placed at the beginning of the sixth century as stated in the *Annales Cambriae* with the adjustments for discrepancies of the Easter Annals as proposed by Alcock, then Camlann's date is right on target, fitting into an era for Arthur at the beginning of the sixth century. That means it can, in fact, be checked in history, using not only at least eight other entries in the *Anglo-Saxon Chronicle* but also verifying it by a check against the Battle of Badon *and* Gildas' reference to Ambrosius Aurelianus. All of this, of course, indicates that Camlann is not hanging in a void.

The second charge, that Arthur's name is not linked with Camlann any time before the annals of the tenth century, is true, but the very fact that a link is made in the tenth century does not make the link false. As an analogy, we can look at Ashe's own claim of linking his fifth century Arthur to Geoffrey of Monmouth's manuscript of the twelfth century, *plus* his linking Arthur with a manuscript of 1019 about Goeznovius. Historically, then, the best entries we still have are the ones from the *Annales Cambriae*, which is a respected entry in a sea of uncertainties.

In the last citation Ashe asks for a belief in two Arthurs in order to fit the time frame he has postulated with *the* Arthur set in the fifth century; his explanation of "Arthur's men" ties in to this, indicating that the memory of Arthur has people of later generations labeling other men of valor, courage, respect, and leadership as being like Arthur, that is, of having Arthur's venerable qualities. However, there is no need to accept a blend with a second Arthur, or even with "Arthur's men," once the premise is accepted that Arthur existed at the beginning of the sixth century and not at the middle of the fifth century.

Other writers have been faced with the same vexations on Camlann; they have alluded to Camlann using terms like mystifying, mysterious, elusive, enigmatic, obscure. Its possible locale ranges from the very far north, where Bromwich and Goodrich set Arthur, to Slaughter Bridge in Cornwall which appears not only in Monmouth but also in Layamon.[26] It seems to be one of those frustrating mysteries, lost in the mists of time, but prior to Ashe's different hypothesis, none of the scholars (except perhaps Dumville) doubted that Camlann was historically attached to King Arthur.

The Camlann entry in the *Annales Cambriae* is much too significant to discard offhandedly. It is one of only two entries which even gives the name of Arthur, supplying not only a time reference for his death, but also adding parameters for Arthur's life span, proposing the culmination to a sequential development of Arthur's career. It is true that no other historical source verifies this, but these entries do allow a direct and circumstantial connection with the prolific literary material. The etymological connection, then, between Camlann and Camboglanna meaning crooked bank is acceptable, plus the possibility of Camlann being Birdoswald. Both must be explored before moving on to the literary contributions.

Gildas, Nennius, John of Glastonbury

Of the four historical manuscripts being used as references in this text, only the *Annales Cambriae* names the Battle of Camlann. Both Gildas and Nennius slide over that major conflict, which is so crucial not only to the pursuit of Arthur, but as a key occurrence in the history of the period.

Gildas makes reference to it only in passing. In the first paragraph of Section 26 he establishes the victory at the siege of Badon Hill, associating it with his own birth. He then begins the very next paragraph: "But the cities of our land are not populated even now as they once were; right to the present they are deserted, in ruins, and unkempt."[27] It has been established that the writing of the *De Excidio* took place in the year 541, Gildas' reference of "right to the present." The Camlann battle, then, would have taken place 23 years earlier, and why Gildas does not concentrate on it is a mystery.

The key, however, is how he begins this second paragraph following the Badon victory, reflecting a total turnabout of atmosphere and mood. By opening the sentence with the word "But," he is implying, "but the Badon victory was then, and this is now." He refers to a "desperate blow to the island" and "that storm," neither of which can refer to the Badon victory and the jubilation which followed. He adds that

All the controls of truth and justice have been shaken and overthrown, leaving no trace, not even a memory, among the orders I have mentioned: with the exception of a few, a very few.[28]

The only possible disaster he could be referring to is the crushing defeat suffered by the Britons. Truth and justice, embodied by King Arthur, have been overthrown, and only a very few even remember that era. Most of the people (including the orders of kings, public and private persons, priests and churchmen) are ignorant of that storm, and the age that followed the Battle of Camlann has experienced only the calm of the present. They are aware only that external wars have stopped but civil ones continue.

Even Gildas' reference to the cessation of foreign wars has strong overtones. There are no longer conflicts with the continental (Germanic) Saxons, but there are still internal squabblings among the victors of Camlann. Gildas then turns to his next subject in sections 27 through 36, the vitriolic attack on the kings, the five tyrants who in his day ruled the five major provinces of Britain. As with so many other items in the *De Excidio*, Gildas does not use a proper name for Camlann, but he describes the event.

Nennius is even more oblique than Gildas about Camlann. He devotes some time to Arthur's 12 victorious campaigns, but then briefly writes that after the Saxons had been defeated in all these battles, they sought help from the mainland, vastly increased their numbers on the island, and imported kings to rule over them in Britain. Hence, about 20 years of history is compressed into one sentence. This sentence, however, takes on an even greater significance later in this chapter in defining the location for Camlann.

John of Glastonbury's *Cronica* is difficult to categorize because it falls into the shadowy realm between history and literary tradition. Its intent is not the same as literature, but at the same time his material draws heavily on Geoffrey of Monmouth, with some flavoring of the *Mabinogion*. In that same shadowy realm, he draws upon material from William of Malmsbury — not considered fiction either — but unfortunately he used a version of Malmsbury's work that had been heavily interpolated at Glastonbury Abbey. Another of his major sources was Adam of Domerham, whom Scott exposed as one of the probable manipulators of Malmsbury's work. He also echoes Nennius, Giraldus Cambrensis, and Ralph Higden.

Of the Battle of Camlann, he writes that King Arthur had sailed to Gaul, leaving Mordred in charge, who then tried to grab the kingdom in Britain. John reports that

> since [Mordred] feared Cerdic alone, in order to gain Cerdic's favor he gave him seven provinces. ... Cerdic agreed upon these, fortified his provinces with newly arriving English, and was crowned in the pagan fashion at Winchester, while Mordred became king over the Britons at London. But King Arthur ... pursued his nephew Mordred ... and killed him.[29]

At a glance, this seems like material which John had borrowed from Geoffrey of Monmouth, but upon closer inspection there are several oddities. For one, Monmouth does not use the name Cerdic; he uses the name Cherdic only once, and that is as a Saxon companion of Octha and Ebissa. To reflect the Monmouth story, John would have had to draw a parallel between Cerdic and Chelric, a Saxon leader different from Cheldric. That seems unlikely, particularly since there are other variations in the story.

Monmouth's Chelric is in league with Mordred, but whereas Chelric's bribe is Kent and Britain from the River Humber to the Scottish border, Cerdic in John's account receives all of the provinces along the southern coast from east to west except Hampshire. It does not seem likely that John would have combined Monmouth and some other source. In addition, there are two other perplexing variations. In John's account Mordred expresses a fear of Cerdic, and John makes no reference to either Cerdic's death or the Saxon's demise at Camblam.

John names Cerdic two more times in conjunction with Arthur. In the second passage he writes that

> The kingdom of Wessex began about the year of grace 495 under Cerdic and his son Cynric. In the eleventh year of Cerdic, when Utherpendragon, the brother of Aurelius Ambrosius, had been killed with poison, his son Arthur, a youth of fifteen years, began to reign over the Britons.[30]

The first sentence could have been borrowed from either the Preface or from the *Chronicle* entry for 495, except that the Preface states explicitly that the kingdom of *Wessex* was established six years after Cerdic's landing in 494, in the year 500. The entry for 519 in the *Chronicle* mentions Cerdic succeeding to the kingdom of *West Saxons*, suggesting that Wessex and West Saxon are two separate kingdoms. Even more unusual is the second sentence, not only linking Cerdic and Arthur but providing some kind of a time frame. The names of Aurelius Ambrosius and Utherpendragon, plus Arthur's being 15 at his coronation, suggests Monmouth's writings. But John supplies the additional information that in Cerdic's eleventh year, Arthur began his reign. If that is applied to floruits for Cerdic established earlier in this text, that means that Arthur began his reign in 461. This in itself piques one's curiosity, since the common date of 460 is given for Ambrosius Aurelianus' successes against the Saxons which turns the tide of destruction.

In a third of John's passages, he again links Cerdic to Arthur:

> King Arthur fought mightily against the Saxons and wore them down; he waged twelve battles against them, conquering and routing them in all twelve instances. Often he struggled with Cerdic, who, if one month Arthur vanquished him, rose up the next fiercer for the fight. Finally, when Arthur tired of the conflict, he accepted Cerdic's fealty and gave him Hampshire and Somerset, which Cerdic called Wessex.[31]

The first sentence here sounds like the introduction to the *Historia*'s battlelist. Only one other early writer, Ralph Higden, makes a connection between Cerdic and Arthur, but John records them as enemies and further adds that Arthur grants the Saxon two territories as part of a truce. Whether or not deliberate, the two territories listed here are the two not included as the other seven provinces which Cerdic received from Mordred later, which would make Cerdic's holdings all of southern Britain.

John does not name a different unknown source or earlier antiquarian for his information, but he conveys a link between Arthur and Cerdic at the battle of Camlann that is not suggested by any other historical document. As a bonus, he provides Cerdic's age at the time of Arthur's coronation.

The Anglo-Saxon Chronicle

In addition to the *Chronicle's* having been used for locking in a date, it can also help determine a *geographic* location for Camlann from two entries which provide place-names, 495 and 519. Two other entries, 508 and 514, were passed over because of their spurious nature. Entry 495 records a landing at *Cerdicesora* in both the Preface and the *Chronicle*, with the latter adding that Cerdic fought against the *Welsh*. Entry 519 lists the landing at *Cerdicesford* and a battle against the *Britons*. The important distinction between "Welsh" and "Briton" has already been discussed, and in this context, entry 495 suggests a battle somewhere in Welsh territory, while entry 519 is interpreted as Charford in the south-central region near Southampton Water.

Most modern scholars — including Morris, Ashe, and Alcock — are silent about Cerdicesora versus Cerdicesford. Ekwall, like all scholars, equates Cerdicesford with Charford but stops short of suggesting the equation of Cerdicesford and Cerdicesora by simply mentioning that both are eponyms of the Saxon king.[32] Ethelwerd accepts Charford as Cerdicesford, but lists Cerdicesora as an "unidentified place."[33] Because Plummer must pay attention to such a myriad of details, he simply observes that *Cerdices ford* for *Cerdices leag* is peculiar to Manuscript E[34]; he does not say, however, that this is a different place mistaken for Charford as a reference. And Wade-Evans sends a mixed message, although he does not confront the issue directly. In a footnote,[35] he writes about Cerdic of the Gewissae at Cerdicesora on the Hampshire coast. Cerdic as a Gewissae would set the locale for Cerdicesora in the Hwicce territories adjacent to *Wales* while Charford on the Hampshire coast would suggest the eponym Cerdicesford.

This text subscribes to the belief that the equations Cerdicesora = Welsh and Cerdicesford = Briton are not attributable to scribal sloppiness. Both are based on a distinction between the two terms that lasted through Arthur's time. This means there is a widespread geographic difference between the Battle of Badon and the Battle of Camlann. Cerdic fits into the milieu of Badon because he would have been a key figure in the midlands, as Cunedda's son and Octha's compatriot. His landing at Cerdicesora could have been anywhere on the shores of the River Severn, perhaps an intrusion into Welsh territory from his homeland in Cornovii.

The distinction between Welsh and Briton leads to the necessity of one other important sidetrack because the term "Saxon" is no longer adequate or accurate. The Romans referred to barbarians from the continent "invariably and indiscriminately as "Saxones,"[36] but at this point in the Arthurian saga, the term has become too generic in referring to Arthur's enemies. Wade-Evans has pointed out the confusion between *continental* Saxons (Germans) and Saxons in Britain (the English).[37] In order to make a distinction, the Welsh invented the term *Saxoniaid* to refer to continental Saxons, while *Saeson* was the normal word for English.[38] The problem is compounded when the "Saxons" (Saeson) are intermixed with the Britons (or more accurately the Welsh) and then referred to as the Gewissae. Historically, Arthur is fighting the Saxons, but no distinction is made between the continental Saxons and the Saxons who had been settled in Britain for several generations, intermixing with the natives. In this text, the appellation German Saxons for continentals, and English Saxons for the mixed race of Roman, Welsh, Briton, Gewissae, or Votadini, including Cerdic, should be workable to denote the difference.

That Badon was fought in the Wroxeter vicinity and that Camlann might have been fought near the Roman fort of Birdoswald seem to support each other. After the English Saxons were defeated at Mount Badon (Wroxeter) and driven out, these expatriated people could have gone to several different possible places. For one, they could have simply *retreated* 150 miles to the north, and settled near Manau Guotodin, suggesting that they were returning to their "homeland" *prior* to the Cunedda migration. However, this location — beyond the Antonine Wall, between the Firth of Forth and the Firth of Tay and almost 250 miles north from Badon battlesite — is not very plausible. This territory would have been Cunedda's initial tribal homeland, but it would not have been the fatherland for his English Saxon compatriots.

A second, more convincing possibility would be that Cunedda and his displaced English-Saxon allies could have settled near Camboglanna at Carlisle, Cunedda's first settlement *after* his southern migration. Material from Taliessin seems to support this contention quite well. In the *Book of Taliessin*, pages 69–70, what is credited as a genuine poem of his relates that Cunedda's name is associated with Kaer Liwelydd, which scholars label as Carlisle.[39] Upon Cunedda's migration from the far northern province of Manau Guotodin, Carlisle becamse his first fortification for driving the Irish from Wales. It would therefore be logical that his progeny (and perhaps his allies) would look to Carlisle, a stone's throw from the Roman fort and Camboglanna, as their homeland, not Manau of the more distant past; Manau in these later years would have blended into Pictish territory.[40]

Camlann equated to Camboglanna seems defensible for another reason. The ancient manuscripts label this battle as a conflict between the Britons (or Welsh) and the Saxons. Camboglanna at first seems unlikely to be occupied by Saxons at this early date, but if the term "Saxon" is limited to mean "English Saxon," then the equation becomes more likely. The English Saxons would have been occupying the adjacent territory of the midlands dating to Vortigern's invitation in the third decade of the fifth century.

A third possibility is Alcock's interpretation. He uses Gildas' reference to the English Saxons' "return to their homeland" as the lands in the east of the island which they had already settled, presumably in Kent and the Isle of Thanet.[41] Based upon all the references supplied (albeit erroneously) by the headings in the *Historia Brittonum*, this retreat would be logical: Hengist and Octha were Kentish kings, Vortigern held power over these kingdoms, and the English Saxons were granted rights to these territories.

Nevertheless, the fourth possibility — that the Battle of Camlann was fought in the vicinity of Charford — is by far the most convincing. The crucial clarification comes from the Nennius manuscript, which is very explicit on this point. In the sentence immediately following the one about the Briton victory at Badon, the *Historia Britonnum* relates that

> When they were defeated in all their campaigns, the English sought help from Germany, and continually and considerably increased their numbers, and they brought over their kings from Germany to rule over them in Britain.[42]

Nennius uses (or, more accurately, copies) the word *Germania*, Germany, twice, plus the term *English* for either Saxons or English Saxons, making the crucial distinction between continental Saxons and English Saxons. The term *Germany* as a reference to the continental Saxons is used in two other places of the manuscript, once in Chapter 31 at the beginning of Vortigern's reign when three keels come from there, and again in one of the spurious chapters, Chapter 43, when Vortimer expels the English Saxons and Hengist must send envoys to Germany to carry back more fighting men.

As further support, the *Chronicle of Æthelweard* reads like a blend of Nennius and the *Anglo-Saxon Chronicle*. Nennius is reflected in Ethelwerd's description of Hengist and Horsa's voyage from a place called Germany, and once the Britons break the treaty, the Saxons send envoys back to their German homeland for reinforcements. Ethelwerd then shifts smoothly to a slightly different version of the *ASC* entry for 449. He writes that the immigrants to Britain came from three provinces of Germany and were called the Saxons, Angles, and Jutes.[43] Then in entry 477 he also records that Ælle came to Britain from Germany with his three sons.[44]

There is no doubt from these manuscripts that after the stunning defeat at Badon, the English Saxons were forced to recruit new allies from across the Channel in their original fatherland. Cerdic was driven from the island, and in the intervening years between Badon and Camlann, he recruited a large army from Germany, the continental Saxon homeland, and assaulted the island, landing at Cerdicesford after sailing up the Southampton Water. A great battle ensued, and Cerdic finally inherited the kingdom of the West Saxons, a territory which extended from the south coast into the midlands.

The second series of solid evidence comes from the *ASC*. One, the distinction between Cerdicesora and Cerdicesford, has already been touched upon. The prelude to the battle of Badon in 495 refers to the Welsh and therefore a location of Cerdicesora which would be along some western sea- or river-shore, which the chronicle by Ethelwerd supports. But the record for 518 lists a battle against the Britons near the Southampton Water on the southern coast. Secondly, the

Chronicle probably would not have listed Cerdic and his progeny as Saxon if he had not had ties to the continental fatherland. If Camlann had been fought near Hadrian's Wall, the great victory would have been listed for the Gewissae in some other island manuscript, but because Cerdic's recruitment was from Germanic kings and warriors, he eked out a niche for himself in Saxon history, chronicled in a Saxon manuscript as a Saxon compatriot and a West Saxon king. As suggested earlier, an interesting contrast can be drawn between entries prior to Badon and those after Camlann. In the 30 years prior to Badon, Saxon conflicts against the *Welsh* are mentioned five times. During approximately the same period of time after the Camlann conflict, the entries, with the notable exception of Ida, shift to the south, naming *Britons* as the enemy and southern geographic locations: the Isle of Wight, Searoburh, Wiltshire. Punctuated by a peaceful reprieve, the atmosphere and mood, in addition to the geographic location, changed from the Britons' decisive victory to their devastating defeat.

Ethelwerd agrees in his chronicle with this viewpoint of a southern Camlann. At the entry for 519 he records:

> ... Cerdic and Cynric attacked the Britons at the place called Cerdicesforda [Charford] on the river Auene [Avon], and in the same year they began to rule.[45]

The addition "on the River Auene" is not part of the *ASC*, leaving no doubt that Cerdicesforda, if equated with Charford on the Avon, must be in the southern heartland. Plummer's verification also lists Charford "below Salisbury on the Wilts and the Hants Avon River."[46]

Being on the banks of two rivers, Charford easily fits the etymological description for *Cambolanda*, "crooked bank," as listed by scholars; the two rivers flow directly south from Salisbury to the English Channel, and even a cursory glance at a map shows how much the rivers meander in their courses. Moreover, its location, in keeping with the Nennius information, shifts the action back to the heartland, where penetration would be made by the continental (German) Saxons.

Alcock's portrayal of Camlann is equally applicable whether the site is Camboglanna or Charford. He writes: "The traditions which grew up around Camlann mark it out as a battle not against invading pagan Saxons, but as an internecine strife of Briton against Briton."[47] The essence of his statement is true; only the terminology is different. The motives for the Battle of Camlann are the same as those of Badon. The enemy is technically not an outside nation, but the internecine English Saxons warring with a faction linked by ancestry, a kind of civil war representing divisive ideologies or opposing motives. By Alcock's use of the word "traditions" he means literary tradition, specifically the Welsh Triads and Geoffrey of Monmouth as the earliest main sources. Alcock's citation, plus details gleaned from literary material, appear in a later segment on Arthur.

Arthur's final battle, then, could have taken place at any of these locations. All of these interpretations of the "homeland" are possibilities, but most likely is reflected in the *Chronicle* entry indicating that *Cerdic* fought the *Britons* at *Cerdicesford*.

Literary Tradition

Alcock believes that "The traditions which grew up around Camlann mark it out as a battle not against invading pagan Saxons, but as an internecine strife of Briton against Briton,"[48] and Ashe thinks the Welsh matter makes Camlann sound more like a domestic feud and downfall of equals rather than a subordinate's rebellion.[49] These beliefs support the tenet that Arthur's enemy was therefore at least quasi–Briton, or stated differently, of English Saxon heritage. Literary tradition focuses specifically upon Cerdic as the leader, a Briton with Saxon predispositions and, similar to Octha, Arthur's former comrade. Camlann, then, is the internal conflict which closes the chapter of post–Roman, Briton history.

When Ashe writes of the "Welsh matter," he is probably referring to the Welsh Triads. Rachel Bromwich introduces the Triads in this way:

> It is the Welsh alone, however, who seem to have made a systematic use of triads as a means of putting the materials of heroic story into catalogue form; several manuscript collections are preserved, containing the names of national Welsh heroes of early times. ... [I]t is clear that the Welsh historical and romantic triads are based on the debris of saga literature, the product of the professional story-tellers known as *cyfarwyddiaid*.[50]

She characterizes them as historical and romantic, a mixture of mythological characters and semi-historical persons, important because "their contents bear marks of a high antiquity."[51] She then gives an explicit description:

> The thirteenth-century MS. Peniarth 16 contains the oldest collection of triads (except for a fragment of "Triads of Horses" in the Black Book of Carmarthen). The White Book of Rhydderch (c.1325) contains a fragment of a much fuller collection, which has been entirely preserved in the Red Book of Hergest (c.1400).[52]

Like O'Sullivan, she cautions against the collections of Iolo Morgannwg, but throughout the reliable versions, the increasing popularity of Arthur and of Arthurian material is evident. In the Red Book of Hergest, some of which shows influences from Geoffrey of Monmouth, two of the triads mention Medraut, who appeared only in the *Annales Cambriae* entry. He becomes a significant figure here because his raid on Arthur's court and his treatment of Gwenhwyfar might have a bearing on Camlann.

Camlann occurs in three distinctive segments called the "Welsh Triads": one of the Three Harmful Blows of the Island of Britain which precipitated the Battle of Camlann, one of the Three Unfortunate Counsels of the Island of Britain which describes Arthur's threefold division of his troops with Medraut at the Battle of Camlann, and one of the Three Futile Battles, the worst because a quarrel between Gwenhwyfar and Gwennhwyfach brought about the Battle of Camlann. In the last citation, Ifor Williams, through a correction in the Three Fierce Handslaps [Three Harmful Blows] suggests that Gwynnhwyfach should be emended to Medraut.

Even though their compilations are a later literary source than *The History of the Kings of Britain*, Monmouth might have had access to some earlier origi-nals, but there is no support for this supposition. Ashe writes that "Geoffrey of Monmouth could have got the bare name of the fatal battle, Camlann, from the Welsh matter."[53] He then guesses that Monmouth "probably did [get the Cam-lann information from Welsh matter], by way of Walter or otherwise,"[54] but it is unclear if Ashe is referring to the very ancient book.

Since there is no evidence that Geoffrey of Monmouth gleaned his infor-mation from an earlier, historical Welsh source, this means that the information comes directly from Geoffrey of Monmouth, as a main literary source. Before briefly recounting the tale, though, some clarifications must be made about Mon-mouth's characters.

Monmouth does not use the name Cerdic anywhere in his manuscript. As he does with Ambrosius Aurelianus becoming Aurelius Ambrosius, and Guitolini (Vitalinus) becoming Guithelinus, and Octha becoming Octa, Cerdic is masked as three possible characters. Cherdic appears only once, as a Saxon companion to Octa and Ebissa who are summoned to Britain by Hengist. This means that Monmouth is the only early source who links Cerdic and Octha as comrades who went to Wall, which is near a wall.

He also makes a distinction between Cheldric and Chelric, who may also blend with Cherdic in Monmouth's confusion of characters. Cheldric is a Saxon leader and Arthur's enemy at the battle at Bath. The events leading up to the Battle of Bath, according to Monmouth, are just as interesting as the battle itself. Arthur besieges the Saxons at Kaerluideoit, the city of Cair Luit Coyt which both John Morris and Graham Webster identify as Wall-by-Lichfield (or Wall-by-the-wall), but which Monmouth places somewhere in Lincolnshire. The Saxons abandon the city and flee, with Arthur in pursuit. Monmouth then inserts the Battle of Caledon Wood, and the Saxons surrender, agreeing to return to Germany with nothing but their boats after relinquishing all their gold and silver (overtones of the tribute of baskets of gold and silver given to Arthur at the Battle of Vaddon in the "Dream of Rhonawby"). During their retreat the Saxons break the treaty, resulting in the Battle at Bath, where the Saxons occupy a neighboring hill. Cheldric is killed in the battle.

For Monmouth, Chelric becomes the Saxon leader at Camlann, in league with Mordred against Arthur. Mordred offers the Saxon all of Kent, plus Britain from the River Humber to the Scottish border. The site for the battle called Camblam is fixed in Cornwall on the River Camel near Slaughter Bridge close to Camelford. Monmouth is equating Camlann with Camel in addition to assuming that the gen-eral locale is Cornwall rather than Cornovii where Arthur, Mordred, and Chelric are killed. This ends the section "Arthur of Britain," which is followed by "The Saxon Domination," implying, of course, the kingdom of the West Saxons.

Conclusion

The geographic shift to the southern part of Britain follows a logistic pat-tern. Once the midlands had been secured and purged of the rebelling English

Saxons, attention turned toward Gaul and staunching the flow of *Saxones* from the mainland. The southern coast became not only the crucial area to protect but the most reasonable for launching attacks. According to Aston, as in all parts of Britain, reoccupied hillforts became focal administrative points in the southern regions during the post–Roman era,[55] and commercial enterprises had continued flourishing under the Romano-Britons who had stayed on the island. Although there were declines in settlements, in Somerset, for instance, there was

> a Romano-British settlement about every one-half mile across the landscape. This is particularly evident around Somerton, but can also be seen in the Bath Area. Over much of medieval Somerset the pattern was similar.[56]

Even in post–Roman times these southern locales were reaffirmed as important centers where "dense settlements were almost continuous down each side of the valleys, and a similar pattern can be seen in south-east Somerset."[57]

The Southern heartland was a significant farming area, one which has undergone a great deal of both natural and man-made changes in the last 15 centuries. Villas likewise accentuated the desirability in this circle of civilian activity. Ilchester, in the northwestern section, was a bustling settlement, connected by a thick pattern of roads to other important parts of the southwest. A further demonstration of this area's importance is the *oppidum* just outside the Roman town of Ilchester itself. *Oppida*, a term evidently coined by Caesar referring to pre–Roman Celtic and Briton settlements, developed from Gallic versions of settlements from across the Channel. In themselves, they contained commercial, social, and religious centers.

If this, then, was the heartland its defense against all invaders would be of primary importance after the wars in the midlands. By using the Wansdyke to the north and Bokerly Dyke/Grim's Ditch to the south, and by taking advantage of other man-made or natural geographic features, the parameters describe a huge area of southern Britain. Within the perimeter is Old Sarum, all of the Salisbury Plain, Charford, Badbury Rings, Roman settlements, Hod Hill and Hambledon Hill, Ilchester, South Cadbury, Glastonbury, and White Sheet Hill, with many of the mining districts still to the northwest protected. No site is more than 25 miles from the next, and in many instances, the distance is fewer than six miles.

Two possible defense systems exist near Charford. The more northerly one takes advantage of Soldiers Ring, Blagdon Hill, and Bokerly Dyke. Soldiers Ring is not an impressive site; on the south and west the ramparts are angular; on the north there are three straight sections but arranged almost like brackets. The bank is not high, but it is obvious. Though at first this site might be rejected as one which might have been used, it is, according to Dyer, of Romano-British construction, a fact strongly in its favor when talking about the immediate post-Roman period. The southerly possibility near Charford follows the Avon River toward the south, then loops to the west to encompass Fordingbridge, crossing the flatland before trailing to the north of Holt Forest and taking full advantage of Penbury Knoll. The height of this tor and its heavily wooded areas and river banks serve as excellent defense barriers. In the Arthurian era, this layout and locale would be consistent with important battles between the Britons and Saxons who encroached from across the Channel. This oval is the "heartland" and could also be what Hengist claimed as "the excellence of the land."

As the history of the Dark Ages unfolded, the series of events leading to the culminating Battle of Camlann required the change of perspective to the southern coast, emphasizing the distinction which the *Historia Brittonum*, the *Chronicle of Æthelweard* and the *Anglo-Saxon Chronicle* all make between the continental (or German) Saxons, the English Saxons, and the generic term of *Saxones* used by the Romans. Once that clarification is recognized, many seeming contradictions of locale dissolve.

The tribes and unknown leaders of the first *Adventus* can properly be termed the pagan Saxons, the Old Saxons, the continental Saxons, or the German Saxons, which would include the Angles, Saxons, and Jutes, called the *Saxones* in Latin. Because Hengist and Horsa overlap the first and the second *Adventi*, they, too, would probably be classified as German Saxons. As the tribes bonded during the second *Adventus* and toward the third, racial lines were less distinct, compounded by the rise of the Gewissae, a mixed tribe with mixed allegiance. This nascent culture — the Hrype, Hwicce, Gewissae, English Saxons — was of Roman, Welsh (or Briton), Saxon, and sometimes even Irish heritage, which gave rise to later historical confusion because of generic terms applied to their origins. One source would seem to indicate that the Britons were engaged in civil warfare, while another source would point to continental invasions as far north as Hadrian's Wall, and a third source would try to unravel the conflicting tangle of archaeological evidence, topographic suggestions, and chronological discrepancies.

Even after clarifying cultural references, other similarities give rise to multiple possibilities. These stem from clusters such as Cornwall, Cornovii, Cornovian Welsh, or Charford, Charlford, Chollerford, or Cerdicesora, Cerdicesford. "Along the Avon River" could be near Salisbury or as displaced as the Avon near Bath; the Severn meanders literally hundreds of miles, almost in a circle; villages named Wall can be found in three widely separated counties. Each choice must be qualified, or the entire historical structure crumbles.

The seeming inconsistency begins with the Gewissae and Cerdic as part of this race of people. Vortigern invites the German Saxons in to defend the Britons against enemies invading from the north. He grants the Saxon allies territory which becomes known as Hwicce, the land of the Saxon compatriots. Cerdic is undoubtedly *not* a Saxon; he is a Briton with a Briton father who migrated from Manau Guotodin to Carlisle. Through the course of events, he aligned himself with the English Saxon compatriots whose new generation has been born on British soil. Once the old division between Saxon and Briton flares up, there is internal strife.

Excluding the one proposed in Geoffrey of Monmouth, two possible sites for Camlann surface: northwestern Wales (Camboglanna near Hadrian's Wall) and Charford near the southern coast. Logistically, Camboglanna is a possibility for three reasons: the name Camlann derives from Camboglanna, it is in the

Historia Brittonum	Hengist invited his son and a nephew, Octha and Ebissa, to Britain and sent them north to Wall, near a wall.
History of Kings	Octa, Ebissa, and a comrade called Cherdic arrived with three hundred boats filled with a fully equipped army.
Historia Brittonum	Vortimer fought against the Saxons on the River Tanat, at Rhyd yr afael (where Horsa was killed), and at the Inscribed Stone near the Irish Sea, all in northern Wales.
Historia Brittonum	Hengist rebelled against Vortigern and massacred the Council.
ASC	Octha came down from the north to rule with his father and fought against Vortigern.
The Cronica of John	In the eleventh year of Cerdic [467] Arthur began to reign over the Britons.
Historia Brittonum	Arthur fought against Octha in those days.
ASC	In 473 Hengist died. Octha became sole ruler of the kingdom.
Historia Brittonum	Arthur fought against Octha during the Battle of Badon.
ASC	In 495 (494 Preface) Cerdic and Cynric came to a place called Cerdicesora in western Britain and fought against the Welsh.
Annales Cambriae	The Battle of Badon is fought in 497, lunar adaptation.
De Excidio	The siege of Mount Badonicus, 44 years after Gildas' birth.
Dream of Rhonabwy	Arthur forded the Severn River with his vast army.
Dream of Rhonabwy	Osla Big Knife occupied the Wrekin, a hill which shadowed Caer Vaddon, the baths at Viroconium.
Dream of Rhonabwy	Four skirmishes at Vaddon ensued, and Arthur granted Osla a truce.
History of Kings	Cheldric and his Saxons occupied a neighboring hill outside Bath and waged war against Arthur and the Britons, and Cador of Cornwall killed Cheldric.
The Cronica of John	Often Arthur struggled with Cerdic in fierce back-and-forth fighting. Finally Arthur tired of the conflict, accepted Cerdic's fealty, and granted him Hampshire and Somerset, which Cerdic called Wessex.
ASC	In 497 Octha died after reigning for 24 years.
Historia Brittonum	When the Saxons were defeated in the campaign at Badon, they sought help from Germany, and recruited German kings to rule over them in Britain.
De Excidio	There was a period of relative peace in Britain.
De Excidio	Then a desperate blow was struck to the Britons, followed by a devastating storm.
Dream of Rhonabwy	Iddawg, the Churl of Britain, by stirring bad feelings between Medrawd and Arthur, wove the Battle of Camlann.
Annales Cambriae	The Battle of Camlann was fought in 518, lunar adaptation, in which Arthur and Medraut perished.
Ethelwerd Chronicle	Cerdic and Cynric attacked the Britons at Charford on the River Avon, and in the same year of 519 they began to rule.
ASC	In 519 Cerdic and Cynric succeeded to the kingdom of the West Saxons and fought against the Britons at Charford, and the princes of the West Saxons ruled from that day onwards.

The Cronica of John	While Arthur was gone, Mordred grasped after the kingdom, and fearing Cerdic, granted him seven provinces in Britain.
History of Kings	Chelric the Saxon was killed at the Battle of Camlann.
Preface of ASC	In 516 Cerdic the West Saxon king died.

Table 14. Events leading to the Battle of Camlann.

vicinity of the events which lead up to it; and Cunedda's first midlands base after his move from Manau Guotodin is at Carlisle.

Although Badon and Camlann are linked in the *Annales* almost as a beginning and an end to Arthur's career, this does not imply contiguity of location. Charford as Camlann, then, is an even more logical choice. First, Camlann has *etymological* ties with the word Cambolanda, "crooked banks," describing Charford on the meandering banks of the Avon River. Second, Nennius is explicit in his distinction between English Saxons, who would consider Carlisle as their homeland, opposed to German Saxons, where the vanquished flee after the Battle of Badon. Third, Cerdic specifically would not have been labeled as a king of the West Saxons or recorded in a Saxon annal unless the link to Germany had been reinforced. Fourth, the term West Saxon is not actually attached to a continental province in the German homeland, but implies that Cerdic was from the western part of Britain, which grew to the vast province of Wessex. And fifth, after the *Chronicle* entry of 495, the centralized geographic emphasis shifts from the midlands of Britain to the southern coast, with succeeding entries showing a pattern of penetration into the heartland, culminating with Ida and Ælle finally acceding to Northumbria.

The progression reflects the increasing popularity of Arthur and Arthurian material, meaning that Arthur had grown beyond his regional roots and had become more of a national hero. As predecessors, Vortigern and Ambrosius Aurelianus, then Arthur himself, engage in military activity in the northern and southern domains of Wales, plus provinces to the east of Offa's Dyke. Alcock's accurate assertion shows that Welsh/English Saxon conflicts were initially in the Irish Sea zone and away from the lowland heart of Roman Britain; he then capsulizes historical events shifting to the south:

> In 530 the Isle of Wight was captured. But the *Chronicle* provides no evidence that the Cerdicingas, the followers of Cerdic, penetrated more than twenty miles inland until 552, when Cynric advanced to Salisbury and defeated the Britons. Four years later Cynric and his son Ceawlin were fighting at Beranbyrig, Barbury Castle in Wiltshire, over fifty miles inland.[58]

Arthur's exploits, then, began in Wales and the midlands but his capabilities as a brilliant leader and savior catapulted him into national renown, which by necessity would require him to widen his field of operations, eventually extending to the southern heartland and the coast of the Channel.

The Camlann entry from the *Annales Cambriae* is important in anchoring

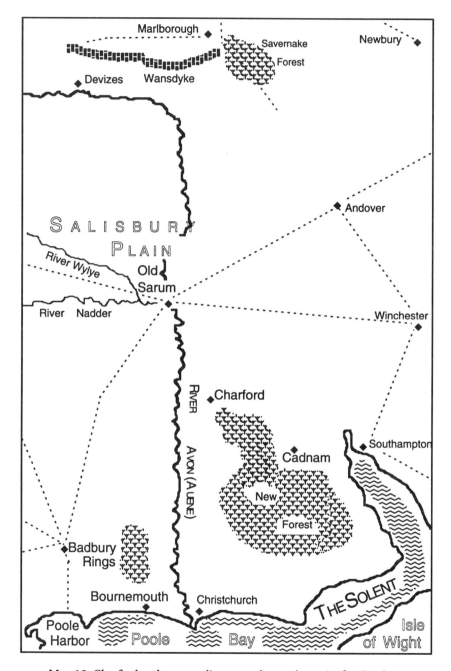

Map 15. Charford and surrounding area, the southern site for Camlann

Arthur to a historical milieu, and to destroy the credibility of one of the most important historical legacies of the period seems impetuous. If this piece of information is ignored, then the only thing left is literary tradition of several centuries later, which becomes more difficult to decipher because of its fictional and legendary exaggeration. There is no need to dismiss the credibility of the Camlann entry; it fits very well into the chronological and geographic information of the historical picture.

Judging from the various versions of the *Chronicle*, the Camlann conflict was a savage battle, running its course through a brutal day until sunset stopped the slaughter. When all the killing had ceased and the din of battle had subsided, the Saxons once again had established a stronghold on the island and succeeded to the kingdom. The Britons' unvanquishable champion, severely wounded, disappeared into the mists of Avalon. The heyday and glory of the Britons defending their homeland after the abandonment by the Romans had come to a bitter and irrevocable end.

Chapter 7
Other Sites:
Camelot and Tintagel

Camelot

Of the numerous Arthurian terms, Camelot is the embodiment of the Arthurian spirit. Although the term was not coined until 1542, over a millennium after King Arthur's time, it has become the object of intense focus in attempts to verify the great king. Just the expression of the "court of King Arthur" kindles the mystique of romanticism which is the core of the Arthurian legends.

Using Alcock's phraseology about this site, however,

> It is as well to say outright that Camelot has no historical authenticity: it is a place that never was. The basis for this assertion is that it is not mentioned in the earliest tradition and the earliest evidence about Arthur.[1]

John Leland, in his famous two-lined passage, was the first to refer to South Cadbury in Somerset as "Camallate" and "Camalat." Whether he assumed a connection between the villages of West Camel or Queen Camel on the River Cam, or whether he used some undisclosed source which stated, or at least suggested, that the fortification near the two Camel villages and the River Cam were in fact known as Camelot in eons past, is uncertain, since Leland does not use any early sources, except for saying that at one point it was a "famose toun or castelle."[2] Alcock's opinion is that Leland alone was responsible for the identification of Cadbury (specifically South Cadbury) with Camelot, and nothing came from either history or local, popular tradition. From the writings of William Stukeley about two centuries later, there was no familiarity with this term by the country people.[3] Leland evidently picked up the term from the late–twelfth century work of Chrétien de Troyes and other French poets who wrote of Camelot, Camalot, Caamalot, and Camahaloth, but these inventions were always vague about location, until John Leland's itinerary.

Because no geographic site with the name of Camelot appears in the ancient documents or in the bardic traditions of the Arthurian age, there are no hidden etymological clues given by its name. Tales such as the *Mabinogion* place Arthur's court in Kelliwic (or Celliwic as another variant), presumed to be somewhere in Cornwall, with some scholars even assigning the names of modern-day sites for it, particularly Killibury or Callington. Geoffrey of Monmouth placed the court in Carleon; Malory in *Le Morte* sets its location in Winchester; Caxton, his publisher, set it in Wales, either at Carleon or at Caerwent, based upon the walls which were still evident during his time

After Leland's assertion, attention shifted to various sites called Cadbury in an attempt to verify Arthur's Camelot. In addition to the heavy concentration on South Cadbury in Somerset, the Cadbury just six miles north of Exeter and Cadbury Camp on the eastern shore of the Mouth of the Severn between Clevedon and Bristol fell under scrutiny. Cadbury Hill near Congresbury joins the ranks, too, as being Camelot because of its association.

Just as there were distinctive sites of "Badbury" and "Bathon" considered as possible locations for Badon, Camelot possibilities fall into that same realm. By far the most common associations made with Camelot are the sites based on the word "Cadbury," but there are others just as logical because of their nature, their location, or both. Each possibility requires consideration, which, as is the case with Badon, may show no link between a Cadbury and Camelot. Unlike Badon, however, the problem for Camelot is much more difficult, since there is no historical base for the latter.

First, there are several sites suggested for Arthur's court which exclude the attribution of Cadbury in the name Camelot. One, Cair Celemion, is included in Nennius' list of important cities of Britain.[4] Neither Stevenson nor Morris writes about its possible location; Morris simply translates it as Celemion Fortress. However, Giles lists the site as "Camalet in Somersetshire,"[5] but lamentably does not go into detail documenting why. Undoubtedly he is referring to the hillfort adjacent to South Cadbury, with a slight variation of spelling. And perhaps if Celemion is a Celtic word and therefore begins with a voiced "c"(just as in "Celtic"), then he might have simply made no more than an anagrammatical connection. More than likely, however, he simply read Leland's description, related the word "Camelot" to "Celemion," and identified it with South Cadbury. No other source, including Eilert Ekwall, gives a clue to its location.

That "Camelot" may stem from "Camelodunum" has also been proposed. This is more alluring, particularly since the first six letters are the same, suggesting the very real possibility that Camelot is the Briton form of the Roman name. If Colchester, its location, is associated with Cair Colun in Nennius' list, then that would be at odds with Cair Celemion. But Cair Colun equated with Colchester is also spurious. Although Colchester is far to the east and not a hillfort, it provides a site of favorable situation according to Morris:

Colchester had obvious advantages as a political centre in reconquered Britain. It was well sited to observe and intimidate the two most formidable English territories, East

Anglia and Kent. Easy roads linked it with the British north and west; and shipping from its harbours might reach Europe without approaching too closely the coast of English Kent. Contact with Europe mattered at the time of Badon, for then the struggle of Goth, Roman, and Frank had not yet finally decided the fate of Gaul. But before the death of Arthur, the victories of Clovis the Frank had permanently turned Gaul into France.[6]

The importance of Colchester and its implications for Arthuriana are evident in this short passage. For one, it had easy access into the western interior of Britain, namely the Cornovian area and eastern Wales while at the same time being situated to monitor Saxon movement. Secondly, it likewise had easy access to the continent, a reminder that literary tradition places Arthur mainly in Gaul and Burgundy. After Badon, attention then shifted to the south of the island and across the Channel; alliance with Rome through Gaul and Burgundy could stop the Saxon incursions at their source. Additionally, Morris himself makes two other important observations, applicable to Colchester as a possible Camelot specifically, and other circumstances generally. First he writes that "Colchester might have been a frequent residence, but Arthur's was not a government that could rule from a single capital."[7] He then concludes:

> If Arthur's central army and administration were of any considerable size, no single area could afford to maintain them for long periods, save perhaps in parts of the west.[8]

Both observations are crucial when considering the possibilities of Camelot. Just as the locus changed from the Battle of Badon in the midlands to the Battle of Camlann near the southern coast, Arthur's court (or more accurately his seat of government) could have changed. Morris' second observation is even more perceptive: the west was capable of supporting a large military force. In specific terms, Viroconium was an ideal center, attested to by its massive rebuilding after Roman abandonment, and Arthur's court would be within easy access. Once emphasis shifted to the south, a similar site could have been established there.

Lastly, literary tradition offers its version of Camelot as Kelliwic, but the name Kelliwic, like Camelot, is lost in history. It, too, is disassociated with the "Cadbury" name, but it aligns itself with frequent references to "Cornwall," a misinterpretation of Cornovii. Several sites, including Kerry, are possibilities. Perceptive, educated postulations can be made, but in the end, because there is no firmly documented historical site, they remain just that — perceptive, educated postulations. Various speculations are intriguing, but there is no evidence to convert them into undeniable fact.

Attention must now turn to the place-name etymology of Cadbury, which gives a flavoring of an area's geographic history in searching for Arthur's stronghold, regardless of its name. *Cadbury* is a Saxon term (Old English) which divides into two affixes. The root -*bury* is not as questionable nor speculative as is its prefix. The variations for -*bury* in this particular instance are -*birie* and -*beria*, both of which stem from -*burgh* with its own variations of -*burg* or -*burh*. This root is a common element in place-names, meaning "a fort," or a "fortified place." Sometimes it may mean "a fortified manor," or simply "manor." It is difficult in each case to decide which meaning is the most exact, unless one is familiar with the physical location. For each of the specific sites considered as "Camelot" with the Cadbury base, there is no doubt that the root means a fort, since they were hillforts from Neolithic times, through the Iron Age, and in some instances, into post–Roman times.

The prefix *Cad-* is not as easily explained. Ekwall lists it as *Cada's Burg*[9] but gives no explanation of whom "Cada" might have been, and suggests a personal name of Cadwy or Cado (Cato) from the Welsh *Life of St. Carannog*. Cato was royalty, perhaps a king or a prince in Dumnonia, but not much more is known of him. Likewise, there is an English name of Cadda (Cada), father of Coenberht, who appears in the 685 entry of the *Anglo-Saxon Chronicle*. There is also a common-noun Celtic affix *cad-* meaning "battle," but it is highly unlikely that the word Cadbury would have been a mixture of Celtic and English.

Several researchers have considered Cadbury Hill near Congresbury as the possible Camelot. This hillfort, about seven miles due east of Weston-Super-Mare, overlooks the River Congresbury Yeo. Several things add to its mystique. For one, it is very near a Roman road that runs along the Mendip Hills, a road which intersects with Foss Way near Shepton Mallet and continues eastward into the maze of roads on the Salisbury Plain. Also, it is in the lead-mining district, an area important to the Roman and post–Roman period. Additionally, Alcock points out that one of the major geographic changes of the Cadbury/Congresbury region is that "Congresbury is now four miles inland, but it is possible that in the fifth/sixth centuries the sea came up to the limestone ridge on which the fort stands."[10]

In common with all others, Cadbury/Congresbury is a hillfort with its beginnings during the Iron Age, over 2,000 years ago. It was not used during the Roman occupation of Britain, but one of its intrigues is that it was subsequently resettled during the Dark Ages, the era of Arthur's reign. One of Alcock's speculations is that "At present it appears that the defences were refurbished on a major scale about A.D. 450."[11] Excavations show that it was probably occupied by the Dobunni Tribe, which, although based mainly in the Cotswolds, seemed to have been in conflict with the Durotriges from Dorset and South Somerset over the possession of the Mendip Hill territory. There have been some excavations of the site, but to date nothing has explained its complex history. The original Iron Age fort was about nine acres, but when it was reoccupied in the fifth or sixth century the established area was only about four and a half acres, compared with South Cadbury which covers about 18 acres of land.

Though much remains to be discovered about this particular hillfort, what has been done so far has uncovered some interesting facts. At the beginning of the Roman occupation of Britain, the Celts who occupied this fort were destroyed because of their poor defense system against the highly skilled Roman Army. The fort itself was abandoned during the Roman occupation, but the region around Congresbury flourished. What Aston writes about fieldwork establishes that this area which was known for its manufacture and distribution of a distinctive grey pottery produced in a large number of lowland settlements.

Coupled with other information in addition to what has already been listed above, these further details support the possibility that Congresbury could be Camelot or at least an Arthurian-age headquarters. If Bath were accepted as the Badon location, then this consideration would make Cadbury/Congresbury a feasible site. Arthur's early connection to Wales has already been established, and this would be familiar territory, within easy access of any conflicts at Bath. The adjacency of Glastonbury is not as strong a factor, because of an inherent implication that Arthur's theater of operation remained constant. Assuming that his stronghold would not have changed during the span of his kingship, then Glastonbury could be a factor, only 15 miles from Congresbury. In opposition, however, South Cadbury is under ten miles from Glastonbury.

Cadbury Camp, a short distance northeast of Tickenham, has been rejected by most scholars as a contender for Arthur's Camelot. It is a multivallate hillfort, surrounded by two ramparts with external ditches. Though it does not appear to be Camelot, in 1922 excavations there uncovered evidence of Romano-British material "demonstrating a probable continuation of occupation." Interestingly, too, "west of the fort it has a line of rampart and ditch cutting off the easy approach of the camp from that direction."[12] But in spite of its seeming continuation of occupation, no archaeological information indicates that it might have been a kingly stronghold.

Cadbury in Devonshire, referred to here as Cadbury-Devon, is also cited as a possible Camelot. It is in the south of Britain, though it is much farther to the west of locales known as the heartland. This particular Cadbury, not to be confused with Cadbury Barton 15 miles directly northwest, is located about seven miles almost due north of Exeter. The River Exe flows north-south just to the east of the hillfort. This hilltop is crowned by a univallate fort, with U-shaped ramparts about 20 feet in height on the southeast, south, and southwest. The slopes to the north and west, the natural contours of the hill, are very steep. There is another ridge forming a concentric circle with a section of the outer rampart. In some places this rampart is about 12 feet high, suggesting that at some point in time it might have been part of the defense system. This hillfort, though, is listed by Dyer as having a shaft excavated in 1847, but nothing revealed Roman or post–Roman habitation.[13] Alcock refers to this particular dig as a ritual shaft; he writes that there was activity in the hillfort "in the third and fourth centuries, but the purpose was religious, not military."[14] He reiterates that defenses in forts such as this were not refurbished for late Roman reuse.

With no other Cadbury site as strong in possibilities, the South Cadbury hillfort in Somerset was further entrenched as Camelot when Leslie Alcock, from 1966 through 1970, did extensive excavations there. He effectively confirmed Camelot's geography through his excavations and elucidative writings, verifying that, if not attached to *the* Arthur, Camelot yielded very convincing evidence of a strong princely fortification and court during the Arthurian era.

In addition to Alcock's contributions, a great deal of the information compiled from a good many sources centralizes the location of Camelot with a great deal of accuracy. One of the important reasons for locating Arthurian events in certain locales is voiced by Collingwood and Myres:

> In the Early Iron Age ... man has left the most impressive evidences of wealth and power in the gigantic hill-forts of the [Salisbury] Plain itself, the downs of Dorset and Hampshire, and the Cotswolds. Thus for two thousand years and more before the coming of the Romans, Salisbury Plain had been a centre to which every new civilization gravitated when it reached Britain, and at which it attained its highest expression of material and spiritual culture.[15]

Therefore, rather than look for Camelot — or Badon and Camlann — in remote places of the far north or in the isolation of southwestern Damnonium, which were sparsely settled military zones, logic dictates that the areas inhabited by Arthur would be located either in eastern Wales including the Cornovii territories, or in the southern heartland.

South Cadbury in Somerset has traditionally become entrenched as an Arthurian stronghold. Alcock's two books, *Was This Camelot?* and *By South Cadbury Is That Camelot* (which is more simply titled *Cadbury/Camelot*) were both first printed in 1972. They are actually the same book with identical color plates, monochrome plates, line drawings and material edited by Sir Mortimer Wheeler. The only difference is that one was published in England and the other in the United States. These two books, in addition to *Arthur's Britain* published in 1971, point to South Cadbury as an Arthurian-age stronghold of royalty. The meticulous excavations and accurate recording of artifacts and data leave little scholarly doubt that this site fits into the Arthurian schemata. Only those scholars who claim a northern Arthur, or those who confuse the several Arthurs from the beginning and the end of the sixth century, disagree with the finds at South Cadbury.

Collingwood and Myres also establish an excellent case in support of South Cadbury as a type of Camelot, although they do not allude to that particular site by its romantic name. Indirectly, but very effectively, they underscore that South Cadbury could not be more ideally situated. In discussing general characteristics about societal development, they write:

> The main development of this culture took place in Dorset and Somerset, whence it spread along the Cotswolds into the midlands. Along the eastern edge of this area it marched with, and in many places supplanted, the earlier south-eastern culture already described, being superior to that culture both in its material equipment and in its political and military organization. Evidences of the character of its daily life have been richly provided by the lake-village at Glastonbury, which proves it by far the most advanced civilization by that time established in this country. ...
>
> The political and military power of this civilization is attested by its hill-forts, which exist in great numbers and far exceed those of the south-east in the massiveness of their structure and the intricacy of their design. Their defences ordinarily consist of stone walls protected by multiple ditches, complicated outworks, and additional defences at the gateways are common features.[16]

The hillforts of this area are contrasted with the ones to the southeast, but the authors mention the cultural continuity between this southern heartland and the midlands, both of which are geographic areas strong in Arthurian history.

Alcock adds a specific reference to South Cadbury, but the generalization which follows it runs a close parallel to what Collingwood and Myres have said of the area. He describes the castle at South Cadbury as setting atop a free-standing hill near the eastern border of Somerset, about 250 feet above the surrounding countryside. There is no water on the hilltop, but at the northeast corner about a hundred feet below the summit of the tor a natural spring was made over and is presently called King Arthur's Well.[17]

His general information, similar to Collingwood's and Myres', concentrates on the Glastonbury area. To the north of South Cadbury is the Somerset Basin, an area of bogs and swamps where there have been extensive excavations of the Somerset levels indicating that in Arthur's time, that area was probably under water from the extension of the Bristol Channel. To the northwest is the imposing landmark of the Glastonbury Tor rising above the plains, only 11 miles away. To the south the far-away hills of South Somerset and Dorset are visible on the horizon on a clear day. To the east are hills higher than South Cadbury, which prevent a true 360-degree view of the surrounding countryside, but with this exception, the panoramic view is unbroken.[18]

Because the findings from the excavations are so complex, a brief synopsis of the hillfort's history is in order, followed by the extraction of only the relevant Arthurian material from the intricate archaeological artifacts recorded by Leslie Alcock. First, it is necessary to reaffirm that the term *Camelot* has no historical authenticity; it is understood that Camelot itself is the euphoric Utopia of the romances, but the search for a principal stronghold or a military base of Arthurian significance is real.

Unlike most of the hillforts located in southern Britain, South Cadbury experienced an unusually long span of human occupancy. Prehistory indicates that the hillfort was first inhabited during the early Neolithic period just prior to 3000 B.C. and was also occupied in the Late Neolithic around 2000 B.C. A long period of abandonment followed until the eighth or seventh century B.C. During this period, people were living permanently on the hilltop, but Alcock states with certainty that the hamlet was not fortified. He explains:

> There is no evidence, whether from air-photography, geophysical survey, or excavation, that it was ever enclosed by a defensive stockade. And it is quite certain that the earliest rampart and ditch of the hillfort are works of later centuries altogether.[19]

By the fifth century B.C., after a hazy transition, a community had arisen and expanded to the status of a large village or town. Alcock concluded from pottery and ornamental pins that during this period the Hallstatt D phase coincided with the early Iron Age period, which is the same time when the first defense system manifested itself at South Cadbury.[20] For some unknown reason, late in the first century B.C. it was abandoned and not reoccupied until early in the first century A.D. by the Celts.[21]

At the beginning of the Roman occupation around five centuries later in A.D. 43, some researchers and historians indicate that the Romans stormed the hillfort and slaughtered its Celtic occupants. Others, including Alcock, set the date at A.D. 70:

From our knowledge of other hillforts in southern England, it was reasonable to suggest that the defenders were the native Celts and their assailants the invading Romans. Those who had not fallen to Roman spears and swords were driven out of the fort, and the hill-top was then demilitarized by pulling down the defences and burning the gates.[22]

Later, however, because of pottery and coins excavated in archaeological digs, he concludes from the evidence that

The Celtic culture of Cadbury was not brought to an abrupt end about A.D. 44. It continued to flourish for a generation or so, accepting a few material objects from the Romans, but basically unchanged from its native ways. The real break comes in the 70s.[23]

For some reason this co-existence between the Celts and Romans was savagely shattered. Because Queen Boudicca's uprising took place ten years earlier in the 60s, her revolt is ruled out as triggering the Roman assault. The whole scene, as it unfolded from archaeological digs, suggested a major battle at the gate, followed by a massacre of men, women, and children. Evidence indicates, however, that although there was a battle and a massacre, the Romans were not guilty of macabre mutilation. Some time later, the Roman troops returned to destroy Cadbury's defenses, and the timber-work of the gate was burned down.[24]

After its early fate during this Roman destruction of the 70s, South Cadbury rose from the ashes again about A.D. 470, and refortifications were completed by about 550. All of these dates are questionable, since no one knows which method of chronology was used, but it sets the general time frame as late– and post–Roman. However, the interesting projection of 470 as the date, points specifically to Arthur's later rule, when his theater of operations would have moved from the midlands to the southern heartland some time shortly after the battle at Badon.

Only South Cadbury, with the excavations which have been presently completed, exhibits such a complete refurbishing of its main line of defense, amounting to nothing less than the complete reconstruction of a new fortification. Some of the later evidence reflects something of the time period. For one, some of the walls indicate that the builders had lost the art of laying masonry with mortar. Secondly, the gate-towers were built with a mixture of dry stonework and timber, suggesting a return to the prehistoric Celtic techniques of fortification.[25]

From this compact historical survey, it is necessary to extract only the Arthurian information from the geophysical surveys and the archaeological evidence, separating the analogous wheat from the chaff in pursuit of the Arthurian quest. The possibility that Cadbury Castle near South Cadbury had connections with Arthur was actually sparked in the 1950s by an amateur collector, a Mrs. Mary Marfield, who systematically recorded all the artifacts she found (unlike many who found relics and simply hoarded them). Dr. C.A.R. Radford, who had access to this data, recognized that some pottery shards found atop the tor at South Cadbury could be dated to the late fifth and early sixth centuries, the period in which the historical Arthur had been active in the south. This led to the subsequent excavation headed by Leslie Alcock between the years 1966 and 1970.

In 1968, Alcock began unearthing Arthurian-age evidence, knowing full well that the name Camelot was a fictional invention. The purpose was not to find Arthur in Camelot; it was to establish a strong intellectual and scientific link between man and his surroundings, both chronologically and geographically. Alcock admitted at the outset that the historical reality of Arthur is in no way linked to that of Camelot and to impugn the authenticity of the one is not to cast doubt upon the other. Arthur is a reality; he fought a battle in 497, and he passed from this life during another battle in 518 at Camlann. Granting those as incontrovertible, the question becomes this: Given the milieu of historical events, how does this south-central site compare to others as principal headquarters for someone of Arthur's stature?

Alcock was able to determine that four large post-holes formed a rectangle about 16 by 13 feet, projecting that this was probably part of a larger building. From the infilling around the post-holes he found several shards of Tintagel-type pottery whose edges had not been worn smooth, indicating that the holes were broadly Arthurian in date. With this to spur him on, he began tracing the entire plan of the building. A slight bulge in the walls suggested "a boat-shaped building which would have been appropriate for a Dark-Age hall."[26] During the next excavating season in 1969, he was able to determine the length and breadth of the building. He eliminated all that was not of Arthurian date, then defined the post-holes. He writes,

> It will always be possible to dispute the attribution of individual holes, but despite this the general pattern of the Arthurian building was clear. Its size, over sixty feet by thirty, and its dominant position on the hill, show that it was the principal building — the feasting hall, in fact — of the Arthurian stronghold.[27]

By 1970 approximately one-fifth of the summit had been excavated, areas signified by rectangles with their irregular protrusions. The probable Roman military buildings are down-slope from the summit and are not of Arthurian date; these remains are likely from the Celtic era when the Romans evacuated the area.

Another noteworthy area was the southwest gate entrance. As part of Cadbury Castle's extensive history, it was also occupied *after* the Arthurian period until about the mid-600s. Then the hilltop lay derelict until Ethelred the Unready rebuilt strong defenses some time during the last several decades of the 900s. This hampered excavation because of the belief that the more recent Ethelredan refortifications had destroyed the evidence of the Arthurian gate. The Arthurian wall-face was evident, but there appeared to be no gate structure or road-way associated with it. After much "painstaking dissection," Alcock concluded that the Arthurian gate had been a timber structure. He writes triumphantly,

> In addition to the timber planks shoring up the rampart ends, there were heavy timber sill-beams or thresholds across the passage at the front and rear of the gate. At

either end of the thresholds, dark stains showed where stout corner posts had decayed. … From this we inferred that the gate had risen to a good height as a look-out tower or fighting platform. Finally, by carefully peeling off the late sixth-century road, we were able to show that this represented a refurbishing or repair to an earlier road. It was a reasonable inference that the first road, the timber gate through which it led, and the dry-stone and timber defensive wall, all belonged to that late fifth- or early sixth-century occupation which was already known from the occurrence of Tintagel-type pottery. Here then, after all our early disappointment, was the Arthurian gateway of Cadbury-Camelot.[28]

The job of disentangling the history of the gate was complicated further by an inverse premise. Because the base of the gate was the original rock of the Iron Age, the rock had been worn down and heavily rutted by cart-wheels, hooves of animals, and centuries of treading feet so that eventually there was a hollow-way about six feet deep. Alcock explains that, "Normally speaking, of course, later structures lie on top of earlier ones, but here the stratification was topsy-turvy: the floor of the earliest guard chamber was at about the level of the eaves of the latest one."[29]

The excavations of the Arthurian gate and wall showed dry-stone walling, signifying that in the interim between the withdrawal of the Romans from the island and Arthur's rise, the art of mortar-making had been lost, and it would not be until thirteen and a half centuries later, in 1756, that this lost art would be reclaimed, ironically by an Englishman named John Smeaton.

Generally, then, what kind of outline can be sketched for South Cadbury? After the Romans had massacred the Celts and torn down the defense system on the tor, the hillfort lay barren until the latter third of the fifth century. At Rampart E Alcock discovered a silver ring or buckle which lay beneath a later road of the southwest gateway. By determining the deterioration on the buckle, and estimating the disintegration of the earthfast timbers, he assessed a date near 500 for the original Rampart E defensive scheme. Going through a similar process with imported pottery, he deduced that the Cadbury hill-top was reoccupied from about A.D. 470

> by a community wealthy enough to take part in the trade which it demonstrates. Of more particular significance, a fragment from a Class B wine-jar was found in or under Rampart E, finally clinching a date in the late fifth or early sixth century for its construction. … Slight though the evidence is, it is just enough to establish that around A.D. 500, Cadbury was once again a fortified place, with a large timber hall as its central building.[30]

The new defenses for this Arthurian period had some protection from the natural landscape, including the four banks and ditches, visible even today along the southeastern section. A timber framework was also added atop the innermost Iron Age rampart, finished off with a dry-stone wall. The southwest gate itself combined its feature with a type of watchtower. Its sturdy earthbound timbers were buried at least three feet into the ground, supporting a threshold beam eight

A blend of enigmatic history and fiction: Glastonbury Tor near Arthur's alleged burial site, viewed from one of the ramparts of the legendary Camelot at South Cadbury.

inches thick. This gate, if it followed the pattern of the Roman forts, which is reasonable, would be topped with an elevated fighting platform.

The size of the enclosure was impressive. It had 3,700 feet of perimeter (almost three-quarters of a mile) with new Arthurian-age ramparts on all sides encircling an 18-acre plateau. Other refortifications of the Roman period commonly enclosed a much smaller perimeter from the original Iron Age site, exemplified by the Hod Hill site, where the Roman camp occupied only a corner. But on the other hand, the entire 18 acres had been refortified at South Cadbury. From this it can be inferred, as voiced by Alcock, that "[the commander of this new fort] had a large garrison to accommodate, and a large labour force to carry out the work."[31] In terms of manpower, Alcock calculates that between a controlled estimate of 300 for the Gododdin army and a Roman field army of 6,000, then "a thousand men might seem right for the armies of Ambrosius Aurelianus and Arthur. And Cadbury itself would be a suitable base for such a body."[32]

The status of Cadbury-Camelot is affirmed by its massive size. Alcock estimates that about 900 stout posts would have been needed to build the front bank of Rampart A, in addition to 70,000 feet of planking for the shoring and breastwork, with even more timber needed for rear posts and cross-ties. This would of course require extensive organization and effort, indicative of the powerful motives for accomplishing the task. The leader of this effort, too, would have to be a powerful and influential individual with a great many resources available to him.[33] Alcock caps his hypothesis by writing:

Local legend can sometimes become engrained as truth. South Cadbury hillfort is much more commonly known as Camelot Fort or Cadbury-Camelot.

> If these generalizations are sound, they emphasize the unusual character of Cadbury-Camelot among British strongholds, in terms both of the strength of its post–Roman refortification and of its large extent. It seems unlikely that this 18-acre fort was intended as a prince's defended homestead, and it is unthinkable that it was a tribal centre on the pre–Roman model. It seems most likely to have served as a base for an army that was large by the standards of the time. Within our present framework of knowledge, it seems plain enough that Cadbury-Camelot played some special part in the warfare of southern Britain in the late fifth and sixth centuries.[34]

Aston, too, conveys the distinctive characteristic of South Cadbury in playing a special role in the protection of southern Britain when he presents this site in a slightly different context. In more detail than given previously, he explains:

> More common, however, are field and place names with *-ford* as a suffix — a crossing place through a stream or a river. Usually this was where particular local topographical features produced a hard bed which could be easily waded. Place-name evidence is difficult, but such names do clearly tell us something of an area, if only that at that point a route crossed a stream or a river. Generally, such places should be seen in a local or regional context and seen together with an assessment of local route ways. In southeast Somerset, for example there are only two *-ford* village names, Mudford and Sparkford; both are significant, as the crossing points of local routes over the Rivers Yeo and Cam respectively.[35]

Topographically, with those two villages as crossing points over rivers, South Cadbury has its defensive position strengthened even further because of the natural protection it affords on its southwestern and northwestern flanks, with

The church at South Cadbury is also steeped in Arthurian legend, particularly since a silver horseshoe found atop the tor can attest to Arthur's ghostly rides around the churchyard during the full moon.

Sparkford only about a mile and a half and Mudford about five miles from the site. Topographically, too, South Cadbury is in a strategic location for the management and protection of the southern heartland. Plotting the centers crucial to Arthur — his court, Glastonbury, and Camlann — the contiguity sustains the logistics of South Cadbury.

As already suggested, just as Viroconium fits into the milieu of the midlands, this site fits into the general schemata of very crucial topographic considerations. Arthur could have had more than one theater of operations and therefore would have relied upon more than a single stronghold. The entire island was in upheaval, with change as the only constant factor. The success at Badon allowed a brief reprieve, but after the expulsion of the English Saxons, there were still incursions from across the Channel. Arthur's Camelot might well have been a Kelliwic such as Kerry when concentration was upon the midlands, but could have relocated to South Cadbury when fighting shifted from central Britain to the southern heartland.

Regardless of its medieval romantic origin, the implausible Camelot has assumed the guise of South Cadbury, and more than likely nothing can shake it from its foundations as Arthur's court. It is well to remember, though, Alcock's admonition that to impugn the authenticity of Camelot is not to cast doubt upon the reality of Arthur. Of the *Annales Cambriae*, he writes

... two references [about King Arthur which] are unimpeachable in terms of the normal rules of historical criticism, and to reject them is to display prejudice, not scholarship. It is impossible to establish any other early source with equal confidence.[36]

Tintagel

Tintagel and Camelot are alike in that neither name appears in the early historical manuscripts. Because these particular terms cast Arthur as a romance figure, they should technically be excluded in a quest for the historic Arthur. However, in deference to their magnified literary importance, Tintagel, too, will be accorded at least a token introduction in conjunction with possible factual Arthurian ramifications, or as a guide to other, parallel historical sites. Geoffrey of Monmouth was the first to provide the roots of literary tradition by narrating Arthur's conception; based upon this, tradition explains that King Arthur assumed the kingship at the early age of 15, but other than that piece of information, there are no *factual* specifics of Arthur between his conception and the appearance of his name in the Badon entry. Literary specifics relate the entire episodes between Gorlois, his wife Ygerna, and Utherpendragon, including Merlin's role in the deception leading to Arthur's conception. Later tradition reveals that Merlin was given charge of the boy's upbringing. The baby was taken from Uther, his father, and Ygerna, his mother, to be raised by Sir Ector. Kay (Sir) was a foster-brother, but Arthur knew nothing of his own origins and heritage until he drew the sword from the anvil. Malory writes that Sir Ector's wife nursed Arthur at her breast. When Arthur was two years old, Uther became ill and died. Arthur's childhood is passed over in one sentence stating that "during the years that followed the death of Uther, while Arthur was still a child, the ambitious barons fought one another for the throne, and the whole of Britain stood in jeopardy."[37]

In two translations of Monmouth, that by Giles and that by Thorpe, Monmouth, like Malory, skips over the first 15 years of Arthur's life. In Book IX Giles describes Uther's death and the bickering between the barons before the crown was set upon Arthur's head. Although he was only 15 years old, Arthur showed a spirit of generosity, munificence, and valor beyond his years after his coronation.[38] Thorpe's divisions and terms describing Arthur are different. Although basically translated the same, he lists the Arthurian section as Part Seven and passes over Arthur's first 15 years. He describes Arthur as a youth of outstanding courage and generosity, with an inborn goodness which gave him grace.[39]

Neither Monmouth nor Malory gives much detail about Tintagel. Readers know that Tintagel is on the Cornwall coast, that it belongs to Duke Gorlois, and that Ygerna is fortified there while her duke is warring against Uther. Malory labels that warring locale as the castle Terrabyl,[40] but Geoffrey identifies it as a fortified camp called Dimilioc,[41] near the village of Pendoggett, about five and a half miles southwest of Tintagel.

These literary references to Tintagel earned it a niche in the romances, but its history does not attach to Arthur. Tintagel is listed in the Domesday Book as property belonging to the monks of Bodmin, with the manor being called Bossiney. After the Norman Conquest, the castle at Tintagel was refortified in the twelfth century, and almost exactly one century after Monmouth's book made its appearance, Richard, Earl of Cornwall, and his younger brother Henry III negotiated with Robert Gervase de Hornicott, who had taken the name of Robert de Tintagel, to repossess Tintagel as part of the earldom in Cornwall. These two eras are much too far removed from Arthur's time for Tintagel to be considered seriously as a possible site for either Arthur's place of conception or his childhood environment.

C.A.R. Radford, supporting the stance as proposed by Henry Jenner, states that the word Tintagel is "Norman French and could not have been taken from an original in the Welsh or British tongue."[42] Likewise, Utherpendragon's seduction of Ygerna and the events surrounding Arthur's birth are more than likely figments of Monmouth's imagination rather than an independent source drawn from ancient tradition, but the setting of this episode at Tintagel, to use Radford's edict, "is an invention by Geoffrey."[43] Radford supports this claim by pointing out that Geoffrey's *History* was published very near the same time that the first castle on the headland was either being contemplated or had just begun construction. The *English Heritage* publication goes into more detail, indicating that Monmouth used the Old Cornish name of *Tin-tagell* with *Tin* or *Din* meaning fortress or fortifiable place, and *-tagell* meaning a constriction or narrows, the neck of the island. Because Geoffrey's description is so detailed and accurate, he had to have known that the builders had unearthed part of the monastic site of centuries earlier. Since much literary tradition, such as the tales in the *Mabinogion*, set Arthur in Cornwall, the discovery of these ruins

> ... would be sufficient inspiration to one whose mind was steeped in the romances of the Celtic race. Here was the Norman Castle of the Earls of Cornwall; here then was the town of his predecessor Duke Gorlois. The story was neatly rounded; and medieval logic could desire no further proof.[44]

Tintagel, then, became engrained in the romances, so that any mention of Cornwall in the ancient bardic stories automatically implied in the later romances Tintagel as its center. Although these ancient tales list Celliwig as Arthur's court, the sheer power of Tintagel on the wild Cornish coast easily captured the imagination of the romanticists, and fit perfectly into the mold of Arthur's milieu of courtly love, knightly virtues, and rugged military prowess. No matter what the Cornwall reference might have been, whether associated with Arthur, or Cador, or Mark in the Tristram and Isolde story, Tintagel became the locus although there is no historical basis for it other than that Tintagel offers the ideal picture of the medieval romances of where Cornish royalty would live. No one, including Leslie Alcock, suggests that the ruins at Tintagel were something different than monastic ruins of the sixth century. Geoffrey Ashe suggests that some subsequent excavations after the Radford explorations "made it more likely that Tintagel was a princely stronghold,"[45] but no other source verifies this.

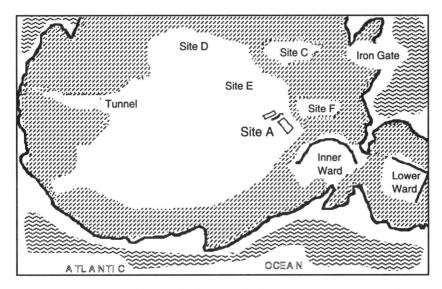

Map 16. Tintagel. Site A is the location of ruins from the Arthurian period.

None of this, however, means that Tintagel (or, more accurately, the area around Bossiney) lay natural and untouched. Cornwall, as with all of the corners of Britain, was directly affected by the Roman occupation. Prior to the Roman invasion, this particular segment of the Cornish coast attracted settlers of the Bronze Age because of pastureland and fields which could be cultivated without the painstaking work of clearing forests and heavy undergrowth. This was part of the era before the coming of Christ, but archaeological finds also attest to Romans being in the area later.

The Romans invaded the area fairly early in the island's conquest. The natives of the area, known as the Dumnoni tribe, were conquered by Rome about a half-century after Christ. As time passed, the Roman influence was naturally stronger to the south and east, with Exeter becoming a fortified Roman city and a thriving metropolis because of the access to the Channel via the River Exe. Still further to the east of Exeter the Roman influence was more wide-spread; bays and coves along the coast led to the development of settlements on or near the shore from Durnovaria and Bournemouth to Southampton and Portsmouth. Cornwall, because of its isolation, retained more of its native cultural ways, and the depth of Roman influence along the northern Cornish coast toward Bristol is still to be disclosed. As Radford points out, Romanized "penetration to Tintagel during the third and fourth centuries is proved by the two Roman milestones found in the parish."[46] He goes on to explain that the purpose for this penetration into Cornwall is uncertain but indicates that an interest might have been antimony, an element sometimes used by the Romans for alloys in metals or for medicinal purposes.

Nevertheless, some archaeological evidence keeps the spark alive that Tintagel

Tintagel showing a segment of the mainland to the left. The interesting things about this particular photo is what locals have dubbed "Arthur's Profile." The left side of the peninsula presents a perfect silhouette of hair, forehead, eye and eyelid, nose, mouth, and even beard.

The headland of Tintagel from the mainland looking west.

just might have been an Arthurian stronghold five to six centuries prior to Monmouth. Radford also writes that evidence of human occupation on the headland ran to about the year 600, which, of course, is of interest to Arthurian scholars. This means that attention focuses on Tintagel ruins at Site A. Two small rectangular buildings occupy Site A, interspersed with walls of other buildings from four different periods. One is a fairly large intact rectangle running north-south, and the other, much more indistinct, runs east-west. A medieval chapel sits between the two older structures. Radford is of the opinion that "these buildings were ruined and probably forgotten by 500."[47]

Cornwall lost contact with the Romans much more quickly than their Briton relatives in the south-central section of the island, probably because the withdrawal affected the more isolated places much more quickly. Yet that does not mean activity at Tintagel came to a halt. Celtic monastic activity continued on the headland, and the hermitages constructed by the founder Saint Juliot and his successors expanded the buildings to about 20 rooms centralized on the headland. An earthen bank and a ditch at the site indicate the possibility of an early defensive rampart or vallum. However, the Rule of Saint Columba states that the monks should "let a fast place with one gate enclose thee." This could suggest that the ditch and vallum was a physical manifestation to symbolically show that the monks were severing themselves from the rest of the community and the world beyond. Radford echoes both possibilities:

> [the vallum enclosing the cashel or settlement] ... seems always to have been a physical barrier, an earthen bank, a rampart of turf or hedge. But it also had a spiritual meaning, separating the city of God from the world outside.[48]

Since no evidence of a castle has been unearthed to suggest a princely stronghold, it is unknown what the vallum might represent. What speaks most strongly against its being Arthur's stronghold in particular is that it is too isolated in relation to the massive evidence showing Arthur's activities centering in eastern Wales and the midlands, and eventually shifting to the central-southern coast. With the midlands identified as Cornovii territory in Arthur's era, this explains additionally the confusion that later generations thought that Arthur was Cornish rather than Cornovian. At that time, Cornwall was still referred to as Dumnonia.

All of these decayed ruins, rebuildings, and additions show that Tintagel had a long and colorful history dating from the Bronze Age, through the Roman occupation, and into the Norman Conquest. For a period before the Conquest, the monastery at Tintagel was abandoned and in ruins. After the Norman victory there was renewed interest in the site and vigorous rebuilding. It was probably during this period that Richard, Earl of Cornwall, had acquired the land upon which the sea had encroached to a point where the gap narrowed from the mainland and Tintagel became almost an island. This would be about a century after Geoffrey of Monmouth, but even earlier, Geoffrey could anticipate the ravages of the sea on the narrow neck of land. The buildings on the headland fell again into disrepair over the next couple of centuries so that by the time the antiquarian John Leland saw the site in the mid–1500s, he saw only desolation and ruin.

Along with Camelot, Tintagel is so engrained in tradition that no logic, no intellectualism, no debate is needed to sanction it as Arthur's conventional birthplace. No amount of evidence to the contrary will persuade medieval romanticists that Arthur's conception occurred in a way different from that proposed by Geoffrey of Monmouth. Under those conditions, Radford aptly defends Tintagel as Arthur's conception place and birthplace:

> Few [people] would desire to see [Arthur's] memory tied to those midland or northern sites where his victories were won, a fate which would condemn his spirit to a peripatetic existence as scholars favour first one and then another identity. For Arthur is above all a Celtic hero and it is fitting that popular memory should picture him in a Cornish setting.[49]

The headland is as enigmatic as Arthur himself. The wild Cornish coast, the low, ominous clouds threatening a coming storm, the forlorn wail of the wind from the sea, the stalwart isolation of the castle — in short, everything as it is described the night that Merlin uses his magic for Uther to gain entry into Ygerna's bedchamber — locks Tintagel into a permanent niche in Arthurian lore. With no facts to contradict the legend, this site is the best for Arthur's beginnings; like the question of Camelot, the enigma of Tintagel does not negate the famous king's historical reality; it is simply a missing piece which in all probability will never be retrieved, adding to the mystique of Arthur. An American Indian maxim perfectly expresses Tintagel's role in the Arthurian legends:

> When the legends die, the dreams end.
> When the dreams end, there is no more greatness.[50]

Chapter 8
The Isle of Avalon:
Arthur's Resting Place

This chapter deals with the most complex geographic site in Arthuriana because of the intricate array of possibilities offered by clues, some supporting a link between Glastonbury and Arthur, others contravening because of some inherent incompatibility. The dilemma is exacerbated by both natural and man-made geomorphic changes, by circumstantial corroboration, and by archaeological discoveries on the one hand, contrasted with vague references, both deliberate and inadvertent deception, hoaxes, and imputations on the other. In the neutral middle ground lies a barrier of imprecise language.

At the beginning of what seems a simple explanation of proper nouns, Glastonbury is connected to the term *Glastonia*, a word of Celtic origin, to which Ekwall gives a couple of meanings. One is the color blue-green, and another is directly associated with woad, the plant from which blue-green dye is made. Hence, Glastonia would be a "place where the woad grows." Glastonbury, then, derived from Glastonia, but when it was later assimilated into Anglo-Saxon as Glaestingabyrig, the prefix became associated with a personal name, the founder of the settlement whose name was Glass, or Glast, or Glaesting,[1] and the suffix was the Saxon dative meaning "fort" or "manor."

Somewhere in the development of its place-names, the word Avalon also became inextricably bound to Glastonbury. Some legendary tales associate Avalon with Glaesting, the founder, and an apple tree signifying the fertility of the land. Different tales of Celtic lore label Avalon as a vague, misty afterworld governed by Avallach, lord of the dead. From this lore springs Avalon, the afterworld, as the Isle of the Dead, a passing ground. One other reference to Avalon (made with no reference to Arthur) is by Richard of Cirencester, who equates Glastonbury and Avalonia as the geographic location of the Hedui tribe covering nearly all of Somersetshire.[2] Monmouth, in an Arthurian context, also records the term

Avalon (Avalonia), dropping an "l," but he does not equate the site with Glastonbury.

One of the major complexities, as shown by Avalon being called the Isle of the Dead, is Glastonbury assuming its "island" titles. With a connection between Glastonia and the personal name Glaesting, the Old English addition of -*ieg* may have been confused with -*ing*, giving Glastonia the name Glaestieg instead of Glaesting. In Old English, -ieg meant "island," associating it, therefore, with Glass Island. Another possibility is that Old English picked up the island motif from the Welsh term *Ynys-witrin*, in which the prefix *ynys*- is also defined as "island." At this point the problem is compounded, because -*witrin*, the suffix of the term, might have been a confusion between -*vitrum* meaning "woad," and -*gutrin* meaning "glass." The former, of course, would make sense as "and where the woad grows," but the latter would lead to one of the many new terms, the Isle of Glass, applied to Glastonbury.

These variations have led to a multitude of names associated with Glastonbury: Glastonia, Glaesting, Glaestingbyrig, Glaestiegbyrig, Glastingbyrieg, Avallon, Avalon, Avalonia, Insula Avalonia, Ynys Avallach, Ynys, Ynys-witrin, Ynesutrin, Insula Vitrea, Isle of Avalonia, Isle of the Dead, Isle of Glass, plus the Isle of Apples and the Fortunate Isles from Monmouth's *Vita Merlini*.[3] How all of these names evolved, and how they all came to be attached to Glastonbury, is buried in the tangle of its etymological roots.

Glastonbury as an Island

Too often the claim that Glastonbury was an island is taken too lightly, under the suspicion that Arthurian scholars claim it to be such only because it wraps the Arthurian geographic locations into a compact packet. However, geotopographers have established that Bridgwater Bay and the Mouth of the Severn stretched extensively inland. With a little sleuthing on one's own, the actual continuation of these channels eastward (which would make Glastonbury an island) can be plotted quite precisely by using any present-day road map and etymologically interpreting some place-names. A shore-line can then be traced around them.

A map of northwestern Somerset shows the present shoreline of the Bristol Channel, the Mendip Hills, the Quantock Hills, and Glastonbury forming a parallelogram. Beginning at the southern base of the Mendip Hills is Nyland Hill. The suffix -*ney* (-*ny*) is an Old English term meaning "island," which etymologically translates "Nyland Hill" as "island hilltop." Almost straight south about five miles is a village named Meare. The affix -*meare*, or -*mere* or *mearc*- is an Old English term defined as "lake," meaning that Meare would be a "lake village." A stone's throw to the east is another village called Godney. The suffix means "island"; the prefix is a personal reference meaning "Goda's," translating to "Goda's Island."

Bypassing Glastonbury, since the term has already been explained, the next

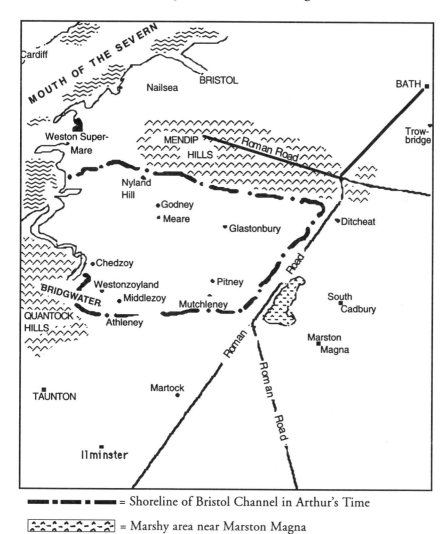

▬ ▪ ▬ ▪ ▬ = Shoreline of Bristol Channel in Arthur's Time

▵▵▵▵▵▵▵ = Marshy area near Marston Magna

Map 17. The encroachment of Bridgwater Bay on Glastonbury.

movement for plotting the points of a shoreline is to the southeast about seven miles, to a location called Ditcheat. Ekwall explains that this means "The gate in the dike," with the dike being part of Foss Way, to the village's western flank. This suggests that the Roman road acted as a barrier to control or confine water, which in turn asserts that Glastonbury, seven miles to the northwest, was an island in the Bristol Channel.

To the south of Ditcheat, and, incidentally, very near South Cadbury, is a village called Marston Magna. The etymology for this is quite straightforward.

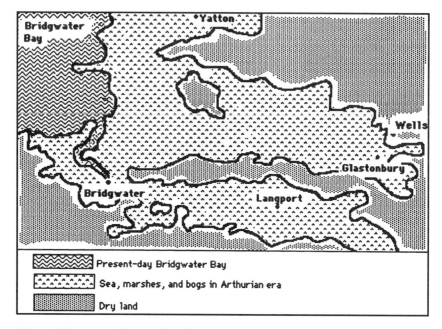

Map 18. The encroachment of Bridgwater Bay, using Map 17 as a base and looking at other professional maps which depict what the Glastonbury area would have looked like in Arthurian times, though this map is still not to scale and not exact. See Map 19 for a more standardized, scaled version of the Somerset Levels in the Glastonbury area, adapted from Coles and Orme.

Mars- is very close to the word "marsh" which derives from Old English *Mersc-*. The root *-ton* (also *-tun*) means "town." The second word for this village means "great," from Latin, thus forming the place-name "town by a great marsh." This explains that Marston Magna is on the swampy edges of the sea, protected from it, just like Ditcheat, by the Roman road called Foss Way.

About ten miles to the southwest of Marston Magna is another village called Martock. Although the prefix seems to have the same history as Marston Magna, meaning "marsh," Martock actually comes from Merkestok recorded in the old Assize Rolls, a document dating to 1265. This means its prefix comes from *mere* (also *mearc*) meaning "place by the lake."

From Martock, three miles due north is Muchelney, which begins a string of islands up to Bridgwater. The etymological derivation for this site, recorded in the Domesday Book in 1084, means "large island." About three miles north of it is Pitney, "Pytta's Island," also recorded in the Domesday Book, in the year 1225. Next in the string, due west of Pitney, is Athelney, "island of the *aethelingas*," the Saxon word for princes, recorded in the *Anglo-Saxon Chronicle* at entry 878.

Due north of it is Middlezoy. A check of Ekwall shows that the ending for this locale was originally *sowi*, with the "i" on the end indicating the Old English

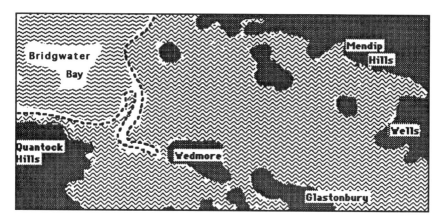

Map 19. Glastonbury as an island, adapted from Coles and Orme. This sketch quite accurately represents what are termed the Somerset Levels in the Glastonbury area. All darkly shaded areas represent islands in what is termed the "Lake District."

-*ieg*, meaning "middle island." In very close proximity to the north is Weston-zoyland, formerly Westsowi, or "west island." Only a short distance from it is Chedzoy, coming from a personal name, "Cedda's Island."

These locations plotted on a modern map with the waterline a short distance on the land side give a very accurate representation of what professional geo-topographers have determined. All that has to be done is fill in minute details, and it is a perfect replication of what the area of Glastonbury looked like in Arthur's day.

In 1982, Coles and Orme, in *The Prehistory of the Somerset Levels*, assert that the Somerset Levels predate Arthur by literally thousands of years. The authors describe the prehistory from 4000 B.C. until the Roman occupation, commenting, "we can see a constant presence of man in the area, always working the land, using forests, the meadows, the islands, and the water marshes."[4] From archaeological evidence they deduced that the natural flooding which occurred from time to time raised the bog level until about A.D. 400. Originally the River Brue skirted Glastonbury Tor, flowing along the ends of the Levels and north into Bleadney Gap. To try to improve drainage, the Glastonbury monks diverted the Brue through an artificial channel just west of the Levels, probably creating Meare Pool, which is today a lake.

Prior to and during the Arthurian era there was a progression when "the marshes were so wet that boat transport was easier to achieve than extensive trackway maintenance."[5] Because of these conditions, two major settlements known as the Lake Villages, Glastonbury and Meare, were established in the Levels. During earlier excavations in 1892, Arthur Bulleid discovered the Glastonbury Lake Village near Godney. Some of the archaeological evidence revealed that Glastonbury Lake Village was built some distance from dry land, with no actual land passage to Glastonbury Tor itself. The Lake Village was surrounded by a fortified structure with a central area of about three and a half acres. Piggott, in his work, describes the Glastonbury area as "a real island in a fresh-water marsh with thick growth," describing the lake villages of Dobunni at Glastonbury as "permanent settlements in a region half-swamp, half actual lake ... [amid] dreary marshes," continuing that these settlements were probably built around 50 B.C.[6]

Three years after Bulleid's discovery of the Glastonbury Lake Village, he uncovered the settlement at Meare, and although he searched for a causeway linking the two villages, he never found one. After an uneventful excavation by Michael Avery in 1965, the Somerset Levels Project in 1978 allowed a fairly comprehensive picture to emerge, although the water table had fallen dramatically and the archaeologists were concerned that valuable evidence might be lost through drying ground conditions. The vicinity was mainly raised bog, sloped gently upwards away from the settlement lying to the north. A little over a hundred yards to the south of the bog was the forested island of Meare, with a low, watery area between, perhaps a stream. According to Coles and Orme, unlike Glastonbury Lake Village, the settlement of Meare Lake Village did not have a palisade, and because of no apparent need for substantial foundations, no evidence of permanent dwellings was found.

Treharne, however, provides a different picture in more detail about the Lake villages by offering this information about the structures:

> On Glastonbury "island" were built eighty-nine circular huts, varying from eighteen to twenty-eight feet in diameter, with small projecting vestibules closed by strong double swing-doors made of oak. Each hut was built on a heavy timber foundation of parallel logs held together by frequently renewed concentric rings of piles driven into the bed of the mere around the edge of the foundation.[7]

This passage makes no distinction between the two villages as proposed by Coles and Orme. Treharne suggests further that there was a combined population of about 1,100 people in these two large communities. He estimates the population of Glastonbury Lake Village at 500; at Meare, because of two crannogs each carrying about 60 huts, he estimates a population of 600 or more, both indicating thriving communities.[8]

Defenses in other sections of Britain were by refortified hillforts and a series of walls and trenches. However, because of different topography at Glastonbury, the fortified defenses suggested by Coles and Orme were different, using a lake, swampy areas, marshes and reeds as protection. The village of Meare, for instance, was an artificial island (crannog or terpen) built in shallow waters near the edge of a large freshwater lake, not far from the higher ground, so that the lake and surrounding swamp offered a natural moat.

> The outer edge of the "island" was defended by a strong palisade of tough wickerwork hurdles ... varying from five to fourteen feet in height above the platform. ... Outside the palisade, on the north-east side, a forty-yard stone and clay causeway ... led to a wooden landing-stage which projected into deeper, open water, thus providing moorings for the canoes.[9]

When the settlements were abandoned at Glastonbury and Meare, evidently because of changing environmental conditions, the area was isolated for several centuries. Coles and Orme establish that in about A.D. 250 there was a "great transgression"[10] of water from Bridgwater Bay which flooded into the northern section of Godney Moor, but then by A.D. 400 the bogs were in effect dead. The only addition they make on the Somerset Levels before ending their search was to say that

> During the cutting of the upper peats, several hoards of Roman coins and other objects have been found; these had been deliberately buried, probably for safekeeping. Otherwise, there is no trace of any substantial interest in the marshlands from the abandonment of the Iron Age villages until the time of the written records of monastic activities.[11]

Certainly none of this verifies Arthur's connection with Glastonbury; the Roman coins and artifacts might suggest immediate post–Roman occupation, but the evidence is much too slim to consider it as substantiation. The purpose of analyzing Glastonbury Lake Village and its neighbor Meare is not to clinch a connection between Arthur and Glastonbury, but to establish the certainty that Glastonbury — more specifically Glastonbury Abbey and the Tor — were on islands surrounded by the waters of Bridgwater Bay which extended quite a few miles inland from its present-day shorelines. This geographic feature would necessarily have impacted Roman, post–Roman and Arthurian times. The extended bay would explain the scarcity of Roman roads in the vicinity of Glastonbury, particularly to the northwest. There is Foss Way to the east, as a type of dike, plus a Roman road which intersects and makes its way into the Mendip Hills for the lead mine which the Romans were operating, but primary civil activity was centered further to the southeast.

With all that is verifiable in claiming that Glastonbury was an island in Arthur's time, topographers have no difficulty in accepting the terrain around Glastonbury in the fifth century as having been under water, a boggy, swampy area of changing scenes, depending upon the moisture and the season. One other item leads to a logical assumption that, although many times a scribe might be ignorant of why ancient manuscripts described events or scenes in a certain way, the scribe recorded the manuscript according to its true form, and did not, as was also frequently done, interpolate the manuscripts so that they made sense to him.

The important geographic feature which emerges is that Glastonbury was an island within memory from Arthurian times, with pinpoints of land connected by a network of causeways going through water and mire, as evidenced by the prehistory of the Somerset Levels unearthed by Coles and Orme. Piggott, too, points out that where causeways were impractical because of water depth, boats were used to maneuver from one site to another.

Archaeological Evidence:
The Abbey and the Tor

One other addition to the complexity of the issue surrounding possible Arthurian connections with Glastonbury is the blend between the Abbey and the Tor; that is, because of the Abbey's contiguity to the Tor, the two sites many times are considered as one. However, because archaeological digs leading to different results have been carried out at both locales, each should be perceived individually.

Archaeological excavations on the Tor have been conducted by Philip Rahtz, who suggests in the Introduction to his study that the Tor is many times ignored because of the overshadowing acclaim accorded to the Abbey. His explorations covered 11 weeks, spread over a three-year span, and the reports of his findings appeared in his article "Excavations on Glastonbury Tor, Somerset, 1964-6," in the *Archaeological Journal* for the year 1970, reprinted in *The Quest for Arthur's Britain*. Of his four major areas of concentration, Period 1 focuses on the Arthurian era, the sixth century A.D. of the Dark Ages. Roughly, there are five categories:

1. Timber buildings, within a perimeter. There were three stake holes along the northern perimeter, and along the east edges of the hollow were several possible stakeholes and two postholes which could represent some sort of fence or protective barrier around the edges of the hollow. Of the timber buildings themselves, there was evidence of timber slots and four major postholes to the west. Rahtz projects five possible buildings, although they might have been joined.
2. Evidence of metal-working. There were several iron and bronze objects, including several ferrules and an iron lamp-holder. Of particular significance were two hearths, which were judged not domestic but used in metal-working because of crucible fragments no more than nine feet away.
3. Evidence of considerable meat-eating.
4. Two graves of seemingly young people, with their heads to the south, more likely to be a non–Christian burial. Prior to Rahtz's excavations, one of his colleagues, C.A. Ralegh Radford, conjectured that there was a Christian monastery at Glastonbury in Arthurian times (the late fifth and early sixth centuries) and that the outer ditch at the perimeter of the abbey ruins represented the pre–Saxon settlement. Rahtz anticipated that, among other things, his search would show the Tor itself might deserve the acclaim that it, rather than the abbey, was the site of the earliest Christian settlement. But no "archaeological proof of this was forthcoming."[12]
5. A mixture of other artifacts, including some imported Mediterranean pottery, local grass-tempered pottery, Roman tiles which might have been inserted in Period 1 but which seems unlikely, Roman Samian, and some bone objects.[13]

From this information, Rahtz considers two possibilities. One is that the Tor could have been a religious community, although the issue of whether it was pagan or Christian remained unresolved. Rahtz felt that a pagan one would historically be unlikely, though there was no archaeological evidence to support this.

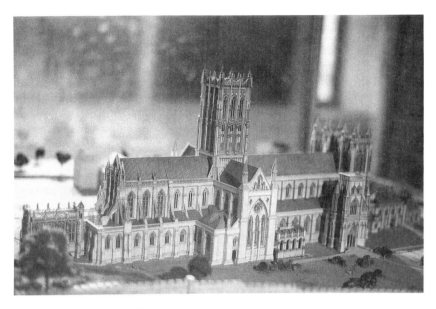

An artist's rendition of Glastonbury Abbey just before the Dissolution. Photo by Frank Reno, with kind permission of the Custodian, Glastonbury Abbey.

Glastonbury Tor as seen from Chalice Hill.

He cites evidence, however, supporting the premise for a religious settlement. First, the number of pottery finds on the Tor are in keeping with the pottery finds of early Christian sites everywhere. Second, metal-working would not be uncommon in a religious settlement, whose inhabitants would be quite self-sufficient. And lastly, the slightly founded buildings would suggest religious occupation. A different find which contradicts the supposition of a religious settlement is the considerable remains of meat-bones.

The second possibility is that the Tor was a defensive or quasi-military establishment. To support this, Rahtz points to its steepness, its panoramic view to warn of invaders, and its likelihood as an outpost, look-out, or signalling station. He conjectures, too, that perhaps it was a settlement of a small local chieftain, but it would not have been the stronghold of Arthur or an Arthur-type figure; instead, it would be the habitat for someone of a lesser stature.

Arthurian Connections with Avalon/Glastonbury

As an Arthurian curiosity, neither Avalon nor its most common synonym Glastonbury can be discovered by a quick check into an index or a glossary of a scholarly text. Like so many other names, either term leads through a maze of etymologies and synonyms. Its location is in the vicinity of other Arthurian by-words, closest to South Cadbury, only 12 miles distant, and about the same mileage to Ilchester, one of the major Roman hubs before Rome began its withdrawal. A hundred miles to the north is Viroconium (Badon), and to the south about 50 miles is Charford (Camlann).

TWELFTH-CENTURY WRITING: WILLIAM OF MALMSBURY

As an impartial antiquarian, William of Malmsbury does not give historical credibility to King Arthur even though he was consigned as a principal authority for the early history of Glastonbury. His book, *De Antiquitate Glastonie Ecclesie*, has not survived the ages without heavily biased interpolations; the edition of Hearne from the manuscript at Trinity College, Cambridge, shows that the book is filled with self-serving and unscrupulous accretions for a hundred years after Malmsbury's death. Luckily, however, Malmsbury himself had included the first part of the *De Antiquitate* in a subsequent edition of another of his works titled *Gestis Regum Anglorum*, which was printed about 1140. The passages from this source, then, come from Malmsbury himself, unencumbered by the interpolations in the *De Antiquitate*.

Before looking at Scott's translation, however, a terse chronology will illustrate the complexity of scrutinizing the Malmsbury material to extract only that material which he truly wrote. William visited Glastonbury Abbey around 1129, commissioned in the specific sense of the term to chronicle an accurate record of the Abbey's long religious history, using manuscripts and charters that were made available to him. William accepted his charge by the abbots and monks, but as a serious historian, he remained remarkably impartial in his recordings, though the pressures to paint a more biased history must have been enormous. He suggests, for instance, that Glastonbury's apostolic origin is a possibility, but he does not wholeheartedly accept that premise, in spite of pressure from his hosts. To borrow some of Scott's words, Malmsbury writes of "fulfilling the monks' expectations, submitting to their commands and following their orders, and offering his work to them as the required token of his obedience."[14] Yet, as another example, William fulfilled only part of the expectations expressed by the monks in validating Saint Dunstan's association with Glastonbury Abbey. A long-standing feud had been going on between Glastonbury and Canterbury over Saint Dunstan's relics, but William omits a great deal of Saint Dunstan's life and the performance of miracles, thus side-stepping the issue without satisfying the Glastonbury contingencies while at the same time avoiding direct insult or denial.

Because of the Saint Dunstan issue, the monks at Glastonbury were dissatisfied with Malmsbury's writings. He offered them the *De Antiquitate*, attempting to convince them that the many things which the manuscript set forth would bring glory and prestige to the monastery, but they remained unhappy with the results. William wrote a *Preface* to the work, and submitted it to the abbot, Henry de Blois, in hopes of mollifying him, but even this appeal did not seem to placate the monks.

As a consequence, Malmsbury's manuscript of the *De Antiquitate* was left in the hands of Henry de Blois and the Glastonbury monks. The offshoot, over the next 150 years, was a manuscript laden with interpolations and rewritten to include material that had not been sanctioned by William, and in most instances did not remotely approach the truth. Modern-day scholars would have been ignorant of Malmsbury's original *DA* and would have forever perpetrated untruths, manipulations, and deliberate deceits, had not William himself included large segments of the *DA* in his revision of *Gestis Regum Anglorum*. We know now, independent of the Glastonbury manuscripts, what Malmsbury left for posterity in writing the *De Antiquitate*.

In all, excluding William's original text, there are at least six major distinctive revisions and rewrites. In addition to a revision around the year 1230, there are manuscripts which bear the initials B, C, L, M, and T. These have nothing to do with an alphabetical chronology but instead indicate abbreviations of where each particular manuscript is housed.[15] There are also hybrids with such labels as CL, indicating that C was written using L as its base. Scott relays some fairly detailed information about these manuscripts, then uses Manuscript T in presenting his translation. Likewise, he is specific about where the deviations from the interpolations occur.

Treharne's scholarly work in 1966 predates Scott's translation by 15 years. On the one hand, Treharne humbly apologizes to the devout believers in the full legends of Joseph of Arimathea and King Arthur at Glastonbury, but indicates that his impartiality as a historian was not meant to be either impious or irreverent. Scott, in Section 4, "Forgery and the Interpolations in the *De Antiquitate*," offers an apology of a different sort. He asks the reader's forgiveness for Glastonbury's transgressions in their deceptive interpolations, defending their actions by saying that "other monasteries [also] tried to bolster their reputations by similarly elaborating stories"[16] and averring that Glastonbury was no different from other abbeys in Britain; the abbeys had to maintain "their places in a world that was increasingly unsympathetic."[17] Both authors, though, display an integrity to the truth and to impartiality of reporting.

William himself writes of his own integrity in what modern-day scholars know to be his untainted version of the *DA*. In addition to it and *Gestis Regum Anglorum*, other manuscripts to his credit are *De Gestis Pontificum Anglorum*, around the year 1125, and *Vita Sancti Dunstani*, probably no later than 1135. What demonstrates his integrity, however, despite his allegiance to the monks and abbot of Glastonbury, is what he writes in the original version of the *De Antiquitate*:

> Since this is the point at which I must bring in the monastery of Glastonbury, let me trace from its very beginning the rise and progress of that church so far as I can discover it from the mass of source-material. … But lest I should appear to deceive the expectations of my readers with trifling fancies, let me come on to narrate facts of solid truth, leaving aside all these discrepancies.[18]

While writing the *DA*, William of Malmsbury stayed at Glastonbury Abbey around 1125. He personally studied the records of the monastery, looking in great detail at the early charters of the church, and gleaning from the monks as many traditional stories as he could. He conveys the feeling that no documents were withheld from him, and he separates the historical data obtained from the written documents and the literary claims of traditional lore. He was aware of claims that the Old Church of Wattles, dedicated to the Blessed Virgin, was the most ancient sanctuary of the island and had been built by missionaries whom the Pope sent from Rome at the request of King Lucius in the year 166. He was likewise aware that an earlier date was claimed for it, allegedly built by the disciples of the Lord. In writing his history, however, he would not commit to any proposition that was merely hearsay or pious opinion.

As relayed by Robinson, who was using the untainted version of the *DA*, Malmsbury claims to have seen a very ancient charter reporting that a king (whose name was illegible) of Domnonia (which then included not only Devon but also the greater part of Somerset) granted to the Old Church (Glastonbury) land in the Isle of Yneswitrin.[19] The interesting term is *Yneswitrin*, linked to Glastonbury. This suggests the same connection made between Glastonbury and Yneswitrin in the Grail manuscripts, but unfortunately it does not make an association between Avalon and Yneswitrin. Therefore, Avalon still does not appear as a synonym for Glastonbury.

In summary, the following items are what Malmsbury thought to be history of credible account:

1. Gildas (no distinction between Albanius or Badonicus) spent several years at the abbey, a place of its sanctity, holiness, and reverence.
2. Glastonbury was a holy shrine which not only attracted many pilgrims but became a coveted resting place for many saints.
3. The shrine was also revered by the conquerors and therefore left intact rather than being destroyed.
4. He accepts the stories about St. Patrick, St. David, and the Lord himself consecrating the Old Church of Wattles.

Malmsbury's "new source of information" refers to the grants and charters given by the Saxon kings and nobles to the Abbey, but until the year 658, Malmsbury's reliable history appears to be as objective as he could possibly make it. He makes no claim that Glastonbury is factually or historically tied to King Arthur. He refers to Gawain as Walwen, the son of Arthur's sister, who "deservedly shared his uncle's fame, for they averted the ruin of their country for many years. But the tomb of Arthur is nowhere to be seen, for which reason the dirges of old relate that he is to come again."[20]

GEOFFREY OF MONMOUTH

Lacy suggests that the name Avalon became attached to Glastonbury because of Arthur; Avalon was Arthur's last earthly destination after his fatal wounding.[21] But Arthur's burial place, like so many other geographical locations attached to Arthur, is not given anywhere in the histories. In Giles' information from *Six Old English Chronicles*, the term Avalon is not even indexed under topographical information. Avalonia or the Isle of Avalon, which is the term synonymous with Glastonbury, appears only twice. Geoffrey of Monmouth, in describing the carnage of the Battle of Camlann, mentions that Cador, Arthur's relative and Duke of Cornwall, along with many thousands of others who died in this fateful battle, ends his passage by saying

> And even the renowned king Arthur himself was mortally wounded; and being carried thence to the isle of Avalon to be cured of his wounds, he gave up the crown of Britain to his kinsman Constantine, the son of Cador... in the five hundred and forty-second year of our Lord's incarnation.[22]

However, Monmouth does not assign the name Avalon to Glastonbury; he might have been thinking of Avalon as the Afterworld, or he might have had in mind a village on the continent by that name. In a different section Monmouth narrates that Arthur girded on his sword, called Caliburn, which was forged in the Isle of Avalon, but again, no indication is given that Avalon is Glastonbury or that Avalon is an earthly place.

Gildas Badonicus, of course, does not name Arthur, let alone his death-site. In addition to Nennius' also remaining silent on Arthur's death and burial-site, he does not list either Glastonbury or Avalon as major Briton cities. The latter might not imply much, however, since Glastonbury was undoubtedly a religious mecca and site for an abbey, not necessarily a prominent commercial, industrial, military, or political location.

THE GRAIL MANUSCRIPTS

At one point in her book attempting to verify King Arthur as a figure of the north, Norma Goodrich dismisses offhandedly walking through, or on, water. In writing about improbabilities found in the Grail manuscripts, Goodrich, questioning why directions to Grail Castle are not in any of the texts, writes:

> One land route runs into another, but the sea intervenes, either from the Solway Firth or from the Wirral Peninsula (adjacent to the modern port of Liverpool). Each text provides the questing hero, his departure on the quest, various recognizable stops along the way, familiar landmarks, and arrival at the Grail Castle, usually at nightfall. Now, if this castle is built upon an island in the sea, and furthermore hidden from sight until the hero stumbles down a steep grade inside a narrow cleft, how did he get there from the mainland?[23]

She answers her own question in the succeeding paragraph by saying, "All along the authors [of the Grail manuscripts] knew of course, that most bridges go *over* water and are not causeways through it, much less under it!" Coles and Orme prove without a doubt that in the Glastonbury area the bridges and trackways did go *through* and *under* the water, not over it.

Goodrich suggests Solway Firth and Wirral Peninsula, because she is attempting to establish Arthur's locale in the north. Wirral Peninsula provides an ironic twist for her reference to the peninsula between the River Dee and the River Mersey outlets near Liverpool. This locale is quite isolated for a northern Arthur, yet if a person simply makes the assumption that the term "Wirral" in the Grail manuscripts refers not to this particular peninsula, but instead refers to Wearyall Hill adjacent to Glastonbury Tor, then the manuscripts take on an entirely different and much more accurate perspective. Among others, Treharne and Carley use the variation of "Wirral Hill" to refer to this famous hill near Glastonbury where Joseph of Arimathea planted his staff which grew into the hollythorn tree. As a matter of fact, John of Glastonbury's original account in Latin reads, "Erat ea tempestate intra insulam Auallonie in Wirale monasterium sanctarum virginum, Petri apostoli nomine dedicatum, in quo rex Arthurus sepius quieuit et mansit loci amenitate illectus."[24] This translates to "In this time, on the Isle of Avalonia, there was on Wirale a monastery of the holy virgins, dedicated by the apostle Peter, in which King Arthur often rested because of its attractiveness." The term "Wearyall Hill" does not appear in any of the ancient manuscripts, but the term used is "Wirral Hill." Ekwall, in his dictionary, indicates that the term "Wirral" comes from Old English *wir* meaning "bog myrtle," with the plural form of Old English *halh* as a suffix. "Halh" is not exactly clear, but it seems to be a variant of "haugh," which means "enclosure." Wirral Hill, just south of the Tor, would be in the correct locale where bridges would, in fact, literally be causeways through or under water.

CARADOC OF LLANCARVAN:
THE LIFE OF GILDAS (ALBANIUS)

Another tale connecting Glastonbury and Arthur centers around the historical figure of Melwas. The principal source for this story comes from *The Life of Gildas*, recorded by Caradoc of Llancarvan, somewhere around 1140. This puts Caradoc quite close chronologically to Henry of Huntingdon and William of Malmsbury, and earlier than Cambrensis and Coggeshall. One of the peculiarities that Carley notes is why Malmsbury, if he were a fairly close contemporary with Caradoc, does not devote more explanation to St. Gildas, quite a prominent figure; Scott even suggests that Caradoc was probably at Glastonbury when William was, or at least soon after. At any rate, in the transmission of his story, Caradoc connects Arthur with Glastonbury; he describes the wicked King Melwas of the Summer Region (Somerset) abducting Guennuvar and holding her at Glastonbury. Caradoc refers to Glastonbury as the "City of Glass," deriving its name from the Welsh Yniswitrin but he gives no hint that this is identical to the island of Avalon. King Arthur travels with all of his forces from Devon and Cornwall to effect Guennuvar's release and exact vengeance. The abbot of Glastonbury, accompanied by St. Gildas, intervene as mediators to prevent a serious conflict; a solution is forged and peace is made, thus restoring the queen to Arthur. As a result of this mediation between the two kings, Glastonbury not only received territories for the Abbey but also extracted promises from both that they would obey Gildas faithfully and not violate the Abbey again. Carley explains that in John of Glastonbury's shorter account, the Latin is made simpler, and "all references to Arthur as *rex rebellis* or *tyrannus* and to the rape of Guinevere by Melwas are removed."[25] As for Malmsbury's silence, Scott suggests that Malmsbury was extremely cautious because of the Arthur connection, and since he, Malmsbury, wanted to report only reliable fact, he avoided the presentation of Gildas.[26]

There is another sidelight to this Melwas connection. Some scholars infer that there was a standing feud between Arthur and Gildas stemming from the death of Gildas' brother, Hueil, at the hands of Arthur. Because of this alleged feud and the bad blood between Arthur and Gildas, Gildas retaliates by not giving credit to Arthur as the leader of the Badon battle. However, the motive behind Gildas' omission of Arthur's name cannot be attributed to personal enmity since this premise is based on misidentification. Gildas' son of Caw is Gildas Albanius, not Gildas Badonicus. In literary tradition, where Gildas Albanius appears, Arthur and he are not on malevolent terms. In "Culhwch and Olwen," for example, as Culhwch invokes Olwen in the name of Arthur's warriors, he enumerates (as part of Arthur's warriors) not only Caw of Scotland, but lists 19 sons of Caw, including Gildas and Hueil. The story affirms that Hueil "never submitted to a lord's hand,"[27] and several pages later relates that a feud developed between Hueil and Arthur because Hueil had stabbed his own uncle Gwydre.[28] But there is no suggestion that this dispute sundered the relationship between Arthur and Gildas Albanius.

In "The Dream of Rhonabwy" Gildas Albanius is listed as one of Arthur's main advisors. Osla Big Knife, Arthur's enemy at Badon, asks for a fortnight's truce, and Arthur calls his council together to seek advice. This means that Gildas Albanius is one of Arthur's high-ranking men. Along with these episodes from the *Mabinogion*, then, the record from Caradoc reinforces that Gildas as a mediator in the dispute between Arthur and Melwas has no animosity toward Arthur. These overtures of camaraderie mandate a different reason if Gildas Badonicus did in truth deliberately shun Arthur as the Badon leader.

The Caradoc story has one other important aspect: that of labeling Glastonbury as the Isle of Glass. In the twelfth century when Caradoc makes this association, the Welsh already had a tradition about *Ynis Witrin*, which was where Melwas lived. It is described as a water-surrounded fortress of glass where nine maidens dwelt perpetually. Carley establishes this connection:

> The Isle of Glass bears a close resemblance to the Isle of Apples described by Geoffrey. It would therefore be possible for someone familiar with both these traditions to make the equation: Glastonbury = Isle of Glass = Isle of Apples = the isle to which the wounded Arthur was conveyed. Certainly it is tempting to think that something similar to this was at least a partial cause for the choice of [Glastonbury as the] excavation site [for Arthur's exhumation]. Moreover, as E.K. Chambers points out, there were probably many places which were known as Avalon in local traditions. Glastonbury was, without a doubt, considered a holy island long before the advent of Christianity and it is quite possible that it enjoyed locally the reputation of being an Isle of Avalon even before the exhumation took place.[29]

In perusing the tales of the *Mabinogion*, one other curiosity emerges regarding a possible equation between Glastonbury and the Isle of Apples. Admittedly it is slight and may dissipate like a phantasm, but there might be a connection and not just a coincidence. That connection is the apple motif on Arthur's mantle and on the mantle of his royal kinsman, Culhwch. Interest has thus far focused upon the *color* of Culhwch's mantle, purple, associated with the Gildas manuscript showing that Ambrosius Aurelianus and his family "wore the purple," a sign of royal Roman stock. Shifting from color to its design, the story describes the cloak: "Culhwch wore a four-cornered purple mantle with a red-gold apple in each corner; each apple was worth a hundred cows."[30] In the tale of Rhonabwy, the apple motif appears again: "This large red-haired man dismounted before Arthur, drew a gold chair and a ribbed brocade mantle from the pack, spread the mantle — there was a red-gold apple in each corner — and set the chair on it."[31] In this second quotation, the bard seems to draw deliberate attention to the red-gold apples. In addition to royalty and authority, both the color and the motif of the mantle states outright a blood-line connection between Arthur and Culhwch specifically, and implies an entire regal lineage. The red-gold apple as a logo may have been inspired by the connection of Arthur's family to the region of Glastonbury, the Island of Apples. The motif is strong enough to warrant attention.

Philip Rahtz has this to say about the connection among Arthur, Melwas, and Glastonbury. As a preface for the immediate post–Roman period, the only finds are those from the Tor. The Tor, if considered a defensive position, would be either a small outpost signaling station as part of a linked system of defensive sites, or, more probably the stronghold of a small local chieftain, which Rahtz favors much more as a permanent residence. He then continues, "If we wish to put a name to the chief of Glastonbury, it should be Melwas, chief of the *Aestiva Regio* [Summer Region] whom Arthur besieged in his Glastonbury stronghold and eventually concluded a treaty with." Rahtz even goes further: "If Arthur was buried at Glastonbury Abbey, he presumably had been a regular visitor there in pursuance of religious duties. However, his impious activities might have made him so much *persona non grata* with the monks at the abbey that he chose not to spend more time there than he had to, and preferred to resort to the Tor where he could eat and drink securely in the company of a few friends."[32] This same line of reasoning could explain why Arthur spent time at Beckery Hill and Wirral Hill rather than at the abbey.

There is one other interesting attachment between Melwas, Arthur, and their connection to Glastonbury. In "Culhwch and Olwen," when Culhwch invokes Olwen in the name of Arthur's warriors in the invocation, one of the names is Maelwys, son of Baeddan, the eighth name in Culhwch's extensive list, surrounded by names borrowed from Irish tales and British deities. No other comment is made of him, and no scholar specifically singles him out, but it is interesting that a tale this old includes him, although it might be nothing more than a bard's listing of any important name he could think of.

GIRALDUS CAMBRENSIS:
THE ARTHURIAN LINK 6½ DECADES LATER

In the year 1190 the abbot at Glastonbury Abbey, while having an ancient cemetery on the abbey's grounds excavated, allegedly discovered the bodies of King Arthur and Queen Guinevere between two ancient inscribed pyramids in an oaken entombment just a little to the south of the Lady Chapel. The site was marked by an inscribed leaden cross, face down.[33] Giraldus Cambrensis is the earliest known person to record this event and, more notably, the earliest source to make a connection between Avalon and Glastonbury. Nevertheless, he was not present during the disinterment, but evidently visited Glastonbury about 1193 and viewed the bones. His account appeared about a year after that in his manuscript *De Principis Instructione*. He writes about King Arthur having a special devotion to St. Mary of Glastonbury and being a generous patron who painted her image on his shield and paid homage to her in the hour of battle. Cambrensis retells the tales about Arthur which by that time had been around for centuries, claiming that these tales related how Arthur's body incarnate had been carried off by spirits to remote regions, how Arthur was not subjected to death, and how Arthur would rise again. These stories had been collected from monks reporting on manuscripts from the monastery, from letters carved on the pyramids, from visions and revelations made to other brethren of the order, and probably most impressively, from King Henry who had heard the story from an ancient historical poet of the Britons.[34]

The Cambrensis passage is fairly long but laden with important material, particularly since it is the original account of how Arthur came to be discovered at Glastonbury:

> Now the body of King Arthur which legend has feigned to have been transferred at his passing, as it were in ghostly form, by spirits to a distant place, and to have been exempt from death, was found in these our days at Glastonbury deep down in the earth and encoffined in a hollow oak between two stone pyramids erected long ago in the consecrated graveyard, the site being revealed by strange and almost miraculous signs, and it was afterwards transported with honour to the Church and decently consigned to a marble tomb. Now in the grave there was found a cross of lead, placed under a stone and not above it, as is now customary, but fixed on the under side. This cross I myself have seen, for I have felt the letters engraved thereon, which do not project or stand out, but are turned inwards toward the stone. They run as follows: "Hic jacet sepultus inclitus rex Arthurus cum Wenneveria exore sua secunda in insula Avallonia." Now in regard to this there are many things worthy of note. For he had two wives, the last of whom was buried with him, and her bones were found together with his, but separated from them as thus; two parts of the tomb, to wit, the head, were allotted to the bones of the man, while the remaining third towards the foot contained the bones of the woman in a place apart; and there was found a yellow tress of woman's hair still retaining its colour and freshness; but when a certain monk snatched it and lifted it with greedy hand, it straightway all of it fell into dust. Now whereas there were certain indications in their writings that the body would be found there, and others in the letters engraved on the pyramids, though they were much defaced by their extreme age, and others again were given in visions and relations vouchsafed to good men and religious, yet it was above all King Henry II of England that most clearly informed the monks, as he himself heard from an ancient Welsh bard, a singer of the past, that they would find the body at least sixteen feet beneath the earth, not on a tomb of stone, but in a hollow oak. And this is the reason why the body was placed so deep and hidden away, to wit, that it might not by any means be discovered by the Saxons, who occupied the island after his death, whom he had so often in his life defeated and almost utterly destroyed; and for the same reason those letters, witnessing to the truth, that were stamped upon the cross, were turned inwards toward the stone, that they might at that time conceal what the tomb contained, and yet in due time and place might one day reveal the truth. ... You must also know that the bones of Arthur were [so] huge. ... For his shank-bone when placed against that of the tallest man in that place, and planted in the earth near his foot, reached, as the Abbot showed us, a good three inches above his knee. And the skull was so large and capacious as to be a portent or a prodigy, for the eyesocket was a good palm in width. Moreover, there were ten wounds or more, all of which were scarred over, save one larger than the rest, which had made a great hole.[35]

Giraldus explains that the unassuming tomb itself was oaken so that the site would not attract attention or be desecrated by the enemy if discovered. Further, he offers that the grave was at a great depth of 16 feet to escape detection, but he makes no reference in this passage that the depth was a direct result of Saint Dunstan in the tenth century raising the level of the cemetery, nor does he give any reason why Dunstan would do this. C.A. Ralegh Radford indicates that a modern trench revealed a major disturbance in the soil, attributing that disturbance to the exhumation in the last decade of the twelfth century. Alcock gives specifics:

> Trenching there in 1962 disclosed firstly a pit apparently about five feet across, from which a great cross might have been removed; then, about ten feet further south, traces of an early mausoleum, which had already been demolished in the tenth century; and third, between the mausoleum and the pit, a large, irregular hole which had been dug out and then shortly afterwards refilled in the 1180s or 1190s.[36]

A second point of interest is the pair of pyramids which Cambrensis describes. Radford suggests that these pyramids "consisted of low partly underground chambers large enough to contain a coffin and marked by lofty standing crosses."[37] Malmsbury describes some of these pyramids at Glastonbury; he is unsure of the meanings of their structures, but he suggests hesitantly that within those hollowed stones are the bones of those whose names can be read on the outside. He then describes the pyramids which stand a few feet from the Old Church. He writes, "The nearer [one] to the church is twenty-six feet high and has five storeys to it. ... The other pyramid is eighteen feet high and has four storeys."[38] Radford, too, proposes that "A man such as Arthur, if resident of Somerset in the sixth century, would probably have been buried at Glastonbury, and a warrior of his fame might be expected to be found buried alongside the mausoleum of a saint,"[39] which he deduces are saints' burial sites marked by pyramids.

The leaden cross, sometimes called the Glastonbury Cross or Arthur's Cross, is one of the most written-about artifacts associated with Arthur's historicity. Cambrensis' information is compact but detailed. He specifies that the leaden cross was affixed to the underpart of a stone in such a way that the inscription was turned inward. The grave, 16 feet below the surface, and the cross concealed face-down on the stone, he explains, was because of a desire to hide the body from the Saxon enemies. He then quotes the inscription on the cross, which he himself had seen, as being "Hic jacet sepultus inclitus rex Arthurus cum Wenneveria exore sua secunda in insula Avallonia."[40] After a silence of centuries, the alleged inscription finally makes the connection between Glastonbury and the Isle of Avalon. Giraldus goes on to say that "what is now called Glastonia was anciently called Insula Avalonia, for it is an island surrounded by marshes, wherefore in the British language it is named Inis Avalon, that is, 'insula pomifera' for at one time the island abounded in apples, for which the British word is 'aval.'"[41] This shows that Giraldus accepts the etymology of the apple motif rather than the Avallach theory. He also uses the terms "inis guitrin" and "insula vitrea," explaining the origin of those references.

According to Alcock, John Leland supposedly saw the cross in 1542, and gave the inscription as "HIC IACET SEPVLTVS INCLYTVS REX ARTVRIVS IN INSVLA AVALONIA."[42] This agrees with the Cambrensis inscription, excluding the reference to the queen. Ralph of Coggeshall's inscription is very similar, except "sepvltvs" comes at the end; that is, it reads, "Hic iacet inclitus rex Arturius in insula Avallonis sepultus."[43] Another minor point is that Leland's inscription has a "y" substitution in the word "inclitus." Alcock is very forgiving of the minor variations, as one should be, explaining that Richard Robinson published an English translation of John Leland's, and though he had Leland's version in front of him, he differed from it at four points. It is very easy, and not at all uncommon, to make errors in transcription.

Camden, however, plays an important role in verifying or nullifying Arthur's burial site as Glastonbury. His drawing of the Glastonbury lead cross has become the prototype for all the modern-day souvenirs, which follows the inscription reported by John Leland with the exception of the spelling for "Inclitus." The "Us" look like "Vs," the "Ns" like "Hs," and the "J" like an "I." The distinction between an actual "H" and an "N" is obvious in the horizontal cross-bar; on the "H" it is thin, while for the "'N" it is thick. This inscription, then, agrees not only with Leland, but also Coggeshall and Cambrensis without the reference to the Queen. Camden is quoted as saying, "Sed ecce crucem illam et inscriptionem,"[44]—"This is the cross itself and the inscription." Robinson points out that Camden's drawing is only an illustration, since in earlier editions the antique letters were shown, arranged as

HIC IACET SEP-
VLTUS INCLITVS
REX ARTVRIUS IN
INSULA AVALO
NIA

Robinson believes that the configuration of the cross is Camden's afterthought and then emphatically asserts that "It is only the antique form of the letters for which Camden expressly vouches."[45] Treharne reports that in 1542 John Leland actually had the cross in his hands and was able to examine it carefully, "giving the height as about one foot."[46]

The last item of importance is Cambrensis' remarks about the size of the bones. His comment about the large size of the shank-bone is vague because he does not provide the height of the "tallest man there." Three inches above a normal man's knee need not be extraordinary, but his comments about the skull are unusual indeed. An eye socket the size of a palm, even the palm of a small man, would indicate a mammoth head. One might expect that the ancient remains of Arthur would be noteworthy, accentuated by Cambrensis using words such as "portent" and "prodigy." Alcock offers the possibility that some historians might go to great lengths to "salt" the grave, but dismisses the speculation by commenting that "no modern archaeologist would know where to dig up such a burial."[47]

In Cambrensis' subsequent writing about the exhumation a quarter of a century later in a book titled *Speculum Ecclesiae*, there are changes and elaboration from his first manuscript. He gives some exhortations about monks, but he omits the details about the King's size. As another variation, in the first he puts "in insula Avalonia" at the end of the inscription, whereas the second inscription reads, "His jacet supultus inclitus Rex Arthurius in insula Avalonia cum Wenneveria sua secunda." However, he does retain the Guinevere account, which is characteristic only in the Giraldus manuscripts.

TURN OF THE 13TH CENTURY:
ADAM OF DOMERHAM

When reading Adam of Domerham (more uncommonly spelled as Damerham) and John of Glastonbury, the two considerations which should be uppermost are that these scribes from the Abbey followed Giraldus Cambrensis by about 100 years and 150 years respectively, plus both of these writers were using the text of Malmsbury's *De Antiquitate* which had been drastically interpolated and modified. As a matter of fact, at the very onset, John states that "If I have followed the lead of the monk William of Malmsbury, I have also followed that of brother Adam of Domerham, another monk of this said monastery of ours."[48] In the next sentence he indicates that William of Malmsbury began Glastonbury's history with the coming of Joseph of Arimathea, which alerts the reader immediately that the version of the *De Antiquitate* he used had been modified, since the Arimathea story was not added to Malmsbury's manuscript until the year 1247. Scott refers to the Arimathea story as "an even later embellishment [to Malmsbury's text],"[49] and Robinson introduces his chapter on Joseph of Arimathea by saying that "William of Malmsbury knows nothing of Joseph of Arimathea."[50]

Malmsbury's *De Antiquitate* underwent a great deal of change during the subsequent century, with the two major additions to it being the exhumation of King Arthur and the Arimathea story, traceable, according to Scott, by the use of different pens, by the use of simplistic grammatical structure contrasted to Malmsbury's more complex use, and by poor Latinity. A great many annotations had been added, leading to a detailed revision which necessarily meant that some scribe would have incorporated these additions into a coherent whole. Scott is confident enough to say that "it can be discerned easily that at least two different monks were involved."[51] Adam of Domerham is the monk who emerges as one of the most likely and obvious candidates for accomplishing this task.

A survey of the bibliography in this text showed that only a handful of scholars referred to Adam of Domerham, and even among those who did, the information was minimal. He had a profound influence on establishing Arthurian ties to Glastonbury, yet his work can be summarized perfunctorily while still maintaining the essence of his effect. Adam of Domerham's *Historia de rebus Glastoniensibus*, written about 1290, showed that the author not only had a vested interest in the well-being of Glastonbury Abbey, but also that he was in a position to help the monastery's cause. He held the positions of cellarer, the person in charge of provisions for the entire monastery, in addition to being the sacristan, the monk in charge of the sacristy, where sacred vessels, ceremonial equipment, and clothes were kept. His other main task was in the transcribing of some of the manuscripts of the Abbey. When he was put in charge of compiling documents into a coherent unit, the Abbey itself was going through a difficult period, including the threat of encroachment by its rival municipality of Wells, just to the north. Thomas Hearne, in reporting on Adam's copy of *Historia de rebus*, states that the monk's "avowed aim is an attempt to incite the manuscript's readers to protect and to increase the prosperity of Glastonbury Abbey."[52]

Adam's account indicates that the newly appointed abbot, Henry de Sully, was admonished concerning a more honorable placing of the famous King, for Arthur had rested near the Old Church between two stone pyramids nobly engraved in former time, for 648 years, and they decided on exhumation and movement into the main church in front of the high altar. He continues:

> When they had dug to an immense depth and were almost in despair, they found a wooden sarcophagus of wondrous size, enclosed on every side. When they had raised and opened it they found the king's bones, which were incredibly large so that one shin-bone reached from the ground to the middle of a tall man's leg, and even further. They found also a leaden cross, having on one side the inscription: "Hic jacet sepultus inclitus rex Arturius in insula Avallonia." After this they opened the tomb of the queen who was buried with Arthur, and found a fair yellow lock of woman's hair plaited with wondrous art, but when they touched it, it crumbled almost to nothing.[53]

Adam relates, too, that curtains (some accounts use the translation of "tents") surrounded the exhumation of Arthur. In 1278 he writes of King Edward I's visit to deposit Arthur's bones in a place of great honor. Like Giraldus before him and John of Glastonbury after him, Adam draws upon the tampered manuscript of Malmsbury's *De Antiquitate*, but whereas his predecessors and successors might not have been aware of the changes to the *De Antiquitate*, Adam was cognizant of the manipulated additions because of his direct involvement.

FOURTEENTH CENTURY: JOHN OF GLASTONBURY

A half-century later, John of Glastonbury finished his manuscript *The Chronicle of Glastonbury*. In his Prologue, he cites two main sources, William of Malmsbury's *De Antiquitate Glastonie Ecclesie*, and Adam of Domerham's *Historia de rebus Glastoniensibus*,[54] as well as excerpts from Giraldus, Ralph Higden's *Polychronicon*, legends of the saints, and "other writings in ancient books." He uses Malmsbury's *Gestis Regum Anglorum* as his source for the general history of any given reign, but then uses the *De Antiquitate* with all of its incorporated interpolations. Carley reports that Malmsbury's *de Gestis Pontificum Anglorum* is not incorporated in any existing Glastonbury records, nor does John of Glastonbury directly quote from it.[55]

This search of the material from John of Glastonbury will naturally focus on any Arthurian material. The first reference to Arthur is in section IX which lists the relics of St. Mary and describes a crystal cross given to the glorious King Arthur by the Blessed Virgin. This cross is mentioned again in section XXXIIII, in a story about two of King Arthur's visions while he was at the monastery of holy virgins on Wearyall Hill. After an ensuing confusing story about the king's squire, Arthur goes to the chapel, sees marvelous things, and has an old man interpret his visions. As an outcome Arthur accepts Christianity, changes his arms in honor of the Lady Virgin and Her Son, and receives the crystal cross to commemorate his conversion. John of Glastonbury says of the relic "to this day [it] is honourably housed and guarded in the treasury of Glastonbury and is carried every year during Lent through the convent."[56] Malmsbury, on the other hand, does not verify this preserved relic, nor does it actually appear in the Abbey's relic lists, which exclude what Carley calls possible romance items. John included this on his list anyway, although the crystal cross is neither observed, commented upon, nor written about.

In section XIII John incorporates material borrowed from Geoffrey of Monmouth: Arthur is fatally wounded by Mordred in Cornwall near the River Camblam. In section XXXV he reaffirms Arthur's pursuing Mordred into the far reaches of Cornwall, catching him and killing him, but the king himself is fatally wounded in the same battle. The king is taken to Avalon (which John explains is now called Glastonbury) where his diseases grow serious. He dies, and is buried deep to prevent the Saxons from desecrating his tomb. John echoes Cambrensis that Guinevere is buried there with him, but in recording the inscription of the cross, he gives only the name of Arthur.

Two other sections echo Geoffrey of Monmouth. In section XX after a reference that King Arthur is associated with Joseph of Arimathea, John talks about Lancelot du Lac, the Round Table, Gawain, the Holy Grail, and Galahad. Section XXXII ties together the date 495 from the *Anglo Saxon Chronicle*, Cerdic, Utherpendragon, his son Arthur, Aurelius Ambrosius, Ygerna, Tintagel, Joseph of Arimathea, Saint Gildas Albanius and the conflict between Hueil and Arthur, concluding with Gildas' sojourn, death, and burial at Glastonbury. This mixture epitomizes Adam of Domerham's interweavings of the myriad of interpolations hooked together to form a web of intriguing mystery shrouding Glastonbury and associating it with every important piece of history and tradition that transpired in south-central Britain.

The next section, XXXIII, borrows the 12 battles from Nennius and links those struggles with Cerdic, who if "one month Arthur vanquished him, rose up the next fiercer for the fight. Finally, when Arthur tired of the conflict, he accepted Cerdic's fealty and gave him Hampshire and Somerset, which Cerdic called Wessex."[57] These suggestions have flavorings from some of the ancient literature, particularly *The Mabinogion*.

In section XIIII John describes Arthur's processional to the Isle of Avalon where he died and was buried, making the claim which by now strongly persists that Glastonbury is in fact the Isle of Avalon. After this connection between Glastonbury and Avalon, in Section XVI John then uses a third synonym, Ynswytryn, describing Glastonbury as once being surrounded with forests, thickets, and marshes, and giving it the Welsh name. Also in section XVI he gives the barest hint of the Joseph of Arimathea story by saying that this island is the same one that was given to Joseph of Arimathea. The Arimathea story resurfaces in section

XXI in a passage headed "This bears witness that King Arthur descended from the stock of Joseph."[58]

He continues with more detail of Arthur's burial and exhumation in section LXXXXVIII, describing Arthur's oaken tomb, detailing Guinevere's burial with him, and giving the same inscription on the cross with no reference to the Queen. He describes the size of Arthur's bones but does not go into Giraldus' graphic detail of the king's skull and its gaping hole. John then recapitulates the removal of the bones into the main church, where they were entombed in front of the high altar. He begins Section CXXVIIII with a dedication commenting one last time on Arthur's exhumation by Edward when the bones were speedily moved and placed before the high altar, with an inscription that King Arthur's bones were placed there in 1278; John adds that only the "heads and knee-joints of [Arthur and Guinevere] were kept out for the people's devotion."[59] At least one other manuscript indicates that the skulls of the two skeletons were displayed, but says nothing of the knee-joints.

As part of the summary on Glastonbury, one other matter deserves attention: the role that Glastonbury plays in some of the Arthurian legends. One of these is the Ider story, recorded in Section XXXIII, which John in turn probably copied from the interpolated version of William of Malmsbury, chapters 34 and 69. In the Malmsbury edition, Arthur is at Caerleon one Christmas when he sends Ider the son of King Nuth to Frog Mountain, now called Brent Knoll, to slay three wicked giants who reside there. Ider precedes Arthur, attacks and kills the giants. Weak from excessive exertion and helplessly lying in a trance, Ider is near death by the time Arthur arrives. Arthur, thinking the young man dead, leaves him unattended and the young man eventually does die. Because Arthur feels himself responsible, when he returns to Glastonbury, he establishes 80 monks there to pray for Ider's soul, and generously grants land, territories, silver, gold, chalices, and "other ecclesiastical ornaments" to the monastery. Chapter 69 of Malmsbury simply affirms that Arthur gave Brent Marsh, Poweldone, and many other lands to Glastonbury for the soul of Ider.

John of Glastonbury inserts more detail, but it is unknown if John was copying Malmsbury and adding details of his own, or if he also had another manuscript available. He relates that at one Christmas festival in Caerleon, King Arthur, after knighting Ider, sends him to Areynes in North Wales where three giants are misbehaving. When the giants are slaughtered, Arthur arrives on the scene and finds Ider, who, "being worn out by his great labor and wholly out of control of his faculties, collapsed unconscious." Arthur leaves Ider as dead, Ider then indeed dies, and when Arthur returns to Glastonbury, he establishes 24 monks there for the sake of Ider's soul, and abundantly bestows possessions, territories, and other items on Glastonbury. The end of the account is the same in both John's version and the interpolated Malmsbury one: the pagan Saxons take away the land given by Arthur, but then, once the Saxons convert to the faith of Christ, they restore these lands along with many other territories.

John's account has an interesting variation. Did an earlier interpolater actually record Frog Mountain/Brent Knoll, and if so, why did John change it to

Wales? Carley explains that there is no specific known romance which connects Ider, son of Nuth, and Arthur, but Arthur has a similar adventure with a giant on Glastonbury Tor. The speculation is that both stories came from the same source, indicating that John's story makes more sense geographically since an adventure on Brent Knoll would be too far from Caerleon, while, if the story is meant to perpetrate a ruse about Arthur's land grants to Glastonbury, then the story loses its logic through the change in location. To complicate matters, the "Mount of Frogs" has metamorphosed into the "Mount of Spiders" through the misreadings of *aranearum* for *renarum*.[60]

A third legend (or, more accurately, a tale or tradition) is the Arthur story directly related to Glastonbury about Arthur's vision of the Virgin Mary. In a fairly long story in section XXXIIII in John of Glastonbury's *Cronica*, while Arthur is sleeping in the monastery of holy virgins at Wearyall on the island of Avalon, he is awakened by an angel of the Lord calling his name. The angel tells him to arise at dawn and go to the hermitage of St. Mary Magdalene of Beckery on that island to see and learn things which are happening there. On Gawain's advice he ignores the vision, but he is visited a second time by an angel, yet the king decides to wait for a third visit. In the interim Arthur's servant has a dream of going to the hermitage, and John relates a confusing story in which the squire's dream turns out to be a reality. Robinson, who actually quotes the entire story, indicates that John has omitted something.[61] At any rate, the squire dies because of his misdeeds at the hermitage, and Arthur visits the hermitage by himself at dawn. He is barred entrance and is terrified because he does not know what prevents him from entering the holy place.

After kneeling, praying and meditating, humbly begging pardon for his sins, he is able to enter. The king observes the sacrifice of mass and afterwards sees a vision of the Holy Mother and her Son. The old priest who had recited the mass explains the vision, and the king vows to believe firmly in the holy sacrament and to do anything asked of him for love of the glorious Mother and her Son. After all of these revelations, according to John's account, Our Lady, the glorious Mother, in testimony of this, gives to the king a crystal cross described above. Arthur changes his shield in their honor, and in lieu of his arms being three red lions, on a silver background, turning their heads over their backs, his blazon becomes a green background with a silver cross, and upon the cross's right arm, an image of the Virgin Mary holding her Son in her arms.

There are two important attachments to this particular story. The first is one which has already been suggested, centered around the opening, which puts Arthur at Wearyall and Beckery, rather than the Abbey proper. Perhaps, as Rahtz suggests, Arthur was uncomfortable at the Abbey and did not like to resort to the companionship of the monks, therefore residing during his sojourns in a more serene spot. The second, more important attachment refers to Chapter LV in Nennius. The eighth battle was in Guinnion fort [castello Guinnion] and in it Arthur carried the image of the holy Mary, the everlasting Virgin, on his shield [humeros].

In order to accept the Virgin Mary and Son blazon on Arthur's shield as verifiable, some explanation has to exist between the entry by Nennius and the one given by John of Glastonbury. If there is no explanation from an independent unbiased source in the intervening centuries, it becomes obligatory to label John's account as an interpolated attempt at deceit, especially since Arthur's new blazon is identical to the one accepted by the abbey on the grounds that vested interest motivated the invention of a legend to explain Nennius' cryptic addition to Arthur's eighth battle. Without that intervening source, it would be very easy for any monk familiar with Nennius to supply a story which explained Nennius' entry in order to extricate the Abbey from its political and or financial straits.

Drawn from the bibliography in this text, only two authors address Nennius' passage of "Arthur carried the image of the holy Mary, the everlasting Virgin, on his shield/shoulders." Fletcher touches upon it and comes up with an intervening legend of sorts. He labels Nennius' statement as clumsy and repetitious, reports that Monmouth restores some sentence logic, and explains that William of Malmsbury (he probably means an interpolator of Malmsbury) reports that Arthur had sewed the image on his arms. Geoffrey of Monmouth is not the intervening unbiased source; although he reports the passage, he does not explain the story behind it. Malmsbury is not that source because Malmsbury, in his original *De Antiquitate*, prior to the later tampering, does not specify Arthur. Unfortunately, Fletcher then sidetracks to an error in translation between "shoulder" and "shield."[62] He quickly redeems himself by giving an explanation of the Cambridge edition of Nennius, which states,

> For Arthur went to Jerusalem, and there made a cross of the size of the true cross, and there it was consecrated, and for three whole days he fasted, watched, and prayed before the cross of the Lord that the Lord would give him victory over the pagans through this rood; which was granted. And he took away with him the image of the Holy Mary, whose fragments are still kept at Wedel in great veneration.[63]

The thrust, however, of Fletcher's inquiry has to do with the Badon entry in the *Annales Cambriae*, including the cross, and the confusion with the Guinnion entry and its mention of the Holy Virgin. The important revelation of Fletcher's conclusion is that even in the tenth century Arthur had become a heroic Welsh figure. In questioning whether or not the Jerusalem myth is the intervening unbiased legend explaining Arthur's blazon mentioned by Nennius, there is, as usual, no simple yes or no. Yes, this myth is disassociated with Glastonbury; yes, it is twelfth century and unattached to Cambrensis, Adam, or John; and yes, it does explain why Arthur would change the blazon on his shield.

But the explanation is shrouded in skepticism. Fletcher indicates that the recorded legend might be from the "genuine" Nennius and may be even older than the time of Nennius. But the specificity of the blazon on Arthur's shield is the image of the Holy Virgin and not the cross. And of course there are some claimed relics, but nothing has ever manifested itself. Lastly, what is most difficult to accept is Arthur's pilgrimage to Jerusalem. There is no historical or literary record, by inference or implication, that Arthur journeyed to the Holy City. The answer to the question does not enter the realm of possibility; it is neither likely nor probable that this story offers a logical explanation of why Arthur changed the blazon on his shield.

Richard Barber, the other scholar who deals with this passage, is more thorough and much more convincing. In *The Figure of Arthur* he deals directly with the Guinnion passage. He demonstrates the difficulty of dealing with the major details in Nennius and sites specifically the image of the Virgin on Arthur's shoulder. He, too, briefly points out the mistranslation of "shield" and "shoulder" but then moves quickly to the more compelling aspects of the entry. He candidly declares that

> A detailed device on a shield of this date has yet to be found, and even in the eleventh century, devices were still extremely simple. ... On the other hand, there is a long tradition of bearing crosses into battle, though even this is rare enough in the west.[64]

The last sentence of the above quotation is what prevents total closure to the concept that Arthur's religious affiliations with Glastonbury were fictitious. The likelihood of Arthur's change of blazon falls into a proper historical framework. The Roman emperor Gallienus who reigned from A.D. 253 to A.D. 268 was much more tolerant of Christianity and refrained from any active repression. Although the later emperor Galerius persecuted Christians with a vengeance during his reign, he asked their forgiveness on his deathbed. Then, when Constantine came to power after A.D. 311 he offered recognition and preferential treatment to the Christian church. Over the next three centuries, close workable relations developed between the church and the empire, suggesting that Arthur's era — the latter half of the fifth century and into the sixth — was a transitional period reflecting the rise of Christianity in Britain.

Recorded history shows that several of the Caesars viewed the island Druids as one of their most formidable threats and hence persecuted them vigorously, eventually driving them from southern England to the far reaches of northwestern Wales and the Isle of Anglesey. The early tales and romances are filled with details suggesting Arthur's Druidic connections. During his reign, Arthur attempted to balance the ways of the Old People and those of the rising Christians, joining the Druidic belief in the Goddess and drawing parallels with the Blessed Virgin and her Son.

Barber's remark about the simplicity of designs in heraldic arms during Arthur's time is logical. Later, the heraldic arms of the twelfth and thirteenth centuries became more elaborate. For example, the emblem of the rampant lion on the shields of Sir Tristram, Sir Pellinor, and Sir Brunor were quite detailed, varying only in color. The two-headed falcons on the shields of Mordred, Gareth, and Gawain are equally artistic, though some of the romance shields are simple designs. Two of Arthur's blazons during the romance period are of simpler design, but the Christian one bearing the Virgin and Her Son — recorded by John of Glastonbury — is complex.

The history of Mariolatry which Barber presents is also accurate[65]; there is no physical evidence, archaeological or otherwise, that can dispute what he offers;

no intervening legends verify that Arthur changed his blazon because of what happened to him at Glastonbury. The question proposed earlier about an intervening legend to explain Arthur's change of blazon because of the Nennius entry still points to an answer of "no." The only conclusion then, is that the story of Arthur's vision that appears in the Glastonbury manuscripts picked up on Nennius' cue and was invented, probably for aggrandizement of the Abbey.

Accepting this conclusion, however, does not mean that any association between Arthur and Glastonbury is automatically non-existent, nor that the recorded history of the period about the decline of Druidism and the simultaneous rise of Christianity can be negated. Specifically, it means that in all probability, Arthur did not change his shield and fight the Battle of Guinnion with the image of his Protectress painted on his shield. Generally it does, however, call into question other possible deceits perpetrated by the abbot or monks of Glastonbury, but each item has to be judged on its own merit.

THE PER CONTRA ARCHAEOLOGICAL EVIDENCE OF GLASTONBURY'S ARTHURIAN EXHUMATION

The task of establishing an accurate composite picture of Glastonbury in Arthurian terms is an extremely complex process attested to by the persistent work of meticulous scholars such as Robinson, Carley, Scott, Sawyer, Treharne, Alcock, Radford, and Ekwall. In spite of these authors' dedication, the picture of Glastonbury remains opaque. Drawing hope from Pandora's box, archaeological evidence of Glastonbury and its surroundings should provide insights to either reinforce or disclaim Arthur's burial there; the expected result is not undeniable proof, for neither the scientific approach of modern archaeology nor the precision of modern scholarship can guarantee that.

As a recapitulation, the following details itemize what some documents have given us about Glastonbury Abbey, six centuries after Arthur's time:

1. An exhumation occurred in the old cemetery of Glastonbury some time in the last decade of the twelfth century.
2. The site for the digging was between two pyramids.
3. The hole dug for the exhumation was about 16 feet deep.
4. The coffin was an oaken entombment.
5. A leaden cross was unearthed.
6. Two skeletons were exhumed.
7. Two contemporaries, but not actual eyewitnesses, write of the exhumation.

The verification of an excavation which was actually carried out comes from the writings of C.A. Ralegh Radford and Leslie Alcock. Alcock writes,

> Trenching there [between the two pyramids mentioned by William of Malmsbury] in 1962 disclosed firstly a pit apparently about five feet across, from which a great cross might have been removed; then, about ten feet further south, traces of an early mausoleum, which had already been demolished in the tenth century; and third,

between the mausoleum and the pit, a large irregular hole which had been dug out and then shortly afterwards refilled in the 1180s or 1190s. The evidence for this precise date is the occurrence in the hole of masons' chippings of the Doulton stone which was used only in building the Lady Chapel in 1184-9. The masons' chippings can scarcely have lain around the area for any length of time. All this points to the irregular hole being the one from which the bones claimed as those of Arthur and Guinevere were exhumed in 1191.[66]

The passage is important, not because it verifies the skeletons as those of Arthur and Guinevere, but because the 1962 archaeological dig verifies an exhumation at that site during the time period when it was claimed. Alcock then goes on to write specifically about the mausoleum, traces of which were also found in the 1962 dig. Of the mausoleum and the pyramidal location, he deduces that "The mausoleum would have held the body or relics of some important saint and burial close beside it would have been a considerable privilege."[67]

From Radford, the primary source, Alcock's paraphrased account is almost identical in wording. Radford indicates that the ordinary graves in the cemetery were rough chests formed by slabs of stone in a box-like fashion with the top stone laid flush with the surface of the cemetery. Of the pyramids, he says,

> This term [pyramid], though originally used to describe a special form of shrine, probably meant in the twelfth century no more than a venerated tomb or shrine, or even, as other accounts of the Glastonbury cemetery suggest, the cross that marked it.[68]

The essence of the information is that given by Alcock: the damaged edges of a hole three to four feet across showed that a large object, probably a monolith, had been dragged from the hole; the mausoleum measured eight feet by seven feet over-all, marked on the surface by a cross; at the bottom of the hole two or perhaps three slablined graves had been destroyed. Radford writes that "Mausolea of this type are rare in Britain. They are rather more common in Gaul and belong to a very early class of burial. At Glastonbury they may be ascribed with some confidence to the period before the Saxon conquest."[69] He then concludes that "One of these destroyed graves was set against the wall of the mausoleum: a position likely to have been granted only to a person of importance."[70]

This relates directly to information about the reported changes made by St. Dunstan as the abbot at Glastonbury:

> At a date before the twelfth century, mausoleum and graves were covered by a bank of clay which still remains to a depth of three feet six inches. On the outer, south side, this bank was delimited by a stone wall of which the foundation trench was found. On the other side, it sloped down towards the Lady Chapel, which stood on the same level as the mausoleum and graves. It is recorded of St. Dunstan that, while he was abbot, in the middle of the tenth century, he enclosed the cemetery of the monks on the south side of the church with a wall of masonry. The area within was raised to form a pleasant meadow, removed from the noise of the passers by, so that it might truly be said of the bodies of the saints lying within that they "repose in

peace." A raising of the level of this whole area would have left the old church of St. Mary half-buried; the formation of an enclosing terrace, as discovered in 1954, is practicable and conforms to the words of the saint's biographer.[71]

Radford's last statement is unequivocal: "It is therefore certain that the large hole discovered in 1962 represents the excavation for the bodies of Arthur and Guinevere."[72] Again, none of this verifies undeniably the skeletons of Arthur and Guinevere, nor does this exhumation verify Glastonbury as Arthur's burial site, but it does confirm an exhumation at this spot and during this period of history, involving some person or persons of importance.

Although stories about the crystal cross given to King Arthur by the Virgin Mary are spurious, the leaden cross, on the other hand, provides interesting speculation, with charges and countercharges about its authenticity. This cross is reported on by Cambrensis, Coggeshall, John, Adam, several antiquarians, and probably all modern scholars. One claim states that the cross is obviously of twelfth century origin. Carley points out, for example, that Stephen Morland claims the word *inclitus* reflects a twelfth century term. Moreover Aelred Watkin states that there is a late twelfth century carving over a doorway of the church in Stoke-sub-Hamdon whose lettering is identical in form to that found on the cross.[73] Another claim indicates that the lettering on the cross is more likely to be of the tenth century rather than of the late twelfth century. Radford, for example, believes that there is no reason to doubt the basic accuracy of the letter forms as engraved by Camden, which would be tenth century.[74] The universal agreement, though, is that the cross is *not* of early sixth century origins.

More important than the wording or the reference to Guinevere is the epigraphic study of the lettering. Robinson expressly points out that Camden does not vouch for either the shape of the cross or for the arrangements of the lettering, but specifically Camden attests to the shape of the lettering. Alcock proposes the most comprehensive explanation of this cross. Although Alcock feels that the accuracy of Camden's drawing is vital and establishes a case as to the 1607 edition of *Britannia* being larger to accommodate a full-scale facsimile, the exactitude of the shape of the cross does not seem to be a crucial issue. As a matter of fact, Alcock states that the scaled facsimile by Camden is six and seven-eighths inches tall, but according to Treharne, the antiquarian John Leland handled the cross and estimated its size as about a foot.

Alcock's hypothesis about the lettering is quite convincing; it is not an inscription contemporary with Arthur's death in the first half of the sixth century, and he points out that various letter forms such as Ns which look like Hs, and square Cs argue against that early date. Similarly, however, those same clues argue against a date in the late twelfth century. Alcock asserts that the best comparisons for the letters are provided by the inscriptions on late Saxon coins, and on these epigraphic grounds he sets a date in the tenth or eleventh centuries.

At first, this seems to complicate matters even further: in the search for a sixth century figure, a cross discovered in the twelfth century has what appears to be tenth century inscriptions. Yet applying what has already been discovered of Glastonbury's history through expert scrutiny of some of the church's reliable records and chronicles, Alcock pieces together this story.

> We know that when St. Dunstan was Abbot of Glastonbury in the years after 945 he enclosed the ancient cemetery with a masonry wall and raised the area itself. Excavations in 1954 and 1962 showed that the raising of the level had been done by laying down a broad low bank of clay. ... The demolition of the mausoleum may well have been part of Dunstan's work. Had there been a monument to Arthur standing just north of the mausoleum it would have been removed at the same time. But it may have been felt that the grave of such a distinguished person should not go altogether unmarked, so a lead cross, inscribed in contemporary tenth-century letters, was placed in the grave. ... Consequently the tenth-century text, improving on its original in the customary manner, added two phrases which could not have been on the sixth-century memorial: INCLITVS REX, "illustrious king," and IN INSVLA AVALONIA, "in the isle of Avalon." These, then were the cross and the burial which were exhumed in 1191.[75]

Alcock admits that this is a hypothesis. Yet quite independent of this passage, the hypothesis does not require a fantastic stretch of the imagination; one is automatically struck by the logistics of what emerges, particularly the connection between St. Dunstan's landscaping of the old cemetery and the tenth century leaden cross. This suggests that other scholars, too, would reach strikingly similar conclusions, and that in itself should merit consideration. Radford cites two instances of the square "C" and three instances of the "N" with a horizontal crossbar as debased and straggling Roman capitals, ending the explanation with "These forms are proper to the eleventh century or earlier, rather than to the twelfth. If the cross was really a fabrication of the late twelfth century, the maker was unusually consistent. It seems more likely that it was a genuine relic of [Norman, 1066] pre–Conquest date."[76]

Other accounts explain that the depth of the grave was a Briton attempt to conceal the body from Saxon discovery. That Arthur's gravesite was discovered accidentally while the monks were burying one of their brethren, as reported in Ralph of Coggeshall's chronicle, can be discounted immediately. Assuming the common burial practice of a grave's six-foot depth, and no historical recording for a burial depth of two-and-a-half times that, the monks would not have conceivably dug a standard grave to a depth of 16 feet.

The depth of 16 feet, however, makes perfect sense when viewed in conjunction with St. Dunstan's elevating the old cemetery by ten feet. Radford affirms that the conditions and arrangements of the gravesite are in keeping with expectations:

> It is clear that, if the hypotheses outlined above (Glastonbury being a Christian sanctuary during the pre–Saxon conquest era, Arthur being a resident of Somerset in the sixth century, and the original monolithic marker being judged the custom in other British lands) are accepted, then the grave of Arthur would have had no distinguishing mark in the early twelfth century. It is equally clear that it was not marked as such in 1190.[77]

Although the depth of the grave can be explained, other events of a suspicious nature surround the knowledge of where to look for the gravesite. Cambrensis indicates that the monks knew where to dig based on some of their writings, on some of the letters engraved on the pyramids, and on visions in dreams. He then adds that above all, the monks knew where to dig based on King Henry II's information from an ancient Welsh bard; this story about King Henry II is adopted by Adam of Domerham and John of Glastonbury.

This leads back to the political motive for wanting Arthur's gravesite discovered. In two of his texts,[78] Carley explores the possibility of Henry II's role in political fraud, and though he admits that "All too easily the deceptive Celtic twilight can descend, obscuring clear logic and sharp, crisp powers of deduction,"[79] he concludes that "the political motive might be weak, since King Henry died in 1189."[80] These uncertainties do, of course, presuppose that Arthur already had Glastonbury connections.

Two other items merit at least a cursory comment. One is the skeletal remains allegedly exhumed from the deep hole, and the other is Adam of Domerham's curious choice of the word "curtains" used at the exhumation. In relation to the first, no historian or archaeologist objectively postulates or remotely suggests that the remains are those of Arthur or his second wife. Treharne wonders with no small amount of sarcasm if the monks had the extreme fortune of unearthing a genuine Celtic burial site or had salted their mine for the "discovery."[81] Alcock, however, provides a response; he prefaces his remark by referring to Treharne's suggestion that the monks had dug up elsewhere a Celtic chieftain and his spouse, and concludes that an event such as this would be as remote and as unlikely as the hoax they were attempting to perpetrate. The skeletal origins remain one of the many frustrating enigmas of the Glastonbury question.

The reference to the use of "curtain" surrounding the exhumation from Adam of Domerham is a curiosity because of its inclusion in his story. He writes that Abbot Henry de Blois on a specific day set curtains round the spot and gave orders to excavate. This would create suspicion because it connotes secrecy and subterfuge. Adam's stance (if in fact a fraud was afoot) was one of complicity, and it seems unlikely that he would be naive or careless enough to insert something which might expose the ruse. If it is false that curtains surrounded the excavation, Adam would not invent such a detail because it would raise suspicions of covert operations in the exhumation, jeopardizing his purpose. As perceptive as Adam was, if he was copying from a manuscript which contained the details of curtains, he would recognize two courses of action. One, he could flaunt his objectivity by incorporating the details into his own manuscript, thus erasing doubts about a hoax. Two, he could omit the matter from his manuscript and by deliberate deception imperil his status if discovered.

The contemplation on these choices affords a couple of suggestions, but nothing that represents a hypothesis. The most evident answer which manifests itself is that no ruse was afoot; Adam might have had nothing to hide, and therefore, from some source other that Cambrensis or Coggeshall which has not survived to present day, he simply recorded that which he thought was the truth. If, however, he was involved in a deception, even though he might have read that passage in an obscure Glastonbury manuscript that has since been lost, it would have been much more prudent for him to simply ignore the passage and not include it in his own writing. Had he been doing more brazen things to perpetrate the deception, certainly this omission would not have bothered his conscience.

Perhaps, as a third possibility, he might have truthfully reported the curtains since so many things of a religious nature are cloaked in the secrecy of sanctity. This is not unusual; many profound things are hidden from the lay public — discoveries as paramount as information from the Dead Sea scrolls not publicized for literally decades, or events more recent yet intriguing like the circles and designs in the English corn and wheatfields not being publicized supposedly because the government is analyzing the results of what has been videotaped. The discovery of Arthur's remains would be an occasion of such magnitude that it would be guarded jealously by the abbot and monks in charge.

LAND GRANTS TO GLASTONBURY ABBEY

The final sources that suggest an Arthurian tie with Glastonbury are sections XVI and XXXIII of John of Glastonbury's *Cronica*, and Chapter LXIX in Scott's book on William of Malmsbury. In these works, both authors describe land grants given to Glastonbury by Arthur.

Studying annotated lists and bibliographies of Anglo-Saxon charters appears at first too divorced from Arthurian matters to be of any significant consequence. These documents are records from various sources compiled for the purpose of tracing land grants throughout British history. Each entry, marked by a coded number, gives the year of the charter, the Saxon king bequeathing the land, the recipient of the grant, the manuscripts which contain the transaction, and comments on the degree of authenticity. In the Glastonbury copy of Malmsbury's *De Antiquitate*, part of an entry explains

> [T]hese lands [Brent Marsh and Poweldone] were fallen upon and taken away by the English when they were pagans but later restored, with many others, after their conversion to the faith.[82]

There is a possibility that, because they are listed by dates, geographic location, and conditions, these historically recorded land grants might be linked to Arthur's pledges. In the tale of Ider, John of Glastonbury writes that Arthur granted Brent Marsh and Poweldone to Glastonbury Abbey as remorse and penance for Ider's death. This passage interfuses three seemingly discrete elements, but upon deeper reflection if a correlation could be established between these historic charters and Arthur's bequests, that correlation could strengthen the genuineness of Arthur and possibly dispel the Glastonbury exhumation as a hoax.

The procedure required four steps. First, a parallel had to exist between lands seized by the Saxons and those self-same lands being regranted to the abbots of Glastonbury; second, the alleged areas donated by Arthur to the Abbey would have to correspond to locations in the charter; third, an etymological check would be required, since Saxon/Briton and ancient/modern place-names varied so drastically; and fourth, the purported dates for Arthur would have to precede the recorded dates in the land grants.

The task was not as overwhelming as anticipated. There were only two specific locales — Brent Marsh and Poweldone — in the Arthurian charter, so there was little to lose and at least something minimal to gain by taking time to determine the possibility of a correlation. The first necessary check was Poweldone for its geographic location and its etymological roots. Possibilities of making such a firm connection seemed slim, but Ekwall, as he tends to do, had an answer already available, as if he had anticipated such a question. Poweldone is not given, but the name Poweldun shows up in various charters and rolls between the years 1235 and 1252. The suffix -*dun* means hill or ridge. The root is from a lost place-name, but its variants, *Pouelt, Poelt, Poholt,* and *Pouholt* occur in a number of charters. The element *holt* is Old English for "wood," but *Pou-*, the Welsh term *pau*, and the Old Welsh term *pou* mean "country." Poweldun is a direct reference to Polden Hill and, by verifying several other entries in Ekwall's work, means "wooded hill by a stream or pool."

Equipped with this information, the next step was to look at charters given to Glastonbury after the Saxon victories, near the end of the sixth century and into the seventh and eighth. This, of course, involved looking not only at entries for Poweldun and Polden Hill, but also at entries with the names of Pauholt, Polden Wood, Pouholt, and Poholt, since these terms were interchangeable in some of the entries. The other site in the King Arthur charters was Brent Marsh.

In all, there are six relevant entries, one which seems to be a repetition. This excludes all other charters given to Glastonbury by Saxon kings but not related to Brent Marsh or Polden during this period. Even with the limitation of six entries, there is too much irrelevant material to include, so that only abbreviated material is given. Peter Sawyer's annotated list of Anglo-Saxon charters is the resource, used also by Carley and Scott in their works. The entries have been cross-referenced and checked with Carley's edition and translation of John of Glastonbury's *Cronica*, and with Scott's edition and translation of Malmsbury's *De Antiquitate*. The charter entries are numbers 238 and its repetition 1671, plus 248, 250, 253, and 1680.

Charter 238 is listed for A.D. 663, but more than likely this date should be A.D. 693. King Ine of the West Saxons, granted to Haemgils, abbot of Glastonbury, land at Brent, Somerset. Five separate scholars — Davidson, Grewsell, Grundy, Turner, and Finberg — all list this charter as having an authentic base. John of Glastonbury, in Chapter XLV, records this entry by saying that King Ine conferred these lands to demonstrate his pious love of Glastonbury, and thus gave to Abbot Haemgils the manor of Brent, which was ten hides. In a footnote, Carley indicates that this charter has an authentic base and adds, "According to the interpolated version of the *De Antiquitate* this territory had belonged to Glastonbury during the British period but had been abandoned by Abbot Beorhtwald. This refers to the supposed donation of Brent Knoll by King Arthur."[83] The charter that looks like a doublet of this one, Number 1671, states that some time between 688 and 726 King Ine granted to Glastonbury Abbey 20 hides at Brentemarais (South Brent, Somerset).

Charter 248 states that in A.D. 705 King Ine of Wessex granted to Abbot Beorhtwald of Glastonbury land by the River Tone at Polden Hill, as well as other sections in Somerset. Scholars vary widely on the genuineness of this charter, labeling it from spurious to dubious to authentic. John of Glastonbury, in Chapter XLVII, amid other charters, lists King Ine giving to Abbot Haemgils 20 hides in a place called "Pouelt." Previously, in Chapter XVI, John writes that King Ine granted 20 hides of land at Brent Marsh, the other alleged site which Arthur had originally granted. Carley, in his notes, points out that Manuscript F identifies Pouelt as Polden Hill and then leans toward the authenticity of this charter by citing Davidson who finds "nothing to condemn its authenticity."[84] Finberg also lists it as authentic.

Charter 250, in A.D. 725, indicates that King Ine gave a grant of land in many places, among them Brent, Meare, and Polden Hill. Of all the charters checked, this is the only one listed by all scholars as spurious. In Chapter XLIX John of Glastonbury quotes a lengthy letter from King Ine to the abbacy of Glastonbury, in which Ine, among other things, declares his piety, affirms Glastonbury's rights to land grants, then donates the land. Of this charter, Carley quotes Davidson as saying "this charter must have been forged considerably later than 909 A.D. when the See of Wells was founded, and that the later forged charter of Edgar was based on it."[85] Scott, on page 99 and following also lists "The great privilege of King Ine," in *The Early History*.

Charter 253 is dated A.D. 729, in which King Aethelheard of Wessex granted to Abbot Coengisl of Glastonbury land at Pouholt. Scholars list this charter as authentic, and Robinson says that even though the form is suspicious, the content may be sound. John of Glastonbury in Chapter LII writes that Coengils (note the spelling; Sawyer's text is a simple transposition) succeeded Abbot Ecgfrith, and Aethelheard is Ine's successor. Aethelheard conceded 60 hides of land in Pohonholt (again, note the spelling variance). Carley explains that the charter is authentic and points out that Manuscript F identifies the land as Polden Wood.

The last charter selected for analysis is 1680, dated as A.D. 754. King Sigebeorht gave to Abbot Tica and Glastonbury a grant of 22 hides in Poholt, Somerset. This appears in John of Glastonbury's work at Chapter LIII. After Abbot Tunberht's death Tyccea ruled the church as abbot, and King Sigebeorht conceded 22 hides of land in the Polden Hills, for a price of 500 gold shillings. Carley indicates that Manuscript F, again, identifies Poholt as Polden Hill. Scott's account is almost identical, using the same spelling for the abbot as Carley, but recording 50 gold solidi as the equivalent of 500 gold shillings.

The relevance of all this information centers around the question, "Even if the abbot and the monks of Glastonbury wanted to persist in perpetuating the ruse of Arthur being buried at Glastonbury, would they have the means or capabilities of carrying out a clandestine sham of such magnitude or complexity that they might risk tainting any association which Arthur had with Glastonbury, even legendarily?" The answer is no; a deception of this proportion would serve no purpose. For instance, the monks would have to invent the tale about Ider and his encounter with the giants at Saint Michael's on Glastonbury Tor so that they could then "invent" a reason why King Arthur would give the Abbey land grants. Additionally, they would have to create a remorseful and humble Arthur so that Arthur could do penance to verify his connection with Glastonbury. This in itself is not unreasonable, but then by the monks' own admissions, they are forced to add that these lands were taken away by the Saxons once the Saxons were victorious and occupied the land. This in turn requires an explanation that after the Saxons occupied the land and had turned from their pagan ways to Christianity, they rededicated the parcels to the Abbey. As a final step, this would require their tampering with a great number of Anglo-Saxon charters. And last, if the monks were going to go to these bizarre and extreme lengths, they would have been much more judicious by avoiding place-names with such obscure and ambiguous variances, or perhaps by selecting charters which were not of such dubious or questionable nature. This scheme is much too complex to succeed as a hoax.

The monks' purpose was to convince the laity that Arthur's burial site was at Glastonbury. They did not want to raise doubts of Arthur's legendary ties to the Abbey nor hazard the possibility that the entire scheme might backfire so that all of Arthur's ties to Glastonbury could be compromised. The monks could have decided upon an intermediate course of action, simply pointed directly to the Anglo-Saxon land grants, charters, and prevented negative focus on Arthur's legendary attraction to Glastonbury. Hence, to this end, the charters on land grants tend to verify the legendary associations between Arthur and Glastonbury.

Other Arthurian sites have either lacked verifiable, reliable, accurate, historical data or have required painstaking reconstruction of diverse sources, but none matches the enigma shrouding the site of Arthur's burial, especially since so much more has been written about it.

Arthurian Connections with the Continental Avallon

When one is immersed in the search for Arthur, it is probable that any one passage may be read literally hundreds of times from some particular source, and the true impact never sinks in until something finally clicks inside the mind and a new perspective emerges. In *The Discovery of King Arthur* Geoffrey Ashe calls this process lateral thinking.[86] In pursuing his theory of Geoffrey of Monmouth's having borrowed his ideas from historical events in Gaul, and thus possibly connecting King Arthur with Riothamus on the continent, Ashe states, "Strangely, I had come within inches of the answer in my early book *From Caesar to Arthur*, published in 1960, but had backed away."[87]

When writing about Glastonbury and its synonymous reference to the Isle of Avalon, Ashe glosses over what can be a very crucial consideration. He explains:

> In Welsh this [paradisiacal "Place of Apples"] is Ynys Avallach. Geoffrey's [of Monmouth] Latin equivalent is *Insula Avallonia*. But this is not really equivalent, since it doesn't correspond to the Welsh. It has been influenced by the spelling of a real place called Avallon. Avallon is a Gaulish name with the same meaning, and the real Avallon is in Burgundy — where Arthur's Gallic career ends.[88]

This passage channels thinking into new directions. The normal pattern indelibly sets King Arthur's departure to the Isle of Avalon as unquestionably a reference to Glastonbury, particularly because vast amounts of evidence can be amassed to show that in Arthur's time Glastonbury was an island. Nothing could be more fitting than to have Arthur's final resting place at this sacred mecca, especially since it, like Tintagel and Camelot, has been engrained from the twelfth century onward.

Ashe's passing statement about Avallon raises several interesting questions. Suppose that the ancient manuscripts were accurate in spelling Arthur's resting place as Avallon rather than Avalon because it was a Gaulish name referring to this particular site in Burgundy? Depending upon the translation, Geoffrey of Monmouth writes that Arthur was "carried off" or "borne away" or "transported." But Malory gets more specific and writes that Bedivere carried the king to the water's edge and there put him into a barge filled with beautiful women, and the barge is rowed away. By combining several speculations, including Ashe's theory that Arthur must be equated with Riothamus, then the Briton king would have a close affinity with Burgundy, where he fought the barbarians on the continent and could conceivably have requested a return to a spot which he loved in his younger days. It would follow also that with the Battle of Camlann being fought at Charford, the barge could have set sail at Southampton Water and crossed the channel to the Avallon of Burgundy.

Again, mind-sets can become so established that the focus blurs the periphery. The emphasis in the instance of Glastonbury has been on the word "isle," which leads to the second interesting question: Could Avallon in Burgundy be referred to as an island? It is quite far inland, and even in Arthur's time the sea did not encroach over 200 miles onto the continent. Nevertheless, looking at some old Atlases of this area provides some interesting conjectures. To the northwest of Avallon in Burgundy/France is a huge area called the Île de France which encompasses an expanse from a village called Vernon, about 50 miles west of Paris, and arcs northeast to Soissons and Reims, about 70 miles northeast of Paris. In this area, the land forms an opposite arc, creating a shape almost like the human eye, curving southwest, with this southwestern curvature called Côte de L'île de France along the Seine River. This Côte de L'île de France lies about 50 miles north of Avallon. Côte d'Or is close to Dijon, about 50 miles from Avallon in a southeasterly direction. This particular Avallon, then, is on the fringes of the highland plateaus, close to an "Isle."

A third question also comes to mind: Is it just coincidental that Avallon in Burgundy/France is in the same general countryside, within 55 miles, of Troyes? Chretien de Troyes was the most well-known master craftsman of the Arthurian legend, and, of course, speculation raises other questions. Was Chretien that absolutely immersed in a nationalistic British figure, or did a deep and abiding interest in Arthur develop because of Arthur's historic and legendary connection to Chretien's native country, including Avallon as the burial site? Did Chretien himself have an unknown ancient source for his romances in the same manner claimed by Geoffrey of Monmouth? Was Chretien aware of—or did he at least sense a connection between—the exploits of Arthur in Britain and Riothamus in Burgundy? Geoffrey Ashe explains his speculative view in this way:

> [Authors who came after Geoffrey of Monmouth] put Arthur on the Continent as well as in Britain. Chretien de Troyes makes him hold court in Brittany. The chief German poet of the Grail, Wolfram von Eschenbach, locates him at the Breton city of Nantes through most of the story, sending him back to Britain only at the close. Romanceers who deal with Arthur's wars show what they think important. Most of them pay little attention to the Saxon-quelling battles in Britain. The warfare in Gaul, now called France, remains.[89]

Conclusions

The search continues for Arthur's burial site, its link to the name Avalon, and its suggestion of Glastonbury. Both of the major possibilities (Avalon and Avallon) offer compelling cases, keeping questions of Arthur's interment open-ended. More and more of Arthur is coming to light, and although the literature seems at times to lead to a dead-end, someone's fresh perspective and new approach will sharpen Arthur's figure even more, although there might be incredibly strong resistance to the time-honored traditions which have linked King Arthur with Glastonbury. In *King Arthur's Avalon*, Ashe befittingly describes Glastonbury, "England's New Jerusalem," as "strong magic, and is not dead merely because the Abbey is ruined."[90] He goes on to say in the first chapter that any story of Glastonbury is plausible, particularly "if you try the experiment of believing while in sight of the Tor."[91]

This has been a comprehensive look at Arthur's association with Glastonbury. The amount of material on geographies, although encapsulated, is massive and the conclusions difficult. Legend and tradition certainly tie Arthur to Glastonbury as the Isle of Avalon or the Isle of Apples, but undeniable evidence is elusive. Archaeological evidence shows that Glastonbury as an island in the true sense of the word was the stronghold of a Celtic chieftain in the Arthurian period and even suggests that the Tor could have been a signaling station or an outpost for Arthur's southwest kingdom, suggesting even more specifically that the Tor was a stronghold for Melwas, and that after the differences and conflicts between Arthur and Melwas were resolved, Melwas was one of Arthur's warriors defending Britain from the

The alleged original burial site for Arthur on the grounds of Glastonbury Abbey. Note the Tor in the background. Photo by Frank Reno, with kind permission of the Custodian, Glastonbury Abbey.

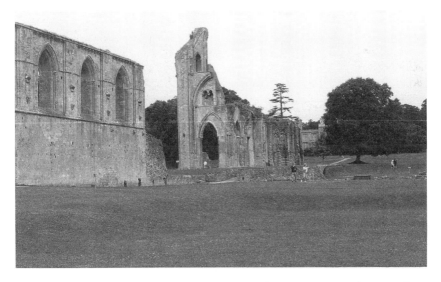

From aside the signpost of the original gravesite, this is a view into the area where the high altar was located. Arthur's new marble entombment, in front of the high altar, would have been approximately at the white marker in the arch of the ruins. Photo by Frank Reno, with kind permission of the Custodian, Glastonbury Abbey.

Arthur's gravesite in front of what was the high altar. Arthur's remains were removed from the original site to inside the Abbey, a distance of about 150 paces. Photo by Frank Reno, with kind permission of the Custodian, Glastonbury Abbey.

View from the high altar to the original gravesite. The signpost is visible just in front of the Abbot's Kitchen. Photo by Frank Reno, with kind permission of the Custodian, Glastonbury Abbey.

onslaught of Saxons. There is little doubt, too, that Glastonbury has a long history as a sacred spot, a religious sanctuary that would attract someone of Arthur's stature, though the location cannot irrefutably claim Arthur's remains or Joseph of Arimathea's visit.

Then comes the silence of centuries, and after this extensive void, reports in the twelfth century flourish with new interest, leading to an entangled, garbled history pieced together over the next several centuries. Geoffrey of Monmouth's *History of the Kings of Britain* appeared about the year 1135 and though Monmouth makes no connection between the story of King Arthur and Glastonbury, he relates that when King Arthur was mortally wounded in the battle on the River Cambula in Cornwall that the injured king was carried to the Isle of Avalon for the healing of his wounds. There is no hint of what is meant by the term, but in *The Life of Merlin*, a Latin poem of Geoffrey's own time which Geoffrey claims to have also written, the bard Taliessin describes the voyage of the

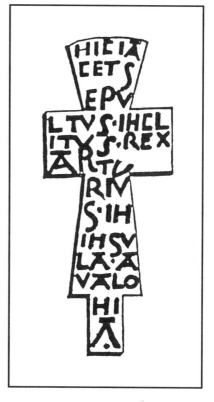

Drawing 3. Arthur's Glastonbury cross.

wounded king. Instead of the island being called Avalon, it is named the "Isle of Apples, the Fortunate Isles," a rich and fertile spot where plants grow naturally without the need for tilling or nurturing. Life was extended there, ruled by nine sisters. The oldest sister Morgen was the most skilled in magic. She had the power to change shapes and to fly like Daedalos. With her supreme knowledge of herbs and medicines, when Arthur was delivered to her, she inspected his injuries and claimed that he could recover if only he would abide a long time under her care.

Geoffrey's description sounds like the afterworld, particularly because of the references to Daedalos, who is specifically tied to myth, and to Morgen, who can change shapes and cure mortal wounds, suggesting the common regeneration motif. Once more, the name of Glastonbury is glaringly absent as Arthur's "resting place"; Monmouth offers no association between the Isle of Avalon or the Isle of Apples or the Fortunate Isles and Glastonbury. If he is using his "ancient book," then the book evidently makes no reference to a connection either.

William of Malmsbury is also silent about the synonymity of Glastonbury and the Isle of Avalon. Giraldus Cambrensis, Ralph of Coggeshall, Adam of Domerham, John of Glastonbury, and Henry of Huntingdon finally express the connection by the thirteenth century. Some claims of the Arthurian connection are couched in nefarious motives; other inquiries are sincere, legitimate, and seemingly objective. Robinson epitomizes the two sides of the coin. On one side, for example, Glastonbury could very well hold claim to the oldest ecclesiastical site in Britain, going back to the very beginning of Christianity on the island. Treharne, too, claims, "There can be no doubt whatsoever that when the West Saxons occupied the district soon after 568 A.D. they found an old and famous Celtic monastery already established and flourishing there, a shrine already venerated by all the Christian British peoples as a place of awesome and holy antiquity."[92] On the other side of that coin, Robinson reminds us, "We can say with practical certainty that the claim of the monks to Avalon and to King Arthur's grave was not put forward before the year 1191."[93] On the perimeter of the dichotomy are all those enticing details which confirm Arthur's connection, punctuated by other, equally convincing contradictions.

The Glastonbury/Arthur paradigm remains a disjointed puzzle of truth, factual historicity, suggestive legend, and fantastic make-believe. The Glastonbury connection has the same mystique attached to it as that of Tintagel and Camelot. Geoffrey Ashe expresses it well in the opening segment of his book on *King Arthur's Avalon*:

> I wrote under the spell ... that Glastonbury, England's new Jerusalem, is strong magic and not dead merely because its Abbey is ruined. That conviction has never deserted me. Whatever the nature of the magic, it is there and it will revive.[94]

Anyone who has ever stood atop the Tor and gazed at the setting sun in all its brilliant and fiery hues knows of Glastonbury's internal spiritual potency; furthermore, when cloudbanks a hundred feet below the summit have created a sea, anyone who has stood atop the Tor knows the dizzying sensation of being transported backwards through centuries of time and experiencing the true mists of Avalon as an island. Glastonbury will never relinquish its magic.

Chapter 9
Ambrosius Aurelianus: History and Tradition

Ambrosius Aurelianus in History and Tradition

Of all figures associated with Arthur, Ambrosius Aurelianus is the most firmly rooted in Britain. Independent of the historic sources cited in Chapter 2, Ambrosius Aurelianus is verified as an authentic figure in Roman history. His ancestry begins with Aurelian, a Roman emperor who ruled from A.D. 270 to 275, whose *praenomen, nomen,* and *cognomen* was Lucius Domitius Aurelianus called by another *agnomen* of *Restitutor Orbis* (Restorer of the City) because of credits for building the Aurelian Wall around Rome. During Aurelian's reign he drove the Goths from Dacia across the Danube and settled Romans in the province of Moesia. He recovered Britain and Gaul from pretenders during the years 271 to 273 but was then killed by conspirators in 275.[1] Not only does the *cognomen* Aurelianus categorize Ambrosius as Roman royalty, but Aurelian's tours took him to Britain, where some of his succeeding generations settled, and to Gaul, which was later divided into provinces including Britanny and Burgundy.

Based upon the typical floruit and assuming that Lucius Domitius Aurelianus was in his prime during his reign when he was assassinated, his life span would have been from circa 245 to 305. Ambrosius Aurelianus was an adolescent in the earlier years of Vortigern's reign, and surmising that he would have been about 12 in Vortigern's twelfth year of reign, then Ambrosius' life span would have been from approximately 425 to 485 and his floruit would have ranged from 440 to 470. The intervening floruits from Lucius Domitius to Ambrosius would be 305 to 335, 335 to 365, 365 to 395, and 395 to 425, making Ambrosius a fourth-removed grandson.

Ambrosius Aurelianus, then, has direct lineage to an emperor of Rome, Lucius

Domitius Aurelianus, known by an abbreviated name of Aurelian. His heritage ties directly to royalty that wore the purple, the color associated with Julius Caesar's standard, and the dragon insignia used by royalty and adopted by Arthur. Through the generations, Caesar's purple dragon was slightly altered to Ambrosius' (and therefore Arthur's) red one, a standard that has become the flag of Wales. Additionally, the shortened name for the Roman emperor Lucius Domitius Aurelianus filtered down to a niche of British tradition as Aurelius Ambrosius in the works of Geoffrey of Monmouth. The equation, therefore, that Ambrosius Aurelianus claims ancestry from Lucius Domitius Aurelianus, and that Aurelius Ambrosius is an offshoot of Ambrosius Aurelianus is irrefutable.

In association with Arthuriana, Ambrosius Aurelianus appears in two of Britain's ancient sources, once in Gildas, and three times in Nennius. In the *De Excidio*, the oldest extant British document with information on the Arthurian period, Gildas provides the one important date which, when used in conjunction with other sources, established the cardinal years given in Chapter 3 of this text.

AMBROSIUS AURELIANUS IN THE *DE EXCIDIO*

Throughout investigations of Arthur's authenticity, Gildas has become the center of controversy revolving around his age when writing the *DE*, his true identity, and his ecclesiastic rank. These unconstructive disagreements cloud the issue and must be set aside; the relevant considerations must deal with rational interpretations and translations of his manuscript, the "reasonable age" concept for Gildas as the author, and his role in the milieu of events.

Thomas O'Sullivan deals with these basic issues and enumerates the pro and con arguments by various scholars, from the *ex eo tempore* passage through the minute scrutiny of individual words.[2] Several possibilities emerge:

1. a host of investigators reckon the *ex eo tempore* Gildas passage as 44 years prior to the penning of the *De Excidio*[3];
2. several base information upon Bede, called the "Adventus" school, that the Badon siege and Gildas' birth took place 44 years after the Saxon dominion[4];
3. others resolve the discrepancy between Gildas and his interpreter Bede by following the lead of Charles Plummer, that the time span between each of the three events is 44 years; that is, 44 years pass from the Saxon dominion to the birth of Gildas/Badon siege, and another 44 years pass from the birth of Gildas/Badon siege to the writing of the *De Excidio*[5];
4. still others redefine the Gildas passage about the Briton challenge to the Saxons as separate victories by Ambrosius and by Arthur at Badon,[6] or that the Saxon *Adventus* and Ambrosian victory are parallel or simultaneous occurrences.[7]

John Morris is the most comprehensive in providing dates. He lists the plain meaning of the *De Excidio* as Ambrosius' rise 40 years prior to the Badon siege, the Badon seige as fought somewhere around 500 or a little before, Gildas penning the *De Excidio* around 540, and Maelgwn dying from the plague several years after Gildas' manuscript. In the *Age of Arthur* he lists Ambrosius' reign from approximately the middle of the fifth decade to 475,[8] interestingly close to the generality of floruit and life span given above. This array of proposals leads O'Sullivan to ask:

> Why emend [Gildas' manuscript] at all? The plain sense of the words "ex eo tempore," as several investigators have noted, is, "from the time of the victory of Ambrosius." The debated passage, then, tells us that the Saxons had risen in revolt, and the nation been saved by the exertions of Ambrosius Aurelianus. In the forty-fourth year thereafter, it says, the Saxons had been decisively defeated at the siege of mons Badonicus, and Gildas had been born.[9]

Coupled with other known events of the period, there can be no other interpretation. Year 497 marks the Battle of Badon; 44 years earlier (in 453, the third Saxon *Adventus*) Briton survivors had rallied around Ambrosius' standard, and 44 years later (in 541) Gildas was writing the *DE*. Chapter 3 has already rounded out the rest of the chronology: Maelgwn's death occurred in 547, Gildas' in 570. Everything else fits into this perspective: Gildas describes the devastation (line 10, Chapter 23 to line 10, Chapter 25) from the second Saxon *Adventus* to the beginning of the third (442 to 453). The survivors rally to Ambrosius Aurelianus from 453 to 497, with minor victories vacillating between the Britons and Saxons until the Battle of Badon, which ended in a *major* victory for the Britons.

This interpretation further explains what has previously been labeled an error in Bede's transcription. Bede's explanation that the Battle of Badon took place 44 years after the Saxon advent (the third *Adventus*) is correct; it is a coincidence that there was also a span of 44 years between the Badon battle and Gildas' birth. Giles' translation is the best:

> After this, sometimes our countrymen, sometimes the enemy, won the field ... until the year of the siege of Bath-hill ... which was forty-four years and one month after the landing of the Saxons, and also the time of my own nativity.[10]

Giles is not suggesting that the Badon battle and the Saxon advent both occurred simultaneously 44 years prior to the penning of the *De Excidio*, but is instead proposing the equation of 453 (third Saxon landing) + 44 = 497 (Battle of Badon) + 44 = 541 (penning of the *De Excidio*). Michael Winterbottom's version of the Gildas original,[11] and his translation,[12] omit "qui prope Sabrinum ostium habetur," thus avoiding the reference to the Saxon landing. Hence, Bede is following the Giles equation.

As an oblique consideration of Ambrosius' battle strategies and the territories he covered, the question about cavalry as a mode of warfare invariably arises, creating controversial stands. Kenneth Jackson writes this of the cavalry:

> The question of the employment of cavalry by the men of the Gododdin has been canvased above and answered in the affirmative. Since the use of cavalry as an organized military tactic was unknown in general in Dark Age Britain but was familiar

to the Romans under the Empire, it has been supposed that this is evidence for the survival of Romanization of the British peoples on the outer border of the Empire in the North.[13]

He points out that the evidence of a Gododdin cavalry shows a Roman origin, but unfortunately his confines for the use of cavalry are too narrow. During the Dark Ages in general (and the latter half of the fifth century coupled with the beginning of the sixth specifically) the use of cavalry was familiar, even though it had not developed into a military tactic, and it was not limited to the outer reaches of the Empire in the north. Roman histories describe the Roman roads, both in the military and the civilian districts, as being able to accommodate both pedestrian and mounted travel. The decline of the Western Roman Empire on the continent is at least partially attributed to the decline of horses, which contradicts the belief that light cavalry was not used in Dark Age Britain. In the immediate post–Roman era an Arthurian cavalry does not necessarily mean that it was as disciplined as the Horse Guards or Dragoons, but the Britons used horsemanship to their highly distinctive advantage in opposing invasions of their country.

Morris supports the viewpoint that the cavalry had an important function in warfare. First, he writes

> The early poetry of the Welsh consistently sings of mounted warriors wearing scarlet [note the color selection of Ambrosius' family mentioned in Gildas] plumes and using swords, riding well-fed horses, who fought an infantry enemy equipped with spears. Their picture of the English is accurate.[14]

He supports his belief that although men fought on foot in the mountainous areas of Wales,

> ... the heroes of the Penine kingdoms and of the west midlands were almost all mounted men; and cavalry was the outstanding arm of the Armorican British.[15]

Not only is it interesting that he mentions "scarlet" plumes, a color of royalty for Ambrosius Aurelianus but also the west midlands (including Cornovii territory), which is where the resistance to the Saxons takes place. He supports the concept of cavalry:

> ... [I]n Gaul, there is first-hand evidence. There, fifth-century success was entirely due to the use of cavalry alone against an infantry enemy. About 471, Ecdicius routed thousands of Goths at Clermont-Ferrand with only 18 mounted men, for the Goths, like most German forces, were poorly armed.[16]

Following this conjecture, he equates the Gallic strategies with Ambrosius Aurelianus' tactics in warfare:

> Ambrosius' resistance [around 460] had begun in Britain some ten years before Ecdicius attacked; and it is not improbable that Ecdicius had himself been fired by stories of Ambrosius. His strategy was the only effective way in which Romans could

fight back with hope of success, and was as valid for lowland Britain as for Gaul. Sixth-century British and late fifth-century Gauls relied on cavalry alone, unencumbered by slow-moving infantry; tradition held that fifth-century British fought in the same manner, and is plainly right.[17]

AMBROSIUS AURELIANUS IN THE *HISTORIA BRITTONUM*

The *De Excidio* in isolation cannot give the full perspective for Ambrosius Aurelianus; whereas Gildas supplies the outline, Nennius fills in some specifics. Ambrosius is first mentioned in Section 31, which relates that Ambrosius' influence must be formidable, since Vortigern fears Ambrosius even more than northern invaders or the return of the Romans. For some reason, Vortigern has become the *superbus tyrannus* prior to Ambrosius' rule, but the usurper knows that Ambrosius is a powerful force to be reckoned with. Nennius relates that the time is just after the end of Roman rule in Britain and prior to the alliance with the Saxons.

The second reference in the *Historia Brittonum*, sections 40 through 42, relates the detailed story of Ambrosius as an adolescent when he confronts Vortigern at Dinas Emrys and is shown to be the Emrys Gwledig whose ancestors were Roman royalty. Although he is just a young boy, Ambrosius intimidates Vortigern and the king's wizards through his supernatural powers. At the end of the tale, after the revelation that Ambrosius is the son of a Roman consul, Vortigern gives the boy the fortress and all the kingdoms of the western part of Britain, and he himself flees to the northern territory called Gwynessi.

Both Sections 48 and 66 (called the *Chronographer*) make only passing references to Ambrosius. In the former, Ambrosius is termed king among kings who, after acquiring the throne from Vortigern, grants permission to Pascent, son of Vortigern, to rule Builth and Gwerthrynion. The *Chronographer* then relates that the discord between Vitalinus and Ambrosius took place 12 years "from the reign of Vortigern," which is interpreted by scholars throughout Nennius as meaning "from the beginning of" a reign. In this instance, it ascribes to a date of 437, the beginning of Vortigern's reign in 425, plus 12 years.

AMBROSIUS AURELIANUS AS VORTIMER

Another enigmatic figure who allegedly existed during the lifetime of Ambrosius/Riothamus/Arthur is Vortimer, whose name is sometimes seen as Guorthemir, with several variations of each. Vortimer historically appears only in Nennius; Gildas does not write of him nor, understandably, does Vortigern's son show up in Bede's writing, since Bede so heavily reflects Gildas. Vortimer likewise does not appear in the *Anglo-Saxon Chronicle* nor in the *Annales Cambriae*. He does, however, show up in later literary writings such as those of Geoffrey of Monmouth, but similar to the Gildas-Bede connection, Vortimer in Monmouth reflects the *Historia Brittonum* as the only ancient manuscript where his name appears. Although it is obvious that there is a strong connection between Gildas and Nennius, the puzzling observation is that Nennius must have also used an independent source. The Nennius manuscript includes a great deal of detail, plus the addition of Vortimer and his battles, which are interwoven with information gleaned from Gildas. There is a possibility that later interpolaters added this material, but because of all the specific details, this would be hard to imagine.

Chapter 2 of this text dealt with Vortimer and his battles, but the emphasis there was upon geographic location; the focus now shifts to the figure of Vortimer and his role in Arthurian matters. R.H. Fletcher comments on the noticeable variance between the Gildas and Nennius manuscripts where, in Nennius, "Guorthemir [Vortimer] practically replaces the Ambrosius of Gildas."[18] Fletcher cites the Chartres manuscript, a fragment pre-dating the Nennius manuscript and lacking the details of the *Historia Brittonum*, which actually stops where a deal is being struck between Vortigern and Hengist for the Saxon's daughter. After some explanation, Fletcher, making comparisons between Nennius' work, the *DE*, and the *ASC*, formulates several observations:

1. The story from Nennius reflects the *Briton* faction, whereby the Gildas story reflects the *Roman*, evidenced by
   a. Nennius speaking of Ambrosius in "subordinate and inconsistent notices," with Ambrosius appearing only dimly in the story as a powerful leader, but Vortimer's battles against the Saxons being reported in much more detail, even though Ambrosius holds the power to give kingdoms to Vortimer's brother.[19]
   b. Nennius viewing Arthur as Briton, and devoting a segment of his writings to the campaigns of Arthur, whereas the Arthurian matter is totally absent in Gildas.
2. Although the Gildas account is more straightforward on one hand, and Nennius reflects more oral and literary legendary tradition on the other, the Nennius manuscript still has a basis in fact, and "it does not seem very reasonable to doubt that Vortigern, Vortimer, Ambrosius, and Arthur were real men who fought against the invaders."[20]
3. The *Chronicle* is of course biased, but it is trying to set down a basis of plain truth, much like the *AC*.
4. The *Chronicle* sets down four battles as fought by Hengist against the Britons, which may have corresponded to the four battles which Vortimer fought against the Saxons.

Alcock makes a similar observation about verifying the authenticity of figures such as Vortigern, Ambrosius, and Arthur. He writes, "Their [Ambrosius, Vortigern, and Arthur] claim to historicity is based on contemporary or near-contemporary notices: of Ambrosius by Gildas Badonicus, of Vortigern in the *calculi* at the head of the British Easter Table compiled in 455, and of Arthur in the British Easter Annals."[21] Glaringly absent, however, is the name of Vortimer, not only from Alcock's work but from most of the other twentieth century scholars. Even though the Nennius document is used frequently, Alcock does not refer to Vortimer as Vortigern's son; Richard Barber bypasses the name Vortimer in *Arthur of Albion* and only refers to him through Nennius in *The Figure of Arthur*; Chambers in

Arthur of Britain gives the name of Vortigern but writes nothing of a Vortimer or a Guothimer.

Morris, on the other hand, treats Vortimer as an authentic character in one of the beginning sections of *The Age of Arthur*, and with Vortimer's battles as reported by Morris, this creates still another round of confusion. Morris quotes Chapter 43 of Nennius in which he translates Nennius' account by saying that Vortimer fought against Hengist and Horsa and expelled them as far as the isle of Thanet, driving them out (of Kent?) for five years.[22] Morris has used the same manuscript as both Giles and Stevenson, but nowhere in the original Nennius manuscript is there any information about the expulsion of the Saxons taking five years. It is a puzzle, too, that when Morris translated that same passage from Nennius in the book *British History*, he does not mention this five-year duration in that text.[23] *The Age of Arthur* was originally printed in 1973, with *British History* published in 1980. Because Morris gives no indication of where he picked up the five-year duration of the expulsion of the Saxons, that piece of information must be disregarded.

Not in the negative sense of the word, Morris "manipulates" dates in *The Age of Arthur* for Vortimer's four battles. He equates three battles from Nennius — Darenth, Episford, and Stone Inscription — with the three entries in the *Anglo-Saxon Chronicle* — 455, 456, and 465 — claiming that "[T]he Saxon Chronicle also lists three battles with the same results, in the same areas, but gives them different names and reverses the order of the first two."[24]

In attempting to trace the historic events for Ambrosius Aurelianus, part of the difficulty here lies in the acceptance of his dates, whereby he claims that the dates from the *Chronicle* "are late additions."[25] Morris has accepted only one coming of the Saxons and has therefore set Vortimer's first battle in the year when Hengist succeeds to the kingdom, the second at the outbreak of the revolt around 442, and the third at Richborough in 452 where the Britons won a victory. Between these last two battles as they are listed in the *Chronicle*, there would be a span of 13 years.

To confuse the issue even more, in *British History* Morris translates Chapter 44 by saying that Vortimer fought four keen battles against the Saxons, but lists only three, giving them in order as Darenth, Episford, and the Inscribed Stone. Giles, however, clarifies Nennius by listing four: the expulsion of the Saxons to Thanet, Darenth, at the Ford where Horsa and Catigern are killed, and near the Inscribed Stone. It is evident from the report by Nennius that the first battle is a Briton victory; the Battle of Darenth has no victor claimed; the third at the Ford where Horsa and Catigern are killed lists no victors; the fourth at the stone is a Briton victory.

Josephus Stevenson, too, explains the oversight by clarifying that because of the omission of five words, *ut supra dictum est; secondum*, supplied by manuscript *a*, there are only three battles which are specified.[26] Likewise, an interpretive reading of the *Historia Brittonum* does unscramble the confusion. Chapter 44 in Nennius has to be viewed with its references back to Chapter 43; Nennius is saying that in Vortimer's first battle with the Saxons the enemy was expelled to the island of Thanet where three more battles then followed (Chapter 43). Then, those other three battles are listed in Chapter 44, with the first being the Saxon expulsion to Thanet, the second on the River Darenth, and the third at Episford. The geography of the fourth by the Inscribed Stone on the shore of the Gallic Sea was discussed at length in Chapter 2, concluding with an emendation of Gaelic, rather than Gallic, Sea

Morris' major variation is the order in which these battles took place. If the first battle is the Saxon expulsion from somewhere in Britain's interior to Thanet, then Morris is expressing the opinion that the second battle is the battle at Episford (Ægelesthrep, Aylesford) which he lists as a Saxon victory, since Hengist "took the kingdom." The third is at Darenth (Darent, Derwen, Darwen, Creacanford, Crayford), fitting Morris' claim that the *Chronicle* reversed the two, where no victory is claimed. The fourth is the battle at Richborough, which he lists as a Briton victory. He dates the Battle of Episford at 442 (455 in the *Chronicle*), the Battle of Darenth about 447, midway between the first and third battle (456 in the *Chronicle*) and The Battle of the Inscribed Stone in 452 (465 in the *Chronicle*).

Morris' interpretation is an interesting speculation, but if Morris' premises are accepted, then during this era Ambrosius disappears mysteriously from the histories, thus negating the time frame given by Gildas. Ashe clarifies Vortimer as an epithet. He writes in his notes:

> In the form Vortigern, the syllable *vor* means "over," the rest is "king" or "chieftain." Vortigern was the overking. While historians accept him as real, his son Vortimer, whom Geoffrey [of Monmouth] portrays as briefly taking his place, is viewed with more skepticism. ... The British original of Vortimer would have been Vortamorix. The *vor* is the same syllable as before, meaning "over"; *tamo* is the superlative suffix like the English "-est"; and *rix*, akin to the Latin *rex*, is another word for "king." So Vortimer means the "over-most" or "highest" king. It is a different expression of the same paramountcy.[27]

This does not mean, however, that Vortimer can be equated with Vortigern, particularly since they embody viewpoints from the opposite ends of a continuum. Vortigern is pro–Saxon, both before and after Vortimer, who is without question anti–Saxon.

The general tenet which views Vortimer as an evocative epithet for Ambrosius Aurelianus in Gildas fits better into the historical details of the period when those details are left intact as they are chronologically proposed in the *Chronicle*. That is, the *Chronicle* proposes that Vortigern invited the Saxons in, and by the year 455 the alliance had disintegrated and Hengist was warring against Vortigern. That is the last entry which names Vortigern, signifying a Saxon victory and implying the death (or at least deposal) of Vortigern. Gildas reflects the general picture that after this stunning Saxon victory, the wretched Briton survivors surrendered to the enemy as slaves, migrated to Brittany, or rallied under the banner of Ambrosius Aurelianus. The succeeding six entries in the *Chronicle*—between 456 and 495, including the three attributed to Vortimer—signify the back-and-forth fortunes of war, right up to the year of the siege of Badon Hill as recorded in Gildas, verified by Nennius that the Saxons would sometimes victoriously advance their frontiers, and would sometimes be defeated and expelled.

The geographic sites for these battles as proposed in Chapter 2 of this text agree with the interpretation that events listed by Gildas and Nennius are also presented in the *Chronicle*. The battles attributed to Vortimer but which more accurately fall into Ambrosius' reign after Vortigern's deposal are all in close proximity to the capital of the Cornovii territory, based on a well-founded assumption that the enemies were necessarily English Saxons and not German Saxons. Considering Viroconium as a pivotal base,

1. the River Tanet, rather than the isle of Thanet would be a border only 30 miles away, opposed to the island, over 150 miles distant;
2. the battle at the River Derwent (derived from Derventio) is approximately 55 miles away, as opposed to Darenth in Kent which is a distance of about 162 miles;
    a. if Darenth is interpreted as Darwen, it is a distance of 75 miles;
    b. if interpreted as Derwen in northern Wales, 40 miles;
3. the battle at Ægelesthrepe, if interpreted as Agglethorpe, is 50 miles from the Cornovii capital, as opposed to Episford in Kent, which, like Darenth, is about 162 miles;
    a. if interpreted as the Welsh Rhyd-y-foel, the distance is 60 miles;
    b. if the reference is to Ryal Ford, a neighbor of Darwen, it is 75 miles;
4. the battle at the Inscribed Stone, a much more general reference, if near a marker such as Eliseg's Pillar, is a distance of about 35 miles, as opposed to Morris' proposal of Richborough in eastern Kent, approximately 175 miles away.

Interestingly, each of these battles, because they do involve the English Saxons, reveal that the enemy is attempting to extend their boundaries from the original Cornovii/Gewissae/Hrype territories, pushing even farther north or into Welsh provinces. When these Saxons "return home," using the term in Nennius and Gildas, they are not retreating to their original homeland on the continent but are withdrawing to the domains granted to them by Vortigern. The Saxons try pushing *outward* to Tanet, to Derwent, and to Agglethorpe, are repulsed, and retreat to their own borders or their "home."

These proposals for the battles (attributed to Vortimer who has no base in the histories of the period) also address some inconsistencies in Morris' approach. First, the *Chronicle* would have to be emended by changing the date from 455 to 445 plus changing the Briton name from Vortigern to Vortimer, by changing the date from 456 to 449 for the battle at Crayford, and by dropping the 465 entry and adding it at 450. In essence, this leaves a blank in the *Chronicle* between 450 and 473.

Because Morris did not leave these entries intact, he overlooks a second important consideration. The *Chronicle* entry for 457 (two years after the Saxon severance of the alliance with Vortigern) is set in Kent suggested by the adjacency of London and by the use of the word "Briton" instead of "Welsh." This directly relates to the Nennius passage that Vortimer expelled the Saxons to Kent, though not necessarily to the island of Thanet. After the Saxons were driven there, they sent envoys to Germany, which led to the later incursions of Ælle and his vast number of warriors to fight against the kings of Britain. In the entries for 465, 473, 477, and 485 the *Chronicle* then reverts to the term "Welsh" instead of "Briton" to describe the Saxon enemies during the battles of that period.

A third key in the sequence centers upon the Saxon massacre of Vortigern's Council. At the end of Section 45 and all of Section 46, Nennius relates after Vortimer's death, the Saxons instigated a treacherous plan to kill Vortigern's council of elders. Under the guise of a peace negotiation, the Saxons slaughter the 300 Seniors and take Vortigern hostage. Morris places the massacre of the *consiliari* (Morris' term is the Council of the Province) at year 458, a Saxon victory in which the Britons were decimated, but makes no connection with the *Chronicle* entry of 456/457 which narrates that the Saxons slaughtered the Britons and the survivors fled in great terror. Morris follows the massacre of the Council by the second migration to Brittany in 459, a sequence which, when pieced together, ideally sets the stage for Ambrosius Aurelianus' entry into the picture.

It must be remembered that Gildas as the original source does not name Vortigern, Vortimer, Hengist, or Horsa; he writes of the *superbus tyrannus*, which was later translated to Vortigern, and of the Saxons also generically but supplies only the name of Ambrosius Aurelianus. Geoffrey Ashe, aware of prolific epithets makes the general statement that

> [v]ery possibly Nennius has lumped together several separate items under the single evocative name of Arthur. But the likelihood of a certain correspondence to fact can scarcely be dodged.[28]

Ashe draws an inferential parallel between epithets and Arthur, but considering Fletcher's statement that Vortimer in Nennius has replaced the Ambrosius of Gildas, Ashe's comment would more accurately state that "Nennius has lumped together several separate items under the single evocative name of *Ambrosius*."

One last problem must be resolved for the Vortimer/Ambrosius equation to make sense. Chapter 2 has already explained the details surrounding all the variable manuscripts of the *HB*, including the misleading headings provided by translations.[29] The battles as listed for Vortimer are no different; the heading of "The Kentish Chronicle, Part 3" must be eliminated for correct interpretation, since Chapter 2 has pinpointed the correct locations other than Kent. Also, the very first word in Section 43 which introduces the battles by Vortimer is a critically important word. In Latin, that word is "interea," which Morris translates as "meanwhile,"[30] and Giles gives as "at length."[31]

The section on Vortimer is interspersed between two sections on Vortigern, indicating that for some reason Vortigern abdicated to Vortimer, but then later reclaimed the throne after Vortimer's "death." If taken sequentially as presented in the *Historia*, then Morris' interpretation of "meanwhile" is sensible. However, Chapter 2 also showed, based upon Stevenson's authority, that the various recensions of the *Historia* are historically valuable but not necessarily chronologically correct, unless verified by some other source.

Fortunately, in this instance there is another source, the *Anglo-Saxon Chronicle*, which can verify a chronology. The *Chronicle* lists Vortigern as king in 455 during the battle in which Horsa was killed, the same battle listed in the *Historia* as the third one fought by Vortimer. Yet Vortimer appears in no other historical source, and Vortigern drops from the histories after 455, at the time when the Briton survivors rally to Ambrosius Aurelianus, according to the Gildas manuscript.

Morris' translation of "interea" therefore is imprecise as "meanwhile," particularly since in an earlier section (31) he translates the word "interea" as "then." Giles' interpretation "at length" is better because it does not connote "during the interlude." But the words "later," or "afterward" are even more accurate. Since Sections 39 ("The Life of Saint Germanus, Part 2") and 47 ("The Life of Saint Germanus, Part 3") are not included in earlier versions of the *Historia*, the applicable parts dealing with Vortigern and the Saxons should be in a sequence of

1. Vortigern barters provinces for Hengist's daughter (Section 37);
2. Hengist sends for more warriors to fight the Irish (Section 38);
3. the barbarians return in force (Section 45);
4. Hengist and his warriors slaughter Vortigern's Council and ransom the king for more territories (Section 46);
5. Vortigern dies sometime after 455 (Section 48);
6. Vortimer fights the Saxons in 456 and 465(?) (Sections 43, 44).

Vortimer makes a debut during the beginning of the period normally attributed to Ambrosius. If the epithet "Vortimer" is an evocative title for Ambrosius, then this chronology suggests that Gildas is writing about the period from 456 to 497 when the wretched survivors rally to Ambrosius as their leader and there are both won and lost battles with the Saxons.

This chronology raises one last curiosity about a parallel not only between Vortimer and Ambrosius, but also one between Vortimer and Arthur. Chapter 43 of the *Historia* describes Vortimer fighting vigorously against Hengist and Horsa and their people. The English send envoys overseas to Germany to summon vast numbers of fighting men, and battles rage back and forth. Horsa is killed in a later battle which suggests that *Vortimer* is also battling against Octha. Chapter 56 relates that the English increased their numbers and *Arthur's* battles were waged against Octha and the Saxons. *Arthur's* battles are back-and-forth conflicts, and after the English were defeated at Badon, they sought help from Germany (German Saxons) and brought over their kings. History does not give detailed information about Ambrosius, but literary tradition, specifically Geoffrey of Monmouth, narrates that *Aurelius Ambrosius* first fights with. "Hengist and Horsa and then with Hengist and Octha. In a later series, *Arthur* fights with Octha and Cerdic. The sequences, Vortimer/Arthur in history connecting to Aurelius Ambrosius in literature, seem suspiciously similar.

In simple, enumerative form, the information about Vortimer can be concluded in the following way:

1. Vortimer is not mentioned in any of the ancient, historical manuscripts, including the *De Excidio, Ecclesiastical History, Annales Cambria*, or the *Anglo-Saxon Chronicle*; the notable exception is his extensive appearance in the *Historia Brittonum*.

2. The vast majority of historians, researchers, and scholars do not refer to Vortimer.
3. The word Vortimer, like Vortigern, is an epithet and not a proper name.
4. Fletcher points out that Nennius strives to give weight and credence to the Briton participation in the conflict for the salvation of Britain, while Gildas stressed the Roman influence in that conflict, leading to Vortimer's replacing Ambrosius in the *Historia*.
5. Leslie Alcock follows the majority of scholars, omitting Vortimer in *Arthur's Britain*, although he verifies the historicity of Ambrosius, Vortigern, and Arthur by citing respectively Gildas, the *calculi* of the *British Easter Table*, and the *Annales Cambriae*.

AMBROSIUS AURELIANUS AS EMRYS

Based on the writings of previous scholars, Vortimer as a mirror image of Ambrosius must be given serious consideration, which in turn requires that other epithets for Ambrosius be analyzed. As suggested earlier Gildas Badonicus should be vindicated for snubbing a national hero such as Ambrosius Aurelianus without "inventing" quarrels between a different Gildas (Albanius) and Arthur. At the end of Chapter 25 Gildas extols this Romano-Briton hero with the highest praise, and it is not presumptuous to assume that Gildas credits Ambrosius with the victory at Badon but felt no need to rename this same hero, since his countrymen already knew that Ambrosius was the leader and victor. Bede, like Gildas, echoes the praise of Ambrosius Aurelianus, "a man of good character and the sole survivor of the Roman race from the catastrophe."[32] Strikingly similar to Gildas, Bede writes that under Ambrosius' leadership the Britons took up arms, challenged their conquerors to battle, and with God's help inflicted defeat on them. From then onward the victories swung back and forth until the Battle of Badon Hill, when the Britons slaughtered the invaders. As shown in the above section, Nennius uses almost identical terms to describe the vacillation of victories by Vortimer: the Saxons fought the Britons, sometimes victoriously advancing and sometimes losing and retreating.

Excluding the name Vortimer as the evocative epithet for Ambrosius, the *Historia Brittonum* provides more information in chapters 41 and 42 about Ambrosius than any of the other ancient manuscripts combined. It is important to keep in mind Josephus Stevenson's admonition that headings within the *Historia* are supplied by some translators, and these headings are superficial and can be misleading. Sometimes Chapter 40 is included as an introduction, with the three chapters headed as "The Tale of Emrys" or "The Tale of Ambrosius." The *cognomen* "Aurelianus" does not appear in any versions of the *Historia* manuscripts, and therefore a heading of "The Tale of Ambrosius Aurelianus" would be deceptive. Similarly, in Chapter 42 the addition of *id est, Embries Guletic ipse videbatur* in parentheses after the name of Ambrosius might be corrupt. On the other hand, material in Chapter 48 which labels Ambrosius as "king among kings of the British people" seems genuine.

For expediency, it seems best to accept the heading simply as "The Tale of Emrys," even though this has led to controversies. This tale is of profound literary

Dinas Emrys, Ambrosius' stronghold in the north of Wales. This site is the reference made in the *Historia Brittonum.*

interest in and of itself but it takes on heightened meaning when it is viewed as a compelling story of contrast between Vortigern the Briton arch-villain and the boy Ambrosius with supernatural powers who confront each other at Dinas Emrys in the far reaches of Snowdonia. The boy's powers reveal that he is the future liberator of Britain. Ambrosius has powers of prophecy, which not only intimidates Vortigern but also prepares the stage for his rise to power as the Romano-Briton savior. The tale as told with its vague clue in Chapter 31, plus the unfolding of the main event in chapters 40, 41, and 42, and then the culmination in Chapter 48 where Nennius links his name to Vitalinus, foreshadows the battlelist for Arthur.

In Chapter 31 the first question requiring an answer is why, above all else, Vortigern has a fear of Ambrosius. He fears, in addition to Ambrosius, invasions by the Picts and the Irish, and a Roman reoccupation of Britain, all of which express an early time frame for his reign. A dread of Ambrosius could stem from one of three possibilities. The first is that Vortigern is a usurper, knowing that Ambrosius has ancestral rights to the throne, even though the Romans have left the island. Of Vortigern's title Ashe writes, " *Tyrannus* is the word used by Gildas for Vortigern, implying power without legitimacy."[33] Morris offers an explanation of how Vortigern came to power, almost as if in response to Ashe's charge that Vortigern's title of *superbus tyrannus* was not legitimate:

> His [Vortigern's] authority rested upon the willingness of the individual regions to obey his government. In the east, where the *federates* lived, their presence gave him

the physical power to enforce payment for the armies, but it was less easy to coerce the states of the south and west, the Belgae, the Durotriges, and the Dubonni, which were the richest areas of Britain.[34]

Based upon the new discoveries already revealed in this text, the only emendation is that Morris places the resistance to Vortigern too far south. Powys becomes a stronghold for the pro–Ambrosian faction, bounded on one side by Vortigern's authority and on the other by Vortigern's Saxon *federates*, but because Ambrosius is still too young to assume the kingship, Vortigern seizes interim power.

The second reason why Vortigern fears Ambrosius is that the usurper was given a sign through an oracle provided by his wizards. He relies on these 12 magis[35] in building a fortified stronghold, and they might well have predicted the king's overthrow by Ambrosius. But when Hengist returns to betray the weak king, Vortigern consorts with his council of elders about which path to take; the *Historia* does not convey the number of wizards whom Vortigern consults.

The third possibility is that Vortigern is infused with fear during his own personal encounter with the boy when he discovers Ambrosius' awesome powers. Again, the *Historia* does not relate Vortigern's intimidation in this confrontation; it simply narrates that Vortigern quickly, without argument, relinquishes a great deal of his territory. It can only be implied that he did it because of fear.

Throughout the three chapters, the words *adolescentem* and *puer* are used, which label Ambrosius as an adolescent, in the stage of pubescence, typically given as a median age of 13. One other chronological clue is Ambrosius' response to Vortigern's question about the boy's father. Ambrosius replies, "My father *is* one of the consuls of the Roman people." Ambrosius' father, therefore, is still alive; he has not yet been killed in the clash recorded by Gildas.

Several bits of information suggest a general time frame. Earlier in this text two facts were established. One was that Vortigern became king in 425. The second was that Hengist was associated with the second (circa 442) and third Saxon *Adventi* (453). Conceding that Vortigern's alliance with Hengist during the third *Adventus* did not deteriorate severely until the year 455 (as provided by the *Chronicle*), Ambrosius' encounter with Vortigern would have occurred between 425 and 455. Ambrosius' median age of 13 added to the year beginning Vortigern's reign would be 438; his age subtracted from the end of Vortigern's reign would be 442. Based upon information so far, then, Ambrosius' encounter with Vortigern would have occurred between 438 and 442.

THE VITALINUS CONNECTION

Vitalinus — referred to in the manuscripts of the *Historia* as Guitolin, Guitolini, or Guitholini and as Vitolinus by Leslie Alcock — is a key figure associated with Ambrosius. Although facts about him are unfortunately scarce, he still unlocks secrets in Arthurian material. Of the ancient manuscripts, only the *Historia* records his name, and among the modern researchers and scholars, only John

Morris and Leslie Alcock refer to him, excluding R.H. Fletcher, who simply reiterates what Nennius gives.

His name appears twice in the *Historia*. Chapter 49 provides this information:

> ... son of Guitolin [Vitalinus], son of Gluoi. Bonus, Paul, Mauron, Guotolin were four brothers, sons of Gloui, who built a major city upon the banks of the river Sabrinae, which the Britons call Cair Cloui, the Saxons Gloecester [Gloucester]. Enough has been said about Guorthigirno [Vortigern] and his clan.[36]

This genealogical string is so tangled, it is no wonder researchers have avoided it. Among the speculations is one by Morris who proposes that Vortigern was the son of Vitalinus, but his passage is as garbled as the original.[37] The various manuscripts of the *Historia* are no help. For instance, one may translate "filii Guorthigirn, Guortheu" as "son of Vortigern the Thin," while another may assume that it should read "filii Guorthigirn, filii Guortheu," thus creating another generation. Because this section does not contribute to the historic search for Arthur (or if it does it is buried too deeply), there is only one item worth gleaning. Gloui is directly related to Vitalinus, and as founder of Gloucester this gives one more verification of geographic location.

The only other passage of significance directly connecting Vitalinus and Ambrosius is the fourth sentence in the *Chronographer*, Chapter 66, which translates to:

> And from the reign of Guorthigirni [Vortigern] to the discord between Guitolini [Vitalinus] and Ambrosius are twelve years, which is Guoloppum, that is, Catguoloph.[38]

Alcock also cites this passage to calibrate a date. Typically, a researcher interprets "from the reign of" to mean "from the beginning of the reign," which was the scribe's intent. In doing so, Alcock reckons the date as 437, 12 years after the beginning of Vortigern's reign. He then cautions that

> ... it is not possible to construe this particular conflict [allegedly between Vitalinus and Ambrosius] in terms of nationalists versus Romanophils, for Vitolinus [sic], unlike Vortigern, bears a name that is as Roman as Ambrosius.[39]

Traditionally scholars have supported the supposition that Ambrosius was allied with a pro–Roman faction while Vitalinus was allied with a pro–Vortigern faction, meaning that Ambrosius and Vitalinus were on opposite sides, a pro-Roman versus a pro–Briton viewpoint. For instance, Morris speculates that in the *Historia Brittonum* passage Ambrosius is an older and different figure from Ambrosius Aurelianus in Gildas. He postulates that

> Ambrosius, who was Vortigern's enemy in the 430s, was too old to be identical with Ambrosius Aurelianus, the resistance leader of the 460s; but the elder Ambrosius may well have been father of the younger, and the father of Ambrosius Aurelianus ruled

for a while as emperor, either in Vortigern's time, as his rival, or before him. Nennius' Chronographer reports that the elder Ambrosius made war on Vortigern in or about 437.[40]

However, there is no evidence which warrants any of these assumptions.

Alcock's commentary, on the other hand, leads to the interesting speculation that Vitalinus and Ambrosius were not necessarily enemies, and may have even been allies. Based on the Latin in the *Historia* documents, the rift between Vitalinus and Ambrosius is described as "discord," some kind of disharmony between Vitalinus and Ambrosius, but not necessarily an out-and-out battle or war between two major adversaries. Nothing in the passage suggests that Vitalinus must be aligned with Vortigern; Vortigern's name is mentioned only as a regnal signpost, just like other emperors listed in that chapter. Further, nothing in the passage signifies that Guoloppum is a battlesite.

This view of the discord between Ambrosius and Vitalinus significantly changes the perspective, which affects the overall chronology of Arthurian history. To begin, between the tale of Emrys and the later entry of discord, there would not be a long time span, thus eliminating the need to "invent" a second, older Ambrosius assumed to be perhaps the father of Ambrosius Aurelianus. It eliminates, too, the need to explain a second Ambrosius in order to establish a workable chronology.

Secondly, it resolves the puzzling issue of having to explain Ambrosius and Vitalinus as enemies. Nennius does not offer any explicit reasons which would suggest that Vitalinus is pro–Vortigern. The deduction is made by translators (and perhaps by Nennius himself) that if a quarrel developed between Vitalinus and Ambrosius, it meant Vitalinus was a representative of Vortigern. A second unfounded deduction is that the quarrel or discord escalated into a full-blown battle. Translators have labeled Wallop as Guoloppum (Catguoloph) and called it a battle, but nowhere in the original is the word battle, conflict, or war, used.

Conversely, both Ambrosius and Vitalinus are names of Roman origin, and although it is possible that Vitalinus might have aligned himself with Vortigern as a Briton because Vortigern was a symbol of the new Britonic wave that was to come, it is much more likely that Ambrosius and Vitalinus were friends and allies, with Vitalinus tied to Ambrosius' family prior to the devastation by the Saxons.

With the great upheaval in Britain during this period, and with many factions at loose ends and opposing each other, it is not unreasonable to assume that one of the contending powers was pro–Roman, and because Ambrosius Aurelianus' parents had been powerful and influential people that Ambrosius himself would ascend to that position of power. Because of Ambrosius' age, Vitalinus would have functioned as a mentor or a protector, and in that capacity, he would have urged Ambrosius to leave the country for fear of reprisals or assassination, particularly from the Briton faction headed by Vortigern. Vitalinus would want the young aspirant to bide his time until the dangerous scramble for the throne had abated. In the fire of his youth, Ambrosius would have wanted to accept the leadership at any cost and confront all opposition, both Saxon and dissenting Briton.

The cardinal year of 437 can therefore be established for Ambrosius Aurelianus through his association with Vitalinus as reported in Nennius. The year of 425 having been established as Vortigern's rise to the throne, and 428 as the first coming of the Saxons, the discord between Vitalinus and Ambrosius occurs between these dates and the years of 440 and 441, the second coming of the Saxons, the Cunedda migration, and Cerdic becoming interpreter for Vortigern. Vitalinus had suggestive connections to Wales and Gloucester through inheritance from his father Gloui. This time frame provides a precise geographic fix in southeastern Wales, directly east of the mouth of the Severn, the same geographic fix for the Hwicca (Gewisse) territory written about by Bede and those who followed him. The discord between Vitalinus and Ambrosius would first necessarily follow Vortigern's encounter with Ambrosius as a boy, and then the death of Ambrosius' father.

Once the premise that Ambrosius and Vitalinus are allies is accepted and the date established, then the question arises, "What could have caused the disagreement between the two?" Unfortunately none of the ancient historical documents offers a direct resolution, but a path through literary tradition can be traced to piece together an answer for Ambrosius.

AMBROSIUS IN *THE HISTORY OF THE KINGS*

Judgments about Geoffrey of Monmouth, both as a historian and as a literary storyteller run from vitriolic contempt to unlimited praise. From a factual point of view, he is praised for the perceptive glimpses he provides for a period almost devoid of history, while at the other end of the continuum he is censured for distorting reality beyond recognition. Literarily, he planted the seeds for one of the most famous legends of all times but at the expense of the facts. He thus irrevocably casts a veil over the truth for a period already destitute of detail.

The dichotomy is most evident in the material on Ambrosius. When Monmouth borrows the accounts from Nennius centuries later, he expands the narrations with some details that coincide with other historical documents, and prove to be accurate. If this is simply a creative gift of interweaving factual detail with literary license, then Monmouth is a genius. Because some details cannot be checked against independent documents, it is impossible to determine in those instances if he is instead a destructive fraud as a historian. Individual judgments have to be made about which are kernels of truth and which are deceptive flights of imagination.

From the onset, Monmouth creates the dichotomy. Gildas provides the name Ambrosius Aurelianus, Nennius uses only Ambrosius, and Monmouth calls him Aurelius Ambrosius. There is, of course, no explanation why Monmouth names him "Aurelius." But as this text revealed in the introduction to Ambrosius Aurelianus in this chapter, Roman genealogies show that one of Ambrosius' ancestors was Lucius Domitius Aurelianus, a Roman emperor commonly referred to as Aurelian. It is beyond coincidence that Monmouth randomly selected the name of Aurelius for his Ambrosius. Aurelius/Aurelian and the entire prefix for Aurelianus is too much to be mere coincidence, particularly since Monmouth supplies so many details about Roman emperors of that period.

In a short space, Monmouth changed history for all succeeding generations. He basically retains the tale of Emrys from Nennius but then combines Ambrosius with Merlin, a person mentioned only once in the *Annales Cambriae*, at an entry dated 573. A new figure, Ambrosius Merlinus, emerges, setting the stage for the Arthur/Merlin bond in the knightly sagas, but in doing so he buries Ambrosius' identity and confuses the search for the authenticity of Arthur.

Since the pursuit of this section is Arthur and any epithet associated with him, the image of Merlin merits attention because of yet another epithet which attaches itself to Arthur. Goodrich expresses a "premonition [that] suggests 'Merlin' was an *agnomen*."[41] Monmouth must have had that same premonition, or perhaps gleaned the information from his ancient book, for in relating the Tale of Emrys according to Nennius, he refers to Ambrosius at two points as *Merlinus qui et Ambrosius dicebur*—Ambrosius Merlinus — before finally clipping that name to Merlin. This suggests that Merlin of the romances of centuries later actually began as an *agnomen* for Ambrosius Aurelianus, denoting another facet of his phenomenal *persona*. As an outgrowth in later epics, Merlin emerged as a separate individual.

Monmouth also assigns to Aurelius Ambrosius the personality of Ambrosius Aurelianus but makes his reign short-lived, compounding the problem by creating a whole new character, Utherpendragon, who finally transfers the reign to his son Arthur. With the power of the pen, Monmouth transfers the magic of Ambrosius Aurelianus as described in the Nennius document to Merlin, creates a brother named Utherpendragon (whether he is cognizant of his error or not) from an epithet for Ambrosius, and passes on to Arthur, another epithet, what should be accorded to Ambrosius as a rightful place in history.

Monmouth compounds the travesty (or perhaps only the extravagance of literary license) concerning the Emrys tale. Chapter 49 in the *Historia* dealing with genealogies unfortunately stops with Gloui, and no historical source provides any specific detail about Vitalinus' ancestry. Monmouth, however, gives a one-sentence clue for Gloius:

> Some, however, say that [the city of Kaerglou or Gloucester] took its name from Duke Gloius, whom Claudius fathered in that city and to whom he granted control of the duchy of the Welsh after Arvirargus.[42]

Only part of this is borrowed from Chapter 49 of the *Historia*, which relates that Gloucester was named after Gloui, father of Vitalinus (Guitholin.)

Checking the other two names provided by Monmouth (Claudius and Arvirargus[43]) is like trying to grasp shadows. The only Claudius possible in this time frame is Claudius II, not Claudius I. Arvirargus, who does not appear in the Roman histories, is listed in Monmouth as a king under Claudius I, over two centuries prior to the Gloui/Vitalinus era.

In spite of his maddening inaccuracies and literary inconsistencies, Monmouth does contribute credible explanations to fill some of the holes in history.

The original *Historia* manuscripts refer to Vitalinus as Guitolin, and as already shown in a previous chapter of this text, this name parallels the name Guithelinus in Monmouth. The addition of the Latin *-us* affix, according to Sir Ifor Williams, was no doubt added to the names for dignity. Monmouth then contributes this information: "The Bishop of Gloucester was promoted to be Archbishop of London."[44] No names are attached at this point, but the word "Gloucester" establishes a tenuous connection with Gloui, Vitalinus' father, as listed in the *Historia*; Caer Gloui was a former name for Gloucester

In Part Four, "The House of Constantine," Monmouth's first sentence is

> The Britons took counsel, and Guithelinus, the Archbishop of London, then crossed the sea to Little Britain, called at that time Armorica or Letavia, to seek help from their blood-brothers.[45]

The purpose of the voyage was the Aetius letter, which is historically assigned to a year late in the fourth decade of the fifth century. Because Monmouth is so unpredictable, it is impossible to conjecture if he made a connection between what he wrote from Part Four and Part Eight, or why he did not supply a name in Part Eight.

Regardless, at this point the lives of Guithelinus and Aurelius Ambrosius entwine. Of Constantine's three sons, Aurelius Ambrosius and Utherpendragon are "given to Guithelinus so that he might bring them up."[46]

After ten years had passed, Ambrosius' father was assassinated by a Pict. This differs from the much more reliable account given by Gildas that Ambrosius' parents were slain by the Saxons. According to Monmouth, however, after the father's death, a disagreement arose among the leaders as to who should be raised to the throne: "Some were in favour of Aurelius Ambrosius, others of Utherpendragon, and still other of various close relatives of the royal family."[47] This could align with the discord between Vitalinus and Ambrosius, suggesting, of course, that Vitalinus was an ally and supporter of Ambrosius, concerned not only with the young boy's right to the throne, but primarily with his safety.

Vortigern, leader of the Gewissae, appears on the scene and seizes the throne. Through deceit, he entices Constans, the third son, to become king by saying, "Your father is dead and your brothers cannot be king because of their youth."[48] Vortigern then plots Constans' assassination and sets the crown upon his own head.

Because Monmouth's story is not presented sequentially, it is impossible, even judging from content, to determine what happens next; it would be even more rash to attempt an accurate historical chronology. In recorded Roman history, the only emperor who could fit into Monmouth's time frame would be Constantius III, who died in 421. This sets the stage for British history when Vortigern assumes the kingship in 425, but Constans was the son of Constantine I (the Great), who dates to the beginning of the 300s. Constans had two brothers, Constantine II and Constantius II, all of which shows that Monmouth has displaced several generations.

There are, however, several events which would fit the sequence. Monmouth writes that

> those in charge of the upbringing of the two brothers Aurelius Ambrosius and Utherpendragon fled with their charges to Little Britain, just in case the two should be murdered by Vortigern.[49]

With the exception of Utherpendragon listed as a brother instead of indicating an epithet for Ambrosius, this is in keeping with what could have transpired after Vortigern had seized the throne and why there was discord between Vitalinus and his ward.

Monmouth then adds that

> [Vortigern] was haunted by the fear of Aurelius Ambrosius and his brother Utherpendragon, who, as explained already, had fled to Little Britain because of him.[50]

This, too, fits historically, whether or not Vortigern had already encountered Ambrosius as related in the *Historia*, again with the realization that the reference to Utherpendragon has to be deleted.

"The House of Constantine," the chapter which supposedly focuses on Ambrosius, is one of Monmouth's more enigmatic chapters, a maze of anachronistic errors.[51] He splits it asunder by driving a wedge titled the "Prophecies of Merlin" between the two parts. At the end of the first half, he retells Chapter 41 from the *Historia* but adds material not found in any versions. According to Geoffrey, Vortigern's wizards come to the village of Kaermerdin (Maes Elleti in the *Historia*) where two boys, Merlin and Dinabutius (unnamed in the *Historia*), are arguing about Merlin not having a father. The wizards question the mother, described as a daughter of the King of Dementia (unidentified in the *Historia*). Geoffrey then adds that Merlin was also called Ambrosius and several sentences later refers to the young boy as Ambrosius Merlinus.

In the "Merlin" section Geoffrey begins the "Tale of Emrys" similarly to the *Historia* version, but then Ambrosius Merlin goes into a trance and gives 15 pages of prophecies. Merlin continues the imagery of the Red and White Dragons, introduces the Boar of Cornwall, and from there adds a great deal of symbology.

When Geoffrey resumes the story on the "House of Constantine," there are several more inventions, or to be kinder, details evidently taken from the alleged "ancient book." Before beginning the narration of Ambrosius, Monmouth opens with more predictions by Merlin again referring to the famous "Boar of Cornwall." Parallel to the *Historia*, Ambrosius is anointed king by the wretched Briton survivors, Hengist slaughters the Council, and battles rage between the Britons and the Saxons, Aurelius urging on the Christians and Hengist encouraging the pagans.[52] Monmouth writes about Hengist's death and Octha's pardon. He also includes Pascent, Vortigern's son, but as Aurelius' enemy, even though the former hates his own father. In the *Historia* this son is portrayed as an ally, who was given permission by Ambrosius to rule two kingdoms.

However, Geoffrey then goes on a tangent about Aurelius requesting more prophecies but being refused, about Merlin moving the Giant's Ring, and about Eopa's assassinating Aurelius by poisoning him. Prophetic signs appear in the heavens, which Merlin interprets. The chapter ends with the fictional Utherpendragon becoming king, Octha breaking the pact he originally had with Aurelius and eventually being killed, the story of Arthur's conception and birth, and Uther's death by poisoning.

Nevertheless, Monmouth discloses cause-and-effect reasons for certain sets of sequences. Vitalinus, a Roman, has already demonstrated his integrity in trying to salvage the Briton empire by seeking aid in Brittany, and as a faithful guardian to Ambrosius, he perceives the dangers for the young boy. Although Ambrosius has a rightful claim to leadership through his father, Vitalinus realizes that because of Ambrosius' age and inexperience, he could easily be deposed or assassinated by those struggling for power within their own ranks. Vitalinus urges the young leader to withdraw and seek refuge in Brittany, but Ambrosius wants to remain on the island where he rightfully belongs. An argument ensues. Vitalinus' sensibilities win out, and Ambrosius is exiled to await a more propitious time to claim his rightful inheritance. Vortigern maintains the kingship, filling the void left by the death of Ambrosius' father and the departure of the proper successor, although the usurper remains in continuous dread of Ambrosius. Somewhere in the interval Vitalinus dies, but other wards for Ambrosius protect him and put him under the sanction of Budic. Figuratively, Ambrosius becomes king at an early age, but because of peril from Vortigern, the rightful king must bide his time.

The Assessment of Ambrosius Aurelianus

For over a thousand years, the notion of multiple personalities and names concealing the sole historic figure has shrouded the aphorism of Arthur's inception. John Morris touches upon the importance of Ambrosius by crediting him with the beginnings of the resistance and its success, but before the final victory of Badon, Morris claims early on in his history that Ambrosius passes the captaincy to Arthur.[53] He follows this later by writing, "Whether Ambrosius was killed, died, or was superseded by a younger general, we do not know."[54] He does not list the possibility that Ambrosius continued living. Thus, in seeking a chronology, Morris does not equate the Ambrosius who was Vortigern's rival with the Ambrosius Aurelianus who was the resistance leader of the 460s, believing that the former would be too old to function as the latter. Although Morris cites a late tradition that exiles Ambrosius to Gaul and brings him back with an army from Europe, he does not consider a time frame which would show that Ambrosius as a young boy during the early reign of Vortigern would not be too old to become a resistance leader in the 460s.

The historical importance of Ambrosius during this period also manifests itself in geographic locales that show spheres of his activities. Ambrosius as the central figure in the search for Arthur also provides further implications about the location of Badon and the subsequent shift in the theaters of warfare. Morris provides a different key:

> The English towns and villages called Ambrosden, Amberley, Amesbury and the like are found only in one part of the country, in the south and south midlands, between the Severn and East Anglia, on the edges of the war zone between the Cotswold heartlands of the Combrogi and the powerful English kingdoms of the east.[55]

Not only does he mention *Combrogi* (the *Cymry* or Welsh), he includes names in Herefordshire, Worchestershire, Gloucestershire, and Oxfordshire, reflecting sites near Wroxeter in the Cornovii province and on the perimeters of Gewissae and West-Saxon territories.

Ekwall gives similar detail about these names in the belt of military activity during the mid fifth century; he also lists Amblecote and Ombersley near Birmingham; Amberley south of Gloucester; Ambrosden, north of Oxford; Emberton east of Northampton; Ambleston, west of Carmarthan; and Emborough, south of Bristol. This area localizes Ambrosius' military activities during a specific period with Caer Vadon centrally located. Morris himself admits that any conclusion about place-names can be no more than inferential, but when amassed with other logical deductions, the historical picture is much more definitive.

The more specific historical picture shows the overlap of Ambrosius and Arthur. The *Historia* relates that Octha came down from the north after Horsa's (emended from Hengist's) death and fought Arthur. Since Horsa died prior to the Battle of the Inscribed Stone, then Octha also fought against Vortimer. Gildas writes that after Vortigern's deposal, Ambrosius directly succeeded to the throne with no other intervening kings. The *Chronicle* records that Octha began his joint reign with his father around 453. Collating this information means that the first of Arthur's battles was fought sometime after 453, that the 12 battles attributed to Arthur were fought between 453 and 497, and that when Octha came down from the north he fought against Ambrosius, Vortimer, and Arthur.

During that span from 453 to 497, Morris calibrates the second migration to Brittany during the year 459.[56] Vortimer is dead, the Council of the Province has been slaughtered, the Saxons have overrun the island, and to escape the devastation, Britons throughout these years of ordeal begin an exodus to Brittany. This, too, fits into the scheme recounted in Gildas, and Ambrosius' counterattack would be "after the British emigration, which can roughly be dated to the late 450s, so that the counterattack itself doubtless began in the 460s."[57]

Of 459/460, Morris writes that "Ambrosius headed the early years of the resistance, but by the time of the final victory Arthur was the 'commander of the kings of the British in the war.'"[58] By 461 the peak of the second migration had passed. Morris is referring to Ambrosius' leadership when he writes, "The counteroffensive was begun by the remnant of the Roman nobility of Britain."[59] After this point, Morris admits "[t]here is no indication of when Ambrosius died or retired,"[60] and "[t]he battles and campaigns of Ambrosius are unremembered."[61]

Ironically, Morris did not realize that Ambrosius might be unremembered because his historic role had been clouded by the use of epithets for this singular figure.

And in order to complete his series of comments about the second migration, one must go full circle to the first part of his text, where Morris writes, "Several contemporary Gauls give reports of the British immigrants, whose fighting force they reckoned at 12,000."[62] Jordanes is the Gaul who writes the history that reports

> The emperor Anthemius heard of it and asked the Brittones for aid. Their king Riotimus came with twelve thousand men into the state of the Bituriges by the way of Ocean, and was received as he disembarked from his ships.[63]

Morris unknowingly prophesies the dissolution of Ambrosius in Britain and the nascence of Riothamus on the continent, leading directly to the second figure of the Arthurian triad, but in reaching this point, he also ties Ambrosius to Arthur, the figure beyond Riothamus. In back-to-back sentences, he writes, "It may be that during the sixth and seventh centuries the name of Ambrosius was as well loved as that of Arthur," followed by "It is also possible that Ambrosius' name survives in England for reasons that owe nothing to legend."[64] Both statements are germane, since Ambrosius and Badon are so closely allied. The latter statement is self-evident: Ambrosius' name *has* survived because of his historical substantiation; he is the cornerstone of Gildas with a name that has not become extenuated in legend nor diluted with exaggeration. Ambrosius is established on a stable, reputable base, and during the sixth and seventh centuries his name was well loved because of his giant stature as a true flesh-and-blood hero. It was only after that, in the succeeding four centuries, that epithets and fantastic tales began emerging so that, as the image of Ambrosius dimmed, the phoenix of Arthur took his place. Morris' statement should to be altered to read, "During the fifth, sixth, and seventh centuries the hero was loved as *Ambrosius*, and thereafter that same figure was loved as *Arthur*."

Chapter 10
Riothamus: The Briton
from Across the Ocean

The Historical Chronology of Riothamus

The history of Riothamus is as brief as a shooting star, but in spite of his instantaneous flash, he plays an indispensable role in the Arthurian saga. His niche in history on the continent, spanning only about ten years, lies between the earlier era of Ambrosius Aurelianus and later escapades attributed to Arthur. Of the antiquarians, only Jordanes, Gregory of Tours, and Sidonius record his actions, and each does it very briefly.

As with Vortimer, most modern scholars have nothing to contribute about Riothamus. John Morris makes passing references to him in his history, but he writes nothing of the name being an epithet. Instead, he identifies Riothamus as a commander named John Reith, who was also called "Regula" and "Riatham," fighting for southwestern Brittany.[1]

Fletcher is another of the few researchers who alludes to Riothamus in a roundabout way. Uriscampum, a chronicler in 1175, interpolated the manuscripts of Sigebert of Gembloux, whose genuine work contained no Arthurian material. Uriscampum, who usually wrote summaries related essentially to Geoffrey of Monmouth, often interpolated, altered, and added to the Sigebert material, using a manuscript that had already been slightly interpolated (between 1138 and 1147) by a monk of Beauvais.[2] The value of the Uriscampum manuscript is not that he distorted historical information. But by questioning Geoffrey's authority rather than blindly accepting the *History of the Kings* as fact, this obscure monk, as early as 1175,[3] makes the suggestion that Riothimir (one of the many variants of the name) should be identified with Arthur.

The most detailed information, however, comes from Geoffrey Ashe who proposes in *The Discovery of King Arthur* that "Maybe Riothamus was Arthur."[4]

But in order to show that the two were one, independent of literary fancy or Geoffrey of Monmouth, there had to be "... evidence that other people ... also spoke of Riothamus and called him Arthur."[5] Chronologically, Ashe is attempting to set Arthur's reign from 454 to 470, but this must be set aside for the more relevant information of Riothamus' theater of operations and relationships with other historical figures. Five major figures play key roles in Riothamus' sphere of activities: Ægidius, his son Syagrius, Anthemius, Euric the Visigoth, and Sidonius. In smaller but by no means unimportant roles there are others such as Avitus, Ricimer, and Arvandus, all of whom help guide the course of continental history.

Difficulties arise in devising a chronology, even prior to interrelating him with figures in the Arthurian saga, because of inconsistencies and contradictions by writers of the period. Morris' caution about the impossibility of an event being dated to a precise year also applies here. For example, in one instance in *The Discovery of Arthur*, Ashe writes that Ægidius established himself about 457,[6] but later he lists Ægidius' reign from 461 to 464.[7] In contrast, Morris writes that Ægidius establishes his kingdom about the same time as the massacre of Vortigern's Council in Britain, which would be around 458, but in providing Ægidius' ascendancy to power he gives the year 455. As a concession, however, both Ashe and Morris fortunately list Ægidius' death in 464, so that date is definitive. An inconsistency arises again, though, when Morris writes that in 467–68 "either Syagrius or Ægidius stationed the British on the frontier where the Gothic attack was expected,"[8] which would be several years after Ægidius' purported death. In this same vein for the years 467–468, Morris says that *Ægidius* evidently enlisted the Saxons to fight against the Goths. Morris and Ashe also differ on another point. Morris writes, "Ægidius found himself transformed to 'king of the Romans,'"[9] but Ashe contends that Syagrius adopts the title "king of the Romans."[10]

The fault, however, lies in the "jumbled list of events [because of the rapidity with which armies changed allegiances] in these years, whose complexity must have dazed contemporaries as much as the modern reader."[11] Two things compound the problem even further; one is that events are related in some detail but no time frame is given, and the other is that many accounts are only local reports and do not give adequate clues of how they fit into the larger scheme of continental occurrences.

The second migration of the Britons to the continent served as a prologue for the insurrections occuring on the mainland:

> Many colonists were drawn from the better-educated and better-off. ... They may simply have been depressed by the prospects [of Saxon rule on the island], but went to Gaul in a more positive spirit, with Ægidius's aid and under his auspices. There was not just a panicked, headlong rush out of Britain; the migration may have contained some of that element, but part of it, too, was Briton movement after debate and consideration. ... Ægidius or his son Syagrius, who succeeded him, may have put the Britons in charge of coastal defense and sponsored these settlements.[12]

The implication is that when the Britons came from the island *en masse* with their leader Riothamus, they were well-organized and ready to build a kingdom for themselves along the coast of Aremorica. Morris asserts that

> The immigrants did not come [to Brittany] empty-handed, receiving their new lands as a charitable gift. There were a fighting force of 12,000 men, whom Ægidius badly needed. ... It was the British who brought aid to Gaul. The survivors of the catastrophe [the massacre of the Council and the Saxon incursions] despaired of their homeland, and sought security in the still Roman dominions of Ægidius. He welcomed them, and gave them estates "north of the Loire," in the "Aremorican Tract" that the *Notitia* extends from the Seine to the Atlantic.[13]

The historical conditions supply the motive for Riothamus' voyage across the Channel toward the end of the second Briton migration. Instead of the migration being viewed as a panicked, headlong flight from Saxons ravishing the island (which would have been the condition approximately a decade earlier), Ambrosius' victories recorded by Gildas could have stabilized sufficiently the Briton kingdoms so that a pact could be hammered out with Roman factions on the continent to deal with the Saxons in their homeland. The *Anglo-Saxon Chronicle* attests to the stabilized Briton kingdoms by its silence on Saxon victories during this period. In 455 and 456 the Saxons are on the offensive and claim major victories, but then there is a silence from 456 until 473, punctuated only by a skirmish in 465 when 12 British chiefs are slain.

Jordanes, in his *Gothic History* of 551, is the major source who provides the motive for Riothamus and his army sailing to Gaul:

> Now Euric king of the Visigoths, perceived the frequent change of Roman Emperors and strove to hold Gaul by his own right. The Emperor Anthemius heard of it and asked the Brittones for aid. Their King Riotimus came with twelve thousand men into the state of the Bituriges by the way of Ocean, and was received as he disembarked from his ships.[14]

Anthemius' request for aid from the Britons shows that the action was not initiated by the Britons, and inherent in that is a reciprocal agreement which would have been beneficial for both parties. By supplying that aid, Riothamus would expect something in return. He might have viewed it as an opportunity to staunch the flow of Saxons to the island by destroying the wellspring. Or he might have been promised territories for displaced Britons, continuing a trend initiated during the first migration. It could have been, too, that Roman victory with Riothamus' aid would shore up a teetering Empire and lead to a resurgence successful enough to have Roman troops reoccupy Britain. Any of the options would have been beneficial enough for Riothamus to gamble his army in return for crushing the barbarian onslaught.

Several events led up to Euric's perception of the decaying Roman civilization. In 455 Valentinian III was murdered, which marked the fall of the Western Empire. Various short-lived successors reigned, but what was left of the provinces was not firmly controlled by Rome. Gaul proclaimed Avitus as emperor, who in turn appointed a fellow-nobleman to take over the armies while he himself went to Rome. He was quickly deposed by Ricimer, a barbarian German *federate* allied to Valentinian's court, who received his training under Aetius, the same individual from whom the Britons had supplicated aid and the same general whom Valentinius murdered. During this time Ricimer installed a puppet emperor for the Frankish empire; a search of history reveals that two "puppets" overlap this era, Majorian and Livius Severus (461-465), the former evidently prior to Ægidius as the crown head of the Franks and Severus as the figurehead who was ignored in favor of Ægidius ruling both empires.[15]

Maintaining loyalty to the remnants of the Roman empire and the Roman way of life, Ægidius of Northern Gaul withheld allegiance to Ricimer, feeling that the German *federate* was not a bonafide emperor of Rome.[16] In 457 the Frankish settlers in that area were in conflict with their king, Childeric, and in order to stop civil infighting they banished him and accepted Ægidius as their leader.[17] At least for a time Ægidius not only ruled Gaul but the Frankish kingdom.

From this information, several items must be emphasized. One is that Riothamus, like Ambrosius, was a product of Roman heritage, aligning himself with the stongest Roman faction (specifically Anthemius) surviving on the continent. The second is that accounts from Jordanes and Gregory of Tours parallel details supplied by Gildas' manuscript. Wretched survivors rallying around Ambrosius match those of survivors rallying around the banner of Riothamus in hopes of acquiring dominions under him in Brittany. The third is that Riothamus' army expected no charitable gifts but contributed to Anthemius' strategy and Ægidius' kingdom in return for their own grants of land.

If indeed Riothamus had a reciprocal pact with Anthemius, it never came to fruition because of the devastating outcome of several battles on the continent. Upon Ægidius' death, Syagrius, his son, became ruler of Gaul, Childeric was reinstated as leader of the Franks, and several other significant events happened in rapid succession. During the period from 468 to 470, a leader named Odovacer (Odoacer), a part of the Roman Army and a member of the Imperial Guard, became dissatisfied during the unrest and switched allegiance to the warring Saxons who were aggressively active in the Loire Valley and around Angers. In a compact history, Gregory of Tours relates that when the rampaging Saxons under Odovacer reached Angers the Romans and Franks fought the Saxons:

> Saxons fled and left many of their people to be slain, the Romans pursuing. Their islands were captured and ravaged by the Franks, and many were slain.[18]

An alliance was then made between Childeric and Odavacer, and they subdued the Alamanni, contributing to the collapse of the Western Empire.

After Leo I appointed Anthemius to rule as the bonafide emperor of the Western Empire,[19] deep rifts occurred. Anthemius supported the Britons and Gauls against Euric, who had murdered his brother Theodoric to become sole king of the Visigoths.[20] However, the new emperor's seditious viceroy, Arvandus, urged Euric not to make peace with Anthemius but to attack the British beyond the Loire, claiming that a treaty had partitioned Gaul between the Visigoths and Burgundians.[21] Arvandus began his treasonous plot against Anthemius and Gaul. His letter to Euric was probably written before the close of 468 and intercepted shortly after Arvandus was recalled to Rome to stand trial. Nevertheless, because the trial was public the essence of the message was still conveyed to Euric, who realized the perfidy at the core of Gaul's empire and attacked the Britons, knowing that the destruction of the king from beyond the Ocean and his host of troops would create the crack in the Roman Empire that would cause it finally to crumble.[22] A second battle followed almost immediately between Riothamus and Euric, with disastrous results for the Roman contingency. In 470, following the Battle of Angers, Jordanes writes,

> Euric, king of the Visigoths, came against them [Riotimus' forces] with an innumerable army, and after a long fight he routed Riotimus, king of the Brittones, before the Romans could join him. So when [Riotimus] had lost a great part of his army, he fled with all the men he could gather together, and came to the Burgundians, a neighbouring tribe then allied to the Romans.[23]

This cataclysmic defeat followed on the heels of the victory over the Saxons at Angers. Roman reinforcements never arrived because of a rebellion by Childeric and the Saxons. The treaty with the Saxons after the Battle of Angers had supposedly made the Saxons and Franks allies and therefore a contingent of the Roman army, but during Euric's siege, both allies rebelled.

Riothamus' army was overwhelmed. Gregory of Tours in the *History of the Franks* adds one more detail: "The Britanni were driven from Bourges by the Goths, and many were slain at the village of Déols."[24] After Riothamus' retreat into Burgundy he drops from the histories.

The letter from Sidonius to Riothamus helps sort out the confusing history of this period by validating at least one date, and in itself provides some personal information about Riothamus. In late 469, Sidonius was installed at Clermont as bishop of the Arverni and was therefore in Gaul at the same time that Arvandus, Anthemius' seditious viceroy, was on trial. As a high-ranking cleric he was asked to make a plea to Riothamus on behalf of a humble rustic whose slaves were being enticed away from him by soldiers of Riothamus' army. In the letter's introduction, he writes:

> Here is a letter in my usual style, for I combine complaint with greeting, not with an express intention of making my pen respectful in its superscription but harsh in the letter itself, but because things are always happening about which it is obviously impossible for a man of my rank and cloth to speak without incurring unpleasantness or to be silent without incurring guilt.[25]

Because Sidonius is in Gaul and had been installed as bishop by 469, his use of the words "rank and cloth" refers to his ecclesiastic position, showing that the letter was written after his appointment.

Sidonius' compliments to Riothamo (the spelling used in his letter) indicate that he has had several contacts with him and knows of the king's impartiality and fair dealings with others:

> However, I am a direct witness of the conscientiousness which weighs on you so heavily, and which has always been of such delicacy as to make you blush for the wrongdoing of others.[26]

The word "blush" can be interpreted to mean the man's intolerance of letting wrongdoings pass unnoticed, or it could mean he is embarrassed or upset that others can tolerate wrongdoing. These praises of Riothamus bring to mind Gildas' praise of Ambrosius Aurelianus.

Drawing parallels leads back to Geoffrey Ashe's theory about Riothamus and Arthur. Ashe's wish — that there would be evidence of other histories speaking of Riothamus and calling him Arthur — is not realized when examining the ancient manuscripts. But that does not void his theory. As Ashe points out, both Jordanes and Gregory of Tours refer to Riothamus as a Briton, or "king of the Britons," not as a Breton, which is a crucial distinction. Riothamus comes "by the way of Ocean" and is not an Armorican king from the first migration. Ashe cites James Campbell as accepting Riothamus as "a British ruler having authority on both sides of the Channel."[27]

He uses two other noteworthy sources. One is by the scribe William, who penned the *Legend of St. Goeznovius* around 1019, a date which Fleuriot labeled as authentic.[28] This would be over a century prior to the Monmouth manuscript and hence not just an echo of Arthur's Gallic compaigns, considered by some as a fictionalized Monmouth account. William writes,

> Presently [Saxon] pride was checked for a while through the great Arthur, king of the Britons. They were largely cleared from the island and reduced to subjection. But when this same Arthur, after many victories which he won gloriously in Britain and in Gaul, was summoned at last from human activity, the way was open for the Saxons to go again into the island.[29]

This, then, is the only account of Arthur's Gallic campaigns, written even earlier than Monmouth. William provides the motive also attributed to Riothamus: the island was secured well enough to allow an army to sail to the continent and fight the Saxons in their homeland. William also refers to Arthur by the epithet "king of the Britons," the same as Jordanes' epithet for Riothamus, which no manuscript up to that date had even done.

The other source Ashe uses is Sharon Turner's *History of the Anglo-Saxons*, published in 1799. Turner argues against an accepted idea in his day that Hengist had completely destroyed the British resistance during the 450s and 460s by pointing out that

> ... at this very period [the 450s and 460s] the Britons were so warlike that twelve thousand went to Gaul, on the solicitations of the emperor, to assist the natives against the Visigoths.[30]

He is of course referring to Riothamus, but the impact is in a footnote where he proffers the idea that Riothamus was Arthur.

Based on these premises, Ashe draws a connection between Riothamus' battle at Angers and the Battle of Agned listed in the *Historia*. The eleventh battle is convoluted in the several manuscripts[31] of the *Historia*, but it is an intriguing parallel for three reasons. For one, as Ashe indicates, no place has been confirmed in Britain; two locations have been suggested (one in Somersetshire and one in Edinburgh) but neither is very convincing. Second, it is a successful Briton campaign against the Saxons, although it does vary from the implied *Historia* account that the Arthurian campaigns were against Octha as the leader. And third, because this eleventh battle is immediately followed by Riothamus' resounding defeat at Bourg-de-Déols, Riothamus could still have collected the remnants of his army, returned to the island, and fought a successful battle against the Saxons at Badon. However, this is contrary to Ashe's theory, which terminates Riothamus' existence at his disappearance into Burgundy, and cancels Badon as attributable to Arthur. Also, accepting Ashe's theory is based upon scribal contraction and corruption from Angers to Agned. Despite pros and cons, it opens up the possibility that if Riothamus is equated with Arthur, then some of the *Historia* campaigns listed for Arthur could have been fought on the continent.

Riothamus' disappearance into Burgundy marks his end historically; his name does not reappear in British or continental accounts. Knowledge, then, of Riothamus dates from the Briton migration of the 460s to his defeat on the Indre and retreat into Burgundy in the 470s. Combined with data about Ambrosius, the two chronologies span two decades, from 450 to 470. If one considers seriously the possibility that Arthur is, in fact, the Briton king Riotimus from across the Ocean, then the quintessence of Arthur must change. Arthur as the next figure will complete the cycle.

Chapter 11
Arthur: Historical and Literary Data

The Historical Arthur

A different approach is required for the third person in this chronological chain. The first two subheadings characterizing Ambrosius Aurelianus and Riothamus aptly described a *historical* chronology, with Arthur, of course, being discussed to some extent, since the theory being extrapolated binds the three figures. Viewed independently, Arthur's existence overlapped that of Vortimer and Ambrosius from the third Saxon *Adventus* to the beginnings of the battlelist recorded in the *Historia*. Riothamus' existence (through speculation) overlapped Arthur's sixth battle on the shores of the Bassas, and also possibly the eleventh battle at Agned. Despite no positive proof for specific dates or battles, however, Riothamus did disappear from history some time during the Arthurian battles.

As a recapitulation of the four ancient historic sources, neither the *De Excidio* nor the *Anglo-Saxon Chronicle* records information under the name Arthur. The *Annales Cambriae* provides only two references. Using the modified dates ascertained in earlier chapters, the two entries are

497 — The Battle of Badon, in which Arthur carried the Cross of our Lord Jesus Christ for three days and three nights on his shoulders (shield) and the Britons were victorious.

518 — The Battle of Camlann, in which Arthur and Medraut fell; and there was plague in Britain and Ireland.

The only other ancient document alluding to the famous king is, of course, the *Historia Brittonum*, where his name appears in two different chapters. First is in Section 73 under the heading "The Wonders of Britain," sometimes delineated as distinctive from the *Historia*, but not applicable here because of its legendary nature. Hence, the two other important references to Arthur are in Section 56, page 35.[1] The first is in the introductory passage, including the emendation from Hengist's death to Horsa's:

> On Horsa's death, Octha came down from the north of Britain. ... Then Arthur fought against [the English] in those days, together with the kings of the British; but he was their leader in battle.

For the 12 battles listed, a connection is thus made between Arthur as the Briton leader and Octha as the Saxon leader.

The second use of Arthur's name is in the entry for the eighth battle:

> ... in Guinnion fort, and in it Arthur carried the image of the holy Mary, the everlasting on his shield ...

This entry is not helpful in attempting either a calibration or a geographic location. John of Glastonbury writes of Arthur's conversion to Christianity and the subsequent change of blazon, but his borrowed material is spurious and not helpful in clarifying Arthur's historicity.

The last appearance of the king's name is attached to the twelfth battle in which

> nine hundred and sixty men fell in one day, from a single charge of Arthur's, and no one laid [the Saxons] low save he alone, and he was victorious in all his campaigns.

With assistance from the *De Excidio* and the *Annales Cambriae*, an accurate calibration was set for the year 497; from parallels drawn in the *ASC*, it was possible to extract the name of one of his adversaries, Cerdic.

The culminating paragraph after the battlelist also gives some extra information:

> The more the [English] Saxons were vanquished, the more they sought for new supplies of Saxons from Germany [i.e., German Saxons]; so that kings, commanders, and military bands were invited over from almost every [German Saxon] province. And this practice they continued till the reign of Ida, who was the ... first king in Bernicia.[2]

At first glance the last passage appears to relay no significant facts, but in reality, it provides important chronological calibrations. The opening clause of the passage relates that the 12 battles have already been fought prior to 497. Up to the battle at Badon in this year, the *Historia* has recorded the coming of the East and South Saxons and set the stage for the West Saxon kingdom. After all the prior English defeats in these battles, they seek help from Germany, always increasing their numbers and importing kings to rule over them. For some unknown reason, the *Historia* omits significant entries between the span of 497 and 547, particularly the Battle of Camlann and Arthur's death in 518, calibrated according to the lunar adaptation. It explains heavy Saxon incursions during a 50-year period, but does not hint why these invasions became possible.

That is the extent of historical material on King Arthur. By itself it is very meager, but if the historic details of Ambrosius Aurelianus, Vortimer, Emrys, and Riothamus are factored in, the information is not as inconsequential as it might first appear. Additionally, a great deal can be gleaned from sources such as John of Glastonbury, Henry of Huntingdon, Gregory of Tours, Geoffrey of Monmouth, Sidonius, Goeznovius, Giraldus Cambrensis, Chretien de Troyes, the *Saints' Lives*, the *Chronica Gallica*, and scores of modern researchers, historians, and scholars. Furthermore, literary tradition, founded upon the historial and factual manuscripts, continues the Arthurian cycle by contributing a massive amount of material.

Literary Data on Arthur

Prior to an appraisal of the contributions which literary tradition makes in refining the image of a historical Arthur, terms — particularly "myth" versus "legend" — must be clarified. Selecting a specific term for literary tradition will provide the platform for launching into literary works whose primary purpose is something other than the simple disclosure of factual data.

Because "myth" is inseparable from religious or allegorical overtones, it is not an appropriate reference to the historic King Arthur, although some scholars have aligned Arthur to mythical beginnings. John Rhys, in the first chapter of *The Arthurian Legend* (titled "Arthur, Historical and Mythical") writes,

> Leaving aside for a while the man Arthur and assuming the existence of a god by that name, let us see what could be made of him. Mythologically speaking he would probably have to be regarded as a Culture Hero; for, a model king and the institutor of the Knighthood of the Round Table, he is represented as the leader of expeditions to the isles of Hades, and as one who stood in somewhat the same kind of relation to Gwalchmei as Gwydion did to Ileu.[3]

As with so much of mythological oral tradition passed down, the ascription of mythological attributes to a real-life figure seems to be a process of one step forward and two steps back. Arthur arises as an epic hero (a Culture Hero in Rhys' terms) from a national catastrophe or from cataclysmic events in the fifth and sixth centuries, but because the emergence of this hero is embedded in the reality of the present, mythological explanations are not fabricated for his exceptional achievements. However, when centuries have dimmed the reality of the catastrophic events (one step forward), exaggerated and embellished stories of the hero minimize or even disregard his human status of eminence (one step back), and elevate him to the supernatural realms of mythology (another step into a deeper past).

For his Culture Hero as applied to Arthur, Rhys places more emphasis on the hero's possible mythological origins based upon clues in medieval romances rather than concentrating on human historical endeavors. Rhys adds to his explanation:

> So here one seems to detect the disturbing influence of a historical fact and to be entitled to regard the death of the Culture Hero in a mythic war with his nephew as suggested by the real death of a man Arthur, at the hands of a real nephew in some such person as that of Maelgwn as already suggested.[4]

The proper emphasis should be *legendary* war rather than *mythic* war. The historic fact during Arthur's existence should be the data which carries the most weight in establishing him as an authentic character. The exaggerations, additions, and supernaturalism should be put into proper perspective when aligned with his heroic but human qualities, which leads more appropriately to the term "legend."

Labeling literary tradition about the historic Arthur does *not* mean the material is devoid of fact. What it does mean is that the historical fact in this section is secondary to aesthetics; factual data gleaned from storytelling and poetry is incidental to the primary purpose of art forms, and because literary tradition is more tolerant of historical manipulations, it is more enigmatic in tracing to its roots. One other specific genre which applies to Arthurian literature is *romance*, defined as "a medieval tale based upon legend." The term *legend* is also common and used in titles such as *The Arthurian Legends* by Richard Barber and *King Arthur and the Legends of the Round Table* by Keith Baines.

"Legend" is an appropriate term, more explicit than "fantasy," "fiction," or "myth." Fantasy implies a free reign of creative indulgence, a chimeric imagination which is unrestrained, and does not fit Arthur or the purpose of this book on his historicity. Fiction, too, denotes an invented or feigned creation of the imagination, connotatively lacking a base in reality, which leaves legend as the best available term. By definition, a legend is a story coming down from the past, regarded as historical although sometimes it is not verifiable by an independent source. Applied here, an inherent connotation states that the legends of Arthur have a kernel of authenticity at their origin, although the stories themselves which have been handed down might not be true in their entirety.

Unlike Rhys' Culture Hero, Bullfinch takes a more general stance of viewing "*mythology as connected with literature.*"[5] [Bullfinch's italics]. He goes on to say that his presentation is not limited to the scholar or philosopher but intended for any reader of English literature who must understand mythological references in order to most fully comprehend the tales of Arthur. Bullfinch, then, uses the term mythology much more loosely, with an aim of supplying "to the modern reader such knowledge of the fables of classical and medieval literature as is needed to render intelligible the allusions which occur in reading and conversation."[6] His design is simply limiting itself to reading and understanding the romances of King Arthur, without trying to establish proof that Arthur descended from the gods.

Later, in his segment on King Arthur, Bullfinch gives a brief background of the Roman withdrawal near the beginning of the fifth century. He then moves immediately to the Age of Chivalry (the twelfth century) to frame an ideal of the heroic character, combining invincible strength and valor, justice, modesty, loyalty to superiors, courtesy to equals, compassion to weakness, and devotedness to the Church; an ideal ... acknowledged ... as the highest model for emulation.[7]

Bullfinch uses the expression "Heroic Character" rather than suggesting a god or demigod such as Hades or Hercules so that the emphasis lies properly with a mortal figure of heroic stature who would function as a role model. The authentic Arthur appeared at precisely the right time in British history to become the Culture Hero/Heroic Character. Arthur takes on larger-than-human characteristics because he emerges as a phoenix from the ashes of the Roman empire in Britain. He is the first Briton to snatch his race from the jaws of barbarism after the might of Romanism is withdrawn from the island. A connection remains between the romantic Arthur and stories tying him to much earlier myths, but the principle of synergism applies here. That is, the total picture of Arthur is greater than the sum of his individual effects as a historic figure. What manifests itself incorrectly is Arthur as a shadowy demigod with no real substance, instead of a genuine mortal hero.

The intent, therefore, is to supply the missing pieces of the jigsaw puzzle not provided by the historical material. Arthur is a central figure in some early literature, so that it becomes reasonable to expect that from these ancient bardic and epic tales evidence can be extracted to authenticate Arthur in a historical setting. The literary material will serve its function by substantiating links between one isolated fact and another so that entire chains of events will emerge.

Unquestionably, there is a distinction between history and literary tradition. Goodrich, though, using Piggott as a spokesman, states, "Piggott, too, saw the gap between history and literature so narrowed in Geoffrey's [of Monmouth] case as to become fused."[8] However, because it is so difficult to accept unquestioningly anything which Geoffrey says at face value, what seems to be literally true is that Piggott saw the gap between history and literature so narrowed in Geoffrey's case as to become *con*fused, not just fused; in Arthurian (and historical) circles, Monmouth is still not exonerated; too many things he writes are confused and cannot be rationalized away, even if a heavily documented, scholarly approach to verification might be employed. His defense is weaker still if a pseudo approach to bonafide documentation is used.

Two prime examples will suffice. A historical figure of the Arthurian age was Ambrosius Aurelianus. Geoffrey "fictionalizes" him as Aurelius Ambrosius by shifting magical powers from Ambrosius Aurelianus to an Ambrosius Merlinus. Monmouth then drops the first name, giving rise to the Merlin of the romances. Second, neither Lancelot nor Utherpendragon is a real person who appears prior to the romances of the thirteenth century. Even Geoffrey Ashe, who in *The Discovery of Arthur* cites Geoffrey of Monmouth often to support the hypotheses of a different Arthurian chronological framework, states that "Uther is neither remote nor unimportant, but he is not real. Before Geoffrey [of Monmouth] he only figures, as 'Uther Pendragon,' in uninformative Welsh verse."[9] Yet Goodrich addresses the authenticity of Monmouth's history as if Utherpendragon and Lancelot were undisputed historical figures. This means that any attempt to verify Arthur by using Uther or Lancelot, whether chronologically, geographically, historically, or any other way, is like trying to build sandcastles during a hurricane.

In the realm of Arthuriana, the scarcity of historical material is polarized by the profuse outpouring of literature; what one lacks in substance is more than adequately atoned for by its counterbalance. Whereas the factual data gave broad general strokes of a reliable historical nature based upon very few resources, literary tradition has such prolific possibilities that it becomes cumbersome. The first requirement in dealing with the deluge of literary material is the necessity to limit the sources in filling the holes left by history. Without limiting the inquiry to only those sources deserving of regard, the task would be insurmountable. The exclusion of a literary source is not meant to impugn its author; in keeping with the philosophy ascribed to the earlier manuscripts, those literary works closest to the Arthurian era will be the focus, with some attention to later works.

This means that the time period covered for Arthur still revolves around the era from the opening decades of the 400s until Arthur's death in 518. Although references may touch upon satellite individuals associated with Arthur in the legends of later centuries, the search centralizes the figure of Ambrosius Aurelianus and his historical attachment to Arthur. The epic tales and bardic poetry do *not* include the romances of later periods; the literary tradition limits itself to the older literature as near to Arthur's lifetime as possible. Hence, all of the romance elements — knights and knightly virtues, courtly love, rescues, quests for adventure, and jousting — do not occupy an important niche in this search.

Although connections between the literature and history of the same era may at times seem nebulous, there are connections with a cause-effect, action-reaction relationship. When, therefore, Lacy and Ashe in their book entitled *The Arthurian Handbook* say, "Romancers not only cared little for originality, they cared little for authenticity either,"[10] this admonition should exclude earlier literary tradition, since they go on:

> [the romance literature] may be the result of updating and medievalizing a tradition that was truly ancient, and have originated in a real person [Arthur]. ... Perhaps the updating, the medievalizing, may seem to make it impossible to break through to an underlying reality. Yet the reality may be there all the same.[11]

Some claims may be made that the ancient literary works such as heroic poetry are not reliable historical sources because, as the name implies, such poetry concentrates on the glorification of heroes. However, the older forms of tradition can supply invaluable information in ascertaining the true figure of Arthur.

SAINTS' LIVES

The *Saints' Lives* relates closely with Irish history, and Irish texts in turn are closely allied with the Welsh versions; it is therefore important to look at this source for historical British information, particularly as it relates to Arthur. The *Saints' Lives* is heavily influenced by the art of storytelling and is perhaps akin to a fable because of an implied moral, yet technically it does not fit into the definition of any specific literary genre. Likewise the accounts cannot be categorized as pure history even though based upon a real figure. Because of the nebulous classification of these stylistic manuscripts, the historical nuggets embedded in them must therefore be extracted only when corroborated by other sources such as annals, genealogies, chronicles, histories, or archaeology.

In context of these manuscripts, saints were not necessarily formally canonized. Many of the monks who founded religious communities were given the title of saints after their death if someone recorded remembrances of them in writing. The *Saints' Lives* are sparse on background material, but instead become moral treatises of how a "saint," through God, becomes superior over a powerful ruler, one who has usually been steeped in sin, so that the ruler is humbled and finally realizes the errors of his ways contrasted to the power of the Lord.[12]

1. Saint *Cadoc* dates to the end of the eleventh century, and includes several passages about Arthur. Cadoc's mother, Gwladys, a princess of Brecknock, was eloping with the man whom she loved and intended to marry at any cost. Gwladys' father was pursuing the couple. As the couple encountered Arthur, he was playing a game with two of his "knights," Cai [who appears in the romances as Kay] and Bedwyr [Bedivere]. At first Arthur wants to seduce Gwladys, but Cai and Bedwyr convince him that he should aid damsels in distress. Arthur concurs, so that when Gwladys' father approaches, Arthur tells him that although he is the girl's father he is outside his jurisdiction and therefore no longer has authority over her. Gwladys ends up marrying her lover, and Cadoc becomes their firstborn.

   Arthur appears again later when, after many years, Cadoc, now the abbot of Llancarfan, gives seven-year sanctuary to a man accused of killing three of Arthur's soldiers. When Arthur discovers that this man is being protected by Cadoc, he goes to the abbey and claims that the abbot has no right to protect the man for that length of time. Arthur is mollified by the compensatory offer of a hundred cattle. Arthur demands that the cattle be red in their forequarters and white in their hindquarters, and Cadoc miraculously meets his demands. However, when Arthur is driving the cattle across a river, the cows change into ferns, and from this Arthur realizes Cadoc's saintly right to grant sanctuary and abandons his attempt at reprisal.

2. The life of *Gildas* (Albanius) as related by Caradoc in the early 1100s tells the story of how Gildas' brother Hueil is captured and put to death by Arthur and the compensation which Arthur must pay for reconciliation. This is the same story related earlier as perhaps an explanation of why Gildas Badonicus did not refer to Arthur by name in the Battle of Badon. In Caradoc's writing, Gildas and Arthur encounter each other once again, when Melwas kidnaps Guinevere and imprisons her in a stronghold near the Glastonbury monastery. Gildas arbitrates a treaty so that Guinevere is reunited with Arthur. This Melwas story seems to supply the first connection of Arthur with his burial at Glastonbury, which carries over into the later legends and romances.

3. The life of Saint *Carannog* relays the story of Arthur stealing the saint's altar. Arthur needs the saint's help to catch a giant serpent laying waste the countryside, and in return, Arthur promises that he will let the saint know where the altar is.

When Carannog triumphs over the serpent and banishes it, Arthur admits that he has had the altar all along, trying to use it as a table. However, every time he sets something upon it, that object is thrown off. He gives the altar back to Carannog and donates a segment of ground to the saint.

4. The life of Saint *Padarn* contains a story in which the tyrant Arthur causes trouble for the poor saint. Arthur takes a tunic from the saint, and as he is carrying it away, Padarn pray's the earth will swallow up the tyrant, whereupon Arthur is immediately buried up to his chin in the earth and must beg the saint's forgiveness before he is released.

Much of this material seems fabricated for the purpose of teaching a moral; Arthur is the strong authority figure, erring in the ways of the Lord, and the saints, with the backing of the Almighty, teach him (and the readers) the errors not condoned by God. By contrast, the *AC* in its entry contradicts this tyrannic image of Arthur, giving him a much more saintly aura of carrying the Cross of our Lord Jesus Christ for three days and three nights on his (shield) during the Battle of Badon.[13]

Nennius, in describing the eighth battle, writes that Arthur bore the image of the Holy Virgin, mother of God, upon his (shield) and through the power of our Lord Jesus Christ, and the holy Mary, put the Saxons to flight.[14] Arthur's image as portrayed in the romances definitely ties into the two entries regarding him as saintly, virtuous, and honorable, rather than the negative portrayal in the stories of the *Saints' Lives*. None of this either affirms or negates Arthur as a historical figure, but it complicates his personality, perhaps pointing up the contradiction between legend and reality, or suggesting a human, multifaceted personality, or posing the possibility of more than one Arthur.

THE MABINOGION

In 1849 Lady Charlotte Guest translated and published a number of Welsh romances drawn from a fourteenth century manuscript called *The Red Book of Hergest*, the only known manuscript dating to the seventeenth century.[15] Gantz, in the introduction to his book on the *Mabinogion*, writes that "*Peniarth 6*, the earliest manuscript to preserve even fragments of the Four Branches, dates only to c. 1225."[16] He then concurs with Ivor John that the earliest copy of the complete *Mabinogion* dates to the *Red Book of Hergest*; an earlier manuscript, the *White Book of Rhydderch*, penned about 1325, is incomplete. Even at the date ascribed for the *Red Book*, Gantz cautions that by this time the transcripts had been greatly altered from the original. Their original form probably evolved somewhere between 1000 and 1250, a span which encompasses Ifor Williams' proposal of 1060 as a likely date for the Four Branches.

A specific date, however, is not as important as the cultural and factual information which can be attached to these other sources for some kind of authentication. In turn, the literary offerings lead to conjectures based upon more than sheer guesswork. Many times geographic locations are too vague to be of any value; even personal names, style of dress, and modes of combat can offer little corroboration. Yet every once in a while there is a flash from a seemingly trivial but fortuitous detail, mentioned apparently in passing, which gives credence to another piece of information in another source. This leads, too, to the speculation (though it is of no real consequence to us here because the French romances themselves might be reworkings of Celtic originals) that the *Mabinogion* might derive from the French romances.

The term "mabinogion" has an interesting history. John Rhys explains,

> The word *mabinogi* is derived from *mabinog*, ... meaning a sort of literary apprentice ... receiving instruction from a qualified bard; and the lowest description of *mabinog* was one who had not acquired the art of making verse.[17]

Confusion of the term stemmed from Lady Charlotte Guest's edition, which she titled the *Mabinogion*. She erroneously formed the plural *mabinogion* from the word *mabinogi*,[18] a term given in the original manuscript. Gantz reiterates that *mabinogion* was a nineteenth century misuse by Lady Guest when she assumed that *mab-* meant "boy" and *mabinogi* was a noun form meaning "a story for children."[19] She then incorrectly formed the plural *mabinogion* to mean "stories for children." Her basic assumption was that the earliest writers who brought this literature to the knowledge of the Welsh world assumed that *mabinogi* meant "youth," and that, as Stephens says in his *Literature of the Cymry*, the tales were "written to wile away the time of young chieftains," suggesting that these stories were nothing more than a collection of medieval Welsh fairy tales. In reality, as Professor Rhys has shown, the term belongs to the Welsh bardic system. The scholar might have been a young person, but the emphasis is more on inexperience than age. The term *mabinogi* meant the "collection of things which formed the *mabinog*'s literary training and stock in trade, so to say."[20] *Mabinogion*, then, is not an authentic Welsh word, although *mabinogi* is indeed a genuine word, used at the beginning of the story of Pwyll, introduced by the sentence, "Llyma dechreu Mabinogi," translating to "Here is the beginning of the Mabinogi."

Although the term *mabinogion* was invented, it has become so engrained in literature that it seems presumptuous to try to change it. This incorrect plural also affected the layout of the stories. In many contemporary publications, the *Mabinogion* simply lists 11 tales; technically, however, there are four which should be labeled "The Four Branches of the Mabinogi," with the remaining seven termed *Other Tales* for a full title of *The Four Branches of the Mabinogi and Other Tales*. Gantz lists its contents as 11 tales in his translation, but explains that the first four make up the Four Branches, with the remainder listed as Other Tales. He points out that "of the three English translations, Lady Charlotte Guest's translation includes a twelfth tale, 'The Story of Talyessin,' not found in the other manuscripts."[21]

Oral tradition, the art of storytelling and performing by bards and scops, is the transmission of information, not through massive verbatim memorization of every tale and song by the performers, but through outlines and sketches. These "transmitters of culture" extemporized the details as they went along. They did not have truth or accuracy as their primary code in a rigid art system. Their main

functions were to entertain and to transmit news. They created interest by sus-
pense, surprise, intriguing plots, and conflicts requiring intense absorption.
Whether wittingly or not, they would sometimes leave out information, confuse
details, or stress the wrong theme. Because accuracy was incidental, this process
explains the elasticity of the information which was passed to the successive generations and why persons, events, places, and sequences are many times inconsistent.

The oral tradition which predates the *Mabinogion* is no different. Once
events were finally recorded, they comprised eclectic tales of myth, legend, folklore, and pseudo-history at one end of the continuum, and factual, sequential
history on the other. In Gantz's own words, "Inasmuch as the Celts tended to
view history as what ought to have happened rather than as what actually did,
fact and fiction in *The Mabinogion* are not easy to distinguish."[22] He adds that
for the Celts many of their harsh realities were softened by wishful thinking.

To complicate matters further, although many of the oral traditions were
finally written down, few manuscripts survived the ravages of the centuries. The
written word sometimes gives the insidious impression that all of man's destiny
has been indelibly etched for future generations to cherish, yet transience in only
five decades can underscore the rapidity of change.

Since the word "myth" is sometimes used to denote the tales in *The Mabinogion*, further clarification of this term is necessary at this point because of its
application to these particular tales. Myth, through its religious and allegorical
overtones, offers supernatural explanations for natural events, taking natural
events (laws of nature) and ascribing those occurrences to a supernatural, omni-
scient being. In *The Mabinogion* the term "myth" is used in a euhemeristic sense.
Euhemerus, a Sicilian philosopher in 3002 B.C., explained mythology as the
deification of earth-born kings and heroes and denied the existence of divine
beings. "Emperor" is the word which Gantz evidently uses deliberately in his
translation to stress that Arthur is a king rather than a hero, and "the heroism
which made him a king is largely in the past."[23] This portrays Arthur much more
accurately; the few recorded historical events which are available to us show that
Arthur was in fact a mortal, an emperor who emerged from the Briton nation
after the withdrawal of the Romans and who became deified in the sense that he
has become immortalized. Again, this is an excellent defense why the term "myth"
should not be applied to Arthur. Other terms describe with keener accuracy
words which should apply to Arthuriana.

Ivor John reaches the conclusion that the Four Branches of the Mabinogi
are "nothing more nor less than degraded and adulterated mythological tales."[24]
But he is unclear on two points. For one, there is no indication of whether he is
accepting the euhemerist theory of mythological formation, or whether he means
Arthur is a human shell with mythical origins. Secondly, in speaking of "degraded
and adulterated mythological tales," Ivor John is seemingly limiting that comment to the Four Branches of the Mabinogi and not the *Other Tales*. Often, Ivor
John's distinction between the Four Branches and two of the other tales of interest here—"Culhwch and Olwen" and "The Dream of Rhonabwy"—are ignored.

He labels "Culhwch and Olwen" as part of a special class of Arthurian Cycle (which in a sense it is), with no affinity to any of the Arthurian romances handed down in French or German. If he is labeling the *Other Tales* differently, and if two of them are in a distinctive class of their own, then Arthur cannot be vaguely labeled as bearing "degraded and adulterated mythological" roots simply because his name appears in "Culhwch and Olwen" and "The Dream of Rhonabwy" in *The Mabinogion*.

Of the *Four Branches* and the other seven tales (excluding the extra tale from Lady Guest's translation) five stories deal with Arthur. All of these come from the *Other Tales*. Two of the five, "Culhwch and Olwen" and the "Dream of Rhonabwy," are important in the search for Arthur. Two others, "Owein" and "Peredur son of Evrawg," are passed over since they so closely resemble the *Yvain* and *Perceval* romances by Chretien de Troyes of later centuries. Both deal with courtly matters, loyalty, trust, kindness and courtesy and even though both refer to Arthur as the emperor and set his court at Caer Llion ar Wysg, neither reveals any other significant historical details. "Gereint and Enid," the last of the tales, although not as important as the Culhwch or Rhonabwy tales, contributes to (or at least reinforces) relevant material.

The information important to the search for a historic Arthur is listed under the stories' headings. Since interest does not coincide with the primary aesthetic purposes of amusement, the fabulous or fantastic detail is culled from the story, allowing the references to become a proper source of valid information.

CULHWCH AND OLWEN

"Culhwch and Olwen," one of the *Other Tales*, is of special interest, since it is the story which introduces Arthur into Welsh prose. Celts inhabited the island for several centuries B.C. and into the period when Roman rule finally became established. The Celts were forced out of south-central Britain and pushed north into Scotland and west into Wales; some migrated to the continent and established themselves as Bretons in Brittany.

This story initiates some romance material of the twelfth and thirteenth centuries. Bedwyr, Kei, Owein, Uwayne, and Gwenhwyvar all make appearances, and additionally, Peredur and Gauvain seem to be forerunners of later figures. Arthur's ship Prydwen, his spear Ron, his knife Carnwennan, his sword Excaliber, and his shield Wynebgwrthucher are all included in the tale. Other information can be listed:

1. Culhwch is Arthur's first cousin.
2. Culhwch wears a four-cornered purple mantle with a red-gold apple in each corner.
3. In his invocation, Culhwch lists Osla Big Knife, a name of Saxon origin, as one of Arthur's important warriors who pursues the boar Twrch Trwyth.
4. Hueil, son of Caw and brother to Gildas, never submitted to a lord's hand.
5. Gormant is the son of Rica, and Arthur's brother on his mother's side.
6. Morvan is the son of Tegid, whom no man struck at Camlann because they thought he was a devil helping.

7. Sanddev Angel Face is one whom no one struck at Camlann because they thought he was an angel helping.
8. Saint Kynwyl is one of the three men to escape from Camlann and the last to leave Arthur.
9. Gwydre, son of Llwydeu by Gwenabwy daughter of Caw, was stabbed by Hueil, which was a source of feud between Hueil and Arthur.
10. Gwyddawg, son of Menestyr who killed Kei, was killed by Arthur in revenge.
11. Gwynn Hyvar, Steward of Devon and Cornwall was one of the nine who planned the Battle of Camlann.
12. For his court, Arthur went to Kelli Wig in Cornwall.
13. Arthur's two uncles, brothers of his mother, Llygadrudd Emys and Gwrvoddw, were killed by Llwydawg, who was then himself killed.

THE DREAM OF RHONABWY

Although this tale directly follows the Cuhlwch story, Gantz indicates that it was the last to have taken shape. Madawg, son of Maredudd is a historical figure who died in 1159, indicating that the framework of the story cannot be much older than 1200. In this tale, Arthur's court is also in Cornwall.

1. Iddawg, the Churl of Britain, was one of the messengers at the Battle of Camlann between Arthur and his nephew Medrawd. He was a high-spirited young man, so eager for battle that he stirred up bad feelings between them. When he was sent by the emperor Arthur to ask Medrawd for peace lest the sons and nobles of the island of Britain be killed, though Arthur spoke as kindly as he could, Iddawg repeated his words to Medrawd in the rudest possible way. That is how the Battle of Camlann was woven.
2. Arthur is called emperor.
3. As he crosses the ford, Avaon, son of Talyessin, splashes water on Arthur and the bishop.
4. There was a huge force which promised to be at the Battle of Baddon by noon in order to fight against Olsa the Big Knife
5. Arthur's first cousin and chief advisor is Caradawg Strong Arm.
6. Another of Arthur's first cousins is March, son of Meirchyawn, who is leading the white troops of Norway to Baddon.
7. The black troops of Denmark join Arthur and his force as they descended below Caer Vaddon, the fortress of Baddon.
8. The emperor Arthur has never fled from battle.
9. Cadwr, Earl of Cornwall, has the task to arm the king on the day of battle.
10. Eiryn, the Splendid, son of Peibyn, Arthur's servant, dismounts and removes from Arthur's pack a gold chair and a ribbed brocade mantle with red-gold apples in each corner.
11. Arthur plays four games of gwyddbwyll with Owein as an opponent, which has the markings of symbolic skirmishes at Badon
12. Twenty-four horsemen come from Osla Big Knife to ask Arthur for a truce to the end of a month and a fortnight.
13. Arthur goes to his advisors about the truce.
14. Gildas, son of Caw, is an advisor to Arthur.
15. A large man with curly auburn hair is identified as Rhun map Maelgwn of Gwynedd, a man whose status is such that everyone comes to him for advice.

16. The advisors began to chant praises to Arthur.
17. Osla Big Knife is granted a truce to the end of a month and a fortnight.
18. Kei invites those who wish to follow Arthur to be in Cornwall, and let everyone else come to meet Arthur at the end of the truce.
19. An unusual ending to this tale states, "This story is called the Dream of Rhonabwy, and the reason is that no one, neither bard nor storyteller, knows the Dream without a book, because of the many colours of the horses and the variety of strange colours of armour and equipment and precious mantles and powerful stones."[25]

Of the entire Rhonabwy tale (14 pages) at least a third of it is devoted to four gwyddbwyll matches between Arthur and Owein which on the surface appears as an insertion of fantasy in the tale. While the two are playing their first game, a page approaches them and complains to Owein that Arthur's young lads and servants are harassing and molesting Owein's ravens, but Arthur refuses to do anything and continues the game. During the second match, a different young lad comes to them and complains to Owein that Arthur's pages are stabbing the ravens, killing some and wounding others. Again, Arthur refuses to interfere and continues playing. During the third game, a third page interrupts and complains to Owein that the noblest ravens had been killed, and those who were not had been molested and wounded badly. For a third time, Arthur continues playing the game and does not interfere.

During that same match a great din arises and a page approaches Arthur and reports that the ravens were killing Arthur's squires and pages. Arthur in turn asks Owein to call off the ravens, but Owein continues playing the game. At the beginning of the fourth match there was a great uproar, a screaming of men and the cawing of ravens. A rider approaches Arthur and angrily complains that the ravens have killed Arthur's retinue and the sons of nobles from the island. Arthur asks Owein to call off the ravens and squeezes the gold pieces (men) on the gwyddbwyll board until they become dust. Owein orders Gwres son of Rheged to lower the banner, and there was peace on both sides.

Historically, Morris explains Reged in some detail as a kingdom evolving at the end of the fifth century in the vicinity of northern Wales.[26] Owein's role is impossible to decipher if his name is considered a variant of Owain son of Urien, or Owain brother of Rhodi ap Hywel, since they both appear in later eras. If the reference is to Owain Finduu, brother to Constantine and Peblig and son of Maxen and Elen,[27] then the time frame is placed before the Roman withdrawal.

An even better clue in the "Dream of Rhonabwy" about the identity of the correct Owein is Owein's orders to Gwres son of Rheged. There is no one named Gwres in the historical manuscripts, but the epithet "Gwyr y Gogledd" appears quite often, meaning "men of the North," a reference to the tribe north of the Humber and south of Hadrian's Wall. Sir Ifor Williams provides a more explicit locale:

> The Men of the North (Gwyr y Gogledd) were the British tribes inhabiting the region between Glasgow and Edinburgh, and down to mid Lancashire on the west and south Yorkshire on the east.[28]

This territory includes all of Cumbria, in itself significant because of Cumbria's association with the Cymry. Sir Ifor also explains the importance of this:

> The dwellers in the three British districts called themselves Britons *(Brython)*. ... The Britons of Wales and Strathclyde, however, for some reason or other, began to call themselves also *Cymry*, the plural of *Cymro*, a compound of *com* a prefix meaning "together" and *bro* "border, coast, district." ... [S]o *Cymro* means ... a fellow countryman. Cornishmen were never known as *cymry*, but the people of *Cumberland* were; ... Cumberland means "the land of the Cymry."[29]

Bromwich clarifies the term by adding that in Welsh tradition, Cumbria is the equivalent of the Old North, which "encompassed a large area of north-west England (Cumberland, Westmorland, and north Lancashire), and Strathclyde as far as the Forth-Clyde line in Scotland."[30]

Although Sir Ifor offers no reason for the Welsh calling themselves Cymry, Wade-Evans not only offers the explanation but also substantiates a significant connection between these "Strathclyde Welsh" (the Cymry) and their allies, the Saxon *federates*:

> ...[T]hese men of the North, Gwyr y Gogledd, became the nucleus of a new powerful English state, formed partly from the disintegrated portions of the Cornovii, under the name of Mercia.[31]

The peoples were a mixture of English Saxons and Brython (Welsh), speaking both languages, while those in the western part of the province also spoke Irish.[32] This mixed race of fellow countrymen consists of Saxons and Britons emerging as a unique culture, which identifies them as Gewissae/Hwicce/Hrype in a territory ruled by Maximus just before Roman withdrawal.

Gwres is listed as the son of Rheged, but Rheged (or Reged) appears in the early manuscripts only as two kingdoms, a north and a south, parts of the Roman province of Brigantes. Southern Rheged was adjacent to northern Wales, part of the area to which Cunedda had migrated when he occupied Carlisle.

With this background for Gwres son of Rheged completed, attention can once again focus upon the name Owein. As mentioned above, there are several Oweins[33] who appear in the genealogies, but only one supplies an even better link to Arthur and the Battle of Badon than Owein Finduu. This is a later generation link, through Cunedda and one of his sons, Enniaun Girt. Enniaun Girt has already achieved prominence in this search as a grandfather to Cuneglasus and Maelgwn; his elder son Eugein Dantguin was Cuneglasus' father, and his younger son Catoglaun Lauhir was Maelgwn's father. Genealogies show that Eugein evolved into the name Owein,[34] which means that Owein Dantguin was a grandson to Cunedda and a nephew to Cerdic. This hub radiates spokes of connections, historically and traditionally. He is part of the Cunedda clan, meaning also part of the Gewissae tribe; geographically placed in the western Cornovii/eastern Wales territory; chronologically separated by only a short span of years from his uncle; in alliance with Cerdic against Arthur; also in league with Octha; one of the warriors at Badon.

Several things support the parallel between the Gewissae and Gwyr y Gogledd. Both tribes were operating in that vicinity, the disintegrated portions of Cornovii territory vacated by the Roman withdrawal. Both became a powerful nucleus for a new Saxon kingdom. Both nascent kingdoms arise in the mid fifth century and continue into the sixth, through periods of the Aetius letter, the Saxon Revolt, the three Saxon *Adventi*, migrations, the Battle of Badon, and the Battle of Camlann. Both align their origins with the gwledig Maxim and mixed Welsh heritage. Both are attached to references about Octha. Both identify with the word Cymry, whether in reference to the Cornovian Welsh or the "Cludwys," "the Gwyr y Gogledd."[35]

If Rhonabwy's dream is interpreted symbolically, it tells a superbly accurate story of the carnage and slaughter during the Badon battle. If Owein (Dantguin) is a symbol of leadership for the Gwyr y Gogledd and allied with Octha Big-Knife (son of Hengist), and his tribe the Gwyr y Gogledd are the ravens (Hræfn) of the Hrype tribe, the Black Warriors, then Owein and Arthur are locked in a deadly battle which will determine the fate of two powerful kingdoms. The Britons are "victorious" in that, against incredible odds, a truce is called by the Hrype tribe.

GEREINT AND ENID

1. Gereint's name brings to mind that of Constantine's general Gerontios, though he himself is not a historical figure.
2. Arthur is referred to as emperor.
3. Arthur holds his court at Caer Llion.
4. One of Arthur's chamberlains is his son Amhar.
5. When Gwenhwyvar is alone during the hunt, Arthur has one of his attendants ask Gildas, son of Caw to accompany her home.
6. Gwallawg, son of Llenawg is one of the historical kings who fought against Hussa at the end of the sixth century.
7. Two Cornwall envoys come from Arthur's uncle Erbin, son of Constantine.

This concludes the section on *The Mabinogion* as a resource for the verification of Arthur's historicity. Three other sources will be enumerated, and once that is accomplished, all the relevant data will be collated.

Arthur in The History of the Kings of Britain

The next essential literary work to consider is Geoffrey of Monmouth's enigmatic *History of the Kings of Britain.* No discussion of King Arthur, serious or otherwise, can deny Geoffrey his rightful position in Arthuriana. No single author has been as quoted, as analyzed, as praised, or as scorned as Geoffrey; scholars have ranged from accepting everything Geoffrey writes as either covert or explicit truth to denouncing him as a fraud; there are very few fence-sitters. A person at the former end of the continuum has to apologize and rationalize for some of the things he writes, while the latter refuse to waste time trying to sort through his distorted claims. But the patient few who are the fence-sitters glean the most from his work.

Norma Goodrich is one of Monmouth's staunch defenders, but in relation to the historicity of Arthur, one of her affirmations that is impossible to accept is the inordinate weight she accords to Geoffrey of Monmouth's *The History of the Kings of Britain* ascribing authenticity to Arthur. She states:

> The defense of King Arthur as a historical figure involves, in a way, the defense of that literary man who first wrote a biography of Arthur, Geoffrey of Monmouth.[36]

Geoffrey offers a wealth of crucial information about Arthur which cannot be discarded, but Arthur's authenticity can be established independently of Geoffrey of Monmouth, and a defense of Arthur's historicity in no way implies an inextricable connection to a defense of Geoffrey's accuracy. The merits of King Arthur's factual origins can stand without the buttress of Monmouth material, although the Monmouth material enhances some chronological detail quite well.

Goodrich continues her specious argument:

> It is therefore imperative that we follow Geoffrey into his mistakes and suggest corrections, for the problem is acute: whoever does not believe Geoffrey of Monmouth cannot believe in the historical King Arthur.[37]

The works of scholarly giants of Arthuriana such as Alcock, Morris, Ashe, Dumville, Jackson, and O'Sullivan, indicate that Arthur can indeed be historically established without Geoffrey of Monmouth. The Monmouth material requires too much mental gymnastics to truly believe that Monmouth must be considered not only as the primary but the *sole* unimpeachable source for verifying the historic King Arthur. One can apologize only so much for Geoffrey of Monmouth by saying "Geoffrey has strayed again ..."; "Geoffrey erred in ..."; "Geoffrey meant to say ..."; "Geoffrey had the wrong notion that ..."; "Geoffrey misinterpreted ..."; "Geoffrey's understandable error ..."; or "Geoffrey must have misunderstood his sources ...." Conversely, lavish praise as a counterbalance must be limited. Describing Geoffrey as "gripping," "brilliant," "grasps the significance of," "marvelous visionary," "apocalyptic," "ardor and enthusiasm," "unassailable Latin" reads more like a modern-day theater billboard. It becomes strained and unrealistic to accept Geoffrey's work as untainted, of which Goodrich is guilty in attempting to situate King Arthur in the north.

Under no circumstances, then, can Monmouth be labeled as a "precise" historian. There has never been any attestation that Geoffrey's "ancient book" ever existed, although it is readily admitted that if Geoffrey's work is purely fictitious, then he is absolutely uncanny in his ability to interweave verifiable historical events from other sources. Even though Goodrich is lavish in her praise and steadfast in her defense, she concedes that "[Geoffrey] made many huge errors in geography."[38]

During his writing, Geoffrey had access to everything available to the modern scholar, and more, even if one discounts the mysterious "ancient book" which he claims as his authoritative source. The misfortune of his work is that it is pawned off as bonafide history rather than being accepted contextually as something like a historical novel. Viewed as fictionalized history, *HKB* offers the same nuggets which embody truth as any of the other works in this section. Because his work is teeming with material on Arthur, *HKB* will be handled in a different way from *The Mabinogion*. A very abbreviated summary will be given, but again, for the sake of brevity, sequences will be enumerated, with important considerations underlined. Additionally, other sources will be cited for clarifications, amplifications, or explanations of passages in Geoffrey.

Before listing the catalogue of events in *HKB*, one association must be reinforced with *The Mabinogion*. As Ivor John points out, there are two tales in *The Mabinogion*, "The Dream of Maxen" and "Llud and Llevelys" which have an "obvious affinity with the legendary history work-up by Geoffrey of Monmouth."[39] Some have even suggested that *The Mabinogion* might be the cryptic "ancient book" which Geoffrey claimed. The character of Maxen in the first story is a composite figure, identified with Maximianus in Geoffrey. The second story chronicles the three plagues, but these do not appear in Geoffrey. There are several scribal errors, in addition to an incorrect etymology tied to the naming of London, but since these have no direct bearing on Arthur, they are not catalogued.

Of Monmouth's entire *History*, approximately 98 of the book's 230 pages is devoted to the Arthurian cycle, excluding Part Five, "The Prophecies of Merlin." Initially, this does not seem much, but when considering that the entire book covers almost two millennia, it means that almost half is devoted to Arthur, preceded by a small slice of his previous generation. "Arthur of Britain" (with perhaps half of it significantly centered on Arthur's exploits on the continent, particularly in Gaul) begins in Part 7, after the death of Utherpendragon, and Part 8 narrates the Saxon domination after Arthur's final battle. Going back no further than Vortigern, Monmouth presents Vortigern, Hengist, Horsa, and Rowena (Hengist's daughter) as accurate representations according to what Nennius describes.

Geoffrey writes of Ambrosius Aurelianus as Aurelius Ambrosius being taken to Little Britain on the continent for protection from Vortigern. Associated with Ambrosius is dragons, the red one signifying the Britons, and the white one signifying the English, which is the fundamental base for the creation of Utherpendragon. Because Ambrosius Aurelianus is a type of wizard in Nennius, Monmouth calls his character Ambrosius Merlinus, shortening it to Merlin in the next section. Not surprisingly, he takes time out from the plot of his story to devote his next chapter to the "Prophecies of Merlin," almost as if he had been stricken with an idea. During Aurelius' reign, Hengist and Aurelius clash in battle; the Saxons might have won in the end, but Aurelius had a cavalry detachment of Armorican Bretons enter the battle, and when they arrived at the scene, the battle turned in Aurelius' favor. Eldol, on the side of the Britons, fought Hengist in hand-to-hand combat, eventually gaining the upper hand and dragging Hengist into the midst of the Britons.

Geoffrey not only assigns Utherpendragon as a brother to Aurelius Ambrosius but gives him an important role in the history as a link between Aurelius

Ambrosius and Arthur. The name Uther is interesting, given its variety of etymological connections: Artu or Uther, meaning head, bear, terrible. Upon Utherpendragon's succession to the throne, more battles with the Saxons follow, and eventually Octa, son of Hengist, is captured. King Utherpendragon falls ill, Octa escapes his imprisonment and goes to Germany, gathers an army, and almost all of the island was devastated. The sick king of the Britons rallied his forces, Octa and Eosa were killed, and the Saxons fled. In celebration of this victory, Uther invites people to his castle, among them Gorlois and his wife Ygerna, followed by one of the most well-known episodes in all of Arthurian material, involving Merlin, Utherpendragon, Ygerna, and the conception of Arthur. Just as Aurelius Ambrosius succeeded Vortigern, and dies from poison, so Utherpendragon succeeded Aurelius and also dies of poison. The Boar of Cornwall emerges as king.

After the chapter on the House of Constantine already mentioned in the Ambrosius section, Monmouth opens "Arthur of Britain," by writing that after Utherpendragon's death, Arthur is crowned king at age 15 and the Saxons "had already over-run all that section of the island which stretches from the River Humber to the sea named Caithness,"[40] which is the extreme northwestern tip of Britain, near the Orkneys. Monmouth then fictionalizes several of the battles from the *Historia*. He skips the battle on the River Glein and begins by blending the second through the fifth as one battle on the River Douglas near York.

Cheldric becomes a major Saxon adversary. Arthur recruits help from King Hoel of Britanny, and the army marches to Kaerluideoit listed historically as Wall-by-Lichfield in Cornovii territory but equated by Monmouth with Lincoln.[41] After a bloody encounter the Saxons retreat to Caledon Wood (which skips the sixth battle at Bassas) where Arthur builds an abatis to entrap the enemy. The Saxons surrender and are granted amnesty, but they break their treaty and assail Bath. Similar to the detail in the Rhonabwy story, they occupy a neighboring hill. Geoffrey goes into detail on Arthur's armour and armaments for the Battle of Badon: a leather jerkin worthy of so great a king; a gold helmet with a crest carved in the shape of a dragon; a circular shield called Pridwen on which was painted a likeness of the Blessed Mary, Mother of God, which forced Arthur to perpetually think of her. Arthur besieges the hillfort, and after great slaughter on both sides, Cheldric flees, is pursued, and killed. Monmouth does not insert the eighth through eleventh battles, respectively at Guinnion Castle, urbe Legionis, Tribruit, and Agned.

At this point the similarities to the *Historia* break down; Monmouth's Arthur meanders through battles at Thanet and Loch Lomond, and then after the king's marriage to Guinevere, he begins his foreign campaigns, including Ireland, Iceland, the Orkneys, Norway, and Gaul. When Arthur finally returns to Britain, he pursues the treacherous Mordred and Chelric (not Cheldric) the Saxon leader, and catches them at the River Camblam. All are killed in the battle and Arthur is carried off to the Isle of Avalon, thus ending the saga of Arthur.

As an intermediary between the ancient literature and the romances, Geoffrey of Monmouth offers an enticing narrative impossible to characterize. It must be underscored that *The History of the Kings of Britain*, in spite of its title, is not historically reliable, considered by some to be pseudo-historical and by others worthless. Nevertheless, in some instances his mixture of authentic characters and fanciful figments of the imagination interwoven into a plot are extraordinarily enlightening. Although the investigation of a character might frequently lead to frustrating anachronisms, some historical figures are bound to Arthur in an uncanny meld of events.

This historical relevancy is borne out by extracting names from various sections of Momouth's *History.* Sometimes the names he uses are variations of factual counterparts, but the parallels are undeniable. When considering the central figures in the Arthurian saga, the analogies provided by Monmouth form the core of Arthuriana:

> Aurelius Ambrosius for Ambrosius Aurelianus
> Ambrosius Merlinus for Emrys
> Cherdic/Cheldric/Chelric for Cerdic
> Cherdic as a companion of Octa and Ebissa
> Hoel
> Budicius for Budic
> Octa for Octha
> Eosa for Ebissa
> Britons liberated from Saxons by Ambrosius, not Arthur
> Glouis for Gloui
> Guithelinus for Guitolin/Vitalinus

Monmouth should be condoned for his legitimate contributions and condemed for his lapses. However, claims against him of habitual scribal errors seem unwarranted, even though that was a common occurrence in copying. As suggested in an earlier chapter, it is possible, for instance, that Monmouth confused Armorica with Armonica, as proponents of a northern Arthur claim, but parts of the Arthurian chronology as he recorded it stand on their own merit. Proponents of a southern Arthur could claim just as feasibly that Arthur's boyhood locale as Caerlaverock in Scotland was mistaken for Caer Laverstock, in the vicinity of Old Sarum. Accepting both the perceptive contributions and the distorted equivocations of Monmouth's manuscript, and being able to differentiate between the two, is an exercise in maintaining the virtues of tolerance and patience.

Poetry of Arthur's Period

According to Celtic bardic tradition, poetry was composed internally, etched in thought without the use of writing. It was recited or sung orally to gathered companies usually in some chieftain's hall, transmitted orally to an apprentice bard who memorized the material, and so passed it on from generation to generation.

There is very little surviving poetry from the period as close to Arthur as possible which allegedly alludes to this legendary king. What few references do exist were selected because of their antiquity in order to minimize the romanticizing influence of intervening centuries, but the pertinent passages from Aneirin and Taliesin which specifically name a warrior called Arthur are very restrictive and uninformative, particularly the Aneirin segments; Taliesin at least plays a role in other Arthurian tales.

1. In section #62 Nennius lists five great poets of the era: Talhaearn Tad Awen, Aneirin, Taliesin, Bluchbard, and Cian known as Gueinth Guaut were "all famous at the same time in British poetry."[42]
2. Talhaearn sings of the praises of Outigern and probably of his wars with Ida, but his works have not survived; there are some allusions in other poems which point to this, plus an allusion to the Battle of Arthuret in 573.
3. Of these five poets, there are surviving remnants from only two, Aneirin and Taliesin.

ANEIRIN

1. Ifor Williams' edition appeared in 1938, called *Canu Aneirin*, published in Welsh, hailed as a major achievement. Because there have not been many changes, modifications, or expansions since then, many obscurities still exist, with no other comprehensive translation having been done.
2. Jackson calls *The Gododdin* "Scottish, though there is a manuscript written in Wales, in the Welsh language, in a Welsh library,"[43] but he believes the nucleus is very likely from Edinburgh in a dialect called "Cumbric."
3. Jackson also says that more than likely, the heroes are Scots, and that Aneirin was also.
4. Tradition conveys that Aneirin lived in the second half of the sixth century.
5. *The Gododdin* story line as presented by Jackson is listed as follows:
   a. A king or chief called Mynyddog, with his troop of picked and disciplined cavalry called Brython (not Cymry), try to smash the growing power of the English on his borders in 588–90.
   b. The name Gododdin comes from the preceding Romano-British period, from the Wotadini. The region is SE Scotland and NE England.
   c. Catraeth is generally accepted as Catterick in northern Yorkshire, assumed even at this time to have been in the hands of the English. The date, according to Jackson, falls between 586 and 605.
6. In answer to Jackson's question, which he asks himself, "Does this fit known history of northern Britain in the Dark ages?" he answers, "Yes."[44]
7. The *Gododdin* fits into the year 600.
   a. Jackson states, "it is most striking that the events described — in so far as any can be said to be described — and all the historical background seen in the poems, suit exactly what we know about the history of the North at the very end of the sixth century. Moreover, the whole tone is contemporary, not harking back to a distant past."[45]
   b. As a parallel to the events, in 603 Aedan, king of the Scots of the Irish Kingdom of Dal Riada in Argyll, led a great army against Æthelfrith at a place which Bede called Degsastan, unidentified by modern scholars. According to the Irish annals the king had help from an Irish prince of the powerful northern O'Neill, and there is some evidence that one of Hussa's sons had joined him as captain of the army. The result, however, was that the Scots were defeated and all except a few were killed. In 605, Æthelfrith made himself master of Deira, expelling King Edwin and fusing the two kingdoms into Northumbria, where he reigned until his death in 617.

8. In the *Gododdin*, Manuscript B, verse 38, there is a reference to Arthur which does not appear in Manuscript A. The passage is about Gwawrddur and his valor. It reads: "He stabbed over three hundred of the finest. ... he behaved worthily in the forefront of the most generous army. ... He glutted (?) black ravens on the rampart of the stronghold, though he was no Arthur."[46] Jackson says, "There is of course no guarantee that [this verse] was in the original *Gododdin*, but if it was, and if the poem was composed about the year 600, it is by far the oldest known reference to King Arthur and dates from a time when people who remembered him would still be alive. Arthur was the great national hero of the entire British people, from Scotland to Brittany, and there is therefore no logic whatever in the idea that this reference can be used to support the theory that he was a Northern leader."[47]

TALIESIN

Taliesin seems to slightly precede Aneirin, perhaps almost a contemporary with him. Aneirin knows of Taliesin as a famous bard, a "master of word-craft" who was perhaps working in the kingdom of Rheged.

1. Taliesin (or at least his offspring) appears quite often in the manuscripts of oral tradition, not only as an author but as a character.
    a. He is one of seven who escaped the conflagration between the Irish and the Island of the Mighty in "Branwen Daughter of Llyr," one of the Four Branches of *The Mabinogion.*
    b. Alcock feels that "Welsh tradition makes the young Taliesin the hero of a conflict with Maelgwn of Gwynnedd."[48]
    c. Chief Bard Talyessin appears on Culhwch's invocation list.
    d. In the "Dream of Rhonabwy" Avaon, son of Talyessin, accidentally splashes water onto Arthur and the holy bishop as they are crossing a river. Later on, Avaon is listed as one of Arthur's advisors.
    e. Taliesin praises Urien of Reged, who emerges as a chief of 13 kings of the north. He supposedly organized his neighbors against the English and emerged victorious in battle. The name of Urien does not appear in the *Annales Cambriae* but his son does, at entry 626: "Edwin is baptized, and Rhun, son of Urien baptized him."[49] In a different poem, Taliesin addresses Urien, at the height of his power about 570, as lord of Catraeth, which means that in his time Rheged still extended not only up the Eden valley but across the Pennines and into the low country.
2. In one of his poems after a reference to "Arthur the blessed,"[50] Taliesin writes
    > From the destruction of chiefs,
    > In a butchering manner,
    > From the loricated Legion,
    > Arose the Guledig, ...[51]
    a. "Loricated Legion" is a reference to a Roman legion wearing the typical leather cuirasses of the period.
    b. This is probably the only reference to Arthur as the Guledig, and suggests that he came from the Roman legion; that is, he was of Roman heritage and rose through the ranks to a guledig, an emperor.
3. In Book XXX Taliesin introduces the selection by praising the supreme king of the island, comments on the prowess of Arthur and also ends several stanzas with references to him:

... And when we went with Arthur, a splendid labour,
Except seven, none returned from Caer Vedwyd.

... Thrice enough to fill Prydwen there went with Arthur,
Except seven, none returned from Caer Golud.

... And when we sent with Arthur of anxious memory,
Except seven, none returned from Caer Vandwy.

... When we went with Arthur of anxious contention,
Except seven, none returned from Caer Ochren.[52]

BLACK BOOK OF CARMARTHEN

One of the poems recorded in the *Black Book of Carmarthen* of about 1200 is an elegy to Gereint, son of Erbin. *The Arthurian Handbook*, page 30, translates one of its stanzas:

In Llongborth I saw Arthur's
Brave men who cut with steel
The emperor, ruler in toil of battle.[53]

The same passage translated by W.F. Skene reads

At Llongborth I saw Arthur
And brave men who hewed down with steel,
Emperor, and conductor of the toil.[54]

There are some controversial interpretations in the translations. The most arguable point is that some scholars, exemplified by Skene, claim that Arthur was present at the Battle of Llongborth and is therefore of the south, while others, similar to Jackson, suggest that Arthur was not at the scene of the battle, that only his brave men were. These distinctions are important in supporting or refuting that Arthur was a figure of the north or of the south. *The Arthurian Handbook*, for instance, identifies Gereint's domain in the southwest, comprising the kingdom of Dumnonia or Dyfeint, from which "Devon" is derived, further adding that this particular Gereint is likely to belong to the late fifth century. "Llongborth" is interpreted as "warship-port" (Gildas Badonicus too speaks of the "long ships" of the Saxons), and the best candidate for the battlesite of Llongborth is Portchester on the Hampshire coast, one harbor east of Southampton Water which has already been shown to play an important role in Arthurian chronology and geography. Additionally, the *Chronicle* entry of 501 puts that contested landing in this area.

The lines about Arthur as a preeminent literary hero in this passage are unlikely to have been added at a later date because

An interpolator would have said more. All we get is the bare reference to his men — to a force fighting under his name alongside Gereint — and the word "emperor," in Welsh *ameraudur*, derived from the Latin *imperator* ... sometimes employed in Ireland to mean a high king.[55]

At any rate, Arthur is viewed as a war-leader, one of the "Kings of Britain," whose troops are highly respected.

Barber ascribes to the same belief that Gereint is usually accepted as the "king of Dumnonia" [i.e., Devon][56] and that Aneirin in *The Gododdin* uses the term "Gereint from the south." Devon as the kingdom is incidentally verified, but it does reflect the basic political situation as that of the sixth or seventh century.[57] Alcock adds that it lacks historical value, saying that when we find Arthur taking part in the Battle of Llongborth, we do not know whether to take this as a historical fact. In a separate segment of *Arthur's Britain*, Alcock cautions "we cannot reasonably argue that because one of our sources of information about Arthur was most probably a Welsh-battle-listing poem, therefore the source itself must necessarily be northern, and so must Arthur."[58] He cautions about accepting other "proofs" that Arthur's activity was confined to the north.[59]

One other of Alcock's quotations goes further than merely stressing Gereint's death; as an appropriate conclusion, it also points out that Gereint was from the southern lowlands and that the poem was a posthumous composition:

> At Llongborth Gereint was killed,
> And brave men from Devon's lowland.[60]

The Collation of Information

In collating the information from literary and oral tradition, similar items are extracted from the various sources and grouped. Since these items appear in more than one source, devising a specific category properly stresses its importance in addition to creating a clearer depiction of the period's conditions by showing a continuum from one manuscript to another. Doing this also demonstrates that certain details were extracted from history and became embedded in heroic lore, sometimes exposing contradictions in an amusing way and thus providing the rationale of why some scribes felt compelled to interpolate what they were copying.

BADON: OSLA BIG KNIFE AND CERDIC

The Culhwch tale does not report on the Battle of Badon, but the entire dream of Rhonabwy is about this conflict and the period of time leading up to it. To properly scrutinize the Rhonabwy tale, concentration must focus upon two separate but equally vital considerations: one is the geographic location for Badon, and the other is Arthur's Saxon adversary who was leader there. First, there are many goegraphic clues given throughout the tale. The onset of Rhonabwy's trek is somewhere in Powys. As soon as he falls asleep, he begins dreaming that "he and his companions were crossing the plain of Argyngrog, and his thoughts and feelings seemed directed toward Rhyd y Groes on the Havern [Severn]."[61] A short time later, "They [had] crossed the plain of Argyngrog to Rhyd y Groes ... and upon reaching the bank they saw Arthur seated on a flat islet below the ford."[62]

Arthur's massive army plans to move on because "they had promised to be at the Battle of Baddon by noon in order to fight against Osla Big Knife."[63] As they begin the march again, "when they reached the middle of the ford Iddawg turned the horse's head round and Rhonabwy looked at the Havern Valley."[64] The main army then reaches its destination: "By the time these troops overtook the host, Arthur and his force had descended below Caer Vaddon."[65]

Arthur's troops are moving, then, from southern Wales across the River Severn to Bath. The spelling of Baddon, with the "double d" pronounced as a "th-" sound, isolates the area as Bathon, disassociated with a connection commonly made with the word "Badbury," as detailed in Chapter 5 on the geography of Badon. Also discussed in that chapter was the engrained acceptance that Caer Vathon (the fortress of Baddon) referred to a hillfort such as Little Solsbury Hill near the modern city of Bath. But the Rhonabwy tale provides irrefutable evidence that Caer Vaddon refers to Viroconium as an ancient Bath in the shadow of the Wrekin. Arthur's army could ford the River Severn and easily reach Caer Vaddon by noon from Wales.

Attention must shift, therefore, from the location of Caer Vaddon to Arthur's destination after a truce is granted to Osla Big Knife, when Kei says that anyone who wants to stay with Arthur should meet in Cornwall for the night. In his introduction Gantz expresses surprise that "As in 'Culhwch,' Arthur's court appears to be in Cornwall and not in Wales."[66] Initially, this is odd, especially since the tales of Owein,[67] Peredur,[68] and Gereint[69] list Carleon as Arthur's main court. Monmouth, too, stresses the importance of Carleon by relating that Arthur's plenary court for all of Europe was held there.[70] In the "Dream of Rhonabwy" the common assumption is that Arthur begins his journey from his court at Carleon, so that his return to Cornwall is strangely out of context. That contradiction was also resolved in an earlier chapter. Antiquarians and modern researchers have erroneously assumed that throughout the Arthurian saga, Cornwall was a reference to the present-day area of that name, but during the Roman and immediate post–Roman period of Arthur's time, the Cornwall area was referred to as Dumnonia. Chapter 5 indicated that Arthur's point of origin is a mystery, but it would not have been somewhere in Cornwall.

Next is a need to come to grips with Arthur's adversaries, beginning with Osla Big Knife. Alcock makes a generic statement about epithets:

> [The passing of certain documents through various phases of transmission] can be shown by the Welsh spelling of Old English personal names — Eoguin or Eadgum for Edwin, Osguid for Wswy, Aedlric for Æthelric, and so on. Then some Angles are given British nicknames — Oswald *Lamnguin*, White-Blade, or Eadfered *Flesaurs*, Æthelfrith the Twister.[71]

Epithets such as "White-Blade" have a direct application here. The name Osla is as jarringly out of place in a Briton context as Cerdic is in a Saxon one. He is correctly equated with Octha, son of Hengist, and even his epithet attests to Saxon heritage. The term *Saxon* literally means big knife, derived from *seax*, meaning "broad sword," a slightly different description for Big Knife.

The peculiarity is that in the Culhwch tale, Osla Big Knife is one of Arthur's favored soldiers, a comrade important enough to be included in an invocation with more than just a mere mention of name. His importance is further magnified in a major role when he is individually identified fighting against Arthur's enemy. While pursuing Twrch Trwyth, Arthur and "the champions of Britain" join the fight, and Osla Big Knife draws near and dunks Twrch into the river "until the currents rolled over him." Some in-fighting goes on, and then we are told Osla Big Knife lost his knife from its sheath in running after the boar; the sheath filled with water, and as Osla was being pulled from the river, it dragged him down to the bottom."[72] This indicates quite distinctly that he was drowned.

For an individual with little persistence, this would without a doubt close the curtains on Osla Big Knife. But there are two curious things which transpire. One has to do with a comrade who drowns alongside Osla in this same scene. This fellow warrior, Cacamwri, a servant to Arthur, is also dragged to the bottom and drowned. But on the very next page, which introduces the next adventure, Cacamwri is miraculously alive, and he and his brother are sent to fight with the Black Hag. The second is that Osla cannot be figuratively buried and forgotten either. He has an even bigger role in the succeeding tale, "The Dream of Rhonabwy," which, according to the scholars, was the last tale of *The Mabinogion* to have taken shape.

In this tale Arthur's huge army of warriors — troops on the Severn lining both sides of the road for a mile before reaching the ford where Arthur is sitting — are on the move to "be at the Battle of Badon by noon in order to fight against Osla Big Knife."[73] Osla is no longer a comrade in Arthur's huge army, but now is an enemy about to be engaged in battle. The massive army indicates that this is not just a minor conflict, but a major battle in a major war, and Osla is more than just a petty figure in a small coup. After Arthur and Owein have played several games of gwyddbwyll, Osla sends 24 horsemen to ask for a truce to the end of a month and a fortnight. Arthur consults with his advisors and grants the truce.

An answer to all the questions revolving around the deterioration of camaraderie to enmity traces back to historical sources. Osla Big Knife was an English Saxon who came to Britain with his father Hengist as a *federate* to help Vortigern, along with Cunedda and his sons who had come down from the north, to drive the Picts and the Irish from Cornovii and Welsh soil. Through this alliance, Cerdic, Octha, and Arthur were, during some point in history, united as comrades-in-arms, companions with the same aspirations. But when the alliance between Britons and the English Saxons was torn asunder, different beliefs and philosophies caused the three figures to choose opposite paths. Cerdic aligned himself with Osla and the English Saxons, and Arthur remained pro–Briton. Incursions and skirmishes continued over a period of years, and even after Osla was killed at Badon and Cerdic was granted Wessex, civil war still tore the country apart.

Only two sources report Octha's death. As already pointed out, in the Culhwch tale as Osla, he drowns by being dragged to the bottom of the River

Severn. By far the most detailed account of his life and death appears in Monmouth; as Octa, he is killed in a conflict with Utherpendragon, just prior to Uther's poisoning and Arthur's succession to the throne. Neither of these literary sources, however, gives reliable information, since he is resurrected from one and killed by a fictional character in the other. Historically, he appears three times in the *Historia*, but each is a brief notice that mentions nothing of his death. Entries about him in the *ASC* present more questions rather than providing answers; in the Parker Chronicle the last entry on Octha is in 488, explaining that he succeeded to the kingdom and ruled for 24 years, while the Laud Chronicle for the same year shows that he succeeded to the kingdom and ruled for 34 years.

CAVALRY

Because of its heavy inclusion in literary tradition, this term deserves more in-depth attention. Although the Culhwch tale does not use the term cavalry even in a loose sense, it gives a surprising amount of detail, describing bridles, saddles, and weapons as Culhwch mounts his steed and begins his journey. Throughout the quest, Arthur's battle-tested warriors are referred to as horsemen, and as part of their task they must obtain the horse of Gweddw and the horse of Moro. Similarly, Rhonabwy's entire dream is about hordes of mounted horsemen moving toward the Battle of Badon. The Gereint material is much more reflective of the Monmouth-style romancers, and much different from Mynyddog's troops of picked and disciplined cavalry in *The Gododdin*; nevertheless, it becomes obvious that horsemen in the late fifth and early sixth centuries are commonplace and militarily invaluable.

At one time or another, all scholars in their study of Arthur have come to grips with the possibility of Arthur using cavalry. Barber, for instance, considered Arthurian cavalry more than once. From one point of view he shows the effectiveness of cavalry against foot-soldiers. In his book *Arthur of Albion*, in a Chapter titled "The Unknown Commander," he states: "Now we know that in Gaul cataphracts, a Byzantine form of heavily-armed cavalry, had been used successfully against the barbarian invaders."[74] Then he adds:

> In Britain, too, the defence of the East Coast was, in the later years of the Roman occupation, mainly dependent on cavalry, which outnumbered the infantry used here by two to one. Either of these two cavalry forces may have given Arthur the idea of forming a small and extremely mobile band of horsemen. ... Such a band ... would explain why Arthur was remembered ... for with such a mobile force, he might well have fought almost anywhere in Britain.[75]

However, he makes a complete turn-about in this respect. In a later book, *The Figure of Arthur*, and in a strikingly similar chapter titled "The Unknown Leader: Badon Hill," he recants:

Cavalry were not a particularly effective weapon against footsoldiers, and the much-quoted Byzantine cataphracts or heavily armed horsemen were not particularly distinguished by their successes.[76]

Rather than "heavily armed horsemen," the definition for cataphracts is armored archers on armored horses, used by the Assyrians and adapted later by the Persians. The weight, of course, encouraged the breeding of large, strong horses, but they were slow in pursuit or retreat. The Roman Empire adapted this Persian method, but because of expense and ineffectiveness abandoned this technique in the Late Western Empire. From the Huns who initially served as mercenaries in the Roman armies, the Empire was impressed with the effectiveness and mobility of the Huns' light cavalry and adopted their style.

Nevertheless, in this vein of reversal, Barber concludes:

> Above all, horses were still for the most part unshod, and the riders had no stirrups. Both these innovations date from the seventh century or later in Britain, and horsemen could neither travel long distances over rough terrain nor charge effectively. Furthermore, the native breed of horses were small-boned ponies rather than chargers; even as a means of transport, they would have been little faster over long distances than footsoldiers. So Badon Hill is unlikely to have been won by a kind of primitive forerunner of knightly cavalry.[77]

However, a person has only to look at the effectiveness of the American Indian to refute this statement. Indian horsemanship was absolutely superb, accomplished with unshod horses and no saddles at all, and definitely without the use of stirrups. It was actually the Plains Indians' horsemanship which allowed them to resist the U.S. Cavalry for so long; the Indians could outmaneuver and outride a great many of their better-equipped enemies. United States history is filled with episodes of a handful of mounted warriors gaining victory over much larger groups of combatants on foot. The American Indians rode ponies rather than chargers, traveled light, and covered distance much faster than their U.S. Cavalry counterparts or, of course, the footsoldiers. This would give mounted warriors on small, agile horses, traveling light, a decided edge.

In Arthur's case, if those troops were traveling the superbly engineered Roman roads — highways in the true sense of the term, six to ten feet high, nine to fifteen feet wide, and cleared of all obstacles, with way-stations every ten to twenty miles — those troops would present a formidable adversary to the Saxons. Like the American Indians, his troops could move much more quickly than footsoldiers and resist invasions because of the very things that Barber lists as disadvantages: small, unencumbered ponies to cover distances quickly as opposed to shod, saddled, lumbering war-horses. Considering the time and the circumstances, this mode of warfare would be far from a primitive forerunner. Perhaps, given the opportunity, Barber might revert to his earlier stance, since his original position is much more accurate.

Literary tradition, verified by history, indicates overwhelmingly that Arthur did employ cavalry tactics, especially since there is evidence that he and other people closely allied to him, such as Ambrosius Aurelianus and Riothamus, were very closely bound to Romanized military strategies, including the use of cavalry. Jeffrey Gantz contributes to the definition of cavalry by offering an explanation:

> It is difficult to trace the first appearance of armour in the *Mabinogion*, or the rise of the concept of knighthood, because the Welsh language did not develop new words for them: *arveu*, originally "weapons," came to mean armour as well, while *marchawg*, "horseman," came to mean "knight," and it is not always clear which is meant.[78]

Even though the word cavalry might be a poor translation, the term means armed (not armored) men, traveling light, mounted on horses, undoubtedly a forerunner of knight-errantry.

ARTHUR'S RELATIVES

1. Culhwch, Caradawg Strong Arm (his chief advisor), March (leader of the white troops of Norway to Badon), and Gereint son of Erbin are Arthur's cousins.
2. Gormant is a brother from his mother's side.
3. Rica (Gormant's father), Meirchyawn (March's father), Llygadrudd Emys, and Gwrvoddw, (brothers of his mother), plus Aurelius Ambrosius, and Erbin of Cornwall who is listed as son of Constantine would be his uncles.
4. Amhar (Arthur's chamberlain), and Llacheu are his sons.
5. Utherpendragon is his father.
6. King Hoel of Brittany is a nephew, son of Arthur's sister.

Of people listed, scholars assure us through other accounts, that Utherpendragon is fictional, making no appearances anywhere until the advent of Geoffrey of Monmouth in the twelfth century. Three others of note make an appearance in the ancient manuscripts of history. One is Mordred, who appears in the *Annales Cambriae* as Medraut, but nothing in that entry gives a hint whether perhaps a father and a son (or uncle and nephew) are fighting on opposite sides in the conflict. Another name, of course, is the variant of Aurelius Ambrosius, who appears in Gildas and later in Nennius.

The third name of historical note is Constantine (Custenhin), listed as Arthur's grandfather and father to Erbin (Arthur's uncle from Cornwall) in *Gereint and Enid*. More than likely, this is not Constantine III, the emperor during the years of 406 and 407, but very probably it could be the Constantine of the sixth century mentioned by Gildas as one of the five Kings of Britain. Gildas speaks of this Constantine as the "tyrannical whelp of the unclean Dumnonian lioness,"[79] which fits this reference since this particular Constantine is listed by Alcock as King of Dumnonia (Cornwall), and his son Erbin is naturally from there also. Peculiar in Gildas' *DE* (if, in fact, both Ambrosius Aurelianus and this Constantine are both from the same royal family) is that one is so highly praised and the other is so castigated. This paradox seems to be resolved by Gildas' earlier passage that Ambrosius Aurelianus was a man who "of all the Roman nation was then alone and ... by chance left alive."[80] This in turn creates a dilemma of how all the relationships in literary tradition can be be resolved.

One other interesting note concerns Arthur's uncle Llygadrudd, in the Culhwch tale of the *Mabinogion*. He has the attachment of what could be a title, Emys. Gantz interprets this as part of a proper name, translated as "stallion." And yet there is the intrigue with the Welsh word "Emrys" as suggested by John Morris, and its variant, "Emhyr," also given by Gantz in writing about Howell son of Emhyr of Britanny, where Gantz mentions that this term is perhaps not originally a proper name. "Emrys" is the term for Ambrosius Aurelianus who passed into Welsh legend with that title. If in fact Arthur's uncle is Emrys instead of "Red-Eyed Stallion," then Arthur, like Ambrosius, would be a *gwledig.*

THE CONNECTION BETWEEEN GILDAS AND ARTHUR

Literary tradition is responsible for answering the question about the alleged, deliberate silence of Gildas in the *DE* ignoring Arthur as the hero of the Battle of Badon. Gildas instead praises Ambrosius Aurelianus but then passes over the name of the Briton leader at Badon, evidently shunning Arthur as the leader, supposedly as a consequence of the feud between the two. There is, of course, in the Culhwch tale a hint of the feud, or at least bad blood which might exist between Gildas and Arthur. The passage indicates that Hueil, son of Caw and therefore brother to Gildas "never submitted to a lord's hand,"[81] and this, combined with the passage two pages later in the Culhwch tale, indicates that because Arthur killed Hueil, a feud ensued between Arthur and Gildas. However, as stressed several times earlier, the life of Saint Gildas by Caradoc refers *not* to Gildas Badonicus, but to Gildas Albanius.

Nevertheless, other passages in literary tradition, though, indicate a civil relationship between Arthur and Gildas Albanius. In "Rhonabwy" Gildas son of Caw is one of Arthur's advisors who is consulted for making a decision about a truce to avert the Battle of Badon.[82] As further indication of an amenable relationship between Gildas and Arthur, in the tale of Gereint, when Gwenhwyvar is alone during the hunt, Arthur has one of his attendants ask Gildas son of Caw to accompany her home.[83] Also, later in Caradoc's story of Gildas, Gildas and Arthur encounter each other once again, when Melwas kidnaps Guinevere and imprisons her in a stronghold near the Glastonbury monastery. Gildas arbitrates a treaty so that Guinevere is reunited with Arthur. This episode does not reflect bad blood between Gildas Albanius and Arthur, but instead suggests a bond.

ARTHUR'S COLORS AND BLAZONS

One important color emerging from the Culhwch tale is in a very brief one-line description of Culhwch's dress. In the text, Culhwch's father tells him to go to his first cousin Arthur and solicit his help. When Culhwch began his quest, he "wore a four-cornered purple mantle with a red-gold apple in each corner; each apple was worth a hundred cows."[84] This seemingly minor piece of information could easily be glossed over, but it is one more tiny piece of the puzzle which links Arthur and his extended family (including Culhwch) to Ambrosius Aurelianus and a fragment of information in Gildas' *DE*. In Chapter 25, where Gildas praises Ambrosius Aurelianus, Gildas also writes that "[Ambrosius'] parents, who for their merit were adorned with the purple, had been slain in these same broils [with the Saxons.]"[85] Ambrosius' parents were high-ranking royalty in Roman circles, and the regal line passed on to Ambrosius. At first this might seem coincidental, with no link intended between Culhwch (and Arthur) and Ambrosius but as a coincidence the hint seems far too subtle. If the bards wanted to establish a royal connection between Ambrosius, Arthur, and Culhwch, there would have been more notice given of the fact.

Gildas does not write about the four red-gold apples as described in the corner of Culhwch's mantle, but this provides us with another link in the *Mabinogion* tale of Rhonabwy. In that story, when Arthur has moved his numerous troops to Badon, they set up tents. After Arthur dismounts,

> A large, red-haired man drew a gold chair and a ribbed brocade mantle from the pack, spread the mantle — there was a red-gold apple in each corner — and set the chair on it.[86]

The worth of the red-gold apples is evident from the Culhwch tale. The color of the mantle is unknown, but inference dictates that if Culhwch and Arthur share the symbols of the red-gold apples, then they would also share the color which sets them apart as royalty. The name of the mantle is Gwenn, translating to white, or pure. However, white is not necessarily its color, but could be more of a name for this particular mantle's peculiar characteristic. One of the properties of this mantle is that "a man wrapped in it could see everyone, but no one could see him, nor would it allow any color on it but its own."[87] The only "color allowed on it" could be purple (royalty), protected by the mantle's magic. If the mantle is named Gwenn (such as Arthur's spear called Ron or his knife called Carnwennan), "white" could be translated as "invisible," which is suggestive of Ambrosius' fabulous wizardry in the Nennius story.

The red-gold motif (not the apples) appears in only one other place. In the mid–1200s, Arthur's blazon consisted of three gold crown on a background of red, but no apples of that color are suggested. In later texts the crowns remain gold but increase to 13 to signify the number of kingdoms under Arthur's domain; the background becomes blue. The apple motif, of course, draws attention to Arthur's possible connection to Glastonbury as the Isle of Apples.

Arthur's blazons give rise to a discussion of the entry on the Battle of Badon from the *Annales Cambriae*. It reads, "Bellum Badonis, in quo Arthur portavit crucem Domini nostri Jhesu Christi tribus diebus et tribus noctibur in humeros suos et Brittones victores fuerunt," translated to, "The Battle of Badon, in which

Drawing 4. Arthur's blazon as described by John of Glastonbury: three lions, red, on a silver background.

Drawing 5. In thirteenth century manuscripts, Arthur's blazon is described as three gold crowns against a blue or a red background.

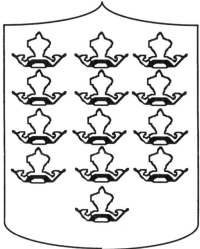

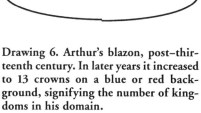

Drawing 6. Arthur's blazon, post–thirteenth century. In later years it increased to 13 crowns on a blue or red background, signifying the number of kingdoms in his domain.

Drawing 7. Arthur's blazon of the Blessed Mary and son in memory of the crystal cross given to him by the Mother. The background was green with a cross of silver.[88]

Arthur carried the cross of our Lord Jesus Christ three days and three nights on his shoulders and the Britons were victorious." For this entry Nennius does not paraphrase the segment about Arthur carrying the cross on his shoulders. However, there is a passage in Nennius for the eighth battle of Guinnion, which reads, "... in quo Arthur portavit imaginem Sanctae Mariae perpetuae virginis super humerous sous ...," translated to "... in which Arthur carried the image of Saint Mary ever Virgin upon his shoulders." In both these instances, *humeros* is interpreted as meaning shoulders. Alcock explains the confusion of this word:

> ... [T]he explanation lies in the confusion between two Welsh words, which led the scribes of the Easter Annals (the *Annales Cambriae*) and the *Historia Brittonum* (Nennius) to mistranslate them into Latin. The Old Welsh word for "shoulder" is scuid but there is a very similar Old Welsh word scuit which means "shield."[89]

This is the explanation given most often. Helen Hill Miller, though, indicates the confusion lies between the Welsh word *yagwydd*, meaning "shoulder," and the Welsh word *yaswyd*, meaning "shield." Whichever translation is accepted, the meaning points to a figurative expression, not a literal one; that is, in the one entry Arthur is bearing the cross of Jesus Christ emblazoned on his shield, and in the other entry the Virgin Mary is painted on his shield.

Interpolations of William of Malmsbury's manuscript confused these two entries, the Battle of Badon and the eighth Battle at the Castle Guinnion. From *The Gesta Regum Anglorum*, translated by E.K. Chambers in *Arthur of Britain*, an interpolater relates, "Finally, at the siege of Mount Badon, relying upon the image of the mother of the Lord which he had sewn on his armour, rising alone against nine hundred of the enemy he dashed them to the ground with incredible slaughter."[90] In actuality, the passage which makes reference to "Our Lord's Mother" is not the Badon passage, but the passage in Nennius describing the battle at Guinnion, in which Arthur is carrying the image of Saint Mary either on his shoulders or his shield.

CAMLANN

The name of Camlann is given several times in the *Mabinogion*. In "Culhwch and Olwen" alone, Camlann appears four times. Fighting on the side of Arthur are Morvan, son of Tegid, Sanddav Angel Face, Saint Kynwl, and Gwyn Hyvar, Steward of Devon and Cornwall. Not much more information can be gleaned from the Morvan and the Sanddav entries, but from the Saint Kynwyl entry there is an addition that the saint was only one of three men to escape and the last to leave Arthur, which attests to the ferocity of the Camlann battle, with carnage on both sides.

The tale of Rhonabwy adds a very interesting highlight about Camlann. Iddawg, called the Churl of Britain, bears the burden of stirring up bad feelings between Medrawd and the emperor Arthur. In this entry Medrawd is listed as Arthur's nephew rather than his bastard son born from an incestuous relationship as other traditions have it, but what this entry supplies is information not given in the *AC*. The *Annales* entry gives no indication of which side Mordred was on; the entry relates only that both Arthur and Medraut were mortally wounded in battle. In later romances Mordred is listed as an adversary, but the Rhonabwy story is one of the earliest traditions that indicates the nature of what transpired at Camlann.

ARTHUR'S COURT

As mentioned earlier, several tales from *The Mabinogion*, plus Geoffrey of Monmouth, set Arthur's court at Caer Llion ar Wysg. Caxton sets Arthur's court somewhere in Wales, perhaps at Caerleon or Caerwent; Malory identifies it with Winchester; and John Leland picked South Cadbury Castle in Somerset. Other guesses have been Killibury, Kerry, Callington, Padstow, and most recently, Viroconium. The general locale has most commonly been given as Cornwall. And yet the survey of early literary tradition is weighted massively to Wales, with only a sprinkling of Cornish references in comparison. Stating a generalization formulated from just this observation leads to the conclusion that Arthur is Welsh; otherwise, the preponderance of Welsh literature would not be about him. The scattered allusions to Cornwall, especially since Cornwall was outside the hub even in Roman times, suggest that the rendition should be Cornovian and not Cornish.

Chapter 12
The Phoenix Arises

Statement of Hypothesis

The quest for the historic Arthur, which has led intricately through a forest of other investigations, is approaching its resolution. Earlier chapters set aside Arthur's role in the romances and instead validated a milieu of historical events and figures spanning Arthur's era. This singularity of purpose stripped Arthur of extraneous associations if they had no relevance to his authenticity. In retrospect, what has been presented so far of his life has the characteristics of a disjointed slide presentation seen through an opaque lens. Arthur himself is still an optical illusion, appearing, dwindling, and reappearing, but never solidifying into a figure of substance or generating a conviction of his historicity. As yet there is no fine-tuned, explicit, clear-cut image which has discretely defined him as a true-to-life hero. Although each entity in the triad — Ambrosius Aurelianus, Riothamus, and Arthur — has been validated as historically accurate, either on the island or the continent or in both places, Ambrosius Aurelianus is the only individual designated by a proper name. The three are locked inextricably to the Arthurian era as pervading influences in Britain and across the Channel, but the scenario of the historic Arthur cannot be completed until the similitude of these three personalities is analyzed. Defining this triad as a single individual eliminates the obscurity of Arthur's rise to the status of Cultural Hero; it fills the void between the second Briton migration to Brittany and the Battle of Badon to give a sequential time frame which makes Arthur a reality; it explains historical developments not only in Britain but also in Little Britain and Gaul on the mainland when the Roman Empire was in its death-throes. The purpose of this final chapter is to replace that opaque lens with a clear one, and splice together those intermittent glimpses so that they create a cinematic sequence of Arthur's chronology, birth to death.

Hence, one last essential theory must be proposed to set the stage for the reconstruction of Arthur, adding the finishing touches to complete his comprehensive portrait and thus provide closure for his eventful lifespan. Geoffrey Ashe postulates in *The Discovery of Arthur* that Arthur and Riothamus were different names for the same individual; the theory here carries that idea one step further, contending that the names Ambrosius Aurelianus, Riothamus, and Arthur *all* refer to the same individual. Stated more explicitly, the terms Riothamus and Arthur are both titles used interchangeably with the proper name Ambrosius Aurelianus. To avoid confusion (since there is enough of that already) it is necessary to coin a name for this triadic individual, even at the risk of sounding arrogant or pretentious. Approached logistically, *rio-* meaning "king" and *-ardd* (with the double-d sounding like an unvoiced -th) meaning "high" can be combined for an epithet of Riardd. Attached to the only proper name, this new phoenix accurately would be called Riardd Ambrosius, one more designation to add to the already overwhelming list.

To that end, the analysis of this hypothesis divides into two segments. The first of the segments concentrates on the definition of titles, epithets, and anonyms, and their application to the three figures. Scholars concur that Riothamus is a title and not a proper name, and Ambrosius Aurelianus has several descriptive titles associated with his name in the histories. The word *Arthur* can be considered either as a proper name with accompanying etymological doubts already cited, or it can can be viewed as a title, much like Riothamus, Vortigern, or Cunorix, among other Roman and Welsh epithets.

The final segment melds the three chronologies sequentially: the first for Ambrosius Aurelianus extending from a birth-year provided by tradition to the second migration, the one for Riothamus covering a decade from the second migration to his defeat at Bourg-de-Déols, and the last for Arthur from 470 until his death in 518. The previous three chapters have already supplied the basics; within a deviation of two years, dates as given by history and literary tradition will appear in an easy-to-read graphics table titled "The Mergence Chronology."

Titles of Rank and Royalty

Histories of the Dark Ages are very much like Russian novels, in which one character can have many different names and nicknames. Added to several possible spellings, epithets have also replaced proper names. To understand references to specific people, one must also understand the distinction between a name and an epithet. Freeborn Romans and Celts customarily bore three names, sometimes four:

1. a *praenomen*, or first name,
2. a *cognomen*, family or last name,
3. a *nomen*, or middle name indicating his *gens* (clan), and sometimes, if a man was very distinguished,
4. an *agnomen*, a surname [an additional cognomen, according to Webster] often bestowed as a title of honor, or fondly as a nickname.[1]

Morris, too, notes these definitions:

> All the [Roman] names are given in the old-fashioned form of *nomen* and *cognomen*,
> family and personal name, that in the later fourth century remained principally in
> vogue among the local nobility of the western *"civitates."* Men so named were not
> native kings to whom Rome granted recognition, but Roman officers placed over bor-
> der barbarians.[2]

Both Morris and Goodrich supply comments about the definitions. Goodrich writes that King Arthur was known as a Romano-Briton, Roman on his
father's side and British on his mother's side, both families being warriors or
commanders of the line. The source of her information is unknown, but her
remark describes Ambrosius Aurelianus; the full name of Ambrosius' recorded
ancestor is Lucius Domitius Aurelianus, who had two *agnomina*, Aurelian and
Restitutor Orbis (Restorer of the City). Ambrosius has a *praenomen* and a *cognomen*;
he additionally has several *agnomina* from the massive evidence in the manuscripts. He is from distinguished Roman stock and, as Morris avers, Rome granted
him recognition. This, of course, does not apply to the singular term Arthur, if
Arthur is viewed as a proper name rather than an epithet.

There are not many titles or epithets describing Ambrosius Aurelianus. In
Chapter 42 of the *Historia* Ambrosius is identified as the son of Roman royalty
and then ascribed the title of Embries Guletic, with its several variations[3] in the
different manuscripts. John Morris describes the term:

> The Welsh coined the title *gwledic*, ruler of the country. ... Bede put it into Latin,
> avoiding the personal title; he lists the men who were held to have "held empire" as
> *imperium* [Imperator, emperor]. The English language gave them the title Bret-
> walda, ruler of Britain; it came near to the imperial title, for a similar word, *Bryt-
> walda*, "wide ruler," was occasionally used of Roman emperors.[4]

Gwledic, a term like *Bretwalda* applied to the Saxons, plays a significant role as a
title or epithet. Morris is affirming that *gwledic* is a Welsh term also associated
with the high rank of Imperator, that Imperator is the equivalent of emperor, and
lastly that emperor is a Latin synonym for the title of king. Ambrosius inherited
that title from his parents; although he is not referred to as *Imperator* or *Emperor*,
gwledic carries the connotative inference of supreme authority.

In Chapter 48 of the *Historia*, the only other title given to Ambrosius is that
of a great king among all the kings on the Isle of Britain. Ascending to the throne
after Vortigern, he is fighting against the barbarians, and Ambrosius has the
power to confer two countries (the term for regions or domains) upon Pascent.
Vortimer is listed as Vortigern's son in this same section, and Chapter 9 of this
text analyzed Ambrosius as the Roman embodiment of this particular son because
the latter is not verified as an authentic person. Although the term Vortimer is
in itself an epithet, it is only speculation that it can be used as such for Ambrosius. The British origin of Vortimer was listed as Vortamorix, *vor-* meaning "over,"
-tamo- as a superlative suffix "-est," and *-rix* as an offshoot of *-rex* meaning

"king." As "most supreme king," the epithet would nevertheless be appropriate for Ambrosius.

Riothamus, the third figure in the analysis of this trilogy, has no list of titles except for "king," or "king of the Britons" in manuscripts by Jordanes and Gregory of Tours. In continental literature and history, the term Riothamus is not used synonymously with references such as gwledig, emperor, or imperator so commonly retained on the island. Lacy's encyclopedia relates that continental documents seem to underlie parts of the account of Arthur in Geoffrey of Monmouth. The explanation is given that

> The Latin form Riothamus, used with slight variants in continental texts, corresponds to the British Rigotamos. Rig, with the added "o" in a compound, meant "king"; tamos was a superlative suffix. As a noun, this word would mean "king-most" or "supreme king" (cf. the modern word generalissimo). As an adjective, it would mean "most kingly," "supremely royal." It appears later as a proper name, becoming Riatham in Breton and Rhiadaf in Welsh.[5]

Lacy explains that as a noun, Riothamus translates to "supreme king." Titles that are more common than proper names exist throughout history: the name Temujin is much more uncommon than his title designation of Genghis Kahn; the epithet Augustus was adopted for Octavian; Basileutatos is the equivalent bestowed upon Minos of Crete. Hence, Riothamus[6] is not a name but a title of honor. Using just superlative degrees to make a point, the epithet Riothamus means "Highest King" and Vortimer means "Highest Overking," an interesting comparison of titles, both which could apply to Ambrosius Aurelianus. The task is to determine the name behind the epithet.

In the source material about Arthur's titles, perhaps ten to fifteen terms describe him, two of the most common being "emperor" in the early literature, and *dux bellorum* in the early chronicles. These are technically called "titles," an attachment to a proper name, signifying honor or distinction. Although a title sometimes drops the proper name, it does so only after there has been an antecedent reference using the *nomen.*

Most commonly, "Arthur" is considered a proper name, offered by several scholars as an common explanation: Arthur is a proper name derived from the Latin Artorius. Kenneth Jackson, for one, writes that

> The name *Arthur* is unquestionably derived from *Artorius*, not rare in the history of Rome since it was the title of the *gens Artoria.* ... We know of one Artorius who really lived in Britain, an officer called Lucius Artorius Castus, apparently a Dalmatian, who led the VIth Legion on an expedition to Armorica in the middle of the second century.[7]

Bromwich, too, writes about the name of Arthur as having a Roman derivative from a proper name:

> The name "Arturus" appears first in the Latin of the Welshman who redacted the *Historia Brittonum* some time in the early ninth century [her way of identifying

Nennius], and as "Arthur" in several Welsh poems which are believed to go back approximately to the same date — one of them indeed, the famous reference to Arthur in the *Gododdin*, may even be considerably earlier.[8]

As support, she indicates that

> Names derived from Latin are by no means rare among the early Welsh genealogies, for men who were born approximately between the dates A.D. 300 and 450: they become less common after that date.[9]

Based upon the floruit most commonly set for King Arthur (470-500), this would put Arthur in Bromwich's latter category, meaning it would be an uncommon name after 450.

Although common assumptions, neither Jackson's nor Bromwich's assertion that King Arthur's name is derived from an early Roman one is particularly convincing. Jackson cites only one Roman officer with the name of *Artorius* during the nearly five centuries of the Roman occupation of Britain; this particular Artorius is chronicled in the middle of the second century (300 years *before* King Arthur's time). Bromwich picks up on the name *Arturus* some time in the early ninth century (400 years *after* King Arthur's historic era).

By separating three distinctive Arthurs reported in the histories of the period, Barber, in *The Figure of Arthur*, clarifies some of the confusion inherent in what Jackson and Bromwich postulate. Yet Bromwich's statement that Latin derivatives are less common after the year 450 contradicts Barber's histories which place the various Arthurs near the beginning of the 600s, nearly 150 years *after* the time when the name of *Arturus* was allegedly common. This shows, then, that between the second century and the end of the sixth, only one proper name, Lucius Artorius Castus, appears in the histories.

Barber is on target by concluding that

> Any connection between Lucius Artorius Castus and the Irish and Welsh Arthurs must be extremely tenuous. We can only conjecture that distant memories of L. Artorius Castus's campaigns ... might have encouraged later writers to embellish the legend of Arthur in otherwise unsuspected ways. To build a bridge of tradition from second-century Roman Britain to ninth-century Wales with no other support is a daring feat of imagination, but not admissible evidence.[10]

A Roman commander with the *nomen* Artorius recorded in the year A.D. 184 seems highly unlikely as a carryover to the fifth century King Arthur as a proper name.

Discounting, then, the far-fetched possibility that the word "Arthur" is a proper name, it is still necessary to examine first the titles of rank and office used in conjunction with Arthur's name. Nennius' reference to Arthur is

> *Tunc Arthur pugnabat contra illos in illis diebus cum*
> *regibus Brittonium, sed ipse dux erat bellorum.*[11]

> Then Arthur fought against them [the Saxons] in those days with the kings of Britain, but he was the leader in battle.

Some researchers have suggested the addition of the word "other," so that the passage would read "Arthur fought against the Saxons with the *other* kings of Britain, but he was the leader in battle." This would then imply that Arthur was a king himself, fighting along with other kings, but he distinguished himself because he was the leader of kings. It seems an unnecessary presumption, however, since there are so many other indications of his royalty.

Stevenson indicates that the passage in the original of Manuscript D was slightly different. He translates it as

> *Et licit multi ipse nobiliores essent, ipse tamen*
> *duodecies dux belli fuit, victorque bellorum.*[12]

> And though there were many more noble than he, he
> was the great leader, victorious in battle.

Neither translation indicates that Arthur was more than a leader in battle, a *dux bellorum*. Such titles do not automatically exclude kings from being leaders in battles — in fact the practice in the Dark Ages was just the opposite, that kings did lead their armies into battles — but nothing in these passages states outright that Arthur himself was designated as High King, or even a king.

In conjunction with the term *dux bellorum*, Fletcher refers to a writer of the first Arthurian *Mirabilia* who calls Arthur by the unassuming title of *miles*, which simply means "soldier" in Latin. Fletcher continues,

> That Arthur was not of royal blood is directly asserted by the tenth-century Vatican version of the *Historia*; but that is too late to have much authority. Taking everything together, it certainly looks as if Arthur owed his position of leader chiefly to his preeminent ability. It may be that his relation to the kings was simply something like that ascribed to Miltiades among the Athenian generals: they may all have given place to him voluntarily, as to the man most capable to command. It seems more likely, however, that there is truth in the theory advanced by Professor Rhys and others, that Arthur owed some of his authority to the fact of holding the office which had belonged to one of the military chiefs under the Roman system of administration in the island. These offices may well have been kept up by the Britons, as least by the Romanizing party, after the departure of the Romans.[13]

One can assert with confidence that Professor Rhys' theory is accurate; Arthur emerges in a period directly after Roman withdrawal, and because the Britons had flourished under four centuries of Roman rule, there was a contingency which clung to Roman heritage. Roman customs did not just abruptly cease; the Britons cherished the life enhanced for them by Roman civilization, and the passing of the Roman way, including military, was gradual over several decades. Fletcher's inference, however, is misleading; Arthur owing his authority to a military chief under a Roman is lamentably misconstrued as Arthur assuming leadership from Ambrosius Aurelianus, since Ambrosius was a descendant of royalty who wore the purple.

Alcock also comments on the title of *dux bellorum* in Nennius:

[W]e must look closely at the words *dux bellorum* for which two alternative translations have been put forward: "Duke," a specific rank or title, or "leader." The late Roman military system had two titles for high-ranking officers, *Dux* and *Comes*, which we may translate as "Duke" and "Count." In Britain, for instance, in the fourth century, there was a *Dux Britanniarum* who commanded the garrison forces of Hadrian's Wall and its supporting forts, and a *Comes Britanniarum* who commanded a mobile field army. ... Even in the late Roman empire a *dux* might command field units as well as garrison troops, and might have administrative duties of a civilian nature as well. In sixth-century Gaul, a *dux* was appointed by the king to administer a tribe or region, especially in an area of military importance, and he also undertook military duties in the field.[14]

He then cautions that the term might be distorted since the Nennius manuscript is not a Latin document which would retain the term's precise meaning:

But when we recall that our ultimate source is not a Latin document in which *dux* might have retained some precise meaning, but a Welsh poem, it becomes doubtful whether this interpretation is valid at all. Our doubts on this point are reinforced when we look at other Welsh evidence. In the elegy on Gereint of Devon, Arthur is called *ameraudur llwiaudir llawus*, emperor, battle-ruler. And in the Llwarch Hen poems, we have *tywyssawc llu* and *tywyssawc cat*, leader of the host or army or, in the second case, since *cat* may mean either "army" or "battle," leader of the battle.[15]

Although the definition might vary, however, it is noteworthy that the title signifies prestige, status, and capabilities in both Roman and Welsh, and its importance cannot be minimized.

John Rhys, a forerunner to both Alcock and Morris, gives the following close interweavings of other titles with the term *dux bellorum*:

Welsh literature never calls Arthur a *gwledig* or prince but emperor, and it may be inferred that this historical position ... was that of one filling after the departure of the Romans, the office of *Comes Britanniae* or Count of Britain. ... The other military captains were the *Dux Britanniarum* ... and the *Comes Littoris Saxonici*. The successors of both these captains seem to have been called in Welsh *gwledigs* or princes. So Arthur's suggested position as *Comes Britanniae* would be in a sense superior to theirs, which harmonizes with his being called emperor and not *gwledig*. The Welsh have borrowed the Latin title of *imperator* "emperor" and made it into *amherawdyr*, later *ameraudur*, so it is not impossible that, when the Roman imperator ceased to have anything more to say to this country, the title was given to the highest officer in the island, namely the *Comes Britanniae*, and that in the words *Yr Amherawdyr Arthur* "the Emperor Arthur" we gave a remnant of our insular history.[16]

This, of course, illustrates the importance of the most common term used in literary tradition, "emperor."

John Morris also equates the Roman word *imperator* and the term emperor, pointing out that *imperator,* a common term throughout the centuries of Roman occupation, was still used after the Romans left. He stresses the uniqueness and peculiarity of the term as it describes Arthur:

Nowhere in Europe is the title emperor used of any ruler but an emperor of Rome before the time of Napoleon; it is confined to the emperors in Constantinople, and to the successors of Charlemagne in the west. But from the time of Arthur, it remained in the political vocabulary of the British Isle. ... One seventh-century Irish writer called an earlier high king of Ireland *Imperator*, and another used the same title of Oswald of Northumbria, calling him "emperor of Britain," not of the English; and in the eleventh century Brian Boru, the last great Irish king, himself asserted the same title. An Aremorican British writer of the ninth century called the Frank king an emperor, and British poets celebrated the emperor Arthur.[17]

In no uncertain terms, he emphatically underscores the importance of the title: Arthur is a leader of leaders; he is king of a country, not just the king of a small domain.

Throughout its tales, *The Mabinogion* uses the title "emperor." Maxen is called the "emperor of Rome," and according to Morris' translation, "This is the dream called the Dream of Maxen Wledig, emperor of Rome."[18] There is once more an equation of *wledig* and emperor, important in this instance because Maxen is a factual historical figure. Five of the eleven tales in *The Mabinogion* specifically include Arthur, and of the five, four of them refer to him continuously as emperor. "Culhwch and Olwen," which does not, has Culhwch refer to his first cousin Arthur as the chief Lord of the island. Maxen was undisputedly a Roman emperor in Britain, and in the early literature Arthur had also acquired this same prestigious title after the Roman withdrawal from the island.

Since all three figures are fused into one, titles for Ambrosius Aurelianus and Riothamus are also important. Ashe concurs with Rhys' "fruitful explanation" of the three Roman military titles retained by the British administration after the Romans left. He adds that when the legions left, the title *Dux Britanniarum* was in abeyance, but the other two persisted, and "Ambrosius Aurelianus may have exercised one of his few rights as king to appoint a *Comes Britanniarum* as Captain-General for the province."[19] Ashe is postulating an Arthur/Riothamus connection, but if an Ambrosius/Arthur/Riothamus connection is made instead, Ambrosius would not *appoint* a *Comes Britanniarum*, he would *be* that leader, fulfilling the dual role of king and military leader, a common practice during this era. In Gildas, when survivors rally to Ambrosius he is called *duce* (dux), the leader. Nennius adds to his titles, terming him *emrys*, *gwledig*, and *rex*.

As with the terms Riothamus and Vortimer, the most plausible explanation is that the name Arthur identifying the great and glorious king of Britain is not derived from either *Artorius* or *Arturus*, but instead is another epithet. This claim is based upon significant clues of what Arthur's true identity is rather than a lone entry suggesting a Lucius Artorius Castus. Some of these clues are provided by statements from several researchers and writers, namely E.K. Chambers, Geoffrey Ashe, and philologist Eilert Ekwall; more subtle clues come from Geoffrey of Monmouth and John Rhys. As suggested at the outset, Ambrosius Aurelianus is the only proper name provided in the triad, and once the term "Arthur" as an epithet is explained in the last section, the triadic chronology will fall into place.

Ambrosius as Riothamus

Chapter 10 of this text showed the excellent foundation which Ashe laid in equating Riothamus with Arthur, but he dismisses too easily the possibility that Ambrosius Aurelianus could be equated to Riothamus. He expresses the peculiarity that Riothamus is labeled as a Briton but never mentioned on the island, leading to the only logical conclusion that he *must* be equated with someone who *is* mentioned. As a researcher should, he considers other possibilities:

Riothamus could have been the title of another royal or prominent Briton. We have to try an elimination. The others who are mentioned are Vortigern, Vortimer, Ceredig, Uther, and (to keep the chief claimant to the last) Ambrosius Aurelianus. We must ask whether the King known as Riothamus could be identical with any of these instead of Arthur.[20]

After eliminating the first four, he writes this of the "chief claimant":

However, the actual equation Riothamus = Ambrosius has not carried conviction. A major obstacle is that Ambrosius is the only fifth-century Briton whom Gildas names or gives any particulars of, and Gildas does not call him a King. He speaks of him purely as a war leader, organizing the Britons for their counteroffensive. Nennius, in a passing phrase, does make him a King, with some sort of paramountcy among the "kings of the British Nation"; but this is legend. Elsewhere Nennius preserves his rank in its Welsh form, calling him Emrys *gwledig*, and those who had this "landholder" office were regional rulers only. Finally, even legend says nothing about Ambrosius's campaigning in Gaul.[21]

Each of these rejections can be approached individually to show that the Riothamus = Ambrosius equation does, in fact, carry conviction. First, rather than an obstacle, the fact that Gildas provides the name of Ambrosius Aurelianus is in itself highly significant. Of the five names Ashe eliminates, only two are proper names: Ceredig and Ambrosius Aurelianus. Ashe concedes that Ceredig is real, but eliminates him because of his "remoteness and unimportance," both of which are untrue. Ceredig, in his triplicate role as Cunedda's son, an interpreter, and finally as the West Saxon king is in the precise location at the precise time to be a primary figure in forging Briton and Saxon history in addition to being a major factor in Arthurian lore.

The earlier section on titles and epithets answers the charge that Gildas does not call Ambrosius Aurelianus a King but refers to him as a war leader. Several of the Gildean manuscripts refer to Ambrosius as "Come,"[22] and a large number of researchers comment on that title. Alcock lists "Come" as one of the two high-ranking officers, one the Comes Britanniarum; John Rhys equates the Comes Britanniae (Count of Britain) with the Welsh term "gwledig" and further suggests that the Comes Littoris Saxonici were succeeded by Welsh gwledigs or princes; Rhys further suggests that a Comes Britanniae would in a sense harmonize with the term "emperor"; even Ashe himself in *King Arthur's Avalon* calls Ambrosius a king who may have exercised his right and appointed Arthur as Comes Britanniarum; and Morris takes "wearing the purple" as meaning Ambrosius' father was an emperor, since in bonafide Roman terms that is how it applies to the Roman emperors.

The third reason Ashe gives for rejecting Ambrosius as Riothamus is because even though Nennius refers to Ambrosius as king and gwledig, Nennius is legend and gwledig is a landholder office for regional rulers only. However, the word legend is an imprecise term for the *Historia*. Although there are some segments such as "The Wonders of Britain" which could be labeled as legendary, and although by definition "legend" implies the inclusion of historical data, the purpose of the *Historia* is different from a literary work such as "The Dream of Rhonabwy." It is unclear, too, why Ashe minimizes the epithets "king"and "king among all the kings of the British nation," particularly since all except two of the *Historia* manuscripts use those expressions, and Manuscript *a* uses the the word *magnus*, the "great king."

Finally, Ashe lists as his last reason for passing over Ambrosius as the equivalent of Riothamus that even in legend Ambrosius does not make a Gallic appearance. It is almost ludicrous that he say this, since he is using Monmouth's work as the base for his theory, and *The History of the Kings of Britain* at best must be termed a pseudo-history. Monmouth relates Ambrosius' warlike deeds in Gaul and in Brittany in the early (and the word "early" should be emphasized) part of his career. And there should be no doubt that Ambrosius Aurelianus is equated with Aurelius Ambrosius because Monmouth himself writes that Gildas praises Ambrosius' victory. Gildas does not use the epithet Riothamus for the same reason he does not use the epithet Arthur: the proper name for these two is Ambrosius Aurelianus, and Gildas knew the High King by his proper name.

A statement by Leslie Alcock about Ambrosius' role in British history after Vortigern's reign also sets Ashe on the wrong path of rejecting Ambrosius as Riothamus. Alcock's actual comment was this:

> So far as Gildas' phraseology allows us to infer anything about Ambrosius, we may cast him in a similar role, as supreme commander of the Britons under the *superbus tyrannus*.[23]

As it stands, this statement is already misleading because the "superbus tyrannus" in Gildas is interpreted as Vortigern, and from the onset in Nennius, Vortigern is in constant fear of Ambrosius, evidenced by the king's flight from Ambrosius as a young boy. Ambrosius is Vortigern's enemy and would therefore never be in a role of supreme commander under King Vortigern.

Ashe then compounds the problem:

> Probably Alcock's view is correct. Ambrosius was a general responsible to a High King, Vortigern's successor; in other words, to Riothamus — whoever he was.[24]

He assigns Ambrosius as a supreme commander under Vortigern's successor, and names that successor as Riothamus. Gildas' phraseology does at times allow a latitude of interpretation, but one of the certainties of what he writes is that *there was no intervening successor* between *the superbus tyrannus* (i.e. Vortigern) and Ambrosius Aurelianus. The wretched survivors turn to Ambrosius immediately after Vortigern's deposal, and that can mean only one thing: Ambrosius Aurelianus is Vortigern's successor not as the supreme commander, but as High King. Ambrosius as Riothamus, then, cannot be dismissed. The equation leads to Leon Fleuriot's belief that the great Briton leader of the fifth century whose title was Riothamus was in actuality Ambrosius, whose exploits in turn went into the making of the Arthurian legend.

Surprisingly, Geoffrey Ashe, who is pursuing the theory that Riothamus is Arthur, is the one who points to Fleuriot's contention that Riothamus is Ambrosius. Of Fleuriot, Ashe writes:

> ... the Britons had a great leader in the third quarter of the fifth century, whose title was Riothamus, and whose exploits went into the making of the Arthur of legend. He [Fleuriot] believes, however, that the ruler was Ambrosius, and his deeds were credited later to somebody else named Arthur.[25]

Fleuriot points to proof by citing a version of a Nennius manuscript dated 1072 which says that Ambrosius was in Brittany. This seemingly insignificant reference places Ambrosius Aurelianus in Brittany where Riothamus is during this same time period. In addition, it gives the bonus of pointing to an *Ambrosian* connection in Britanny rather than an Arthurian one, whether Monmouth missed the connection or chose to ignore it.

Ambrosius, therefore, is the important anchor for the triad. After the Roman withdrawal from Britain, Ambrosius' father, a product of Roman aristocracy, remained on the island and continued to have direct, first-generation ties with Rome. As continuously suggested,

> From the late fourth century on, the word "king," rex, was used colloquially of emperors, though never officially; and the letter of Honorius legitimized emperors who ruled in Britain alone. One of them is known. The parents of Ambrosius Aurelianus, who headed the resistance of the 460's had "worn the purple"; the words mean that his father was emperor, for no subject "wore the purple."[26]

When Ambrosius succeeded to the kingdom after Vortigern's reign, he would have retained the prestigious carry-over from his parents. Because Rome was having difficulties protecting its frontiers from barbarians in Europe, the Romans (specifically Anthemius) negotiated a pact during these desperate times with Ambrosius, the successful Briton king, who was a bastion of hope. Rome made alliances with those powerful families who had allegiance to Rome, and in return, once the Empire was secured on the continent, aid would again be forthcoming on the island. The Briton king from across the Ocean would have been an epic hero in the true sense of the word.

Riothamus as Arthur

Two other sources which Ashe uses are noteworthy. One is Sidonius and the other is Jordanes, whom Ashe writes are "the bedrock proofs of [Riothamus'] existence referring to [Arthur] by that title or honorific."[27] Neither scribe, however, uses the name Arthur, but they write of Riothamus, a title which Ashe theorizes is an epithet for Arthur. Ashe is correct in his connection, but to be more accurate, he should have added the extension that Arthur is also a title or honorific for Ambrosius Aurelianus.

Geoffrey Ashe devoted his entire book, the *Discovery of King Arthur*, to the postulation that Arthur is Riothamus. From his first premise he does a radical reversal from articles published in *The Quest for Arthur's Britain*. Instead of viewing Geoffrey of Monmouth as a fanciful, untrustworthy, unreliable historical source, he suggests another closer look with a different slant to see if *The History of the Kings of Britain* had "realities behind it,"[28] rather than rejecting the book because of preconceived notions of what Geoffrey of Monmouth had to offer.

Despite knowing Monmouth's serious flaws in chronology of the early fifth century, he had the insight to perceive Monmouth in an innovative way, which he termed lateral thinking. Rather than view Monmouth with heavy misgivings, he construed the inverse proposition that on the whole, Monmouth was historically accurate.[29] By daring to tread on hallowed ground protected by traditionalists, Ashe encouraged new avenues for exploration.

The Discovery of King Arthur contains logical proposals supporting his hypothesis that Riothamus is Arthur. However, it has one major shortcoming with forks branching off the main stem. The main flaw is that it ignores all the ramifications of chronology. Two sources Ashe cites are a William of 1019[30] who puts Arthur in the latter half of the fifth century immediately after the Saxon Revolt, and Jacques de Guise, a scribe who also places Arthur in the mid–fifth century during the reign of Emperor Leo and Ægidius,[31] fighting Huns, the Goths, and the Vandals in the area of Hainaut. An intriguing divergence here is that de Guise gives the name of Arthur for events that are attributable to Riothamus during this time span, especially important because de Guise is not motivated to prove Arthur in a certain context, but is instead focusing on the history of Hainaut. Even if these sources are used as substantiation, however, Geoffrey of Monmouth still cannot be accepted unconditionally at the expense of the *Annales Cambriae*, the *Historia Brittonum*, the *De Excidio*, the *Ecclesiastical History*, and the tales in *The Mabinogion*.

By offsetting the chronology for Arthur in the sixth and seventh decades of the *fifth* century rather than the dates for Arthur as suggested by the *AC* in the second and third decades of the *sixth* century, one of the inconsistencies Ashe overlooks seems obvious: in actuality he is equating Ambrosius with Riothamus, since all of those dates belong to the Ambrosian era, yet for some disconcerting reason, he just elides Ambrosius, probably because he was focused too intently on proving the Arthur/Riothamus theory.

Ashe approaches the Aurelius Ambrosius sequence in Monmouth this way:

> And when [the chroniclers] speak of Arthur they could all be referring to our High King [not Ambrosius], with a reign running from about 454 to 470. The *Anglo-Saxon Chronicle* has Vortigern still living in 455, but this is his last appearance.[32]

The crucial affirmation Ashe makes here is that no intervening leaders arise between Vortigern and Arthur; that is, the kingship passes directly from Vortigern to Arthur. This implies that a leader like Ambrosius Aurelianus (not Monmouth's Aurelius Ambrosius) must be erased from the histories of Gildas and Nennius. On the contrary, however, because Ambrosius Aurelianus is an indispensable link between the decay of Roman Britain and the rise of a Briton empire, this means that Ashe should have made one further assertion that Riothamus/Arthur must be equated with Ambrosius Aurelianus, and the kingdom passes from Vortigern directly to Arthur Ambrosius.

Morris, discussing a fragmented story about a second Budic as ruler of Quimper,[33] hints indirectly of a Riothamus-Ambrosius connection, but offers no definitive proof. He writes that

> Riothamus, leader of the second migration, was regarded as the founder of the dynasties of eastern Domnonie, and the later rulers of Quimper also claimed descent from his "son" Daniel Dremrud, who left Gaul to become "king of the Alamanni."[34]

A historical link is thus made between Riothamus and one of the later rulers of Quimper, that is, Budic. That does not seem particularly surprising, but Geoffrey of Monmouth makes the same connection. No one else in the surveyed literature even mentions Budic. Fletcher is the only one who (again) suggests that Monmouth must have had another source. It falls into the realm of impossibility that Monmouth just happened to pick randomly the name of Budic to associate with Arthur in that particular time frame.

Other curiosities arise in relation to Hoel, whom Monmouth lists as Budic's son, a detail which does not appear in the histories. Morris equates Hoel (Howel) with Hueil, son of Caw and Gildas' brother, but tradition denies this. Caw is entrenched in Scotland and Scottish lore but is not linked with Quimper or Brittany. In Culhwch's invocation,[35] a great many of Caw's sons (including Hueil whose name appears twice) are listed, but there is no indication that this son goes by another name. Hueil's name is given only in the Culhwch tale, but Howel's name appears in three of the succeeding tales, first in the list of Arthur's advisors in the Rhonabwy tale, then in the Peredur episode, and last in "Gereint and Enid." In each instance he is identified as "Howel son of Emhyr of Brittany." Brittany ties him to Quimper, and his father's epithet of Emhyr ties him to Wales. In Monmouth Howel appears in a major role as Arthur's ally. Monmouth, then, gives this view in literary tradition, and Gregory of Tours and the annals of early Welsh genealogical tracts verify it historically.

Arthur as Ambrosius Aurelianus

Titles given in the introductory segment of this chapter are important in signifying Arthur's position, but they are not the major emphasis for this chapter. The more important designation in this chapter is "epithet," to draw attention to the term "Arthur" as a descriptive word replacing a proper name. The term "anonym" as it applies to Arthur's name might also work; the emphasis here would be on Arthur's epithet referring to an anonymous person; that is, it explains that "Arthur" is not a proper name, but instead a substitute for that individual, and the anonym, which in Arthur's case has been hidden for so long, must be revealed as a known historical personage.

Chambers, in his chapter on "The Historicity of Arthur," explains how modern writers construct "confident pedigrees for Arthur," but he does not strongly support those proposals because they are based mainly on Geoffrey of Monmouth or at best upon medieval Welsh attempts to reconcile Geoffrey with native genealogies. He continues:

> We do not even know what were [Arthur's] relations to Ambrosius Aurelianus, who is so important in Gildas, and about whom Nennius is so far from explicit. I have sometimes thought that they might be doublets of the same personality, reaching Nennius through two name-forms of which one had undergone scribal corruption from Aurelianus into Arthur. But on the whole, this does not seem very probable.[36]

Unfortunately, in the last sentence he backs away from an impressive, credible postulation. It would have been very interesting if he had followed through to substantiate his intuitive insight that Arthur and Ambrosius were doublets. It is also surprising that no one picked up on his speculation to conduct a serious, in-depth investigation.

Chambers' mention of Geoffrey of Monmouth is interesting because something in Monmouth's own writing leads in this exact direction. At one point in the "Arthur of Britain" section of his *History*, Monmouth's writing becomes confusing in regard to who is who. In order to retain the context as much as possible, the following passage is given as Monmouth reported, with the pertinent segment italicized. He writes that

> Arthur accepted the advice of his retainers and withdrew into the town of London. There they convened the bishops and the clergy of the entire realm and asked their suggestion as to what it would be best and safest for him to do, in the face of this invasion of pagans. Eventually a common policy was agreed upon and messengers were dispatched to King Hoel in Brittany to explain to him the disaster which had befallen Great Britain. *This Hoel was the son of Arthur's sister; and his father was Budicius, the King of the Armorican Britons.*[37]

Only a few pages earlier, however, on page 209 there is a contradiction that Arthur's sister Anna had been given by their father, King Uther, to Loth of Lodonesia.[38] A later passage states that she has two sons, Gawain and Mordred, by Loth but at that point she is listed as Ambrosius' sister.[39] Hence Monmouth conveys that Anna is sister to two different men, and additionally is married to two different kings; the latter paradox is unsolvable unless she is considered bigamous, divorced, or widowed and remarried. She would nonetheless have three sons, Hoel, Gawain, and Mordred. Lewis Thorpe, the translator of this particular edition, corrects the passage so that it reads, "For Arthur's sister" we must read "the sister of Aurelius Ambrosius."[40] The newly coined name of Riardd Ambrosius makes part of the confusion a moot point: it makes no difference if Anna is sister to Arthur or Ambrosius.

This slip, if it is such, on Monmouth's part is the interesting segment. Monmouth also refers to Hoel as Arthur's nephew rather than his cousin. This dual error invites speculation that Geoffrey indeed might have had a mysterious ancient book. If so, did it equate Arthur and Ambrosius, or perhaps at least imply it? Geoffrey might have either misunderstood the connection between Arthur and Ambrosius, or he might have understood the connection and rejected it because of overwhelming disapproval and wrath he would incur from all Britons if he were to destroy their national epic hero, their British savior and demigod, Arthur, in favor of Ambrosius Aurelianus, who was of Roman heritage rather than Briton. The rest of the puzzle is outside the realm of this inquiry.

However, the references to Budicius and his son Hoel remain important. Fletcher also hints at this ancient book in reference to the episode about Hoel. He writes that Monmouth had a source outside the histories of Gildas and Nennius but does not suggest whether the source is of historical or pseudo-historical tradition, nor does he indicate outright that it is the ancient book. He is sure, however, that Monmouth owes something to that material because of "the mention of Budicius of Britanny, to whom Aurelius and Uther are sent."[41] The connection is between Hoel and Aurelius, *not* between Hoel and Arthur, an implication that Geoffrey had access to some unknown source. Viewing the character as Riardd Ambrosius resolves the issue, and Monmouth's further implication supports the contention that discord existed between Ambrosius Aurelianus and Vitalinus and that, Vitalinus sent the young Emrys to Budicius of Brittany to protect the rightful inheritor of the throne.

Budicius, whom Monmouth connects to Arthur, appears as two Budics in Morris' *The Age of Arthur*. Akin to the name provided by Monmouth, Morris verifies a King Budic of Armorica through a "story preserved only in disjointed morsels," but he pieces together this information:

> The brothers Budic and Maxentius, heirs to the British kingdom of Quimper in south-western Brittany, are said [by Gregory of Tours] to have returned from abroad at the beginning of the sixth century, and to have recovered their patrimony from a ruler named Marcellus. ...
> The quite independent traditions of south-east Wales connect the dynasty of Brittany with [Dementia]. ... [A]fter killing Marcellus, the brothers divided the kingdom of Quimper, Maxentius expelled Budic and seized his portion of the kingdom, and Theodoric, commanding Agricola's Dementian fleet, restored Budic.[42]

Surprisingly, Ashe does not pick up on Morris' "tradition anchored to reality," although he was using Monmouth as a touchstone to verify the connection between Arthur and Riothamus. Chambers directly asserts that Ambrosius and Arthur are the same individual, and Fleuriot also claims that Riothamus and Ambrosius are the same individual, even suggesting that Arthur was given the identity of both. All of these contentions strung together denote that Ambrosius is Riothamus, and Riothamus is Arthur, supporting Ashe's two sides of the triangular hypothesis given here.

Arthur

Other researchers offer little information about the term "Arthur" being an epithet or anonym. John Rhys traces the word Arthur to "Airem" with the genitive forms of "Ariomanos" or "Airomonos," which in Gaulish is a man's name, "Ariomanus." Nothing more emerges other than an anagrammatical arrangement of Ariomanus in Rhys, Aurelianus in Gildas, and Aurelius in Monmouth. Because Rhys was attempting to bind a Brythonic god named Artor (genitive of Artoros) with Arthur and thus yield a familiar form of Arthur in Welsh, his search goes through an impressive philological maze from agricultural possibilities to orator, to bard, to friend or companion, but leads to nothing substantial.[43]

Anagrammatical arrangements direct one to Ashe's postulation that Riothamus = Arthur and his insertion of Utherpendragon into a bonafide historical chronology. By doing so, Ashe gives Monmouth's total Arthurian chronology credence, although, by his own admission, "Geoffrey's chronology seldom hangs together."[44] He writes that "Uther[pendragon] is neither remote nor unimportant, but he is not real,"[45] but still he works from a detailed outline of Monmouth[46] that shows a mixture of historical data and literary fiction. Ashe suggests the possibility that "[t]he Welsh *uthr* means 'terrible' and the phrase 'Arthur the terrible' could have been misconstrued as 'Arthur son of Uthr.'"[47] He does not, however, follow through on the conjecture. Utherpendragon, then, is one of Monmouth's inventions, perhaps tied to Rhys' Uthr Ben of mythology, perhaps an etymological slip from Uthr meaning terrible, or perhaps a distorted anagram of Arthur. Regardless, this figure is not an authentic person. Eliminating him from a factual chronology eliminates the chaff, and what remains are the three names recurring in history: Ambrosius Aurelianus, Riothamus, and Arthur, with Utherpendragon as yet another epithet.

With Uther eliminated from the Monmouth chronology, and with Aurelius Ambrosius in the Monmouth saga killed after ruling only two years, there would be a gap left between Aurelius Ambrosius' short reign and Arthur, a span of 16 years if Alberic's dating is used. Alberic, a Cistercian monk, attempted to chronicle Arthur's era by coordinating French information with Geoffrey of Monmouth. According to Ashe, Alberic lists Arthur's reign as beginning in 459 and running for 16 years until 475.[48] This is surprisingly close to the era of Riothamus, with Riothamus' name arising around 459–60 and dropping from the histories around 470. If Riothamus fills the gap in Alberic's calibration, this leads properly to a chronology showing no successor between Arthur and Vortigern.

Fletcher also lists all of the variations for the term "Arthur," including Arthoure, Arthure, Arthurus, Arturus, Artus, and, from the Spanish annales, Zitus, but he does nothing more than relate the theories from some of the earlier writers such as Rhys. Obviously, there are a great many possibilities other than the name Arthur being a proper name derived from a Latin root of Artorius, or Arthur as a namesake of Lucius Artorius Castus.

Lindsay makes a possible connection between Arthur and the Celtic artos, meaning "bear." Graham Phillips and Martin Keatman, in their text first published in 1992, build their case of Arthur on this interpretation, giving Arthur a tribal title of "Bear," by using not only "the Brythonic word *Arth*, but also the Latin word for bear, Ursus. His original title may therefore have been Arthursus later being shortened to Arthur."[49]

This is distinctively different from what Rhys was alluding to when he referred to Artos as a mythological god, although the spellings for the mythical god and the Welsh derivative are the same, with the difference being a common versus a proper noun.[50] No researcher has proposed the possibility of the god Artos as a bear symbol. Viewing the word Arthur as an epithet, however, opens up other interpretations, with the root artos meaning bear as only one possibility.

Ekwall suggests a different interpretation for the affix arth- which can explain the evolution to the name Arthur, though he does it very tersely, with just enough cryptic tinge to offer an intriguing clue. In citing the etymology for Arthuret, Cumberland, he gives this information: "...has been identified with Ard eryd in the Chron. of the Picts and Scots. If that is right, the first el[ement] is identical with Welsh ardd 'height' or early Welsh Arth 'high.'"[51]

Anderson and Anderson also shed some light on ardd- as an affix. In doing an analysis of Adomnan's manuscript on the life of Saint Columba, they explain the strange mixture of Old Irish stems, compounds and spellings with Latin affixes, a linguistic technique which was common at that time and applies to Arthurian material:

> The exact form of Irish words in Adomnan's time is important for the history of the Gaelic language. When he conceals that form by latinizing Irish names, it is necessary to reconstruct the Old-Irish from the Latin form; ... [h]is practice was to produce a Latin noun by adding a Latin case-ending (such as -us, -a) to an Irish noun, and rarely a Latin adjective by adding a Latin case-ending to an Irish adjective. ... When he wished to produce a Latin adjective from an Irish noun, he did so by adding to the Irish noun the Latin adjectival endings -icus, -ica, or -ensis.
> ... When Adomnan turned a masculine noun of this declension into Latin, his practice was to add the Latin nominative ending -us to the nominative singular, and to inflect the word as a noun of the Latin second declension.
> ... The neuter substantive ardd ["height"] receives the Irish plural inflection of a neuter O-stem ... genitive art.[52]

As in Welsh there is an Irish adjective "ardd" — the adjectival form meaning "high" — conjoining the Latin neuter substantive, plus the genitive "art." What this translates to when applied is that if "ardd" or "arth" as a masculine noun of this declension is turned into Latin, the practice would be to add the Latin nominative ending of "-us" which would give the word "arddus " (in which the "double d" would be pronounced as a "th-") or "arthus."

Sir Ifor Williams also clarifies this postulation. In discussing the name Maelgwn as it appears in the *Historia Brittonum*, he writes

> [Nennius] refers to Maelgwn Gwynedd at the beginning of the paragraph as Mailcunus, but the -us need not be taken seriously: it is the Latin ending tacked on to a Welsh name to give it dignity.[53]

The process by which Welsh genitives became Welsh epithets is the same as with Welsh names acquiring a -us suffix. Earlier, Sir Ifor explains that

> The significance of this fact has not been fully realised. It proves that the old British declension system had gone to pieces in Wales long before 540, or whatever date we ascribe to Gildas. British grammar must have been in a very bad way when a king's name was only known in the genitive case![54]

This means, therefore, that "arthus" or "arddus" could have been considered proper noun forms of Arthus/Arddus, disconnected from the proper name Artorius, taken directly from Latin, with which they are confused. As a Welsh genitive epithet, "arth" evolved into "arthus" as a genitive epithet with a Latin suffix to increase its stature. From there it became a genitive used in a nominative position, giving birth to the *cognomen* "Arthus," which became confused with Artorius and its translation Arthur. Sir Ifor summarizes his proposition of Latin absorption into the Welsh language:

> [In any pedigree] the first name is in the nominative; every other name is in the genitive, whether you talk in Latin, Celtic, Old Irish or Old Welsh. In the course of centuries these genitives would tend to become fixed. People forgot that they were genitives. ... The old nominatives became obsolete, or survived here and there as doublets.[55]

The progressive development would hence be arth, arthus, Arthus, and Arthur as an epithet for an unnamed person, namely Ambrosius Aurelianus. This is particularly interesting because so many sources list Arthur with a Welsh descendancy rather than just a Roman one.

It is not imperative, therefore, to accept Artos, or Arturius, or Lucius Artorius Castus as roots for Arthur's name, but instead, the list of Arthur's epithets can be extended to a different title/title combination. "Rex Arthur" as title/name is simple in its translation of "the king Arthur," but on a recondite level, it could be "rex arth" or "rex ardd" or "rex arthu" as a title/title arrangement translating to "high king," a term which is already quite frequently used to refer to Arthur, a mixture of Roman and Welsh. Affixing these epithets to the only proper name provided by the early Briton manuscripts, Ambrosius Aurelianus, would result in the title/title/name of "rex arthus Ambrosius Aurelianus," or the "high king Ambrosius." This is what led to the coining of the term "Riardd," also translating to "high king."

THE LONGEVITY OF ARTHUR

With the historical data examined, the remainder of the Arthurian puzzle must be complemented with literary tradition and contemporary scholarship (a much more subjective process) to provide the details not supplied by the ancient manuscripts. The historical manuscripts contain exaggerations, but literary material requires a more wary eye. With a blend of caution and scientific inquiry, however, the combined information allows the more comprehensive picture of events, persons, or geography to emerge.

One of the key concepts from literary tradition that must be addressed is Arthur's life-span. To do this, only two dates are needed, a birth-year and a death-year. His death-year was calculated earlier through historical sources, beginning with the *AC*. Clues were traced through several manuscripts, and relying on contemporary events, Arthur's final passing from human activity at the Battle of Camlann was ascertained as 518, the 19-year lunar adjustment subtracted from what was provided in the *Annales* for the year 537.

Now a birth-year for Arthur must be calibrated, first as a single individual and then as part of the Riardd Ambrosius triad. Geoffrey of Monmouth supplies information about Arthur's conception but gives no clues of chronology. Of the names he uses — Merlin, Gorlois, Utherpendragon, and Ygerna — only Merlin appears in the histories, in the *Annales Cambriae* under entry 573, which is outside the realm of Arthur's era. There have been other synonyms attached to his name, but the only other reference of note is Monmouth's epithetic attachment of Ambrosius Merlinus to Ambrosius Aurelianus.

Monmouth does, though, give one clue of Arthur's age at his coronation:

> He [Dubricius] called the other bishops to him and bestowed the crown of the kingdom upon Arthur. Arthur was a young man only fifteen years old; but he was of outstanding courage and generosity, and his inborn goodness gave him such grace that he was loved by almost all the people.[56]

Writers who succeeded Monmouth and used his work as a base have echoed this passage. Wace, whose writing appeared almost 20 years after Monmouth's, wrote that "Arthur at the time of his coronation was a damoiseau of some fifteen years, but tall and strong for his age."[57] Together, these two pseudo-histories (with Wace of course drawing upon Monmouth as his principal source) function as the forerunners for the majority of details that follow in the romances. Arthur's age at his coronation does stimulate a search on the importance of this date, but neither writer helps solve the mystery of Arthur's birth-year.

Layamon,[58] however, who flourished shortly after Wace, adds what turns out to be the only clue about Arthur's birth.

As soon as [Arthur] came on earth fays took him.
They enchanted the child with magic right strong:
They gave him the might to be the best of all knights;
They gave him another thing, that he should be a mighty king;
They gave him a third — his death would be long deferred.[59]

The first three lines (which give a tinge of Druidism) seem more applicable to Ambrosius Aurelianus as the child prodigy Emrys in the *Historia*. The fourth could apply to either Ambrosius or Arthur, but the fifth gives a covert hint about Arthur. Layamon does not list the actual number of years for Arthur, but there is finally a clue that Arthur's lifespan was extraordinarily long, something incorporated in the later romances.

In the 1250s, an anonymous interpolator of Malmsbury's *De Antiquitate* is cited by J. Armitage Robinson:

Arthur, in the year of our Lord's Incarnation 542, was wounded fatally by Modred in Cornwall, near the river Camba; and thence he was carried for the healing of his wounds to the island of Avallon; and there he died in the summer, about Pentecost, being well nigh a hundred years old or thereabout.[60]

The first line supplies the date 542 for Arthur's death, which is the same one used by Monmouth; the Mordred, Cornwall, and Camba material also come from Monmouth. The last segment perhaps echoes Layamon, but is more specific. Arthur's death is long deferred; he was almost a centigenarian when he sailed away to the Isle of Avalon and hence exempt from the "reasonable age" concept applied to other prominent figures associated with the Arthurian quest.

Literary tradition, then, relates two important things, one of which is Arthur's age at his coronation. This, of course, is applicable whether Arthur is accepted as an individual or as part of the triad postulated in this text. As a separate entity Arthur is commonly assigned a floruit, as reflected by John Morris, of 475 to 505 and a lifespan from 460 to 520. If he became king at age 15, then he succeeded to the throne in approximately 475. It has already been shown that there were no successors between Vortigern and Ambrosius Aurelianus, which means that Ambrosius could possibly have ruled from approximately 461 (after the massacre of Vortigern's Council) to 475. All of the following would still be valid for Arthur as a single individual:

1. He was born in 460 and his father could have been Ambrosius Aurelianus, age 38 at his birth;
2. he was coronated in 475 when his father passed away, at age 53;
3. he was victorious at the Battle of Badon in 497 at age 35;
4. he died at the Battle of Camlann in 518 at age 58.

Considering Arthur as a separate individual, however, negates almost all of literary tradition, the contents which, of course, could be viewed as make-believe anyway. Based on the kernels of truth embedded in any literary tradition, however, it seems rash to totally reject any historical relevance which can be gleaned from it as a valid source. Viewing Arthur as part of a triad adds, in addition to those items listed above, other pieces of information to fill in the void. From literary sources, Arthur as a triadic figure explains Arthur's

1. Gallic warfare involving Leo, Anthemius, Ægidius, and Euric, all of whom are prior to Arthur's reign as a separate individual;
2. rise to Culture Hero/legendary status because of his seeming invincibility; and
3. long-deferred death, that is, extended lifespan.

If justifications of statements from tradition can be provided on Arthur's lifespan or his Gallic warfare, then the literature of the era fulfills its secondary function, since its base is reality. If there is no authentic base, then essentially there is still nothing lost, though nothing new is gained either. Without concern yet about specific years and dates, and without synchronizing the dates in tradition with those in the reality of history, it is possible to extrapolate the possibilities but postpone acceptance or rejection. One curiosity concerns the coronation of Arthur in Monmouth and Wace. If these references can be accepted as based in historical accuracy, is there any date within Arthur's time-span that would offer a clue when Arthur was chosen as king? Combined with what this text has already established about Arthur being an epithet for Ambrosius Aurelianus, this means that Ambrosius' history must also be considered.

THE REGENERATION MOTIF

Another notion merged with the question of Arthur's longevity is the concept of the regeneration motif. John Rhys asks, "How then did Arthur become famous above [others] and how came he to be the subject of so much story and romance?" then answering, "Besides a historic Arthur there was a Brythonic divinity named Arthur."[61] By endowing Arthur with these mythological beginnings, Rhys retarded the exploration of other avenues of Arthur's misty origin. Based upon the belief that Arthur evolved from mythology, there is the automatic assumption that the regeneration motif ties in to those possible assertions, leading to the idea that regeneration, rebirth, and resurrection belong in the nebulous realm of religious doctrine. Assigning a religious context to a concept unfortunately puts that concept beyond the normal capabilities of inquiries, not really in the mortal domain, but something which must be accepted spiritually.

Putting all the spiritual and mythological ramifications aside, however, modern as well as folk and bardic tales still carry an inherent and pervading ascription that Arthur is not dead or at least a belief that, if he is dead, he will be resurrected to rule Britain and drive its enemies from the land. The term "death" is not applied to Arthur; some accounts indicate he has been summoned from human activity but will again return in human form; other accounts relate that he is sleeping in the deep recesses of a hill, perhaps Camelot, biding his time until his call to return; still others tell the tale that, though severely wounded, he sailed to Avallon to be cured so that he might one day return. The figure of Arthur, his passing, the regeneration motif, and the mystique of where he goes all lead to vague connections with the Otherworld.

Wace's writing offers an example of the shroud of mystery cloaking Arthur's death:

> He is yet in Avalon, awaited of the Britons; for as they say and deem he will return from whence he went and live again. Master Wace, the writer of this book, cannot add more to this matter of his end than was spoken by Merlin the prophet. Merlin said of Arthur — if I read aright — that his end should be hidden in doubtfulness.[62]

But for Arthur there are two other explanations that manifest themselves when the chronology merges factual data and literary tradition. For the figure of Arthur, that means the explanation for the regeneration motif must shift its emphasis. As Ambrosius, Arthur could have perpetrated the regeneration motif invented by later generations because of his disappearance upon Vitalinus' insistence when he goes to Britanny but resurfaces again later to take the kingship from Vortigern. This absence and subsequent reappearance could be construed as a rebirth.

A second explanation is offered by Arthur/Ambrosius as Riothamus. Ambrosius Aurelianus is a hero in the true sense of the word, not a god nor even a demigod who could claim either a goddess as a mother or a god as a father. Gildas tethers Aurelianus to earth and gives him earthly parents. Later, in the "Tale of Emrys" there are hints or overtones of an immaculate conception or an incubus for a father. But even in the *Historia* passage, when Vortigern asks Ambrosius from what family he comes, the boy replies that his father is one of the consuls of the Roman people. Ambrosius' parents are mortal, and they die in the conflicts with the barbarians. If Ambrosius was mortal, the belief which transcended his invincibility might easily have come from the tales of an era just prior to Gildas' time. There were people who knew that Ambrosius Aurelianus was the same hero known on the continent as Riothamus, and later known on the island of Britain after his return from the wars on the continent as Arthur. Riothamus suffers a stunning defeat at the hands of Euric the Visigoth, after which Riothamus retreats into Burgundy and disappears from history.

Yet there is no verification of Riothamus' death. If this Riothamus resurfaced in southern Britain with the remnants of his troops and rallied new support, he could regenerate once more as High King who continues on from the mid-470s until his "death" in 518. Because Ambrosius had been "reborn" as Riothamus, and Riothamus had been "reborn" as Arthur, then that would lead to the belief that Arthur himself could be resurrected once again after his defeat in the Battle of Camlann in 518. Riardd Ambrosius, then, carries on the tradition that when his country beckons to him in a time of need, he will rise once again. These heroics of a savior with supernatural powers take place in a mortal realm, outside religion or mythology. Riardd Ambrosius survived the *Adventi* of the Saxons and the Saxon revolt, the Saxon massacre of the Council, the battles in Brittany and Gaul; he survived the Battle of Badon on his return to his native soil, and he managed to keep peace for the next two decades. All of this reinforces the merging of Ambrosius Aurelianus, Riothamus, and Arthur; the movement from one title to another is itself significant of regeneration and rebirth. In this light, Riardd Ambrosius is elevated beyond heroic heights to divine and supernatural stature.

This is the process by which Culture Heroes are created. The hope of another resurrection lingers on, and in the romances Arthur's "summons from this life" suggests not Arthur's death but a respite until Britain finds urgent need for a mighty king who will arise from his sleep and vanquish the enemy. Cerdic inherits the kingdom of the West Saxons, and Riardd Ambrosius enters the mystical realm not only of resurrection, but of legendary Ascension; since he had in a sense risen from the dead at least twice before, he will rise again.

CERDIC, ARTHUR'S ADVERSARY

Because the *ASC* and its Genealogical Preface are not considered works of fiction, the distinction between "Welsh" and "Britons" must be critically noted. Upon checking Whitelock's translations, none of the manuscripts — A, B, C, D, E, F, or G — make any differentiation between the two terms although manuscript E, like manuscript Ā, consistently uses the term "Welsh" in its entries rather than "Briton." In the entries 456 through 556, Whitelock uses the term "Briton" 17 times, when "Welsh" should have been used seven times. Specifically, in entries for 465, 473, 477, 485, 495, and 508 the term should be "Welsh." This is crucial because it distinguishes between two widely separated geographic regions. Although many of the specific geographic names provided by the *Chronicle* cannot be pinpointed, it is a safe deduction that if a geographic name is used in an entry with the term "Welsh," then it is in Welsh territory or the borders of the midlands, whereas if used in an entry with "Briton," it is near the southern coast.

This generalization is borne out by several known specifics. In entry 491, Andredesceaster is accepted as the Roman Anderida, near Pevensey, and following the logic of the generalization, because Andredesceaster occurs in an entry with the word Briton, then it is along the southern coast; Pevensey is on the southeastern coast near Eastbourne. In entry 456, Britons are driven from Kent; hence Kent is on the southern coast. As a contrast, in entry 465 Hengist fights the Welsh, which means Wippedesfleot is in Wales or the borders of the midlands. Entry 477 also supports the generalization. In addition to the word "Welsh" being used in manuscripts Ā and E, the entry gives other clues; Cym- in Cymen and Cymenesora is an affix meaning Welsh, exemplified by Cumberland (land of the Welsh), Cymry (Welsh), and Cymru (Welshman). There are two pairs of exceptions, 495/514 and 508/527, which seem to be doublets, each separated by a 19-year lunar difference. Yet even so, Cerdicesora signifies a location in Wales, while Cerdicesford signifies the southern coast up Southampton Water; not even Plummer or Rhys try to explain Cerdicesleag.

Material about Cerdic must also be accepted at face value. According to the *Chronicle* he lands at Cerdicesora, fights the Welsh on the same day, and 24 years later succeeds to the kingdom of the West Saxons. According to the Genealogical Preface he lands at Cerdicesora and six years later he conquers the kingdom of the West Saxons. It is natural to assume, too, that progressive movements of the Saxons initiated in the *east* (in the Thames Valley and in Kent), along the *southern* coast and eventually to Southampton Water, the *western* part of the southern coast, thus giving rise to the generic label of the East, the South, and the West Saxons. Once those terms and that pattern become engrained in the thought processes, the malaise of "mind-set" paralyzes the brain, setting up shields which are almost impenetrable to protect the patterns which are almost indestructible.

The traditional pattern is expressed by Alcock in several different ways: "In 495, according to the *Anglo-Saxon Chronicle*, two ealdormen ('chieftains'), Cerdic and his son Cynric, came to Britain with five ships and landed apparently on the shore of Southampton Water"[63]; "... the Battle of Badon is likely to have been fought at that period in southern England"[64]; "[w]e can nevertheless believe that at the end of the fifth century or early in the sixth a small band of Saxon adventurers land on the south Hampshire coast."[65] Once the southern locale is accepted, lethargy evidently hampers Saxon invasion, perhaps because "it was the fear engendered among the English by the slaughter of Badon which held the *Cerdingas* to their beach-head for about fifty years"[66]; so "For some decades they achieved little more than a conquest of Wight and the securing of a bridgehead on the mainland"[67]; and "... the *Chronicle* provides no evidence that the *Cerdingas*, the followers of Cerdic, penetrated more than twenty miles inland until 552."[68] Finally, however, the West Saxons begin their invasion in earnest: "but in the second half of the sixth century they erupted into the heartland of Wessex."[69]

With that mind-set, what is accepted as truth is more far-fetched than a new proposal. Gildas relates that after Badon external wars stopped, but even up to his time civil wars were still raging. This labels Cerdic as an internal (or English Saxon) and therefore he would not be part of a patterned entry into Britain from the southern coast. As progeny from a mixed race stemming from the Saxon recruitment and Votadinian migration orchestrated by Vortigern, Cerdic was already in Britain's heartland.

In addition to patterns as obstacles, terms, crammed into short passages and seemingly obvious, present other major hurdles because of their diverse implications, each of which crucially controls the results of interpreting outcomes. Excluding any reference to chronology, the following terms were touched upon in earlier chapters: *Cerdicesora, Welsh, English Saxon, German Saxon.* Others require further explication: *Gewissae, West Saxon, Wessex,* and *conquered.*

The malaise created by patterned thinking and sundry definitions is most evident in relation to Cerdic. Most Arthurian researchers agree that Cerdic is not a Saxon name, but in spite of this he is persistently labeled as one. Part of Chapter 3 delved into Morris' incorrect assertion that Cerdic's ancestry as reported in the *Chronicle* are "patent inventions," and instead accepted Ashe's perception that Cerdic's father is Elesa, which is like the Eliseg in the Powys dynasty, that the West Saxons are referred to as Gewissi or Gewissae in early sources, and that there was a phase of British-Saxon fraternization and intermarriage in the fifth century. Many times in the fifth century two and sometimes three names referred to the same individual, one British and one Roman according to Ashe's observation,[70] plus a third, Saxon, since the three cultures overlapped during this era. In this instance, it applies to Cunedda/Eliset as a Briton/Saxon connection, but it also generally affiliates with Cerdic/Ceretic/Ceredig or Octha/Osla/Æsc.

The earlier Camlann chapter distinguished between English and German Saxons, explaining that the English Saxons were the mixed race of Old Saxons, Roman, Welsh, Briton, Gewissae and Votadini. The term English Saxon applies to Cerdic, but he is still erroneously viewed as a German Saxon, implying his homeland is the continent rather than Cornovii. This text embraces the innovative theory that Cerdic the (English) Saxon king is the same person as Cunedda's son and Vortigern's interpreter, and despite that, mind-set raises its ugly head. Cerdic landed at Cerdicesora, but it must not be inferred that this site is on the shore of Southampton Water. The Genealogical Preface shows the incorrect assumption of Cerdicesora near Southampton Water by recording that the "West Saxons [Cerdic and his son] were the first kings who conquered the land of Wessex from the Welsh."[71]

That single sentence requires further explanation. The key term describing Cerdic is Gewissae, which in all of its ramifications labels him a Briton whose homeland is the midlands, bordering Wales, in the vicinity of Llangollen where an inscribed stone commemorates his ancestors. The genealogical entries in the *Anglo-Saxon Chronicle* also provide a clue. The listing for Cerdic's great-great grandfather is Gewis, and as a root it is much too close to Gewissae for a coincidence. Cunedda/Elesa could be a Briton/Saxon distinction, just as Æternus/Esla might refer to a Roman/Saxon difference, after which the genealogy drifts into mythology. Cerdic is labeled in the Genealogical Preface as West Saxon because he is truly of the western midlands and because his allegiance is to the English Saxons, *federate* settlers initially invited in as allies by Vortigern. He acquires his title of West Saxon not because he came from the continent to the western part of the south coast but because he relinquished his Briton associations and allied himself with the Saxon settlers already in Britain.

Another clarification must be made: the terms "West Saxon" and "Wessex" are not synonymous. In the *Chronicle* all domains attached to Cerdic are called West Saxon, and in two manuscripts Cerdic and his son are referred to as "the princes of West Saxon," a peculiar title unless interpreted that Cunedda is king and therefore his offspring would be princes. Nevertheless, Cerdic's West Saxon territories are those parts of the Gewissae domains in the midlands he inherited from his father, plus his namesake in western Wales. However, the term Wessex does not appear in the *Chronicle* until entry 560, the year in which Ceawlin (Cerdic's great-grandson) succeeded to the kingdom in Wessex and Ælle to the kingdom of the Northumbrians.[72] Ceawlin seemingly inherits a part of the West Saxon empire, Wessex. The only other time the term Wessex is used is in the Genealogical Preface. John of Glastonbury explains Wessex:

> King Arthur fought mightily against the Saxons and wore them down; he waged twelve battles against them, conquering them and routing them in all twelve instances. Often he struggled with Cerdic, who, if one month Arthur vanquished him, rose up the next fiercer for the fight. Finally when Arthur tired of the conflict, he accepted Cerdic's fealty and gave him Hampshire and Somerset, which Cerdic called Wessex.[73]

The massive tracts of land called Hampshire and Somerset, then, become known as Wessex. Basing his representation on archaeological evidence, Alcock describes the nucleus of this area later termed Wessex as a peasant settlement going back a generation before Cerdic's landing.[74] These lands were added to Cerdic's existent dominions, all of which was incorporated as the West Saxon kingdom. Wessex is only a segment of Cerdic's holdings.

John of Glastonbury's account offers two additional clarifications. There are obvious echoes from Nennius (and parallels from Geoffrey of Monmouth's narrative of the battle between Arthur and Cheldric), but the Cerdic/Arthur equation is one of the important segments of the passage, not totally explained from either of the above sources but indicating an extended connection between Arthur and Cerdic; there was a long-term disagreement and conflict between the two, which in its later stages was resolved by Cerdic's pledge of fealty in return for territories to the south of his homeland.

John then offers a different perspective of the Genealogical Preface and its use of the word "conquered." Whereas the Preface points to war and an outcome of victory, John of Glastonbury states outright that Wessex was given by treaty. What Ethelwerd records in his chronicle points to John's interpretation. Ethelwerd writes that "in the sixth year from their [Cerdic and his son] arrival they encircled [circumierunt] that western area of Britain now known as Wessex."[75] What Ethelwerd wished to express by "circumierunt" is unknown, but "encompass" as a synonym meaning "to include" could convey the impression that six years after first squabbling with the Welsh, Wessex was included as Cerdic's West Saxon territory, being granted according to John's account. The word *circumierunt* neither denotatively or connotatively matches the word *conquered* to describe the West Saxon acquisition of Wessex; there are no deaths, defeats, or victories recorded.

And last, the Genealogical Preface states that the West Saxons took Wessex from the *Welsh*. The answer to Ashe's "unsolved riddle" revolving around the synonymity of Welsh and Gewissae is answered by Eliseg's Pillar connecting Vortigern, Cunedda, and Cerdic.[76] The Welsh context is given several times: near Llangollen, the kingdom of Powys, east-central Wales and part of Shropshire. Vortigern is the first of the ancestral line ascribed with the term Gewissae, but Ashe, even though he is focused upon the word "Gewisse" and elsewhere makes a suggestive connection between Cerdic the interpreter and Cerdic king of the West Saxons, does not consciously perceive the name Cerdic lurking behind the context of Vortigern. Similarly, Morris suggested the connection between Cerdic son of Cunedda and Cerdic the interpreter but misses the connection of Cerdic as the Saxon king because his focus is on *Cunedda* as Welsh royalty. Cunedda drives the

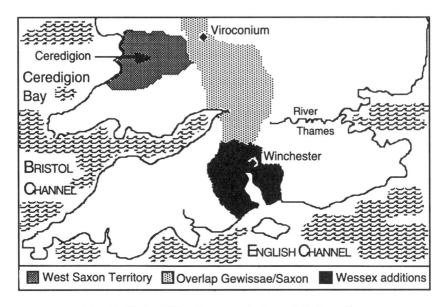

Map 20. Hwicce/West Saxon territories and their overlap.

Irish from Wales; Cerdic as royalty inherits part of Wales when his father dies; and Cerdic as a *Gewissae* West Saxon becomes a powerful king on the island. There is no need for elaboration on this point, since most of the explanation appears in Chapter 2. It should now be obvious, though, how much explication is needed for short passages in any of the ancient manuscripts. At this time, it is possible to turn to Cerdic's *literary* impact, which continues the Arthurian saga and enhances the images of Arthur and Cerdic even more.

"Culhwch and Olwen" tells of Arthur's initial friendship with the Saxon *federates* which transects into a rivalry in the Rhonabwy tale. Octha (Osla Big Knife), Cerdic, Owein Dantguin, and the Gwyr y Gogledd (the men of the North) make a stand on the Wrekin in their Gewissae homeland near Caer Vadon (Viroconium). The beleagured Saxons ask for a truce to the end of the month and a fortnight, which Arthur grants. Arthur withdraws after instructing his troops that they may follow him now, or meet again here, at the same site of the truce. When "The Dream of Rhonabwy" ends, neither history or legend tells what happens immediately after the negotiation. The only logical deduction, of course, is that just as with their fealty, Octha and Cerdic break the conditions of the truce and remain at Vadon.

Arthur returns with his massive army and routes Cerdic, killing Octha (*Chronicle* death-year: 497) in the battle. John of Glastonbury describes the next segment, which comes *after* the 12 battles from the *Historia* list. Even after Vadon, the twelfth battle, John records that Arthur and Cerdic fought continuously with defeats and victories on each side, until the two leaders finally negotiate a treaty that grants Cerdic the vast territory of Wessex on the condition that he contain his expansion. Cerdic does not honor that pledge, and after great slaughter, Cerdic is driven out of Britain.

Under the name of Chelric, Geoffrey of Monmouth continues the story in which Cerdic[77] conscripts a massive army of Germans (German Saxons), and fights the devastating Battle of Camlann 21 years after Vadon. There is "immense slaughter" on both sides:

> Everywhere men were receiving wounds themselves or inflicting them, dying or dealing out death[;] ... all the leaders on both sides were present and rushed into the fight at the head of their troop.[78]

By the battle's end, Mordred (Medraut in the *AC* entry 537), Cerdic (Genealogical Preface: death-year, 494 + 6 + 16 = 516, coinciding with Battle of Camlann, *AC*, entry 537, minus 19 years for lunar adjustment = 518) and Arthur are killed. Creoda then inherits the West Saxon kingdom and reigns until 534.

Even if Arthur is viewed as a single individual, other concepts in this text explain his historicity. In addition to the brief enumeration just above, the premises dealing directly with Arthur which still remain valid are these:

1. the locales of Arthur's activities, including the Badon and Camlann sites;
2. Cerdic and Octha as his initial comrades who become his mortal enemies;
3. all of the cardinal and ordinal years established in Chapter 3, including the principal years of Badon and Camlann, the three *adventi* of the Saxons, and the floruits of Cerdic, Octha, and Cunedda;
4. the role of Owein Dantguin (son of Enniaun Girt, grandson of Cunedda, and nephew of Cerdic) and the men of the North in the Arthurian drama.

The historical events of the Dark Ages provided as satellite information in establishing the milieu of the Arthurian age which also remain valid are these:

1. Cerdic's three roles as Cunedda's son, Vortigern's interpreter, and finally the West Saxon king;
2. the reconciled dates for the West Saxon dynasty in the *ASC* and the Genealogical Preface, from Cerdic's reign in 500 through Queen Seaxburh's one-year term in 671–72;
3. Octha's role as a Saxon leader after Horsa's death;
4. the reconciled dates for Hengist's death, Octha's joint succession with his father in 455, Octha's sole succession in 473, and Octha's subsequent length of reign ending in 497.

If, on the other hand, Arthur is part of a triad and legend was accurate in labeling him as a centigenarian, then his representation is even more comprehensive. His renown endures and explains the following:

1. why Gildas did not use the term Arthur in the *De Excidio*;
2. Arthur's mission in Gaul;
3. the discord between Ambrosius Aurelianus and Vitalinus;

4. the connection between Vitalinus of history and Vitalinus of tradition;
5. the historical reasons for Arthur's popularity not only on the island but on the continent, especially in France, Brittany, Gaul, and Burgundy;
6. Riothamus' role as a Briton in Gaul during the seventh decade of the fifth century;
7. the origins of the regeneration motif in Arthurian legend in his transformation from Ambrosius to Riothamus to Arthur;
8. the origins of his legendary magical powers;
9. Arthur's Welsh connections;
10. Arthur's parents and Roman connections;
11. Arthur's birth-year;
12. Arthur's known connections with other authenticated figures such as Aurelianus, Leo I, Ægidius, Anthemius, Budic, Hoel, Euric, and Sidonius.

Hence, the merits of this text do not rest solely on the belief that Arthur is one name of a triad. Unlike the proverbial foundation for a house of cards, the entire Arthuriad structure will not crumble if that one premise is altered. The scope for Arthur is certainly more comprehensive based upon the triad, but even without that extension, the perception of Arthur is much sharper than before.

The Triumvirate Chronology

This completes the trilogy of separate chronologies. The Ambrosian era is a general span from the beginning of Vortigern's reign around 425 to the second Briton migration in 460. If one accepts the possibility that Ambrosius is in reality Arthur, then a portal to his childhood in the late 430s is finally opened, and he can accurately be viewed as an imposing figure even as an adolescent, strong in leadership, bearing the assurance and confidence of an aristocrat, and precocious in assuming responsibility as evidenced by his contact with Vortigern and by his status as Emrys. At the end of his career, he is not named by Gildas as the leader of the Badon battle because Gildas had given the proper name Ambrosius Aurelianus in the preceding sentence; the name "Arthur" does not appear because that epithet had not yet been coined to identify Ambrosius Aurelianus.

The Riothamus chronology, second in the sequence, covers approximately 10 years, from the second British migration in 460 to his disappearance after the battle at Bourges in 470. Riothamus is itself a title, supreme king, also referred to as king of the Britons, but confused as Breton. Rachael Bromwich writes that although Bretons clung to traditions inherited from insular Britain, the legends of the Breton kingdoms did not have a reverse impact on native Welsh tradition. She then adds one disclaimer:

> The only minor exception to this ... is the appearance in Welsh sources of that indeterminate figure "Emrys Llydaw," whose name means merely "an emperor (ruler) of Brittany."[79]

The exception should not be considered minor, nor should the epithet of Emrys Llydaw be translated as "merely" an emperor. This, too, was an insular (not Breton) traditional title inherited from the Welsh, borne originally by Ambrosius and carried by Riothamus to Brittany.

The era of Arthur (the last Roman emperor, but also the first medieval king[80]) begins not with a single year as a postulation, but a chronological fix based upon the reign of Leo I, between 457 and 474, narrowed to 468–474, and reduced even further by Sharon Turner to 469–470.[81] Averaging this last figure with Morris' date of 475 gives an "Arthurian" span of 473 to 518, the latter marking his death at the Battle of Camlann. After the compilation of all data, the evidence points to the "Arthur of Dyfed," if retaining Richard Barber's trichotomy. More accurately, however, the term should be a "western" or a "west-midlands" Arthur combined with the southern. There is no credibility for a "far northern" Arthur, though some of his escapades could have taken him as far as Hadrian's Wall. After a circular pattern from southern Wales to northern Wales, and then eastward to the Cornovian territory, the movement during the latter part of his life was southward, but not with the same intense concentration on the heartland as heretofore assumed. Arthur is last in the triad; the title of prince is never given to him because he had risen beyond that. He is most often called emperor, and by the end of his career, he acquired a list of titles: chief lord of the island, war-leader, leader of battles, leader of the armies, commander, general king, high king, and supreme ruler.

These three separate figures meld surprisingly well to supply a persuasive, single chronology. Although David Dumville brazenly ravages the use of Welsh matter as historical evidence for Arthur, he does not postulate a better theory. Ambrosius Aurelianus has unequivocal Roman ancestry. This claim is made not just because of what he tells Vortigern as Emrys in the *Historia*, but because he is linked with Lucius Domitius Aurelianus in Roman history; his heritage carries through Wales and the midlands just to the east. Riothamus is also Roman, tied to the Roman allies on the continent; Vitalinus is to Ambrosius what Ægidius is to Riothamus. And Arthur carries on the Roman tradition: the purple mantle, his title of emperor, Cornovian associations, prominence in Welsh literature, Gallic enterprises, and Breton allies.

The hypothesis given at the beginning of this chapter was that the end of the era for Ambrosius marked the beginning of the era for Riothamus, and that the end of the era for Riothamus marked the beginning of the era for Arthur, a sequence which substantiates phases of the same person and which demonstrates why the title of this chapter referring to Riardd Ambrosius as a phoenix makes sense. Ambrosius Aurelianus drops from sight in the 460s and from his ashes, Riothamus arises on the continent; when Riothamus vanishes from history in Burgundy, Arthur rises from his ashes and again becomes a victor, this time at Badon in Britain. As the decades pass, Ambrosius Aurelianus' escapades on the continent and his successful return to Britain are remembered, no longer assigned to him by a proper name, but instead by epithets which still reflect his power as high king.

There is one remaining task prior to melding the three separate historical chronologies into one. The major key is the word *transition* in combining these three historical chronologies. During the century between 420 and 520 there is still enormous impact from Roman influence. Many archaeologists and historians, including Alcock and Morris, emphasize the slowness of the deterioration of the Roman effect in all aspects of British life. Closely aligned with the gradual Roman decline was the need for the Britons to begin fending for themselves, setting up a parallel with (but a distinction from) the Roman way of life, borrowing some things, discarding others. The Saxon encroachment, too, added its own flavoring to an island in turmoil. With the entire island of Britain in transition from Roman to Briton, plus a complicating factor of Saxon influence, events took on three different perspectives, each with pockets of truth and accuracy.

The superimposition of these three major layers makes it extremely difficult to determine what transpired and how certain events were reported by the three different cultures. Each would have its own unique viewpoint and its own biased slant, but likewise, each would reflect some element of truth. Although certain details might be exaggerated simply to increase prestige or honor or national pride, there would necessarily be some underlying, accurate details for an event to maintain its credibility. For example, if one culture did not want to admit a military defeat, it would not just out-and-out lie about a victory; instead, it would just avoid recording a defeat or victory and perhaps concentrate upon a segment of the battle which would put it in a more favorable light.

The more discerning researchers maintained a critical vigil for biased reporting in the available documents. Many times the biases of the scribes might not be evident or even conscious, with distortion occurring only in the selective process of reporting or in the subtle connotation of words used. Personal and place-names might have been in Latin, therefore giving a Roman tinge to the report; another might subconsciously prefer a descriptive Welsh term for a geographic name to give more credence to that influence as it broke away from Roman dominion; a third report could be from a Saxon viewpoint, simply reporting that in a certain year they fought a battle against the Britons. All three could be reporting on the same persons in the same events at the same times and in the same geographic locations. The clues might be minute and unless some careful researcher uncovered them, the variances of viewpoint for a large-scaled, expansive, more comprehensive picture would be lost.

As that process applies to the merging of chronologies here, an earlier chapter corrected inconsistencies in some of the ancient manuscripts. For one, the age-old discrepancy between the *ASC* and its Preface has been reconciled so that all the dates for the West Saxon royal house match. In the *Chronicle* specifically, a generation is missing; Cerdic and Cynric were not father-son, but grandfather-grandson, requiring that some of the entries listing Cynric must be changed to Creoda, and some entries identifying Cerdic should name Creoda. Secondly, some entries for Hengist were incompatible. Hengist's death-year and Octha's length of reign (contingent upon his father's death) both had to be set properly in the year 473, settling the dispute of one version of the *Chronicle* claiming that

Octha had reigned 24 years while the other claimed 34 years. Third, because of doublets, some of the entries after the turn of the sixth century had to be eliminated or rearranged.

There were also changes in the other manuscripts, some just as significant or innovative. In the *Historia*, one modification (not interpretation) was in the introductory paragraph of Chapter 56, which should have read, "On *Horsa's* death, Octha came down from the north"; Vortimer's battle by the Inscribed Stone should have been located on the shore of the *Gaelic* Sea rather than the *Gallic* Sea, to refer to the ancient Irish form of writing called *ogam* or *ogham* chiseled on commemorative monuments such as the Inscribed Stone; third, the titles and headings supplied for the *Historia* by a later scribe should be eliminated since they create confusion about Hengist's genealogies and the territories he occupied. In the *Annales Cambriae*, there were two changes applicable to Arthurian history: the Battle of Badon and the Battle of Camlann were adjusted according to a lunar adaptation.

The penning of the *De Excidio* in 541 was also established earlier in Chapter 3 of this text. Wood and Dumville agree:

> Gildas knows of the descendants in his own day of Ambrosius Aurelianus, the victor of the first battle against the Saxons, which occurred [during?] an uncertain period (although I conjectured, above, that it was brief) before Mount Badon. ... These descendants are in fact [Ambrosius'] grandchildren (*auita* makes the relationship clear). ... [T]hey are the third generation of now presumably hereditary rules in the area.[82]

What Dumville states is affirmed by the chronology established earlier in this text. If Gildas wrote the *DE* in 541, then Ambrosius' grandchildren would be contemporaries of Gildas; those grandchildren might not have had direct contact with Ambrosius' first victory, but they would be one generation removed from it, which could account for their not being as honorable as their grandfather. If Riardd Ambrosius is set aside and if Alcock's rule of thumb about generations is used — that one generation equals about 20 years — then two generations prior to 541 would be very close to the Badon era. Much of western England was in Anglo-Saxon hands in Gildas' day, once again in accord with the findings of this text. Ambrosius — i.e., Arthur or Riardd Ambrosius — had been killed at the Battle of Camlann in 518, which established the kingdom of the West Saxons; after that year the Saxons no longer encountered resistance as they moved inland, since the legendary leader had passed from this life. This too answers Dumville's question about why Gildas did not have a free and open "westerly land-route to Caerleon."[83]

Dumville affixes a chronology to Gildas, and warns about the "risk of foolish over-simplification." Sensitive to that admonition, part of that chronology is quoted here:

ca. 490?	Extent of the war. Destruction of urban life
	Fates of survivors (including overseas migrations).

	Tempore aliquanto interueniente, return home to the northeastern Britain of Saxon rebels.
	Reorganization of Britons, under Ambrosius Aurelianus.
ca. 495?	First successful British battle against Saxons won by Ambrosius &c.
ca. 495 × *ca.* 500+	Changing fortunes of war.
ca. 500+	Battle of Mount Badon. Slaughter of the Saxons.
ca. 500 × *ca.* 545	Gildas' lifetime. Up to his 44th year, that of writing.[84]

If Ambrosius Aurelianus' name were to be deemphasized, Dumville's chronology would offer some interesting parallels to what has been established in this text. Both his date for Ambrosius' victory (*ca.* 495) and his date for the Badon battle (500+) are close to the year 497 established by this text for the Badon battle, in itself suggesting a doublet in Dumville's chronology. If those two events are a doublet, then it is strengthened even more by the postulation of this text that Arthur is an epithet for Ambrosius Aurelianus. Judging from the Genealogical Preface of the *Chronicle*, the "changing fortunes of war" which Dumville sets in the year 500+ could refer to Cerdic's acquisition of Wessex (Hampshire and Wiltshire), the time period shortly after Badon but almost two decades before the Camlann battle. This interim (495 to 500) is only 5 years, and as shown earlier, the acquisition was not by conquest but by treaty, accounting for the 18 years of uneasy peace before the ravages of Camlann.

Dumville's chronology by its nature must be conservative, particularly since he is using only Gildas as his source for supplying dates of reckoning. In his text he recommends that

> ideas of the place of Vortigern, Hencgest and Horsa, Ambrosius Aurelianus, the battle of Mount Badon (and a consequent casting back of Anglo-Saxon settlement and a reverse migration to the Continent) in the development of southern English history must be abandoned, completely and at once.[85]

He may make this recommendation because of his meticulous approach to research, but the statement is overly conservative and if taken at face-value would discourage any theories, innovations, or ingenious inventiveness. Conversely, Morris' stand *encourages* rather than *discourages* advancement of new avenues to be explored. Dumville must realize the importance of flexibility and exploration, or otherwise he would not have used the term "new approaches" as part of the title for the book he co-edited with Michael Lapidge on Gildas.

The following chronology which merges the three individuals has already been comprehensively presented as three separate components. The remaining task is to combine the information with other details extracted from all sources to clarify the continuum of Arthur.

The quest for the historicity of King Arthur — in truth a historical inquiry into the Dark Ages — must be a continuous one. As Steinbeck wrote, the subject of King Arthur is so huge that the deeper one delves, the more profound the subject becomes. Like Percival's quest for the Holy Grail in the later romances, the mood is sometimes that of forlorn desolation. There is a *(continued on page 364)*

Table 15. The Riardd Ambrosius Chronology

Date	Event	Comments
409–410	At this time, because the strength of the Romans was weakened in the five Britains, the Britons were ravaged by an incursion of *Saxones*. (The beginning of Roman abandonment.)	*Chronica Gallica a CCCCLII:* Year I of Theodosius II. Hac tempestate prae valentudine Romanorum vires funditus attenuatae Britanniae Saxonum incursione devastatae.[86]
413–415	Birth of Hengist.	Floruit: 428–458. Life-Span: 413–473.
422	Birth of Ambrosius Aurelianus.	*HB:* Chapter 66, discord between Ambrosius and Vitalinus, 437 minus 15, *Arthur's age at* coronation = 422.
		Throughout the centuries many names and epithets will come to be associated with him, particularly Riothamus and Arthur, to give him an accurate title of Riardd Ambrosius.
425	Because of Rome's process of withdrawal and subsequent English Saxon devastation, only Ambrosius Aurelianus is left as a successor. By virtue of his heritage, he rightfully inherits the title of king, but because of his youth and the fear for his safety, Vortigern assumes the kingship as a Briton usurper.	*HB:* Chapters 31, 36. *DE:* Chapters 22, 23. *ASC:* 423, 449.
428	Saxon Adventus One. Vortigern solicits Saxon help to defend the island from the Picts and the Irish.	*DE:* Chapter 23.3–4. *HB:* Chapter 31.
434–435	Ambrosius, son of a Roman consul, has an encounter with Vortigern and his wizards. Vortigern gives the boy Emrys the kingdoms of western Britain and flees to Dementia, a stronghold of Cunedda's.	*HB:* Chapters 40–41. This story of Emrys in *HB* gives rise to Geoffrey of Monmouth coining the name of Ambrosius Merlinus, subsequently dropping the name of Ambrosius and creating the birth of a new character in Arthurian romances, thus adding another epithet to Riardd Ambrosius.
437	The quarrel between Vitalinus and Ambrosius.	*HB:* Chapter 66. Both Vitalinus and Ambrosius as representatives of Romanitas are opposed to Vortigern as an usurper.

Table 15, continued

Date	Event	Comments
437 (cont.)	Ambrosius taken to Gaul.	*HKB:* Part Four, The House of Constantine. Although Riardd Ambrosius is named king, instead of ascending to the throne in place of Vortigern, he takes refuge in Gaul; Vitalinus (Guithelinus) as the guardian of Riardd convinces him to cross the Channel so that he will not be assassinated.
	Birth of Octha.	Floruit: 452–482. Lifespan: 437–497.
442	Because of motives shrouded in history, Cunedda migrates to the south of Hadrian's Wall.	*HB:* Chapters 14 and 62.
	The Saxon Revolt: Britains are subjected to the dominion of the English.	*Chronica Gallica a. CCCCLII:* 19th year of Theodosius after the death of Honorius: Death of Honorius Flavius, 423 + 19 = 442. Brittanie usque ad hoc tempus variis cladibus eventibusque la[cera]tae in dicionem Saxonum rediguntur.[87]
	Saxon Adventus Two.	*Chronica Gallica a. DXI: XVI: Britanniae a Romanis Amissae in dicionem Saxonum cedunt.* *DE:* Chapter 23.4.
		The second major coming of the Saxons is commanded by Hengist and Horsa.
446	The plea to Aetius for help.	*DE:* Chapter 20, Manuscript V, Polydore Vergil. *ASC:* Entry 443, Parker, Laud Chronicle.
		This plea for Roman intercession is based on the conflicts between Romanitas and Barbaria, not between Ancient Britons and invading German Saxons. This dispute links Arthur's name to Octha in the later decades.[88]
449	Saxon Adventus Three: Hengist and Horsa, invited by Vortigern, king of the Britons, came to Britain at first to help the Britons.	*ASC:* Entry 449. *DE:* Chapter 23.5.

Date	Event	Comments
450	The birth of Cerdic, fifth son of Cunedda, who plays a major role in the history of the time, including being an interpreter for Vortigern and rising to a kingship of the West Saxons in his later life.	Floruit: 465–495. Lifespan: 450–510. These three individuals — Octha, Cerdic, and Riardd Ambrosius — become comrades and friends with Briton salvation as a common cause. The relationship deteriorates into powerful rivalry when Cerdic switches allegiance and sides with Octha, becoming a West Saxon leader. Their rivalry continues to the Battle of Badon when Octha is killed and culminates at the Battle of Camlann where Cerdic and Riardd both die.
451	Aetius' last great Roman victory over Attila and the Huns near Chalons-sur-Marne.	
455	In this year Hengist and Horsa fought against Vortigern at Ægelesthrep, and his brother Horsa was killed there.	*ASC:* Entry 455, Parker and Laud chronicles. Ægelesthrep = Agglethorpe, on the border of Britannia Maxima.
	Octha comes down from the north.	*HB:* Chapter 56.
	Hengist and his son Octha succeeded to the kingdom and jointly rule until 473.	*ASC:* Entry 455.
457		Leo I becomes Emperor of the East.
458	Hengist and his Saxons massacre Vortigern's council.	*HB:* Chapter 46, Essex, Sussex, Middlesex, and other districts are ceded to Hengist.
459–460	The second migration to Brittany: Some survivors of the internal struggles made for lands beyond the sea; others held out, though not without fear, in their own land.	*DE:* Chapter 25.1–2.
460–461	The victories of Ambrosius Aurelianus.	*DE:* Chapter 25.3, 26.1. *HB:* Chapter 48, ¶ 2.
	In the eleventh year of Cerdic, Arthur (i.e., Ambrosius Aurelianus) began to rule over the Britons.	John of Glastonbury: *CsAGE:* Ch. XXXII.
467	Anthemius appointed Emperor of the West by Leo I.	Jordanes, *Gothic History.*

Table 15, continued

Date	Event	Comments
469–470	Riothamus and the Battle of Angers: Odovacer and the Saxons came to Angers, and when Odovacer reached the city, Childeric, King of the Franks, arrived the next day and took the city. The Saxons and Romans then fought each other. The Saxons turned tail and many of them fell to the Roman pursuit.	Gregory of Tours, *Historia Francorum*.
	Sidonius' letter to Riothamus, Riardd Ambrosius.	*Sidonius: Poems and Letters.*
	Euric the Visigoth after a long fight routed Riotimus, king of the Britons, before the Romans could join him. The Britons were expelled from Bourg-de-Déols, and when Riotimus had lost a great part of his army, he fled to the Burgundians, a neighboring tribe allied to the Romans.	Jordanes: *Gothic History.* Gregory of Tours: *Historia Francorum.*
	Riothamus' disappearance into friendly territory gives rise to the resurrection/regeneration motif. When he resurfaces again in England as Arthur, another epithet attaches itself to Ambrosius Aurelianus.	During the period of time before Ægidius' death, he and his son Syagrius are strong in Gaul, while Euric is dealing with internal struggles, which means that the Visigoths are not threatening invasions until the later half of the decade. After Ægidius' death during the great plague, Syagrius assumes the kingship and continues, with Riardd as an ally, the battles against the Saxons and Visigoths.
473	In this year Hengist and Octha fought against the Welsh.	*ASC:* Entry 473.
	In this year Hengist died.	Last mention of Hengist: Entry 473.
	In this year Octha became sole successor to the kingdom and reigned for 24 years.	Emendation of 488 to 473: Æsc entry in the middle of South Saxon kingships.
475	The year traditionally set for Arthur's rise to the throne, ostensibly because this year occurs 15 years after Ambrosius' victory, and legends tell of Arthur's being coronated at 15.	Ambrosius Aurelianus' victory and last mention in history: 460 + Arthur's age of 15 at succession = 475.

Date	Event	Comments
475 *(cont.)*		This is the year in which the epithet "Arthur" is coined to refer to the regeneration of Riothamus on the island after his defeat on the continent. In essence, Ambrosius Aurelianus becomes first Riothamus and then Arthur.
494– 495	In this year Cerdic and his son [Creoda] landed at Cerdicesora with five ships.	Genealogical Preface: separate document Manuscript Ā: 494. *ASC:* Entry 495.
497	Battle of Badon: Viroconium: Riardd Ambrosius fought against Octha and Cerdic at the Wrekin and Octha is killed there. Cerdic is granted amnesty.	*AC:* Entry 516 minus 19 years lunar adjustment = 497; *De Excidio:* penning the manuscript, 541 minus 44 = 497; *ASC:* equated with entry 495, Cerdic's battle against the Welsh.
	Birth of Gildas.	*De Excidio:* penning the manuscript, 541 minus 44 = 497
	Death of Octha, reign of 24 years.	*ASC:* Parker Chronicle, 473 = last entry for Hengist, implying his death, Octha's second succession; Octha's 24-year reign: 473 plus 24 = 497; DOR Osla Big Knife fights at Badon; *HB,* Octha involved in all twelve of Arthur's campaigns; *HKB,* Octa and Chedric are companions in Britain.
500	Six years after Cerdic and his son Creoda landed, they acquired the land of Wessex (Hampshire and Somerset) and those territories become part of Cerdic's West Saxon kingdom in Wales and the midlands.	Genealogical Preface: separate document Manuscript Ā: 500. Ethelwerd: *CÆ:* Entry 500. John of Glastonbury: *CsAGE,* Ch. XXXIII.
508+	In this year Cerdic and his son Creoda kill a Welsh king and 5,000 men with him.	*ASC:* Parker and Laud Chronicles: Entry 508.
	Cerdic evidently breaks his fealty with Riardd Ambrosius, and when routed a second time, the Saxons, with reinforcements from the continent, began a new series of incursions in the typical pattern.	*HB:* Chapter 56, last ¶.
516– 519	The Battle of Camlann: Charford.	*AC:* Entry 537 minus 19 years lunar adjustment = 518.

Table 15, continued

Date	Event	Comments
516–519	Death of Riardd Ambrosius [Arthur].	*AC:* Entry 537 minus 19 years lunar adjustment = 518.
(cont.)	Death of Cerdic.	Genealogical Preface: Entry 500 + Cerdic's reign of 16 years = 516. *ASC:* Entry 534 minus Creoda's reign of 18 years = 516.
	Cerdic and Creoda obtained the kingdom of the West Saxons, and from that day on the princes of the West Saxons have reigned.	*ASC:* Entry 519, Parker and Laud chronicles.
534	In this year [Creoda], son of Cerdic, died.	*ASC:* emendation of Entry 534 and insertion of lost generation; Creoda inherits kingdom in 516 + reign of 18 years = 534.
	Cynric succeeded to the kingdom and ruled for 26 years.	*ASC:* Entry 534, Parker and Laud chronicles.
541	Gildas writes the *DE*.	
560–561	In this year Cynric died and Ceawlin succeeded to the kingdom in Wessex.	Genealogical Preface *ASC:* Entry 560, Parker and Laud chronicles.

(continued from page 358) sense of satisfaction in piecing together any facet of Arthuriana, yet this satisfaction is tempered by a pervading sense of elusiveness, a melancholy hollowness that counterbalances the challenge and any ensuing accomplishment. Although the goals of a sharper image for this renowned king have been attained, Arthur remains more than a phoenix of Britain; his presence permeates the post–Roman period in Gaul, Brittany, and Burgundy as well as on the island, which more accurately describes him as a phoenix of the Dark Ages, not just a phoenix king of Britain.

This text has journeyed through several mazes that are seemingly dead ends. Other relevant quests — such as the *Historia* battlelist in its entirety and Mordred's historical role in his association with Arthur — were not undertaken. The other *Historia* battles demand much more investigation, both on the island and on the continent, since they might significantly clarify Arthur as a triadic figure. In conjunction with this, Mordred's connection with Cerdic (Chelric in literary tradition), his role at Camlann, and the possible motives behind the decline and fall of the Briton Empire could cast more light upon the Arthurian saga. The mood of hopeless elusiveness will diminish even more when these exciting perplexities and entanglements are pursued by future Arthurian scholars. Arthur is an immortal phoenix, a historical figure entrenched in reality so bound to legend that the dream will never end, nor will the King's greatness ever die.

Appendix A:
The Arthurian Chronology

The purpose of this particular addendum is to give the panoramic view of a thousand years of history that shaped the Arthurian legends based upon the Arthurian fact. The first column listing the date does not use question marks to suggest approximations; it is already an accepted condition that these dates are estimations and must be accepted as such. In some instances where there are barren spots in history, longer time-spans are given. Whereby the Riardd Ambrosius Chronology in Chapter 12 summarized the postulations directly related to Arthur and his milieu, the Event column here provides information of a more general nature but is still applicable to Arthur. Hence the Riardd Chronology and the Arthurian Chronology should supplement each other, eliminating extensive repetition while at the same time allowing an expanded, pervasive essence of Arthur.

Table 16. The Arthurian Chronology

Date	Event
54–55	Julius Caesar invades Britain.
60	Boudicca's rebellion against the Romans and her defeat.
381	Maximus succeeds to the throne.
383	Maximus proclaimed emperor by British army.
417–421	Constantius III (not to be confused with Constantine the Usurper who was executed in 411 at Ravenna) is sometimes listed as the father of Ambrosius Aurelianus. Constantius III, who rescued Galla Placidia, Honorius' sister, from the Visigoths and married her in 417, was appointed co-emperor by Honorius in February 421. He died a short time after the appointment, *circa* September 421. Because the time frame is right, and because Constantius was active in Gaul, Ambrosius Aurelianus could be the son of Constantius and Galla Placidia. However, according to the *De Excidio*, Ambrosius' parents were killed in the Saxon conflicts in Britain; in contrast, Constantius III allegedly died in Ravenna,

Date	Event
417– 421 *(cont.)*	and history does not record Galla Placidia in Britain or more than her one son, Valentinian III. Several researchers refer erroneously to a Constantine III of 406–7 in Britain and Gaul, but the reign of Constantine III was from 612 to 641. Constantine the Usurper, who stole the emperorship in 406–7, was captured and executed in Gaul before Ambrosius' time. Geoffrey of Monmouth lists Constantine II (killed by his brother Constans in 340) as Ambrosius' father, but according to all the other historical data that would place Ambrosius almost a century too early. In addition to Constans, Constantine II had another brother, Constantius II, but he died in Gaul in 361, still six decades too early for the Ambrosian era.
409– 410	The beginning of Roman abandonment; the *Chronica Gallica a CCCCLII* records a savage incursion by Saxones of the continent. Goths take Rome.
455	Valentinian III is murdered and Ægidius, who later becomes Riothamus' ally, eventually becomes king of the Northern Gauls, and a temporary leader of the Franks.
464	Ægidius dies; Syagrius, also an ally with Riothamus, becomes ruler of Gaul.
466	Euric, adversary of Syagrius and Riothamus, murders his brother Theodoric and becomes king of the Visigoths.
467	Leo I, Emperor of the East, appoints Anthemius as Emperor of the West, who aligns the Roman army with the Gauls, the Bretons, the Britons, and the Burgundians.
469	Sidonius is in Gaul when Arvandus is summoned to Rome for treasonous collusion with Euric. Euric still proceeds with plans to attack Gaul.
470	Riothamus is expelled from Bourges by Euric before the Romans can send reinforcements, retreats into Burgundy, and disappears.
471+	Arthur, the phoenix of Riothamus, makes his appearance in Britain.
475	The reign of Ambrosius/Riothamus comes to an end.
486	Clovis the Frank drives the Visigoths towards Spain, and Gaul becomes Frankish.
500+	Leslie Alcock excavations at South Cadbury verify Arthurian-age occupation during the end of the fifth and beginning of the sixth centuries.
549	Death of Maelgwn. Great Plague.
586	In this year Ceawlin died after 25 years of reign and Ceol succeeded to the kingdom.
c. 600	Arthur is mentioned by name in the *Gododdin*. Barber writes that there are three Arthurs: one of the north (Arthur of Dalriada), one of the west (Arthur of Dyfed), and one of the south who appears in history three-quarters of a century earlier than the first two.
601	One of the earliest factual tracings of land grants from the kings of the West Saxons back to Glastonbury Abbey. These early land grants could be indicative of Arthur's original donation of lands to the Abbey as recorded by John of Glastonbury.

731	Bede completes his book, *A History of the English Church and People*, supplying among other things, the term Hwicce as a synonym for Gewissae.
735	Death of Bede.
858	Much of the *Historia Brittonum*, including the Arthurian material, is commonly marked as late tenth century, but Stevenson, in his Preface, writes that one of the Prologues assigns it to this year, though he adds the disclaimer that there are no copies of the Prologues anterior to the twelfth century. See Appendix B for the *Historia*'s niche in *Harleian Manuscript 3859*.
940–957	St. Dunstan lengthens Ine's church and adds a tower; raises the level of the cemetery at Glastonbury Abbey.
977–980	*Annales Cambriae* compiled, preserved as part of the *Harleian 3859* manuscripts, folios 190A through 193A.
990s	Reversals in Glastonbury Abbey's fortunes.
1050	*The Mabinogion* appears; an invaluable resource for Arthurian literary tradition.
1066 (+/-)	*Anglo-Saxon Chronicle*: Seven manuscripts are extant: (1066 +/-) Manuscript $\overline{A}$, *The Parker Chronicle*, is introduced by a Genealogical Preface. 1066(-) Manuscript A, (G, W), transcript of $\overline{A}$, except for a few leaves, was destroyed in the Cottonian fire of 1731. 977 Manuscript B, *Abingdon Chronicle*, is an eleventh century copy (year 1000). 1066 Manuscript C, *Abingdon Chronicle*, like its sister copy B, is an eleventh century duplicate, adding dates from 977 to the middle of Entry 1066. 1050/1079 Manuscript D, *Worcester Chronicle*: A close link to Manuscript E until 1031, when Manuscript D begins to record interest in northern affairs. The original was a north-country, not a West Midland chronicle. 1153 Manuscript E, *Laud (Peterborough) Chronicle*. 1066(+) Manuscript F.
1120	Eadmer, a Canterbury monk, counters the Glastonbury claim that St. Dunstan's relics are there instead at Glastonbury.
1125	William of Malmsbury writes *de Gestis Regum Anglorum*.
1126	King Henry complains about the sad state of affairs at Glastonbury.
1127	Henry de Blois, nephew of King Henry, appointed as abbot of Glastonbury.
1129	William of Malmsbury completes *De Antiquitate Glastonie ecclesie* (On the Antiquity of the Church of Glastonbury).
1135	Geoffrey of Monmouth completes the *Historia Regum Brittaniae*, a pseudo-history which becomes the forerunner to the romances of King Arthur. By this year, Henry of Huntingdon had completed seven of the eight books of his *History*. In Book II he mentions Arthur and his battles, and vaguely suggests Cerdic as Arthur's arch-enemy, something also suggested several times in *The Mabinogion*. Most of Book II is founded upon Bede, with some material from the *ASC*. William of Malmsbury writes Book II on St. Dunstan, which indicates his visit to Glastonbury fell within the ten years from 1125 to 1135.
1135–1140	William of Malmsbury issued revised second and third versions of his *de Gestis Regum Anglorum* which have much more information of Glastonbury's early

Date	Event
1135– 1140 (cont.)	history. They also include parts of the *De Antiquitate*, thus giving future generations his untainted version which makes no factual or historical claims to Arthur.
1140+	Caradoc of Llancarfan writes the *Life of St. Gildas* in which an Arthurian connection is made with Glastonbury. An association between Glastonbury and Yniswitrin is also made, but not carried further to a connection between Glastonbury and Avalon. A further link is established between Arthur and the historical figure of Melwas.
1150	Earliest probable date for "The Dream of Rhonabwy" in *The Mabinogion*, considered the latest of the tales, with "Culhwch and Olwen" considered the earliest. This date, however is misleading, since the Celtic sources it draws upon are much more ancient than that. Of the seven "Other Tales" of *The Mabinogion*, "Culhwch" and "Rhonabwy" draw upon early Celtic myth and folklore which already portray Arthur as an established hero. The later series of tales dealing with Arthur are more linked with the romances.
1155	Wace makes the first mention of King Arthur's Round Table.
1184	A large part of Glastonbury Abbey is destroyed by fire.
1190	Layamon writes about King Arthur.
1191	The "discovery" of Arthur's tomb in the cemetery of Glastonbury Abbey.
1192/3	Giraldus Cambrensis writes of Arthur's exhumation, allegedly viewing the Glastonbury Cross.
1194	Giraldus Cambrensis revises the *De Instructione Principis*, but leaves the cross inscription the same.
1216	Giraldus Cambrensis dies.
1230	Much revision and interpolation of William of Malmsbury's *De Antiquitate* which includes material on Arthur.
1247	The story of Joseph of Arimathea is added to the *De Antiquitate*, linking Joseph with King Arthur. Manuscript "T," Trinity College, scribe recopies Malmsbury's *D. A.* and Adam's history.
1265	Manuscript "L," Malmsbury's *DA*.
1400s	Manuscript "M," British Library MS Additional, c. 1313, copy of Malmsbury's *DA*. Manuscript "C," Cotton Cleopatra, *DA*. Manuscript "B," Oxford Bodliean, *DA*.
1278	King Edward I and Queen Eleanor visit Glastonbury and oversee the transfer of King Arthur's remains.
1290	Adam of Domerham, monk of Glastonbury, writes his history, which includes Arthurian material.
1342	John of Glastonbury finishes his *Cronica* which likewise includes all of the Arthurian material.
1542	John Leland, of South Cadbury renown, examines the Glastonbury cross, relating its inscription and estimating its size as about a foot in height.

Appendix B:
Harleian MS 3859

Table 17 — *Harleian MS 3859* is a miscellany which includes the *Historia Brittonum* attributed to Nennius, and the *Annales Cambriae*. Column 1 gives the folio numbers for **3859**, Column 2 gives the section numbers of the *Historia Brittonum*, and Column 3 provides specifics. The boldface type indicates those folios which constitute the base of the *Historia Brittonum*.

Folio	Section	Comments
174B	1–6	The Six Ages of the World.
174B–177A	7–18	British Origins. Sec. 14 (folio 176A) names Cunedda; Sec. 16 explains lunar cycles.
177A–179B	19–30	Roman Conquest and Occupation of Britain.
179B–185B	**31–49**	**The first independent section of *Historia Brittonum*. The Fifth Century, Vortigern, Germanus 1-2-3, Kentish Chronicles 1-2-3, Emrys Ambrosius, Vortigern genealogy.**
185B–187A	**50–55**	**Patrick.**
187A–B	**56**	**Campaigns of Arthur.**
187B–188B	**57–62**	**Anglican Genealogies, Anglican-Mercian source in late eighth century, English to Welsh. Sec. 62 = Maelgwn.**
188B– 189B	**57, 62–65**	**Diverse sources. Northern Histories = preponderance of English, not British.**
189B–190A	**66**	**Vortigern's reign, recapitulation of 31–49.**
190A–193A		*Annales Cambriae* (Welsh Annales)
193A–195A		Welsh Genealogies, Cunedda and Sons, late fourth-early fifth century territories.
195A–195B	66a	Cities of Britain.
195B–198A	67–76	The Wonders of Britain, Mona, and Ireland.

369

Glossary

abatis— A defensive obstacle formed by felled trees with sharpened branches facing the enemy. Pitt-Rivers suggests these were used in Bokerly and Wansdyke when these lines of defenses ran into thickly wooded areas.

Adam of Domerham— The scribe of *Historia de rebus Glastoniensibus* dated around 1290, a cellarer and sacristan of Glastonbury in charge of compiling the Abbey's documents into a coherent unit. Adam gives an account of Arthur's grave at Glastonbury.

Aetius— A crucial historical figure used to determine the date of the Saxon Revolt and the ascendancy of Ambrosius Aurelianus. Gildas gives his name as Agitius, but Bede evidently emended it to the correct person, since Ægidius of Gaul was never a Roman consul.

agger— A reference to Roman roads, normally raised three feet above the surrounding terrain in accounts given by Vitruvius. The layers for these roads, from the base up, were termed *pavimentum, statumen, ruderatio, nucleus,* and either *summen dorsum*, which was hard stone, or *summa crusta*, pounded lime, dependent upon the materials available in the district.

Agned— Also referred to as Breguoin, Cat Bregion, and Agned Cathregonion, the eleventh of twelve battles attributed to Arthur in the *Historia Brittonum*. Geoffrey Ashe postulates that this battle might be Angers in Gaul.

alae— Roman term for cavalry.

Albion— An ancient term used by the Roman Pliny and picked up by Bede for Great Britain, White Island, related to Latin Albus, meaning "white."

Ambrosius Aurelianus— In the *De Excidio* Gildas praises this last surviving son of Roman royalty who eventually brings Briton victory against the Saxons. In the *Historia Brittonum* Ambrosius appears first as a young boy, Emrys Gwledig, and later as a great king among kings succeeding Vortigern. Ambrosius' reign is traditionally assigned to the fifth century, a span between the end of the fourth decade through the fifth. (*See* Aurelius Ambrosius.)

Amherawdyr, Ameraudur— The Welsh term for Imperator, Emperor.

Ancient Book— Geoffrey of Monmouth's undisclosed source in his writing of *The History of the Kings of Britain.*

Aneirin— Identified as a sixth or seventh century poet whose major writing was *The Gododdin*. His work offers a background for Arthur, and is one of the earliest literary source to mention Arthur by name, supposedly not an interpolation of a later time. However, the earliest surviving manuscript for Aneirin is just after Taliesin's of the 1200s. (*See* Taliesin.)

Anglo-Saxon Chronicle— Dovetailed with Gildas, Nennius, and the *Annales Cambriae*, reconciled with the Genealogical Preface, and emended in its entries on Hengist and on the West Saxon House, this indispensable document gives credence to a series of events which create an accurate chronology for Arthur's era.

Anglo-Saxon Chronicle: Genealogical Preface— An important part to the *Chronicle*. Previously perceived to bear major discrepancies with the body of the *Chronicle*. This text has resolved the discrepancy of those dates by inserting the correct generations and reigns for Cerdic, Creoda, Cynric, Ceawlin, and Ceol. (*See* Cerdic, Creoda, Cynric, Ceawlin, Ceol.)

Annales Cambriae— "The Welsh Annals." There are two entries pertinent to Arthur's historicity. The first reads, "an. Bellum Badonis, in quo Arthur portavit crucem Domini nostri Jhesu Christi tribus diebus et tribus noctibus in humeros suos et Brittones victores fuerunt," translated as "The Battle of Badon in which Arthur carried the cross of our Lord Jesus Christ three days and three nights on his scuid and the Britons were victorious." The second reads, "an. Gueith Camlann in qua Arthur et Medraut corruerunt, et mortalitas in Brittannia et in Hibernia fuit," translated as, "The Battle of Camlann, in which Arthur and Medraut fell, and there were many deaths in Britain and Ireland." These two entries in the *Annales* have different dates from those postulated by this book, which establishes the date for Badon at 497 and the date for Camlann at 518.

Two other entries applicable to Arthur's historicity give a time frame for the appropriate chronology. The first is the death of Maelgwn, King of Gwynedd, and the second is the death of Gildas, Wisest of Britons.

De Antiquitate— William of Malmsbury's manuscript written for Glastonbury as its history, heavily interpolated after his death. (*See De Gestis Regum Anglorum*, William of Malmsbury.)

Apocrypha— A literary term referring to writings of dubious authenticity. Because of obscure beginnings, this literature is accepted as having a historically genuine base, but no solid verification from other sources exists. This term could very well apply to a great deal of Arthuriana.

Armonica— A Stuart Piggott suggestion that this term is Latin for *Arfon* sometimes called Gwynedd of North Wales, confused by Geoffrey of Monmouth with Armorica, a term for Brittany.

Armorica— The earlier term for Brittany, the large area of northwestern France forming a peninsula into the Atlantic Ocean to the west and the English Channel on the north. This area lies between the Loire and Seine rivers, and the Celtic derived from the Roman "ar-" and "-mor," "on the sea." In the fifth century Britons, driven out of the islands by the Saxon raids and warfare, migrated to this area. "Aremorica" is sometimes listed as a variant spelling.

Arthur— Successor as King of Britain after Ambrosius Aurelianus' and Riothamus' "deaths." His ascension to kingship is traditionally listed as the middle of the seventh decade in the fifth century. (*See* Titles for Arthur.)

Atavus— A Latin term in a general sense meaning "ancestor," but in a more specific sense can refer to an ancestor two generations removed.

Aurelius Ambrosius— Geoffrey of Monmouth's parallel to Ambrosius Aurelianus. His reign, according to Geoffrey is very short, with his successor as Utherpendragon, a fictional character not mentioned anywhere in the histories. Henry of Huntingdon uses the name Aurelius Ambrosius in his chronicle. (*See* Ambrosius Aurelianus.)

Avalon— An ancient term applied to Glastonbury in Somerset. At one point, Glastonbury was in fact an island, surrounded by water from the Bristol Channel, and attested to by tracks and walkways. The book *Prehistory of the Somerset Levels* describes in detail

Glastonbury as an island. The Isle of Avalon occupies a major niche in the romances. Avalon has attached to it an "other-worldliness."

 Avallon on the continent might also be a possibility as Arthur's burial site. (*See* Glastonbury.)

Badon— The last battle in the *Historia's* battlelist attributed to Arthur, assigned to the date of 497 in this text and geographically set at the Wrekin near Viroconium. Arthur's major adversaries were Octha and Cerdic.

Bath— One of the logical possibilities for the location of the Battle of Badon. The Latin word Badonis has the "d" sound as "th-" and its locale would not be in the city itself, but on the hillfort somewhere on the outskirts. (*See* Badon, Caer Vadon.)

Bath-Hill— A term used in reference to Badon, but not necessarily a reference to modern-day Bath, which was called *Aquae Sulis* by the Romans.

Bede— Listed as the scribe for the *Historia Ecclesiastica Gentis Anglorum*, written during the middle to late eighth century, with some sources indicating the completion of the *History* in 731. His work, much of which was based upon Gildas, does not mention Arthur by name, but he does refer to Ambrosius Aurelianus and Mount Badon, and he gives some genealogies of Saxon kings, including Hengist and Horsa.

Bossiney— The original term for Tintagel, since the latter is the term which only appears in Geoffrey of Monmouth. The term breaks into two affixes, *bossi-* and *-ney*. The prefix comes from "the monks of Bodmin," with *bod* or *bot* meaning "house or dwelling," and *-min* meaning "of monks." *-Ney* or *-ny* means island. Pieced together, then, Bossiney would mean "the island dwelling-place of monks."

Bretwalda— A Saxon term meaning "ruler of Britain" or "Britain-ruler." It implies an imperial title, but it was mainly honorific because the Bretwalda did not coordinate regional kingdoms. The title Brytwalda is an offshoot of this, but John Morris indicates that this offshoot means "wide ruler."

Britanni— A synonymous term with Britannians, the provincials of Roman Britain. Most commonly the term refers to the pre–Roman inhabitants called the Ancient Britons, used by Gildas, but the term can also apply to all the inhabitants of southern Britain, no matter what origin.

Britons— Before the advent of the term "Welsh," this term distinguished the (English) Saxons to the east of Wales, and the Britons to the west, in what became the country of Wales. Once the Welsh language emerged, "Welsh" was applied to the territories of the west, "English Saxons" referred to those Britanni who occupied parts of Britannia Secunda and Britannia Maxima, and "Britons" referred to those native inhabitants of Britannia Prima.

Brittany—*see* Armorica, Llydaw.

Brittones— The Latin term for Britons.

Brue (River)— River near the base of Glastonbury Tor. Its meaning is related to the Welsh *bryw* meaning "brisk, vigorous," supporting Michael Aston's stance of great landscape changes which have occurred over the last 1,500 years, since today the river is very small and sedate. This is purportedly one of the sites where Sir Bedivere returned Excalibur to the Lady of the Lake after the Battle of Camlann.

Budic— An heir to the Breton kingdom of Quimper in southwest Brittany. His importance lies in his connection with Riothamus, the King of the Britons who crossed the sea with 12,000 warriors.

Cabal, Cavall— Arthur's dog, as listed in the *Historia Brittonum*, with the latter as a spelling variant in *The Mabinogion*, "Culhwch and Olwen."

Cadbury-Camelot— The traditional romance setting for King Arthur's court established by Leslie Alcock's excavations of South Cadbury.

Cadbury-Congresbury— A commonly proposed site for the Camelot of Arthurian times.

Cadbury, Dorset—Another contender for the title of Camelot. It is located a short distance from Exeter, and therefore near the mouth of the River Exe; Exeter is connected by Roman roads to all of the important central coastal areas. Its one drawback as a serious contender is that it is too far west of the "heartland of Britain."

Cadnam—An actual probable geographic site for Arthur's last battle, the Battle of Camlann. Although much has been written about the possible locale of Camlann, this book uses etymological derivatives to suggest that there may have been a scribal confusion between Cadnam and Camlann. Cadnam can be selected on three major counts: first, the similarity in pronunciation and visual representation could easily lead to confusion by scribes whose interest lay more with ecclesiastical matters; second, Cadnam fits the etymological derivative for Camlann, being between the Hants and the Avon Rivers; third, Cadnam is only two to three miles inland, to the west of Southampton Water and close to Charford, which is listed in the *Chronicle* as the Saxons' major re-entry into Britain. (*See Annales Cambriae*, Camlann, Charford.)

Caer Vadon—Another term for Bath. (*See also* Badon.)

Caliburn—The early term for Arthur's sword. (*See* Excalibur.)

Camelot—Arthur's main stronghold and living residence, glorified in the later romances. (*See* Cadbury-Camelot, Cadbury-Congresbury, and Cadbury, Dorset.)

Camlann—Arthur's last battle, not included in Nennius' list of the 12 battles, but listed in the *Annales Cambriae*. The specific year in which it was fought, as proposed by this book, was 516. The entry does not indicate whether Arthur and Medraut were on the same side or whether they were enemies. Later tradition and romances set them up as enemies, with the traitorous Medraut joining the Saxons.

    Much has been written about Camlann in an attempt to fix the site geographically, mainly using etymological information of Camboglanna = crooked bank, and Cambolanda = crooked enclosure. (*See Annales Cambriae*, Cadnam, Charford.)

Carannog—In the life of this early Welsh saint, there is a segment which mentions Arthur, who has stolen the altar for his own purposes. Because Carannog helps rid the land of a giant serpent, Arthur returns the altar to him.

Caratacus—son of Cymbeline (Cunobelinus), leader of the resistance to the Roman conquest of Britain from southern and northern Wales during the reign of Claudius I. He was captured by pro–Roman Queen Cartimandua and turned over to Claudius, who supposedly spared his life. (*See* Coroticus.)

Cardinal Year—A term coined in this text to give credence in establishing a chronology for the historic King Arthur. A cardinal year must derive implicitly or explicitly from one of the ancient manuscripts listed in Chapter 2, it must be verified from a separate historic source, and it must have a direct bearing on Arthur. (*See also* Ordinal Year.)

Carlisle—*See* Ligualid, Luilid: a principal city as listed by Nennius, Cunedda's homeland after his southern migration.

Carnwennan—Arthur's knife in the Culhwch tale of *The Mabinogion*.

cashel—A synonym for a hillfort, but distinctive from a rath. Cashels have a normally circular enclosure, but the enclosure is a dry-built stone wall usually without an accompanying ditch. (*See* hillfort, rath.)

Celemion—One of the cities listed by Nennius, often interpreted as Camalet, Somersetshire, and mentioned as such by Giles. (*See* Camelot and the various Cadburies.)

Celli Wig—A story in *The Mabinogion*, "Culhwch and Olwen," labels this place, interestingly in Cornwall, as Arthur's main residence. In Welsh this means "wooded land" and it, like so many other geographic locations, is difficult to pinpoint. The *Triads* mention that this site is where the deep discord arises between Arthur and Medraut, which eventually leads to the Battle of Camlann. Kerry is one of its possible locations.

Cerdic—A major Saxon leader who permeates the Arthurian material. In the histories he makes appearances as 1) an interpreter for Vortigern, 2) Cunedda's fifth son; and 3) the West Saxon king appearing in the *Chronicle* entries for 495, 508, 519, 527, 530, and 534. This book offers two major postulations on Cerdic. One is that the interpreter, the son, and the West Saxon king are all references to the same individual. The second is that Cerdic is a close comrade of Octha's in the literary references. Like Octha, his association with Arthur is an initial friendship which then deteriorates into a rivalry of leaders warring for supremacy in Britain. The two battles between Arthur and Cerdic are the Battle of Badon in which Osla is killed and Cerdic after defeat pledges fealty to Arthur, and the final destructive battle at Camlann. (*See* Badon, Bath, Vadon, Creoda, Cynric, Osla, Camlann.)

Cerdicesford— As recorded in the *Anglo-Saxon Chronicle*, one of Cerdic's landing sites in Britain, identified as Charford.

Cerdicesora— As recorded in the *Anglo-Saxon Chronicle*, one of Cerdic's landing sites in western Britain.

Charford— The site of several battles listed in the *Chronicle*. It is located west of Southampton Water, and South of Salisbury and Old Sarum, very near Cadnam, a common route for the Saxons landing in Southampton Water. It, like Cadnam, is located near the banks of the Hants and Avon rivers. Since Charford is listed as the actual site for the battle in the *Chronicle* during the year 519, it is aligned with Camlann.

Cheldric— Geoffrey of Monmouth's Saxon leader who is killed by Cador at the Battle of Bath; one of the equivalents of Cerdic in the histories.

Chelric— Geoffrey of Monmouth's Saxon successor to Cheldric, in league with Mordred against Arthur, killed at the Battle of Camlann; another equivalent to Cerdic in the histories.

Cherdic— From Geoffrey of Monmouth, a Saxon comrade who accompanied Octa and Ebissa to northern Britain.

cohort— one of ten divisions of an ancient Roman legion.

combe— a deep, narrow valley or basin on the flank of a hill, in reference to a natural defense system incorporated in the construction of the Dykes in England, specifically the Bokerly.

Comes Britanniae— A Roman title meaning "Count of Britain," a leader who commanded the mobile field armies of Britain.

Comes Littoris Saxonici— A Roman title for the leader commanding the forces in southern Britain against the Saxons.

Constantine— In literary tradition, Constantine III is listed as the father of Aurelius Ambrosius and Utherpendragon. In tales such as *The Mabinogion*, Constantine is referred to as Cuestenhin. Historically, approximately between 410 and 460, Constantine (III) was proclaimed by the British as a native emperor who crossed over to Gaul and, with his son Constans and a Briton general named Gerontius, attempted to expel the invading barbarians, eventually failing in his attempts, with the Britons renouncing Constantine and turning back to Honorius for help.

Coroticus— A name appearing only once, in the manuscripts *Confessio* and *Epistola* attributed to Saint Patrick. Most scholars (cf. A.W. Wade-Evans, John Morris, Leslie Alcock) consider Coroticus another name for a Ceretic, king of Strathclyde, but there is no connection made with Caratacus of the first century. An interesting postulation, however, is that the name Coroticus refers to a smaller kingdom (named in honor of Caratacus) within the domain of Strathclyde, under the leadership of "Ceretic Guletic," a reasonable assumption since the letter is directed to the soldiers of Coroticus (a province) under the leadership of a gwledig (Ceretic). This Ceretic could very well be the son of Cunedda, thus showing an ancestry of Cunobelinus/Cunedda/Caraticus/Cerdic. (*See* Caraticus.)

crannog—An artificial fortified island constructed in a lake or a marsh.

Creoda—Son of Cerdic, mentioned in few of the *Chronicle* entries and genealogies, and in the *Chronicle's* Genealogical Preface; he is listed as Cerdic's son, often confused with Cynric, Cerdic's grandson; Creoda supplies the missing generation which helps reestablish the accuracy in dating entries in the *Chronicle*. (*See* Cerdic, Cynric.)

Culhwch and Olwen—One of the tales in *The Mabinogion* which centers on Arthur, a relative of Culhwch, whose mission with Arthur is to kill the giant Ysbaddaden and win the giant's daughter.

Cunedda—A powerful warrior of the north, who, with his eight sons, migrates south and has some important connection with Vortigern and the Saxons. One of his sons, Cerdic, has an enigmatic relevancy with Arthurian material. (*See* Cerdic, Osla.)

Cunobelinus—Another name for Cymbeline, a Roman ruler ca. A.D. 5–A.D. 50 posted at Camelodunum (Colchester), titled by Seutonius as *Britannorum rex*, lordship over southeastern Britain. The prefixes of his names, *cuno-*, *cym-*, show an early origin for successors such as Cunedda and Cunorix, and a base for words such as Cymry and Cymru. (*See also* Caratacus, one of his sons.)

cursus—An extended roadway having on either side a ditch and a bank, an example of which is the Stonehenge Cursus. The term was coined by William Stukeley, but the purpose for the structure was unknown.

Custenhin—A Welsh name for Constantine III. (*See* Constantine.)

cyfarwydd—An Early Welsh term meaning "storyteller."

Cymbeline—*See* Cunobelinus.

Cynric—Grandson of Cerdic and son of Creoda. His name is mentioned often in the *Chronicle* in conjunction with Cerdic. After Creoda's death, the kingship passes to him. (*See* Cerdic, Creoda.)

Darent(h)—The location of Vortimer's second battle against the Saxons. Morris equates this with the battle at Crayford near London. However, Darenth has the same etymological root as Derwen, Derwent, and Darwen, all more logistically located in northern Wales or immediately to the east in the upper midlands.

Dinas Emrys—A Welsh hillfort in Snowdonia, literally meaning "Emry's Fort." According to Nennius in the *Historia Brittonum*, Vortigern wants to sacrifice Ambrosius, the boy-prophet, to build a stronghold on this spot. The boy-prophet foils Vortigern's soothsayers and frightens Vortigern so that Vortigern not only refrains from sacrificing the boy but flees from the site, granting that territory and others to the boy.

Dionysiac Table—A method for giving the date of Easter proposed by Dionysius Exiguus in 525, introducing an era starting from the Incarnation of Christ, rather than from the Passion. This method of reckoning creates a 28-year discrepancy according to the Passion. (*See* Easter Annals, Victorian Table, Lunar Cycle.)

Dundadgel—*See* Tintagel.

Dux Bellorum—A title assigned to Arthur by Nennius, literally translated as "Duke of Battles."

Dux Britanniae—A title used by the Romans meaning "Duke of Britain," a leader who commanded garrison forces of Hadrian's Wall.

Easter Annals—Part of the compilation of *Harleian 3859*, Folios 190A–193A. They cover 533 years, the Great Cycle, and are important ecclesiastical and historical documents used for pinpointing chronologies more accurately than other available sources. Coupled with the present knowledge of the Victorian Table of reckoning, the Dionysiac Table of reckoning, and the discrepancies of lunar cycles possible in the Easter Annals, a precise (in terms of sixth century) determination can be made for dates. (*See Annales Cambriae*, Dionysiac Table, Victorian Table, Lunar Cycles.)

Easter Tables— Year-by-year compilations used by the church to determine Easter, since it was a moveable feast. In addition to these manuscripts recording church matters, a blank space in the right-hand column allowed scribes to record important historical information. These were then consolidated into a Great Cycle in the Easter Annals.

Ecclesiastical History— *See* Bede.

Elesa— According to the *Anglo-Saxon Chronicle*, an ancestor of Cerdic the West Saxon king, associated with Eliset/Eliseg, a Welsh royal family during the same era. (*See* Eliset.)

Eliset, Eliseg— A name appearing on an inscribed pillar near Llangollen in Wales. It is associated with the name "Elesa" in the *Anglo-Saxon Chronicle*, a listing for Cerdic's father in the genealogy.

Embresguletic— The British term for Ambrosius Aurelianus, according to Nennius. (*See* Ambrosius Aurelianus, Emrys, Gwledig, Wledig.)

Emrys— Sometimes spelled Emhrys. The Welsh epithet meaning "emperor" for Ambrosius Aurelianus. (*See* Ambrosius Aurelianus.)

English Saxons— Those Saxons who had been settled in Britain for several generations, intermixing with the Britanni. Sometimes a synonymous term with Gewissae.

englynion— Early Welsh metrical three-line, rhyming stanzas used as a preface to prose. They were forerunners to the eleventh and twelfth century Triads.

epaulement— A descriptive, figurative term suggesting a line at right angles or near right angles, to another line. Specifically, Pitt-Rivers uses this term to describe an entrenchment and a bank which angle off from the major entrenchments and ramparts of Bokerly Dyke.

Episford— Vortimer's third battle against the Saxons. This is referred to as Aylesford. In this battle Horsa is killed and Hengist and his son succeed to the kingdom.

escarpment— A man-made entrenchment to steepen a hillside, usually of a hillfort, particularly to increase its defensibility.

Eubonia— A term used by Nennius for the Isle of Man.

Euric— The Visigoth who attains leadership by murdering his brother Theodoric. He defeats Riothamus at the Battle of Bourg de Déols and Riothamus disappears into Burgundy.

Eusebius— A prominent scribal scholar who wrote the *Historia Ecclesiastica* and was one of the first devisers and synchronizers of the 19-year lunar systems tables.

Excalibur— The late medieval term for Arthur's sword, in earlier centuries called Caliburn, Caliburnus.

De Excidio et Conquestu Britanniae— The title of Gildas' work. (*See* Gildas.)

Fleuriot, Leon— Professor and distinguished Breton historian and author of *Les Origines de la Bretagne* who judged that the term Riothamus was a title meaning supreme king, and not a name. Further, Professor Fleuriot maintained that the Britons had a great leader during the last segment of the fifth century, whose title was Riothamus, and whose successes helped make up Arthuriana. He equated Riothamus with Ambrosius Aurelianus, and claims, as this book does, that Ambrosius' deeds were credited later to somebody else named Arthur. Geoffrey Ashe minimizes that equation on the grounds that Gildas does not refer to Ambrosius as "a King."

floruit— A generational measure used to signify a 30-year time span. To determine a lifespan, 15 years are added onto both ends of the floruit.

German Saxons— A reference to the continental Saxons.

De Gestis Regum Anglorum— William of Malmsbury's work fortunately preserved and which shows the interpolations added to the *De Antiquitate* at Glastonbury Abbey. Both this work and the *De Antiquitate* are extremely reserved in references to King

Arthur, since Malmsbury is writing from a conservative historic perspective. (*See De Antiquitate*, William of Malmsbury.)

Gewissi—A crucial term in tracing Arthurian connections. The word "Gewis" is used in the *Anglo-Saxon Chronicle* ancestry of Cerdic, and appears as Hwicci in Bede, as Gewissi, Gewissie, Gewisse, Gewissae in other contexts of early Welsh literature. Its reference is to an early Briton territory in western-central Wales and its inhabitants of mixed cultures. The term aligns itself with the West Saxon king Cerdic, Elesa, and Eliseg. (*See* each of the names given.)

Gildas Albanius—A different Gildas, a near-contemporary with the author of the *De Excidio*. He was born ca. 425 in Scotland and at age 13 moved to France where he later founded the monastery of Ruys. He died ca. 512.

Gildas Badonicus—One of the primary sources for historical information gleaned about the sixth century. His manuscript, the *De Excidio*, his birth date, and his death date are crucial in calibrating chronology and pinpointing geographic sites for Arthur's historicity and authenticity, although Arthur's name is nowhere in Gildas.

His background on the Saxons, the Briton-Saxon conflicts, Vortigern, Maelgwn, Ambrosius Aurelianus, and the profligate kings of Britain all lead to an indispensable scenario for Arthur's emergence. Likewise, references to him in the *Annales Cambriae* help construct a panorama of the period. Further, Bede and Nennius borrow from him in depth. Gildas is one of the singular most important connections for the establishment not only of Arthur but, just as important, the establishment of Ambrosius Aurelianus. (*See* Ambrosius Aurelianus, *Annales Cambriae*, Arthur, Badon, Bede, *De Excidio*, Nennius.)

Giraldus Cambrensis—In *De Instructione Principis*, Giraldus gives a detailed description of Arthur's exhumation at Glastonbury. (*See* Glastonbury.)

Glastonbury—Giraldus Cambrensis indicates that Glastonbury (Glaestingabyrig, "the fort of glass") was the legendary Avalon, Arthur's burial site. Purportedly, in the early years of the 1190s monks of Glastonbury Abbey claimed that they exhumed the bodies of Arthur and Guinevere south of the Lady Chapel of the Abbey church. In 1278 in the presence of Edward I and Queen Eleanor, the remains were transferred inside the Abbey to the front of the high altar. In 1539 the dissolution of the monasteries instigated by Henry VIII destroyed and irretrievably scattered what was entombed in front of the high altar. (*See* Giraldus Cambrensis.)

Glastonbury Cross—Beneath the coffin cover (some reports say beneath a stone slab, with the inscribed face downwards, above the coffin) was a leaden cross. After the dissolution of the monasteries, the cross was reportedly seen by John Leland in 1542, who claimed that it was approximately one foot high and bore the inscription "HIC IACET SEPVLTVS IHCLITVS REX ARTVRIVS IH IHSVLA AVALOHIA," with the J looking like an I, the N's looking like H's, and the U's looking like V's. This translates to "Here lies buried the famous King Arthur in the Isle of Avalon." The cross thus makes a connection between Glastonbury and the legendary Isle of Avalon, the Isle of Glass. It allegedly was traced into the eighteenth century in Wells, about six miles from Glastonbury, but thereafter disappeared. (*See* Glastonbury.)

Glastonbury Tor—The Tor, very near the Abbey, can be seen from any direction from a distance of approximately 20 miles, including Cadbury-Camelot to the south and west. The entire area of Glastonbury, the Abbey, Chalice Well, Wearyall Hill, and the Tor with its suggested maze and its shrine on top, has acquired a solemn, reverent, religious atmosphere, undoubtedly a carry-over from the "other-worldliness" of legend and Christian attachments through Joseph of Arimathea and the Holy Grail.

Gododdin—See Aneirin.

Gododdin—A territory in northern Britain, near the Antonine Wall.

Gregory of Tours—A continental scribe of the sixth century who writes about matters unrelated to Arthur, but provides some implicit connection with Riothamus and his victory over the Saxons at the Battle of Angers. (*See* Ambrosius Aurelianus, Riothamus.)

Guaul—The Roman name for Wall, spelled Gwawl in Welsh, sometimes associated with Wall, the village near Hadrian's Wall. However, it may also refer to Wall-by-Lichfield (Caer Luit Coyt) where Octha was sent on his mission north.

Gurthrigern, Gwrtheyrn—The name used by Nennius. (*See also* Vortigern.)

Gwrthefyr—*See* Vortimer.

Gwyr y Gogledd—Literally "men of the North" who occupied the territories between the two Walls. The tribes were of mixed origins, not only people from the Valentia province beyond the Antonine Wall, but those tribes called the English Saxons, the Gewissae, and the Britons, later known as Welsh. Cunedda, Cerdic, Octha, and Owein Dantguin emerged as the four major leaders.

Harleian 3859—The identification tag for a miscellany of materials located in the British Museum. The longest portion of the collection is the *Historia Brittonum*, ascribed to Nennius, followed by Chronicles usually called the *Annales Cambriae* (*The Welsh Annals*) and some genealogies of Welsh families. Leslie Alcock, in his works, refers to this collection as the British Historical Miscellany. (See Appendix B.)

hectare—A metric measurement approximating 2.47 acres of land. As an example, South Cadbury–Camelot encloses 8.0 hectares of land, which would be approximately 19.75 acres. Conversely, one hide of land would be slightly over 48.50 hectares. (*See* hide.)

herepath—a local name referring to an "army road."

hide—An Old English unit of land measurement equaling 120 acres.

hillforts—The term for third millennium B.C. strongholds that dot the British countryside. After a period of abandonment, some were reoccupied by the Romans shortly after they conquered and occupied Britain. Some of these Roman hillforts were abandoned later, only to be reestablished in the third through seventh centuries. Some of the common hilltop strongholds are Old Sarum, Solsbury Hill, Badbury Rings, Glastonbury Tor, Cadbury-Camelot, Cadbury-Congresbury, Tintagel(?), Cadbury-Dorset, Castle Dore, Dinas Powys, and Dinas Emrys. (*See* multivallate, univallate, rath, cashel.)

Historia Brittonum—The work attributed to Nennius. (*See* Nennius.)

Historia de Rebus Glastoniensibus—(*See* Adam of Domerham.)

Historia Ecclesiastica Gentis Anglorum—The Latinized title for Bede's work.

A History of the English Church and People—(*See* Bede.)

Hueil—One of the sons of Caw, brother to Gildas. Hueil appears in two stories, "Culhwch and Olwen" and "The Life of St. Gildas" by Caradoc. His connection to the search for Arthur's historicity is important in one aspect: as Gildas' brother, who was killed by Arthur, this suggests one reason Gildas does not mention Arthur by name in the *De Excidio.*

Hwicci—Bede's variant term for Gewisse.

imperator—A Latin term associated with the word "emperor." (*See also* ameraudur.)

John of Glastonbury—The Glastonbury Abbey monk who penned the *Cronica sive Antiquitates Glastoniensis Ecclesie,* ca. 1342. Much of the work is repetitive copy, but segments indicate sources other than the common ones.

Jordanes—Continental scribe of *Gothic History* who writes about the king "Riotimus." In his manuscript this king was not just a local chieftain, but a great king who came by way of the Ocean with 12,000 men. This number is probably an exaggeration, but the army must have been large enough to be considered a major force hoping to check Euric the Visigoth.

This king had to have been a strong power on either side of the Ocean, a king with ties and loyalty to the center of Rome. (*See* Riothamus, Ambrosius Aurelianus.)

Kaerluideoit—Geoffrey of Monmouth's version of Caer Luit Coyt, Wall-by-Lichfield, Octha's stronghold as postulated by this text.

Kelliwic, Kelli Wig—*See* Celli Wig.

lagg—A low area or depression of land, many times filling up with water.

lias—A bluish rock, the oldest strata of the Jurassic period, found particularly in Britain.

Ligualid, Luilid—A major city of Britain as listed by Nennius, interpreted by both Morris and Giles as Carlisle.

Llamrei—Arthur's horse, recorded several times in the Culhwch tale.

Llydaw—The Welsh name for Brittany. (*See* Brittany, Armorica.)

lunar cycle—Easter Tables covering a 19-year period devised by the church to calculate the date for Easter. The tables are governed by the phases of the moon, creating what is called 19-year lunar cycles. In misidentifying lunar cycles, a scribe could place an event exactly 19 years too late. (*See* Dionysiac Table, Easter Annals, Victorian Table.)

lynchet—Contoured and terraced ploughing associated with early farming techniques.

Mabinogion—The composite title for 11 medieval prose tales: the Four Branches, titled "Pwyll, Lord of Dyved," "Branwen Daughter of Llyr," "Manawydan, Son of Llyr," and "Math Son of Mathonwy," and the rest labeled as "Other Tales." Of the seven others, one of significance in relation to Arthur is "Culhwch and Olwen," Arthur's first appearance in Celtic lore. The second is the "Dream of Rhonabwy."

Maelgwn—King of Gwynedd, mentioned in Gildas' *De Excidio* and in the *Annales Cambriae*. Maelgwn's life and death aid in determining when Gildas wrote of the *De Excidio*, and that in turn helps to calibrate a chronology for Arthur. He is additionally important because his reign sets the time frame of Cunedda's migration to the south.

Maglocunus—The name used by Gildas, referring to Maelgwn.

Mailcun—The name used by Nennius referring to Maelgwn.

Man, Isle of—*See* Eubonia: one of the three large Isles of Britain.

Manau Guotodin—The northern section of the early Roman territory called Votadini, Cunedda's province prior to southern migration. Also spelled Manaw Guotodin, Manau Gododdin, Manaw Gododdin.

marchawg—Old Welsh term meaning "horseman." However, because Welsh did not develop new words, this also came to mean "knight."

Mervin—Merfyn, Mermin, Mermini, Mermenus, Meruin, Meruini refer to the King of the Britons mentioned by Nennius in his Prologue and in Chapter 16, and in the *Annales Cambriae* at entry 844. The mention of this king helps establish a reckoning for Nennius' *Historia Brittonum*.

Modred, Mordred—Derivatives of Medraut, the individual mentioned in the Camlann entry. Later romances list him as Arthur's traitorous son.

multivallate—(Of a hillfort) having more than one rampart and ditch.

Nennius—Listed as the writer of *Historia Brittonum*. Nennius, like Bede, borrows heavily from Gildas, but two of his segments — the listing of cities and the listings of battles attributed to Arthur — are important in the quest for the legendary and historical king. Nennius claims that "he has made a heap of all he has written," but his style is not that difficult or unpleasant to read.

His work is also commonly titled in its translated form, *The History of the Britons*. His writings occur later than Bede's — most scholars place his composition around the beginning of the ninth century — and are used often by Geoffrey of Monmouth.

Nymet—An ancient term for the River Yeo, commonly interpreted as "River at a holy place."

Oppidum, =*da*— The chief settlement of the British tribes prior to the Roman conquest. The term was used by Caesar to refer to pre–Roman hillforts or flatland villages, many times defended by dykes and ditches.

Octha, Octa, Æsc— names ascribed to Hengist's son; Nennius and Geoffrey of Monmouth use the spelling of Octa, Bede uses Oisc and Oeric.

Ordinal year— A term coined in this text very similar to a cardinal year. Two conditions are the same: a date must be implicitly or explicitly given in one of the four major manuscripts listed in Chapter 2, and that date must have a direct bearing to Arthur. The variant, however, is that unlike the cardinal year which needs a confirmation from a separate historic source, an ordinal year uses confirmation from an ancient *literary* source. (*See* cardinal year.)

Osla Big Knife— Arthur's ally in the tale "Culhwch and Olwen" and his adversary in the tale the "Dream of Rhonabwy," both from the *Mabinogion.*

Ossa— The son of Octha; Hengist's grandson.

Pridwen— Arthur's shield.

rath— A synonym for a hillfort, distinctive from a cashel. A rath has a circular enclosure surrounded by an earthen bank made by excavating an external ditch. (*See* hillfort, cashel.)

Riardd Ambrosius— The name coined by this text to refer to the triumvirate of Ambrosius Aurelianus, Riothamus, and Arthur, stemming from the postulation that neither Riothamus nor Arthur are proper names but epithets which apply to Ambrosius Aurelianus.

Riothamus (Riotamus, Rigotamus)— A title rather than a name. "Rig(o)-" means "king," with the suffix "-tamos" being a superlative such as "supreme," a title, therefore, such as Supreme King. This is the title given to the King of the Britons who came with 12,000 men into Bituriges by way of the Ocean. Riothamus fights against the Saxons at Angers and Euric's Visigoths at Bourges de Déols, then disappears from history around 470. (*See* Ambrosius Aurelianus, Riardd Ambrosius, Arthur.)

Roman occupation of Britain— The Romans occupied Britain from the time of Julius Caesar around 50 B.C. until early in the fifth century A.D., when they withdrew to the continent to try to protect their crumbling empire. For an incredible span of approximately three and a half centuries, their culture molded a civilized Britain. Roman ruins create a stark contrast between life under the Roman rule and the perversity of the surrounding barbarians. Literally thousands of sites around the island attest to the quality of life offered to the Britons under Roman dominion.

   When the time came for Roman withdrawal, Britons tried to entice the Empire to once again help them repel the barbarians and prevent them from engulfing the Island. Because the Empire had serious problems of its own, no reciprocal help was forthcoming, and the Britons were left to their own defenses.

Roman roads— One of the legacies left by the Romans to the Britons. Several of the maps in the body of this text attest to the advanced technology of Roman roads — tracks built up sometimes to a height of approximately ten feet, accurate surveying capabilities, and distances between towns and villages covered by straight lines, seldom deviating except to avoid a rapid descent or intersect with another road, making travel easy and fast. Roman legions on foot could cover 20 miles a day on these roads, with a station or fortification approximately every 20 miles (sometimes only ten) for overnight rest if the need arose.

   Modern-day surveyors were initially thrown off by the measurement of Roman miles, since the distances seemed inaccurate and variable, until they realized that the Romans measure only the horizontal distances without regarding the irregularities of the surface. The miles bear a regular proportion to the English miles on the plains but fall short on hilly ground.

Ron—The shortened name of Arthur's spear, Rhongomynyad.

Rowena—Sometimes seen as Renwein, Hengist's daughter given to Vortigern in return for Briton territories.

Saesons—A synonym for the English, all Frisian-speaking people settled in Britain. For the most part, these English occupied Britannia Secunda. (*See* English Saxons.)

Saxones—A third century Latin generic term for strangers who had arrived from the continent, not in reference to a single nation, but considered more as an alliance of Germanic tribes including the knife-men (Saxons), the Angles, and the Frisians. An accurate synonym would perhaps be Old Saxons.

Saxoniaid—A Welsh term synonymous with German Saxons or continental Anglo-Saxons. (*See* German Saxons.)

Saxons—A generic term borrowed from Latin "Saxones" by the British/Welsh as "Saeson," meaning the English, for all the Frisian-speaking people in Britain. Unfortunately the ancient manuscripts often do not distinguish between Britanni, Briton, Welsh, German Saxons, English Saxons, or Angles. The term is sometimes used synonymously with "English," distinguished from the Britons of Britain and the Bretons of Bretagne (Brittany).

scuid—Old Welsh word meaning "shoulder." (*See* yagwydd.)

scuit—Old Welsh word meaning "shield." (*See* yaswyd.)

Sidonius—A Continental born at Lyons around the year 430. His importance in the Arthurian pursuit focuses upon his letter to the king "Riothamo." The letter is about a wrongdoing against a humble farmer by certain Bretons, the subject unimportant, but the tone suggesting the character and ethics of the king Riothamo. The king has a conscientiousness that weighs heavily on him, a delicacy which makes him blush for the wrongdoings of others, and an impartiality, all of which rings with overtones of Gildas' praising Ambrosius Aurelianus in the *De Excidio*, calling him meritorious, worthy, and honorable. (*See* Ambrosius Aurelianus.)

superbus tyrannus—The Roman title meaning "supreme ruler."

Taliesin, Talyessin—A bard of the early sixth century. The earliest surviving manuscript for Taliesin's work is in the 1200s, in the *Black Book of Carmarthen*. Nennius lists five bards in his work, with only manuscripts from Taliesin and Aneirin surviving. The other bards are Talhaern, with only references to his praises of King Maelgwn, and two others, Cian and Bluchbard.

Tanat, Tanet—A term often confused with the Isle of Thanet. Both have the same etymological root. This book rejects Vortimer's battle as having been fought on the Isle of Thanet, placing instead the site near the River Tanet in northern Wales.

Thanet—The island given to the Saxons by Vortigern in their first coming. This site, too, is listed as the location of Vortimer's first battle against the Saxons after their revolt. (*See* Tanat.)

Tintagel—A fortress on the northern coast of Cornwall; was not connected until recently to the sixth century or the Arthur of that time; it was an outgrowth, allegedly fictional, of Geoffrey of Monmouth of the twelfth century, until archaeological excavations in the 1930s by C.A. Ralegh Radford revealed it had late fifth and early sixth century connections. At first the earlier structures were thought to be a monastery, but pottery and other artifacts indicate that it might have been a chieftain stronghold. Its local form is Dundadgel, a name with obscure roots. (*See also* Bossiney.)

Titles for Arthur—Dux Bellorum, Dux Britanniarum, Ameraudur, Imperator, Commander-in-Chief, Emperor, Leader of Battles, British High King, Chief Lord of the Island.

toises—Roman units of distance. The Roman mile was approximately 755 toises or 1,593 yards, English measure. (*See* Roman Roads.)

tor— A British term for a high, craggy hill, a common site for hillforts.

Tywyssawc Cat— A Welsh term meaning "leader of the battle."

Tywyssawc Llu— A Welsh term meaning "leader of the army."

univallate—(Of a hillfort) containing only one rampart and ditch as a perimeter defense system.

Uther— The clipped name for Utherpendragon is a figment of the later romances; Uther as Arthur's father is not found in the histories. The term Uther, however, has an interesting etymology which can be connected to Arthur. As an aside, Uther is nearly a perfect anagram for Arthur. In Welsh "uthr" means "terrible"; if this were used to describe Arthur's ferocity in battle, it could have been misconstrued as Arthur, son of Uthr. "Pendragon" probably comes from the Latin root *draco*, which was later incorporated into Old Welsh as *dragwn, dragon*, which meant "war leader." *Pen-* meant prime, or main, or head. Thus Pendragon would be "head war leader." The banner for Caesar was likewise a purple dragon, the color signifying royalty.

Vadon, Vathon, Caer Vadon— A term referring to Bath, Bath-hill, and Badon, since the double-d arrangement is pronounced as a *th-* sound.

vallum— A Roman rampart consisting of the *agger* (a mound of earth) and the *sudes* (palisades driven into the ground) to secure and strengthen the rampart.

Victorian Table— A method for determining the date of Easter proposed in 457 by Victorius of Aquitaine based upon the Passion of Christ. In the process, he discovered that Easter would fall on the same day of the month and at the same phase of the moon as in the year of the Passion itself, which came to be known as the Great Cycle of 532 years. There is a discrepancy of 28 years between this Table and the Dionysiac Table, and a 19-year discrepancy between this Table and miscalculations of the Lunar Cycle. (*See* Easter Annals, Dionysiac Table, Lunar Cycle.)

Vortigern— The predecessor of Ambrosius Aurelianus, also called Gurthrigern or Gwrtheyrn, the arch-villain of all Britons, blamed for inviting the Saxons into Britain to try to contain the Picts and the Irish. He seizes the kingship until he is dethroned some time near the year 455.

Vortimer— Son of Vortigern, named only in the *Historia Brittonum* and noted for fighting four main battles against the Saxons. Another name for him is Gwrthefyr.

Walas— A synonym for Britanni in Gildas. The English used this term to apply to the offshoot Britons, the Welsh, which also gave rise to the term Wales. Disparagingly, they also used the term for Romans.

Wall— The Roman city of Letocetum, also known as Wall-by-Lichfield and Cair Luit Coyt, postulated in this text as Octha's stronghold. (*See also* Kaerluideoit, Guaul.)

William of Malmsbury— Scribal historian commissioned to write the *De Antiquitate* for Glastonbury Abbey. His straightforward, no-nonsense manuscripts are important in giving reliable historical information of the period, in the mid-quarter of the 1100s. (See *De Gestis*.)

Wrekin, the —Ancient hillfort adjacent to Wroxeter, occupied in the late fifth and early sixth century, postulated in this text as the site for the Badon battle.

Wroxeter— The Roman city of Viroconium or Uriconium, the fourth largest city in Britain in Roman times, the main stronghold of the Cornovi territory.

Wynebgwrthucher— Arthur's shield in the Culhwch tale. (*See* Prydwen.)

yagwydd— Welsh word meaning "shoulder." (*See* scuid.)

yaswyd— Welsh word meaning "shield." (*See* scuit.)

Yeo (River)—*See* Nymet.

Notes

Preface

1. John Steinbeck, *The Acts of King Arthur and His Noble Knights*, Appendix of letters, page 354.
2. Steinbeck, page 356.
3. Steinbeck, page 361.
4. Steinbeck, *A Life in Letters*, page 607.
5. Charles Plummer, *Two of the Saxon Chronicles Parallel*, page 3.
6. John Morris, *The Age of Arthur*, page xv.

Chapter 1— Introductory Background

1. Kenneth Jackson, *The Gododdin,* page 112.
2. Richard Barber, *The Figure of Arthur*, page 31.
3. Barber, page 31.
4. Barber, page 36.
5. Leslie Alcock, *Arthur's Britain*, page 59.
6. Alcock, page 294. See also the preceding section leading up to this, pages 287–294 and Map 9, page 288.
7. Barber, *The Figure of Arthur,* page 50.

Chapter 2 — The Ancient Manuscripts

1. For a compact summary, see G.N. Garmonsway, *The Anglo-Saxon Chronicle,* pages xxxii–xlii.
2. John Morris, *The Age of Arthur,* page 39.
3. J.A. Giles, *Six Old English Chronicles*, page vii.
4. Alcock, *Arthur's Britain*, discusses this on page 22; Thomas O'Sullivan, in *The De Excidio of Gildas,* also mentions versions of later centuries, page 3.
5. Thomas O'Sullivan, *The* De Excidio *of Gildas,* page 3.
6. O'Sullivan, page 7.
7. O'Sullivan, page 6.

8. O'Sullivan, page 9.

9. O'Sullivan, page 11.

10. Geoffrey Ashe, "The Arthurian Fact," *The Quest for Arthur's Britain*, page 30.

11. Alcock, *Arthur's Britain*, page 22.

12. Alcock, page 53.

13. Leslie Alcock, *Was This Camelot?*, page 216. Forty-three years were added to the date of A.D. 499, arriving at a date of A.D. 442 for the penning of the *De Excidio* instead of 542. At another point, in *Arthur's Britain*, there is an unfortunate transposition of 452 + 12 = 437 instead of A.D. 425 (the beginning of Vortigern's reign) + 12 years later (discord with Vitalinus) = 437. Although detectable in our century because of modern technology, these errors indicate how easily scribal mistakes could have occurred in manuscripts.

14. Morris, *The Age of Arthur*, page 35.

15. Giles, *Six Old English Chronicles*, page 310.

16. Giles, pages 312–313.

17. Giles, page 313.

18. Alcock, *Arthur's Britain*, page 359.

19. Ashe, "The Arthurian Fact," *The Quest for Arthur's Britain*, page 48.

20. Leo Sherley-Price, trans. *Bede: A History of the English Church and People*, page 66.

21. Betram Colgrave and R.A.B. Mynors, eds., *Bede's Ecclesiastical History*, page xxi.

22. Colgrave and Mynors, pages 54–55.

23. John Morris, *British History*, page 85.

24. Morris, page 85.

25. Morris, page 85.

26. Morris, page 86.

27. Kathryn Grabowski and David Dumville, *Chronicles and Annals of Medieaval Ireland and Wales*, page 209.

28. Grabowski and Dumville, page 210.

29. Alcock, *Arthur's Britain*. Tables 1, 2, 3, and 4 in this text show the different formatting for each table.

30. Grabowski and Dumville, page 209.

31. Thomas O'Sullivan, *The* De Excidio *of Gildas*, page 40.

32. O'Sullivan, page 46.

33. Sherley-Price, *Bede: A History of the English Church and People*, pages 315–324.

34. Sherley-Price, page 323.

35. Morris, *The Age of Arthur*, page 144.

36. Morris, page 563, footnote 144.2.

37. Charles Plummer, *Two of the Saxon Chronicles Parallel*, page xxi, footnote 1.

38. O'Sullivan, page 79, footnote 11.

39. Alcock, *Arthur's Britain*, page 131.

40. Morris, *The Age of Arthur*, page 145.

41. E.K. Chambers, *Arthur of Britain*, page 171.

42. O'Sullivan, page 40.

43. Alcock, *Arthur's Britain*, pages 45–49.

44. Alcock, *Arthur's Britain*, page xvii.

45. John Morris, ed. and trans., *Nennius: British History and the Welsh Annals*, page 44. This small volume contains *The Annales Cambriae* and *Historia Brittonum* plus their translations, *The Welsh Annals* and *British History*. Because the text is referred to most commonly as *British History*, the footnotes here follow that pattern; see the bibliography for its full title. O'Sullivan, in *The* De Excidio *of Gildas*, indicates that *an. i* of the *Annales* is conventionally A.D. 445 but can vary as widely as A.D. 449, the date commonly used as the first Saxon *Adventus*.

46. Michael Lapidge and David Dumville, eds., *Gildas: New Approaches,* page 54.

47. See the Preface in Josephus Stevenson's *Nennii: Historia Brittonum,* for details of Prologues and manuscripts, pages v and xxi–xxx.

48. Josephus Stevenson, *Nennii: Historia Brittonum,* page xv.

49. Stevenson, pages xvii–xviii.

50. Stevenson, page xx. The manuscript is referred to as *Harleian MS 3859,* folio 135 b, listed as A.

51. Morris, *British History,* page 21.

52. Morris, page 21.

53. Giles, *Six Old English Chronicles,* page 383.

54. Giles, page 384.

55. Morris, *British History,* pages 1 through 3 of Morris' Introduction, with two references to Chapter 16. The difference between the dates of 857 and 829 is a span of 28 years, the exact difference between Dionysiac and Victorian reckonings, unlikely to be just a coincidence. Perhaps a 19-year lunar cycle adjustment is needed because of a miscalculation by Nennius or a copyist, but the date would not be 829.

56. Morris, *British History,* page 48.

57. Stevenson, *Nennii,* page v.

58. Stevenson, page xviii.

59. Rachel Bromwich, *The Beginnings of Welsh Poetry,* Chapter 1, "When Did British Become Welsh?," page 11.

60. Bromwich, *The Beginnings of Welsh Poetry,* page 10.

61. Bromwich, page 150.

62. Bromwich, pages 126–127.

63. Giles, Chapter 47, page 406.

64. Giles, Chapter 42, page 404.

65. Giles, Chapter 41, page 402.

66. Eliert Ekwall, *The Concise Oxford Dictionary of English Place-names,* page 311. See Maesbrook and Maesbury. Maesbrook, twelve miles south of Llangollen, and Maesbury Marsh, in the same vicinity, are the only two east of Offa's Dkye, though only by a minimal distance. In Wales are Maesglas, just outside of Newport, on the shores of the Mouth of the Severn; Maeshafn, ten miles west of Chester in northern Wales; Maesmynis, three miles southwest of Builth; Maesteg, five miles from Swansea Bay; Maesybont, fifteen miles northwest of Swansea; Maesycrugiau, five miles east of Maesllyn; and Maesycwnmer, seven miles north of Cardiff.

67. Stevenson, *Nennii,* page 31, footnote 22.

68. Stevenson also states that "The orthography of the text is supported by Asser's Life of Alfred," page 31, footnote 24.

69. Stevenson, page 31, footnotes 3 and 5.

70. Giles, end of Chapter 42, pages 403–404.

71. Giles, end of Chapter 42, page 404.

72. Alcock, *Arthur's Britain,* pages 358–359.

73. Alcock, page 103.

74. Giles, Chapter 37, page 400.

75. Ekwall, page 86.

76. Stevenson, *Nennii,* page 28, footnote 25.

77. Stevenson, page 29, footnote 1.

78. Giles, end of Chapter 38, page 400.

79. Stevenson, *Nennii,* page 30, footnote 1.

80. Stevenson, page 50, note 22.

81. Giles, beginning of Chapter 43, page 404.

82. Ekwall, page 459.

83. Ekwall, page 139.

84. Ekwall, page 143.

85. Giles, Chapter 44, page 404. Stevenson in *Nennii,* page 35, elaborates upon this, spelling the name as Rit Hergabail, and giving the variation of Satheneghabail in manuscripts D and H, Sateneghabail in Manuscript E, and Set Thergabail in Manuscript *a.*

86. Ekwall, pages 468–469.

87. Giles, Chapter 44, page 44.

88. Alcock, *Arthur's Britain,* page 246.

89. Alcock, page 246. Refer to the entire discussion of the Ogham stones. Alcock writes not only that "The immigrant tribe or dynasty of the Dési would have had the chief responsibility for the introduction of these Irish customs to Britain," (page 241) but adds "The greatest concentration of Ogham inscriptions and of vertical Latin inscriptions is certainly in Dyfed, where the influence of the ruling dynasty of the Dési was obviously responsible. It means too that the Dési would have found certain familiar elements in the Dementian landscape where they came across in the late fourth century" (page 268).

90. Ekwall, page 388.

91. Ekwall, page 385.

92. Ekwall, page 386.

93. Morris, *The Age of Arthur,* page 214.

94. Peter Clayton, *Guide to the Archaeological Sites of Britain,* pages 139–140.

95. Ashe, *The Discovery of King Arthur,* page 197.

96. Morris, *The Age of Arthur,* page 294.

97. Morris, *The Age of Arthur,* footnote 294.1, page 581 and footnote 324.2, page 588.

98. Morris, page 319.

99. Plummer, *Two of the Saxon Chronicles Parallel,* pages xvii–xviii.

100. Plummer, page cxiii.

101. Morris, page 145.

102. Morris, page 145.

103. See Plummer's material on the growth of the *Chronicle,* pages cxiv and cxv.

104. Plummer, pages civ, cv.

105. Plummer, page cvi.

106. Plummer, page cvi.

107. Plummer, page cviii.

108. Plummer, page cx.

109. Plummer, page cxxv.

110. Plummer, page xxiii.

111. Plummer, page cii.

112. Plummer, page cxvii.

113. Plummer, pages cxxii, cxxiii.

114. Plummer, page xxvii. A range from 892 to 900 is given, since Plummer gives the date as approximately 892 but then mentions in a footnote that Mr. C.F. Warner listed the date as 900.

115. Plummer, page xxviii.

116. Plummer, page xxxv.

117. Plummer, pages cii, ciii.

118. Plummer, pages ciii, civ.

119. Dorothy Whitelock, et al., *The Anglo-Saxon Chronicle,* page xviii.

120. Alcock, *Arthur's Britain,* page 43.

121. Garmonsway, Manuscript $\overline{\text{A}}$, the Parker Chronicle, *The Anglo-Saxon Chronicle,* page 14.

122. Whitelock, page 11.
123. Garmonsway, page 2.
124. Plummer, page 2.
125. Whitelock, pages 11, 12.
126. Plummer, page 13.
127. Plummer, page cxii in conjunction with footnote 3.
128. For discussions on Stuf and Wihtgar, see Plummer, entry 514, page 13, and entry 544, page 14. See also Ethelwerd's chronicle in Giles, entry 514 on page 7 and entry 534 on page 8. Ethelwerd does not include an entry for 544 and does not mention Wihtgar's death.
129. Plummer, page cxii, in conjunction with footnote 2.
130. Plummer, pages ci–cii.
131. Plummer, page cvi.
132. Plummer, page cx.
133. A. Campbell, *The Chronicle of Æthelweard*, page 11.
134. Campbell, page 11.
135. Campbell, page 12. Campbell claims that 56 years should read 66, evidently to align with the year of 449 as listed in the *ASC*.
136. Campbell, page 12.
137. Plummer, page 6.
138. See Plummer, individual entries, plus material in the index, particularly all the variations of Bryttas and Bryttisc, versus all the variations of Wilsc and Wealas.
139. Giles, page 7.
140. Campbell, page 11.
141. Whitelock, *Anglo-Saxon Chronicle*, page 206.
142. Garmonsway, page 2.
143. See Garmonsway, page 2, as an example of this insertion.
144. Plummer, page 2.
145. Plummer, pages 2–3.
146. Plummer, page 3.
147. Alcock, *Arthur's Britain*, page 20.
148. Plummer, pages 4 and 5.
149. Whitelock, page 206.

Chapter 3 — Cardinal/Ordinal Years

1. Alcock, Leslie, *Arthur's Britain*, page 3.
2. Alcock, page 6.
3. Alcock, page 18.
4. Alcock, page 39.
5. Alcock, page 45.
6. Alcock, page xvii.
7. Leslie Alcock, *"By South Cadbury Is That Camelot...,"* page 216.
8. Alcock, *Arthur's Britain*, page 41.
9. Alcock, page 39.
10. Alcock, page 49.
11. Alcock, page xvii.
12. Alcock, page 45.
13. Ashe, *The Quest for Arthur's Britain*, page 38.

14. Alcock, *Arthur's Britain,* pages 110–111.

15. Alcock, page 111.

16. Alcock, *By South Cadbury,* page 216.

17. Ashe, *The Discovery of King Arthur,* page 118.

18. Giles, *Six Old English Chronicles,* page 313.

19. Morris, *The Age of Arthur,* pages 512–513.

20. Sherley-Price, *Bede,* page 55.

21. O'Sullivan, *The* De Excidio *of Gildas,* page 139.

22. Morris, "Britain and Rome," *Essays,* pages 156–157.

23. O'Sullivan, pages 177–178.

24. Alcock, *Arthur's Britain,* pages 53–54. As related in Chapter 2 of this text, Alcock reasons that by calibrating the year 9 as A.D. 455, one arrives at 518 as the year for the Badon battle and 539 for the Battle of Camlann. Based upon an obscure passage, Gildas writes that he was born in the year of the Battle of Badon, which in turn means that Gildas wrote the *De Excidio* in 561.

25. Alcock, page 55, writes, "It is not impossible that in the process of copying from one Easter Table to another the dates of both Badon and Camlann have suffered a twenty-eight year dislocation." This is the discrepancy between the Victorian and the Dionysiac chronologies, as explained in the present chapter of this text.

26. Alcock, pages 110–111, states, "But when all allowance is made for the chronological vagueness of the *De Excidio,* it is difficult to believe that there was any long interval between the initial Ambrosian victory some time before 475 and the triumph of Badon. If this view is sound, then it becomes difficult to think of Badon as late as 518. In other words, a consideration of the possible dates for Ambrosius leads us to favor the alternative earlier date for Badon, namely A.D. 490."

27. Alcock, page xvii, adjusts his two previous dates by writing, "I now think that my discussion of the irreconcilable dates which the Welsh Easter Annals give for Badon and Maelgwn Gwynedd ... is too elaborate. Confusion between Incarnation and Passion dating is not the only way in which chronological errors can occur in the records of the period; another cause of error is confusion between successive nineteen-year Easter cycles. *If we assume such an error here, then the date of Badon might be corrected to A.D. 499, leaving the death of Maelgwn unaltered at A.D. 549.*" (Italics mine.)

28. Lapidge and Dumville, *Gildas: New Approaches,* page 83.

29. Geoffrey Ashe, *The Quest for Arthur's Britain,* pages 38–39.

30. Kenneth Jackson, "The Arthur of History," Roger S. Loomis, ed., *ALMA,* page 5.

31. O'Sullivan, page 146.

32. Alcock, *Arthur's Britain,* page 92.

33. Sherley-Price, *Bede,* page 56.

34. Whitelock, *The Anglo-Saxon Chronicle,* page 10.

35. Giles, *Six Old English Chronicles,* page 311.

36. Alcock, *Arthur's Britain,* pages 104–105. Additionally, see Chapter 3, Sections I and II in this text for explanations of the Victorian and Dionysiac chronologies.

37. Morris, *The Age of Arthur,* page 512.

38. Stevenson, *Nennii: Historia Brittonum,* page 55.

39. Alcock, *Arthur's Britain,* pages 105, 110, and 358 respectively.

40. Stevenson, page 55.

41. *Oxford Dictionary of English Etymology.* See page 203 for *conflict,* page 272 for *discord.* Chambers in *AoB* on page 16 mentions the term *discordia,* but does not commit to its definition; he mentions the term again on page 174 and then suggests that *quod est Guoloppum, id est, Catguoloph* was an interpolation added later.

42. Morris, *The Age of Arthur,* pages 54–55, page 74.

43. Alcock, *Arthur's Britain,* page 106; Morris, *The Age of Arthur,* page 43; Wade-Evans, *The Emergence of England and Wales,* page 17.

44. Manuscript A is of the thirteenth century, belonging to the Public Library of the University of Cambridge, and Manuscript B dates to the end of the fourteenth or the beginning of the fifteenth century, also at Cambridge. See Stevenson, *Gildas,* page xvi.

45. Josephus Stevenson, *Gildas: De Excidio Britanniæ,* page xvii.

46. For the Alcock material, see *Arthur's Britain,* pages 107–108, and page 352. The material from Morris' *The Age of Arthur* is more complicated. At one point, in talking about the Gaulish chronicler, Morris gives the date as "in or about the year 442," (page 38, then giving that same date again on pages 75, 81, and in his chronology chart on 513). But on page 77, in describing the Britons' reaction to the devastation by the Saxons, he writes, "The immediate reaction of the British is known. They sought help from Gaul, in or soon after 446." If the Britons' reaction was immediate, which it certainly would have been, they would not have waited four years to seek help. The date of 442, therefore, seems to be a more reliable date; 446 might be no more than an oversight on Morris' part, or perhaps a reminder that events in the fifth and sixth centuries cannot be dated to an exact year. Morris also explains Bede's inheritance of the error on pages 39–40 of *The Age of Arthur:* "... [Bede] placed the letter among the events of the 430s. Six years later, in the *History,* he had discovered its date, and entered it at 446; but he had no evidence that could help him correct Gildas' mistake; he had to preserve Gildas' order of events, although the intervals were plainly wrong, giving a very few years where Gildas had written "a long time," and placing many years between events that Gildas made consecutive."

47. Wade-Evans, *The Emergence of England and Wales,* pages 3–4.

48. Wade-Evans, page 15. The author also earlier clarified the term *Saxones* in footnote 3, page 6. Part of his explanation is that the "use of the term 'Saxons' in Britain is ambiguous, it being the general and literary name in Latin for the Angles and Frisians in the island, adopted as such in British and Irish."

49. Wade-Evans, page 18 and footnote 1, also page 110.

50. Wade-Evans, page 19.

51. Sherley-Price, *Bede,* page 55.

52. Alcock, *Arthur's Britain,* page 92.

53. Giles, Chapter 31, page 396.

54. Garmonsway, *The Anglo-Saxon Chronicle,* page 13.

55. Alcock, *Arthur's Britain,* page 101. For others who also concur with this viewpoint, see James Dyer and Michael Aston.

56. Morris, *British History,* page 45.

57. Barber, *The Figure of Arthur,* page 115, quotes the passage from William of Malmsbury's *Deeds of the Kings of Britain,* about the province of Ros, as does Fletcher, page 104. O'Sullivan tells of the Taliesin tale where Vad Velen came to Rhos and doomed Maelgwn to death, page 82. On the following page, in footnote 28, O'Sullivan points out the important niche that Maelgwn had in history and in medieval folklore and then cites Manuscript B of the *Annales Cambriae* which records the "long sleep of Maelgwn in the court of Rhos."

58. Lapidge and Dumville, *Gildas: New Approaches,* page 58.

59. John O'Donovan, *Annals of the Kingdom of Ireland,* page 186, footnote, bottom of column one.

60. O'Sullivan, pages 81–86. Procopius, during the reign of Justinian, describes the Bubonic plague as creating a swelling in the groin, the armpits, and the ears, but O'Sullivan then turns his attention to the Yellow Pestilence, traces how it can be identified, and indicates that Maelgwn very likely died of the Yellow Pestilence. John Morris refers to this as the Yellow Plague.

61. Taliesin Williams, *Iolo Manuscripts,* page 78.

62. J. Gwenogvryn Evans, "De Vita sancti Teiliavi," *The Book of Llan Dav,* page 107.

63. Sir Ifor Williams writes that Iolo Morganwg was "the greatest forger of Welsh documents that Wales has ever known. The mischief that that man has done! Perhaps he was mad — let us be charitable. Any way, if any one should persist in using Iolo's faked manuscript to support any theory or thesis, he does so at his own risk and peril." See Sir Ifor Williams, *Lectures on Early Welsh Poetry,* pages 60–61.

64. O'Sullivan, page 85, plus footnotes 36, 37, 38, and 39.

65. Wade-Evans, *The Emergence of England and Wales,* page 132.

66. O'Sullivan, page 22, footnote 90.

67. Sherley-Price, *Bede,* page 146.

68. Morris, *The Age of Arthur,* pages 192–197.

69. O'Sullivan, pages 113–114.

70. O'Sullivan, page 133.

71. Alcock, *Arthur's Britain,* page 125.

72. Sherley-Price, *Bede,* Chapter 2, page 101, Chapter 13, page 227, and Chapter 23, page 331.

73. Giles, *Six Old English Chronicles,* page 43.

74. Geoffrey of Monmouth, *The History of the Kings of Britain,* Lewis Thorpe, ed. Geoffrey first uses the term on page 133 when he indicates that Octavius is the Duke of Gewissei just prior to Roman abandonment. He then indicates that it is the territory ruled over by Vortigern, on page 151 and again on page 181 in "The Prophecies of Merlin." He gives a further clue on page 195 that the Galabes Springs is in the territory of the Gewissei.

75. Morris, *The Age of Arthur,* pages 226 and 282, plus footnote 41.3, page 552.

76. Morris, page 581, footnote 294.1.

77. Morris, page 588, footnote 324.2.

78. Plummer, *Two of the Saxon Chronicles Parallel,* page 398.

79. Whitelock, et al.,*The Anglo-Saxon Chronicle,* entry 755, page 31, is the most detailed genealogy. There is also information in Table 1, page 206 and Table 7, page 212. Editor Simon Taylor, *The Anglo-Saxon Chronicle: A Collaborative Edition,* Volume 4, D.S. Brewer, Cambridge, 1983, page 26, gives basically the same information.

80. Morris, *The Age of Arthur,* page 298.

81. Morris, page 513.

82. These are the names assigned to Cerdic's ancestors in *The Anglo-Saxon Chronicle,* in Preface A and entries 552, 597, and 855–858.

83. Eliseg's Pillar is mentioned by several historians and researchers but described in some detail by Jack Lindsay in *Arthur and His Times,* page 67, and by Geoffrey Ashe in "Extending the Map," *The Quest for Arthur's Britain,* pages 158–159.

84. Ashe, *The Discovery of King Arthur,* page 198.

85. Clayton, *Guide to the Archaeological Sites of Britain,* page 174.

86. Grabowski and Dumville, *Chronicles and Annals of Mediaeval Ireland and Wales,* page 225.

87. Grabowski and Dumville, page 226.

88. Whitelock, et al., page 11.

89. Whitelock, page 12.

90. Ashe, *The Discovery of Arthur,* page 207.

91. Plummer, Notes, page 4.

92. Plummer, pages 4–5, footnote 4.

93. Plummer, Index, page 356.

94. Whitelock, page 206.

95. Whitelock, page 228.

96. Garmonsway, *The Anglo-Saxon Chronicle*, page 66, footnote 2.
97. Alcock, *Arthur's Britain*, page 125.
98. Alcock, page 126.
99. Alcock, page 36.
100. O'Sullivan, page 131. See also pages 124–130 which explain how the conclusion was reached.
101. O'Sullivan, page 129.
102. Alcock, *Arthur's Britain*, page 127.
103. Ashe, "Extending the Map," *The Quest for Arthur's Britain*, page 159.
104. See O'Sullivan, pages 116–123. Not only does Cunedda directly relate to the importance of Maelgwn in one direction, but in the other he is directly tied to the next section, Cerdic of Fact.
105. Giles, Chapter 14, page 389.
106. Giles, Chapter 62, page 414.
107. Alcock, *Arthur's Britain*, page 125.
108. Morris, *The Age of Arthur*, page 66, and *British History*, page 79.
109. Stevenson, *Nennii*, page 53.
110. Alcock, *Arthur's Britain*, pages 126–127.
111. O'Sullivan, page 117.
112. Alcock, *Arthur's Britain*, page 126. O'Sullivan cites other scholars who have grappled with this complex problem. Thomas O'Rahilly abandons the 146-year figure and like Alcock goes by a genealogical rule of thumb which indicates that Cunedda flourished about a century prior to Maelgwn; Tolstoy ties Cunedda to Germanus, claiming that they were acting together in Wales and hence the migration was in 429; a great deal of analysis then falls to Cerdic as one of Cunedda's sons, a separate complex issue. See *The De Excidio of Gildas* page 118 plus footnote 180 for the O'Rahilly information, pages 119–120 for the Tolstoy details, and pages 124–131 for the Cerdic/Cunedda connection.
113. See Alcock, *Arthur's Britain*, page 128. For detailed explanations, see also pages 125–129, 342, and 354.
114. Graham Webster, *The Cornovii*, pages 125–126. Morris explains that Roman officers, titled "praefecti gentium," were placed over border barbarians. These border barbarians did not have their own kings, but they were pacified by an understood amnesty which protected them as Roman citizens. In the transitional period when Roman power declined, the praefecti, sometimes called kings in addition to their Roman epithets, passed on their authority and title to heirs. The titles and authority were retained by the natives as Roman influence faded. See *The Age of Arthur*, pages 17–18.
115. See Wade-Evans, page 50 of *The Emergence of England and Wales*, and Morris, *The Age of Arthur*, page 226.
116. Wade-Evans, page 93.
117. Morris, *The Age of Arthur*, page 98.
118. Morris, *The Age of Arthur*, pages 68–70.
119. Alcock, *Arthur's Britain*, page 127.
120. Morris, *British History*, pages 20–21.
121. Vortipor, mentioned in Gildas, occupies approximately the same floruit as Maelgwn, somewhere around 517–547. His father, Agricola (Aircol, King of Dyfed), would have flourished around 475, only about one generation removed rather than two, as suggested by Morris.
122. Morris, *The Age of Arthur*, page 158. See also note 158.2 page 565, note 125.3 page 561, and page 384.
123. Plummer, page 12.
124. Morris, *British History*, page 28.

125. Stevenson, *Nennii: Historia Brittonum,* page 28.
126. Giles, pages 399–400.
127. Barber, *The Figure of Arthur,* page 86.
128. Giles, Chapter 50, page 409.
129. Thomas Forester, ed. and trans., *The Chronicle of Henry of Huntingdon,* page 48.
130. See Michael Winterbottom, ed. and trans., *Gildas: The Ruin of Britain and Other Works,* pages 5 and 6 of his Preface, and "The Complaint of the Kings," pages 29–36.
131. Winterbottom, *Gildas,* page 30.
132. O'Sullivan, page 139.
133. Morris, "Dark Age Dates," *Britain and Rome,* pages 150–157. See also his Introduction in Winterbottom's book, *Gildas,* page 1, opening sentence.
134. Alcock, *Was This Camelot?,* page 216. Unfortunately, there is a transcriptional error in the text which actually reads "442," but it is obvious that the date should be 542. Similarly, it records Maelgwn's death at 449 when it should be 549.
135. O'Sullivan, page 178.
136. Lapidge and Dumville, *Gildas: New Approaches,* page 78.
137. Lapidge and Dumville, page 78.
138. Lapidge and Dumville, page 82.
139. Giles, page 313.
140. Alan O. Anderson and Marjorie O. Anderson, *Adomnan's Life of Columba,* pages 105–109.
141. Anderson and Anderson, page 67.
142. Anderson and Anderson, page 66.
143. *Encyclopedia Americana,* Volume 8, page 530.
144. Morris, *British History,* page 45.
145. John O'Donovan, *Annals of the Kingdom of Ireland,* page lii and footnote n.
146. O'Donovan, page 147, footnote t.
147. Grabowski and Dumville, *Chronicles and Annals of Mediaeval Ireland and Wales,* page 216.

Chapter 4 — Hillforts and Roman Roads

1. R.G. Collingwood, *Roman Britain,* page 11.
2. F. Haverfield, *The Romanization of Roman Britain,* page 26.
3. Collingwood, page 20.
4. Haverfield, page 26.
5. Collingwood, page 20.
6. Haverfield, page 26.
7. Haverfield, page 57.
8. Collingwood, page 21.
9. Collingwood, page 14.
10. Haverfield, page 46.
11. Haverfield, page 30.
12. Haverfield, page 46.
13. Haverfield, page 34.
14. Collingwood, pages 18–19.
15. Thomas Codrington, *Roman Roads in Britain,* page 11.
16. Alcock, *Was This Camelot?,* page 117.

17. Alcock, *Arthur's Britain,* page 255.
18. Janet and Colin Bord, *A Guide to Ancient Sites in Britain,* page 9.
19. Alcock, *Arthur's Britain,* page 255. Alcock footnotes this information with: M.J. O'Kelly, "Problems of Irish Ring-Forts," *The Irish Sea Province in Archaeology and History,* edited by D. Moore, Cardiff, 1970, pages 50–54.
20. Alcock, *Arthur's Britain,* page 255.
21. Alcock, *Was This Camelot?,* page 118.
22. Morris, *The Age of Arthur,* page 43.
23. Alcock, *Arthur's Britain,* page 347.
24. Alcock, pages 347–348.
25. Clayton, *Guide to the Archaeological Sites of Britain,* page 131.
26. Ekwall, page 515.
27. Clayton, page 174.
28. C. Musson, "Two Winters at the Breiddin," *Current Archaeology,* pages xxxiii, 263, 1972.
29. Codrington, page 253.
30. Codrington, page 255.
31. Giles, *Six Old English Chronicles,* page 473.
32. Giles, page 475.
33. Giles, page 475.
34. See Codrington, pages 12–14 for one technique of Roman road-building, as analyzed by Palladio who recorded roadbuilding in Italy. Codrington gives details on materials used, techniques of packing and layering, widths, and heights. On page 251, for a second technique of construction, he cites Bergier in France who described the interior composition of the roads. The remains suggest the Romans evidently followed no hard-and-fast rule but constructed roads according to the situation and the materials available.
35. R.G. Collingwood and J.N.L. Myres, *Roman Britain and the English Settlements,* page 314.
36. Collingwood and Myres, pages 315–316.
37. Alcock, *Arthur's Britain,* page 294; for details see pages 282–294.

Chapter 5 — The Geography of Badon

1. Pitt-Rivers, *Excavations in Bokerly and Wansdyke, Dorset and Wilts,* 1888–1891, Volume I, page 60.
2. Pitt-Rivers, Volume III, page xi of the Preface.
3. Webster, *The Cornovii,* pages 19–20.
4. Morris, *The Age of Arthur,* pages 68–69.
5. R.G. Collingwood and J.N.L. Myres, *Roman Britain and the English Settlements,* page 317.
6. Collingwood and Myres, pages 317–318.
7. Collingwood and Myres, page 318; see pages 316 to 320 for more detailed information.
8. James Dyer, *Southern England: An Archaeological Guide,* page xxx.
9. Michael Aston, *Interpreting the Landscape,* page 65.
10. Aston, page 83.
11. Lapidge and Dumville, *Gildas: New Approaches,* page 75.
12. Lapidge and Dumville, page 75.
13. Eilert Ekwall, *The Concise Oxford Dictionary of English Place-names,* page 20.

14. Ekwall, page 20.

15. Ekwall, page 20.

16. Alcock, *Arthur's Britain*, page 71.

17. Alcock, page 70.

18. Ekwall, page 145.

19. Ekwall, page 29.

20. Alcock, *Arthur's Britain*, page 346. On page 16, the Parker Chronicle, at entry 547, states that Bamburgh was "enclosed by a stockade and thereafter by a rampart."

21. Giles, Chapter 63, page 414.

22. Ashe, *King Arthur's Avalon*, page 77.

23. Ashe, page 77.

24. Ashe, page 77.

25. Alcock, *Arthur's Britain*, pages 349–350.

26. Pitt-Rivers, Vol. III, page 29. He originally stated that "We must not overlook the possibility of such an entrenchment having been thrown up during the troubles of the year 208, when the Caledonians penetrated far into South Britain, necessitating the presence of the Emperor Severus himself, to put a stop to the inroads.

27. Pitt-Rivers, Vol. III, page 30.

28. M.W. Thompson, *General Pitt-Rivers*, page 102. In Volume III, page 28, Pitt-Rivers himself explains that "Section excavation proves that the Wansdyke was Roman or post–Roman, and that the entrenchment was on the ground before it. Under those circumstances (nowhere near the number of coins found at Wansdyke as at Bokerly) we were unable to fix the date of the Wansdyke with the same certainty as that of Bokerly, although its Roman or post–Roman origin has been satisfactorily determined."

29. Pitt-Rivers, Vol. III, page 27.

30. Pitt-Rivers, *Excavations in Bokerly and Wansdyke, Dorset and Wilts, Vol. III, 1888–1891*, page 25.

31. Pitt-Rivers, Vol. III, page 25.

32. Pitt-Rivers, Vol. III, page 29.

33. Pitt Rivers, Vol. I, page xii.

34. Pitt-Rivers, Vol. III, page 29.

35. Pitt-Rivers, Vol. III, page 29.

36. Geoffrey Ashe, *King Arthur's Avalon*, page 72.

37. Pitt-Rivers, Vol. III, page 57.

38. Pitt-Rivers, Vol. III, page 58.

39. Pitt-Rivers, Vol. III, page 58.

40. Pitt-Rivers, Vol. III, page 59.

41. Pitt-Rivers, Vol. III, page 63.

42. Pitt-Rivers, Vol. III, page 64.

43. Pitt-Rivers, Vol. III, page 66.

44. Pitt-Rivers, Vol. III, page 9.

45. Pitt-Rivers, Vol. III, page 14. Pitt-Rivers goes into great detail about Bokerly as a defense system. In Volume III, page 293 of Appendix A, recording its surprising height, he writes, "Neither does it really appear to me probable that a work of such high relief as the center and left-center portion of the [Bokerly] Dyke, which before it silted up, could have not been much less than 40 feet from the bottom of the ditch to the crest of the rampart," and then concludes that it "could not have been thrown up for any other purpose than defence." He also suggests (Volume III, pages 60–61) that "The Bokerly Dyke appears to have run from the high hilly ground in Martin Wood ... continuous with the forest of Holt ... to the forest of Cranborne Chase ... and to have been intended to defend the open and accessible country between these two forest districts. ... No one who has

examined the whole line from a military point of view, can I think, doubt its being a defensive work. There is evidence that … the whole line as it approached from the direction of Salisbury seems marked out as a defensive position." He concludes by asserting that "Taking all the circumstances into consideration, the most reasonable supposition appears to be that, it was a defensive position taken upon the Roman road for the defence of the country to the westward."

46. Pitt-Rivers, Vol. III, page 8.

47. Pitt-Rivers, Vol. III, page 293. He explains that "Animal remains prove that the inhabitants of the Romano-British villages fed almost entirely on domesticated animals, and such large entrenchments, for the purpose of driving game, could therefore have never been thrown up for their benefit."

48. Codrington, *Roman Roads in Britain,* page 253.

49. Codrington, page 255.

50. Thompson, page 101.

51. Morris, *The Age of Arthur,* page 113.

52. Morris, page 113.

53. Alcock, *Arthur's Britain,* page 71.

54. Alcock, page 359.

55. Plummer, *Two of the Saxon Chronicles,* page 16 of Notes, and page 337.

56. Barry Cunliffe, *Iron Age Communities in Britain,* page 7.

57. W.A. Dowden, "Proceedings of the Spelæological Society: 1956–1957," Volume 8, page 28, and Dowden, "Proceedings of the Spelæological Society: 1958," Volume 9, page 182.

58. Dowden, Volume 8, page 28.

59. Morris, *British History,* page 40.

60. Alcock, *Arthur's Britain,* page 70.

61. Morris, *British History,* page 40.

62. Morris, page 81.

63. Stevenson, *Nennii,* page 56.

64. Stevenson in *Nennii* lists the variables as Gleguissing, Gleuisincg, and Gleuesingi. This is a tract of land between the Rivers Usk and Rumney in Monmouthshire. *Nennius,* footnote 24, page 31.

65. Graham Webster and Phillip Barker, "Wroxeter: Roman City," page 3.

66. Webster and Barker, page 18.

67. Webster and Barker, page 18.

68. Webster and Barker, page 21.

69. Webster, *The Cornovii,* page 32. See Figure 13, "Distribution of military sites in the Canton."

70. Giles, *Six Old English Chronicles,* "Richard of Cirencester," page 476.

71. Stevenson, *Nennii,* page 29.

72. Wade-Evans, *The Emergence of England and Wales,* page 67.

73. Webster, *The Cornovii,* page 89. Caer Lwytgoed is a Welsh form meaning "grey wood," the name having been transferred to Lichfield.

74. Webster, pages 89–91.

75. Alcock, *Arthur's Britain,* page 59.

76. Alcock, pages 81–82.

77. Morris, *The Age of Arthur,* page 68.

78. Morris, page 75.

79. Webster and Barker, page 7.

80. Webster and Barker, page 12.

81. Webster and Barker, page 10.

82. Webster and Barker, page 21.
83. Webster, *The Cornovii,* page 91.
84. Webster and Barker, page 26.
85. See page 27 of "Wroxeter: Roman City."
86. Webster and Barker, page 28.
87. Alcock, *Arthur's Britain,* page 246.
88. Webster and Barker, pages 28–29.
89. Webster and Barker, pages 28–29.
90. Webster, *The Cornovii,* page 4.
91. Webster, page 4.
92. Webster, page 63.
93. Webster, page 64.
94. Webster, pages 18–19.
95. Sabine Baring-Gould and John Fisher, *The Lives of the British Saints,* Vol. III, page 89.
96. O'Sullivan, page 158.

Chapter 6 — Geography of Camlann

1. Entries 455 (Agælesthrep), 465 (fought Welsh, killed Welsh nobles), 473 (fought the Welsh, the Welsh fled), 477 (Cymen, Cymenesora, slew many Welsh), 485 (fought the Welsh), and 495 (Cerdicesora, fought the Welsh).
2. Entries 449 (Vortigern = Welsh name, Ypsinesfleot = indistinguishable) and 508 (Welsh king, but location of Cerdicesford).
3. Entries 456 (fought the Britons, the Britons fled), 491 (all the Britons killed at Andredesceaster), and 501 (came to Portsmouth, slew a Briton).
4. Entries 527 (Creoda and Cynric fight the Britons), 530 (Creoda and Cynric obtain the Isle of Wight), 552 (Cynric fights the Britons at Searoburh), and 556 (Cynric and Ceawlin fight the Britons in Wiltshire).
5. Entry 547 (Ida reigns in Northumbria).
6. Entries 534 (Creoda passes away and Cynric rules, but no kingdom is mentioned) and 560 (a split between Ceawlin succeeding to the kingdom of Wessex and Aelle becoming king of Northumbria).
7. Plummer, page 10.
8. Morris, *The Age of Arthur,* page 94.
9. Morris, page 271.
10. Morris, page 113.
11. Plummer, page 14.
12. Plummer, page 6.
13. Whitelock et al., footnote 10, page 40.
14. Morris, *British History,* page 85. Fletcher (page 32), Morris (page 45), and Chambers (page 15) translate *corruerunt* as "fell," but Alcock, *Arthur's Britain,* page 45, prefers the word "perished."
15. Alcock, *Arthur's Britain,* page 67.
16. Alcock, page 67.
17. Alcock, page 67.
18. Ashe, Geoffrey, ed., *The Quest for Arthur's Britain,* "Extending the Map," page 150.
19. Ashe, page 151.
20. Ashe, *The Discovery of King Arthur,* page 73.

21. Ashe, page 84.
22. Ashe, page 84.
23. Ashe, page 85.
24. Ashe, page 119.
25. Ashe, page 123.
26. Richard Brengle, ed., *Arthur, King of Britain,* "Layamon," page 140.
27. Michael Winterbottom, ed. and trans., *Gildas,* page 28.
28. Winterbottom, page 28.
29. James Carley, ed., *The Chronicle of Glastonbury Abbey,* page 81.
30. Carley, page 73.
31. Carley, page 75.
32. Ekwall, column 2, page 95.
33. Campbell, *The Chronicle of Æthelweard,* column 2, page 59.
34. Whitelock, page 13.
35. Wade-Evans, *The Emergence of England and Wales,* footnote 3, page 2.
36. Wade-Evans, page 6.
37. Wade-Evans, page 1, footnotes 1 and 2. He explains that the term "Saxons as applied to Angles and Frisians in Britain (the English) was not a native one, but Roman. The term was borrowed by the British/Welsh as Saeson, 'the English,' for all the Frisian-speaking folks in Britain. These people referred to themselves mainly as Angles, leading to the name of their country, Angleterre, England."
38. Wade-Evans, page 4, footnote 2.
39. Alcock, *Arthur's Britain,* page 110.
40. Wade-Evans, page 104, footnote 6.
41. Alcock, *Arthur's Britain,* page 126, points out that "There is no serious dispute about where Cunedda [originally] came from, Manua Guotodin — to distinguish it from Manaw, the Isle of Man — was a small district around the head of the Firth of Forth, on the northern limits of the tribal region or kingdom of the Guotodin, Gododdin, or Votadini." Other scholars are equally specific about its location. Wade-Evans writes, "Manaw is known to have been a small portion beyond the Wall of Antonine facing Fife of the old (second century) territory of the Votadini (i.e., Gododdin in later Welsh)" (page 7, footnote 1), and Kenneth Jackson relates that "Manaw of Gododdin ... was a small province on the far northwestern boundaries of Gododdin" (O'Sullivan, page 120, footnote 190).
42. Morris, *British History,* page 36.
43. Campbell, *The Chronicle of Æthelweard,* pages 8–9.
44. Campbell, page 11.
45. Campbell, page 12.
46. Plummer, page 13.
47. Alcock, *Arthur's Britain,* page 67.
48. Alcock, page 67.
49. Ashe, *The Discovery of King Arthur,* pages 141 and 191.
50. Rachel Bromwich, "The Welsh Triads," in *ALMA,* R.S. Loomis, ed., page 44.
51. Bromwich, page 46.
52. Bromwich, page 46.
53. Ashe, *The Discovery of King Arthur,* page 89.
54. Ashe, page 89.
55. Aston, page 44.
56. Aston, page 83.
57. Aston, page 101.
58. Alcock, *Arthur's Britain,* page 116.

Chapter 7 — The Geography of Camelot/Tintagel

1. Alcock, *Was This Camelot?*, page 14.
2. Lucy Toulmin Smith, ed., *The Itineraries of John Leland*, Vol. 1, page 151.
3. Alcock, page 12.
4. Morris, *British History*, includes the 28 cities in a special section labeled as 66a, page 40 of his translation. Josephus Stevenson provides the list at the end of Section 76, page 62 of his text. J.A. Giles places the list in Section 7, page 386 of his Nennius translation. The number of cities likewise varies; Morris and Stevenson list 28, Giles 33.
5. Giles, page 386.
6. Morris, *The Age of Arthur*, page 138.
7. Morris, page 138.
8. Morris, page 139.
9. Ekwall, *Dictionary of English Place-names*, page 75.
10. Alcock, *Arthur's Britain*, page 219.
11. Alcock, page 219.
12. Dyer, *Southern England: An Archaeological Guide*, page 243.
13. Dyer, page 58.
14. Alcock, *Arthur's Britain*, page 180.
15. Collingwood and Myres, *Roman Britain and the English Settlements*, page 10.
16. Collingwood and Myres, pages 24–25.
17. Alcock, *Was This Camelot?*, page 24. Because this chapter relies so heavily on Leslie Alcock's work as the sole comprehensive resource on Cadbury-Camelot, all material which cites Alcock will be listed by name and page number only on condition that the reference is to the text *Was This Camelot?* If there is a citation to a different book by Alcock, then the reference will be by name, book and page.
18. For direct information of the topographical information given by Alcock, see pages 24 and 25.
19. Alcock, page 117.
20. Alcock, page 122.
21. Alcock, page 162.
22. Alcock, page 159.
23. Alcock, page 161.
24. Alcock, page 106.
25. Alcock, *Arthur's Britain*, pages 220–223.
26. Alcock, *Was This Camelot?*, page 75.
27. Alcock, page 79.
28. Alcock, pages 104–105.
29. Alcock, page 107.
30. Alcock, page 175.
31. Alcock, page 193.
32. Alcock, page 193.
33. Alcock, page 129.
34. Alcock, *Arthur's Britain*, pages 348–349.
35. Aston, *Interpreting the Landscape*, pages 141, 143.
36. Alcock, *Was This Camelot?*, page 17.
37. Keith Baines, *Le Morte d'Arthur*, Bramhall House, page 24.
38. Giles, *Six Old English Chronicles*, page 230.
39. Lewis Thorpe, trans., *Geoffrey of Monmouth*, page 212.

40. Baines, *Malory's* Le Morte D'Arthur, page 21.

41. Thorpe, *Geoffrey of Monmouth*, page 206.

42. C.A. Ralegh Radford, "Tintagel in History and Legend,"*Journal of the Royal Institution of Cornwall*, page 38.

43. Radford, page 38.

44. Radford, page 38.

45. Ashe, *The Discovery of King Arthur*, page 79.

46. Radford, page 25.

47. Radford, page 26.

48. Radford, "Romance and Reality in Cornwall," Geoffrey Ashe, ed., *The Quest for Arthur's Britain*, page 66.

49. Radford, "Tintagel in History and Legend," *Journal of the Royal Institution of Cornwall*, page 41.

50. Hal Borland, *When the Legends Die*, page vi.

Chapter 8 — The Isle of Avalon

1. Ekwall, page 198. But Reaney, in *English Place-names*, page vii, cautions about guessing at place-names, exemplified by assuming that Oxshott derived its name from "where the ox was shot," even though the locale had nothing to do with an ox, and shott was a piece of land.

2. Giles, page 440.

3. Lacy, *The Arthurian Encyclopedia*, page 33.

4. Coles and Orme, *Prehistory of the Somerset Levels*, page 2.

5. Coles and Orme, page 51.

6. Piggott, *British Prehistory*, page 173.

7. Treharne, *The Glastonbury Legends*, page 14.

8. Treharne, page 15.

9. Treharne, page 14.

10. Coles and Orme, page 63.

11. Coles and Orme, page 63.

12. Philip Rahtz, "Glastonbury Tor," Geoffrey Ashe, ed., *The Quest for Arthur's Britain*, page 119.

13. Rahtz, "Excavations on Glastonbury Tor, Somerset, 1964–6," *The Archaeological Journal*, Volume CXXVII, 1970, pages 12 through 18 give specific finds.

14. Scott, *The Early History of Glastonbury by William of Malmsbury*, page 4.

15. Malmsbury's Manuscript B, written in the 1400s, is located at the Oxford Bodleian Library; C (also 1400s) is in the British Library Cotton Cleopatra; L (c. 1265) is at the Oxford Library, catalogued as MS Laud. Misc.; M (c. 1313) is the British Library MS Additional; and T (c. 1290) is at Cambridge, Trinity College.

16. Scott, page 29.

17. Scott, page 33.

18. Treharne, *The Glastonbury Legends*, pages 34–35.

19. Robinson, *Two Glastonbury Legends*, pages 3–4.

20. Barber, *The Figure of Arthur*, page 115, quoted from William of Malmsbury, *Gesta Regum Anglorum*, London, 1894, page 127.

21. Lacy, *The Arthurian Encyclopedia*, page 238.

22. Giles, *Six Old English Chronicles*, page 271.

23. Goodrich, *King Arthur*, page 30.

24. Carley, *The Chronicle of Glastonbury Abbey*, page 76.

25. Carley, page xxxix.

26. Scott, page 24.

27. Gantz, "Culhwch and Olwen," *The Mabinogion*, page 142.

28. Gantz, page 144.

29. Carley, *The Chronicle of Glastonbury Abbey*, page l (Roman Numeral 50).

30. Gantz, page 137.

31. Gantz, page 185.

32. Rahtz, "Glastonbury Tor," *The Quest for Arthur's Britain*, Geoffrey Ashe, ed., page 121.

33. Alcock, *Arthur's Britain*, page 74.

34. Robinson, pages 8–9.

35. James Carley, *Glastonbury Abbey: The Holy House at the Head of the Moors Adventurous*, pages 148–149. With few exceptions, H.E. Butler, in *The Autobiography of Giraldus Cambrensis*, pages 119–121, translates the passage in the same way.

36. Alcock, *Arthur's Britain*, page 75.

37. Ashe, *The Quest for Arthur's Britain*, Illustration 66–69, unnumbered page.

38. Scott, *The Early History of Glastonbury by William of Malmsbury*, page 85.

39. Radford, "Glastonbury Abbey," *The Quest for Arthur's Britain*, Geoffrey Ashe, ed., page 108.

40. Carley, *Glastonbury Abbey*, pages 148–149.

41. Robinson, page 9, footnote 53.

42. Alcock, *Arthur's Britain*, page 77.

43. Barber, *The Figure of Arthur*, page 129.

44. Alcock, page 77. See cross in Camden's *Britannia*, page 65, trans. by Edmund Gibson.

45. Robinson, *Two Glastonbury Legends*, page 59.

46. Treharne, *The Glastonbury Legends*, page 103.

47. Alcock, *Arthur's Britain*, page 76.

48. Carley, *The Chronicle of Glastonbury Abbey*, page 7.

49. Scott, *The Early History of Glastonbury*, page 7.

50. Robinson, *Two Glastonbury Legends*, page 28.

51. Scott, *The Early History of Glastonbury*, page 35.

52. Carley, *The Chronicle of Glastonbury Abbey*, page xxxvi.

53. Robinson, *Two Glastonbury Legends*, page 12, reporting on Adam of Domerham's account in the *Historia de rebus*.

54. Carley, *The Chronicle of Glastonbury Abbey*, page xxxv.

55. Carley, page xlv.

56. Carley, page 79.

57. Carley, page 75.

58. Carley, page 55.

59. Carley, page 245.

60. Carley, page 284.

61. Robinson, *Two Glastonbury Legends*, page 20.

62. Fletcher, *The Arthurian Material in the Chronicles*, page 32.

63. Fletcher, page 33. Stevenson, *Nennii*, page 49, footnote 4, provides the Latin version, explaining on page xxv of his Preface that the Jerusalem story is peculiar to Manuscript K, written in the thirteenth century, with many additions interpolated in the margins and later introduced into the text of other copies.

64. Barber, *The Figure of Arthur*, page 101.

65. Barber, pages 102–103.

66. Alcock, *Arthur's Britain*, page 77.

67. Alcock, page 79.

68. Radford, "Glastonbury Abbey," *The Quest for Arthur's Britain,* Geoffrey Ashe, ed., page 107.

69. Radford, page 106.

70. Radford, page 107.

71. Radford, page 108.

72. Radford, page 108.

73. Carley, *Glastonbury Abbey,* page 178.

74. Radford, "Glastonbury Abbey," *The Quest for Arthur's Britain,* Geoffrey Ashe, ed., page 100.

75. Alcock, *Arthur's Britain,* page 80.

76. Radford, "Glastonbury Abbey," *The Quest for Arthur's Britain,* Geoffrey Ashe, ed., page 100.

77. Radford, page 109.

78. See James P. Carley, *The Chronicle of Glastonbury Abbey: An Edition, Translation, and Study of John of Glastonbury's Cronica Sive Antiquitates Glastoniensis Ecclesie,* and *Glastonbury Abbey: The Holy House at the Head of the Moors.*

79. Carley, *Glastonbury Abbey,* page 159.

80. Carley, *The Chronicle of Glastonbury Abbey,* pages xlix, footnote 6.

81. Treharne, page 102.

82. Scott, *The Early History of Glastonbury,* page 141.

83. Carley, *The Chronicle of Glastonbury Abbey,* pages 93 and 286, footnote 152.

84. Carley, pages 93 and 286, footnote 155.

85. Carley, page 287, footnote 165.

86. Ashe, *The Discovery of King Arthur,* pages 86–92.

87. Ashe, page 96.

88. Ashe, page 95.

89. Ashe, page 91.

90. Ashe, page 7.

91. Ashe, *King Arthur's Avalon,* page 24.

92. Treharne, *The Glastonbury Legends,* page 24.

93. Robinson, *Two Glastonbury Legends,* page 17.

94. Ashe, *King Arthur's Avalon,* page 7.

Chapter 9 — Ambrosius Aurelianus: History and Tradition

1. A brief *vita* for Lucius Domitius Aurelianus can be found in any standard encyclopedia, such as *Americana,* the Roman Empire (27 B.C. to A.D. 476).

2. See O'Sullivan, last paragraph on page 141, to the end of that chapter, page 157.

3. O'Sullivan surveys each of the following who equate Gildas' birth and the seige of Badon occurring 44 years prior to the *De Excidio:* Henrich Zimmer and Theodor Mommsen, page 135; A.W. Wade-Evans and J.N.L. Myres, page 136; Michael Hughes, page 137; Arthur De la Borderie, page 138; and G.H. Wheeler, page 139.

4. Sherley-Price, *Bede,* page 58. O'Sullivan then provides a summary of those who subscribe to Bede's premise: C.E. Stevens and C.F.C. Hawkes, page 141.

5. O'Sullivan records Charles Plummer, page 139, with variations by Frederic Seebohm and W.B. Nicholson, page 142, and John Morris, page 137.

6. O'Sullivan presents the Baring-Gould/Fisher proposal which refers to Ambrosius as Aurelius, page 142.

7. See O'Sullivan, Nikolai Tolstoy, page 143.

8. Morris, *The Age of Arthur,* pages 37, 513.

9. O'Sullivan, page 155.

10. Giles, page 313.

11. Winterbottom, *Gildas,* page 98.

12. Winterbottom, page 28.

13. Jackson, *The Gododdin,* Appendix, page 84.

14. Morris, *The Age of Arthur,* page 96.

15. Morris, page 96.

16. Morris, page 96.

17. Morris, page 97.

18. Fletcher, *The Arthurian Material in the Chronicles,* page 18.

19. Fletcher, pages 18–19.

20. Fletcher, page 23. For more detailed information, read Fletcher's entire account, pages 8–30.

21. Alcock, *Arthur's Britain,* page 359.

22. Morris, *The Age of Arthur,* page 80.

23. Morris, *British History,* page 31.

24. Morris, *The Age of Arthur,* page 81.

25. Morris, page 81.

26. Stevenson, *Gildas,* page 35, footnote 1.

27. Ashe, *The Discovery of King Arthur,* page 203. *Tamos* here would be the same affix in the word Riothamos.

28. Ashe, *King Arthur's Avalon,* page 74; *The Discovery of King Arthur,* page 98.

29. See again Stevenson, *Nennii,* page 34, where Section 43 immediately follows Section 42 without an introductory heading.

30. Morris, *British History,* page 31.

31. Giles, page 404.

32. Sherley-Price, *Bede,* pages 57–58.

33. Ashe, "The Arthurian Fact," *The Quest for Arthur's Britain,* Geoffrey Ashe, ed., page 48.

34. Morris, *The Age of Arthur,* page 73.

35. According to Manuscript *a,* footnote 24, page 30 in Stevenson's *Nennii.*

36. Translated from Stevenson, *Nennii,* Chapter 49, pages 40–41.

37. Morris, *The Age of Arthur,* page 55; see also pages 73–74.

38. Stevenson, *Nennii,* page 55.

39. Alcock, *Arthur's Britain,* page 105.

40. Morris, *The Age of Arthur,* page 71.

41. Goodrich, *Merlin,* page 8.

42. Lewis Thorpe, trans., *Geoffrey of Monmouth: The History of the Kings of Britain,* page 121.

43. James Carley records this name as Arviragus.

44. Thorpe, *Geoffrey of Monmouth,* Part Eight, page 262.

45. Thorpe, page 149.

46. Thorpe, page 151.

47. Thorpe, page 151.

48. Thorpe, page 152.

49. Thorpe, page 155.

50. Thorpe, page 155.

51. The first set of errors is that Monmouth places Constantine at the same time when Saint Daniel (Deinielo) of Bangor dies, along with Saint David of Menevia dying at this

same time. The *Annales Cambriae* lists Saint Daniel's death in 584, and as mentioned in Chapter 3 of this text on ordinal years, Saint David's death occurred in 598. Additionally, if Monmouth is writing about Constantine III, then he is off in his calculations by literally decades, since Constantine III was born in 612 and died in 641. John Morris is also off in his calculations because in his "Table of Dates" (*The Age of Arthur,* page 512), he lists Constantine III as emperor of the West from 407 to 411, when in reality the emperor of the West during that time is Flavius Claudius Constantinus, also known as Constantine the Usurper. Constantine the Usurper has no connection with Constantine I (Constantine the Great) nor with any of the Constantinian dynasty. The Constantine whom Geoffrey is writing about, therefore, is misplaced by almost exactly two centuries. In order to accurately describe his sequence of events, Constantine would have to be replaced by Constantius III and this tie-in to Guithelinus should be set in his chapter on the coming of the Romans, in the segment which Thorpe labels "Rome Helps Britain for the Last Time," page 145.

52. Thorpe, *Geoffrey of Monmouth,* page 191.
53. Morris, *The Age of Arthur,* page 43.
54. Morris, page 95.
55. Morris, page 100. See also the map on page 101 of *The Age of Arthur* which shows the strip of land with Ambrosian place-names. Morris further lists some Ambros place-names on page 625 of his text when talking about the war zone.
56. Morris, *The Age of Arthur,* page 513.
57. Lacy, *The Arthurian Encyclopedia,* page 5.
58. Morris, *The Age of Arthur,* page 95.
59. Morris, page 98.
60. Morris, page 103.
61. Morris, page 103.
62. Morris, page 38.
63. Charles C. Mierow, *Jordanes: The Origin and Deeds of the Goths,* page 74.
64. Morris, page 100.

Chapter 10 — Riothamus: The Briton from Across the Ocean

1. Morris, *The Age of Arthur,* page 92.
2. Fletcher, *The Arthurian Material in the Chronicles,* pages 170, 172.
3. Fletcher, page 185.
4. Ashe, *The Discovery of King Arthur,* page 100.
5. Ashe, page 100.
6. Ashe, page 48.
7. Ashe, pages 109–110.
8. Morris, *The Age of Arthur,* page 92.
9. Morris, page 90.
10. Ashe, *The Discovery of King Arthur,* page 52.
11. Morris, *The Age of Arthur,* page 91.
12. Ashe, *The Discovery of King Arthur,* page 49.
13. Morris, *The Age of Arthur,* page 90.
14. Charles C. Mierow, *Jordanes: The Origin and Deeds of the Goths,* page 74.
15. Ashe, page 48.
16. Morris, *The Age of Arthur,* pages 89–90.

17. Ashe, *The Discovery of King Arthur,* page 48.

18. Ernest Brehaut, trans, Gregory of Tours, *History of the Franks,* page 35.

19. Ashe, *The Discovery of King Arthur,* page 52; Anderson on Sidonius, Volume I, page xxvii.

20. Anderson, Volume I, page xxvii. Anderson gives the date of 467 when Leo I appointed Anthemius, and Euric's murder of his brother Theodoric one year previously in 466, but this does not coincide with Ægidius' also being in league with Riothamus, since Ægidius' death year is listed as 464.

21. Morris, *The Age of Arthur,* page 91; Ashe, *The Discovery of King Arthur,* pages 55–56.

22. Anderson, Volume I, page xli.

23. Mierow, *Jordanes: The Origin and Deeds of the Goths,* page 74.

24. Brehaut, Gregory of Tours, *History of the Franks,* page 35.

25. Anderson, Volume I, page xlii; Book III, section IX, page 35.

26. Anderson, Book III, section IX, page 35.

27. Ashe, *The Discovery of King Arthur,* page 53.

28. Ashe, pages 102–103.

29. Ashe, page 103.

30. Ashe, page 100.

31. Josephus Stevenson, *Nennii,* lists all of these variations in his footnote, page 49: Agned Catbregomion, Bregnion, Cathbregyon, Agned Thabregomion, and Agned Cathregonnon.

Chapter 11— Arthur: Historical and Literary Data

1. For each of the specific battles cited below, see Section 56, pages 35 and 36 in *British History.*

2. Giles, Chapter 50, page 409.

3. John Rhys, *The Arthurian Legend,* pages 8–9.

4. Rhys, page 18.

5. Thomas Bullfinch, *Mythology,* page vii.

6. Bullfinch, page ix.

7. Bullfinch, page 367.

8. Goodrich, *King Arthur,* page 46.

9. Ashe, *The Discovery of King Arthur,* page 113.

10. Lacy and Ashe, *The Arthurian Handbook,* page 5.

11. Lacy and Ashe, page 6.

12. See Morris, *The Age of Arthur,* and his comment from Fustel de Coulanges, pages 164–165.

13. Morris, *British History,* page 45.

14. Giles, *Six Old English Chronicles,* page 408.

15. Ivor John, *Popular Studies in Mythology, Romances, and Folklore,* No. 11, "The Mabinogion," page 3.

16. Gantz, *The Mabinogion,* page 21.

17. Rhys, pages 1–2.

18. Ivor John, page 3.

19. Gantz, page 31.

20. Rhys, page 2.

21. Gantz, page 33.

22. Gantz, page 13.

23. Gantz, page 20.

24. Ivor John, page 7.

25. Gantz, page 191.

26. See Morris, *The Age of Arthur,* pages 214–215, and Map 13, page 209.

27. Wade-Evans, *The Emergence of England and Wales,* page 102, footnote 11.

28. Bromwich, *The Beginnings of Welsh Poetry,* page 70.

29. Bromwich, page 71.

30. Bromwich, page 71, footnote 4. She adds even more history of the term: "The earliest occurrence of Cymry in reference to the Welsh is probably that in *Moliant Cadwallon.* It occurs also in the Llywarch Hen poetry, and in *Armes Prydein,* though it is not found in the poetry of Aneirin and Taliesin, who invariably employ *Brython.* In reference to the inhabitants of Cumbria the earliest occurrence is in Ethelwerd's Chronicle (circa 1000), where[as] both Asser and the Anglo-Saxon Chronicle refer to the Picts and the Strathclyde Welsh. ... In older Welsh usage *cymry* denoted both the country and the people; later *Cymru* came to be the name for Wales, and *cymro,* pl. *Cymry* the name for the people of the country."

31. Wade-Evans, page 60.

32. Wade-Evans, page 5.

33. Of importance here is the line beginning with the son of Maximus who was named Owain and became king of Buallt (see Wade-Evans, page 102), through Owain map Hywel Dda, one of the Welsh nobles who died in 988 (see O'Sullivan, pages 90–91, 102).

34. John Morris exemplifies Owain as a derivative from Eugein in his *British History* translation, at entry 811.

35. See Wade-Evans, *The Emergence of England and Wales,* pages 5, 18, 20, 47–48, 60, 94, and 111.

36. Goodrich, *King Arthur,* page 36.

37. Goodrich, page 42.

38. Goodrich, page 42.

39. Ivor John, page 3.

40. Thorpe, *Geoffrey of Monmouth,* page 212.

41. As mentioned earlier, Kaerluideoit (Cair Luit Coyt) appears in the *Historia* as one of the major cities in Britain and is identified among others by John Morris and Graham Webster as Wall-by-Lichfield, postulated in this text as the locale where Octha was sent.

42. Giles, Chapter 62, page 414.

43. Jackson, *The Gododdin,* page ix.

44. Jackson, pages 8–11.

45. Jackson, page 56.

46. Jackson, page 112.

47. Jackson, page 112.

48. Alcock, *Arthur's Britain,* page 14.

49. Morris, *British History,* page 46.

50. W.F. Skene, "Book of Taliessin XV," *The Four Ancient Books of Wales,* page 259.

51. Skene, page 261.

52. Skene, pages 265–266.

53. See Lacy and Ashe, *The Arthurian Handbook,* page 30, and Kenneth Jackson, "Arthur in Early Welsh Verse," *Arthurian Literature in the Middle Ages,* ed. R.S. Loomis, page 13. Jackson writes, "At Llongborth I saw belonging to Arthur / Bold men who hewed with steel / The emperor, the ruler in the toil of battle."

54. W.F. Skene, *The Four Ancient Books of Wales,* page 267.
55. Lacy and Ashe, *The Arthurian Handbook,* page 30.
56. Barber, *The Figure of Arthur,* page 67.
57. Alcock, *Arthur's Britain,* page 14.
58. Alcock, page 82.
59. Alcock, page 83.
60. Alcock, page 14.
61. Gantz, page 180.
62. Gantz, page 181.
63. Gantz, page 183.
64. Gantz, page 183.
65. Gantz, page 184.
66. Gantz, page 177.
67. Gantz, "Owein, or the Countess of the Fountain," *The Mabinogion,* pages 193 and 209.
68. Gantz, "Peredur Son of Evrawg," *The Mabinogion,* pages 235, 240, and 248.
69. Gantz, "Gereint and Enid," *The Mabinogion,* pages 259, 263, and 274.
70. Thorpe, *Geoffrey of Monmouth,* page 226.
71. Alcock, *Arthur's Britain,* page 36.
72. Gantz, *The Mabinogion,* page 174.
73. Gantz, page 183.
74. Barber, *Arthur of Albion,* page 11.
75. Barber, page 11.
76. Barber, *The Figure of Arthur,* page 52.
77. Barber, page 52.
78. Gantz, Introduction to *The Mabinogion,* pages 23–24.
79. Giles, page 314.
80. Giles, page 312.
81. Gantz, page 142.
82. Gantz, pages 190–191.
83. Gantz, pages 269–270.
84. Gantz, page 137.
85. Giles, *Six Old English Chronicles,* page 312.
86. Gantz, page 185.
87. Gantz, page 185.
88. Drawing 7, Arthur's blazon, page 323. Exhaustive research has shown that the arms of this shield are generally regarded as those adopted by Glastonbury Abbey for its own use. There has not, however, been any official representation of the Arthurian blazon, except for one done by J. Armitage Robinson, which is an inaccurate depiction. According to a memo by D.R. Orchard in 1993, the cross should be blazoned as botonée, with the ends similar to a clover leaf, rather than Robinson's rendition of a fleurs-de-lis design, which is perhaps based upon sculptors' work contracted by Abbot Bere. Likewise, judging from the Glastonbury insignia, the Virgin and Child should be in the dexter canton of the cross with the Mother holding a scepter in Her left hand and the Child in Her right, unlike the reverse as shown by Robinson. The Arms of Glastonbury Abbey has a gold crown in each of the other cantons, whereby the Arthurian blazon does not include the crowns.
89. Alcock, *Arthur's Britain,* page 52.
90. Chambers, *Arthur of Britain,* page 17.

Chapter 12 — The Phoenix Arises

1. Goodrich, *Merlin,* page 8.
2. Morris, *The Age of Arthur,* page 17.
3. Depending upon the manuscript, Ambrosius' title is also spelled Embries Gluetic, Embres Gulethic, and Embreis Gleutic. See Stevenson, *Nennii,* page 34, footnote 3.
4. Morris, *The Age of Arthur,* page 329.
5. Lacy, *The Arthurian Encyclopedia,* page 454.
6. Riothamus has these variations of spellings: Riothamos, Riotamos, Rhithamos, Rhiothamus, Rigotamos, Rigotamus, Rigothamos, Rigothamus, and Riothimir, which makes the search for him difficult.
7. Kenneth Jackson, "Arthur in Early Welsh Verse," *Arthurian Literature in the Middle Ages,* ed. R.S. Loomis, page 2.
8. Bromwich, "Celtic Elements in Arthurian Romance: A General Survey," *The Legend of Arthur in the Middle Ages,* edited by P.B. Grout et al., page 42.
9. Bromwich, page 42.
10. Barber, *The Figure of Arthur,* pages 37–38.
11. Morris, *British History,* page 76.
12. Stevenson, *Nennii,* page 48, footnote 2.
13. Fletcher, *The Arthurian Material in the Chronicles,* pages 28–29.
14. Alcock, *Arthur's Britain,* page 60.
15. Alcock, page 61.
16. Rhys, *The Arthurian Legend,* page 7.
17. Morris, *The Age of Arthur,* page 329.
18. Morris, page 419.
19. Ashe, *King Arthur's Avalon,* page 76.
20. Ashe, *The Discovery of King Arthur,* pages 112–113.
21. Ashe, pages 113–114.
22. Stevenson, *Gildas,* page 33, footnote 12.
23. Alcock, *Arthur's Britain,* page 358.
24. Ashe, *The Discovery of King Arthur,* page 114.
25. Ashe, page 113.
26. Morris, page 48.
27. Ashe, *The Discovery of King Arthur,* page 111.
28. Ashe, page 15.
29. Interspersed with the summaries from Monmouth, Ashe has included some of his strategies and procedures incorporating the Monmouth material into his theoretical use of lateral thinking. See specifically pages 24–26, and 86–111.
30. Ashe, *The Discovery of Arthur,* pages 102–106.
31. Ashe, page 109.
32. Ashe, page 110.
33. Morris, *The Age of Arthur,* page 259.
34. Morris, page 256.
35. Gantz, *The Mabinogion,* page 142.
36. Chambers, *Arthur of Britain,* page 169.
37. Thorpe, *Geoffrey of Monmouth,* page 214.
38. Thorpe, page 209.
39. Thorpe, page 221.
40. Thorpe, page 214, footnote 1.
41. Fletcher, *Arthurian Material in the Chronicles,* page 75.

42. Morris, *The Age of Arthur,* pages 130–131.

43. For the detailed etymological possibilities, see Rhys, *Studies in the Arthurian Legend,* Chapter I, "Arthur, Historical and Mythical," and Chapter II, "Arthur and Airem." See also Chambers' condensed explanation of Rhys, *Arthur of Britain,* pages 210–211.

44. Ashe, *The Discovery of King Arthur,* page 92.

45. Ashe, page 113.

46. A modified outline given by Ashe is as follows:
> I. Constantine III — reigned 10 years beginning 407, page 30.
> > — In 410 were the Saxon assaults, page 30.
> II. Vortigern reign begins in about 425, page 39.
> > — kills Constans by having him assassinated by a Pict.
> > — invites Hengist and Horsa to Britain about 428, page 41.
> > — marries Hengist's daughter in 429, page 36.
> > — Vortimer rebels.
> III. Aurelius Ambrosius [not to be confused with Ambrosius Aurelianus] crowned king when Vortigern is killed, somewhere between 455–460, page 50.
> > — poisoned.
> IV. Uther — reigns for 15 years after Arthur's birth.
> > —(Alberic, 442; rules for 17 years), page 107.
> V. Arthur — coronated.
> > —(Alberic, 459; reigns 16 years,), page 108.
> > —(Gregory of Tours, 470), page 110.
> VI. Arthur — presence in Gaul.
> > —(Goeznovius via Wilson, late 460s), page 105.
> VII. Arthur — summoned from human activity.
> > —(Alberic, 475), page 108.
> > —(Gregory of Tours, 470), page 110.

47. Ashe, *The Discovery of King Arthur,* page 113.

48. Ashe, page 108.

49. Phillips and Keatman, *King Arthur: The True Story,* page 128.

50. Lindsay, *Arthur and His Times,* page 220.

51. Ekwall, *The Concise Oxford Dictionary of English Place-names,* First Edition, 1936, page 12.

52. Anderson and Anderson, *Adomnan's Life of Columba,* pages 132–133.

53. Bromwich, *The Beginnings of Welsh Poetry,* page 10.

54. Bromwich, page 10.

55. Bromwich, page 6.

56. Thorpe, *Geoffrey of Monmouth,* page 212.

57. Brengle, *Arthur, King of Britain,* page 115.

58. More correctly, Lazamon or Lawman, who flourished in the late tenth/early eleventh century. His original manuscript did not survive, but the two copies in the British Museum date from about 1205 and 1275.

59. Brengle, *Arthur, King of Britain,* page 128.

60. Robinson, *Two Glastonbury Legends,* page 18.

61. Rhys, *Studies in the Arthurian Legend,* page 8.

62. Brengle, "Roman de Brut," *Arthur: King of Britain,* page 126.

63. Alcock, *Arthur's Britain,* page 116.

64. Alcock, page 69.

65. Alcock, page 117.

66. Alcock, page 117.

67. Alcock, page 117.
68. Alcock, page 116.
69. Alcock, page 117.
70. Ashe, *The Discovery of King Arthur*, page 97.
71. Garmonsway, page 2.
72. The second half of this entry is an oddity. The oddity here about Ælle is that he is viewed as a South Saxon judging from entries 477, 485, and 491, since scholars have identified Cymenesora, Andredeslea, and Andredescaster as southern locations, respectively at Selsey Bill, the Weald, and the Roman Anderida near Pevensey. Mearcredesburna in entry 485 is not identified. And yet entry 560 indicates that Ælle (a grandson?) inherits Northumbria from Ida, far to the north. In entry 477 one of Ælle's sons is named Cymen, and the site where they land is called Cymenesora, both proper names looking suspiciously like they have roots based upon Cymry, meaning Welsh and suggesting Cumbria, which is named after Cymry. The name Andredesleag seems to have a different root in Andreas, associated with the Isle of Man, as opposed to Andredescaster. These two items point to Ælles' being in the north, in or near Cumbria. This is borne out by entries 477 and 485 recording that Ælle fought against the *Welsh*, while entry 491 relates a battle at Andredescaster fought against the *Britons*.
73. Carley, *The Chronicle of Glastonbury Abbey*, page 75.
74. Alcock, *Arthur's Britain*, page 294.
75. Campbell, *The Chronicle of Æthelweard*, page 11.
76. Ashe, *The Quest for Arthur's Britain*, page 158. Morris also writes of the same connection between Cunedda and the inscriptions on the cross near Llangollen: "One group of inscriptions seems to concern a Votadinian family who moved to north Wales, and implies that the immigrants also brought settlers from the Clyde." Continuing this line of reasoning, he proposes that Cerdic inherited segments of the West and that Cardigan was named after him. *The Age of Arthur*, page 67.
77. There is a striking similarity in four of Monmouth's battles: Albans, where Octa and Eosa are killed; Badon, where Hoel becomes ill and Cheldric is killed; Saussy, where Auguselus, Aschil, Loth, Hoel and Gawain are Arthur's allies; and Camlann, where Auguselus, Gawain, Mordred, Chelric, and Arthur are killed. The Battle of Saussy shows the feasibility that Loth, Hoel, Gawain, and Auguselus are Arthur's allies contemporaneous with and polarized by Octha, Cheldric, Chelric, and Chedric, this latter who appears only once as a companion of Octha and Ebissa, page 161. For the Battle of Albans, see pages 209–211; for Badon, pages 216–218; for Saussy, pages 247–249; for Camlann, pages 258–261.
78. Thorpe, *Geoffrey of Monmouth*, page 261.
79. Bromwich, "Celtic Elements in Arthurian Romance: A General Survey." *The Legend of Arthur in the Middle Ages*, ed. by P.B. Grout, et al., page 49.
80. Morris, *The Age of Arthur*, page 506.
81. Lacy, *Arthurian Encyclopedia*, page 25.
82. Lapidge and Dumville, *Gildas: New Approaches*, page 77.
83. Lapidge and Dumville, page 78.
84. Lapidge and Dumville, *Gildas: New Approaches*, page 83.
85. Lapidge and Dumville, page 79.
86. Theodor Mommsen, *Chronica Minora*, Vol. 1, page 660. According to Wade-Evans, *The Emergence of England and Wales*, page 7, footnote 2: "This was the last attack, as recorded by any contemporary writer, of hostile oversea Saxones on Roman Britain, a fact generally overlooked."
87. Mommsen, *Chronica Minora*, Vol. 1, page 660. Wade-Evans, page 17, interprets this passage as "Britains up to this time torn by various disasters and other occurrences

are reduced under the jurisdiction of the English," while Alcock, *Arthur's Britain,* page 106, writes "Britain, which up to this time had suffered manifold devastations and accidents, was subjected to the domination of the Saxons."

88. The Aetius letter is perhaps the most controversial issue in Gildas. In the two surviving Gildean manuscripts, the name of Agitium appears rather than Aetius, but in Manuscript V, ascribed to Polydore Vergil who used copies of unknown antiquity, the name is Aetium. (See Josephus Stevenson, *Gildas,* page xix.)

Selected Bibliography

Ackerman, Robert, Frederick W. Locke, and Carleton W. Carroll, trans. *Chretien de Troyes' Ywain: The Knight of the Lion.* New York: The Ungar Publishing Company, 1977.

Alcock, Leslie. *Arthur's Britain.* New York: Viking Penguin, Inc., 1987.

_____. *"By South Cadbury Is That Camelot ...": The Excavation of Cadbury Castle 1966–1970.* Hazell Watson and Viney Ltd., Aylesbury, Great Britain: Thames and Hudson, 1972.

_____. "Wales in the Arthurian Age." *The Quest for Arthur's Britain.* Edited by Geoffrey Ashe. Chicago, Ill.: Academy Chicago Publishers, 1987.

_____. *Was This Camelot? Excavations at Cadbury Castle, 1966–1970.* New York: Stein and Day Publishers, 1972.

_____, and Geoffrey Ashe. "Cadbury: Is It Camelot?" *The Quest for Arthur's Britain.* Chicago, Ill.: Academy Chicago Publishers, 1987.

Anderson, Alan Orr, and Marjorie Ogilvie Anderson. *Adomnan's* Life of Columba. Toronto and New York: Thomas Nelson and Sons Ltd., 1961.

Anderson, W.B., ed. and trans. *Sidonius: Poems and Letters, Volume 1.* Cambridge, Mass.: Harvard University Press, reprinted 1956, 1963.

_____, ed. and trans. *Sidonius: Poems and Letters, Volume 2.* Cambridge, Mass.: Harvard University Press, reprinted 1956, 1963.

Ashe, Geoffrey. *Camelot and the Vision of Albion.* New York: St. Martin's Press, 1971.

_____. "'A Certain Very Ancient Book': Traces of an Arthurian Source in Geoffrey of Monmouth's History," *Speculum* 56, 1981.

_____. *The Discovery of King Arthur.* New York: Henry Holt and Company, 1987.

_____. *The Glastonbury Tor Maze.* Glastonbury, Somerset: Gothic Image, 1979.

_____. *King Arthur: The Dream of a Golden Age.* New York: Thames and Hudson, 1990.

_____. *King Arthur's Avalon: The Story of Glastonbury.* Glasgow: William Collins Sons and Co. Ltd, copyright 1957, tenth impression, 1987.

Ashe, Geoffrey, ed. *The Quest for Arthur's Britain.* Chicago: Academy Chicago Publisher, 1987.

Aston, Michael. *Interpreting the Landscape: Landscape Archaeology in Local Studies.* London: B.T. Batsford, 1985.

Baines, Keith. *Malory's* Le Morte d'Arthur. New York: New American Library, 1962.

_____. "A Rendition in Modern Idiom." *Sir Thomas Malory's* Le Morte D'Arthur. New York: Bramhall House, 1957.

Barber, Richard W. *Arthur of Albion.* London: Barrie and Rockliff with Pall Mall Press, 1961.

_____. *The Arthurian Legends: An Illustrated Anthology.* U.S.A.: Littlefield Adams and Company, 1979.

_____. *The Figure of Arthur.* London: Longman Group Ltd., 1972.

Baring-Gould, Sabine, and John Fisher. *The Lives of the British Saints.* 4 vols. For the honourable Society of Cymmrodorion: London, 1907–1913.

Blunt, John Henry. *The Annotated Book of Common Prayer, Forming a Concise Commentary of the Devotional System of the Church of England.* New York: Pott, Young, & Company, 1876.

Bord, Janet and Colin Bord. *A Guide to the Ancient Sites in Britain.* London: Paladin Books, Granada Publishing Ltd., 1979.

Brehaut, Ernest, trans. Gregory of Tours. *History of the Franks.* New York: Columbia University Press, 1916.

Brengle, Richard L., ed. *Arthur, King of Britain: History, Romance, Chronicle, & Criticism.* New York: Meredith Publishing Company, 1964.

Bromwich, Rachel. "Celtic Elements in Arthurian Romance: A General Survey." *The Legend of Arthur in the Middle Ages.* Edited by P.B. Grout, et al. Cambridge: D.S. Brewer, an imprint of Boydell and Brewer Ltd., 1983.

_____, ed. *The Beginnings of Welsh Poetry: Studies by Sir Ifor Williams.* Cardiff: reprinted by permission of University of Wales Press, 1972.

Bullfinch, Thomas. *Bullfinch's Mythology.* "King Arthur and His Knights" and "The Mabinogion." New York: Avenel Books, Crown Publishers, 1989.

Burrow, J. A., ed. *Sir Gawain and the Green Knight.* Middlesex, England: Penguin Books, 1972.

Butler, H.E., ed. and trans. *The Autobiography of Giraldus Cambrensis.* London: Johnathan Cape, 1937.

Campbell, A., ed. *The Chronicle of Æthelweard.* Edinburgh: Thomas Nelson and Sons Ltd., 1962.

Canby, Courtlandt. *A Guide to the Archaelogical Sites of the British Isles.* New York: Hudson Group, 1988.

Carley, James P. *The Chronicle of Glastonbury Abbey: An Edition, Translation and Study of John of Glastonbury's Cronica Sive Antiquitates Glastoniensis Ecclesie.* Translated by David Townsend. Woodbridge, Suffolk: The Boydell Press, 1985.

_____. *Glastonbury Abbey: The Holy House at the Head of the Moors Adventurous.* New York: St. Martin's Press, 1988.

Chambers, E.K. *Arthur of Britain.* Cambridge: Speculum Historiale, 1964.

Clayton, Peter. *Guide to the Archaeological Sites of Britain.* London: B.T. Batsford Ltd., 1985.

Codrington, Thomas. *Roman Roads in Britain.* New York: The Macmillan Company, 1919.

Coles, J.M., and B.J. Orme. *Prehistory of the Somerset Levels.* Hertford, England: Stephen Austin and Sons Ltd., 1982.

Colgrave, Betram, and R.A.B. Mynors, eds. *Bede's Ecclesiastical History of the English People.* Oxford: Clarendon Press, 1969.

Collingwood, R.G. *Roman Britain.* London: Oxford University Press, 1923.

Collingwood, R.G., and J.N.L. Myres. *Roman Britain and the English Settlements.* Oxford: Clarendon Press, 1937.

Cook, Elizabeth. *The Ordinary and the Fabulous: An Introduction to Myths, Legends and Fairy Tales.* New York: Cambridge University Press, 2nd edition, 1976.

Cornell, Tim, and John Matthews. *Atlas of the Roman World.* New York: Facts on File Publication, 1982.

Cowan, Janet, ed. *Sir Thomas Malory's Le Morte D'Arthur, Volume I.* Middlesex, England: Penguin Books, 1969.

_____, ed. *Sir Thomas Malory's* Le Morte D'Arthur, *Volume II*. Middlesex, England: Penguin Books, 1969.

Cross, Tom Peete, and Clark Harris Slover, eds. *Ancient Irish Tales*. New York: Henry Holt and Company, 1936.

Cunliffe, Barry. *The City of Bath*. New Haven: Yale University Press, 1986.

_____. *Iron Age Communities in Britain*. London: Routledge and Kegan Paul Ltd., 1974.

_____. Selector and Introducer. *Heywood Sumner's Wessex*. Wimbourne, Dorset: Rox Gasson Associates, 1985.

Darrah, John. *The Real Camelot: Paganism and the Arthurian Romances*. London: Thames and Hudson, 1981.

Doble, Gilbert Hunter. *Lives of the Welsh Saints*. Edited by D. Simon Evans. Cardiff: University of Wales Press, 1971 (1984 printing).

Dowden, W.A. "Little Solsbury Camp.," *Proceedings of the Bristol University Spelaeological Society* 8 (1957):18–29; 9 (1962):177–182.

Dumville, David, and Simon Keynes, gen. eds.; Janet M. Bately, ed. *The Anglo-Saxon Chronicle: A Collaborative Edition. Volume 3, Manuscript A*. Cambridge: D.S. Brewer Ltd., 1986.

_____; Simon Taylor, ed. *The Anglo-Saxon Chronicle: A Collaborative Edition. Volume 4, Manuscript B*. Cambridge: D.S. Brewer Ltd., 1983.

Dyer, James. *Southern England: An Archaeological Guide: The Prehistoric and Roman Remains*. London: Faber and Faber Ltd., 1973.

Ekwall, Eilert. *The Concise Oxford Dictionary of English Place-names*. Oxford: Clarendon Press, 1936.

_____. *The Concise Oxford Dictionary of English Place-names*, 4th ed. Oxford: Clarendon Press, 1991.

Evans, D.H. "Valle Crucis Abbey." *Valle Crucis Abbey*. Cadw: Welsh Historic Monuments, 1987.

Evans, J. Gwenogvryn. *The Text of the* Book of Llan Dav, *Reproduced from the Gwnsaney Manuscript*. Oxford, 1893.

Evans, Sebastain, trans. *Geoffrey of Monmouth's* History of the Kings of Britain. New York: E.P. Dutton and Company, 1958.

Fletcher, Robert Huntington. *The Arthurian Material in the Chronicles*. New York: Burt Franklin, 1966.

Forester, Thomas, ed. and trans. *The Chronicle of Henry of Huntingdon, Comprising the History of England, from the Invasion of Julius Caesar to the Accession of Henry II*. London: Henry G. Bohn, York Street, Covent Garden, 1853.

Gantz, Jeffrey, trans. *The Mabinogion*. New York: Viking Penguin Books, 1987.

Garmonsway, G.N., ed. and trans. The *Anglo-Saxon Chronicle*. London: J.M. Dent and Son Ltd., 1990.

Gibson, Edmond, trans. *Camden's Britannia, Newly Translated into English with Large Additions and Improvements*. Printed by F. Collins, for A. Swale, at the Unicorn at the West-end of St. Paul's Church-yard, and A. & J. Churchil, at the Black Swan in Pater-noster-Row, 1695.

Giles, J.A., ed. *Six Old English Chronicles*. London: George Bell and Sons, 1885.

Glennie, J.S. Stuart. *Arthurian Localities,* 1869.

Goodrich, Norma Lorre. *King Arthur*. New York, Toronto: Franklin Watts, 1986.

_____. *Merlin*. New York: Franklin Watts, 1987.

_____. *Myths of the Hero*. New York: The Orion Press, 1962.

Grabowski, Kathryn, and David Dumville. *Chronicles and Annals of Mediaeval Ireland and Wales*. Woodbridge, Suffolk: The Boydell Press, 1984.

Grant, Michael, with cartography by Arthur Banks. *Ancient History Atlas*. 3d ed. London: Weidenfeld and Nicolson, 1971.

Grout, P.B., et al., eds. *The Legend of Arthur in the Middle Ages.* Cambridge: D.S. Brewer, an imprint of Boydell & Brewer Ltd., 1983.

Hamilton, Edith. *Mythology.* New York: Mentor Books, Little, Brown and Company, 1942.

Haverfield, F. *The Romanization of Roman Britain.* Oxford: Clarendon Press, 1926.

Hill, David. *An Atlas of Anglo-Saxon England.* Toronto and Buffalo: University of Toronto Press, 1981.

Historical Maps on File. New York: Facts on File, Inc., (460 Park Avenue South, New York, New York, 10016).

Hogg, A.H.A. *British Hillforts: An Index.* Oxford, England: BAR British Series 62, 1979.

Howard, Don, and Christian Zacher, editors. *Critical Studies of* Sir Gawain and the Green Knight. South Bend, Ind.: Notre Dame University Press, 1968.

Hughes, Kathleen. *Celtic Britain in the Early Middle Ages: Studies in Scottish and Welsh Sources.* Woodbridge, Suffolk: Boydell Press, 1980.

Jackson, Kenneth. "Arthur in Early Welsh Verse." *Arthurian Literature in the Middle Ages.* Edited by R.S. Loomis. Oxford: Clarendon Press, 1959.

_____. "The Arthur of History." *Arthurian Literature in the Middle Ages.* Edited by R.S. Loomis. Oxford: Clarendon Press, 1959.

_____, ed. and trans. *A Celtic Miscellany.* London: Routledge & Paul, 1951.

_____. The Gododdin: *The Oldest Scottish Poem.* Edinburgh: The University Press, 1969.

Jarman, A.O.H. "The Arthurian Allusions in *The Black Book of Carmarthen.*" *The Legend of Arthur in the Middle Ages.* Edited by P.B. Grout, et al. Cambridge: D.S. Brewer, an imprint of Boydell and Brewer Ltd., 1983.

John, Ivor B. *Popular Studies in Mythology, Romances, and Folklore, No. 11.* "The Mabinogion." Long Acre London: Sign of the Phoenix, 1901.

Jones, Major Francis. *A Catalogue of Welsh Manuscripts in the College of Arms.* Gloucester: Alan Sutton Publishing Ltd., the Harleian Society, 1988.

Jones, J. Graham. *A Pocket Guide: The History of Wales.* Cardiff: University of Wales Press, 1990.

Jones, Thomas. "The Early Evolution of the Legend of Arthur," *Nottingham Medieval Studies 8*, translated by Gerald Morgan.

Knight, Jeremy. "The Pillar of Eliseg," *Valle Crucis Abbey.* Cadw: Welsh Historic Monuments, 1987.

Knight, Stephen. *Arthurian Literature and Society.* New York: Peter Bedrick Books, 1986.

_____. *The Structure of Sir Thomas Malory's Arthuriad.* Hampshire and London: Macmillan Press, 1983.

Lacy, Norris J., ed. *The Arthurian Encyclopedia.* New York: Peter Bedrick Books, 1986.

Lacy, Norris J., and Geoffrey Ashe. *The Arthurian Handbook.* New York & London: Garland Publishing Inc. 1988.

Lapidge, Michael, and David Dumville, eds. *Gildas: New Approaches.* Dover, N.H.: The Boydell Press, 1984.

Lindsay, Jack. *Arthur and His Times: Britain in the Dark Ages.* London: Fredrick Muller Ltd., 1958.

Loomis, Roger Sherman, editor. *Arthurian Literature in the Middle Ages: A Collaborative History.* Oxford: Clarendon Press, 1959.

Microw, Charles C. *Jordanes: The Origin and Deeds of the Goths.* Princeton, N.J.: Princeton University Press, 1908.

Miller, Helen Hill. *The Realms of Arthur.* New York: Charles Scribner's Sons, 1969.

Mommsen, Theodor, ed. *Chronica Minora saec. IV. V. VI. VII.* Volume I, Berlin, 1892–1898.

Morris, John. *The Age of Arthur: A History of the British Isles from 350 to 650.* London: Weidenfeld and Nicolson, 1989.

_____. "Dark Age Dates." *Britain and Rome: Essays Presented to Eric Birley.* Edited by M.G. Jarrett and Brian Dobson. Kendal, 1965.

_____, ed., trans. *Nennius: British History and the Welsh Annals.* London and Chichester: Phillimore and Co. Ltd., 1980.

Muir, Richard and Nina. *The National Trust Rivers of Britain.* London: Bloomsbury Books, 1986.

Nitze, William A. "Yvain and the Myth of the Fountain." *Speculum* 30 (Jan.–Oct. 1955).

O'Donovan, John. *Annals of the Kingdom of Ireland by the Four Masters, from the Earliest Period to the Year 1616.* New York: AMS Press, Inc., 1966.

O'Faolain, Eileen. *Irish Sagas and Folk-Tales.* Retold by Eileen O'Faolain. Illustrated by Joan Kiddell-Monroe. London: Oxford University Press, 1954.

O'Sullivan, Thomas. The De Excidio *of Gildas: Its Authenticity and Date.* Reprinted with permission of the Trustees of Columbia University Press, 1978.

Phillips, Graham, and Martin Keatman. *King Arthur: The True Story.* London: Century Random House, 1992.

Pickford, C.E., and R.W. Last, *The Arthurian Bibliography,* Volumes 1–3. Cambridge: Boydell and Brewer, 1981–1988.

Piggott, Stuart. *British Prehistory.* Oxford: Home University Library, Oxford University Press, 1949.

Pitt-Rivers (Fox-Pitt-Rivers), Lieutenant-General. *Excavations in Cranbourne Chase Near Rushmore on the Borders of Dorset and Wilts, 1880–1888, Volume II.* Printed privately, 1888.

_____. *Excavations in Bokerly and Wansdyke, Dorset and Wilts, 1888–1891, with Observations on the Human Remains by J.G. Garson, M.D. Volume III.* Printed privately, 1892.

Plummer, Charles, and John Earle, eds. *Two of the Saxon Chronicles Parallel with Supplementary Extracts from the Others.* Oxford: Clarendon Press, 1899.

Publications of the English Historical Society. *Nennius: Historia Brittonum.* Germany: Kraus Reprint Ltd., 1964.

Radford, C.A. Ralegh. "Glastonbury Abbey." *The Quest for Arthur's Britain.* Edited by Geoffrey Ashe. Chicago, Ill.: Academy Chicago Publishers, 1987.

_____. "Romance and Reality in Cornwall." *The Quest for Arthur's Britain.* Edited by Geoffrey Ashe. Chicago, Ill.: Academy Chicago Publishers, 1987.

_____. "Tintagel in History and Legend." *Journal of the Royal Institution of Cornwall.* Volume 25. Truro, England: Workers of Cornwall, Ltd., 1942.

Rahtz, Philip. *Book of Glastonbury.* London: B.T. Batsford, Ltd./English Heritage, 1993.

_____. "Excavations on Glastonbury Tor, Somerset, 1964-6." *The Archaeological Journal.* Volume CXXVII (for the year 1970) 1–81. Leeds, England: W.S. Maney and Son Ltd., published by the Royal Archaelogical Institute, London, 1971.

_____. "Glastonbury Tor." *The Quest for Arthur's Britain.* Edited by Geoffrey Ashe. Chicago, Ill.: Academy Chicago Publishers, 1987.

Reaney, P.H. *The Origin of English Place-names.* London: Routledge and Kegan Paul, 1960.

Rees, William. *An Historical Atlas of Wales from Early to Modern Times.* London: Faber and Faber, 1951, reprinted 1966.

Rhys, John. *Studies in the Arthurian Legend.* Oxford: Clarendon Press, 1890.

Rivet, A.L.F., and Colin Smith. *The Place-Names of Roman Britain.* Princeton, New Jersey: Princeton University Press, 1979.

Robinson, J. Armitage. *Two Glastonbury Legends: King Arthur and St. Joseph of Arimathea.* Cambridge: The University Press, 1926.

Rolleston, T.W. *Myths and Legend Series: Celtic.* London: Bracken Books, the Bath Press, Imprint of Studio Editions, 1986.

Salway, Peter. *The Oxford Illustrated History of Roman Britain.* Oxford: Oxford University Press, 1993.

Sawyer, Peter H. *Anglo-Saxon Chargers: An Annotated List and Bibliography*. London: Offices of the Royal Historical Society, University College London, 1968.

_____. *Domesday Book: A Reassessment*. Victoria, Australia: Edward Arnold Ltd., 1985.

_____. *From Roman Britain to Norman England*. New York: St. Martin's Press, 1978.

Scott, John. *The Early History of Glastonbury: An Edition, Translation, and Study of William of Malmsbury's* De Antiquitate Glastonie Ecclesie. Woodbridge, Suffolk: The Boydell Press, 1981.

Sherley-Price, Leo, trans. *Bede: A History of the English Church and People*. New York: Dorset Press, 1985.

Simpson, D.P. *Cassell's Latin Dictionary*. New York: Macmillan Publishing Company, 1968.

Skene, William F. *The Four Ancient Books of Wales Containing the Cymric Poems Attributed to the Bards of the Sixth Century*. Volume I. Edinburgh: Edmonston and Douglas, 1868.

Smith, Lucy Toulmin, ed. *The Itinerary of John Leland in or About the Years 1535–1543*. "The Laboriouse Journey and Serche of John Leylande for Englandes Antiquitees, given of him as a Newe Yeares gyfte to King Henry viii, in the xxxvi year of his raygne." Volumes 1–5. Carbondale, Ill.: Southern Illinois University Press, 1964.

Steinbeck, Elaine, and Robert Wallston, eds. *Steinbeck: A Life in Letters*. New York: Viking Press, 1975.

Steinbeck, John. *The Acts of King Arthur and His Noble Knights*. New York: Del Rey Ballantine Books, 1976.

Stevenson, Josephus. *Gildas: De Excidio Britanniæ*. Vaduz, Liechtenstein: Kraus Reprint Ltd., Reprinted from a copy in the collections of the the New York Public Library, 1964.

_____. *Nennii: Historia Brittonum*. Vaduz, Liechtenstein: Kraus Reprint Ltd., 1964.

Stewart, Mary. *The Crystal Cave*. New York: William Morrow and Company, 1970.

_____. *The Hollow Hills*. New York: Ballantine Publishing, 1974.

_____. *The Last Enchantment*. New York: William Morrow and Company, 1979.

Stone, Brian, trans. *Sir Gawain and the Green Knight*. Middlesex, England: Penguin Books, 1959.

Sumner, Heywood. *Wessex*. Selected and Introduced by Barry Cunliff. Wimbourne, Dorset: Rox Gasson Associates, 1985.

Tatlock, J.S.P. *The Legendary History of Britain*. Berkeley: University of California Press, 1950.

Taylor, John. *The Universal Chronicle of Ranulf Higden*. Oxford: Clarendon Press, 1966.

Thompson, M.W. *General Pitt-Rivers: Evolution and Archaeology in the Nineteenth Century*. Bradford-on-Avon, Wiltshire: Moonraker Press, 1977.

Thorpe, Lewis, trans. *Geoffrey of Monmouth: The History of the Kings of Britain*. Middlesex, England: Penguin Books, 1966.

Tolkien, J.R.R., trans. *Sir Gawain and the Green Knight, Pearl, and Sir Orfeo*. New York: Ballantine Books, 1975.

Treharne, R.F. *The Glastonbury Legends: Joseph of Arimathea, the Holy Grail, and King Arthur*. London: Cresset Press, 1967.

Wacher, John. *The Towns of Roman Britain*. Berkeley and Los Angeles: University of California Press, 1974.

Wade-Evans, Arthur W. *The Emergence of England and Wales*. Cambridge: W. Heffer & Sons Ltd., 1959.

Walker, David. *Medieval Wales*. Cambridge: Cambridge University Press, 1990.

Warren, Fredrick Edward, ed. The Leofric Missal, *as used in the Cathedral of Exeter during the episcopate of its first bishop, A.D. 1050–1072*. Oxford: The Clarendon Press, 1883.

Webster, Graham. *The Cornovii.* Stroud, Gloucester: Alan Sutton Publishing Ltd., 1991.

____, and Phillip Barker. "Wroxeter: Roman City." London: English Heritage, 1993.

Welch, Martin. *Discovering Anglo-Saxon England.* University Park, Pennsylvania: Pennsylvania State University Press, 1992.

Whitelock, Dorothy, David Douglas, and Susie Tucker, eds. *The Anglo-Saxon Chronicle.* New Jersey: Rutgers University Press, 1961.

Williams, Ifor. *Lectures on Early Welsh Poetry.* Dublin: Dublin Institute for Advanced Studies, 1944.

Williams, Taliesin, ed. and trans. *Iolo Manuscripts, a selection of ancient Welsh manuscripts in prose and verse from the collection made by Iolo Morganwg (Edward Williams).* London: The Welsh MSS Society, Llandovery (sold by Longman), 1848.

Winbolt, S.E. *Britain Under the Romans.* Middlesex, England: Penguin Books, 1945.

Winterbottom, Michael, ed. and trans. *Gildas:* The Ruin of Britain *and Other Works.* Chichester, England: Phillimore and Co., Ltd., 1978 and Totowa, New Jersey: Rowman and Littlefield, 1978.

Wright, Thomas. *The Celt, the Roman, and the Saxon: A History of the Early Inhabitants of Britain.* London: Arthur Hall, Virtue, and Co., 1861.

Index

CBA

FEB 19 1997